LITERARY THEMES
for Students

LITERARY THEMES

for Students

Examining Diverse Literature to Understand and Compare Universal Themes

THE AMERICAN DREAM

VOLUME 1

Anne Marie Hacht, Editor

Foreword by Margaret Brantley

GALE
CENGAGE Learning

Detroit • New York • San Francisco • New Haven, Conn • Waterville, Maine • London

Literary Themes for Students: The American Dream

Project Editor
Anne Marie Hacht

Editorial
Ira Mark Milne

Rights Acquisition and Management
Robbie Mc Cord, Lista Person, Kelly Quin,
Andrew Specht

Manufacturing
Rita Wimberley

Imaging
Lezlie Light and Robyn Young

Product Design
Pamela A. E. Galbreath and Jennifer Wahi

Vendor Administration
Civie Green

Product Manager
Meggin Condino

LIBRARY OF CONGRESS CATALOGING-IN-PUBLICATION DATA

Literary themes for students : the American dream : examining diverse literature to
understand and compare universal themes / Anne Marie Hacht, editor ; foreword by
Margaret Brantley.
    p. cm. – (Literary themes for students)
Includes bibliographical references and index.
ISBN-13: 978-1-4144-0433-2 (set : alk. paper)
ISBN-10: 1-4144-0433-6 (set : alk. paper)
ISBN-13: 978-1-4144-0285-7 (vol. 1 : alk. paper)
ISBN-10: 1-4144-0285-6 (vol. 1 : alk. paper)
[etc.]
1. American literature–History and criticism. 2. American literature–Themes, motives.
3. National characteristics, American in literature. I. Hacht, Anne Marie.
PS169.N35L58 2007
810.9'358–dc22   2007005602

ISBN-13:
978-1-4144-0433-2 (set)
978-1-4144-0285-7 (vol. 1)
978-1-4144-0286-4 (vol. 2)

ISBN-10:
1-144-0433-6 (set)
1-4144-0285-6 (vol. 1)
1-4144-0286-4 (vol. 2)

This title is also available as an e-book.
ISBN-13: 978-1-4144-2931-1
ISBN-10: 1-4144-2931-2
Contact your Gale sales representative for ordering information.

Printed in the United States of America
2 3 4 5 6 7 14 13 12 11 10 09 08

Table of Contents

Volume 2

Foreword

Each volume of *Literary Themes for Students* brings together dozens of renowned works of literature that share a specific theme. The theme for this volume of *Literary Themes for Students* is The American dream.

The settlement of the New World brought strange, exciting experiences and ideas for the people who were destined to call it "home." Unfamiliar civilizations, animals, plants, climates, and landscape became familiar quickly enough, but new ideas and ideals are still the hallmark of the New World, even six centuries after the first Europeans lay claim to it. Those ideas—of a new home, new opportunities, new freedoms, and a new life—are at the heart of the American dream. While the concept of the American dream is well known at home and around the world, the definition may be as varied as the individuals who attempt to define it. As the literature shows, all who pursue the American dream have aspirations; what they aspire to spans the breadth of human experiences.

If it is human nature to hope, dream, and progress, what, then makes the American dream peculiar to the United States? The promise of opportunity, equality, and dignity, in a land that rewards hard work and respects the individual give the dream its shape; the array of stories of triumph and success from people of every background give the American dream its power. The literature of the American dream serves to shape, chronicle, and examine Americans' aspirations, both as persons and as a people. It is not one thing to all people, although that they aspire is one thing those people have in common. The difficulty of defining the dream is part of its strength and beauty. Walt Whitman captures the feeling of that vague yet vast power in his seminal poem, "Song of Myself":

> The past and present wilt—I have fill'd
>   them, emptied them,
> And proceed to fill my next fold of the
>   future.
>
> Listener up there! what have you to confide
>   to me?
> Look in my face while I snuff the sidle of
>   evening,
> (Talk honestly, no one else hears you, and I
>   stay only a minute longer.)
>
> Do I contradict myself?
> Very well then I contradict myself,
> (I am large, I contain multitudes.)
>
> *(Whitman, Walt, "Song of Myself," Leaves
> of Grass, Signet Classics, 1980, pp. 49–96;
> originally published in 1892.)*

Some of the selections in *Literary Themes for Students* are chronicles of the experiences of different Americans. Alvar Núñez Cabeza de Vaca's *Chronicle of the Narváez Expedition* introduced the New World and its possibilities to Europeans in the mid-1500s. His descriptions of the land's natural wealth inspired others to explore, settle, and make new lives as the first American dreamers. Native Americans, people all but exterminated by the Europeans who followed Cabeza de Vaca, found little voice for their experience with the American dream until the twentieth century, when chronicles like *Black Elk Speaks* (1932) emerged speak for those so long voiceless. Laura Ingalls Wilder's *Little House on the Prairie* (1935) tells of life as a white pioneer in the nineteenth century. Henry Roth's *Call it Sleep* (1934), was published about the same time as Black Elk's and Wilder's stories, and offers a third, completely different, perspective. While a work of fiction, Roth's novel is based on the author's own experiences as a young Jewish immigrant to New York in the early twentieth century and captures the feeling of the experience for a large segment of American dreamers.

Such chronicles are but a small part of the literature of the American dream. Literature has given the dream form, and continues to refine, reshape, and refresh it. Nonfiction, like John Winthrop's 1630 address "A Model of Christian Charity," Thomas Paine's revolutionary "Common Sense," Benjamin Franklin's *Autobiography,* and the Declaration of Independence helped the fledgling country establish its ideals and identity. Later nonfiction, like Emerson's "Self-Reliance" (1841) and President Kennedy's 1961 inaugural speech refreshed established ideals of the American dream and even introduced new tenets into the philosophy of Americanism. Fiction and poetry have also shaped the American dream for many, creating new examples and expressions of the individual pursuit of happiness. Whitman's "Song of Myself" written after the Civil War, boldly celebrates the individual—every individual—in a wholly original American style and voice. Jack Kerouac's masterpiece of modern disillusionment, *On the Road* (1957) served as the model for generations of Americans seeking their own version of the dream.

Perhaps literature's most important role is to examine ideologies as they exist in the world, expose their flaws, and explore higher ideals that might yet be reached. Writers may question society's values, as do Henry James in "Daisy Miller" (1878) and F. Scott Fitzgerald in *The Great Gatsby* (1925). The tone of a call for a national change in course may range from mocking, as with Stephen Colbert's 2006 speech at the White House Correspondents' Association Dinner, to outrage, as with John Steinbeck's *The Grapes of Wrath* (1939). Langston Hughes's *Montage of a Dream Deferred* (1951), Tomás Rivera 's . . . *And the Earth Did Not Devour Him* (1971), N. Scott Momaday's *House Made of Dawn* (1968), and Marie Lee's *Finding My Voice* (1992) bring the hopes and struggles well known within some American subcultures to the broad awareness of Americans in general. The works that prompt self-examination may be gentle and slightly melancholy, such as Robert Frost's "Mending Wall" (1915) and Thornton Wilder's *Our Town* (1938). Some writers try to shock their readers out of complacency with darker takes on the human condition, such as Arthur Miller in *Death of a Salesman* (1949) and John Updike in *Rabbit, Run* (1960).

The works explored in this volume represent the gamut of genres, tones, and reactions, but all prompt readers to re-examine their notion of the American dream. *Literary Themes for Students* cannot take the place of experiencing firsthand the books it presents. This overview of the topics, points-of-view, and critical interpretations is meant to guide readers who want to explore more on their own. By celebrating the variability and mutability of the American dream, it encourages all individuals—not just Americans—to define the dream for them selves, pursue their own goals, and aspire to creating a better life.

Margaret Brantley
Brantley is a literature critic and a literary reference editor.

Introduction

Purpose of the Book

The purpose of *Literary Themes for Students (LTfS)* is to provide readers with an overview of literary works that explore a specific theme. The volumes analyze poetry, plays, short stories, novels, and works of nonfiction that address the theme in some capacity, and the reader discovers how that theme has been treated in literature at different times in history and across diverse cultures. Volumes Five and Six, *Literary Themes: The American Dream in Literature*, include "classic" political and historical texts, as well as more contemporary accounts of race and prejudice and works by minority, international, and female writers.

These volumes begin with an overview essay that introduces the theme of race and prejudice in literature. This essay is followed by fourteen sub-essays, which break these themes down further into subthemes that correspond to recurring ideas in the literature of the American dream. Sub-essays examine particular titles that exemplify the subthemes and by treating them the volume can thus track how that subtheme has developed over time.

Each work is discussed in a separate entry. These entries include an introduction to the work and the work's author; a plot summary, to help readers understand the action and story of the work; an analysis of themes that relate to the subject of the American dream, to provide readers with a multifaceted look at the complexity of the aspirations, obstacles, and inspirations of American dreamers; and a section on important historical and cultural events that shaped the author and the work, as well as events in the real world (from the time of the author or another time in history) that affect the plot or characters in the work.

Additionally, readers are presented with a critical overview discussing how the work was initially received by critics and how the work is presently viewed. Accompanying the critical overview is an excerpt from a previously published critical essay discussing the work's relation to the theme of race and prejudice. For further analysis and enjoyment, an extended list of media adaptations is also included, as well as a list of poems, short stories, novels, plays, and works of nonfiction that further address the theme of race and prejudice, and thus students are encouraged to continue their study of this theme.

Selection Criteria

The titles of each volume of *LTfS* were selected by surveying numerous sources on teaching literature and analyzing course curricula for a number of school districts. Our advisory board provided input, as did educators in various areas.

How Each Entry is Organized

Each chapter focuses on the ways in which an entry relates to the theme of the American dream. Each entry heading includes the author's name, the title of the work being discussed, and the year it was published. The following sections are included in the discussion of each entry:

Introduction: a brief overview of the work being discussed. It provides information about the work's first appearance, any controversies surrounding its publication, its literary reputation, and general details about the work's connection to the theme of the American dream.

Plot Summary: a description of the events that occur in the work. For poems, some additional insight into the context and interpretation of the poem—and discussion of symbols and elements—is provided. The plot summary is broken down by subheadings, usually organized by chapter, section, or stanza.

Themes: a discussion of how the work approaches the issue of the American dream through various themes. Each theme is addressed under a separate subheading. Several of the major recurring themes are discussed at more length in individual sub-essays.

Historical and Cultural Context: a discussion of the historical and cultural events that appear in the work or that affected the writer while the work was being written. This can include large-scale events such as wars, social movements, and political decisions, as well as smaller-scale events such as cultural trends and literary movements. If the work is set during a different time period from that in which the author wrote it, historical and cultural events from both periods are included.

Critical Overview: a discussion of the work's general critical reputation, including how it was initially received by reviewers, critics, and the general public. Any controversy surrounding the work is treated in this section. For older works, this section also includes information on the ways that views of the work have changed over time.

Criticism: a previously published critical essay discussing how the work addresses the issues of race and/or prejudice. When no appropriate criticism could be found, *LTfS* commissioned essays that deal specifically with the work and are written for student audiences.

Sources: an alphabetical list of sources used in compiling the entry, including bibliographic information.

In addition, each entry includes the following sidebars, set apart from the rest of the text:

Author Biography Sidebar: a brief biography of the author, including how he or she was affected by or led to write about the American dream.

Media Adaptations: a list of film, television, and/or stage adaptations, audio versions, and other forms of media related to the work. Source information is included.

Other Features

LTfS includes "We Contain Multitudes: The Literature of the American Dream" by Mo Brantley, a writer and editor of language arts reference books. This is a foreword about how the literature of the American dream can help contemporary readers appreciate the history, the varieties, the vagaries, and the universality of the many forms the American dream may take.

Each entry may have several illustrations, including photos of the author, depictions of key elements of the plot, stills from film adaptations, and/or historical photos of the people, places, or events discussed in the entry.

Fourteen sub-essays discuss various focuses of the literature of the American dream: in different time periods, including the colonial era, the nineteenth century, the twentieth century, and the modern day; for different populations of Americans, including African Americans; Asian Americans, Native Americans, Hispanic Americans; American Immigrants; as it relates to certain specific experiences, such as among frontiersmen, Southerners, feminists, foreigners and expatriates, and public figures. Each sub-essay addresses approximately a dozen works that deal directly with the subtheme, and discusses how treatment of that theme has changed over time.

A Media Adaptation list compiles more than seventy films, plays, television series, and other media that deal with the subject of the American dream. The adaptations are organized by subtheme for easy access.

The *What Do I Read Next?* section provides over one hundred plays, short stories, poems, novels, and nonfiction works on the subject of the American dream. These works are also organized by subtheme.

An overview essay on the theme of the American dream in literature discusses how the American dream represents many things to many people. It goes on to argue that its pervasive allure and power come from the capacity for it to encompass so many aspirations. Discussion of key poems, plays, short stories, novels, and nonfiction works reflect the continuing evolution of the American dream.

Citing Literary Themes for Students

When writing papers, students who quote directly from any volume of *Literary Themes for Students* may use the following general formats. These examples are based on MLA style. Teachers may request that students adhere to a different style, so the following examples should be adapted as needed.

When citing text from *LTfS* that is not attributed to a particular author (i.e., from the Themes or Historical Context sections), the following format should be used in the bibliography section:

"O Pioneers!." Literary Themes for Students. Ed. TK. Vol. TK. Detroit: Thomson Gale, 2007. TK–TK.

When quoting a journal or newspaper essay that is reprinted in a volume of *LTfS*, the following format may be used:

Heddendorf, David, "Rabbit Reread," in the *Southern Review*, Vol. 36, No. 3, Summer 2000, pp. 641–47; excerpted and reprinted in *Literary Themes for Students*, Vol. TK, ed. TK (Detroit: Thomson Gale, 2007), pp. TK–TK.

When quoting material reprinted from a book that appears in a volume of *LTfS*, the following form may be used:

Schubnell, Matthias, *N. Scott Momaday: The Cultural and Literary Background*, University of Oklahoma Press, 1985, pp. 101–39; excerpted and reprinted in *Literary Themes for Students*, Vol. TK, ed. TK (Detroit: Thomson Gale, 2007), pp. TK–TK.

We Welcome Your Suggestions

The editorial staff of *LTfS* welcomes your comments, ideas, and suggestions. Readers who wish to suggest themes and works for future volumes, or who have any other suggestions, are cordially invited to contact the editor. You may do so via email at ForStudentsEditors@gale.cengage.com or via mail at:

Editor, *Literary Themes for Students*
Gale
27500 Drake Road
Farmington Hills, MI 48331-3535

Acknowledgments

COPYRIGHTED EXCERPTS IN *LTSAD*, VOLUMES 1-2, WERE REPRODUCED FROM THE FOLLOWING PERIODICALS:

American Drama, v. 2, fall, 1992. Copyright (c) 1992 American Drama Institute. Reproduced by permission.—*American Heritage*, v. 47, July-August, 1996. Copyright 1996 American Heritage, A Division of Forbes, Inc. Reproduced by permission of American Heritage.—*American Transcendental Quarterly*, v. 19, September, 2005. Copyright (c) 2005 by The University of Rhode Island. Reproduced by permission.—*Atlantic Monthly*, v. 289, February, 2002 for "Sheer Data" by Benjamin Schwarz. Reproduced by permission of the author.—*Children's Literature*, v. 24, 1996. Copyright (c) 1996 by Yale University. All rights reserved. Reproduced by permission.—*College Literature*, v. 20, October, 1993. Copyright (c) 1993 by West Chester University. Reproduced by permission.—*CRITIQUE: Studies in Contemporary Fiction*, v. 47, fall, 2005. Copyright (c) 2005 by Helen Dwight Reid Educational Foundation. Reproduced with permission of the Helen Dwight Reid Educational Foundation, published by Heldref Publications, 1319 18th Street, NW, Washington, DC 20036-1802.—*Cross Currents*, v. 43, fall, 1993. Copyright 1993 by Cross Currents, Inc. Reproduced by permission.—*Early American Literature*, v. 35, fall, 2000. Copyright (c) 2000 by the University of North Carolina Press. Used by permission.—*FindLaw's Writ*, May 9, 2006. Copyright (c) 2006 FindLaw, a Thomson business. This column originally appeared On FindLaw.com. Reproduced by permission.—*Kenyon Review*, summer-fall, 2002 for "Deadpan Huck" by Sacvan Bercovitch. Copyright 2002 Kenyon College. All rights reserved. Reproduced by permission of the author.—*The Massachusetts Review*, v. 14, autumn, 1973. Copyright (c) 1974 by The Massachusetts Review, Inc. Reproduced by permission.—*MELUS*, v. 8, fall, 1981; v. 27, winter, 2002. Copyright MELUS: The Society for the Study of Multi-Ethnic Literature of the United States, 1981, 2002. Both reproduced by permission.—*Modern Fiction Studies*, v. 49, fall, 2003. Copyright (c) 2003 by Purdue Research Foundation, West Lafayette, IN 47907. All rights reserved. Reproduced by permission of The Johns Hopkins University.—*The New York Review of Books*, v. 38, October 10, 1991. Copyright (c) 1991 by NYREV, Inc. Reprinted with permission from The New York Review of Books.—*Philosophy and Literature*, v. 21, 1997. Copyright (c) 1997 The Johns Hopkins University Press. Reproduced by permission.—*Prologue*, v. 22, spring, 1990 for "The Stylistic Artistry of 'The Declaration of Independence'" by Stephen E. Lucas. (c) 1989 Stephen E. Lucas. Reproduced by permission of the author.—*Southern Review*, v. 36, summer, 2000 for "Rabbit Reread" by David Heddendorf. Copyright (c) 2000 by Louisiana State University. Reproduced by permission of the author.—*Southwest*

Review, v. 48, autumn, 1963. Copyright (c) 1963 Southern Methodist University. All rights reserved. Reproduced by permission.—*Studia Anglica Posnaniensia*, v. 41, 2005. Copyright 2005 Adam Mickiewicz University Press. Reproduced by permission.—*Studies in Short Fiction*, v. 25, fall, 1988. Copyright (c) 1988 by North Texas State University. Reproduced by permission.—*Studies in the Novel*, v. 23, spring, 1991. Copyright (c) 1991 by North Texas State University. Reproduced by permission.—*Texas Studies in Literature and Language*, v. 43, summer, 2001 for "Peasant Dreams: Reading 'On the Road'" by Mark Richardson. Copyright (c) 2001 by the University of Texas Press. Reproduced by permission of the publisher and the author.

COPYRIGHTED EXCERPTS IN *LTSAD*, VOLUMES 1-2, WERE REPRODUCED FROM THE FOLLOWING BOOKS:

Brown, John Mason. From *Dramatis Personae: A Retrospective Show*. Viking Press, 1963. Copyright 1929, 1930, 1934, 1938, 1940, 1944, 1946, 1948-1955 inclusive, (c) 1957, 1958, 1962, 1963, renewed 1991 by John Mason Brown. Used by permission of Viking Penguin, a division of Penguin Group (USA) Inc.—Conder, John J. From *Naturalism in American Fiction: The Classic Phase*. University Press of Kentucky, 1984. Copyright (c) 1984 by The University Press of Kentucky. Reproduced by permission of The University Press of Kentucky.—Couser, G. Thomas. From *Altered Egos: Authority in American Autobiography*. Oxford University Press, 1989. Copyright (c) 1989 by Oxford University Press, Inc. All rights reserved. Reproduced by permission of Oxford University Press, Inc.—Goldstein, Malcolm. From *The Art of Thornton Wilder*. University of Nebraska Press, 1965. Copyright (c) 1965 by the University of Nebraska Press. (c) renewed 1993 by the University of Nebraska Press. All rights reserved. Reproduced by permission of the University of Nebraska Press.—Kennedy, Rick. From "Building a City on a Hill," in *Events that Changed America Through the Seventeenth Century*. Edited by John Findling and Frank Thackeray. Greenwood Press, 2000. Copyright (c) 2000 by John E. Findling and Frank W. Thackeray. All rights reserved. Reproduced by permission of Greenwood Publishing Group, Inc., Westport, CT.—The Massachusetts Review, v. 14, autumn, 1973. Copyright (c) 1974 by The Massachusetts Review, Inc. Reproduced by permission.—Schubnell, Matthias. From *N. Scott Momaday: The Cultural and Literary Background*. University of Oklahoma Press, 1985. Copyright (c) 1985 University of Oklahoma Press. Reproduced by permission.—Singal, Daniel Joseph. From *William Faulkner: The Making of a Modernist*. University of North Carolina Press, 1997. Copyright (c) 1997 by the University of North Carolina Press. All rights reserved. Used by permission of the publisher.—Sloane, David E. E. From *Sister Carrie: Theodore Dreiser's Sociological Tragedy*. Twayne Publishers, 1992. Copyright (c) 1992 by Twayne Publishers. All rights reserved. Reproduced by permission of Thomson Gale.—Weisbuch, Robert. From *New Essays on Daisy Miller and The Turn of the Screw*. Cambridge University Press, 1993. Copyright (c) 1993 Cambridge University Press. Reprinted with the permission of Cambridge University Press.

National Advisory Board

Contributors

Margaret Brantley: Brantley is a literature critic and a literary reference editor. Foreword.

Ann Guidry: Guidry is a freelance writer and editor with a B.A. in English from the University of Texas. Major Work on the *Autobiography of Benjamin Franklin*, *The Grapes of Wrath*, John F. Kennedy's Inaugural Speech, *O Pioneers!*, *Rabbit, Run*, and "Song of Myself," as well as the essays "The Colonial American Dream," "The American Dream in the Nineteenth Century," "The Immigrant American Dream," "The American Political Dream," and "The Southern American Dream."

Jonathan Lampley: Lampley is a doctoral candidate in English at Middle Tennessee State University and is a freelance writer. Major work on the Declaration of Independence and the White House Correspondents' Association Dinner 2006 Speech, as well as the essay "The American Dream Today."

Michelle Lee: Lee has been a freelance writer and editor for the past 15 years, and is working toward a Ph.D. in English literature at the University of Texas. Major Work on *The Big Money*, *The Great Gatsby*, "Mending Wall," and *Our Town*, as well as the essays "The American Dream," "The American Dream Abroad," "The American Feminist Dream," "The Asian American Dream," and "The Frontier American Dream."

Ray Mescallado: Mescallado holds a master's degree in English and is a freelance writer. Major Work on *Sister Carrie*

Annette Petrusso: Petrusso is a freelance writer and editor with a B.A. in history from the University of Michigan and an M.A. in screenwriting from The University of Texas at Austin. Major work on *Absalom, Absalom!*, *Adventures of Huckleberry Finn*, *... And the Earth Did Not Devour Him Autobiography of My Dead Brother*, *Cane*, *Chronicle of the Narváez Expedition*, *Daisy Miller*, *Death of a Salesman*, "Elbow Room," *Finding My Voice*, *House Made of Dawn*, *Little House on the Prairie*, *Main Street*, and "My Kinsman, Major Molineux.

Laura Baker Shearer: Shearer holds a Ph.D. in American literature and works as an English professor and freelance writer. Major work on "Common Sense" and "Self-Reliance."

Greg Wilson Wilson is a freelance literature and popular culture writer. Major work on *Black Elk Speaks*, *Call It Sleep*, *Lonesome Dove*, "A Model of Christian Charity," *Montage of a Dream Deferred*, and *On the Road*, as well as the essays "The African American Dream," "The American Dream in the Twentieth Century," "The Hispanic American Dream," and "The Native American Dream."

Literary Chronology

1485: Alvar Núñez Cabeza de Vaca is born between 1485 and 1492, probably in Jerez de la Frontera, Spain.

1555: Cabeza de Vaca's *Chronicle of the Narváez Expedition* is published.

1559: Cabeza de Vaca dies in 1559 or 1560 in Spain.

1588: John Winthrop is born on January 12 in Suffolk, England.

1630: Winthrop's "A Model of Christian Charity," is published.

1649: Winthrop dies on March 26.

1706: Benjamin Franklin is born on January 17 in Boston, Massachusetts.

1737: Thomas Paine is born in England.

1743: Thomas Jefferson is born on April 13 in Virginia.

1776: Paine's *Common Sense* is published.

1776: Jefferson's *The Declaration of Independence* is adopted on July 4.

1790: Franklin dies on April 17 in Philadelphia, Pennsylvania.

1803: Ralph Waldo Emerson is born on May 25 in Massachusetts.

1804: Nathaniel Hawthorne is born on July 4 in Salem, Massachusetts.

1809: Paine dies in June in New York City, New York.

1819: Walt Whitman is born on May 31 in West Hills, New York.

1826: Jefferson dies on July 4.

1832: Hawthorne's "My Kinsman, Major Molineux" is published.

1835: Samuel Langhorne Clemens (Mark Twain) is born on November 30 in Florida, Missouri.

1841: Emerson's "Self-Reliance" is published.

1843: Henry James is born on April 15 in New York City, New York.

1864: Hawthorne dies on May 19 from cancer.

1867: Laura Ingalls Wilder is born on February 7 in Pepin, Wisconsin.

1871: Herman Theodore Dreiser is born on August 27 in Terre Haute, Indiana.

1873: Willa Sibert Cather is born on December 7 in Back Creek Valley, Virginia.

1874: Robert Lee Frost is born on March 26 in San Francisco, California.

1878: James's *Daisy Miller* is published.

1882: Emerson dies on April 27.

1885: Twain's *Adventures of Huckleberry Finn* is published.

1885: Harry Sinclair Lewis is born on February 7 in Sauk Centre, Minnesota.

1886: Franklin's *The Autobiography of Benjamin Franklin* is published.

1891: John Gneisenau Neihardt is born on January 8 near Sharpsburg, Illinois.

1892: Whitman's "Song of Myself" is published.

1892: Whitman dies on March 26 in Camden, New Jersey.

1894: Nathan Eugene Pinchback (Jean) Toomer is born on December 26 in Washington, D.C.

1896: John Dos Passos is born on January 14 in Chicago, Illinois.

1896: Francis (F.) Scott Fitzgerald is born on September 4 in St. Paul, Minnesota.

1897: William Faulkner is born on September 25 in New Albany, Mississippi.

1897: Thornton Wilder is born on April 17 in Madison, Wisconsin.

1900: Dreiser's *Sister Carrie* is published.

1902: John Ernst Steinbeck is born on February 27 in Salinas, California.

1902: James Langston Hughes is born on February 1 in Joplin, Missouri.

1906: Herschel (Henry) Roth is born on February 8 in Tysmenica, Galicia, Austria-Hungary (now part of the Ukraine).

1910: Twain dies of heart disease on April 21 in Redding, Connecticut.

1913: Cather's *O Pioneers!* is published.

1915: Frost's "Mending Wall" is published.

1915: Arthur Miller is born on October 17 in New York City, New York.

1916: James dies on February 28 of edema following a series of strokes in London, England.

1917: John Fitzgerald Kennedy is born on May 29 in Brookline, Massachusetts.

1920: Lewis's *Main Street* is published.

1922: Jean-Louis Lebris de Kerouac (Jack Kerouac) is born on March 12 in Lowell, Massachusetts.

1923: Toomer's *Cane* is published.

1925: Fitzgerald's *The Great Gatsby* is published.

1932: John Hoyer Updike is born on March 18 in Shillington, Pennsylvania.

1932: Neihardt's *Black Elk Speaks* is published.

1934: Roth's *Call It Sleep* is published.

1934: Navarre Scott Mammedaty (N. Scott Momaday) is born on February 27 in Lawton, Oklahoma.

1935: Tomás Rivera is born December 22 in Crystal City, Texas.

1935: Wilder's *Little House on the Prairie* is published.

1936: Faulkner's *Absalom, Absalom!* is published.

1936: Dos Passos's *The Big Money* is published.

1936: Larry McMurtry is born on June 3 in Wichita Falls, Texas.

1937: Walter Milton Myers (Walter Dean Myers) is born on August 12 in Martinsburg, West Virginia.

1937: Wilder dies on February 10 in Mansfield, Missouri.

1938: Wilder's *Our Town* is published.

1939: Steinbeck's *The Grapes of Wrath* is published.

1940: Fitzgerald dies on December 21 of a heart attack in Hollywood, California.

1943: James Alan McPherson is born on September 16 in Savannah, Georgia.

1945: Dreiser dies on December 28 of a heart attack in Los Angeles, California.

1947: Cather dies on April 24 of a cerebral hemorrhage in New York, New York.

1949: Miller's *Death of a Salesman* is published.

1951: Lewis dies of a heart attack on January 10 near Rome, Italy.

1951: Hughes's *Montage of a Dream Deferred* is published.

1957: Kerouac's *On the Road* is published.

1960: Updike's *Rabbit, Run* is published.

1961: Kennedy delivers his inaugural address on January 20.

1962: Faulkner dies on July 6 in Byhalia, Mississippi.

1963: Kennedy is assassinated on November 22 in Dallas, Texas.

1963: Frost dies on January 29 in Boston, Massachusetts.

1964: Marie G. Lee is born on April 25 in Hibbing, Minnesota.

1964: Stephen Colbert is born on May 13 in Charleston, South Carolina.

1967: Toomer dies on March 30 in Doylestown, Pennsylvania.

1967: Hughes dies on May 22 of congestive heart failure in New York, New York.

1968: Steinbeck dies on December 20 of heart disease in New York City, New York.

1968: Momaday's *House Made of Dawn* is published.

1969: Kerouac dies of cirrhosis of the liver and internal bleeding on October 21 in St. Petersburg, Florida .

1970: Dos Passos dies on September 28 in Baltimore, Maryland.

1971: Rivera's *. . . And the Earth Did Not Devour Him* is published.

1973: Neihardt dies on November 24 in Columbia, Missouri.

1975: Wilder dies of a heart attack on December 7 in Hamden, Connecticut.

1977: McPherson's "Elbow Room" is published.

1984: Rivera dies on May 16 in Fontana, California.

1985: McMurtry's *Lonesome Dove* is published.

1992: Lee's *Finding My Voice* is published.

1995: Roth dies on October 13.

2005: Miller dies on February 10 of heart failure in Roxbury Connecticut.

2005: *Autobiography of My Dead Brother* is published.

2006: Colbert delivers his speech at the White House Correspondents' Association Dinner on April 29.

Overview Essay

THE AMERICAN DREAM

The American Dream: Overview

Introduction

In 1965, "The Impossible Dream," theme song from *Man of La Mancha*, a Broadway musical based on the novel *The Adventures of Don Quixote* (1604) by Miguel de Cervantes, reflected not only the undying optimism of protagonist Don Quixote, but also an ideology shared by its American audience. At a time when the fight for civil rights knocked down both social and political boundaries and the war in Vietnam was escalating, the lyrics, "To dream the impossible dream," written by Joe Darion, spoke to an individual quest and a united hope.

The notion that every man and woman in America, amid national and international chaos, could still persevere, achieve, and become successful was more important than ever. As protesters called for peace, and African Americans and women demanded equality, America was literally and figuratively reaching for the moon. As promised with the birth of the nation, Americans were entitled to life, liberty, and the pursuit of happiness. "The Impossible Dream" illustrates that deep-seated sense of entitlement and ownership of certain unalienable, constitutional rights, particularly the rights to pursue any and all opportunity, even those that seem impossible.

American history demonstrates that the reasons behind the pilgrims' escape to the New World differ from the reasons behind suffrage,

or even the robber barons' controversial business practices. However, social and political motivations aside, the same American dream connected them all: the opportunity to create something from virtually nothing, to "right the unrightable wrong," to follow whatever "star" they chose. This loose interpretation of the American dream allowed a variety of manifestations, and over the centuries, though born from a group of white forefathers, the American dream has taken a multicultural, multidimensional shape. With native, ethnic, female, young, and old voices added to the mix, the American dream was challenged and ultimately began to change.

As a result, the idea of the "impossible dream" became, in some ways, exposed as the American nightmare. The myth of "equal opportunity for all" no longer held up. Once a melting pot, America seemed to be harkening back to its late nineteenth and early twentieth century history and questioning immigration practices. Women in business still kept an eye toward the glass ceiling. America's super-power came at the expense of other countries around the world. But these cracks in the American dream dogma allowed room for amendment and revolutionary action as Americans realized that more than one version of the dream, of happiness, of liberty, exists. American literature tracks the American dream's historical and ideological arc from sanctuary and settlement to rights and respect. This essay follows that trajectory, focusing on the birth of the American dream, the dream united "under God," the dream as icon, those barred from the dream, those who revolutionized the dream, the high cost of the dream, a new definition of the dream, and finally, the dream's future.

Birth of the American Dream

William Bradford, American forefather and one of the first Puritans to arrive in the New World, signed the Mayflower Compact in November 1620, a contract that established a government determined by the settlers. The Compact, a response to near mutiny on the ship among disgruntled Church of England members, united these "Strangers" and "Separatists," or pilgrims, in a binding pact. No one could simply do their own will or, as Bradford writes in chapter 11 in *Of Plymouth Plantation*, "use their own liberty." Instead, they would come together as a "Civil Body Politic," for "better ordering and preservation." This act would be for the "general good of

the colony," and the American dream became a joint hope and quest for survival. John Carver, who had been appointed governor, guided the group in building homes and establishing laws, and as Bradford observes,

> In these hard and difficult beginnings they found some discontents and murmurings arise amongst some, and mutinous speeches and carriages in others; but they were soon quelled and overcome by the wisdom, patience, and just and equal carriage of things, by the Governor and better part, which clave faithfully together in the main.

More than a century later, in 1776, "discontents and murmurings" arose after the British imposed new taxes and laws on the colonies. While some demanded independence from England, the Tories, or Loyalists, resisted. The Tories did not believe separating from the motherland would be beneficial. However, revolutionaries, or Patriots, rallied much of the "national" community and battled the British for their rights and territory. On July 4, 1776, after the colonists abolished the royal governments and formed locally elected legislative assemblies, the Declaration of Independence was written by John Adams, Benjamin Franklin, and Thomas Jefferson, and then signed by the members of the Second Continental Congress. This document, like the Mayflower Compact, ensured the government to be controlled by those governed yet, more importantly, established the foundation for the individual American dream:

> We hold these truths to be self-evident, that all men are created equal, that they are endowed by their Creator with certain unalienable rights, that among these are Life, Liberty, and the pursuit of Happiness. That to secure these rights, Governments are instituted among Men, deriving their just powers from the consent of the governed.

Benjamin Franklin not only helped establish the foundation for the individual American dream but also was a model, a living example, of how to achieve the American dream. Born one of seventeen children, Franklin completed only two years of education by age ten. By age twenty-two, however, he had opened his first printing office. Through his curiosity, love of learning, and hard work, he would become a brilliant statesman, printer, scientist, inventor, and diplomat. But in his role as author, Franklin shared his views on how to achieve the American dream. In his famous *Poor Richard's Almanack*, Franklin dispensed such pearls of wisdom as this:

In short, the way to wealth, if you desire it, is as plain as the way to market. It depends chiefly on two words, industry and frugality; that is, waste neither time nor money, but make the best use of both. Without industry and frugality nothing will do, and with them everything. He that gets all he can honestly and saves all he gets (necessary expenses excepted), will certainly become rich.

Franklin's notion that the only true way to wealth was through hard work became the soul of the "American dream," which naturally fed the idea that each person has the same opportunity to achieve success.

As the colonies cemented their right to personal pursuits and powers, some explorers headed west to live the dream. The legendary Daniel Boone was the epitome of an adventuresome woodsman, particularly after his bold experiences were published in 1784 in *Daniel Boone: His Own Story*. Known for settling Kentucky and surviving both on his wits and off the land, Boone was a lieutenant colonel in the Revolutionary War and a representative elected to the Virginia General Assembly. Boone's life was the perfect example of living the American dream, as the man made his own way across unexplored land and helped build a new nation. In fact, Boone became a symbol of the future "manifest destiny," a term made popular in the 1840s to describe the territorial expansion of the United States.

On the surface, Daniel Boone and Walt Whitman appear dissimilar, one a beloved national hero, the other a beloved national poet. Though Whitman was born in 1819, the year before Boone died, Boone's free spirit and passion for America echoes in Whitman's work. Whitman writes in the preface to the 1855 edition of *Leaves of Grass*,

> The United States themselves are essentially the greatest poem.... Here are the roughs and the beards and space and ruggedness and nonchalance that the soul loves.... One sees it must indeed own the riches of the summer and winter, and need never be bankrupt while corn grows from the ground or the orchards drop apples or the bays contain fish or men beget children upon women.

He goes on to say that as a poet, "his spirit responds to his country's spirit," but although "he incarnates its geography and natural life and rivers and lakes," ordinary people like "hunters, woodmen, early risers, cultivators of gardens and orchards and fields" acknowledge nature's power just as well. Whitman respects and honors men and women like Boone as shown in one of the last lines of his preface, "An individual is as superb as a nation when he has the qualities which make a superb nation."

Robert Frost, like Whitman, is one of America's most revered poets, known for celebrating nature and humanity in an ordinary fashion. Frost's signature, colloquial tone characterizes the quintessential language of the American dream: Through his poetry, the common man offers his simple yet profound view of the world. In 1942, Frost wrote "The Gift Outright," a poem that echoes Whitman's idea that the "United States themselves are essentially the greatest poem." "The Gift Outright" not only recognizes the beginning of America's history, but also acknowledges "our" growing relationship to America. The first three lines, "The land was ours before we were the land's. / She was our land more than a hundred years / Before we were her people," emphasize that the American dream began a century before "we" officially became Americans. We began to claim the land in the Virginia and Plymouth colonies, growing settlements, villages, and communities. But because we still lived under English rule and were "still colonials," we existed in a limbo world, not quite "unpossessed by," "possessed by," or even possessing the land; the land was not ours until we stopped "withholding from our land of living." We "found salvation in surrender[ing]" to the land, which unfortunately meant fighting, for our "deed of gift" required many "deeds of war." We charged to our manifest destiny, "to the land vaguely realizing westward," a land untouched, "unenhanced." With the last line, Frost muses at the cost of the birth of the American dream: Though we would finally possess the land from coast to coast, she would not be "storied," made artful, or improved. In a sense, our "salvation" would be born from her "surrender."

Emma Lazarus's sonnet, "The New Colossus," embraces those who grew the nation. In 1883, Lazarus donated "The New Colossus" to a fundraising auction for the Statue of Liberty's pedestal. Like Boone's autobiography and Whitman's poetic epic, Lazarus's poem symbolized the strength, promise, and beauty of America, in addition to the people responsible for growing the new nation. The Statue of Liberty speaks and "Glows world-wide welcome" to those fulfilling their dreams by reaching American shores. "Give me your tired, your poor, /

Your huddled masses yearning to breathe free," she says to "ancient lands." Named "Mother of Exiles," she offers a new chance for those immigrants who seek liberty, those who appreciate the boundlessness of a new land. Emma Lazarus's words are etched onto a plaque mounted in the base of the Statue of Liberty, commemorating the place where dreams simultaneously came true and were shattered. For some newcomers to America, the quintessential American dream would never be within reach, but Lazarus's sonnet would forever offer hope.

One American Dream Under God

In both the Mayflower Compact and the Declaration of Independence, the American dream is determined by God. Specifically, the signers of both documents sheltered the individual and communal rights of citizens, "with a firm reliance on the protection of divine Providence" and "by the grace of God." In other words, only God's will could alter the pact, because no person had more power than God. Those of the Plymouth Plantation had "undertaken" their journey "for the Glory of God and advancement of the Christian faith," and this commitment would continue to appear throughout the rhetoric of the American dream.

In 1630, at age eighteen, Puritan Anne Bradstreet sailed for the New World with her family. At first, Bradstreet was taken aback by the customs of the New World, but she saw the differences as "the way of God," as she would tell her children years later. Though books were rare and female authors rarer still, Bradstreet recorded her feelings about this godly "New England" in poetry and was the first American woman to have her works published. "A Dialogue Between Old England and New, Concerning their Present Troubles, Anno 1642" extols the virtues of "New England" as compared to "Old"; "New England" tells "Old" that she will soon become as worthy as her young daughter, because "the day of [her] redemption's nigh / The scales shall fall from [her] long-blinded eyes / And Him [she] shall adore who now despise." Old England has lost her way with God and country, and New England, as her virtuous daughter, will heal her because, of course, New England is rich in spirituality. New England promises, "So shall thy happy Nation ever flourish, / When truth and righteousness they thus shall nourish." Bradstreet instructs that righteousness is the key to salvation.

Cotton Mather, as a third-generation Puritan minister, certainly adhered to that belief. Mather published over 450 books and pamphlets, with which he influenced the new nation's morality. With the idea that people were drifting away from their faith, Mather called for a return to the theological roots of Puritanism and used the language of the Bible to persuade his readership. To achieve the ultimate dream of meeting God, Mather suggests life on Earth must be lived in a righteous way in his text, *What Must I Do to Be Saved?*: "Briefly, You must Deny all Ungodliness and Worldly Lusts and Live godily and soberly and righteously in the World. This is that Holiness without which no man shall see the Lord." The American dream was earthly preparation for the hereafter.

Phyllis Wheatley looked to the same spiritual guide. Wheatley was brought to America from Africa as a slave in 1761. As a house servant, she was given her name, as well as lessons in reading, writing, astronomy, geography, history, and Latin. Incredibly, at the age of thirteen, she wrote verse, and in 1773, her book *Poems on Various Subjects, Religious and Moral* was published—the first book published by an African American. Wheatley took her inspiration from the Bible and felt blessed to be brought into the Christian fold from pagan beginnings. Her poem, "On Being Brought from Africa to America," clearly illustrates this gratitude in the opening lines: "'Twas mercy brought me from my Pagan land, / Taught my benighted soul to understand / That there's a God, that there's a Saviour too." Wheatley, like Bradstreet and Mather, thought earthly virtue and goodness could lead her into "endless life and bliss," as demonstrated in this excerpt from her poem, "On Virtue":

> Attend me, Virtue, thro' my youthful years!
> O leave me not to the false joys of time!
> But guide my steps to endless life and bliss.
> Greatness, or Goodness, say what I shall call
> thee.

Wheatley believed that life in America had been her first step heavenward.

Nathaniel Hawthorne, descendant of Puritan settlers, wrote the short story "Young Goodman Brown" in 1835 to challenge the old religious ways. Haunted, in a sense, by his ancestors' religious tenets, Hawthorne uses the story to question the Puritans' strict moral code and show how believing in the sinfulness of humanity creates distrust. In the woods, confronted by a devil figure and townsfolk turned evil, Goodman Brown realizes that even good, respected people can become sinful, and he subsequently loses his faith in others:

> Had Goodman Brown fallen asleep in the forest and only dreamed a wild dream of a witch-meeting? Be it so if you will; but alas! It was a dream of evil omen for young Goodman Brown. A stern, sad, darkly meditative, a distrustful, if not a desperate man did he become from the night of that fearful dream.

In the end, Goodman Brown obviously dies miserable. New England's righteousness, as in Bradstreet's poem, is not his salvation. In showing that one man's virtue is another man's sin, Hawthorne demonstrates that perhaps religion does not always direct what is right and wrong; thus, how can one live "by the grace of God" or rely on the "protection of divine Providence"? At the same time, man cannot live suspicious of others or devoid of faith; if so, he will lead an empty, unproductive life, in essence, the anti-American dream.

In 1892, nearly 120 years after the Declaration of Independence was signed, Francis Bellamy was commissioned by *The Youth's Companion* magazine, circulated to schools nationwide, to write a patriotic saying for students to recite on Columbus Day. At first, this "Pledge of Allegiance to the Flag" did not contain religious reference, but simply reflected nationalism: "I pledge allegiance to my Flag and the Republic for which it stands—one nation indivisible—with liberty and justice for all." However, decades later, in 1954, President Dwight D. Eisenhower signed off on an amendment adding the words, "under God," to "reaffir[m] the transcendence of religious faith in America's heritage and future.... [and] strengthen those spiritual weapons which forever will be our country's most powerful resource in peace and war."

In 1995, Tim LaHaye and Jerry B. Jenkins launched the first of a series of books echoing not only the notion to "reaffirm faith in America's heritage and future," but also the idea that humanity should be one "under God." *Left Behind: A Novel of the Earth's Last Days* plays into evangelical beliefs as a story about the Rapture of the Saints, when those who are faithful to Jesus are taken to Heaven. At the same time, as punishment for their non-belief, sinners remain on Earth, essentially "left behind." The response to the "Left Behind"

Title page book illustration for Ragged Dick, *written by Horatio Alger, Jr* © Corbis

series was overwhelming; the books have sold more than 50 million copies and have inspired spin-offs into different genres, including graphic novels, music albums, nonfiction, and several other fiction series. Sales fairly skyrocketed after the World Trade Center attacks on September 11, 2001, even among more secular Americans. "Apocalypse Now," an article by Nancy Gibbs in a *Time* magazine devoted to "The Bible and the Apocalypse," provides the results of a Time/CNN poll: "more than one-third of Americans say they are paying more attention now to how the news might relate to the end of the world, and have talked about what the Bible has to say on the subject. Fully 59 percent say they believe the events in Revelation are going to come true."

Interestingly, the "Left Behind" series was not the first spiritual bestseller to affect American society at large. In 1662, Michael Wigglesworth, Puritan minister, wrote America's first bestseller, *The Day of Doom*, which circulated nearly two thousand copies in its first year of publication. Like the "Left Behind" series, this long poem compelled readers to embrace religion by pointing out the dire consequences of their neglect. In stanzas 1–25, sinners are awakened from sleeping off a night of "sloth," "song," and "cups" by the "son of God" who has come to judge them. They run and hide in fear but cannot escape the "Judge's" wrath. His angels scour the land, looking for the sinners. The faithful stand by Christ's side, "in long white Robes yclad [*sic*], / Their countenance full of pleasance, / appearing wondrous glad." But the sinners have a different fate in store:

> Ye sinful wights, and cursed sprights,
>   that work Iniquity,
> Depart together from me for ever
>   to endless Misery;
> Your portion take in yonder Lake,
>   where Fire and Brimstone flameth:
> Suffer the smart, which your desert
>   as it's due wages claimeth.

The sinners are forever doomed to hell and "flames of Burning Fire," not "to be released, or to be eased, not after years, but Never." This poem was recited doctrine for over 200 years, essentially a guide to living on Earth and reaching the hereafter. Wigglesworth, like LaHaye, was attempting to unite his readers by prophecy and to illustrate the penalty for their religious indifference. The American dream was, in a way, simply preparation for another "new world."

The Iconic American Dream

Like the "Pledge of Allegiance," the "Star-Spangled Banner" was written innocuously, without the intent of becoming a national lyric. In 1814, Francis Scott Key wrote the poem after watching the British attack Fort McHenry during the Battle of Baltimore. Originally called "The Defence of Fort McHenry," the poem was published, circulated, and performed widely; in 1916, President Wilson even ordered the song be played during formal military events. The first stanza of the poem became the national anthem in 1931, and still stands as a monument to the nation's patriotism and is used to commemorate sporting, military, and other public occasions.

The "Star-Spangled Banner" represents pride, nationalism, and the idea that all Americans are united through Key's unique and moving experience. Laura Ingalls Wilder is as much an American icon as the national anthem, as her books are read by children all over the world and her experiences are vivid enough to be real. Wilder shaped the American dream with her first

book published in 1931, the same year the anthem became official. The novel, *Little House in the Big Woods*, began the eight-book autobiographical chronicle of Wilder's journey west in the late nineteenth century. Her adventures and tales of everyday life on the prairie show that young America relied on the gumption, commitment, and tenacity of families and communities, of individual dreams coming together for common goals: settlement and survival. Wilder exemplifies the free-spirited, hard-working pioneer and has become a role model for young girls, though she did have her bold, tomboyish tendencies, as shown in this scene when she meets Mr. Edwards in *Little House on the Prairie*:

> He was lean and tall and brown. He bowed to Ma and called her "Ma'am," politely. But he told Laura he was a wildcat from Tennessee. He wore tall boots and a ragged jumper, and a coonskin cap, and he could spit tobacco juice. He could hit anything he spit at, too. Laura tried and tried, but she could never spit so far or so well as Mr. Edwards could.

Another free-spirited representative of the American dream is Huckleberry Finn, protagonist of Mark Twain's classic, *Adventures of Huckleberry Finn*, published in 1884. Young Huck is Everyboy, or at least a boy every boy wants to be. Bold, reckless, and confined by civilized life, Huck escapes from his drunken father and, in the company of Jim, a runaway slave, heads down the Mississippi River to freedom. "We said there warn't no home like a raft, after all," Huck says. "Other places do seem so cramped up and smothery, but a raft don't. You feel mighty free and easy and comfortable on a raft." In contrast to Daniel Boone's purposeful trek into the wilderness, Huck's devil-may-care expedition offers another version of what the American dream looks like. Huck, unlike Boone, does not care to help build America, but instead seeks to break free of imposed boundaries. In addition, through Huck and Jim's escapades, Twain challenges American "civilization" with regard to slavery, portraying it as morally inferior.

As Mark Twain's contemporary, Horatio Alger also contributed to the iconic definition of the American dream, but with his narrative style rather than specific characters. Most of his 135 dime novels, written in the late nineteenth century, follow a rags-to-riches plot, essentially a formula for young male readers to achieve success in the form of a modest income and security;

with hard work, pluck, and compassion, the young men in the novels set themselves up with a solid future. This image of the self-made man combines the determination and courage of Daniel Boone with the energy and daring of Huck Finn and presents a man willing to chisel his own space in the business world. But, in connection with the devout American dream of Bradstreet, Wheatley, and Mather, these men must also have goodliness and godliness to succeed. As Rychard Fink suggests in the introduction to a two-novel set, *Ragged Dick and Mark the Match Boy*,

> Alger's image of the self-made man demanded more than the chance to be just lucky or shrewd. A self-made man also had to be deserving of good fortune, to be the kind of man whom the Lord could favor. If he were not on His side, he could still succeed, but the flaw in his manhood would be there for all to see.

In *Ragged Dick* (1867), one of Alger's most popular novels, Richard Hunter, a poor orphaned bootblack from New York City, learns that honesty, integrity, hard work, and even luck, lead to personal triumph when he comes to the aid of those more fortunate than himself. At first, Dick doubts he will succeed, but his friend Frank assures him, through a rags-to-riches story about wealthy businessman Mr. A. T. Stewart who changed his direction, that his dream can be achieved:

> When he first came to New York as a young man he was a teacher, and teachers are not generally very rich. At last he went into business, starting in a small way, and worked his way up by degrees. But there was one thing he determined in the beginning; that he would be strictly honorable in all his dealings, and never overreach any one for the sake of making money. If there was a chance for him, Dick, there is a chance for you.

Alger's rags-to-riches stories mark a turning point as the definition of the American dream began to expand. As America was parceled, claimed, and legalized into the vast United States, man could no longer find his freedom in the woods or on rafts. Resources belonged to someone, and those resources were being used to develop a new nation. With industrialization and mass transportation came cities, and to cities people flocked for new opportunities. Thornton Wilder's *Our Town* (1938) also indicates this turning point. Set between 1899 and 1913, the play emphasizes the need to value heritage and family, particularly in the face of industrialization, which brings with it social decline and personal separation. Grover's Corners appears to be the last of a certain kind of idyllic small town in America, and its isolated, protected world is becoming infiltrated by progress. The outside world, depicted by war, automobiles, and even baseball, offers the strong potential for tragedy. In the middle of act 1, the audience of the play interrogates the characters while the Stage Manager mediates. A "Man at Back of Auditorium" asks, "Is there no one in town aware of social injustice and industrial inequality?" His question, plus references throughout the play to the town's forefathers and history, shows that this town remains a romantic symbol; in reflecting the ideals of the seventeenth century, Grover's Corners demonstrates how community is truly the center of life and how love and appreciation make people rich. In addition, at the end of act 1, when Rebecca mentions a friend's letter to George, she describes Jane Crofut's ultimate address as in "the Universe; the Mind of God." The minister who sent the letter represents the church-going people of Grover's Corners as a whole, and like Wheatley and Bradstreet, sees the town in relation to a higher power. *Our Town*, in this way, serves as a testament to a place that once existed, and at the same time, a dream of what might exist if people stopped acting solely for personal gain and material wealth.

Unlike Thornton Wilder, Arthur Miller turned the decay of the American dream into a national emblem through two of his plays, *The Crucible* and *Death of a Salesman*. Published in 1953, *The Crucible* provides a commentary on the 1950s-era McCarthy hearings, veiled by the metaphorical retelling of the famous Salem witch trials in Massachusetts. Much like the Salem trials, the modern-day Senator Joe McCarthy held hearings through the House Un-American Committee (HUAC) to uncover suspected Communists. This unjustified prosecution was completely against the American ideals of democracy, or equality for all. Based on hearsay and neighbors bearing false witness against neighbors, testimonies stripped the American dream from those suspected as Communists as their basic rights were taken away; specifically, those accused were blacklisted and could no longer make a decent living because their reputations lie in ruin. Arthur Miller himself was called to testify in front of the HUAC. Beforehand, he made an agreement with the committee, which agreed to not pressure him to reveal names. However, once Arthur Miller appeared on the stand, he was forced to relinquish names of suspected Communists. But Miller refused, much like John Proctor in the *Crucible*. Proctor finally concedes defeat and confesses to witchcraft but spares others of his fate: "I speak my own sins; I cannot judge another. Crying out, with hatred: I have no tongue for it." For his refusal to implicate others, Miller was found guilty of contempt, fined, sentenced to prison, blacklisted, and denied a U.S. passport. The McCarthy hearings show how fragile the American dream truly is and how quickly our "unalienable rights" can be forcibly removed by a government gone awry.

Through his portrayal of Willy Loman in the play, *Death of a Salesman*, written in 1949, Miller makes a statement about the social and economic corruption of morality, exposing the reality of capitalism and free enterprise. America is not the land of easy opportunity, and affability does not automatically determine social position. The play focuses on Willy Loman, a hopeless, struggling salesman, who still sees the American dream within easy reach. Willy has worked all his life to become a respected, successful businessman, but his quest for popularity has only led him to failure, proving an interesting comparison to the lives of Alger's various protagonists. Despite his shortcomings, Willy still blindly believes in the rags-to-riches notion and tells his sons they can achieve everything he did not. But Happy and Biff will share their father's fate, as they wish for opportunity to drop into their laps instead of making their futures happen. "All I can do now is wait for the merchandise manager to die," Happy says with regard to his prospects, while Biff looks for money, with no strings attached, to bankroll his dream: "If I could get ten thousand or even seven or eight thousand dollars I could buy a beautiful ranch." Through the Loman family, Miller also predicts the effect consumerism and technological inventions will have in the 1950s, offering commentary on how the more modern America becomes, the more obsolete and expendable humanity becomes. As a traveling salesman, Willy belongs to a breed of men slowly falling from existence.

Herman Melville, in "Bartleby the Scrivener" (1853), also positions his protagonist as a man gradually losing his identity because of his occu-pation. Bartleby has become the example of what might happen when a person does not rise against America's capitalist society or does not strive for individuality. Bartleby works in a law office on Wall Street copying legal documents. He is a human copier, his spirit deadened by repetitive work on the white collar assembly line. He practically lives at his desk, where he keeps "a tin basin, with soap and a ragged towel; in a newspaper a few crumbs of gingernuts and a morsel of cheese." The narrator, Bartleby's boss, upon realizing Bartleby resides in the office, sympathizes; "His poverty is great," he muses about his employee, "but his solitude, how horrible!" Melville also emphasizes Bartleby's meager existence by setting the story on Wall Street, a canyon of buildings where no sun can reach; for example, the narrator's office has a view of "a lofty brick wall, black by age and everlasting shade." Despite these conditions, however, Bartleby resists in his own passive fashion, and each time the narrator asks him to do something, Bartleby refuses quietly by saying, "I would prefer not to." The narrator cannot understand this mild rebellion, but is intrigued, for they have "the bond of common humanity" as "the sons of Adam." When Bartleby decides he will no longer copy documents, the narrator fires him, but Bartleby will not leave. In time, the narrator, irritated by Bartleby's presence, decides if Bartleby will not "quit" him, then he must "quit" Bartleby. "Bartleby the Scrivener" is a modern story about alienation from the outside world as well as from the person within. Nature cannot exist in a world where the horizon is made of "dead brick walls." Both the narrator, a successful businessman, and Bartleby are victims of progress and cannot connect with each other.

Barred From the American Dream

The tragic ruin of Bartleby and Willy Loman notwithstanding, they were not physically excluded from pursuing the American dream. But since the beginning of the nation, certain groups have been denied the right to life, liberty, and the pursuit of happiness, regardless of laws demanding the contrary. In the 1850s, Isaac Stevens, governor and commissioner of Indian Affairs of the Washington territory, worked hard to encourage Native Americans, through treaty and violence, to relinquish their lands to the federal government. In 1854, he asked for a large tract of land in the Washington territory and promised to relocate the people to a reservation. Chief

Seattle, head of the Suquamish and Duwamish tribes and a converted Catholic, had previously compromised with the "white man" over property and takes Stevens's offer, but not before expressing his disappointment, disapproval, and disgust. Chief Seattle addresses the proposal with an understatement:

> The great, and I presume also good, white chief sends us word that he wants to buy our lands but is willing to allow us to reserve enough to live on comfortably. This indeed appears generous, for the red man no longer has rights that he need respect, and the offer may be wise, also, for we are no longer in need of a great country.

The "red man" neither had "rights" nor "need" for space because the members of their race had been run off or killed by the white man. Chief Seattle said,

> The Indian's night promises to be dark. No bright star hovers above the horizon. Sad-voiced winds moan in the distance. Some grim Nemesis of our race is on the red man's trail, and wherever he goes he will still hear the sure approaching footsteps of the fell destroyer and prepare to meet his doom, as does the wounded doe that hears the approaching footsteps of the hunter. A few more moons, a few more winters, and not one of all the mighty hosts that once filled this broad land or that now roam in fragmentary bands through these vast solitudes will remain to weep over the tombs of a people once as powerful and as hopeful as your own.

The speech, translated years later in the October 29, 1887, edition of the *Seattle Sunday Star*, keenly illustrates that the Native Americans were not treated as Americans; Chief Seattle used religious rhetoric to emphasize that point:

> Your God seems to us to be partial. He came to the white man. We never saw Him; never even heard His voice; He gave the white man laws but He had no word for His red children whose teeming millions filled this vast continent as the stars fill the firmament.

Because the Native Americans had their own religious belief system, they could not possibly partake of anything in the "great country." They were not godly or goodly, in thinking back to the Puritanical faith of Wheatley, Mather, and Bradstreet, particularly because they "could never remember nor comprehend it." Thus, the Native American dream of liberty, "gather[ed] around them like a dense fog floating inward from a midnight sea."

A decade later, in November 1863, the nation continued to establish itself "under God" as President Abraham Lincoln, in the "Gettysburg Address," reaffirmed the government's commitment to the idea that "all men are created equal." In a speech dedicating the Soldiers' National Cemetery in Gettysburg, Pennsylvania, where the Union army had won the Battle of Gettysburg, Lincoln declared that this nation "under God, shall have a new birth of freedom—and that government of the people, by the people, for the people, shall not perish from the earth." Lincoln does not directly use the word slavery in his proclamation or even mention the South, but the references to the Declaration directly address anti-slavery proponents who adopted the Declaration of Independence as evidence to support their argument, though more than likely slaves had not been considered part of "all men" when the document was originally written.

Though the Emancipation Proclamation freeing slaves went into full effect in early 1863 and the "Gettysburg Address" underscored the individual right to American liberty, African Americans would fight for civil rights and equality for more than a century. In 1932, Langston Hughes wrote "I, Too," a poem in which the speaker rejects socially imposed restrictions to develop and declare his worth, not to mention claim his entitlement to an American identity: "I, too, sing America." At first, the speaker is relegated to the kitchen "when company comes." He cannot be seen or heard; he cannot exist. But the speaker resists invisibility by "eat[ing] well" and "grow[ing] strong." In the near future—tomorrow—he will be confident enough in himself to "be at the table / When company comes"; he will be seen as a human being and no one will "dare" tell him to "Eat in the kitchen." In the near future, others will recognize him for the "beautiful" person he is and will regret the way they treated him. He, like everyone else, is part of America.

Elizabeth Cady Stanton, suffragette and spokesperson for the women's movement in the middle of the nineteenth century, addressed the New York State Legislature in 1860. She, along with other members of the movement, made abolition a priority as they actively campaigned for women's rights. However, during this particular speech, Stanton used the "black man's [newly won] right to suffrage" to shine light on women's limitation in that regard. "Certain rights and immunities, such and such privileges are to be secured to white male citizens," Stanton put forth this argument:

> What have women and Negroes to do with rights? What know they of government, war, or glory? The prejudice against color, of which we hear so much, is no stronger than that against sex. It is produced by the same cause, and manifested very much in the same way.

Stanton goes on to claim that both "Negroes" and women "were intended to be in subjection to the white Saxon man," yet with the black man given the right to vote, "it is evident that the prejudice against sex is more deeply rooted and more unreasonably maintained than that against color." Stanton calls for society to allow women to take care of themselves and declares, "We do not ask man to represent us." Stanton continued for decades to push for women's suffrage, but women did not receive the vote until 1920.

In 1911, Charlotte Perkins Gilman published "Women Do Not Want It," a poem included in the collection *Suffrage Songs and Verses*, to draw attention to women's own confinement:

> Did we ask for veils and harems in the Oriental races?
> Did we beseech to be "unclean," shut out of sacred places?
> Did we beg for scolding bridles and ducking stools to come?
> And clamour for the beating stick no thicker than your thumb?
> Did we ask to be forbidden from all the trades that pay?
> Did we claim the lower wages for a man's full work today?
> Have we petitioned for the laws wherein our shame is shown:
> That not a woman's child—nor her own body—is her own?
> What women want has never been a strongly acting cause,
> When woman has been wronged by man in churches, customs, laws;
> Why should he find this preference so largely in his way,
> When he himself admits the right of what we ask today?

Though Gilman fought for suffrage for American women, she uses the plight of women across the world to illustrate her point. To her, women are extremely limited, living behind veils, inside harems, outside sanctuary. With the "ducking stool," she references women being dunked in water to determine if they were witches, and with the "beating stick," she draws

attention to those women trapped in situations of domestic abuse. She attacks women's unfair salaries, challenges the limitation of menial, dead-end jobs, and even addresses abortion in asking if a woman's body is not "her own." Women, Gilman announces, have rights that have been ignored or dismissed—wronged.

Native Americans, African Americans, and women represent only part of a large, multicultural, multiracial community that fought individually and collectively to claim their civil liberties. Immigrants from all over the world landed on American shores in search of better lives. Unfortunately, although the Statue of Liberty offered her "world-wide welcome," newcomers to the United States would often find prejudice, fear, and hatred waiting for them.

In 1882, for example, Congress passed the Chinese Exclusion Act, restricting immigration and naturalization for the next sixty years. The strong Chinese work ethic fueled jealousy and subsequently inspired anti-Chinese sentiment— a "Yellow Peril" that virtually threatened American economy. For the same reason, the Tydings-McDuffie Act passed in 1935, limiting the annual number of Filipino immigrants to fifty. Eight years later, in 1943, Filipino poet Carlos Bulosan describes his difficult journey from the Philippines to America in his book, *America is in the Heart*. Though classified as an autobiography, Bulosan's novel combines his first-hand experiences with stories he was told, providing a history recounted more from the voices of the Filipino American community than from his own. A poor boy in his homeland, Bulosan becomes a migrant worker in the United States with virtually no rights; stereotyped as criminals or animals, Filipinos were often exploited by employers and exposed to violent manifestations of racism and prejudice, as shown when he tries to get a job and is "beaten upon several occasions by restaurant and hotel proprietors." Bulosan opens chapter 29 by offhandedly explaining the situation: "It was now the year of the great hatred: the lives of Filipinos were cheaper than dogs. They were forcibly shoved off the streets when they showed resistance." Through hard-fought battles for daily survival, Bulosan champions reform for Filipino Americans and holds tight to his brother Macario's inspiring words about the American dream, words that remind a reader of Walt Whitman and Langston Hughes:

New York Giants celebrate after Bobby Thomson hits a three run homer in the 1951 playoffs between the NY Giants and Brooklyn Dodgers © *Bettmann/Corbis*

America is the illiterate immigrant who is ashamed that the world of books and intellectual opportunities is closed to him. We are all that nameless foreigner, that homeless refugee, that hungry boy, that illiterate immigrant and that lynched black body. All of us, from the first Adams to the last Filipino, native born or alien, educated or illiterate—We are America! The old world is dying, but a new world is being born. It generates inspiration from the chaos that beats upon us all.

At the turn of the century, despite the fact that Irish immigrants were not physically distinct from America's majority-white society, Irish were also denied employment opportunities in major cities such as New York and Boston because of their heritage. This cold reception makes these sincere lyrics from Helen Selina's "Lament of the Irish Emigrant" (circa 1848), though written in sentimental folk style, highly ironic:

I'm biddin' you a long farewell,
   My Mary—kind and true!
But I'll not forget you, darling!
   In the land I'm goin' to;
They say there's bread and work for all,
   And the sun shines always there—
But I'll not forget old Ireland,
   Were it fifty times as fair!

In 1893, Stephen Crane self-published *Maggie, A Girl of the Streets*, a novel about the dark and hopeless existence for those Irish immigrants who fled the potato famine and ended up in the Bowery district of New York. The book was condemned in its time, perhaps for its realistic portrayal. The second section of the novel describes the Bowery conditions without censor:

A wind of early autumn raised yellow dust from cobbles and swirled it against a hundred windows. Long streamers of garments fluttered from fire-escapes. In all unhandy places there were buckets, brooms, rags, and bottles. In the street infants played or fought with other infants or sat stupidly in the way of vehicles. Formidable women, with uncombed hair and disordered dress, gossiped while leaning on railings, or screamed in frantic quarrels. Withered persons, in curious postures of submission to something, sat smoking pipes in obscure corners. . . . The building quivered and creaked from the weight of humanity stamping about in its bowels.

Crane's story, combining the style of a mock epic with naturalism, is often compared to Thomas Hardy's *Tess of the D'Urbervilles* (1891); saintly Maggie, whose name was a socially accepted synonym for Irish prostitute, desperately tries to care for her younger siblings when her parents take to drinking, but her mother, violently and emotionally abusive, casts her out on the streets. In a world of poverty, sweatshops, and over a million people crowded into tenements, Maggie falls into prostitution, accepting the occupation that her name implies to survive. In the end, Crane keeps her death murky, either murder or suicide. The community calls the death "an affliction" and blames Maggie for being sinful, a "disobed'ent chile."

But even people whose families had settled in America for generations could not escape racial and/or cultural bias. During World War II, Japanese Americans were torn from their homes and jobs and placed in internment camps across the United States. John Okada's *No-No Boy* (1978), tells the story of American-born Ichiro who refused to serve in the U.S. Army and was placed in a camp for two years. The story does not focus on his internment but rather on his personal struggle to put his life back together following his release. Ichiro must deal with his status as a no-no boy, those young Japanese American men who answered no to two questions: "Are you willing to serve in the armed forces of the United States on combat duty wherever ordered?" and

Will you swear unqualified allegiance to the United States of America and faithfully defend the United States from any or all attack by foreign or domestic forces, and forswear any form of allegiance or obedience to the Japanese emperor, to any other foreign government, power or organization?

Ichiro cannot come to terms with his heritage and his birthright and finds himself trapped between two worlds, both a part of him: "But it is not enough to be American only in the eyes of

the law and it is not enough to be only half an American and know it is an empty half. . . . I wish with all my heart that I were Japanese or that I were American." Unfortunately, Ichiro is forced to choose in order to lead a normal life.

Revolutionizing the American Dream

In some ways, Ichiro practiced what Henry David Thoreau preached in his essay, "Civil Disobedience" (1849). "Under a government which imprisons unjustly," Thoreau states,

the true place for a just man is also a prison. . . . It is there that the fugitive slave, and the Mexican prisoner on parole, and the Indian come to plead the wrongs of his race should find them; on that separate, but more free and honorable, ground, where the State places those who are not *with* her, but against her.

Thoreau also suggests that "action from principle, the perception and performance of right, changes things and relations; it is essentially revolutionary." "Civil Disobedience" became the touchstone for future efforts of passive resistance, advocating for people to let their conscience, and not the government, dictate their actions. Thoreau saw the American government as doing more harm than good and calls for Americans to be "men first, and subjects afterward." He also believed that "the character inherent in the American people has done all that has been accomplished; and it would have done somewhat more, if the government had not sometimes got in its way." Thoreau wanted a better government, one run by "just men" acting on their "just ideals"; to him, that was the ultimate dream.

Over one hundred years later, Martin Luther King Jr. employed Thoreau's rhetorical, social, and political strategies to gain momentum and attention for the civil rights movement. In 1963, on his quest for racial equality, King and his followers protested in Birmingham, Alabama, where local officials attacked the peaceful marchers. King was arrested, but he managed to organize a march to be held in Washington, D.C., on August 28. On the steps of the Lincoln Memorial, King gave the infamous "I Have a Dream" speech, which galvanized even more supporters and led to the Civil Rights Act, passed in 1964. King, as Thoreau suggests of his readers, calls his audience to action with his "just" ideology. He considers the government defaulting on their "sacred obligation" to allow all Americans the equal pursuit of life, liberty, and the pursuit of happiness. He encourages people to act, to join forces with each other, to rise up for what they believe in:

> We must forever conduct our struggle on the high plane of dignity and discipline. We must not allow our creative protest to degenerate into physical violence. Again and again we must rise to the majestic heights of meeting physical force with soul force. The marvelous new militancy which has engulfed the Negro community must not lead us to distrust of all white people, for many of our white brothers, as evidenced by their presence here today, have come to realize that their destiny is tied up with our destiny and their freedom is inextricably bound to our freedom. We cannot walk alone.

King's dream is a truly unified nation "under God"; he says,

> And when this happens, when we allow freedom to ring, when we let it ring from every village and every hamlet, from every state and every city, we will be able to speed up that day when all of God's children, black men and white men, Jews and Gentiles, Protestants and Catholics, will be able to join hands and sing in the words of the old Negro spiritual, "Free at last! Free at last! Thank God Almighty, we are free at last!"

The same year King made the speech that mobilized a movement to succeed, Betty Friedan rallied women with *The Feminine Mystique*. The book challenged social constructs by attacking women's prescribed roles and exposing women's inner conflicts and true desires. She introduces the book with the central issue:

> The problem lay buried, unspoken, for many years in the minds of American women. It was a strange stirring, a sense of dissatisfaction, a yearning that women suffered in the middle of the twentieth century in the United States. . . . [S]he was afraid to ask even of herself the silent question—"Is this all?"

The Feminine Mystique sparked the second wave of feminism and called for a new feminine belief system: one in which women did not have to define themselves by their husbands, home, and children. Friedan encouraged women to be independent, emotionally and financially. She ends the book with a powerful, compelling question of her reader: "Who knows what women can be when they are finally free to become themselves?"

Freidan's female empowerment reveals itself in a novel that created waves in 1973: *Fear of Flying*. Erica Jong's first novel was considered revolutionary, even shocking, as heroine Isadora Wing owns and delights in her independence and sexuality. Freethinking and free-spirited, Isadora searches for creative freedom, personal validation, and life's answers through one erotic affair after another. After decades of women fighting to acknowledge their inner selves and genuine aspirations, Jong's book provided a symbolic shedding of social trappings, traditions, and taboos. At fourteen, when Isadora visits a psychiatrist, she thinks to herself, "I don't want to be a woman. Because it's too confusing. Because Shaw says you can't be a woman and an artist. Having babies uses you up, he says. And I want to be an artist. That's all I ever wanted." As an adult, she still wrestles with her identity as a woman and resists the expected mold:

> I was already a hostage. The hostage of my fantasies. The hostage of my fears. The hostage of my false definitions. What did it mean to be a woman, anyway? . . . If it meant seething resentment and giving lectures on the joys of childbearing, then I didn't want it. Far better to be an intellectual nun than that.

Through Isadora, Jong was providing a physical manifestation of Friedan's feminist doctrine.

Lucille Clifton's poem, "My Dream About Being White" (1987), celebrates pride in both a female and an African American identity, showing the power gained from the efforts of bold activists in the decades following King and Friedan.

Though the speaker of the poem imagines a white identity, a "perfect line of a nose," she ends up owning her true self, her true history. She does not see a "future" in "those clothes" belonging to a white past, to a white someone else; she is no longer inferior. She has the power to succeed, shown through the final image of her dancing, without false, put-on whiteness. The speaker exemplifies the American dream of acceptance, both by self and society. Her "dream" is more than "about being white"; it is about finally being seen for who she is.

The High Cost of the American Dream

But the American dream, whether it meant a battle for land, freedom, identity, or human rights, came at a high price, often demanding more than an individual, society, or the nation could sacrifice. In addition, the pursuit of the dream frequently led to moral, ethical, and socioeconomic corruption, all in the name of progress.

Many authors exposed this dark side, shining a light on the pitfalls and poisons of personal and professional evolution. Rebecca Harding Davis wrote "Life in the Iron-Mills" (1861), tackling the beasts of industrialization: poverty, labor abuse, and environmental pollution. Though Davis published the work anonymously, the short story in the *Atlantic Monthly* drew attention from important literary newsmakers such as Louisa May Alcott, Nathaniel Hawthorne, and Ralph Waldo Emerson because of its realistic naturalism. Through her fiction, Davis sympathizes with the exploited industrial workers at a metal foundry, but does not shy away from depicting them as they are. "Life in the Iron Mills" confronted its readers with its raw portrayal of mill life and shows the hopelessness and impossibility of ever rising above an impoverished existence, both in body and soul. Davis writes,

> I look on the slow stream of human life creeping past, night and morning, to the great mills. Masses of men, with dull, besotted faces bent to the ground, sharpened here and there by pain or cunning; skin and muscle and flesh begrimed with smoke and ashes; stooping all night over boiling cauldrons of metal, laired by day in dens of drunkenness and infamy; breathing from infancy to death an air saturated with fog and grease and soot, vileness for soul and body. What do you make of a case like that . . . ?

In the "Iron-Mills," Davis creates a world where "money has spoken," where the cost of America's growth is a "reality of soul-starvation, of living death, that meets you every day under the besotted faces on the street."

In 1897, Edwin Arlington Robinson, a poet with an impoverished background, wrote "Richard Cory," a poem from the point of view of one of the "people on the pavement." The object of their frequent attention is "gentleman" Richard Cory, "clean favored and imperially slim." At first, the speaker's admiration for Cory is unmistakable: "And he was always quietly arrayed, / And he was always human when he talked; / But still he fluttered pulses when he said / 'Good-morning,' and he glittered when he walked." The speaker believes Cory's life is "richer than a king" as he was "schooled in every grace"; in fact, the speaker sees Cory as everything he, and the others on the street, wish to be. But life for the impeccable Cory is not the happy fantasy they surmise, and the final verse of the poem shows that despite the speaker's less-than-opportune existence, he is better off than a "gentleman from sole to crown":

> So on we worked and waited for the light,
> And went without the meat, and cursed the
>   bread;
> And Richard Cory, one calm summer night,
> Went home and put a bullet through his head.

"Richard Cory" shows that prosperity demands something from everyone, and the American dream may not be as enticing or rewarding as promised, for any of society, from the "masses of men" to those "fine" and "clean favored."

Three decades later, John Dos Passos also comments on the rise and fall of the "Richard Cory"-type in his "U.S.A. Trilogy." In *The 42nd Parallel* (1930), *1919* (1932), and *The Big Money* (1936), Dos Passos employs newspaper clippings, biographical material, and autobiographical experiences to accurately portray contemporary American society, culture, and politics. Dos Passos criticizes the political and economic direction of the United States, and few of the characters—rich, poor, male, female, immigrant—manage to hold onto their ideals through World War I. All of the novels, but particularly *The Big Money*, represent the American dream as corrupt. Dos Passos uses stories about real American businessmen to frame the novel, including the biography of Samuel Insull, who worked for Thomas Edison as an assistant. Not long after Insull grew the company's reputation in electricity, he took on gas; "when politicians got in his way, he bought them, when laborleaders got in his way he bought them." Eventually, he controlled the light and power companies, "coalmines and tractioncompanies" and owned "a twelfth of the power output of America"; however, with the stock market crash, he crawled "on his knees to the bankers" and had no choice but to surrender his power. Insull fled to Canada, Europe, and Greece, but was extradited to the United States where he stood trial. Insull played to the jury's compassion with his Horatio Alger story and received a "not guilty" verdict. Though Insull does not kill himself like Cory, his track from apprentice to utilities mogul shows good intentions and young ambition leading to greed and unethical practices, which ultimately pave the way for Insull's financial ruin and court case. Insull is only one "character" among many in the trilogy who begins with the simple dream of success and ends up sacrificing everything he so carefully built. Most characters tragically end up dead.

In the 1930s, John Steinbeck also used his novels to comment on social and economic ills. With a resume of jobs ranging from laborer and seaman to newspaper reporter and bricklayer, he based his stories on first-hand experiences. One of his most popular books, *Of Mice and Men* (1937), tells the story of two itinerant ranch hands and their shattered dream of owning a small farm. Eager to become independent, George Milton and Lennie Small find work and start a nest egg, but when simple, strong Lennie is provoked into breaking the ranch foreman's arm and accidentally kills the ranch owner's daughter-in-law, their dream becomes impossible to reach. In the end, George shoots Lennie before he can fall into the hands of a posse bent on revenge. "Let's do it now," Lennie urges before he dies. "Let's get that place now." But for George and Lennie, as for many men and women affected by the Great Depression and the Dust Bowl, the fantasy of being your own boss and purchasing a piece of land was an impossible dream, and the socio-economic reality an unbeatable foe. The plains and prairies emptied as the drought continued for several years, and those with once prospering farms and secure employment jockeyed for pennies or even biscuits. The American dream, for a time, blew away in the dry, Midwest wind, leaving thousands of people jobless, homeless, and hopeless.

In the years following *Of Mice and Men*, the national economic outlook improved tremendously, but achieving the American dream still is not easy. In "Cannery Town in August," poet-activist Lorna Dee Cervantes, a Californian of Mexican andNative American descent, writes about exile in society and the workplace, and about how the American dream leaves women laborers like walking ghosts.

Published in 1981, this poem captures an intimate moment between speaker and cannery workers leaving for the night, a moment that probably occurs regularly, at the end of each day. The women are "bodyless uniforms," zombie-like as they "drift" down streets that are violently "moon-possessed." They do not speak in the "clamor" of the cannery; their voices are lost. These women "walk like a dream," but a dream of emptiness, disconnection, even death. Unlike Steinbeck, whose 1945 novel *Cannery Row* told the story of a worker community during the Great Depression, Cervantes joins these women in numbness—"dumbness"—but provides no other bond. These women need to be "palm[ed] back to living" from a job that has left them walking alone.

Joy Harjo captures the isolation and anesthetization of the Native American population in her short prose poem, "Autobiography," published in 1990 as part of *In Mad Love and War*. A member of the Creek, or Muscogree, nation, Harjo begins by connecting recent events to history: "We lived next door to the bootlegger, and were lucky. The bootlegger reigned. We were a stolen people in a stolen land. Oklahoma meant defeat. But the sacred lands have their own plans, seep through fingers of the alcohol spirit. Nothing can be forgotten, only left behind." In the sixteenth century, the Creek nation's agrarian populace spread across most of what are now the southeastern states. Ultimately, the Cherokee and European settlers pushed them west to Oklahoma, or "Indian Territory." This displacement and essentially "defeat" led people to let the "bootlegger reign" and alcohol rule their lives. Though alcohol was used to numb the pain, the "sacred lands" could not be "forgotten."

Harjo goes on to weave together past, present, and future, commenting on the state of dreams:

> Last week I saw the river where the hickory stood; this homeland doesn't predict a legacy of malls and hotels. Dreams aren't glass and steel but made from the hearts of the deer, the blazing eye of a circling panther. Translating them was to understand the death count from Alabama, the destruction of grandchildren, famine of stories. I didn't think I could stand it. My father couldn't. He searched out his death with the vengeance of a warrior who has been the hunted. It's in our blood.

In a world of progress and consumerism, Harjo holds on to the America of Walt Whitman, the "river," the "hickory," the "deer," and "panther." She defines her dream with nature, future generations, and tales to tell. Yet she identifies herself and her father, her people, as "the hunted." She, like her people, has paid for her future by sacrificing her innocence and childhood; she writes, "At five I was designated to string beads in kindergarten. At seven I knew how to play chicken and win. And at fourteen I was drinking." Yet Harjo ends the poem with promise, suggesting that she has begun to physically and spiritually recoup her losses:

Yesterday there was rain traveling east to home. A hummingbird spoke. She was a shining piece of invisible memory, inside the raw cortex of songs. I knew then this was the Muscogee season of forgiveness, time of new corn, the spiraling dance.

The marginalized and oft-ignored lower class of America is not always so fortunate to recover, spiritually, physically, or emotionally. In 2001, journalist Barbara Ehrenreich decided to investigate how the lower class makes ends meet by living as a low-paid, low-skilled worker. Ehrenreich, with $1,000 in seed money, a car, and her laptop computer, took a variety of jobs across the country over a two-year period, from waitressing in Florida and serving as a nursing home aide in Maine, to working as a Wal-Mart associate in Minnesota. *Nickel and Dimed: On (Not) Getting By in America* details her experiences; in the book, Ehrenreich comes to this conclusion:

> Something is wrong, very wrong, when a single person in good health, a person who in addition possesses a working car, can barely support herself by the sweat of her brow. You don't need a degree in economics to see that wages are too low and rents too high.

Through her personal study, Ehrenreich sees the futility of the American dream as her various co-workers desperately attempt to break through their social strata and leave the life of the "working poor" behind. But housing and transportation costs, medical bills, and the price of basic needs create obstacles that are often insurmountable. Though Ehrenreich still sees hope and a strong drive to succeed within this community, she fears a future uprising as people "are bound to tire of getting so little in return and to demand to be paid what they're worth. There'll be a lot of anger when that day comes, and strikes and disruption."

Redefining the American Dream

Exploring the origins, limits, promises, and worth of the American dream ultimately leads to a conversation about what problems the myth evokes, and about how that dialogue leads to change. Authors such as e. e. cummings, Edna St. Vincent Millay, Allen Ginsburg, and Sandra Cisneros, among others, make their readers question the quintessential image of America by showing history in a new context, offering emotional liberation from the trap of tradition, shining new light on both material resources and

consumerism, and providing new representations of what the American dream looks like.

In 1925, e. e. cummings wrote "next to of course god america i," a sonnet that uses the nation's pilgrim heritage to jumpstart a stream-of-consciousness speech to America, as witnessed in this excerpt:

> why talk of beauty what could be more beautiful than these heroic happy dead
> who rushed like lions to the roaring slaughter
> they did not stop to think they died instead
> then shall the voice of liberty be mute?
>
> He spoke. And drank rapidly a glass of water

The poem's lack of punctuation, purposeful line breaks, and fragmented language splinters the speaker's patriotic intentions and emphasizes the fact that the speaker is not really saying anything profound at all. Instead, he is merely regurgitating bits and pieces from various nationalistic lyrics, clichés, and famous quotations. Brian Docherty, in "e. e. cummings," suggests that "while anyone who dared to criticise any of these concepts would be labelled un-American and a commie subversive, [cummings believed] it is politicians like this who have muted the voice of liberty." The last line of the sonnet, set apart from the rest, shows the speaker downing "rapidly a glass of water," possibly trying to wash away the bad taste in his mouth, left from meaningless jibberish and erroneous images emphasizing glory and honor in war. Rather than "rush[ing] like lions to the roaring slaughter," cummings says that Americans should think about the message they are conveying; is America simply acting on impulse, out of some past custom or because of some ancient belief system? Does America know what it is fighting for and why? Cummings's satire, written after his experiences as an ambulance driver overseas during World War I, inspires an assessment of American participation in and motivation for war, not to mention a serious contemplation of what liberty means to a twentieth century nation.

Edna St. Vincent Millay also used satire in her poem, "Apostrophe to Man," published in 1934, to reflect on the possibility of a second world war. She also uses a sonnet to directly address her readers, this time the public at large, starting with the line, "Detestable race, continue to expunge yourself, die out." Unlike cummings, Millay does not mince words and unabashedly points to man's flaws and foibles

Sue Lyon in a scene from the film Lolita © *Corbis*

as the cause of his fetid future. Though not framed specifically for Americans, Millay certainly was active in social and political causes, advocating for labor rights and championing democracy. The sonnet does more than wag a finger at humanity; it blasts humanity. But the poem also directly aims its punch at the growing pains of America. Dos Passos's fictional trilogy comes to mind, with its images of crowded American cities, people encroaching on each other's territory, and "hopeful bodies of the young." Charley Anderson, in Dos Passos's *The Big Money*, builds airplanes, while Valentino and Margo Dowling get photographed and are "all but overcome" by life in the fast lane. Millay could be addressing American society, as it expunges itself with its furious pace and disconnection to each other. In the end, if humans continue to act as they are, they will expand far too much and "die out."

Poet Allen Ginsberg is also famous for his controversial rhetoric as part of the Beat Generation, a term introduced in 1948 by Jack Kerouac to describe an anti-conformist counterculture. His social and political commentary is immediately obvious in poems such as "America" and "Howl," both published in 1956. The first line of "America" is undeniably angry and defeated: "America I've given you all and now I'm nothing," while the first line of "Howl" rings with a bitter poignancy: "I saw the best minds of my generation destroyed by madness, starving hysterical naked." Ginsberg, through his poetry, acts as the voice of America and Americans, together and solitary.

In a 1996 interview, Ginsberg declared that "the national soul, the national spirit...has been violated by our government's actions. I think we, as a nation, need to apologize." Ginsberg also told the interviewer,

> [S]ince the government's going into a tailspin, morally and economically, with the elimination of the safety net for the poor in health, money and housing, the majority of people are restless and their restlessness isn't lucidly communicated through the government or media; but it is lucidly communicated through the poetry. Poets are presenting their restlessness, their sense of justice and injustice, their sense of beauty and their sense of environmental ugliness...government is manipulative and full of

hypocrites who are avoiding the real issues of ecology, overpopulation, underclass suffering, medical bankruptcy, homelessness, malnutrition, race divisions, the issue of drugs.... [P]oetry can stand out as the one beacon of sanity: a beacon of individual clarity, and lucidity in every direction—whether on the Internet or in coffee houses or university forums or classrooms. Poetry, along with its old companion, music, becomes one means of communication that is not controlled by the establishment.

In "America," Ginsburg interrogates and charges the nation, "America why are your libraries full of tears?" and concludes, "Your machinery is too much for me."

The poem's rhythm turns on rhetorical questions, as if the speaker expects an answer. Yet as the speaker bombards America with one statement, one contest after another, America cannot get a word in edgewise. America is silenced by the issues raised; there are too many to solve. America is overwhelmed by its to-do list, its responsibilities. This is not Whitman's America.

Edward Albee, in 1961, produced *The American Dream*, a one-act absurdist play that is critical of the American middle class. "*The American Dream*," Albee said in an article in *South Coast Repertory Play Insights*, "is the substitution of artificial values for real values, the acceptance of appearance for content, the slow drift of accommodation. People try so hard to escape being touched by unpleasantness that they wind up being unable to feel anything or to communicate anything." Albee believes a playwright "has a responsibility in his society, not to aid it, or comfort it, but to comment and criticize." Through his satire, Albee shows the American dream as empty, immoral, violent, meaningless. The cast offers an interesting, dark portrayal of the American family, with the controlling Mommy, ineffectual Daddy, and wry Grandma. Mommy and Daddy adopted a son many years before but tortured and murdered the child because of its deformed appearance. A "clean-cut, midwest farm boy type, almost insultingly good-looking.... typically American" Young Man, arriving at the house in search of work, turns out to be the child's twin and is dubbed "The American Dream" by Grandma. After vicariously experiencing the pain of his brother's torture, he remains an emotional husk who will "do almost anything for money." This muscular Young Man is "perfect" for Mommy and Daddy,

unlike their first "bumble of joy." In the preface to the play, Albee calls the work "a picture of our time," helping to define American life more accurately, but many critics disagreed, thinking the play too defeatist and nihilist. Albee's play forces readers to examine the American quest for "perfection," not to mention to question a society founded on appearance, acquisition, excess, and disposability.

Sandra Cisneros, first-generation Mexican American, centers the American dream in bicultural America, divining a life that is not one thing or another. Just as Ichiro's conflict came from standing on the edge of two cultures in *No-No Boy*, Cisneros offers the borderland where Mexico and the United States meet as a frame for plot and character to develop. In a chapter called "Mericans" included in the novel *Woman Hollering Creek* (1991), three children play outside a church as they wait for their "awful grandmother." Two strangers, a woman and a man, wander by and ask, in garbled Spanish, to take the older boy's picture. The woman offers gum and he accepts, then calls to his siblings:

> "Hey, Michele, Keeks. You guys want gum?"
>
> "But you speak English!"
>
> "Yeah," my brother says, "we're Mericans."
>
> We're Mericans, we're Mericans, and inside the awful grandmother prays.

Through this short, simple vignette narrated by the girl, Cisneros acknowledges the prevalent problem of racial and cultural stereotyping, as well as the conflict of social identity. Despite the brother proclaiming their nationality, the girl's repetition of "We're Mericans" juxtaposed with the image of the grandmother praying to La Virgen de Guadalupe shows she is torn between two worlds. But in writing stories where the protagonists represent a non-white side of America, Cisneros positions America in between different cultures as well. The American dream is speaking two languages, praying, and chewing gum at the same time.

Conclusion: The Future of the American Dream

The American dream began to evolve as the myth was reassessed and revolutionized. The promise of second chances still glimmers, but the shine is a bit tarnished and perhaps a bit more realistic. Margaret Atwood, in her 2003 "Letter to America," published in the newspaper the *Nation*, wants America to wake up to its flaws and return to its ideals. She sees America as straying from its origins but believes it can regain its integrity, as framed by this excerpt:

> You're gutting the Constitution. Already your home can be entered without your knowledge or permission, you can be snatched away and incarcerated without cause, your mail can be spied on, your private records searched. Why isn't this a recipe for widespread business theft, political intimidation, and fraud? I know you've been told all this is for your own safety and protection, but think about it for a minute. Anyway, when did you get so scared? You didn't used to be easily frightened.
>
> You're running up a record level of debt. Keep spending at this rate and pretty soon you won't be able to afford any big military adventures. Either that or you'll go the way of the USSR: lots of tanks, but no air conditioning. That will make folks very cross. They'll be even crosser when they can't take a shower because your short-sighted bulldozing of environmental protections has dirtied most of the water and dried up the rest. Then things will get hot and dirty indeed.... If you proceed much further down the slippery slope, people around the world will stop admiring the good things about you. They'll decide that your city upon the hill is a slum and your democracy is a sham, and therefore you have no business trying to impose your sullied vision on them.... The British used to have a myth about King Arthur. He wasn't dead, but sleeping in a cave, it was said; in the country's hour of greatest peril, he would return. You, too, have great spirits of the past you may call upon: men and women of courage, of conscience, of prescience. Summon them now, to stand with you, to inspire you, to defend the best in you. You need them.

According to Atwood, America has a chance, if it turns to its noble origins, if it looks to its "great spirits of the past" and resurrects its "courage and conscience." America can once again be a new world.

The American dream, since the first settlers arrived in the New World, has remained fundamentally the same. A "new" world presented the chance to start over, spiritually, economically, personally. It offered a chance to create a new government, with new laws, new freedoms, new limits. This world was unclaimed, leaving ample room for newcomers to make their mark, however they desired. Some sought a different identity, others an adventure. Still others looked toward heaven. But all had equal opportunity to set forth on the quest, no matter where they were from, what language they spoke, or the

amount of money they saved. At least that was the prevailing philosophy signed by American forefathers. Unfortunately, the words were not in stone.

A land so vast and beautiful, honored by Boone, Whitman, Thoreau, and Frost, was gradually parceled, pieced, bordered, "possessed." It was traversed by wagons, bloodied by prejudice and greed, and industrialized in the name of material success. Life, liberty, and the pursuit of happiness all came with amendments and demands. "One Nation under God" turned into "Every Man for Himself." The strong American work ethic was replaced by the mantra "Get Rich Quick." Equality had a definite color, as did entitlement. As Chief Seattle illuminated the criminal loss of "red man's rights," Langston Hughes dared take pride in his racial identity, and Elizabeth Cady Stanton demanded national representation for women, icons such as Huck Finn, Horatio Alger's protagonists, and Grover's Corners were moved aside to reveal the secreted symbols of America. Irish prostitutes such as Crane's Maggie and Japanese American "no-no boys," together with the workers in the iron-mills and the marchers who followed Dr. King, chose not to be silent.

SOURCES

Albee, Edward, *The American Dream and Zoo Story*, New American Library, 1963; reprint, Plume, 1997, pp. 54, 107, 109.

Alger, Horatio, *Ragged Dick and Mark the Match Boy*, Scribner, 1962, p. 20; originally published in 1868.

Atwood, Margaret, "A Letter to America," in the *Nation*, March 27, 2003, www.thenation.com/doc/20030414/atwood (January 9, 2007).

Bellamy, Francis, "The Pledge of Allegiance," *U.S. Flag.org*, www.usflag.org/history/pledgeofallegiance.html (December 20, 2006).

Bradford, William, *Of Plymouth Plantation*, in *Concise Anthology of American Literature 5th ed.*, edited by George McMichael, et al., Prentice Hall, 2001, pp. 62–63; originally published in 1856.

Bradstreet, Anne, "A Dialogue Between Old England and New, Concerning Their Present Troubles, Anno 1642," Old South Leaflets, Vol. 7, *Hanover Historical Texts Project*, pp. 169–76, history.hanover.edu/texts/BRADDIAL.html (December 20, 2006).

Brame, Gloria G., "An Interview with Poet Allen Ginsberg," *ELF: Eclectic Literary Forum*, Summer

1996, loria-brame.com/glory/ginsberg.htm (December 20, 2006).

Bulosan, Carlos, *America Is in the Heart*, University of Washington Press, 2000, pp. 143, 189.

Cervantes, Lorna Dee, "Cannery Town in August," in *Norton Anthology Literature By Women 2d ed.*, edited by Sandra Gilbert and Susan Gubar, W. W. Norton, 1996, p. 2349; originally published in 1981.

Chief Seattle, "Chief Seattle's Reply," 1854, *History Link. org*, www.historylink.org/essays/output.cfm?file_id = 1427 (December 20, 2006).

Cisneros, Sandra, "Mericans" in *Woman Hollering Creek*, Random House, 1991; reprinted in *Concise Anthology of American Literature 5th ed.*, edited by George McMichael, et al., Prentice Hall, 2001, p. 2272.

Clifton, Lucille, "My Dream About Being White," in *Norton Anthology Literature By Women 2d ed.*, edited by Sandra Gilbert and Susan Gubar, W. W. Norton, 1996, p. 2139; originally published in 1987.

Crane, Stephen, *Maggie, A Girl of the Streets and Other New York Writings*, Modern Library, 2001, p. 6; originally published in 1893.

cummings, e. e., "next to of course god america I," in *Concise Anthology of American Literature 5th ed.*, edited by George McMichael, et al., Prentice Hall, 2001, p. 1722; originally published in 1925.

Darion, Joe, Mitch Leigh, and Dale Wasserman, *Man of La Mancha*, Random House, 1966.

Davis, Rebecca Harding, "Life in the Iron-Mills," in *Norton Anthology Literature By Women, 2d ed.*, edited by Sandra Gilbert and Susan Gubar, W. W. Norton, 1996, pp. 920–25; originally published in 1861.

"Declaration of Independence," on *NARA: The National Archives Experience*, www.archives.gov/national-archives-experience/charters/declaration_transcript.html (January 8, 2007).

Docherty, Brian, "e. e. cummings," in *American Poetry: The Modernist Ideal*, edited by Clive Bloom and Brian Docherty, St. Martin's Press, 1995, reprinted in *Modern American Poetry*, www.english.uiuc.edu/maps/poets/a_f/cummings/nexttoofcourse.htm (December 20, 2006).

Dos Passos, John, *The Big Money*, Harcourt, Brace, 1936; reprint, Mariner Books, 2000, pp. 420–26.

Ehrenreich, Barbara, *Nickel and Dimed: On (Not) Getting By in America*, Owl Books, 2002, pp. 199–221.

Fink, Rychard, "Introduction" in *Ragged Dick and Mark, the Match Boy*, Macmillan, 1962; reprint, Touchstone, 1998, p. 20

Franklin, Benjamin, *Poor Richard's Almanack*, in *Benjamin Franklin's the Art of Virtue: His Formula for Successful Living*, edited by George L. Rogers, Acorn Publishing, 1996, p. 178.

Friedan, Betty, *The Feminine Mystique*, W. W. Norton, 2001, pp. 15, 378; originally published in 1963.

Frost, Robert, "The Gift Outright," in *The Poetry of Robert Frost: The Collected Poems, Complete and Unabridged*, edited by Edward Connery Lathem, Henry Holt, 1969, p. 348.

Gibbs, Nancy, "Apocalypse Now," *Time Magazine*, July 1, 2002, www.time.com/time/magazine/article/0,9171,1002759,00.html (January 9, 2007).

Gilman, Charlotte Perkins, "Women Do Not Want It," in *Suffrage Songs and Verses*, The Charlton Company, 1911, pp. 21–22, digital.library.upenn.edu/women/gilman/suffrage/su-want.html (December 20, 2006).

Ginsberg, Allen, "America," in *Concise Anthology of American Literature 5th ed.*, edited by George McMichael, et al., Prentice Hall, 2001, p. 2039; originally published in 1956.

———, "Howl," in *Howl and Other Poems*, City Lights Publishers, 1956; reprint, in *Collected Poems 1947–1980*, Harper & Row, 1984, p. 126.

Harjo, Joy, "Autobiography," in *In Mad Love and War*, Wesleyan University Press, 1990, p. 14.

Hawthorne, Nathaniel, "Young Goodman Brown," in *Concise Anthology of American Literature 5th ed.*, edited by George McMichael, et al., Prentice Hall, 2001, p. 694; originally published in 1835.

Hughes, Langston, "I, Too," in *Concise Anthology of American Literature 5th ed.*, edited by George McMichael, et al., Prentice Hall, 2001, p. 1867; originally published in 1932.

Jong, Erica, *Fear of Flying*, Holt, Reinhart, and Winston, 1973; reprint, Signet, 1995, pp. 47, 156.

Kiger, Jennifer, "Edward Albee's *A Delicate Balance*," in *South Coast Repertory Play Insights*, www.scr.org/season/00-01season/snl00-01/snlms3.html (January 9, 2007).

King, Martin Luther, Jr., "I Have a Dream," August 28, 1963, www.americanrhetoric.com/speeches/mlkihaveadream.htm (December 20, 2006).

La Haye, Tim, and Jerry B. Jenkins, *Left Behind: A Novel of the Earth's Last Days*, Tyndale House Publishers, 2000, p. 243.

Lazarus, Emma, "The New Colossus," in *The Poems of Emma Lazarus*, Vol. 1, 1889; reprinted at www.libertystatepark.com/emma.htm (December 20, 2006).

"Left Behind Series Featured in Time Cover Story," *Left Behind Series*, www.leftbehind.com (December 20, 2006).

Lincoln, Abraham, "The Gettysburg Address," November 19, 1863, showcase.netins.net/web/creative/lincoln/speeches/gettysburg.htm (December 16, 2006).

Mather, Cotton, *What Must I Do To Be Saved?*, www.spurgeon.org/~phil/mather/whatmust.htm (December 20, 2006); originally published in 1721.

Melville, Herman, "Bartleby the Scrivener," in *Concise Anthology of American Literature 5th ed.*, edited by George McMichael, et al., Prentice Hall, 2001, pp. 728, 729, 737; originally published in 1853.

Millay, Edna St. Vincent, "Apostrophe to Man," in *Norton Anthology Literature By Women 2d ed.*, edited by Sandra Gilbert and Susan Gubar, W. W. Norton, 1996, p. 1512.

Miller, Arthur, *The Crucible*, Viking Press, 1953; reprint, Penguin, 2003, p. 141.

———, *Death of a Salesman*, Viking Press, 1953; reprinted in *Concise Anthology of American Literature 5th ed.*, edited by George McMichael, et al., Prentice Hall, 2001, pp. 1938–39.

Okada, John, *No-No Boy*, C. E. Tuttle, 1957; reprint, University of Washington Press, 1978, p. 16.

Robinson, Edwin Arlington, "Richard Cory," in *Concise Anthology of American Literature 5th ed.*, edited by George McMichael, et al., Prentice Hall, 2001, p. 1563; originally published in 1897.

Selina, Helen, "Lament of the Irish Emigrant," in *A Victorian Anthology: 1837–1895*, edited by Edmund Clarence Stedman, www.bartleby.com/246/200.html (January 18, 2007); originally published in 1895.

Stanton, Elizabeth Cady, "Address to the New York State Legislature, 1860" in *Norton Anthology Literature By Women 2d ed.*, edited by Sandra Gilbert and Susan Gubar, W. W. Norton, 1996, pp. 467–68.

Steinbeck, John, *Of Mice and Men*, Covici-Friede, 1937; reprint, Penguin, 1993, p. 106.

Thoreau, Henry David, "Civil Disobedience," in *Concise Anthology of American Literature 5th ed.*, edited by George McMichael, et al., Prentice Hall, 2001, pp. 811, 812, 816, 818; originally published in 1849.

Twain, Mark, *Adventures of Huckleberry Finn*, 1885; reprint, Prestwick House, 2005, p. 105.

Wheatley, Phyllis, "On Being Brought from Africa to America," in *Concise Anthology of American Literature 5th ed.*, edited by George McMichael, et al., Prentice Hall, 2001, p. 379; originally published in *Poems on Various Subjects, Religious and Moral*, 1773.

———, "On Virtue," in *Concise Anthology of American Literature 5th ed.*, edited by George McMichael, et al., Prentice Hall, 2001, p. 378; originally published in *Poems on Various Subjects, Religious and Moral*, 1773.

Whitman, Walt, "Preface" to *Leaves of Grass*, 1855; reprinted in *Concise Anthology of American Literature 5th ed.*, edited by George McMichael, et al., Prentice Hall, 2001, pp. 1018–19, 1022, 1032.

Wigglesworth, Michael, *The Day of Doom*, Kessinger Publishing, 2003, pp. 6, 60; originally published in 1662.

Wilder, Laura Ingalls, *Little House on the Prairie*, HarperTrophy, 1953, p. 63; originally published in 1935.

Wilder, Thornton, *Our Town*, Coward-McGann, 1938, pp. 19, 36.

Major Works

Absalom, Absalom!

WILLIAM FAULKNER
1936

William Faulkner's *Absalom, Absalom!* (1936) is considered by many critics and scholars to be one of the most important and influential American novels by one of the greatest authors of the twentieth century. It is one of a series of great novels by Faulkner exploring the South, southern families, and effects of Civil War on southerners, such as *The Sound and the Fury* (1929) and *As I Lay Dying* (1930). Like many of Faulkner's works, a number of critics appreciated *Absalom, Absalom!* at the time of its publication, but its reputation as a major American novel did not come for some years.

The novel's title was inspired by the Biblical story of David and his son Absalom who turned his people against him. In *Absalom, Absalom!*, Faulkner emphasizes the centrality of the relationships between father and son in his gothic saga of Thomas Sutpen and his family. Using a number of narrators, including Sutpen's former sister-in-law and the grandson of his only friend, Faulkner allows each character to offer his or her point of view, adding to an understanding of the central, complex story. The result is an emotionally intense, chaotic psychological portrait that reflects the complexities of the South and human understanding of the idea of truth.

Emerging from a poor, uneducated, white family in Virginia, Sutpen became rich in the West Indies and later establishes a plantation, Sutpen's Hundred, outside of the fictional

Jefferson, Mississippi. Marrying an upstanding local store owner's daughter, Ellen Coldfield, Sutpen becomes somewhat respectable and has two children, Henry and Judith. Sutpen's past, however, comes back to tear apart his family. Sutpen had a wife and son in Haiti, only to repudiate them after he learned his wife had some black ancestry.

Charles Bon, the Haitian son, becomes friends with Henry at college, and he comes to the Sutpen home one Christmas as his guest. Bon becomes engaged to Judith, but it is unclear if he knows who Sutpen really is. Henry rejects his father after Sutpen tells him about Bon the following Christmas. After serving together for four years in the Confederate Army during the Civil War, Henry kills his half-brother after learning about his black ancestry—more distressed that his sister might marry a black man than he is at the prospect of her marrying a close relative—and then runs away.

His wife already dead, Sutpen becomes desperate for another male heir, and he offers to marry Rosa, his former sister-in-law, if she produces a son with him first. First engaged to and later rejected by Rosa, Sutpen impregnates the young granddaughter of Wash Jones, a poor white plantation hand on his property. Sutpen abandons her when she bears a daughter. Wash kills Sutpen as well as his granddaughter and her child. Years later, Henry returns to Sutpen's Hundred and lives with Clytie, Sutpen's daughter by a slave, for four years as he waits to die. Fearing Henry's imminent arrest when Rosa learns of his presence and returns to care for him, Clytie sets the house on fire and kills them both.

The novel ends with Quentin, a Harvard student and the grandson of Sutpen's only friend General Compson, and his Canadian roommate Shreve trying to make sense of the story and the South. Each does so in his own way. In the end, the only remaining Sutpen is Jim Bond, the black grandson of Charles Bon.

Many critics see the story and structure of *Absalom, Absalom!* as a metaphor for the South. Critics have also noted that Faulkner explores the ideas of racism through Sutpen's rejection of Charles Bon and his mother because of her partially black ancestry, a concept that drives the narrative. The way the story plays out is also one of the many metaphors for race relations in the South, and indicative of its citizens' difficulties accepting blacks as equals. This racism undermines Sutpen's American dream: His grand design—his ruthless

BIOGRAPHY

WILLIAM FAULKNER

William Falkner was born on September 25, 1897, in New Albany, Mississippi, the oldest son of parents who came from formerly wealthy families ruined financially by the Civil War. A great-grandfather, Colonel William C. Falkner had penned a popular book in the 1880s; Faulkner's father was a small business owner and university business manager. Though Faulkner enjoyed reading complex literature as a teenager, he only attended school regularly through fifth grade and dropped out of high school. After briefly serving in the Canadian Air Force during World War I, he spent a year as a special student at the University of Mississippi. Stints working in New York City and at the University of Mississippi were short-lived as he soon focused primarily on writing poetry and fiction.

Faulkner published his first novel in 1926, and he found success in the early 1930s with *Sanctuary*, a novel written solely to earn money. While continuing to produce what would be considered some of the greatest American novels, including *Absalom, Absalom!* (1936), Faulkner also worked in Hollywood writing movie scenarios and acting as an advisor, solely for the paychecks. After World War II, critical acclaim for Faulkner's work grew, culminating in his winning the 1949 Nobel Prize for literature. He died in July 1962 in Byhalia, Mississippi.

plan for wealth, respectability, and a legacy—compels him to jettison anything that does not fit in his narrow definition of success.

Distilling the importance of *Absalom, Absalom!*, Gail Caldwell of the *Boston Globe* writes,

> With its central themes of incest, miscegenation and familial betrayal, the Sutpens' story alone is as searing as any novel ever written about the South.... Faulkner constructed a myth that transcends Thomas Sutpen to take on so much

more: the Civil War, the impenetrability of time and memory, the smoldering ashes of the South.

PLOT SUMMARY

Chapter 1

Absalom, Absalom! opens in Jefferson, Mississippi, in 1909. Elderly Miss Rosa Coldfield has summoned Quentin Compson, a local nineteen-year-old bound for Harvard, to her home. She wants to tell him a story she wants written about events that happened years before, claiming that he may want to write about the story if he decides to "enter the literary profession." He thinks she has other reasons for wanting to tell him about the "demon" Colonel Thomas Sutpen:

> *It's because she wants it told* he thought *so that people whom she will never see and whose names she will never hear and who have never heard her name nor seen her face will read it and know at last why God let us lose the War: that only through the blood of our men and the tears of our women could He stay this demon and efface his name and lineage from the earth.*

Though Quentin did not really know her before, he did know about some of the violence in her family, including tragicdeaths. These events were linked to a man, Thomas Sutpen, who appeared in their town out of nowhere in June 1833. Sutpen married Rosa's sister Ellen and had two children. Their son, Henry, killed the betrothed of their daughter, Judith, just before they were to marry. Quentin does not understand why Rosa chose to tell him this story until his father explains the link in their families. Mr. Compson tells his son that they even bear some responsibility because Quentin's grandfather, General Compson, befriended Sutpen, helping him establish himself in the town of Jefferson.

As Quentin listens to Rosa tell her story, he hears the hatred in her voice. Rosa tells him about Sutpen's past and the respectability he gained by marrying her sister and becoming a gentleman. Yet after Ellen's marriage, there was distance between Ellen and her family, which included her father, her aunt, and Rosa. Sutpen was never part of a social relationship with Ellen's family, and he acted in ways that greatly offended Ellen and her kin. He liked to stage, and even participate in, fights and races with his slaves. Rosa also tells him that Ellen and her children paid a price because of Sutpen's actions. Yet Rosa agreed to marry Sutpen herself after her

William Faulkner Getty Images

sister died. She lived on his plantation, Sutpen's Hundred, after her sister's death because she had no other family alive. Rosa was to protect Judith, though Rosa was younger than her niece, because Ellen asked this favor on her death bed.

Chapter 2

One evening in the summer of 1909, Quentin waits for the time to perform some errand. While he waits on the porch, his father tells him more of the story. When Sutpen came to Jefferson at the age of twenty-five, he was completely unknown but seemed driven by a secret. Quentin's grandfather became friends with the mysterious wild man, although Sutpen seemed to be without the time or the money for socializing over drinks. Sutpen bought one hundred square miles of virgin land, left for two months, and came back with a French architect and a crew of slaves. He took two years to build the house, and the plantation took three more years to establish; then he decided to marry.

Sutpen wanted respectability, and he believed a wife would make him respectable. Sutpen went away to get fixtures for the home, such as chandeliers and mahogany. He built a relationship with Coldfield, who owned a store in town. Sutpen raised the suspicions of the townspeople, so much so that the "vigilance committee" paid him a visit, detained him once, and grew to a group of fifty men who followed, watched, and disapproved of Sutpen. Sutpen married Coldfield's daughter Ellen in June 1838, in a wedding that was a fiasco. "When they were married, there were just ten people in the church, including the wedding party, of the hundred who had been invited," with Quentin's grandparents among the handful who attended. When the couple came out of the church, a few people threw things at them.

Chapter 3

Quentin learns more about the Sutpen family from his father. When Coldfield died in 1864, Rosa, then twenty, went to live with her niece and fulfill her sister's death-bed request. Clytie, Sutpen's daughter by one of his slaves, also lived on the plantation with them, along with Wash Jones, a servant. Rosa's mother, then past forty years old, had died in childbirth with her. The aunt who raised her generally kept Rosa separated from Ellen. After her aunt eloped with a horse trader, Rosa and her father visited Ellen once a year. They stopped going when Judith and Henry, Ellen's children, were nearly adults. Rosa then visited Judith and Ellen often. In this time period, Judith met Charles Bon, Henry's college friend from New Orleans, and became engaged to him. Bon visited the following summer on his way to New Orleans, "the summer in which Sutpen himself went away, on business, Ellen said," Quentin's father tells him.

The sisters' relationship grew more complicated after Ellen told everyone Judith was engaged to Bon. Ellen and Rosa did not visit each other any more. Rosa never met Charles Bon, who seemed to come out of nowhere. Rosa tried to help by making garments for Judith's trousseau—"those intimate young girl garments which were to be for her own vicarious bridal"— with cloth she stole from her father's store. Because Rosa did not see Ellen, she learned through town talk that following Christmas eve, Henry left with Bon and renounced his birthright.

When the Civil War started, Sutpen left in 1861 to serve in the Confederate Army. Rosa's father hated the war so much that he closed his store so he would not have to sell to soldiers and

their families. He would not let Rosa look at soldiers, nor would he take back her aunt (his sister) whose husband was also serving. After the store was ransacked by soldiers, Coldfield locked himself into his attic for three years. While he lived in his attic, Rosa fed him with what was left in the store and wrote poetry about the soldiers. Coldfield died there, leaving Rosa a poor orphan. By this time, Ellen had been dead for two years. For some unknown reason, Rosa does not go to live with her niece at Sutpen's Hundred yet. One day, Wash Jones comes to Rosa's house.

Chapter 4

Quentin is still waiting for the right time to start his errand with Rosa. His father brings him an old letter—from Charles Bon to Judith—but will not let him read it. Mr. Compson continues the story. He tells his son that Henry loved Bon and rejected his father because of something his father told him: Compson believes that Sutpen had learned about Bon's black mistress and child in New Orleans. Henry went to New Orleans to find out the truth, even though Compson believes Henry must have known it was true. Mr. Compson believes that Henry probably knew that he was destined to kill Bon. Sutpen intended to prevent the marriage.

Quentin's father explains more about Bon. Henry renounced his family after his father forbade the marriage between Bon and Judith, claiming that Bon was already married to another woman and had a child with her. Henry refused to believe his father and went with his friend, but learned that Bon did have a wife in New Orleans who was also his slave. Mr. Compson also points out that Judith and Bon were never alone when they were engaged. There was no courtship, and he even wonders if the engagement was real. Yet Henry killed Bon to prevent Judith and Bon from marrying. Quentin's father finds the situation odd and believes some information is missing:

> Judith, Bon, Henry, Sutpen . . . There they are, yet something is missing. They are like a chemical formula exhumed along with the letters from that forgotten chest . . . you bring them together again and again nothing happens: just the words, the symbols, the shapes themselves, shadowy inscrutable and serene, against that turgid background of a horrible and bloody mischancing of human affairs.

Mr. Compson tells Quentin about the Christmas when Henry brought Bon home for the first time. Sutpen, Ellen, and Judith saw him for the first time during the twelve days Bon stayed there. He believes that the engagement was in Ellen's mind before Bon ever came to their home; it started for her when Henry wrote home about his new friend. The couple then had two days together at the beginning of summer vacation. Sutpen said nothing about the situation.

At Christmas the following year, 1860, Sutpen and Henry had their confrontation. Henry and Bon left afterward and went to New Orleans. Mr. Compson says that Bon knew what Sutpen had learned in New Orleans, and Henry knew what his father said was true at the time. Henry did not ask Bon if it was a lie so that Bon did not lie to him. Henry went to New Orleans to find out for himself. During the four-year period in which Henry prevented Bon from writing to Judith, Judith did not even know if Bon was still alive. Mr. Compson believes that Henry learned of Bon's part-black wife and child, and Henry gave him that time to renounce the woman and child. Bon did not do so.

Instead, Henry and Bon joined a Confederate Army company organized at their university. While they were away fighting, Judith never learned why her father objected to the marriage. Henry wrote her that Bon was alive but he would not let him write her. Judith did not ask Henry or her father for an explanation.

During the Civil War, Sutpen also served in the Confederate Army. His wife and daughter remained at Sutpen's Hundred. His slaves left when Union troops passed through the area for the first time. Ellen stayed in her bed, dying, while Clytie and Wash Jones helped Judith run the household. At the time, Wash lived on Sutpen's property with his daughter and granddaughter.

Ellen died two years after Sutpen left. Coldfield died soon after. After Bon was killed, Judith brought a letter to Quentin's grandmother. Judith told her she could keep or destroy the letter, even read it if she wanted to. Mr. Compson gives this letter to Quentin, who reads it. It is from Bon to Judith, and although it mentions neither love nor marriage, it prompted her to make a wedding dress and look for his return to Sutpen's Hundred. He never married her; Henry killed him at the gates of the plantation before he entered. Wash brought Rosa to the plantation after Henry killed Bon.

Chapter 5

The events are now explained primarily from Rosa's first-person point of view. When Rosa

went to Judith after Henry killed Bon, she had not been to Sutpen's Hundred for two years. Her last time there was when Ellen died. Rosa found the house in better shape than she expected. At the house, Clytie did not want Rosa to go upstairs and touched Rosa to stop her. Rosa is deeply offended by the black woman's touch. Rosa finally sees Judith holding a picture of herself that she had given Bon. Judith calmly made preparations for the funeral, and Rosa never saw Bon's body. Rosa stayed for dinner as the coffin for Bon was being made. She helped bury him.

Rosa stayed on with Judith and Clytie, waiting for Sutpen to come home. Rosa helped keep house and maintain a garden for food. Clytie, Judith, and Rosa slept in the same room for safety. She tells Quentin why she stayed:

> I waited for him exactly as Judith and Clytie waited for him: because now he was all we had, all that gave us any reason for continuing to exist, to eat food and sleep and wake and rise again: knowing that he would need us, knowing as we did (who knew him) that he would begin at once to salvage what was left of Sutpen's Hundred and restore it.

When Sutpen returned from the war in January, he and Rosa became engaged. There was no real courtship as Sutpen essentially told her he would be married to her. Three months after his return, Rosa realized that she could go home and he would not have missed her. She left after two months and returned to her home in town. Judith brought her food from time to time. As Rosa concludes her story, she tells Quentin that Clytie still lives at Sutpen's house and she believes that something is hidden there.

Chapter 6

At Harvard in January 1910, Quentin has a letter from his father, which says that Rosa was in a coma for two weeks, then died on January 7. Quentin remembers back to the previous September when he visited Rosa and drove her out to Sutpen's Hundred. She believed someone was hiding there. Quentin's roommate is a Canadian named Shreve, who, like all his other schoolmates, is curious and fascinated by tales of life in the South. Quentin shares the story of Sutpen and his extended family.

Based on what Quentin has told him, Shreve tries to understand the story and recaps what has been told thus far. He also adds that Rosa rejected Sutpen and left Sutpen's Hundred because he wanted her to have a child before he would marry her. If it was a boy, he would go through with the wedding. After Rosa left, he found someone else. As Shreve speaks, Quentin sees a resemblance between his father and Shreve.

When Shreve is finished, Quentin thinks back on more of the story. Sutpen survived by running a country store. He slept with Wash Jones's fifteen-year-old granddaughter, Milly, and she became pregnant. As a result, Wash then believed that his relationship with Sutpen had changed and now would come into Sutpen's house. She delivered a daughter, not a son, and Sutpen put her aside. Sutpen told her, "*Well, Milly, too bad you're not a mare.... Then I could give you a decent stall in the stable.*" Wash then killed Sutpen with a scythe, and Judith buried him. Judith and Clytie kept living at the plantation house.

Quentin tells Shreve of a time he went quail hunting with his father and a black servant named Luster. They saw the headstones and burial places of Sutpen, Ellen, Bon, and Bon's son from New Orleans who died in 1884. Sutpen had bought the first two—of fine Italian marble—when he was in the army. Judith bought the other three after she sold her father's store: Charles Bon's, her own, and one for Bon's son. Quentin's father revealed that Bon's wife had come once with her then eleven-year-old son to visit Bon's grave. They stayed for a week in the house with Judith and Clytie.

When Bon's wife died, Clytie brought Bon's son to the Sutpen home. He was twelve years old and only spoke French. He was told that he was had black ancestry, and no one outside of the Sutpen home could talk to him as he grew up. Clytie taught him to plow and farm. As a young man, he was arrested for getting into a fight at a "negro ball." Quentin's grandfather paid his fine and gave him money to disappear. He returned a year later married to a black woman. He had been beaten badly and could barely sit up, but he threw his marriage license into Judith's face. He had a son, known as Jim Bond, lived with his family in a former slave cabin, and rented land from Judith where he lived.

Judith offered to sell some land to send Bon's son north, and to care for his wife and son after he was gone. She pleaded with him to accept her help so he could escape his blackness:

We will have General Compson sell some of the land; he will do it, and you can go. Into the

North, the cities, where it will not matter even if—But they will not. They will not dare. I will tell them that you are Henry's son and who could or would dare to dispute—

He refused. He stayed and worked the land. He was arrested several times for drunkenness. About four years later, he contracted yellow fever. Judith cared for him during his illness and became sick as well. They both died of the disease in 1884. After Charles's son died, Clytie raised Jim Bond. On Judith's headstone, Rosa had these words inscribed: "Pause, Mortal; Remember Vanity and Folly and Beware."

The chapter ends with Shreve eager to learn what Quentin and Rosa found when they went to Sutpen's Hundred the previous fall.

Chapter 7

At Harvard, Quentin tells Shreve what his grandfather learned about Sutpen the first time the French architect disappeared from Sutpen's work site. Sutpen chased the architect down with dogs and slaves. General Compson, Quentin's grandfather, helped with the search and learned about Sutpen's past.

Sutpen was born into a large, poor, white family in the area that would become West Virginia. When his mother died, his alcoholic father was left with many children and moved them to a plantation where he found employment.

> That's the way he got it. He had learned the difference not only between white men and black ones, but he was learning that there was a difference between white men and white men not to be measured by lifting anvils or gouging eyes or how much whiskey you could drink then get up and walk out of the room.

The young Sutpen was fascinated by the rich man who owned the plantation. The wealthy owner had a slave attendant who was better dressed than poor Sutpen. Still naïve about the conventions of social status, young Sutpen went to the front door of the plantation house with a message from his father one day. The slave who answered the door told him to go to the back door. Embarrassed and unsure what to do, Sutpen first ran to a cave, then home to wait for the consequences of his actions.

Sutpen left his family that night and never saw them again. He went to Haiti, a destination he chose because he heard that the West Indies were where poor men could become rich. Sutpen arrived there when he was fourteen years old and eventually became the overseer on a sugar plantation. When Sutpen was twenty years old, he spent eight days during a slave rebellion barricaded in the main house of a French sugar plantation with its owner, his daughter, and servants for eight days. The fields were being burned, and those inside used muskets to defend the property. Sutpen became engaged to the daughter.

General Compson wanted to hear the rest of the story, but Sutpen stopped as they caught the architect. The architect finished the house, then left. Quentin tells Shreve that Sutpen did not finish his story for thirty years. When Sutpen continued the story in General Compson's office, Sutpen told him that he repudiated his first wife, the plantation owner's daughter, and their child. His conscience had bothered him at first, but he was angry at them for withholding information. He only learned this information after his son was born, and it ruined his plan. He worked out a deal with her, paid her off, gave her and her son new names, and left.

Then Henry brought home Bon for Christmas and Sutpen was forced to face the son he abandoned twenty-eight years earlier. Quentin's father believes that Sutpen was shocked to see him again and did not react, but he probably told Henry about Bon's parentage. Quentin tells Shreve, "Father said that he (Sutpen) probably knew what Henry would do too and counted on Henry doing it because he still believed that it had been only a minor tactical mistake" in his life plan. They speculate that Sutpen went to New Orleans to visit Bon and his mother, and wonder if Bon knew at that time that Sutpen was his father. Sutpen did nothing about the situation between Judith and Bon, but let the situation work itself out.

After the war, Sutpen tried to rebuild his dynasty with Rosa. When that failed, he used Wash, a hand on the plantation who idolized Sutpen. Sutpen seduced and impregnated Wash's granddaughter. When Sutpen rejected her and their daughter, then used his whip on the protesting Wash's face, Wash became angry at the betrayal. He killed Sutpen with his scythe. When the town sheriff and others came to his door to confront Wash, he killed his granddaughter and her child as well.

Chapter 8

Shreve speculates about what Henry and Sutpen said in their confrontation when Sutpen told Henry that Bon was his brother. Shreve thinks that Sutpen said Bon knew the whole time he was Henry's brother, but really believes that Bon did not know. Shreve also guesses about what Bon's mother did, when, if, and how she told her son about his father, and the role their lawyer might have played. Shreve wonders if she was trailing Sutpen to know if he was alive.

Shreve also considers the relationship between Bon and his mother, and what Bon was thinking as he went to the University of Mississippi to attend school. He speculates about her reaction to her son's marriage to a black woman and their child. Bon perhaps wondered why he was compelled to attend this school.

Continuing his speculation, Shreve wonders if Bon cultivated a relationship with Henry and saw himself in Henry. When Bon went home with Henry for Christmas, he came face to face with the man who could be his father, but he did not see a sign of recognition in his face. Shreve also wonders about Bon's relationship with Judith, and believes that Bon knew what would happen. Quentin and Shreve debate whether Bon and Judith were truly in love.

Delving further into Bon and Judith's relationship, Shreve considers how Bon rationalized romance with his sister and how he proceeded in the relationship. Shreve also wonders how the engagement came to be, believing it was from Ellen's imagination at first. When Bon came back a second time for a few days at the start of summer vacation, Sutpen was gone and Bon probably knew where he went. He still had no word for Bon when he came back for the second Christmas.

Shreve and Quentin are thinking the same thoughts and telling the story, excited as the drama (as they imagine it) unfolds. They think that when Henry and Bon were riding to the steamboat after the confrontation, they had nothing to say to each other. In their version, "Henry who knew yet did not believe." Bon could have taken Henry to visit his mistress-wife and child.

The Harvard students speculate that Henry and Bon grapple with the ideas of incest and love and family and revenge—and honor, as they imagine Bon killing Henry in a friendly fire incident during the war. They imagine that Bon wants only recognition from Sutpen, and he waited to decide about marrying Judith, hoping that Henry would do it for him, simply by acknowledging him and asking him not to marry his sister.

They picture Henry being called into his father's tent. Sutpen tells his son that Henry will not let Bon marry Judith, and he tells him that Bon is part black through his mother, a fact he only learned after the child was born. It is the reason he repudiated Bon and his mother. This information changes Henry, the students believe. In the brothers' confrontation over the revelation, Bon says, "*So it's the miscegenation, not the incest, which you can't bear.*" Bon tries to provoke Henry into killing him on the way to Sutpen's Hundred, but he does not. Sherve imagines that Bon was found with the picture of his wife and child as a sort of admission of guilt to Judith, a message that she should not grieve over his death.

Chapter 9

In their beds, Quentin and Shreve continue to talk. Shreve disparages the South with comments like, "I didn't know there were ten in Mississippi that went to school at one time." Quentin tells him he has to be born there to fully understand it.

Quentin thinks back to the late-night trip he took with Rosa to Sutpen's Hundred. When they reached the gate, she made him stop and he did not know what to do. Quentin tried to get Rosa to go back to town, but she would not. Nor would she let him drive to the house, but she had him escort her there. At the house, Rosa had Quentin break down the door. Clytie appeared and told him not to let Rosa go upstairs. Rosa knocked Clytie down. Jim Bond was there as well. Later at home after taking Rosa to her house, Quentin remembered that Henry was there. He had lived there for four years, having come home to die.

Three months later, Rosa went back with an ambulance to get Henry to a doctor. Thinking it was the police coming to arrest Henry for Bon's murder, Clytie set the house on fire. Rosa tried to get into the house but collapsed. Clytie and Henry were killed in the fire. Only the mentally challenged Jim Bond escaped. The story complete, Shreve tells Quentin, "I think that in time the Jim Bonds are going to conquer the western hemisphere," and asks Quentin why he hates the South. Quentin denies these feelings, but he seems to be trying to convince himself, rather than Shreve, that he does not hate his homeland.

> YOU SEE, I HAD A DESIGN IN MY MIND. WHETHER IT WAS A GOOD OR BAD DESIGN IS BESIDE THE POINT; THE QUESTION IS, WHERE DID I MAKE THE MISTAKE IN IT, WHAT DID I DO OR MISDO IN IT, WHOM OR WHAT INJURE BY IT TO THE EXTENT WHICH THIS WOULD INDICATE."

THEMES

Striving for Success at Any Cost

In *Absalom, Absalom!*, the central figure, Thomas Sutpen, is reviled by many other characters because of his plan for success, a significant part of the American dream, and followed that plan no matter what the cost. Inspired by a teacher telling him that poor men who went to the West Indies could become rich there, fourteen-year-old Sutpen leaves his family and goes to Haiti. By the age of twenty, he was married to the daughter of a plantation owner there, fulfilling a plan he had for his life to become rich and successful. Yet he felt he had to repudiate her and their son because she did not tell him she had some black ancestry, a fact that would have changed everything if he had known from the beginning.

In chapter 7, while telling the story of his background to General Compson, Sutpen mentioned this plan that helped him fulfill the American dream of overcoming an impoverished background to become rich. In a discussion centering on his repudiation of his first wife and child, Sutpen tells Quentin's grandfather,

> You see, I had a design in my mind. Whether it was a good design or bad design is beside the point; the question is, where did I make the mistake in it, what did I do or misdo in it, whom or what injure by it to the extent which this would indicate. I had a design. To accomplish it, I should require money, a house, a plantation, slaves, a family—incidentally of course, a wife. I set out to acquire these, asking no favor of any man.

That Sutpen's plan essentially failed in Haiti did not deter him. He returned to the United States and started over in Jefferson, Mississippi, drawing on funds he acquired in the West Indies. Sutpen married again, had a daughter and son, and became a rich cotton plantation owner. He owned one hundred square miles of land. Sutpen was even able to purchase some respectability through his wife's family, the Coldfields. While his past again interfered with his long-term plan—his first son showed up as the college friend of his second son and became engaged to his daughter—Sutpen persevered. Even being renounced by his son, the Civil War, and the death of his wife could not stop Sutpen from again trying to leave his legacy to the world.

After Henry left after murdering his half-brother Charles Bon, Sutpen sought to replace him by marrying again. Sutpen decided to marry his wife's younger sister, Rosa, who left when his conditions for marriage included bearing him a son. Sutpen had better luck with the fifteen-year-old granddaughter of Wash Jones, a poor white squatter he allowed to live on his land. When she gave birth to his daughter, Sutpen insulted her and refused to have anything to do with her. This action resulted in the end of his plan and his death. His legacy only lived on through his repudiated son's African American grandchild, Jim Bond, the only survivor of Thomas Sutpen's line.

Racism

A darker side to the American dream is the racism that runs throughout the story, endemic of life in the South for Faulkner. Set primarily in Mississippi from the pre–to post–Civil War period, most of the characters exhibit racist attitudes and regard them as an expected, acceptable way of life. African Americans are secondary characters and regularly dismissed or regarded as lessers by white characters.

In *Absalom, Absalom!*, racism is not depicted as particularly right or wrong but an accepted way of life in the South; the Civil War only changed the terms, not the institution itself. Shreve, a Canadian, finds such Southern attitudes odd, but Quentin tells him one cannot really understand the South unless one was born there. In a society largely defined by racism, being held back by or rising above people of a different race is at once a motivator and an obstacle in the American dream for many in the South.

Sutpen, a native of Virginia, repudiates his first wife and son after his birth because he learns that she has black ancestry. He cannot be married to someone with this heritage and fulfill his life's plan for success. Sutpen has no problem having sex with slaves. He has a daughter, Clytie, by a slave. Clytie lives at Sutpen's Hundred and works as a servant there. But Sutpen refuses to have any African American blood in his legitimate bloodlines.

Sutpen is not the only racist character. His son Henry stands by his half-brother Bon and disavows his father the second Christmas he brings Bon home. Henry even considers allowing Bon to marry Judith, though Bon is married to a woman with one-eighth black ancestry and has a son with her. However, Sutpen tells him that Bon is part black himself, Henry murders Bon to prevent the marriage.

Rosa, although portrayed as the victim of Sutpen's evil, is every bit as racist herself. At the beginning of chapter 5, Rosa describes being taken aback by Clytie calling Rosa by her given name when Rosa goes to Sutpen's Hundred after Bon is murdered. Rosa's outrage grows deeper when Clytie touches her as she tries to prevent Rosa from going upstairs. Rosa explains,

> *I know only that my entire being seemed to run at blind full tilt into something monstrous and immobile, with a shocking impact too soon and too quick to be mere amazement and outrage at that black arresting and untimorous hand on my white woman's flesh. Because there is something in the touch of flesh with flesh which abrogates, cuts sharp and straight across devious intricate channels of decorous ordering.*

Rosa uses a racial epithet to tell Clytie to remove her hand, and then describes how she would not even play with the same toys that Clytie had touched when they were children. Judith and Henry shared toys with Clytie, and Judith even slept in the same bed as her half-sister. Rosa understands that she was raised to think this way. She says, "*that warped and spartan solitude which I called my childhood, . . . also taught me not only to instinctively fear her and what she was, but to shun the very objects which she had touched.*"

HISTORICAL OVERVIEW

Pre–Civil War Mississippi

Absalom, Absalom! stretches from the pre– to post–Civil War period, beginning as early as the 1820s. At the time, Chickasaw Indians still lived in northern Mississippi, where the novel is set. This Native American tribe, as well as the neighboring Choctaws, were forced by the federal government to leave the area in the 1820s and early 1830s. Whites came to Mississippi and bought the abandoned Indian land, as Thomas Sutpen does in the novel.

Thus, the 1830s saw a boom in the economy of the state. Some plantations were founded and an economy based on cotton as the primary cash crop was established. Mississippi also saw a vast increase in the use of slave labor, though the state had not had many slaves before this time period. By 1840, black slaves were a majority of the population at 52 percent. While the small number of plantations were significant in Mississippi, most farms were small and these farmers owned only a few, if any, slaves.

Yet slavery was the primary reason for Mississippi's secession from the union in 1861, under the banner of states' rights along with other southern states. However, many whites who lived in the state, including some plantation owners with investments in the North, did not want Mississippi to secede. Many Mississippians saw themselves not as southerners but as westerners only a few years before the war broke out.

Post–Civil War Mississippi

Immediately after the Civil War, Mississippi saw Reconstruction being managed with input from both black and white politicians. Between 1865 and 1877, Reconstruction saw the former Confederate states reorganized under the control of the federal government. These states were eventually restored to the United States.

This situation changed in Mississippi by the mid-1870s. Racist whites wrested political power away, often by using violence and intimidation. Their policies led to an end to any political power held by black Mississippians for nearly a century. By the 1890s, the rights of African Americans were curbed by such policies as poll taxes and literary tests administered before being allowed to vote. Though such laws were supposed to be given to all voters, they were given to favor whites, even if illiterate, and to ensure that qualified black voters could not cast ballots. Racism against blacks dominated politics in Mississippi for many years.

Economically and socially, the state suffered because of such racial policies. The farm-based economy became one of sharecropping, a system in which a tenant farmer works land owned by someone else and is paid only a portion of what his crop yields. The sharecropping system essentially created another system of servitude for African Americans, though poor whites became an increasing large percentage of sharecroppers. Over time, into the early twentieth century, Mississippi remained an agriculture-based economy and relatively poor compared to the rest of the United States, which was becoming more wealthy, urban, and industrialized. Cotton remained the primary crop.

Mississippi During the Great Depression

When Faulkner was writing *Absalom, Absalom!*, the United States was in the midst of the Great Depression. This was a period of great economic decline, not just in America but in the whole world. Beginning with the stock market crash of 1929, the United States saw massive unemployment and widespread poverty. Mississippi was especially hard hit during the Great Depression and became even poorer. It was one of the poorest states in America before the Depression, and the situation grew worse in the 1930s. Because the state's economy was dependent on cotton, the plummeting price of the crop devastated the Mississippi's economy. Such economic problems compelled many African Americans to move to northern states, changing the racial face of the state. In 1900, about 60 percent of Mississippi's population was black; fifty years later, the percentage was barely 33 percent.

CRITICAL OVERVIEW

When *Absalom, Absalom!* was first published in 1936 by Random House, the novel received some positive reviews from a number of critics who found it powerful and saw Faulkner as a gifted artist. Many critics gave *Absalom, Absalom!* mixed or negative reviews. Such critics found the novel challenging and ineffective, primarily because of its demanding, even confusing structure. The book was also controversial with some readers because it touched on the idea of incest. In addition, the novel suffered from some unpopularity because of its dark themes, out of favor during the dark times of the Great Depression. Though *Absalom, Absalom!* initially had some scholarly and critical support, the novel had poor sales and was out of print by 1944 in the United States. Faulkner found a more receptive audience in Europe.

Pebble Hill Plantation House near Thomasville, Gerogia © *Kevin Fleming/Corbis*

Beginning in the post–World War II period, *Absalom*, like the rest of Faulkner's major works, gradually became more popular among critics and literati in the United States. Faulkner also came to be seen as a powerful and gifted writer. Scholars praised the way he portrayed the South and considered the book one of his most effective treatments of the South and all its racial and social complexities. Referring to *Absalom, Absalom!* as well as two other great novels by Faulkner, *The Sound and the Fury* and *As I Lay Dying*, Michiko Kakutani of the *New York Times* writes,

> William Faulkner irrevocably changed the geography of American literature.... [H]e also made the postage stamp-sized piece of Mississippi soil he called home yield fresh and enduring myths—myths that would define both the predicament of the post–Civil War South and the condition of America as it entered the turbulent 20th century.

Critics came to praise *Absalom* for its structure, style, and tone, which they considered complex, interesting, and experimental, if not breathtaking, for its time. They lauded the prose, which was tormented and dramatic. Also, they saw Faulkner's experimentation with form as purposeful, related to the loose concepts of knowledge and interpersonal understanding. Critics believed Faulkner showed that one cannot really know facts and truth from letters and conversations; such ideas are relative. Faulkner's construction also uses mythology as part of its creation. In *American Writers*, William Van O'Connor argues, "Sutpen's story, told in a series of anecdotes, guesses, and inferences, represents the South to Quentin. His investigation of Sutpen's rise and fall and the family's subsequent destruction is also an investigation of his own heritage."

Absalom continued to be highly regarded for many years, eventually seen as one of the best novels produced by an American writer. Cleanth Brooks in *William Faulkner: The Yoknapatawpha Country* asserts,

> *Absalom, Absalom!*, in my opinion the greatest of Faulkner's novels, is probably the least well understood of all his books. The property of a great work, as T. S. Eliot remarked long ago, is to communicate before it is understood; and *Absalom, Absalom!* passes this test triumphantly. It has meant something very powerful and important to all sorts of people.

There is some debate over which is Faulkner's best novel, with some regarding the earlier novel *The Sound and the Fury* as a better, more important, masterwork than *Absalom*. Other critics believe that Faulkner's contribution to American literature with the novel was underappreciated. In 1997, Luke Salisbury of the *Boston Globe* surmises, "Faulkner knew what America's original sin is and wrote about it before any other major white writer. He knew what had to be acknowledged. That acknowledgement hasn't come yet."

Despite continuing deliberation, most critics believe in the might of Faulkner's words. Faulkner scholar Diane Roberts tells Jonathan Yardley of the *Tampa Tribune*, "He reminds us powerfully (though we may not need it) of the weight of the past, he reinvented the Southern Gothic so thoroughly that we can never look straight at a ruined plantation house again."

CRITICISM

Daniel Joseph Singal

In the following excerpt, Singal argues that in Absalom, Absalom!, *Faulkner creates a modernist Southern man, more interested in looking forward than looking back.*

The task of constructing what Robert Dale Parker calls the "preferred explanation"—preferred because "it matches the incidental details that need explaining"—falls to Quentin and Shreve in the second half of the book. Sitting in their frigid dormitory room at Harvard, the two young men together function like Faulkner's conception of the ideal Modernist novelist, immersing themselves in the story until the characters live again within their minds. In a process governed by the integrative impulse lying at the heart of Modernist culture, things that had previously been separated by time and space are now fused together in a white heat of literary creation to form a nearly seamless whole, a kind of hermeneutic epiphany in which "there might be paradox and inconsistency but nothing fault nor false." Not only do Shreve and Quentin become interchangeable, "both thinking as one, the voice which happened to be speaking the thought only the thinking become audible," but the two soon fuse with their subjects to the point where the distinction between past and present completely dissolves: "Because now neither of them was there.

They were both in Carolina and the time was forty-six years ago, ... since now both of them were Henry Sutpen and both of them were Bon, compounded each of both yet either neither, smelling the very smoke which had blown and faded away forty-six years ago." In this way, as Bernhard Radloff formulates it, "their minds do not create a vision" but rather "give themselves up to one" that has been inscribed in the written and oral evidence passed down to them. "Listening," Radloff writes, "they are allowed to see."

Essential to that exercise is the contribution of Shreve. A Canadian, and therefore even more removed from the traumas of southern history than a Yankee would be, he provides an indispensable measure of critical detachment that Quentin could not conceivably muster on his own. At the same time, in his mounting fascination with the Sutpen tale, Shreve prods his roommate to further exploration, forcing Quentin to confront the more anguishing implications of the story and generating interpretive momentum until the final portrait of interracial fratricide becomes inescapable. However, one must never forget that Shreve originated not as a real person but as a voice within Faulkner's consciousness. He speaks, Ruth Vande Kieft rightly tells us, "for the Faulkner who had traveled, read, seen through other than Southern eyes the fantastic facts and fictions of his homeland," just as Quentin represents the traditionalist Faulkner "who had lived and felt the Southern past and accepted its full burden of guilt." Shreve, in other words, stands for the Modernist Faulkner that often sparred with its alter ego inside the psyche that held them both. On this occasion, though, the two have merged, making possible a moment of supreme vision."

For Quentin, the other half of that collaboration, things are far more complicated. All his life he has heard the Sutpen story until it has become an elemental part of his cultural memory as a southerner, yet at the outset he would much rather retreat into the comfort of obliviousness than seek out its significance. "Why tell me about it?" he asks his father in the novel's opening pages, shortly after Rosa Coldfield has summoned him. "What is it to me that the land or the earth or whatever it was got tired of him at last and turned and destroyed him?" At the same time, something within him, reinforced later by Shreve, wants to know the "truth" about the problematic past he has inherited, leading to his titanic struggle during the balance of *Absalom, Absalom!*, as Faulkner once put it, to "get God to tell him why." The internal conflict waxes and wanes, with the decisive moment coming in the final chapter during the visit that he and Miss Rosa pay to Sutpen's Hundred. "I just dont want to be here," he thinks to himself as they approach the house; "I just dont want to know about whatever [is] . . . hidden in it." But an hour later when Rosa descends the stairway in shock, having seen the secret residing in the upstairs bedroom, Quentin cannot stop himself from going up as well: "I must see too now. I will have to. Maybe I shall be sorry tomorrow, but I must see." His decision to pursue knowledge whatever the cost is no small matter, qualifying as an act of Faulknerian heroism comparable to those of Judith and Bon.

That heroic act would strongly suggest that the Quentin of *Absalom, Absalom!* has undergone a substantial transformation from the pathetic soul who committed suicide in *The Sound and the Fury*. The earlier Quentin, who dreamed of transcendent purity and struggled to stop the flow of time, had been derived primarily from Faulkner's former post-Victorian self. By contrast, this new Quentin displays no obsession with purity and, thanks to his alliance with Shreve, is able to comprehend and accept the fluid medium of history, even making his peace with the fact that things never finish themselves:

> *Maybe nothing ever happens once and is finished. Maybe happen is never once but like ripples maybe on water after the pebble sinks, the ripples moving on, spreading, the pool attached by a narrow umbilical water-cord to the next pool which the first pool feeds, has fed, did feed, let this second pool contain a different temperature of water, a different molecularity of having seen, felt, remembered . . . , it doesn't matter: that pebble's watery echo whose fall it did not even see moves across its surface too at the original ripple-space, to the old ineradicable rhythm.*

Existence may have no more intrinsic pattern to it than the surface of a body of water, but once people act, the consequences of their actions will reverberate across the "narrow umbilical" to future generations, creating a pattern. At odds with his father's teaching, Quentin now realizes that no external fate controls human destiny; rather, we generate fate by what we do, setting in motion an "ineradicable rhythm" much as Thomas Sutpen did when he put aside his first wife and child. In short, in this Quentin a post-Victorian sensibility has gradually and reluctantly become Modernist, if just barely, during the course of the novel.

The question immediately arises of whether Quentin's progress is enough to save him. Should we as readers assume that he is able to "work through" the Sutpen story in a Freudian sense and so free himself from its awful psychic burden, or are we to conclude that it crushes him, causing him to fall back into fin de siècle gloom and pushing him toward the suicidal choice he makes in *The Sound and the Fury*?

Here the evidence is incredibly mixed. There can be little doubt that Quentin experiences great agony during his extended séance with Shreve. At first he responds to the more troubling revelations by staying silent; later, after recalling his meeting with Henry Sutpen, he begins "to jerk all over, violently and uncontrollably." It is not clear, however, how we should interpret these convulsions. Are they a sign of his heroic initiative in carrying the narrative forward, equivalent to the body movements that sometimes take place during psychoanalytic sessions when a patient successfully combats his or her personal demons? Or do they signify a neurotic stasis that he cannot overcome, an inner blockage giving rise to the Poe-like "Nevermore of peace" refrain that runs through his mind at the end? Again, it is hard to tell. We do know that Faulkner chose to cut a reference to Quentin's death that had originally opened the second chapter, a possible indication that this reconceived Quentin may not be destined to plunge into the Charles River. Still, we cannot overlook Quentin's morbid complaint on the novel's penultimate page of how he is "older at twenty than a lot of people who have died," followed shortly by the entry in the genealogy that has his life end later that year in Cambridge. As with Joe Christmas, Faulkner leaves the ultimate disposition of his protagonist unresolved.

Also deliberately left opaque is Faulkner's prognosis for the racial future of southern society. *Absalom*'s final haunting passages, many of them added during the last stages of revision, engage that subject through the enigmatic figure of Jim Bond, Charles Etienne Bon's "idiot negro" son and thus the "scion, the heir, the apparent (though not obvious)" of the dynasty Thomas Sutpen had sought to found. A clear-cut successor to Benjy Compson, whose horrific bellow in the concluding pages of *The Sound and the Fury* registered Faulkner's otherwise inexpressible judgment on the history of his region, Bond dwells amid the ruins of the Sutpen estate howling incessantly at the moral outrage that has attended its rise and fall. What makes Bond so intriguing, however, is the prediction that Shreve hazards concerning him. Though they may be outcasts today, Shreve informs an astonished Quentin, in time "the Jim Bonds are going to conquer the western hemisphere" through interracial procreation with whites. Their offspring, it is true, will likely "bleach out" over the succeeding generations, but "it will still be Jim Bond," so that "in a few thousand years I who regard you will also have sprung from the loins of African kings."

Once more Faulkner masks his intent. Some critics have seen these remarks as no more than Shreve's callow attempt to tease his distressed southern roommate as they disengage from their intense narrative partnership. Supporting that reading is the highly pejorative treatment of miscegenation in many of Faulkner's other works, where it is portrayed as resulting inevitably in degeneracy and misfortune. Bond, with his "slackmouthed idiot face," would seem to offer evidence for that point of view. But such an approach must contend with the insert that Faulkner composed for *Intruder in the Dust* in 1949, which refers favorably to Shreve's remark (calling it the "tag line" of the novel) and speeds up the timetable for racial amalgamation from "a few thousand" to "five hundred years or perhaps even less than that." Moreover, the entire thematic thrust of *Absalom, Absalom!* would lead one to believe that that "tag line" conveys Faulkner's own position on racial mixing. Why, Charles Bon comments in regard to his octoroon mistress, should anyone care about "a little matter like a spot of negro blood," a phrase drenched with irony when one realizes that it was just such a "spot" that caused Bon's father to disown him, setting in motion the train of events that not only doomed the family but became "the land's catastrophe too." Faulkner, it would appear, was saying that a mentality obsessed with racial purity was primed for destruction.

To be sure, from the vantage of the late twentieth century, some have argued that Faulkner, in calling for blacks to "bleach out," was surrendering to the venerable white dream-wish that people of African descent would simply vanish, but that is inexcusably anachronistic. During the 1930s when *Absalom, Absalom!* was written, the vision of an integrated society that Shreve sets forth could only be understood as a fundamental challenge to the South's sacred system of genealogical accounting. From the colonial era onward, perhaps the most potent force motivating southerners first to preserve slavery and then, in the decades following emancipation, to devise a system of legal racial separation had been their fear of a possible "mongrelized" society. Under these circumstances, the importance of Faulkner's attempt to forecast a posterity in which racial blending would be both inevitable and essentially benign must not be discounted. What he was engaged in, writes James Snead, was no less than "a radical attempt to integrate" that which his society had "sundered" by illustrating the "futility of applying strict binary categories to human affairs." Indeed, that a white Mississippian raised during the apogee of segregation would see fit in 1936 to substitute Jim Bond (the very name effuses integration) for Jim Crow might stand as an act of Faulknerian heroism dwarfing all the others.

Source: Daniel Joseph Singal, "The Dark House of Southern History," in *William Faulkner: The Making of a Modernist*, University of North Carolina Press, 1997, pp. 189–334.

SOURCES

Brooks, Cleanth, "History and the Sense of the Tragic," in *William Faulkner: The Yoknapatawpha Country*, Yale University Press, 1963, pp. 295–324.

Caldwell, Gail, "Going Deeper into Yoknapatawpha," in the *Boston Globe*, July 22, 1990, p. B17.

Faulkner, William, *Absalom, Absalom!*, Random House, 1936; reprint, *The Corrected Edition*, Vintage International, 1990.

Kakutani, Michiko, "Books of the Times: A New Work on Faulkner, Linking His Life and His Art," in the *New York Times*, May 26, 1989, p. C25.

O'Connor, William Van, "William Faulkner 1867–1962," in *American Writers*, Vol. 2, Charles Scribner's Sons, 1974, pp. 54–76.

Salisbury, Luke, "Faulkner and the Power of Words," in the *Boston Globe*, September 24, 1997, p. A23.

Yardley, Jonathan, "Faulkner at 100: Wallflower at His Own Party," in the *Tampa Tribune*, October 26, 1997, p. 6.

Adventures of Huckleberry Finn

MARK TWAIN

1885

With *Adventures of Huckleberry Finn* (1885) Mark Twain developed an archetypal American hero. Huck Finn, the natural boy, resistant to civilization and hungry for adventure, morally right and often legally wrong, is as vivid and familiar a personality to readers as any childhood friend. The novel is a classic of American literature, and, many believe, the greatest work of a great author. Since *Huckleberry Finn*'s publication in 1885, it has appeared in over 150 American editions alone and 200,000 copies are sold each year. *Huckleberry Finn* has also been translated into over 50 languages and at least 700 editions have been published worldwide. The novel has also been controversial since its publication, primarily because of its racial content, and it has been repeatedly banned by various libraries and schools.

Twain introduced the character of Huck Finn in his 1876 novel *The Adventures of Tom Sawyer* as a partner in Sawyer's adventures. Like many of the characters and events in the novels, Huck Finn was based on someone Twain knew while growing up in Hannibal, Missouri. Twain began writing what became *Adventures of Huckleberry Finn* soon after publishing *Tom Sawyer* with ideas left over from the novel. *Huckleberry Finn* took him nearly seven years to complete as he struggled to finish the story several times and let the manuscript rest while working out the story's direction.

Set in the 1830s or 1840s, *Adventures of Huckleberry Finn* features Huck as the first-person narrator of the novel. He is running from the Widow Douglas's attempt to turn him into a respectable citizen, as well as from his alcoholic, abusive father. With Huck on his journey is Jim, a runaway slave owned by Miss Watson, the widow's sister who also tries to civilize Huck in the early chapters of *Huckleberry Finn*.

As Huck and Jim travel along the Mississippi River by raft and canoe, they encounter a variety of people from many social classes, from con artists to kind-hearted wealthy families. Both seek total freedom and enjoy the liberty they have along the way. Huck eventually ends up at the Phelps farm where Jim is held as a runaway slave. In the end, both Jim and Huck remain free as Huck will not let himself be adopted and changed by the Phelpses. He plans to continue his journey.

Huckleberry Finn satirizes society's hypocrisy as it demonstrates the positive results of moral action. Twain explores these ideas as Huck deals with issues of right and wrong and wrestles his conscience several times over helping Jim escape in the book. As Hamlin Hill explains in the *Dictionary of Literary Biography*, "*Huckleberry Finn* explores whether any human being can transcend his society, violate his training, achieve independence from external pressure and judgment."

Twain also uses *Huckleberry Finn* to explore issues of slavery and race relations. The novel as a whole has been interpreted as an attack on racism, something supported by Twain's own opinions on the subject. Huck comes to see that though Jim is black and a slave, he is also a person and loyal friend who repeatedly protects Huck. While many critics have praised his take on racism, a significant number have taken issue with what they consider to be Twain's stereotypical depiction of Jim. *Adventures of Huckleberry Finn* has been seen as racist because the word "nigger" is used more than 200 times. This racial content is one of the primary reasons why the book has been banned from certain schools and libraries. Despite such controversies, *Adventures of Huckleberry Finn* remains among the most important and beloved American novels. Richard Lemon of *People Weekly* wrote on the occasion of the novel's centennial, "Huck Finn's overriding virtue is that he stays simple: He is a boy who loves freedom and the American land and can instruct us in both."

BIOGRAPHY

MARK TWAIN

Born Samuel Langhorne Clemens in Florida, Missoiri, on November 30, 1835, the author was raised in Hannibal, Missouri. This town along the Mississippi River later served as a source of inspiration for his novels, including the early chapters of *Adventures of Huckleberry Finn*. As a boy, Clemens's limited formal education ended when his father died and he was apprenticed to a printer at the age of twelve. By his early twenties, Clemens was fulfilling a childhood dream by working as a steamboat pilot on the Mississippi. It was there that he first heard the boating term "mark twain," which he would adopt as a pen name. The Civil War ended Clemens's work on the river but led him into his journalism career. Clemens traveled west with his brother Orion, who was the territorial secretary of Nevada.

Clemens first took the name Mark Twain while writing for the Nevada-based *Territorial Enterprise*. Twain launched his book publishing career by the mid-1860s with humorous nonfiction, first with a collection of previously published pieces entitled *The Celebrated Jumping Frog of Calaveras County*. In 1876, Twain introduced the character of Huckleberry Finn in the novel *The Adventures of Tom Sawyer*, based on real people and events in Hannibal and his uncle's Florida farm. Twain published his best-known novels, including *Huck Finn* (1885), in the 1880s, and earned a reputation as one of the greatest living American writers. Twain continued writing humorous nonfiction until his death from heart disease on April 21, 1910, in Redding, Connecticut.

PLOT SUMMARY

Chapters 1–3
Adventures of Huckleberry Finn opens with Huck introducing himself and explaining what has

Mark Twain © Corbis

happened to him since the end of the last book by Twain, *The Adventures of Tom Sawyer*. He and Tom split the $6,000 they found, and the Widow Douglas took Huck in. She forces him to live by rules, quit smoking, and go to school. Her sister, Miss Watson, teaches him about religion and contributes to his education. One night, Huck slips out of the house and finds Tom Sawyer waiting for him. After creating mischief with Jim, an adult slave owned by Miss Watson, Huck and Tom meet other boys. They form a gang of highwaymen headed by Tom. Miss Watson tries to teach Huck to pray, but he decides there is nothing to it. Huck tells readers that he has not seen his father, Pap, in over a year and he is glad about it. After playing with Tom's gang for a month, Huck resigns. The most mischief the gang gets into is breaking up a Sunday school picnic.

Chapters 4–6

A few months later, Huck has learned to read a little and grown to tolerate his new lifestyle. He sees tracks outside, which makes him run to Judge Thatcher's. Huck sells him the $6,000 plus interest from his *Tom Sawyer* adventure

for $1. Huck later finds Pap in his room. Pap threatens to beat Huck if he continues going to school. Pap tells him, "You've put on considerable many frills since I been away. I'll take you down a peg before I get done with you." He tells his son that he heard about the money. Huck tells him that the money belongs to Judge Thatcher now. The widow and the judge go to court to gain guardianship of Huck, but the new judge in town refuses to give it to them. Under the threat of violence, Huck gets his father money, which he spends getting drunk. The new judge tries to help by cleaning Pap up and putting him up in a spare room in his home. Pap persists in his legal fight for Huck's money, and occasionally beats his son for continuing to attend school. As Huck reasons, "I didn't want to go to school much before, but I reckoned I'd go now to spite pap." He takes Huck to a cabin on the Illinois shore. Although Pap gets drunk and beats him, Huck enjoys not having rules again. He refuses to go back to the widow's, though she tries to rescue him. The beatings and his father's drunken behavior compel Huck's decision to run away.

Chapters 7–9

While checking the fishing lines for his father, Huck finds a canoe and hides it. When Pap leaves for town to sell part of a raft they found, Huck loads everything from the cabin in his canoe. He also makes it look like there was a robbery and Huck was killed. After ensuring his father has returned to the cabin, Huck takes his canoe to Jackson's Island where he hides and goes to sleep. The next morning, Huck sees a ferryboat float by with Pap, the widow, and others looking for Huck's body. While enjoying life on the island, Huck comes across Jim. Jim thinks Huck is a ghost until Huck convinces him otherwise. Huck shares the story of what happened to him, and Jim tells him that he has been hiding on Jackson's Island since Huck allegedly died. Jim ran off because Miss Watson had been picking on him and seemed finally ready to make good on her threat to sell him. Huck and Jim hide the canoe and move the supplies into a cavern on a ridge in the middle of the island. Huck is content and enjoys exploring the island's shore in the canoe during the day. During his travels, Huck catches part of a lumber raft. He also comes across a house floating by. Huck finds a dead man inside, but Jim will not let him look at the body. Huck and Jim take all the goods of value from inside the home.

Chapters 10–13

Among the goods, Jim and Huck find money. Huck decides to trick Jim by putting a dead rattlesnake on his blanket. Another rattlesnake later joins it and bites Jim. Huck feels guilty, believing that he had brought bad luck by handling a snake skin. Jim takes care of the bite and recovers in a few days. Bored, Huck decides to disguise himself as a girl and find out what is going on in town. Huck he goes to the home of newcomer Mrs. Judith Loftus, pretending to be Sarah Williams. He learns from her that some in town think that Huck staged his own death, while others believe that Jim killed him. There is also a reward for turning Jim in. Still others believe that Huck's father killed him and made it look like a robbery so that he could get his hands on his son's money. Mrs. Loftus thinks Jim is on Jackson's Island. Huck learns that her husband and another man are going to the island that night to look for Jim. Huck returns to the island, sets up a decoy camp, and takes off with the raft and canoe with Jim.

Huck and Jim drift down the river, passing St. Louis. They stop each night and buy food. Passing a steamboat wrecked on a rock, Huck insists they check it out, though Jim is reluctant. On board, Huck finds two men stealing what is aboard and arguing about a killing. When Huck sends Jim to set the men's boat adrift, Jim returns and tells Huck that their own raft is gone. Worried, Huck steals the men's boat and they take off after the raft. They get their raft back after a storm and put the stolen items from the men's boat on board. While Jim takes care of the raft, Huck finds a riverboat and convinces the operator to go back to the crashed ferryboat with a fake story. Huck believes the widow would be proud of what he has done, "because rapscallions and dead beats is the kind the widow and good people takes the most interest in."

Chapters 14–16

Huck and Jim enjoy the loot from the wreck. Huck reads some of the books they found to Jim, which leads to a conversation about what kings do. When the talk turns to the biblical King Solomon, Jim tells Huck that he does not think Solomon was wise because he was going to cut a child in half, arguing, "You take a man dat's on'y got one or two chillen; is dat man gwyne be waseful o' chillen? No, he ain't; he can't 'ford it. *He* know how to value 'em." Huck tells Jim that he missed the point of the story, but Jim will not listen.

Huck and Jim decide to go to Cairo, Illinois, sell the raft, and take a steamboat up the Ohio River to the free states. On the second day of their journey, a fog comes up, throwing off their plans. Huck is in the canoe and gets separated from Jim on the raft for a long time. When Huck finally catches up with Jim, Huck pretends like nothing had happened. Jim finally realizes Huck was fooling him and gets angry:

> When I got all wore out wid work, en wid de callin' for you, en went to sleep, my heart wuz mos' broke because you wuz los', en I didn' k'yer no' mo' what become er me en de raf'. En when I wake up en find you back ag'in, all safe en soun', de tears come, en I could 'a' got down on my knees en kiss yo' foot, I's so thankful. En all you wuz thinkin' 'bout wuz how you could make a fool uv old Jim wid a lie.

Huck feels guilty and apologizes, noting, "I didn't do no more mean tricks, and I wouldn't done that one if I'd 'a' knowed it would make him feel that way."

While Jim is excited because he is nearly free, Huck feels like he has done wrong to Miss Watson. Huck thinks, "I got to feeling so mean and so miserable I most wished I was dead." As Jim makes plans for his freedom, Huck feels even worse. He decides to go ashore at first light and tell on Jim in the town they think might be Cairo. Huck tells Jim that he is making sure it is Cairo. Huck feels conflicted because Jim says Huck is his friend, and he winds up protecting Jim from some runaway slave catchers. They learn that they have floated far south of Cairo and continue to travel, but they lose the canoe. They take the raft downstream looking for a canoe to buy. The raft is apparently destroyed by a steamboat in the fog, and Huck cannot find Jim. Huck takes hold of a plank and finds a house onshore.

Chapters 17–18

Huck is taken in by the Grangerford family. He makes up a story about his background, and the Grangerfords offer him a permanent home. While Huck has problems remembering his fake name at first, he likes the house, the books, the artwork, and the food. Huck admires the family patriarch, Col. Grangerford, and finds the family large and beautiful. The Grangerfords have been feuding with the similarly wealthy Shepherdsons for thirty years. One day, Sophia Grangerford asks Huck to go back to church as a favor for her to get her New Testament, which she left there. Huck finds a slip of paper inside with a time on it. She is happy to get her book.

Jack, the slave assigned to Huck, leads him to Jim, whom the Grangerford slaves had been hiding in the nearby woods. Jim has been repairing the raft and buying supplies. The next day, Sophia has been found to have run off and married a Shepherdson son. This event leads to a gunfight that Huck watches from a tree. The colonel and two sons are killed as are several Shepherdsons. Huck feels guilty for contributing to the incident. He finds Jim, who is glad to see him. Jack had told Jim that Huck was dead. The pair continues their travels on the Mississippi River.

Chapters 19–20

While ashore one day, two men beg Huck to let them join him and Jim on the raft. Both men are con artists who have been run out of town; though they had not known each other before, they decide to join forces. The younger man claims he is a duke, while the elder says he is the missing dauphin and rightful Louis XVII, the son of the French King Louis XVI. Jim is excited to treat them like royalty; Huck soon decides they are fakes, but keeps up the act anyway.

The duke and king decide they will put on a play though the dauphin has not acted before. With Huck, the duke and the king go into a small town. The whole community is at a revival camp meeting two miles outside town. Huck and the king go to the meeting, where the king bilks people out of money. In the meantime, the duke goes to the print shop to make up posters promoting his schemes and a runaway slave poster with Jim's description on it. So they can travel during the day, the duke says they can tie up Jim as needed and claim he is a runaway slave they are taking downstream.

Chapters 21–23

As the raft travels both day and night, the duke and the king work on their performance for the production they plan to put on. Reaching a small town in Arkansas, Jim stays with the raft while Huck, the duke, and the king go ashore. The con artists rent the town courthouse and prepare for the show. At the show, only twelve people show

up. They laugh at the duke's and king's interpretation of certain Shakespearean scenes. The duke promises a new, funny show, and he prints up handbills for the event. Ladies and children will not be admitted.

A house full of men shows up at the production. It is short: just the king naked and painted prancing on all fours for a few moments. While the audience laughs, they feel taken but do not want everyone else in town to know they have been. They decide to let the rest of the town see it so everyone is equal. The duke and king do well on the second night as well. On the third night, the audience consists of men who have seen the show and come loaded with rotting produce to throw at them. The duke and Huck run to the raft before the show started; the king is already there. The next morning, Huck finds Jim upset by thoughts of his wife and children. Huck finds Jim's feelings odd, thinking, "I do believe he cared just as much for his people as white folks does for their'n. It don't seem natural, but I reckon it's so."

Chapters 24–26

Traveling a little farther, the king and the duke decide to work two towns on opposite sides of the riverbank with Huck's help. So he will not be bothered or questioned, they leave Jim on the raft, painted blue and in the King Lear costume, with a sign that says "Sick Arab." From a man going aboard a steamboat, the king learns about a recently deceased citizen. The king decides to pose as a reverend, the England-based brother of the deceased man who had hoped to see his minister brother before his death. The duke poses as the reverend's other brother, a deaf-mute.

The townspeople, including the deceased man's daughters, believe the con men. Dealing with $6,000 in cash the dead man left behind for his brothers in his cellar, the king and the duke are surprised to find that the stash is more $400 short. The duke decides they should make up the difference and give the money to the daughters, to prove they are honest men. Their con is nearly exposed when the town doctor believes the men are frauds and tells everyone so. No one will believe it, and Mary Jane, one of the deceased man's daughters, gives the $6,000 back to the king to invest.

The king, the duke, and Huck, who acts as their valet ("valley"), stay in the family home. Huck grows fond of the daughters and feels guilty about helping to steal their inheritance. Huck decides to rectify the situation by stealing the money back for them.

Chapters 27–30

Late at night, Huck puts the money in the coffin; it is buried with the dead man the next day. The king tells the group after the funeral that he would settle the estate immediately and return home. He auctions the house and property right away. The king even sells the slaves though the daughters did not want it done. When the king and duke learn the money is missing, Huck blames it on the slaves and they believe him. He tells Mary Jane everything that has happened, even though telling the truth seems to him "so kind of strange and unregular."

The deceased man's real brothers arrive and have trouble getting people to believe that they are who they say. There is a public confrontation over which set of brothers to believe. The investigators decide to dig up the body to see if he has a tattoo described differently by each pair. When the coffin is opened, everyone is surprised to see the missing money there. Huck runs away in the excitement. As he leaves with Jim, he sees the duke and king coming toward them fast in a rowboat. Huck reports, "So wilted right down onto the planks then, and give up; and it was all I could do to keep from crying." They come aboard.

Chapters 31–33

As the duke and the king grow more broke and desperate, Huck and Jim worry about what they will do next. In Pikesville, the king and the duke get distracted, and Huck decides he and Jim will run. When Huck gets back to the raft, he finds that Jim has been sold as a runaway slave and is being sent to New Orleans. Huck does not know what to do other than steal Jim back. In town, Huck uses an emotional story to learn from the duke where Jim.

Huck debates what he should do; he knows that "the right thing and the clean thing" is to write a letter to Miss Watson, telling her the location of her runaway slave. However, when he thinks of what a great friend Jim has been, he decides to follow the path of "wickedness" and help Jim escape. As Huck surveys the Phelps farm, where Jim is being held, he is spotted by one of the family's slaves and is mistaken for a visiting nephew. Huck plays along, and he soon discovers that the "nephew" he is impersonating is none

other than Tom Sawyer. Tom's Aunt Sally and Uncle Silas welcome the boy into their home as their nephew.

When he hears the steamboat coming, Huck goes to head Tom off. After convincing Tom that he is not a ghost, Huck tells him about the immediate situation, and Tom agrees that Huck should continue to pretend to be him. Tom also agrees to help Huck steal Jim back. At the Phelpses' plantation, Tom tells Sally that he is Sid Sawyer, Tom's brother. Huck and Tom learn that Jim told the townspeople about the king and duke being frauds. When Huck and Tom sneak out of the house at night, they fill each other in on their lives. Huck and Tom pass the king and duke, who are being tarred and feathered.

Chapter 34–39

Tom and Huck plan to free Jim. Tom objects to Huck's straightforward plan, saying, "What's the good of a plan that ain't no more trouble than that? It's as mild as goose-milk." Instead, Tom devises an elaborate plan reminiscent of a popular adventure novel. The boys decide that, instead of lifting up the leg of the bed to slip Jim's chain off, they should saw through the leg of the bed—only after Huck convinces Tom that sawing through Jim's leg is not a good option. Instead of using the door to escape Jim's cabin prison, Tom decides they will tunnel their way out.

Chapters 40–43

On the night of the planned escape, Aunt Sally catches Huck in the cellar and is suspicious. She tells him to go to the parlor where armed farmers were gathered. Afraid, Huck answers her questions. After he is sent upstairs to bed, he goes out again, finds Tom and Jim, and they escape. The men shoot at them, and while Jim is free, Tom gets shot in the leg. Huck and Jim insist on going for a doctor for him, though Tom does not want it. Jim hides while Huck convinces a doctor in town to come to treat Tom and not say anything. Huck runs into Uncle Silas, who sends Huck home to appease Aunt Sally.

By breakfast, the doctor has brought Tom home on a mattress with Jim tied up behind them. Sally is happy that Tom is alive. While the men argue about whether to hang Jim, the doctor stands up for him, telling how he helped with Tom. When Tom recovers, he tells his aunt that Jim is already free; Miss Watson has died

> " THE WIDOW DOUGLAS SHE TOOK ME FOR HER
> SON, AND ALLOWED SHE WOULD SIVILIZE ME; BUT IT
> WAS ROUGH LIVING IN THE HOUSE ALL THE TIME,
> CONSIDERING HOW DISMAL REGULAR AND DECENT THE
> WIDOW WAS IN ALL HER WAYS; AND SO WHEN I
> COULDN'T STAND IT NO LONGER I LIT OUT. I GOT INTO
> MY OLD RAGS AND MY SUGAR-HOGSHEAD AGAIN, AND
> WAS FREE AND SATISFIED."

and freed him in her will. Tom's Aunt Polly shows up and reveals the truth about the boy's identity and confirms that Jim is free.

In the final chapter, Tom reveals that he planned for them to free Jim, have adventures on the river, and return home to celebrate Jim as a hero and a free man. Tom gives Jim $40 for the trouble he caused. Huck worries the money he had at home is gone, but Tom says it is all still there. Jim tells Huck his father is dead; Pap was the man in the floating house. The Phelpses offer to take Huck in. Tom suggests that he, Huck, and Jim head for the Indian Territories to have some adventures. Huck ends his story, saying,

> But I reckon I got to light out for the Territory ahead of the rest, because Aunt Sally she's going to adopt me and sivilize me and I can't stand it. I been there before.

THEMES

Freedom

Both Huck Finn and Jim are on a quest for freedom, trying to escape the rules of society. By declaring their independence in this manner, the two are fulfilling an American dream of living as they choose to without being subject to the restraints and restrictions they do not embrace. They find life most agreeable on their raft and canoe on the river, despite many mishaps along the way.

Huck avoids efforts to "sivilize" him by the Widow Douglas, Miss Watson, and others he meets along the river. In the first few chapters of

Adventures of Huckleberry Finn, Huck goes to school, quits smoking and swearing, and learns how to pray. While Huck uses these life skills down the line—his reading skills entertain Jim— and does care about doing the right thing—he does not like the duke's and king's plans for bilking Mary Jane and her sisters—he cherishes his freedom to choose where he goes and how he lives.

Huck enjoys living in the cabin with Pap more than with the widow, though Pap beats him, insults him, and only wants his money. There, Huck can swear and smoke. It is only when this situation becomes too difficult that he runs away, meets up with Jim on Jackson Island, and begins his quest in earnest. By the end of the novel, not much has changed. The Phelpses want to adopt Huck, but he plans to continue his journey before any more rules of society can be thrust upon him.

Jim's quest for freedom is more complex than Huck's. He ran away from Miss Watson because he believed she was finally going make good on her threat to sell him in New Orleans. Huck and Jim initially head toward free states where Jim can escape the bonds of slavery. Jim hopes to buy his family's freedom once he is free. While Huck feels some conflict over helping a slave escape, Huck ultimately sees Jim as a friend and helps him escape from difficult situations over and over again.

Equality

Huck Finn explores another tenet of the American dream: equality, or rather its absence. Set in Missouri and the South in the pre–Civil War United States, Twain makes the concept of African American personhood more acceptable to his post–Civil War readers by offering an innocent child-hero who understands it instinctively. Twain illustrates the depth of racism in this time period while showing that characters like Huck can overcome them and look at African Americans as people with feelings, families, and friendships, even with whites. Though Huck and other characters uses the word "nigger" to describe black slaves, Huck is also surprised to learn how much Jim really means to him over the course of their travels. No one questions the use of this racial epitaph in the book, though modern readers often find it troublesome and distracting. Huck sees Jim as a friend and a person and so cannot return him to slavery, even though he does not question the larger institution of slavery.

Mickey Rooney as Huck Finn in the 1939 film of The Adventures of Huckleberry Finn *© Bettmann/Corbis*

However, in addition to showing that Huck can achieve personal growth in how he regards Jim, Twain also shows that characters, such as the doctor who tends to Tom Sawyer after he is shot, can stand up for the runaway slave as a man of character. Twain also uses people's racism to protect Jim as part of the story. The duke comes up with several plans so that people leave Jim alone while the con artists bilk townsfolk. The primary one involves printing up fake posters about Jim being a runaway slave so they can leave him tied up during the day. Another plan also plays on racist feelings when the duke dresses up Jim in the King Lear costume, paints him blue, and labels him a sick Arab so people will avoid him when he is alone on the raft.

Righteousness

As the story in *Huck Finn* progresses, Huck develops a conscience about what is right and what is wrong, and acts accordingly. He uses his moral sense to expose hypocrisy in others and to try to correct such situations when he can. It is a moral code of the American dream. While Huck almost always does the "right" thing from a moral perspective, because of his upbringing he cannot help but feel that his actions are actually wicked and immoral. When Huck first finds Jim,

he promises not to reveal Jim's secret: "People would call me a low down Abolitionist and despise me for keeping mum—but that don't make no difference. I ain't agoing to tell." Later, when Huck tries to convince himself that the right thing to do is to turn Jim in, he cannot defy his conscience:

> It made me shiver. And I about made up my mind to pray, and see if I couldn't try to quit being the kind of a boy I was and be better. So I kneeled down. But the words wouldn't come. Why wouldn't they? It warn't no use to try and hide it from Him. Nor from me, neither. I knowed very well why they wouldn't come. It was because my heart warn't right; it was because I warn't square; it was because I was playing double. I was letting *on* to give up sin, but away inside of me I was holding on to the biggest one of all. I was trying to make my mouth *say* I would do the right thing and the clean thing, and go and write to that nigger's owner and tell where he was; but deep down in me I knowed it was a lie, and He knowed it. You can't pray a lie—I found that out.

Even though he feels that he is the wicked one, not the institution of slavery, Huck embraces his "wickedness" and makes peace with it. In doing so, Huck demonstrates to Twain's post-Emancipation readers that the right thing and the traditional thing may not be the same.

Although Huck is not above stealing for survival, he does have standards. In chapters 12 and 13, for example, he ensures that the men he overheard talking about a killing and stealing have a chance to come to justice, an action of which he is sure that the Widow Douglas, his standard for morality, would be proud.

When Huck and Jim take up with the duke and king, Huck does not mind taking part in their schemes. He does not protest about the shows they put on that sucker a village of men into paying to watch a naked, painted king prancing around. But when they claim to be the uncles of Mary Jane and her sisters and try to control their wealth, Huck takes issue with their deceit. Huck helps the men because he feels he has to, but he also feels guilty and thinks of a way for Mary Jane to retain what is rightfully hers.

HISTORICAL OVERVIEW

Slavery in Pre–Civil War America

By the 1840s, the era in which *Adventures of Huckleberry Finn* is set, the issue of slavery was very divisive in the United States. The agrarian states of the South relied on slave labor, especially on large plantations, and did not want to give up the right to own slaves. However, only a third of white Southerners owned slaves, primarily those who were wealthy land owners. The rest of the white population in the South was generally poor, often living in conditions comparable to many slaves with little chance of advancing economically and socially. Many of them embraced slavery and racism as a way to feel superior to someone and endure their hard lives. Pressure from northern abolitionists did not change these attitudes, so every time a new territory was admitted to statehood a battle broke out between northern and southern states in the U.S. Congress.

Missouri played a prominent role in this struggle between South and North. In 1818, the territory petitioned for statehood. Members of Congress from the North protested because slavery was practiced there, putting off Missouri's statehood for a time. It was not until Kentucky Representative Henry Clay devised a compromise in 1820 that Missouri was admitted to the Union. To keep the balance of slave and free states—and thus assure that slavery would still be allowed in the South—Clay proposed admitting Maine as a free state at the same time. Clay also put forth that slavery also not be allowed in other territories acquired with the Louisiana Purchase north or west of Missouri.

Clay's proposal was accepted, and Missouri was admitted to the United States in 1821. Despite the compromise, new wrinkles ensued as more territories were acquired. In 1845, for example, Texas, a slave state, was annexed. The balance between slave and free states continued to be precarious in Congress. Clay continued to play a prominent role in creating compromises to avoid internal war. His Compromise of 1850 involved Congress passing the Fugitive Slave Act, which forced the return of slaves who made it to free areas of the United States to be returned to their rightful owners. In return, the western part of the United States would be free of slavery. The standoff continued until the Civil War erupted in the early 1860s.

The Post–Civil War South

When Twain was writing *Adventures of Huckleberry Finn* in the late 1870s and early 1880s, the South was undergoing another change. As the Civil War ended in 1865 and the Confederate states surrendered to the Union, the South faced a time of physical, political, and emotional reconstruction. During Reconstruction, slavery was erased from the South and the federal government helped integrate the newly freed blacks into their new lives with increased civil rights.

While the radical reconstructionists tried to punish former Confederates in the late 1860s and early 1870s, so-called redeemers, supported by white supremacy groups such as the Ku Klux Klan, were in charge of all former Confederate states by 1877. Redeemers, often conservative Democrats, passed legislation that undermined federal Reconstruction in the South. Southern states passed laws that led to fewer political and civil rights for blacks. While public discrimination was still illegal according to an 1883 U.S. Supreme Court decision, private discrimination was legal.

Even so, blacks faced many forms of segregation and discrimination in their public lives as well. Jim Crow laws and poll taxes affected the ability of many African Americans to vote, for example. Thus thousands of blacks left the South beginning in 1877. The so-called exodusters left southern states in this time period looking for a better life in Kansas, only to encounter more racial hostility. Those blacks who remained in the South often faced conditions no better than during slavery, with many remaining poor as sharecropping farmers or domestic workers. By 1880, about 90 percent of African Americans living in the South made their living in these professions—about the same proportion as before the Civil War.

CRITICAL OVERVIEW

Adventures of Huckleberry Finn is arguably the best known and most iconic novel by Twain, but it is one mired in controversy since its publication. Some writers see it as the most influential American novel, including Pulitzer and Nobel Prize–winning author Ernest Hemingway, who, in *Green Hills of Africa*, offers *Adventures of Huckleberry Finn* its most well-known and enduring compliment:

> All modern American literature comes from one book by Mark Twain called *Huckleberry Finn*.... All American writing comes from that. There was nothing before. There has been nothing as good since.

MEDIA ADAPTATIONS

An abridged audio adaptation narrated and adapted by Garrison Keillor was released by Highbridge Audio in 2003. This version is currently available in both audiocassette and CD format.

An unabridged audio adaptation, narrated by Dick Hill, was released in 2001 by Brilliance Audio. It is currently available in both CD and audiocassette format.

An electronic version of the book was released for Microsoft Reader by Amazon Press in 2000. This version features an introduction by John D. Seelye and is available through amazon.com.

A film based on the book was released in 1939 by MGM, directed by Richard Thorpe and starred Mickey Rooney in the title role. It was released in VHS format by MGM in 1999.

A full-color film adaptation of the novel was released by MGM in 1960. The film was directed by Michael Curtiz and starred Eddie Hodges as Huck and Tony Randall as the king. It is currently available on DVD through Warner Home Video.

A filmed musical adaptation of the novel was released by MGM in 1974, directed by J. Lee Thompson and featuring songs by Richard and Robert Sherman (famous for their work in movies such as *Mary Poppins* and *Chitty Chitty Bang Bang*). This version is currently available on DVD through MGM.

An adaptation of the novel was released by Disney in 1995; this version starred Elijah Wood as Huck Finn and Courtney B. Vance as Jim and was directed by Stephen Sommers. Although every film adaptation has been criticized to some degree for not staying true to the book, this version in particular features a radically altered ending. This version is currently available on DVD from Walt Disney Video.

The novel has been adapted for television several times: first in 1955, then again in 1975 (with Ron Howard in the title role), yet again in 1981, and once more in 1985. The 1975 version was released on VHS by Twentieth Century Fox in 1996, and the 1985 version was released on VHS by MCA Home Video in 1992. None of these versions is currently available.

An animated television adaptation of *The Adventures of Huckleberry Finn* was created by Koch Vision in 1984. This version was released on DVD in 2006.

Big River: The Adventures of Huckleberry Finn, a stage musical version of the novel, began its run on Broadway in 1985 and remained there until 1987. This version featured music and lyrics by legendary country musician Roger Miller, with performances by John Goodman and René Auberjonois, among others; a soundtrack of the original cast recording was released by Decca U.S. in 1990 and is currently available in CD format.

Others regard the novel as an unorganized mess that is highly overrated. It has been subject to bans by schools and libraries for being harmful to young readers because of its apparently racist leanings.

When *Huckleberry Finn* was originally published in 1885, the novel generally received harsh reviews from contemporaries. Famous author Louisa May Alcott was one prominent voice dismissing the book. Jonathan Yardley of the *Washington Post* quotes her as writing, "If

Mr. Clemens cannot think of something better to tell our pure-minded lads and lasses, he had best stop writing for them." The novel was also deemed unsuitable for young audiences by a number of critics and promptly banned by the public library in Concord, Massachusetts.

Huckleberry Finn did received some initial positive reviews as well. Writing in London's *Saturday Review* in 1885, Brander Matthews declares that the novel is not as good as *Adventures of Tom Sawyer* but also finds that "the skill with which the character of Huck Finn is maintained is marvellous." Matthews goes on to praise the character himself:

> Huck Finn is a genuine boy; he is neither a girl in boy's clothes like many of the modern heroes of juvenile fiction, nor is he a "little man," a full-grown man cut down; he is a boy, just a boy, only a boy.

The acclaim grew louder by the twentieth century when the novel began being seen as a masterwork. Biographer Albert Bigelow Paine writes in his 1912 book *Mark Twain, a Biography: The Personal and Literary Life of Samuel Langhorne Clemens*, "The story of Huck Finn will probably stand as the best of Mark Twain's purely fictional writings. A sequel to *Tom Sawyer*, it is greater than its predecessor; greater artistically." Focusing on Huck himself, Waldo Frank lauds the character in 1919 in *Our America*, "Huckleberry Finn is the American epic hero. Greece had Ulysses. America must be content with an illiterate lad. He expresses our germinal past. He expresses the movement of the American soul through all the sultry climaxes of the Nineteenth Century."

While Huck Finn's popularity reached its height by the middle of the twentieth century, some controversies still remained about the book even at century's end. The loose structure of the novel is often considered a major flaw. Richard Lemon of *People Weekly* makes this assessment: "there's hardly a plot worth speaking of, only a series of adventures." One long-standing source of controversy is the way the novel ends, which in many eyes does not match the power of the rest of the book. When Huck reaches the Phelps farm and finds the family expecting his friend, Tom Sawyer, many critics find the set-up too coincidental. Also problematic for critics is the way Huck regresses in this section. Huck goes along with the elaborate, if not torturous, schemes devised by Tom to help Jim escape without much protest. For some critics, this change in Huck seems unexpected considering the way he had evolved over the course of the novel.

More controversial than the novel's structural or stylistic shortcomings are Twain's depictions of slavery, racism, and race relations. While many accept that Twain had anti-racist intent when he wrote *Huckleberry Finn*, it is this aspect of the book that is often the source of modern day bannings. Yardley quotes John H. Wallace, a member of the Human Relations Committee of Mark Twain Intermediate School, considering a

ban in 1982: "The book is poison. It is anti-American; it works against the melting-pot theory of our country; it works against the idea that all men are created equal." The American Library Association, which tracks the number of "challenges" leveled at controversial books in libraries nationwide, lists *Adventures of Huckleberry Finn* as the fifth most-challenged book in libraries between 1990 and 2000.

Despite such continuing tumult and bannings, the *Adventures of Huckleberry Finn* is still used in classrooms, and its reputation is still strong. A 1995 *Washington Post* article sums up the ongoing debate: "*Huckleberry Finn* will always attract the attentions of the bowdlerizers and the censors, and every so often some dimwitted or fainthearted school administrator will see fit to suppress it, but like the great river by and upon which it is set, it just keeps rolling along."

CRITICISM

Sacvan Bercovitch

In the following excerpt, Bercovitch examines how Twain's novel is a watershed achievement in deadpan humor, and how that approach makes the work open for various interpretations of a hypothetical American ideal.

Mark Twain's humor is deadpan at its best, and *Huckleberry Finn* is his funniest book, in all three senses of the term. Accordingly, in what follows I use the terms tall tale, con man, and deadpan reciprocally, fluidly, on the grounds that Twain's deadpan—the third, sinister, "odd or curious" sense of funny—incorporates (without submerging, indeed while deliberately drawing out) the other two forms of humor.

His method involves a drastic turnabout in deadpan effect. In order to enlist the tall tale and con game in the service of deadpan, Twain actually reverses conventional techniques. That is to say, the novel overturns the very tradition of deadpan that it builds upon. As a rule, that tradition belongs to the narrator. Huck has often been said to speak deadpan-style; but the funny thing is, he is not a humorist, not even when he's putting someone on (as he does Aunt Sally, when he pretends to be Tom Sawyer). In fact, he rarely has fun; he's usually "in a sweat," and on the rare occasion when he does try to kid around (as when he tells Jim they were not separated in the fog) the joke turns back on itself to humiliate him. Huck's voice may be described as pseudo-deadpan; it sounds comic, but actually it's troubled, earnest. The real deadpan artist is Mark Twain of course, and what's remarkable, what makes for the inversion I just spoke of, is that this con man is not straight-faced (as Huck is), but smiling. To recall Twain's distinction between the English comic story and the American humorous story, the author is wearing the Mask of Comedy. He hides his humor, we might say, behind a comic facade. The humor, a vehicle of deceit, is directed against the audience. The tale itself, however, is constantly entertaining, often musing, sometimes hilarious; apparently the storyteller is having a wonderful time, laughing through it all—and actually so are we.

So here's the odd or curious setup of *Huckleberry Finn*: the deadpan artist is Mark Twain, wearing the Comic Mask, doing his best to conceal the fact that he suspects that there's anything grave, let alone sinister, about his story, and he succeeds famously. Then, as we laugh, or after we've laughed, we may realize, if we're alert, that there's something we've overlooked. We haven't seen what's funny about the fact that we've found it funny. This artist has gulled us. He has diverted our attention away from the real point, and we have to go back over his story in order to recognize its nub.

The nature of re-cognition in this sense (understanding something all over again, doing a double take) may be simply illustrated. Consider a culture like the late nineteenth-century Southwest, which was both racist and egalitarian. The minstrel show was a genre born out of precisely that contradiction. So imagine a deadpan minstrel act that goes like this. The audience hears a funny story about a stereotype "darkie" and they smile and laugh along. The nub of course is that they are being laughed at; they've been taken in and made the butt of a joke. Once they see that, if they do, they understand what's truly funny about the story, and they're free to laugh at themselves for having laughed in the first place. That freedom may be compared to the shock of the funny bone. It's a complex sensation, engaging all three meanings of funny, not unlike the odd tingling, vibration you feel when you're hit on the funny bone. A light touch might mean no more than a bit of healthy fun—say, the wake-up call of the tall tale (the joke reminds you of your egalitarian

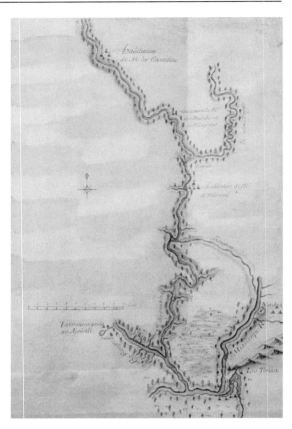

The Confluence of the Mississippi and Red Rivers is shown in this hand-drawn map from a French manuscript, 1766 © *Corbis*

principles). A sharp touch might be unnerving— a satire directed against the system at large (you recognize that this self-proclaimed egalitarian society is fundamentally racist). A direct and vicious cut would be painful, a sensation of violence, as in the sinister sense of "funny" (you realize that egalitarianism itself is a joke and that you're a sucker for having believed in it).

Twain's humor, to repeat, spans all three forms. *Huckleberry Finn* is the apotheosis of American deadpan, a masterfully coordinated synthesis of all three layers of the meaning of funny, with the emphasis on the sinister. It is worth remarking that the novel is unique in this regard. Twain achieved this feat only once. His earlier works are rarely sinister, not even when they're brimful of violence, as in *Roughing It* (1872), or for that matter *Tom Sawyer* (1876). His later works are rarely funny, not even when they're brimful of jokes, as in *Puddn'head Wilson* (1892) or the tales of terror collected posthumously as *The Great Dark*. *Adventures of Huckleberry Finn* is Twain's great synthetic work, incorporating every stage of his development as "America's Humorist," from the unalloyed cheer of "The Celebrated Jumping Frog of Calaveras County" through the fierce satire of The Gilded Age to the David Lynch— (or Robert Crum—) like world of "The Man Who Corrupted Hadleyburgh" Twain's mode of coordination in *Huckleberry Finn*, the dialectic behind his fantastic synthesis, is a drastic reversal of effect: the deadpan artist with the Comic Mask. And the procession of nubs or snappers he delivers constitutes the most severe shocks in our literature to the American funny bone.

As Huck tells the story we come to feel that his conscience is the object of Twain's expose. It's conscience that makes Huck a racist, conscience that keeps leading him astray, and we interpret his conscience, properly, as an indictment of the values of the antebellum Southwest. But there was no need in 1885 to indict slave society. Primarily Twain's deadpan is directed against his readership, then and later, even unto our own time—against, that is, the conscience-driven forms of liberal interpretation. To a certain extent, his project here reflects the frontier sources of tall-tale humor that I quoted at the start of this essay: the storyteller's "pleasure in dethroning the condescension of gentility at the thickly settled Eastern core, while at the same time reproducing the radical discrepancies and incongruities at the root of all American experience," Eastern-intellectual as well as roughneck-Southwest. What better, and more cutting, way to accomplish these ends than to get the Eastern gentility to identify condescendingly with this con-man's outcast-redneck hero?

And it's precisely in this sense, I submit, that a distinct liberal theme permeates the discourse about the novel, a critical main current that runs through virtually all sides of the argument (provided that the critic does not dogmatically, foolishly, condemn the book for being racist). To judge from a century of Twain experts, Huck is "self-reliant," "an Adamic innocent," "exemplifying the . . . strong and wholesome [individual that] . . . springs from . . . the great common stock," exemplifying too the heroics of "the private man . . . [for whom] the highest form of freedom [resides in] . . . each man's and each woman's consciousness of what is right," and thereby, in its absolute "liberation," "ultimately transcend[ing] even anarchy as

confinement"—in sum, an independent spirit," "the affirmation of adventure," "enterprise," and "movement," the soul of "toleran[ce], and common sense." More than that: Huck and Jim on the raft have been taken as an emblem of the ideal society. In contrast to the settlements, they represent the "spiritual values" of "individualism compatible with community"—not just the proof of "Twain's commitment to black civil rights" (and his appeal to "compensate" the blacks on "the national level" for "injuries" done them during the slavery era), but his summons to the "cause of freedom" in general. Huck and Jim together forecast "a redeeming hope for the future health of society"; they stand for the very "pinnacle of human community"; they provide "a utopian pattern of all human relationships." Critics have reiterated these "great redemptive fact[s] about the book" over and again, with what can only be called reflexive adoration. As Jonathan Arac observes, "it is as if 'we' uttered in self-congratulation: 'Americans have spiritually solved any problems involved in blacks and whites living together as free human beings and we had already done so by the 1880s.'" I would add that, beyond smugness, what this attests to is the process of interpretation as self-acculturation—a striking example of what I called the literary enterprise of socialization, in compliance with the charge bequeathed to "teachers of American literature" (society's "special custodians"), to inculcate the values of "enterprise, individualism, self-reliance, and the demand for freedom."

More interesting still, this process of interpretation reveals just how socialization works. The abstractions I've just rehearsed are admittedly "American ideals" but they are applied as universals, as though Huck represented not just what America but what all humanity ought to be. Thus a particular cultural vision—individualism, initiative, enterprise, and above all personal freedom ("What *Huckleberry Finn* is about is the process . . . of setting a man free")—becomes a sweeping moral imperative. And as moral imperative it is then reinstated, restored as it were from heaven to earth, from utopian "alternative world" to actual geographical space, as a definition of the quintessential American. As Norman Podhoretz, editor of the conservative journal Commentary, has written: "Sooner or later, all discussions of *Huckleberry Finn* turn into discussions of America." Or in the words of the late Irving Howe, writing in his leftwing journal Dissent: "Huck is not only the most American boy in our own literature, he is also the character with whom most American readers have most deeply identified." Or once again, according to the centrist Americanist scholar Eric Sundquist, *Huckleberry Finn* is "an autobiographical journey into the past" that tells the great "story of a nation." Harold Bloom accurately summarizes the tone of his collection of "best critical essays" on the novel when he remarks that the "book tells a story which most Americans need to believe is a true representation of the way things were, are, and yet might be."

That "need to believe," is the core of the "American humor" of *Huckleberry Finn*. It may be true that in its magnificent colloquialism the novel marks "America's literary declaration of independence...a model of how one breaks free from the colonizers culture." But as a deadpan declaration the model it presents is, mockingly, the illusion of independence. It reveals our imprisonment within what Lewis Hyde, in his sweeping overview of the Trickster figure, calls the "joints" of culture. For Hyde, this concept involves a heroic view of the possibilities of interpretation. He pictures the Trickster's cultural work in physiological terms, as an assault upon the vulnerable parts of the social body, most tellingly its "flexible or movable" joints, where variant spheres of society (home, school, church, job) intersect. At these anatomical weak points, he writes, Tricksters come most vividly to life, unsettling the system, transgressing boundaries, exposing conflicts and contradictions—thus freeing us, he contends, as sympathetic interpreters of their subversion, from social constraints. If so, Mark Twain is a kind of laughing anti-trickster. It's not just that he's mocking the tricksters in the novel: Tom, the Duke and King, Huck himself. It's that he's mocking our would-be capacities for Trickster criticism. What's funny about our interpretation of the novel—both of the narrative and of its autobiographical hero—is that what begins as our independent assessment, and often our oppositional perspective, leads us happily, of our own free will, into the institutions of our colonizing culture.

Thus it was all but inevitable that in our multicultural era, Huck should be discovered to be (in addition to everything else that's positively American) multicultural. This is not the place to discuss Huck's blackness—or for that matter the possibility of his ethnic Irish-Americanness— but it's pertinent here as elsewhere to recall Twain's warning that interpretation may be a trap of culture. He speaks abundantly of the nature of that trap in his later writings—in letters to friends, for example, reprimanding them for presuming that "there is still dignity in man," whereas the plain fact is that "Man is...an April-fool joke played by a malicious Creator with nothing better to waste his time upon"; and in essays protesting that he has "no race prejudices...[nor] color prejudices, nor creed prejudices...I can stand any society. All that I need to know is that a man is a human being; that is enough for me; he can't be any worse"; and in journals documenting how "history, in all climes, all ages, and all circumstances, furnishes oceans and continents of proof that of all creatures that were made he [man] is the most detestable...below the rats, the grubs, the trichinae...There are certain sweet-smelling, sugarcoated lies current in the world...One of these...is that there is heroism in human life: that he is not mainly made up of malice and treachery; that he is sometimes not a coward; that there is something about him that ought to be perpetuated." In his posthumously published novel, *The Mysterious Stranger*, Twain exposes the nub itself—lays bare the mechanism of the trap of hope. Here his stand-in deadpan artist, Satan, pairs up with a poor-white, innocent, sound-hearted little boy, a boy not unlike Huck—befriends him and conjures up for him a variety of alluring spectacles and promises, only to reveal, at the end, the absurdity of each one of them. "You perceive now," Satan declares, that it "is all a Dream, a grotesque and foolish dream." And then the boy's epiphany: "He vanished, and left me appalled: for I knew, and realized, that all that he had said was true."

That's the humorous point of *Huckleberry Finn*, if we're alert. The novel's underlying moral and motive, its deadpan plot, is that this grand flight to freedom—black and white together, the individual regenerated by nature—was all a dream. Not a grotesque dream, to be sure, but a foolish one because it is a dream that befools. Recall the image of the novel with which critical tradition has left us. The plot is a river story, the style is a flow of humor, and our interpretation is a raft that promises protection (from conscience, from civilization, from all the slings and arrows of outrageous adulthood). Now consider the facts. The river keeps returning us again and again and yet again to the settlements, the raft proves to be a con-man haven, and on this "raft of trouble," on this river that betrays and kills, we're left with two mock-symbolic figures. One is Huck Finn, bond-slave to society, mostly scared to death, speaking a language we don't trust, and (as Pap puts it, in a drunken flash of insight) an Angel of Death. The other is Jim, the fugitive black who need never have run off, and who leads Huck into what Jim himself, early in the novel, calls the Black Angel's hell's-pact. So the nub is: the Angel of Death and the Black Angel, on a deadpan raft-to-freedom, drifting deeper and deeper into slave territory. It makes for a savagely funny obituary to the American dream.

Source: Sacvan Bercovitch, "Deadpan Huck," in *Kenyon Review*, Summer–Fall 2002, pp. 90–134.

SOURCES

Frank, Waldo, *Our America*, Boni and Liveright, 1919, pp. 13–58.

Hemingway, Ernest, *Green Hills of Africa*, Scribner's Sons, 1935; reprint, 1987, p. 22.

Hill, Hamlin, "Samuel Langhorne Clemens," in *Dictionary of Literary Biography*, Vol. 12: *American Realists and Naturalists*, edited by Donald Pizer and Earl N. Harbert, Gale Group, 1982, pp. 71–94.

"Huck Finn and the Ebb and Flow of Controversy," in the *Washington Post*, March 13, 1995, p. D2.

Lemon, Richard, "Huckleberry Finn," in *People Weekly*, Vol. 23, February 25, 1985, p. 67.

Matthews, Brander, Review of *Adventures of Huckleberry Finn*, in the *Saturday Review*, Vol. 59, No. 1527, January 31, 1885, pp. 153–54.

Paine, Albert Bigelow, *Mark Twain, a Biography: The Personal and Literary Life of Samuel Langhorne Clemens*, Vol. 2, Harper & Brothers Publishers, 1912, pp. 793–98.

"The 100 Most Frequently Challenged Books of 1990–2000," American Library Association, www.ala.org/ala/oif/bannedbooksweek/bbwlinks/100mostfrequently.htm (December 9, 2006).

Twain, Mark, *Adventures of Huckleberry Finn*, Harper & Brothers, 1885; reprint, Pocket Books, 2004.

Yardley, Jonathan, "Huck Finn Doesn't Wear a White Sheet," in the *Washington Post*, April 12, 1982, p. C1.

...And the Earth Did Not Devour Him

TOMÁS RIVERA

1971

Originally published in Spanish as . . . *y no se lo tragó la tierra*, . . . *And the Earth Did Not Devour Him* is a seminal work of Chicano literature and one of the first books in the emerging literature of Mexican Americans. Its success made author Tomás Rivera a leading figure in this genre. Written in 1967 and 1968, the book was awarded the premiere Quinto Sol Prize for literature in 1970. . . . *Y no se lo tragó la tierra* was first published in 1971 in a bilingual edition, with an English translation by Herminio Ríos. A later translation by Evangelina Vigil-Piñón, first published in 1988, is considered the definitive English version.

From its first publication, . . . *And the Earth Did Not Devour Him* has been praised by critics for its depiction of the harsh life of migrant agricultural workers in the United States, its sense of realism that had previously not been a part of Chicano literature, and its innovative literary form. Rivera was himself the son of migrant workers and a migrant worker himself until he completed junior college. Drawing on his background and own experiences, he explores many aspects of this lifestyle and how it affects those directly involved.

Set after World War II, from about 1945 to 1955, the stories and vignettes that make up . . . *And the Earth Did Not Devour Him* show the racism and discrimination Chicano migrant workers encountered, even among their peers.

BIOGRAPHY

TOMÁS RIVERA

Rivera was born in Texas in Crystal City, Texas, on December 22, 1935, to Mexican parents who immigrated to the United States and worked as migrant farm workers. Though he was raised migrating between agricultural locations in Texas and the Midwest, he graduated from high school and went on to college. Rivera earned his bachelor's degree in English from Southwest Texas State College in 1958. After finding it difficult to obtain work as a high school teacher because of his race, Rivera returned to Southwest Texas for his master's degree in education, graduating in 1964. In 1969, he earned his Ph.D. in Spanish literature from the University of Oklahoma.

While working as a college instructor and publishing some stories and poems in the late 1960s, Rivera wrote his first book, *. . . y no se lo tragó la tierra* (*. . . And the Earth Did Not Devour Him*) (1971). The success of the book cemented his place as a leading Chicano author. While Rivera continued to write short stories, poetry, and essays in the 1970s, he focused more on his career, which had shifted to college administration where he felt he could be more influential. In 1979, he was named the president of chancellor of the University of California, Riverside. He held this position until his death on May 16, 1984, in Fontana, California.

Rivera explores the effects of economic and social injustice. While there is much suffering and uncertainty in many of the stories, Rivera also emphasizes the resilience and determination of the migrant workers. Religion and faith play important roles in their lives as do family and community. In addition, Rivera underscores the importance of education as a means of liberation for farm workers and their children. Several stories in the book are specifically about education, unsurprising considering the author's primary

career was working at various universities as an instructor, professor, and administrator.

Critics agree about the strength of the stories Rivera tells in *. . . And the Earth Did Not Devour Him.* In *Book Report,* Sherry York claims "while [the stories] seem simple, they are powerful tales that portray a dignity in the face of adversity." However, there is critical division over whether the book is a collection of related short stories or a novel. The stories are tied together by a young male narrator who is trying to understand who he is and remember things he does not necessarily completely understand, culminating in the last story of the book, "Under the House." Many of the stories are subjective, involve characters that change from story to story, and lack a definite chronology. A number of them function as anecdotal glimpses into opinions, mentalities, and lives of migrant workers and their families while revealing deeper concerns.

Whether *. . . And the Earth Did Not Devour Him* is a collection of short stories or a novel, most critics believe it reveals the realities of Chicano social history. Some of them see it as political, but Luis Leal, writing in *Dictionary of Literary Biography,* believes, "Rivera transcended the political. He had a deep sympathy and respect for humanity, especially for the migrant workers from whom he drew his inspiration to write and work building a better society in the Americas."

PLOT SUMMARY

The Lost Year

. . . And the Earth Did Not Devour Him opens with the introduction of the recurring, unnamed young male character in the book. He is trying to come to terms with a lost year, including when and how it began. He is falling asleep, not sure if he is awake or dreaming, and experiences a flood of memories and images.

Vignette 1

Every night he drank the glass of water his mother put under his bed for the spirits. Though he thought about telling her at one point, he decided to do so when he was an adult.

The Children Couldn't Wait

It is unusually hot for early April. Their boss only brings them a bucket of water twice a day,

Cover of the book . . . And the Earth Did Not Devour Him Reprinted with permission from the publisher, Arte Publico Press/Recovery Project Archive Files, (Arte Publico Press—University of Houston)

but it not enough. Though the adult workers can wait, the children generally cannot and take to drinking from a tank for the cattle. They pretended to be relieving themselves nearby to disguise their frequent breaks for water, but the boss caught on. He does not want them to do drink this water because they are being paid by the hour and drinking the water takes away from the labor. Because one child in particular would drink regularly from the tank, the boss decides to scare him. He shoots at the child when he drinks there, but he accidentally hits the child in the head and kills him. Workers talking about him well after the incident report that he began drinking, lost his ranch, and tried to kill himself. One says, "I think he did go crazy. You've seen the likes of him nowadays. He looks like a beggar." Another replies, "Sure, but that's 'cause he doesn't have any more money."

Vignette 2

A group is gathered to consult a medium who is in a trance. A mother worries about her son, Julianito, who is in the military overseas. She has recently been told that he has been missing in action. The medium assures her that he will becoming back soon.

A Prayer

A mother is praying for the safe return from her son in Korea for the third Sunday in a row. She begs God, Virgin Mary, and other Catholic saints for their assistance. She asks, "Shield his body, cover his head, cover the eyes of the Communists and the Koreans and the Chinese so they cannot see him, so they won't kill him." The mother promises to give her own heart if he returns to her alive.

Vignette 3

Two migrant workers are talking. One worker asks the other if he is going to Utah, in part because he does not believe such a place exists and he does not trust the contractor. The first worker tells him that though he has not been there, he believes it is near Japan.

It's That It Hurts

This first-person story focuses on a child from a migrant family in the North walking home from school. He has just been expelled for hitting a white boy who taunted him, and hit him first. He is worried about telling his family what happened because education is important to them. He is sure he will be beaten. He thinks about a number of things, including how he dislikes how the schools treat him, humiliating him at times. The school nurses have forced him to strip naked to be inspected for lice, although he knows why they feel like they do about members of his community:

> On Sundays they sit out in front of the chicken coops picking lice from each other's heads. And the gringos, passing by in their cars, looking and pointing at them. Dad is right when he says that they look like monkeys in the zoo.

It is also not the first fight he has gotten into at school, but the first one was broken up without incident. He worries about his future, as his father wants him to be a telephone operator like he saw once in a movie. He debates about how to explain his school troubles to his parents, thinking, "It's that it hurts and it's embarrassing at the same time."

Vignette 4

One child asks another, "Why do y'all go to school so much?" The student tells him his father makes him go in case there is an opportunity. The first one tells him not to worry about such things because "The poor can't get poorer."

Hand in His Pocket

This first-person story focuses on a young boy who stays with Don Laíto and Doña Bone, acquaintances of his family, while he completes the last three weeks of school. The couple is popular with migrants and whites alike, selling food, clothes, and toys, then giving away what they cannot sell. The couple is nice to him at first, feeding him well but with rotten meat that made him sick.

While there, he has to sleep in an overstuffed storage room, which makes him uncomfortable. As he stays with them, he learns where some of this stuff comes from: They steal things down-town. Though his father paid his room and board, the couple wants him to steal flour, but he refuses because it is wrong. As he is put to work in the yard, more is demanded of him and his food grows worse.

He also sees an old "wetback" without family connections going into the house who visits Doña Bone while Don Laíto is away, and always pays her for services. The boy is not allowed inside when the wetback is inside with Bone. One day, The couple makes him dig what they tell him will be a small cellar. That night when he goes to bed, he finds the body of the wetback in his room, and "The old couple burst into laughter." The couple makes him help them bury the dead man. When his parents come for him a few weeks later, he recalls:

> Don Laíto and Doña Bone squeezed me and told me in loud voices, so that Dad could hear, not to say anything or they would tell the police. Then they started laughing and I noticed that Dad had taken it as a joke.

They later send him the dead man's ring, which he carries with him.

Vignette 5

The boy decides to get a haircut before going to a movie, but the barbers at the shop near the the-ater refuse to serve him. He is told by the barber "That he couldn't cut his hair." They even shoo him from in front of the theater, at which point he goes home to find his father.

A Silvery Night

A boy is enthralled by the idea of the devil. One night, in defiance of his parents, he stays awake while everyone in his family goes to sleep. Leaving just before midnight, he walks to a knoll and tries to summon the devil. Though he tries every verbal trick he can think of, nothing happens. When he goes to sleep that night he comes to a conclusion: "Those who summon the devil went crazy, not because the devil appeared, but just the opposite, because he didn't appear."

Vignette 6

A Protestant minister comes to the farm and tells the migrant worker men that another man will come out to them to teach them manual skills, primarily carpentry. Learning the skills will free them from fieldwork. When a man comes two weeks later, he has the minister's wife with him and the pair does not teach any skills to the laborers. The couple later run off together.

And the Earth Did Not Devour Him

The eldest son of a farm labor family is angry because of the illnesses that have devastated his family. First his aunt and uncle die from tuber-culosis, and his father suffers from severe sun-stroke working in the fields. His father might die from the illness. The son prays to God for assis-tance, but he grows frustrated and furious when God does not intervene. While his mother still believes God will help, the son is not so sure. He tells his mother, "I tell you, God could care less about the poor."

Because his mother stays home to take care of his father, the son is in charge of his siblings as they work in the fields. He tells them the plan for the working but escaping from the worst heat of the day, emphasizing that they should stop if they feel faint. In the heat of afternoon, the youngest boy gets sunstroke symptoms. The son worries about his little brother dying as he carries him to the house. He curses God aloud, then worries that the earth will swallow him for the sacrilege he has just committed. Nothing happens, a fact that gives him a sense of peace that night. Both his father and brother start to improve by morning, and, "He thought of telling his mother, but decided to keep it secret. All he told her was that the earth did not devour any-one, nor did the sun."

Vignette 7

A paralyzed grandfather asks one of his visiting grandsons what he wanted most in life. The grandson says for the ten years to pass immediately so he will know what will happen in his life when he is older. "The grandfather told him he was very stupid and cut off the conversation," and the grandson only understands his grandfather's words when he is an adult.

First Communion

A first-person male narrator looks back at the day of his First Communion, and can recall every detail. He could not sleep the night before the event because he was trying to remember all his sins to confess beforehand. He recalls, "The real truth was that we practiced a lot telling our sins, but the real truth was that I didn't understand a lot of things."

He remembers getting up early that day and going to church earlier than his mother anticipated. When he arrived at church, it was closed. As he walked around the church, he saw a couple having sex on the floor of the cleaners next door. He remembers, "I couldn't get my mind off of what I had seen. I realized then that maybe those were the sins we committed with our hands."

Back at church, he felt guilty, believing he committed a sin of the flesh. When he went to confession, he told the priest two hundred sins, but not what he had seen at the cleaners. After the ceremony, he went home and saw things had changed. He saw the adults, including his parents, naked and laughing. He left the house as soon as he could, though his relatives found it to be disrespectful, and ran to a thicket. While thinking, he found he enjoyed remembering what he saw and that his world had not changed.

Vignette 8

The boy tears a button off his shirt when his teacher needs one for a class project. His action surprises her because of his poverty, and "She didn't know whether he did this to be helpful, to feel like he belonged or out of love for her." She is especially amazed by "the intensity of the child's desire."

The Little Burnt Victims

The five members of the García family, parents, two young sons, and a young daughter, come home from seeing a movie about boxing. The father, Efraín, is inspired to turn his children into boxers, hoping one might be a champion. He buys boxing gloves and rubs a little alcohol on their chests like the boxers in the movie. On Monday, the parents go and work in the fields, leaving their sleeping children home. Don Efraí tells his wife, "I love my children so much, like you. . . . I was thinking about how much they also like to play with us."

That morning, field workers see flames coming from near the farm. The Garcías' shack family home is on fire, and only the oldest son survives the blaze. He had put the boxing gloves on his young siblings and rubbed alcohol on their chest. When he made them food, the kerosene tank exploded, young ones caught on fire and the blaze quickly spread. The gloves survive the fire.

Vignette 9

Before a wedding, the groom and his father decorate the bride's family's backyard. They put water down on the soil so that dust will not blow when people dance under the canvas tent. After the couple is married in the church, the couple walks down the street with their godparents and children announce their approach.

The Night the Lights Went Out

One night, the lights go out in a town for no obvious reason. There had been a dance, which ended when the electricity went out. The next day, people talk about what happened.

Ramón was in love with Juanita. Before she traveled to Minnesota to work in the fields with her family, she promised to marry him and not see anyone else while she was away. She spent time with another boy there, a "smooth talker" named Ramiro from San Antonio, while telling Ramón that she was faithful. His friends who were there told him what was going on.

Ramón was devastated by the news and began drinking. He vowed that when they were together again, he would take her away with him. Juanita rationalized her behavior because she was just talking to Ramiro and she still loved Ramón. She went to a dance with Ramiro, and she danced with him the whole night and promised to see him again when they returned south.

Ramón confronted her when she came back, and they broke off their relationship. He told her not to dance with anyone if she was planning to go to the dance that night. Juanita went with some of her friends and when Ramón arrived, she danced with the first boy she saw. She then argued with Ramón, who threatened to kill himself. He left, and the lights blacked out. He had gone to a nearby power plant and held on to a transformer, where the power workers found him. Others agreed that it was because they were so in love.

Vignette 10

There is an accident on the freeway in which a white woman who is driving drunk hits a truck transporting field workers early in the morning. Immediately, a number of workers are thrown from the truck and the rest become trapped inside as it catches on fire. Sixteen people die in the accident.

The Night Before Christmas

As Christmas nears, Doña María wants to buy her children presents. Her husband would bring them candies and nuts, and when they asked for toys, she always told them to wait until January 6, the day of the Magi: "Why don't you wait until the day of the Reyes Magos. That's when the toys really arrive." These gifts never come, and she always reassured them that they were good children.

Because her husband works long hours at a restaurant, she has to go a few blocks by herself to buy the toys. She is afraid to do so, having previously gotten lost in Wilmar, Minnesota, because she never goes anywhere by herself. Doña María is determined to make this Christmas special.

The next day, she starts walking to the store. Once downtown, her ears are ringing. She wants to go back but feels caught up in the crowd. She finally finds the store, which is also crowded, and feels disoriented. She finds some presents, puts them in a bag, and walks to the exit. Outside, she is accused of theft and collapses.

At jail, her husband takes care of things with the help of a notary public. They explain about her anxiety attacks, and she is freed. Doña María worries that she will be forced to go to the mental hospital and they will lose everything. Her husband reassures her and tells her to stay home from now on, and wants to tell the children there is no Santa Claus so they will not bother her about it. He agrees to maintain the myth of the Magi, saying, "I suppose it's always best to have hope." Their children overhear this conversation and do not say anything when presents do not show up in January.

Vignette 11

For five dollars each, a priest blesses the cars of workers before the travel north to work. With the money he makes, he is able to travel home to Spain to visit his family. He puts postcards of a modern Spanish church by the entrance of his parish, suggesting that they could have a nicer church. He does not understand why people deface the images.

The Portrait

A portrait salesman from San Antonio works a neighborhood. He sells a package with an enlargement and a wood frame for thirty dollars. Don Mateo and his wife have only one picture of their son who died in the Korean War. They buy the package and let the salesman take the picture. When the salesman does not return in a month, they become suspicious. Some children playing in the tunnels after a heavy rain finds the salesman's suitcase full of damaged and destroyed pictures, including their son's. Don Mateo goes to San Antonio to find the swindler who took advantage of him and his neighbors. When Don Mateo finds the salesman, he confronts him and demands he complete the work. The salesman does so from memory. Though Don Mateo does not remember what his son looks like anymore, he is sure the resulting portrait looks like him.

Vignette 12

Some people talk about Figueroa, who has just gotten out of prison but is ill with an odd sickness. Figueroa went to jail because he was involved with a seventeen-year-old white girl who came with him from Wisconsin. They believe that a white person turned him in and he had no one defending him. They expect he "won't last a year" because of his "strange disease."

When We Arrive

A truck carrying migrant workers breaks down at four o'clock in the morning. Inside the truck, the workers think about what has been happening to them and what they plan to do in the future. One man hopes to buy a car so his family can travel in more comfort while another worries about work and debt. One likes the driver, while the driver plans to drop them off with the growers and letting the workers find their own way back to Texas. He thinks, "Each one to fend for himself." Together, they focus on what they will do when they arrive at the destination as dawn breaks.

❝

**THEY CARRIED SUITCASES PACKED WITH
SAMPLES AND ALWAYS WORE SHIRTS AND TIES. THAT
WAY THEY LOOKED MORE IMPORTANT AND THE
PEOPLE BELIEVED EVERYTHING THEY WOULD TELL
THEM AND INVITE THEM INTO THEIR HOMES WITHOUT
GIVING IT MUCH THOUGHT. I THINK THAT DEEP DOWN
THEY EVEN LONGED FOR THEIR CHILDREN ONE DAY TO
BE LIKE THEM.❞**

Vignette 13

The boy remembers Bartolo, a poet who incorporates the names of locals in his work. He sells his poems in December when people return home from working in the north with cash. Bartolo tells the people to read them aloud "because the spoken word was the seed of love in the darkness."

Under the House

The boy hides under a house instead of going to school. While he enjoys it at first, the fleas that are soon biting him move. As he lies there, he remembers things his father said about events involving himself and others. Included are bits of information about some of the tales in ... *And the Earth Did Not Devour Him* such as the night the lights went out and Doña María's attack. He thinks, "I would like to see all of the people together. And then, if I had great big arms, I could embrace them all.... I think today what I wanted to do was recall this past year. And that's just one year."

He is jerked into the present when children from the house start throwing rocks at him. Their mother pushes at him with boards. They do not know who it is until he comes out from under the house. The mother thinks he might be mentally incapacitated like his mother, but he is content and sure that he still has everything.

THEMES

Education

Throughout ... *And the Earth Did Not Devour Him*, Rivera emphasizes the importance of education as a means to a better life, a bedrock principle

of so many American dreams. Though "Hand in His Pocket" is not exclusively about education, the reason the protagonist is staying with the fiendish Don Laíto and Doña Bone for three weeks is to finish the school year. The narrator says, "All that my parents wanted was for me to finish school so I could find me some job that wasn't so hard."

The fourth vignette of the book focuses exclusively on school in similar terms. In a dialogue between two young Latinos, one asks the other the reason for his or her regular attendance at school. The reply underscores education as an opening: "My Dad says it's to prepare us. He says that someday there's an opportunity, maybe they'll give it to us." Vignette 8 looks at education from a teacher's point of view when a poor boy removes a button from what she believes is his only shirt for a school poster. She is deeply moved by the gesture of her enthusiastic student.

The loss of an educational opportunity can be devastating. In "It's That It Hurts," the young male protagonist has been thrown out of school for hitting a white student who hit him first. While the protagonist does not like the discrimination he faces, he is more immediately concerned with how he is going to explain his expulsion to his parents. They want him to finish school so he can become a telephone operator and lead a better life. Walking home, the boy tries to think of how to explain what happened and how he must live with the disappointment of his extended family.

Racism

Rivera also catalogs many forms of discrimination his Latino and Latina characters face in their every day life and work. The central character in "It's That It Hurts" talks about several incidents at school in which he is treated poorly because of his race and migrant status. He recounts to his parents one particularly embarrassing incident in which he is forced to strip naked in front of the school nurse to be checked for lice. When the migrant workers' children enter schools in the North, they are always checked for lice, which humiliates them.

Later in this same story, Rivera outlines more explicitly stereotypical generalizations. The central character says that he was picked on for being Mexican, with one student saying to him "I don't like Mexicans because they steal." Even the fight that gets him expelled was started by this white boy, who hits him without warning. One school

Migrant Mexican workers picking strawberries in the Salinas Valley © *Bettmann/Corbis*

administrator says of the protagonists' people, "they could care less if I expel him . . . They need him in the fields."

Not all the incidents of poor treatment are accepted quietly. Another act of discrimination is the focus of Vignette 5: refusal of service. A young man of indeterminate age goes to a barbershop to get his hair cut before seeing a movie. The barbers ignore him, then tell him that they could not his hair. The racism continues after he is told to leave the barbershop. One barber told him to leave again when he waited outside for the theater to open. Unlike the young character in "It's That It Hurts," this one is not afraid to tell his father what happened. Likewise, when a portrait salesman hustles a whole Spanish-speaking neighborhood in "The Portrait," Rivera shows one man, Don Mateo, going after him and getting the picture of his only son, which he had already paid for. The characters' resistance to second-class treatment is a part of their striving for something better in life.

Survival

In *. . . And the Earth Did Not Devour Him*, many characters do what they have to survive their circumstances in ways big and small. These stories generally focus on work and the effects of conditions of migrant labor on their families. In "The

Children Couldn't Wait," for example, the children of the migrant workers on the ranch do what they must to get the water they need. The boss of the ranch will only allow them to drink water twice a day, though it is extremely hot, to ensure their productivity. The children start sneaking drinks from a tank for cattle to get enough water to drink. While this defiance ultimately leads to the death of one of the children, the boss who kills the youngster suffers for his actions. The boss loses status, livelihood, and sanity for going to extremes to deny people water.

Not every act of survival leads to a balanced outcome in Rivera's book. In "The Little Burnt Victims," Don Efraín and Doña Chona are a migrant couple with three young children. They are forced to leave their children alone while they work in the fields. They worry about their children's safety, but this work is their only means of survival. Don Efraín's enthusiasm for boxing as a potential means of a better life literally goes up in smoke as the children's imitation of his actions leads to a fire. Two of the children die in the blaze, and the family grieves for the loss caused, Rivera implies, by their life circumstances.

HISTORICAL OVERVIEW

Chicano Farm Workers in the 1940s and 1950s

. . . And the Earth Did Not Devour Him is set after World War II, reflecting the period when the author lived the life of a child of migrant farm workers. Millions of Mexican Americans came to the United States during and after World War II to work as farm laborers. Though a significant number were illegal immigrants, many stayed in America and made it their home. In the early 1950s, the U.S. government tried to curb the immigration though the federal program called Operation Wetback. This program called for several coordinated agencies to find and deport illegal Mexican immigrants. Many Chicanos, both legal and illegal immigrants, settled in urban environments, often in barrios (Spanish-speaking enclaves).

Many Chicanos continued to work as migrant farm laborers in the 1940s and 1950s. Picking crops was an intense labor process involving many long hours of hard, back-breaking work. Workers were put in direct contact with pesticides and pesticide-laden crops, which could lead to health problems. Not every grower provided sanitary water and/or living quarters. The conditions under which migrant farm workers lived and labored were often appalling and contributed to continued, deep poverty. Some farmers treated their migrant farm laborers well, but others treated them poorly or devised reasons to not pay them at all. Another reason for their poverty was federal legislation. During the New Deal, legislation passed such as the Wagner Act and federal farm programs benefited farmers who owned their land. Migratory farm workers were but one category of laborers who were not covered by minimum wage or Social Security requirements, leaving them with little federal wage protection or long-term support.

Chicano Labor Movement

When Rivera was writing his book, primarily from 1967 to 1968, Chicano labor struggles were a leading social issue in the United States. Influenced by the black civil rights and Black Power movements, many Hispanics became politically active. One of the best-known Chicano activists was César Chávez, who was the son of farm workers and who worked as a produce picker himself as a teenager. While the migrant farm workers had tried to organize a union in the 1920s and each decade afterward, it was not until Chávez became a leader in the movement in the 1960s that victories were achieved.

Chávez was a head of what became the United Farm Workers union, which was the first Hispanic-led group to garner attention on a massive scale. This union wanted to organize farm workers, making their plight the center of national attention. One of Chávez's first labor successes came in 1965. He led a strike against grape growers while demanding higher wages for grape pickers. Chávez also encouraged Americans to boycott grapes as a means of supporting the union. The strike lasted for five years, leading to a federal inquiry, and a victory for the union. The United Farm Workers achieved other victories in the early 1970s via strikes and boycotts, winning higher wages for workers who were employed by certain other growers. Chávez's political activities with the United Farm Workers also led to the founding of other farm worker unions and more marches in support of the rights of farm workers.

Farm workers were not the only politically active Hispanic Americans in this time period.

Chicano activists seized land in northern New Mexico. In cities like Los Angeles and Denver, urban Chicano movements were organized. National meetings of Chicano students were held in Denver in 1969 and 1970, which led to a number of publications that emphasized cultural nationalism. A group with militant leanings called the Brown Berets worked to feed preschoolers. They also taught Chicano studies and raised the cultural and political consciousness of older Chicano students.

Crystal City, Texas

In the1960s, Rivera's native Crystal City, Texas, was the focal point of several important incidents of Mexican American politics. The majority of the population in the city was Latino, many of whom were migratory farm workers who went to the Midwest to harvest crops every year. In 1963, the Chicano majority won five seats on the city council and held this majority for five years. This political victory helped start the Chicano movement of political and social activism. A few years later, Crystal City saw the founding of La Raza Unida, a radical political party led by Mexican Americans. In 1969, the party won a majority of offices in Crystal City and the surrounding Zavala County, taking over from a white minority population. Eventually, La Raza Unida established local power bases throughout the Southwest and California.

CRITICAL OVERVIEW

. . . And the Earth Did Not Devour Him has been recognized as a significant piece of Hispanic American literature since it was published in a bilingual edition in 1971. Writing in the *Modern Language Journal*, William H. González calls it "One of the outstanding examples of this new literature," referring to Chicano literature. The critic goes on to claim that "This book is a summary of the past, a living present, and a base for the future of Chicano literature."

By 1988, when another translation of the book was published, *. . . And the Earth Did Not Devour Him* was called "a classic Chicano novel" by *Booklist*. Believing this translation, by Evangelina Vigil-Piñón, is superior to the 1971 version by Herminio Ríos, Carl R. Shirley in *Western American Literature* writes, "This book is a landmark in Chicano letters, one of the best and most famous, and it should be read by anyone hoping to learn the least bit about the field."

Among other things, critics of . . . *And the Earth Did Not Devour Him* comment on how Rivera drew his characters and depicted their often difficult circumstances. Ralph F. Grajeda of *Hispania* explains, "Throughout the book some tension is created between the opposing values of resignation and rebellion as the people are shown enduring the repetitive hardships of the present, and as they anticipate their future." Similarly, Donaldo W. Urioste, in his essay "The Child's Process of Alienation in Tomas Rivera's . . . *y no se lo trago la tierra*," claims,

> If . . . Rivera's explicit objective was to critically document migrant life, he has indeed been successful. By the novel's end not only have we been made aware of that existence with its many degradations, but we are also in a position to make critical judgments about the different forces that have caused and perpetuated such oppressive conditions.

Rivera's unique narrative technique also garnered critical attention. Don Graham of *Texas Monthly* asserts "the work owes more to James Joyce than to realistic American novels that deal with similar material—a people dispossessed of land and forced to take to the road to earn a living." Graham is one critic who weighed into the debate over whether . . . *And the Earth Did Not Devour Him* is a collection of short stories or a novel, arguing for the former. Writing in the *Dictionary of Literary Biography*, Luis Leal explains: "The fragmented structure of Rivera's novel has led some critics (Daniel P. Testa and Juan Rodríguez, for example) to consider the work as a collection of short stories, yet there are unifying elements." Leal is one of many critics who regards the book as a novel.

In addition, . . . *And the Earth Did Not Devour Him* is also praised for its dialogue. In *Voice of Youth Advocates*, Delia A. Culberson reviews a Spanish edition of the book and finds Rivera's use of language inspiring. She says, "With dialogue rich in idiomatic expressions and popular slang, Rivera's powerful prose brings to life memorable characters." She also believes of the book as a whole, "this enlightening, unforgettable book conveys a feeling of great spiritual strength, an innate zest for life, and the constant hope of a better tomorrow."

MEDIA ADAPTATIONS

. . . *And the Earth Did Not Swallow Him* (1995) is an adaptation of the classic work of Chicano fiction . . . *y no se lo tragó la tierra* (. . . *And the Earth Did Not Devour Him*). Directed and written by Severo Perez, the adaptation stars Jose Alcala, Rose Portillo, and Marco Rodriguez. Originally filmed for KPBS–TV (San Diego, California) and aired on *American Playhouse*, the work was eventually released as a film. . . . *And the Earth Did Not Swallow Him* is available on VHS from Kino International.

SOURCES

Culberson, Delia A., Review of . . . *y no se lo trago la tierra*, in *Voice of Youth Advocates*, Vol. 19, June 1996, p. 104.

González, William H., Review of . . . *y no se lo trago la tierra*, in *The Modern Language Journal*, Vol. 57, No. 4, April 1973, p. 229.

Graham, Don, "Don Graham's Texas Classics," in *Texas Monthly*, Vol. 29, No. 3, March 2001, p. 26.

Grajeda, Ralph F., "Tomás Rivera's . . . *y no se lo tragó la tierra*: Discovery and Appropriation of the Chicano Past," in *Hispania*, Vol. 62, No. 1, March 1979, pp. 71–81.

Leal, Luis, "Tomás Rivera," in *Dictionary of Literary Biography, Volume 82: Chicano Writers*, edited by Francisco A. Lomeli and Carl R. Shirley, Gale Group, 1989, pp. 206–13.

Review of . . . *y no se lo trago la tierra*, in *Booklist*, Vol. 84, January 15, 1988, p. 84.

Rivera, Tomás, . . . *And the Earth Did Not Devour Him and Related Readings*, translated by Evangelina Vigil-Piñón, 1987; reprint, Glencoe McGraw-Hill, 2000.

Shirley, Carl R., Review of . . . *y no se lo trago la tierra/ And the Earth Did Not Devour Him*, in *Western American Literature*, Vol. 23, No. 4, Winter 1989, pp. 388–90.

Urioste, Donaldo W., "The Child's Process of Alienation in Tomas Rivera's . . . *y no se lo trago la tierra*," in *The Chicano Struggle: Analyses of Past and Present Efforts*, Bilingual Press/Editorial Bilingüe, 1984, pp. 178–91.

York, Sherry, Review of . . . *y no se lo trago la tierra*, in *Book Report*, Vol. 15, No. 2, September–October 1996, p. 45.

Autobiography of My Dead Brother

WALTER DEAN MYERS

2005

Autobiography of My Dead Brother (2005) is a vivid, wrenching, and hopeful look into the confusing and scary lives teen boys face in poor, violent, urban worlds. Through innovative illustrations and honest characterizations, Walter Dean Myers captures the conflicts—internal and external, hopeless and hopeful—that less-privileged Americans face pursuing the American dream. A finalist for the 2005 National Book Award in the young people's division, *Autobiography of My Dead Brother* explores life in a Harlem neighborhood through the eyes of fifteen-year-old Jesse Givens.

Jesse is a gifted artist whose drawings (illustrated in the book by Myers's son Christopher) are an integral part of the text. Jesse uses his art to make sense of events around him, including the deaths of several friends, drive-by shootings, the threats of gang life, and the changes in his long-time "blood brother," Rise. Jesse tries to understand what Rise has become as Rise chooses to become involved in drugs and gangs. Jesse and his friends must also walk the fine line of seeking peer acceptance while remaining true to their own ideals.

Like Jesse and his friends, Myers grew up on the streets of Harlem and got in trouble while a high school student. Though he was always interested in reading and later in writing, Myers did not have hope for his own future by the time he was in his teens. He worked as a drug courier and

BIOGRAPHY

WALTER DEAN MYERS

Walter Dean Myers, a prolific author of books for children and young adults, was born Walter Milton Myers on August 12, 1937, in Martinsburg, West Virginia. After his mother died when he was two years old, he went to live with family friends, the Deans, in New York City's Harlem neighborhood. Myers was an avid reader with a speech impediment who got into fights with those who teased him. Despite becoming involved in street life and essentially dropping out of high school by his senior year in 1954, Myers was inspired by a teacher who encouraged his writing. He graduated from Empire State College in 1984.

After serving in the army and working as a book editor, Myers focused on writing full time beginning in 1977. Drawing on his own childhood experiences in Harlem, Myers began publishing picture books in the late 1960s and early 1970s before focusing on fiction for children and young adults in the mid-1970s. Often putting young black males at the center of his fiction, Myers has been praised for consistently producing quality books and helping change how African Americans were portrayed in young people's literature. The prolific Myers—who sometimes produces several books in a single year—writes in other genres, including nonfiction and poetry, and the bulk of his work depicts the difficulties of life in Harlem while emphasizing its residents' humanity and dignity. He published *Autobiography of My Dead Brother* in 2005. As of 2006, Myers lives with his family in Jersey City, New Jersey.

became involved in gangs. Myers never completed high school, though he later earned a college degree. He drew on this background when writing books such as *Autobiography of My Dead Brother*.

In the novel, Myers uses authentic-sounding dialogue and plot developments to expound his themes. He emphasizes the importance of loyalty and friendship as well as the support of family and other trusted adults, while realistically depicting the tensions and traumas faced by teens in contemporary Harlem. Though Myers shows that the lure of drugs and violence is hard to escape and affects everyone, he also underscores the importance of trying to rise above one's circumstances using one's talents. With characters like Jesse and C. J., finding their identities and being true to themselves are critical steps toward a successful life.

Myers also highlights the power of self-expression—that is, defining one's self through one's abilities—in the novel. Characters like Rise, Little Man, and Mason have no such outlets and become victims of the streets. Emphasizing personal abilities also gives teens a means of escaping from their environment and hoping for a better future as they reach adulthood.

One of Myers's goals as an author of books such as *Autobiography of My Dead Brother* is to realistically depict this world he knows so well to affect the lives of his readers. He told Toni Brandeis of the *Wisconsin State Journal*,

> If they can read about a problem, for example, with drugs, sex, or gangs, they can think about them before they meet these problems in the street, when it's much more difficult to make a good decision. What I want them to do with my books is to engage these problems.

PLOT SUMMARY

Chapter 1

Autobiography of My Dead Brother opens at the church funeral for fourteen-year-old Bobby Green, who was killed in a random drive-by shooting. The attendees include Jesse Givens, a fifteen-year-old friend of Bobby and the novel's first-person narrator; Jesse's mother; Jesse's fifteen-year-old friend C. J., who plays the organ at the service; and Rise, Jesse's seventeen-year-old friend. After the church service ends, Jesse, C. J., and Rise go to a nearby park.

Rise informs them that Calvin has called a meeting of the Counts, a social club the boys belong to. He also tells them, "Bobby G. was good people and everything, but that's why you have to make your life special every day. You never know when your time is up." When Rise leaves, C. J. and Jesse agree that they do not want to get shot. Jesse admits to himself that he has been nervous and jumpy all the time since the shooting, even at home, and that "It was a drag, and I didn't want to talk to anybody about it."

At home the next day, Jesse's mother tries to get Jesse and his father to spend time together. Jesse reveals that his mother is upset about the violence in the neighborhood and thinks about moving to the suburbs. He tells about when they first moved to the area. Rise's mother babysat one-year-old Jesse while Jesse's parents worked. Jesse and Rise grew up together. "He was more than a best friend—he was really like a brother. So when we saw an old movie on television about these two guys cutting themselves and mixing their blood to become blood brothers, we thought it was a good idea," he explains. When they were seven and nine years old, they became blood brothers

Rise's and Jesse's lives have been intertwined for years. Both boys collected comic books, until Rise's grandmother, Aunt Celia, threw Rise's collection away and he decided it "was a stupid thing to do, anyway." By this time, Jesse had discovered his own artistic skills and was drawing his own comics. Jesse also notes that Rise changed about the time he was a junior in high school. Though Rise had plans to go to college, he soon started getting in trouble and ditching school. About the time Rise changed, Jesse and C. J. became friends.

Chapter 2

At the meeting of the Counts, the members vote on collecting dues and inviting women to join the group. They also discuss taking in a new member, a tough kid they believe to be an elementary school student, "Little Man." He gets angry when they refuse to decide right away on admitting him.

A seventeen-year-old named Mason Grier, a member of the Counts, has been arrested for robbing a bodega owned by Mr. Alvarez. Calvin, a leader of the Counts, relays a message from Mason, who says that he is innocent of the crime. "He wants the Counts to rough up the bodega store owner. Send him a message," Calvin says. Rise is in favor of backing up Mason, while the rest do not want to be involved. Rise leaves, then the others ask Jesse about his friend. Jesse admits that he and Rise may not be as "tight" friends anymore.

When Rise and Jesse hang out later at Rise's apartment, Sidney Rock stops by. He is a local police detective who was raised in the neighborhood. Sidney has heard about the call for the assault on Alvarez and implicitly warns them about the consequences of their actions, saying that in jail, "We got too many snitches, too many nonsnitches, and way too may young brothers trying to figure out how they got there." After Sidney leaves, Rise makes fun of him, but tells Jesse that he is not going to do anything on Mason's behalf. Rise suggests that Jesse write his biography, starting with a portrait of him that shows his strength. He explains, "when these street dudes do their muscle hustle, they got to lose, because sooner or later they're going to run into something stronger than they are." He wants "to be bigger than life."

Chapter 3

Jesse and C. J. are hanging out at church, where "C. J. was doodling over the keys" of the organ. Jesse tells C. J. that Rise has changed and he does not know him as well as he did before. Walking home, Jesse thinks that C. J. is easy to spend time with, like Rise used to be. He thinks, "Now I was getting the feeling that when Rise was saying one thing, there was something else going on behind the words." At home, Jesse draws Rise from memory. His mother compliments the drawing before asking who it is. "Mom was right," Jesse thinks, "it didn't look like Rise."

Chapter 4

Benny, a member of the Counts, organizes C. J., Jesse, and others into a Cuban music band to play for money at an adolescent's birthday party. Benny looks at the party as a break for them. Though C. J. agrees, both Jesse and C. J. doubt that C. J.'s mother will approve. Later, C. J. tells Jesse that he loves all music, but his mother wants him to play only in church. C. J. wants Jesse to get Jesse's mom to talk to C.J.'s mom about playing with the band.

Jesse tells C. J. that Rise wants a biography, to which C. J. responds, "He wants a biography, he should write it. He knows what he did." Jesse replies, "I know what he did too." While he and C. J. talk and walk, Jesse notices a beat-up doll that they had seen a skinny, disheveled little girl play-abusing earlier. He would have drawn it, but he stopped carrying his sketchbook around with him because some older men destroyed it when they thought he was sketching them.

Chapter 5

Benny calls Jesse on Saturday morning and tells him that the bodega was firebombed and he heard that two white cops are looking for Jesse as a suspect. His parents overhear the conversation and are concerned, though Jesse assures them he had nothing to do with it. Jesse's father asks if he should call a lawyer and says, "I don't like messing around with the police." Jesse then calls C. J.'s mom and tries to convince her to let him play in the band. C. J.'s mom and Jesse's mom talk about the band. Later, Jesse and C. J. walk to the bodega, which is destroyed. They see Sidney there, and Jesse agrees to go with him to tell the still-incarcerated Mason about the bombing. Sidney has also convinced Rise to come.

Chapter 6

On Monday night, Sidney takes Jesse and Rise to visit Mason. Jesse is annoyed by Rise's precautions and attitude; "Can't have people seeing me dealing with the Man," Rise says. Sidney asks them to emphasize to Mason the difference between armed robbery and homicide, and to leave the bodega owner alone. Sidney also tells the boys how easily armed robbery can turn into murder. Inside, Rise tells Jesse, "You can put in my book that when the Man was dealing lies, I was real-a-lizing what he was trying to put down." Jesse thinks, "maybe what Rise was doing was putting marks in the air, the way I did on paper, trying to do a self-portrait that I would believe and copy. . . . [but] I was looking for what was the truth behind the real thought he was keeping."

Chapter 7

When Mason comes into the room, he is limping. He does not say anything to Jesse and Rise for a while, and finally accuses his friends of "pimping for the Man." Jesse does as Sidney asked, telling Mason that he "ought to cool it, because if somebody died [he] would get homicide." Mason replies, "They can give you anything they want to give you," because evidence can be planted. Mason is angry that the Counts did not do as he asked. Rise tells him, "You don't send out no messages, you send out *requests*" because he is powerless in jail. Mason and Rise nearly come to blows, and Mason tells Rise he has "nothing to lose." The encounter leaves Jesse afraid and befuddled.

Chapter 8

After drawing some scenes from Rise's life as cartoons, Jesse brings his creations to Rise's apartment. Rise likes the work and is amazed that Jesse can remember so many events from their childhood. "You got the art thing going on good," Rise says. He also says he will be moving into his own place soon, and that he will pay for it dealing drugs. Shocked, Jesse tells his friend, "That doesn't even sound like you. All the time you talking about not doing drugs and how that stuff is sucking the life out of the hood." Rise reminds him that they are blood brothers, then goes on to explain how his perspective changed:

> One day I seen me standing in the cold by the side of the track waiting for my train to come. All I was getting was colder and colder and my train never did come. What I'm thinking now is that I need to get out of the cold.

Walking home, Jesse thinks, "I told myself that if I did his autobiography right, if I did a really good job, maybe I could change him back to what I knew."

Chapter 9

Jesse introduces his comic strip "Spodi Roti and Wise," through which he sometimes processes and expresses the things that are hard to deal with in his life. Jesse reflects on how he is close to his parents, but less so as he gets older because it was "like their brains were in a different place than [his] sometimes." He wishes he could talk to them about Rise, but he cannot imagine how. Jesse plays the congas at the Cuban band gig. The band does well, primarily because of C. J.'s talent. Going home, Jesse learns that C. J.'s mom let him play because the party was being given by a Wall Street executive, and that she hopes her son will turn away from music and go to college and have a good career.

Chapter 10

Jesse sits on the stoop with Benny, White Clara, and Gun, talking about guns. A school bus drives down the street, which is odd because it is summer. Some men on the bus start shooting as they drive past Jesse and his friends. Benny gets shot in the hand, and a cab driver who had gotten in the bus's way is also shot. The incident upsets Jesse very much. He later learns that the Diablos, an uptown gang, were probably responsible. There is another drive-by later in the week that is payback against the Diablos. Sidney later informs him that the drive-bys were probably over drugs. Jesse talks to C. J. about Rise, and C. J. expresses his concern. Rise calls Jesse and invites him to meet some new people.

Chapter 11

Jesse is uncomfortable when he meets Rise at the Ras Uhuru Social Haven. Jesse shows Rise more pictures for his autobiography and Rise explains it to the woman doing his nails: "My man here is writing my autobiography. I'm living the life and he writing it down like I tell him." Rise also lets Jesse know that his having "dropped the word" led to the retaliation drive-by against the Diablos. Though Rise and Jesse talk about memories of their shared past, Jesse is annoyed by Rise's gangster act. Jesse grows even more perturbed when Rise tells him where his drug-dealing territory is:

> My mind was going blank. The whole thing was too heavy for me. I couldn't even think straight, but Rise wanted to keep going over the pictures as if him "dropping the word" for a drive-by wasn't any big thing. If it wasn't big to him, it was sure big to me.

Before Rise leaves, he gives Jesse a fourteen-year-old girl named Tania as his "old lady." Jesse is attracted to her. Tania takes him to a Chinese restaurant for food, then they go to Tania's apartment so Jesse can draw her. Though Tania offers to be naked for him, Jesse declines. Tania also tells Jesse to tell Rise that they had sex. Tania loves her picture, and they kiss. At home, Jesse is confused by Rise and what he has become.

Chapter 12

C. J. informs Jesse that Rise is now a drug dealer, Rise's employers did the second drive-by shooting, and that Little Man carries a gun. Both Jesse and C. J. are puzzled by what is going on. While eating dinner with his parents, Jesse thinks about Rise telling him not to tell anyone about his new life though Rise told Calvin the same information. Jesse still hates drugs and what they do to people.

Jesse remembers a time a few years earlier in which Rise mouthed off to an adult in the neighborhood, Drew, and seemed ready to fight him. Drew pulled a straight razor and the boys ran away. Jesse recalls wondering "why Rise was so upset that he had to step to a hard dude like Drew," and thinks, "When I thought back to that, I wondered if maybe I didn't know Rise the way I thought I did."

Chapter 13

Jesse is hanging out on the stoop with Gun, C. J., and White Clara. Talking about the funeral for the member of the Diablos who was killed in the second drive-by, Gun tells them that the gang might take revenge in their neighborhood. Calvin joins them, and agrees that everyone should lie low. When a car drives up, Jesse and the others believe it might be another shooting, so they run and hide. It turns out to be white police officers, who pat them down because they ran. The policemen ask about the drive-by, but the boys say nothing. "It was a big thing because I was sitting on the stoop, copping an attitude that was chill to the world while inside I was, like, shaking," he says. He goes home and falls asleep.

Chapter 14

Jesse's mother wakes him up to talk to Sidney on the telephone, who offers him baseball tickets. Sidney asks how the book about Rise is coming, revealing it in a way that lets Jesse know Sidney knows about Rise's recent activities. Jesse is suddenly inspired to draw Rise in a pose he had once seen in a photograph of Black Panthers leader Huey Newton looking regal. Jesse becomes frustrated because he cannot get the picture right, but he finally comes up with an interesting, exaggerated, stylized version that pleases him. When he asks his mother who she thinks it is, she replies, "Well, it could be Bizarro, the mad villain of Gotham City, Stinky Scourge of the Underworld."

Chapter 15

Though it is morning, Jesse feels that he must show Rise the picture right away. Waiting for Rise to get out of the shower, Jesse feels doubts about the picture and how Rise will react. Rise loves the picture, telling him, "This is me, man! Truth rules, little brother. Truth rules!"

Chapter 16

Tania calls Jesse and says that she is his girlfriend, but he does not have to do much. Jesse likes having her as a girlfriend. Then C. J. calls, upset. When Jesse meets him at the church, C. J. is sitting with Little Man at the piano. Little Man implicitly mocks the piano, the church, and C. J. and Jesse, and then leaves. C. J. is distressed, and Jesse waits as he plays "Amazing Grace" and cries. When C. J. and Jesse walk home, Jesse learns that Little Man called him "a faggot." C. J. is upset by Little Man's actions and his own reaction. Jesse is supportive, telling his friend,

> We can't let fools drag us down to their level. If that's all they got, then that's all they got. We

got something else. . . . You got the music thing going on, and that's important to me, because what you're doing makes me surer about what I'm doing.

Chapter 17

Jesse's dad reads an article about Mason in which the Counts are described as a gang, not a social club. Jesse's dad tells him that he cannot be a member of the group anymore. Jesse's father is clearly worried about the bad influences around his son, but when Jesse talks back, his father hits him in the face. "He was yelling, something about how he hadn't raised a child to be going to prison." Before he can hit his son again, Jesse's mother comes home and stops him. Later, Jesse cannot open one of his eyes, so she insists on taking him to a doctor.

When they arrive home, Jesse wants to stay on the stoop with Calvin and Benny, but his mother wants him to go inside. Because he stays outside, his mother sits down and joins them. Calvin and Benny soon leave. His mother tells him that a policeman at the hospital asked if a report should be filed, but she asked that nothing be done. They are both upset, hurt, and angry because of the situation at home, as well as in the rough neighborhood in general. After she leaves, Jesse thinks, "My eye was hurting; I was mad at Dad for being afraid for me, even though in my heart I knew I was afraid, too."

Chapter 18

On Sunday, Jesse is still angry with his parents and declines to go to church with them, though the decision leaves him feeling bad. While trying to decide what he wanted to do for the day, Sidney calls. Sidney tells him that he has heard of an upcoming showdown between the Counts and Diablos. Jesse tries to maintain his anger at his father, and he tries to find ways to pass his day, without much luck. Rise calls Jesse later and tells him that there is a meeting with the Counts and some the Diablos to discuss territory, and that he expects Jesse to come to help the Counts show their numbers.

Chapter 19

Jesse is painting in his room, deciding what to do about the meeting. He did not commit to going, but he feels like he is being drawn in in spite of himself. Jesse calls C. J. to talk about it. He is surprised to learn that C. J. plans to go to the meeting, saying, "I can't be hiding in church all

my life." Calvin and Gun also plan to attend. Still unsure about what to do, Jesse asks C. J. if they can watch out for each other, but C. J. will not commit. Jesse was hoping that C. J. would not go so he could back out, but now he is even more torn. After remembering an incident from childhood when Rise desperately wished he had a father, Jesse decides to call Rise, who tells him that everything will be okay. Jesse lets him think he will come to the meeting.

Chapter 20

Jesse walks toward the meeting, still unsure about going. When he gets there, C. J., Gun, Rise, and Rise's girlfriend, Junice, are there. Rise tells them the situation with the Diablos and acts like he is in charge. He says all he wants to do is get the Diablos and their drug dealing out of their neighborhood and not bring attention to themselves. Jesse wonders why Rise seems so wise and philosophical, while just a year earlier he was only a kid. C. J. and Gun seemed soothed by Rise. When Gun asks where the Diablos are, Rise tells him that they are not really organized. The meeting breaks up shortly thereafter.

Rise, Junice, and Gun take a cab, while C. J. and Jesse walk home. They talk about the changing Rise. While C. J. is ordering street food, police cars and emergency vehicles pass by. They guess about what has happened, then go to check it out. A young girl tells them about the shooting that killed at least one man and injured a pregnant woman.

Chapter 21

In the middle of the night, Jesse's mom wakes him up. She tells him, "Some boys were shot on 144th Street. Two died and one is in bad condition." Sidney is in the apartment to question Jesse about the shooting. Jesse tells them that he and C. J. walked by it, but did not see anything. Sidney still has to take him downtown. Though the family lawyer tells Jesse not to say anything while riding with Sidney, Jesse tells him about the meeting. Sidney informs him that there was another meeting, and the meeting Jesse went to was part of a setup: The Counts and Diablos were apparently both sent to different locations for the meeting. Jesse and everyone else who was at the meeting is being questioned.

At the station, the family's lawyer believes the police understand that those at the meeting were just there to provide a cover for the real

> "I WAS LIVING IN A HOOD WITH A LOT OF DRUGS AND SHOOTINGS, BUT I DIDN'T WANT IT TO BE EVERYDAY NEWS. I FIGURED ME AND MY PEEPS ALL HAD SOMETHING ELSE GOING ON THAT KEPT US OUT OF THAT "EVERYDAY NEWS" CATEGORY. NOW RISE LOOKED LIKE HE WAS ANXIOUS TO GET INTO IT."

meeting and shooting. The lawyer also tells them that Jesse and C. J. should stay away from Rise. Sidney soon tells them they can leave. As they go home, dawn is breaking.

Chapter 22

In his room, Jesse looks at his drawings of Rise, realizing that the Rise he knew is gone. He tries to draw this Rise again, but cannot. About a week later, Jesse hears from Rise, after he was released from police custody. Rise tells him that he is moving to Miami, wants the drawings for his book, and will stop by before he leaves. Jesse says,

> I took out the book I was doing and thumbed through it, looking at the photographs and pictures I had drawn, thinking how hard it was going to be to say good-bye. . . . Then, suddenly, it came to me—the book was coming out wrong, and I knew why it was wrong.

Jesse decides that Rise can have his book of drawings but Rise has to finish his autobiography himself. When Jesse goes outside to say goodbye to Rise, C. J. and Benny are there, too. Arriving in a white limo, Rise is dressed in a suit and shows off. Little Man shows up and shoots Rise with a gun hidden in a brown paper bag. After running and hiding during the gunfire, Jesse holds Rise, who says, "Yo, Jesse, I'm scared, man, I'm so scared!" and dies in Jesse's arms.

Chapter 23

The funeral is a week later. Jesse is upset and apologizes to Rise's body. Jesse does not go to the cemetery but stays at the church as C. J. plays jazz. Jesse thinks, "It wasn't just the tiredness, the deep-in-the-bone weariness that kept me sitting. It was the feeling of not knowing how to go on anymore."

Jesse thinks about how Little Man was crying when he was arrested, just like Rise was crying when he died. When C. J. finishes playing, he and Jesse walk home. C. J. tells Jesse that while he is sad that Rise is gone, he is happy not to have to deal with gangs anymore. Jesse agrees and listens to C. J. talk about a music project and not about Rise. In his mind, Jesse promises Rise to finish his autobiography.

THEMES

Self-Expression

One of the primary ideas explored in *Autobiography of My Dead Brother* is the importance and power of constructive self-expression. Freedom of thought and expression are cornerstones of the American dream, are promised and protected in the First Amendment, and are one of the aspects of life in the United States that draws dreamers from around the world. For Americans in hard situations, such as Jesse and several of his friends and acquaintances, their talents help them define who they are and who to be above the sometimes-harsh realities of life in Harlem. Such gifts also provide a potential means of escape from this urban life. Some of those who do not have such a means of self-expression, such as Rise and Little Man, end up as victims of violence.

This outlet buoys Jesse, an artist whose talent is recognized by his peers, parents, and others. He draws to process what is happening around him, but also as a source of comfort when facing difficulties. Much of his art revolves around Rise, as Jesse tries to understand how his blood brother could change from someone who once aspired to go to college and hated drugs to a posturing drug dealer who uses his friends. Rise has Jesse create Rise's autobiography through Jesse's drawings, which allows Jesse to work through the transformation of Rise's character.

Others in Jesse's circle are defined by their means of self-expression. Gun is a gifted basketball player who is working toward playing the sport in college. Myers explores C. J.'s talent as a musician more deeply. C. J. plays organ and piano in the church for services and funerals. He also takes musical charge of the Cuban band Benny organizes to play at a girl's birthday party. C. J.'s mother encourages his music as a way of staying off the streets but worries that any form other than church music, such as jazz and blues, can be

Bill Clinton shakes hands with teenagers in Harlem, New York AP Images

dangerous. Like art for Jesse, music is C. J.'s refuge. C. J. is deeply wounded when Little Man calls him names and makes fun of his musical interests. Yet like Rise, Little Man can only express himself through swagger and violent action, and he ends up murdering because of it.

The Man versus the Street

The concept of "The Man," primarily policemen, versus the lure of renegade street life is a source of tension between characters in the novel. The Man is not trusted. The jailed Mason tells Rise and Jesse, "They got everything on their side. . . . They got the power in here, and they jacking up people on the street."

The Man is not a monolithic entity in *Autobiography of My Dead Brother*. Sidney Rock is a police detective who grew up in the neighborhood and now works cases there. He tries to help the kids who live there as much as possible, though some have doubts about him because he represents a distrusted outside authority. White

police, on the other hand, are not as respected in the neighborhood. During a discussion about guns, White Clara declares, "If a white cop sees you with a cap gun, he's going to use it as an excuse to shoot you."

While Jesse and his friends are definitely leery of unknown white police officers, most of them are much less suspicious of Sidney. Jesse in particular listens to Sidney about the situation with Mason, the drive-bys, and other happenings in the neighborhood. Jesse can joke about not sitting with a cop at a baseball game, and he trusts Sidney enough to tell him what happened at the meeting at Earl's Antiques though his lawyer advises otherwise.

Older kids like Mason and Rise do not share Jesse's sentiments. Rise's opinion of Sidney has changed dramatically, especially after he gets drawn into drug dealing. While Rise once shared Jesse's opinion that Sidney was acceptable, if not a friend, he now mimics the detective's voice and dismisses nearly everything Sidney says. Rise will not even let Sidney pick him and Jesse up in the neighborhood to talk to Mason. Like Mason, Rise wants to establish his own authority on the streets.

Escaping and Improving Circumstances

Two related themes underscored in *Autobiography of My Dead Brother* are escaping and improving the circumstances of life. While none of the characters moves out of the neighborhood, many are trying to improve their lots in life. C. J.'s mom looks to music and the church as a way to keep her son safe and enable a better life later on. Benny puts together the band to play at the birthday party and looks at it as the start of something bigger. C. J.'s mom only lets him play at the party because of this potential for something good to happen for her son. Even Rise starts working as a drug dealer in another part of the city as his own means of escaping his environment and making his life better. However, his attempt to leave New York for Miami after the arrest never comes to fruition; Little Man guns him down before Rise has a chance to become the only character who leaves the neighborhood by choice. Though no character actually leaves the neighborhood, many still have plans to escape or improve their circumstances at the novel's end.

HISTORICAL OVERVIEW

Gang Violence in New York City

In 2002, the National Youth Gang Center estimated that there were approximately 731,000 members of gangs in the United States. Gangs and gang-related violence was a problem on the increase in specifically New York City in the early 2000s. In the city in 2003, there were approximately 15,000 people in gangs, though only 3,600 were believed to be active, non-incarcerated gang members. There were a number of active gangs in New York City including the Bloods, the Crips, the Latin Kings, the Mexican Boys, and Los Pitufos (the Smurfs), among many others.

Murder rates, as well as that of other crimes in New York City, had generally fallen in the late 1990s and early 2000s. In central Harlem by 2005, the overall rate for crimes such as murder, rape, robbery, and burglary had dropped significantly over several years. The crime rate in this neighborhood was similar to the best neighborhoods in cities like Santa Monica, California.

However, in the whole of New York City, killings caused by or related to gang violence remained high. In 2003, for example, murders involving gangs were up 80 percent over the previous year; in 2002, there were twenty-nine gang-related murders, while in 2003, the number increased to fifty-two. Of all the murders in New York City in 2003, one in six were gang-related.

Life in Harlem

Harlem is a neighborhood in the Manhattan borough of New York City, and it has been a center of African American culture as well as high rates of poverty and crime since at least the 1920s. The unemployment rate was often twice as high as the rest of New York City, and many teens lived in single-parent homes. By 1990, a fifteen-year-old black male in Harlem had only a 37 percent chance of surviving to the age of sixty-five, while a fifteen-year-old black female had a 65 percent chance of making it to the same age. These figures are comparable to Angola and India, respectively.

In Central and East Harlem, the two parts of Harlem with the highest concentration of African Americans, there were approximately 20,500 adolescents between the ages of twelve and nineteen, according to the 2000 U.S. Census. Compared to their counterparts in other areas of New York City, these teens had much higher rates of sexually transmitted diseases and pregnancy. In addition to non-life-threatening diseases, a much higher percentage of teenagers living with HIV/AIDS reside in Harlem than the rest of Manhattan. The top causes of deaths for adolescents living in Harlem in the early 2000s were asthma, complications related to pregnancy, depression-related disorders, and homicide. Harlem had one of the highest rates of asthma in the United States.

CRITICAL OVERVIEW

Like many of Myers's novels, *Autobiography of My Dead Brother* was generally praised by critics for its engaging depiction of Jesse's struggles, conflicts between friends, and violent reality of life in Harlem. Francisca Goldsmith of *School Library Journal* comments, "This novel is like photorealism; it paints a vivid and genuine portrait of life that will have a palpable effect on its readers."

Critics noted a number of the book's strengths, including Myers's use of language and his characterizations. Writing in *Booklist*, Gillian Enberg notes, "What will affect readers most is Jesse's sharp, sometimes poetic first-person voice and the spirited, rhythmic dialogue of other vivid characters."

Other reviewers gave the author critical kudos for his deft handling of the novel's themes. In a review of *Autobiography*, as well as several other novels by Myers, Herbert Kohl of *Rethinking Schools Online* writes, "I realized how skillfully Myers places the human heart at the center of troubling stories and turns what could be stories about violence into tales of hope and redemption."

Another aspect of the book on which many reviewers focused praise were the timely illustrations created by Myers's son, Christopher. Noting the power of the drawings, the critic in *Kirkus Reviews* comments, "The innovative illustrated novel format is effective, essential to Rise's autobiography and to Jesse's own quest for understanding."

Summarizing the book's appeal for many critics, Alexis Burling of teenreads.com called the novel "a true-to-life story that is profoundly moving and one that boldly addresses many of the prevailing conflicts confronting urban youth today."

CRITICISM

A. Petruso

Petruso is a freelance writer with degrees in history and screenwriting. In this essay, Petruso examines Myers's depiction of authority figures in the novel Autobiography of My Dead Brother.

In an interview with *Black Issues Book Review*, Walter Dean Myers tells interviewer Grace L. Williams,

> I write about urban settings because you see that there is a negative public image. People use code words like "inner city" or say things like "ghetto," but you can't feel good about your home and if you never see urban areas depicted as anything but negative, it tells you that where you come from is crap.

While Myers was referring to the settings of his books such as *Autobiography of My Dead Brother*, this statement could also apply to his depiction of parents and authority figures who live in this urban locale and who help to raise teens like Jesse, C. J., and Rise. While the media often downplay the role of adults in poor, urban settings, Myers quietly celebrates it in this novel.

THOUGH IT IS ULTIMATELY JESSE, C. J., RISE, AND THE OTHER TEENS WHO MAKE THEIR OWN DECISIONS, MYERS REPEATEDLY EMPHASIZES THE IMPORTANCE OF ADULT AUTHORITY FIGURES ON THEIR LIVES AND CHOICES."

The critic in the *Publishers Weekly* review of *Autobiography of My Dead Brother* wrongly dismisses Myers's presentation of certain authority figures, claiming "Jesse's parents seem vague." Though the book is written from Jesse's point of view, Myers offers a complex depiction of urban parental figures and other authority figures as a subtext to the novel. Because Jesse's parents are still married and both work to support their family financially and emotionally, Myers underscores the importance of having two active parents in a young person's life. C. J. has a similar situation, though his mother is the dominant partner and the one depicted as having the most influence in her son's life.

Caring police detectives and adults in the church also play significant roles in supporting the teens at the novel's core. Though it is ultimately Jesse, C. J., Rise, and the other teens who make their own decisions, Myers repeatedly emphasizes the importance of adult authority figures on their lives and choices. When this direction is lacking, the situation can turn ugly. Rise was raised by a single mom with the help of her parents; he decides to drop out of school and deal drugs, and ends up dead. Myers clearly is implying that guidance of parents and other authorities is important to positively affecting younger people.

This fact can most clearly be seen in the relationship between the novel's first-person narrator, Jesse Givens, and his parents. His parents are married, live with their son in an apartment, and have a very close and interested relationship with him. Jesse explains, "I was tight with my folks in a way. I could say things to them, and they would try not to get too crazy about if even if they were nervous." But he understood why their relationship was sometimes tense. He continues, "It wasn't as if they were stupid or anything—it was like their brains were in a different place than mine sometimes."

Throughout *Autobiography of My Dead Brother*, Jesse's mother in particular is depicted as a caring, loving woman who stays involved in her teenage son's life and activities from the first chapter of the book. She attends the funeral of both Bobby Green and Rise with her son. She helps him to say goodbye at the casket of the latter's funeral, something Jesse could not do at Bobby G.'s church service. Mrs. Givens also plays a big role in Jesse's day-to-day life, supporting his artwork by getting him a desk for his art supplies and allowing him to look into summer art classes at the Cooper Union. She also pushes her husband and Jesse to be close and communicate more openly with each other.

Jesse's father does care, but this relationship is more complicated. As Myers states in an interview published in the *Wisconsin State Journal*,

> What happens is that parents feels that [they] have to have a certain moral stance and they lose the ability to talk to the children because when I'm talking to the child, I have to be the parent. . . . In the book, I think Jesse's father wants to say to his son, "Look, I don't know who you are and I'm at a loss," but he needs to sit down and say exactly that to him.

Instead, Jesse's father is somewhat distant. He reluctantly gives into his wife's entreaties to be open with Jesse and spend time bonding with him after Bobby G.'s funeral, though Jesse's meeting with the Counts stymies their plans to go bowling that night.

Yet when Mr. Givens realizes that Jesse has not told him about Mason being arrested and Jesse potentially being identified as the person who firebombed the bodega, he shows his true feelings. Jesse's dad tells him, "It involves my son, it's important. . . . You got that?" Jesse also describes his father's physical reaction while speaking these words: "There was a catch in his voice, and I could see he was getting real emotional." Jesse's father wants to be involved, but he does not always know how to express this desire well, which eventually leads to a physical altercation with his son.

Jesse's father acts out in violence when he is confronted with information that terrifies him about influences on his son. In an article in the *Amsterdam News* about Mason's sentencing for his armed robbery of the bodega, Mr. Givens reads that the Counts are described as a street gang. Jesse tries to explain to his father that Mason is making himself sound bigger than he really is, but his father demands that Jesse remove himself from the Counts. This statement leads to a tense showdown between them, with Jesse asking, "Why don't you hit me? Maybe you're as tough as Mason," and his father hitting him in the face.

While it is clear that Jesse's father is acting out of worry for his son, he has let anger and fear drive his actions. Jesse's mother gets between them and ensures her son receives medical care for his injured eye. She also makes sure that the police do not become involved in the matter because she knows it will make the situation worse. Myers includes this key scenario in the novel to show that even involved parents are not perfect, but make mistakes, sometimes big ones, too. Even Jesse realizes this, as Myers writes, "I was mad at Dad for being afraid for me, even though in my heart I knew I was afraid, too." Though Jesse and his father do not get along well for a while, Jesse continues to act in accordance with his parents' moral upbringing and tries to make sense out of the changes he sees in Rise and other situations around him.

Another character who expresses herself physically is C. J. Europe's mom, though not to the same degree as Mr. Givens. With her more playful whacks, Mrs. Europe plays a role in her son's life similar to Jesse's mom. While there is a Mr. Europe who apparently lives with his family, Myers emphasizes that it is Mrs. Europe who is primarily concerned with actively protecting her son from the violence of the streets. C. J. finds solace in music and is a talented musician. His mother tries to guide every choice he makes, including the kind of music he plays. She wants him to stick to classical music and gospel for his own good, though he wants to play jazz. Mrs. Europe was once a blues singer herself, but she could not make a living at it.

Mrs. Europe tries to direct C. J.'s life to ensure his future will be positive and include his attending college. C. J. tells Jesse that she even considers moving away from the neighborhood but she thinks that his playing piano for the church keeps him interested in music and off the streets. Mrs. Europe also allows him to play in Benny's Cuban band not because he gets paid, but because the band is playing at a children's birthday party for the daughter of an important businessman. She hopes this opportunity could get her son somewhere later on. Mrs. Europe's guidance seems to work, for C. J. is very focused on his music and where he could go in life. He easily sees through Rise's posturing before even Jesse does. C. J. is also careful in the choices he makes on the street, and he does not deliberately put himself in jeopardy.

Rise Davis's family situation is more complicated. Myers makes it clear that Rise's father has not been a particularly active part of the family for many years. Rise was raised by his mother, Mrs. Davis, and his maternal grandparents, the Johnsons. Rise's mother and grandmother did not have jobs when Rise was young, but they stayed home and covered expenses by babysitting other children. Jesse and Rise have been close since they were toddlers, because Rise's mother and grandmother cared for Jesse while his parents were working. Jesse even says he was envious of Rise's family situation for a time when he was younger, but he came to see how advantageous it was to have a father in the home.

Yet even though the information comes through Jesse, Myers does not depict Rise's family as particularly influential or involved in Rise's life. Rise still lives at home and has his own room, but he does not have the same kind of guidance that Jesse and C. J. receive. One factor in this situation may be the illness of his grandmother, who has suffered from Alzheimer's disease for some years. Such an illness can distract and drain a family, another reality of life Myers touches on. Though his grandmother is incapable of actively caring about Rise's choices in life, his mother and grandfather can fill that role, but they are not depicted as doing so.

One man who tries to guide Rise is Sidney Rock. A police detective who grew up on the block where Jesse lives, Sidney is a guiding, helpful force to all the teens in the novel. He has built this relationship with them up over a number of years. Jesse explains, "He kind of looked out for all the brothers he knew and that were straight with him. He'd also bust you if he had to, but at least he did it with respect." Sidney worked to avoid having to bust as many of the young men he knew as possible.

While Rise once listened to Sidney, he now dismisses the detective's words and importance. Rise has already decided to cross the line into illegal activities, and allowing a policeman to have any kind of positive relationship goes against what Rise has come to stand for. As Rise tells Jesse when they visit Mason in jail, "He looks like a brother and sounds like one, but he's still the Man." Though Rise does not care much about Sidney and what he says, Jesse and C. J., in particular, allow Sidney to play a positive role in their lives, reinforcing the good choices they make. Jesse and C. J. respect him and what he says. Jesse even tells him exactly what happened when he went to the meeting Rise called at Earl's Antiques between the Counts and the Diablos, though his father tells Jesse to say nothing. Sidney helps the two out when they are unfairly accused of being involved in the setup of the shooting of several gang members because of their attendance at that meeting.

Another place where adults guide the young people in *Autobiography of My Dead Brother* is in the church. While the church plays an even smaller role than Sidney, Myers begins and ends his novel there. The author subtly shows its importance in the community and to Jesse and C. J., who both attend regularly. Myers even names the church's minister Pastor Loving. The church is depicted as something of a sanctuary, especially for C. J., as it is where he can practice piano and organ. He also plays during services.

When Little Man violates this haven by coming in and insulting C. J. there, both Jesse and Elder Smitty, an active member of the church, comfort him. Elder Smitty demonstrates the power of positive action and words by complimenting Jesse's handling of C. J.'s distress over Little Man's harassment. Elder Smitty tells him, "Old as I am, I've never learned to deal with people like [Little Man] without bloodshed. You did real good, Jesse." Such small moments of positive reinforcement show how important the understated weight of even the barely significant authority figure can be to sometimes-unappreciative adolescents.

Source: A. Petruso, Critical Essay on *Autobiography of My Dead Brother*, in *Literary Themes for Students: American Dream*, Gale, 2007.

SOURCES

Brandeis, Toni, "Book Talk: Award-Winning Author Walter Dean Myers Chats with a Madison Writer and A Local School Librarian," in the *Wisconsin State Journal*, November 15, 2005, p. D1.

Burling, Alexis, Review of *Autobiography of My Dead Brother*, in *teenreads.com*, www.teenreads.com/reviews/006058291X.asp (September 6, 2006).

Enberg, Gillian, Review of *Autobiography of My Dead Brother*, in *Booklist*, Vol. 1001, Nos. 19–20, June 1, 2005, p. 1787.

Goldsmith, Francisca, Review of *Autobiography of My Dead Brother*, in *School Library Journal*, Vol. 51, No. 8, August 2005, p. 132.

Kohl, Herbert, "The Work, Not Just the Book," in *Rethinking Schools Online*, www.rethinkingschools.org/archive/20_02/good202.shtml (September 6, 2006).

Myers, Walter Dean, *Autobiography of My Dead Brother*, Harper Tempest, 2005.

Review of *Autobiography of My Dead Brother*, in *Kirkus Reviews*, Vol. 73, No. 13, July 1, 2005, p. 740.

Review of *Autobiography of My Dead Brother*, in *Publishers Weekly*, Vol. 252, No. 37, September 19, 2005, p. 68.

Williams, Grace L., "At Their Level," in *Black Issues Book Review*, Vol. 7, No. 6, November/December 2005, pp. 39–40.

The Autobiography of Benjamin Franklin

BENJAMIN FRANKLIN

1886

The Autobiography of Benjamin Franklin is a blueprint for the prototypical American, chronicling Benjamin Franklin's life as a printer, diplomat, statesman, patriot, scientist, inventor, and writer. Published posthumously in various forms over several years, first in French and then in English, Franklin's autobiography is a literary achievement worthy of the epic U.S. founding father. Franklin originally intended the document of his life and works to be for the sole use and enjoyment of his son, William. The first part, written in 1771, addresses his eldest child, but parts 2–4, written in 1784, 1788, and 1790, reflect its subject's hope that the book would find a wider audience, for the benefit of mankind. Franklin writes,

> Having emerg'd from the Poverty and Obscurity in which I was born and bred, to a State of Affluence and some Degree of Reputation in the World, and having gone so far thro' Life with a considerable Share of Felicity, the conducing Means I made use of, which with the Blessing of God so well succeeded, my Posterity may like to know, as they may find some of them suitable to their own Situations, and therefore fit to be imitated.

As much a historical account of eighteenth-century America as a guide to being virtuous, *The Autobiography of Benjamin Franklin* follows in the tradition of "conduct books" made popular by statesmen, soldiers, and noblemen before Franklin. His straightforward, no-nonsense writing style

BIOGRAPHY

BENJAMIN FRANKLIN

Benjamin Franklin, the eighth child and youngest son of his parents' ten children, was born on January 17, 1706, in Boston to Josiah and Abiah Franklin. Although his father hoped Franklin would become a member of the clergy, he was only able to pay for two years of schooling, ending his son's formal education at the age of ten. At the age of twelve, Franklin became a printer's apprentice to his brother, James. By 1730, Franklin had his own print shop, started his own newspaper, and was well on his way to becoming a honored member of Philadelphia society. He married Deborah Read, fathered three children, and soon began publishing his famous collection of quotations, *Poor Richard's Almanack*, from which the adage "A penny saved is a penny earned" is taken.

Once his financial standing was secure, Franklin began to indulge in his passion for scientific inquiry. He investigated the phenomena of electricity and invented the lightning rod, bifocals, the Franklin stove, and the flexible urinary catheter, among other things. He held many public offices, was awarded honorary degrees by both Harvard and Yale universities, and was selected to serve on the committee to draft the Declaration of Independence. In 1776, Franklin was sent to Paris, France, where he served as America's first ambassador. He lived outside of Paris, in a town called Passy, for nine years and became one of its most beloved residents. He returned to America in 1785 and became president of the abolitionist society in 1787. Franklin died at the age of 84 on April 17, 1790, in Philadelphia and was buried beside his wife, Deborah. An estimated 20,000 mourners attended his funeral on April 21, 1790. His autobiography was published nearly a century later, in 1886.

---

reveals much about the man who readily admits "that were it offer'd to my Choice, I should have no Objection to a Repetition of the same Life from its Beginning." Much of Franklin's contentment in life lies in his striving to achieve moral perfection. His father planted the seed of that goal early in the author's life; he approached the project with scientific clarity later. Of his father, Franklin writes,

> I remember well his being frequently visited by leading People, who consulted him for his Opinion in Affairs of the Town or of the Church he belong'd to and show'd a good deal of Respect for his Judgment and Advice. He was also much consulted by private Persons about their Affairs when any Difficulty occur'd, and frequently chosen an Arbitrator between contending Parties. At his Table he lik'd to have as often as he could, some sensible Friend or Neighbour, to converse with, and always took care to start some ingenious or useful Topic for Discourse, which might tend to improve the Minds of his Children. By this means he turn'd our Attention to what was good, just, and prudent in the Conduct of Life.

Franklin's account of life as an English American, as a subject of England's king in one of the British Empire's many colonies, is a fascinating glimpse into a nation at the time of its birth. More fascinating, still, is the fact that Franklin himself had much to do with the construction of the emerging nation. Like his father, Franklin's opinion on a variety of matters was highly sought after by intelligent, respectable colonists. Due to his reputation, the printer-turned-statesman was able to influence his colleagues to pursue industry, knowledge, economy, and sobriety as a way of becoming successful. These traits, along with his love of reading and flourish with language, are responsible for his success in the many and varied endeavors he undertook in his lifetime. The long list of Franklin's achievements includes inventing the first room-warming stove, the postal service, the public library, the lightning rod, and bifocals. He was also elected to represent the American colonies on trips to England and the Continental Congress, and he was selected to become a member of the committee that drafted the Declaration of Independence.

According to Edmund S. Morgan in his foreword to the second Yale University Press edition of the book,

> [*The Autobiography of Benjamin Franklin*] became itself the most widely read autobiography ever written by an American. It has served many Americans as it may have served Franklin—to define what it meant, what it had meant, and what it ought to mean to be an American.

PLOT SUMMARY

Part 1

Part 1 of *The Autobiography of Benjamin Franklin* begins as a letter with the salutation, "Dear Son." The setting and date noted at the top, "Twyford, at the Bishop of St. Asaph's 1771," mark the location of Franklin's week-long vacation, a respite dedicated to setting down his memoirs for his son William, then royal governor of New Jersey. He writes that he enjoyed "obtaining any little Anecdotes of my Ancestors" and so believes William might like to "know the Circumstances of *my* life." Franklin writes that if he could, he would repeat his life, correcting the errors he had made along the way. Acknowledging the impossibility of such an experience, he writes, "the next Thing most like living one's Life over again, seems to be a *Recollection* of that Life; and to make that Recollection as durable as possible, the putting it down in Writing." He thanks God for the good life he has had and begins to recount a bit of his family's ancestry.

Franklin writes, "The Notes one of my Uncles (who had the same kind of Curiosity in collecting Family Anecdotes) once put into my Hands furnish'd me with several Particulars relating to our ancestors." According to these notes, the Franklins lived in Ecton, Northamptonshire, England, for at least three hundred years. Franklin himself was the youngest son of the youngest son for five generations. His father, Josiah Franklin, left England for America in 1682 with his first wife and three children. After settling in their new home, they had four more children. After the first wife died, Josiah married Abiah Folger, Franklin's mother. Josiah had ten more children with Abiah, making Franklin the fifteenth of Josiah's seventeen children.

Josiah Franklin wanted his youngest son to become a member of the clergy. This meant he would have to go to school, unlike his other brothers who became apprentices in various

Benjamin Franklin The Library of Congress

trades. Franklin proved a failure at math, but showed great promise in reading and writing and quickly rose to the top of his class. Because of the family's financial situation, though, Franklin was made to leave school after only two years to become an assistant in his father's soap- and candle-making business. Franklin admired his father and writes of how the man, though lowly in station, was well respected by his neighbors and friends. Josiah taught his son much, including right virtues and the art of debate. The latter would come to serve Franklin especially well in his later life.

Franklin became an apprentice in his brother James's print shop at the age of twelve. Indentured by contract to work there for the next eight years, Franklin was able to pursue his love of reading and books due to his new station. He read the works of Cotton Mather and Daniel Defoe and, around this time, began imitating the writing style of professional writers in an effort to improve his own. He discovered a book "by one Tryon, recommending a Vegetable Diet," which Franklin pursued for a brief time. He became skeptical of religion, attempted to become less arrogant, and began writing anonymous articles that were published in his brother James's newspaper, the *New England*

Courant. James printed the pieces, not knowing his younger brother had penned them. Franklin's brother was a severe master to his brother/apprentice Benjamin, who notes, "I fancy his harsh and tyrannical Treatment of me, might be a means of impressing me with that Aversion to arbitrary Power that has stuck to me thro' my whole Life." His unexpected success in writing gave Franklin the confidence to quit the print shop and secretly move to Philadelphia.

In 1723, seventeen-year-old Franklin found work with a man named Keimer who ran a Philadelphia print shop. He received a letter from his brother-in-law, Robert Holmes, who asked Franklin to return home to Boston. Franklin's eloquently written reply was read by Pennsylvania Governor William Keith, who was impressed by Franklin's writing ability. Franklin recounts that Keith said, "I appear'd a young Man of promising Parts, and therefore should be encouraged: The Printers at Philadelphia were wretched ones, and if I would set up there, he made no doubt I should succeed." Keith visited Franklin at Keimer's print shop and offered to help the young man set up his own printing business. Franklin first decided to travel to England to make connections with professionals in bookselling and stationery businesses there. He asked Deborah Read to marry him, but she refused because of his upcoming travels. Franklin asked his friend James Ralph, a fellow writer and lover of debate, to accompany him to England.

In London, Franklin wrote a pamphlet titled *A Dissertation on Liberty and Necessity, Pleasure and Pain*. He also broke off his friendship with Ralph over a misunderstanding with Ralph's girlfriend. Though Franklin found some measure of success in London as a writer, he returned to Philadelphia in 1726, after eighteen months abroad. He took over Keimer's print shop and started his own newspaper. He began practicing Deism and formed a group called the Junto. Members of the group convened every Friday night to discuss topics related to morality and philosophy. He fell out with Keimer and opened his own printing shop in 1728. Franklin became the official printer for the Pennsylvania assembly and began making a substantial amount of money, which he used to expand his newspaper operation. After writing a pamphlet called *The Nature and Necessity of a Paper Currency*, Franklin was chosen by the legislature to print

the money, which brings in even more income. Franklin married Deborah Read and began a subscription library, his "first project of a public nature."

Part 2

Part 2 begins with letters urging Franklin to finish and publish his memoirs. The first, from Abel James, was written in 1782. The second, from Benjamin Vaughn, is dated January 1783. Vaughn, after having read the outline and sections of early text, encourages Franklin to finish the book because it would offer direction to people hoping to better their lives. He also points out that wide publication of the *Autobiography* would show the British how industrious and virtuous the Americans were. Further, it would prove that America held great economic promise. Franklin writes in 1784, "It is some time since I receiv'd the above Letters, but I have been too busy till now to think of complying with the Request they contain." Writing from Paris immediately after the American Revolution, Franklin is seventy-eight years old by the time he picks up where he left off.

The library he started in 1730 was a huge success. He writes that "Reading became fashionable," as a result of people's access to books. He hesitated to take full credit for the system, sensing some resentment about his growing good fortune. He and his wife started a family that Franklin supported by continuing to be frugal and industrious. Around this time he embraced a personal challenge:

> I conceiv'd the bold and arduous Project of arriving at moral Perfection. I wish'd to live without committing any Fault at any time. ...
> As I knew, or thought I knew, what was right and wrong, I did not see why I might not *always* do the one and avoid the other. But I soon found I had undertaken a Task of more Difficulty than I had imagined.

This project involved listing thirteen virtues, to be mastered in order, perfecting each one before moving on to the next. Franklin decided that temperance, silence, order, resolution, frugality, industry, sincerity, justice, moderation, cleanliness, tranquility, chastity, and humility are the most important virtues. Once he began his project, he was not troubled by realizing just how many faults he had, noting, "A benevolent Man should allow a few Faults in himself, to keep his Friends in Countenance." He hopes those who read *The Autobiography* "may follow the Example and reap the Benefit" of his experiment.

Part 3

Part 3 begins, "I am now about to write at home, August 1788[,] but cannot have the help expected from my Papers, many of them being lost in the War." He picks up from 1731, the year he started planning *"a great and extensive Project."* He quotes from a paper ("accidentally preserved") from 1731, in which he outlines a "Party for Virtue," organized "by forming the Virtuous and good Men of all Nations into a regular Body, to be govern'd by suitable good and wise Rules, which good and wise Men may probably be more unanimous in their Obedience to, than common People are to common Laws." The party would be called "the Society of the *Free and Easy*" and would be based on the essential principles of major religions. All party members would have to subscribe to Franklin's thirteen virtues and come to each meeting prepared with a plan for bettering the human race. Because of his devotion to several public and private occupations, he did not have the time or energy to establish the party.

A year later, Franklin began writing *Poor Richard's Almanack*, which featured information typical of annual almanacs, but which also contained the author's aphorisms—adages or memorable words of wisdom. He recalls that "I endeavor'd to make it both entertaining and useful, and it accordingly came to be in such Demand that I reap'd considerable profit from it," during its twenty-five-year run. Franklin considered the *Almanack* a means with which to instruct the common people; this same interest drove Franklin to dedicate parts of his newspaper, the *Pennsylvania Gazette*, to educational purposes as well.

As he aged, Franklin became more politically motivated and began to advocate the education of women. He learned several languages and played chess regularly. He made amends with his brother, James, in Boston. In 1736, his four-year-old son died of small pox, a fate he hoped to spare other parents from enduring:

> I long regretted bitterly and still regret that I had not given it to him by Inoculation; This I mention for the Sake of Parents, who omit that Operation on the Supposition that they should never forgive themselves if a Child died under it; my Example showing that the Regret may be the same either way, and that therefore the safer should be chosen.

In 1736, the original twelve members of the Junto decided that each should go and start his own group to increase their "Power of doing Good." Franklin became Clerk of the General Assembly of Pennsylvania that same year, and the year after, Deputy Postmaster of Philadelphia; he allows that both official posts enhanced his private businesses. Through the Junto, he advocated a property tax to better fund the police and formed the Union Fire Company, the first American fire department. With these many successes under his belt, Franklin became famous.

Franklin invented a room-warming stove in 1742 and refused to patent it in hopes that it would more widely proliferate. He wrote *Plain Truth* (1744), a pamphlet calling for colonial unity. Franklin became Commissioner of the Peace and a member of the Pennsylvania Assembly and advised the construction of a Presbyterian meeting house. In 1749, he wrote a pamphlet titled *Proposals Relating to the Education of Youth in Pennsylvania*, which launched interest in planning an educational academy. Franklin chose members of the Junto to become a board of trustees and the Academy (now the University of Pennsylvania) opened in 1753. He organized a street-sweeping system, set a street paving initiative into action, and designed street lights, all because he believes "Human Felicity is produc'd not so much by great Pieces of good Fortune that seldom happen, as by little Advantages that occur every Day." Franklin was awarded honorary degrees from Harvard and Yale. During this time, he also rose to the rank of Postmaster General of America.

In 1754, the Seven Years' War erupted in Europe and the French and Indian War erupted in America. This set Franklin to the task of drawing up plans to defend the colonies and for setting up a wartime government. He developed a plan to fund the armed forces, which began to cause great concern among the English government. They saw the colonies becoming self-sufficient and so they began sending British forces to the colonies. Franklin implored those with extra horses and wagons to relinquish them to the war effort, and he began preparing care packages for fighting soldiers. He spent a good deal of time in the field and became a financial commissioner in charge of distributing funds to organize a militia. He spent any extra time, effort, and money on keeping the troops supplied.

Franklin focuses the end of part 3 less on his military experiences and more on his scientific experiments, which he conducted at home in

"

I WAS NOT DISCOURAG'D BY THE SEEMING
MAGNITUDE OF THE UNDERTAKING, AS I HAVE ALWAYS
THOUGHT THAT ONE MAN OF TOLERABLE ABILITIES
MAY WORK GREAT CHANGES, AND ACCOMPLISH GREAT
AFFAIRS AMONG MANKIND, IF HE FIRST FORMS A GOOD
PLAN, AND, CUTTING OFF ALL AMUSEMENTS OR OTHER
EMPLOYMENTS THAT WOULD DIVERT HIS ATTENTION,
MAKES THE EXECUTION OF THAT SAME PLAN HIS SOLE
STUDY AND BUSINESS."

Philadelphia. He published a paper "on the Sameness of Lightning with Electricity," which caused much debate and notoriety:

> M. Delor...undertook to repeat what he call'd the *Philadelphia Experiments,* and after they were performed before the King and Court, all the Curious of Paris flocked to see them. I will not swell this Narrative with an Account of that capital Experiment nor the infinite Pleasure I receiv'd in the Success of a similar one I made soon after with a Kite at Philadelphia.

He was awarded a medal of honor from the Royal Society and became a member. As a member of the Pennsylvania's legislative assembly, he often settled disputes between the "Proprietary"— those who the king had granted property and appointed to govern in the colony—and local interests. With such success and repute in that role, Franklin was elected as the assembly's agent to go to England and petition the king against the over-reaching power of his deputies in America. He arrived in London on July 27, 1757.

Part 4

The shortest segment of *The Autobiography*, part 4 recounts Franklin's trip to London in 1757. Lord Granville, the president of the King's Privy Council, informed Franklin that "the King is the legislator of the colonies." Franklin realized the English view is at odds with the colonial view of their relationship:

> I had always understood from our Charters, that our Laws were to be made by our Assemblies, to be presented indeed to the King for

his Royal Assent, but that being once given the King could not repeal or alter them.... [Granville] assur'd me I was totally mistaken. ...[H]is Lordship's Conversation...a little alarm'd me as to what might be the Sentiments of the Court concerning us.

He tried to argue for fairness in England's taxation in the colonies, but the trip was mainly unsuccessful. Upon his return to Philadelphia, the Assembly acknowledged his efforts to promote American interests abroad. Franklin dies before he is able to finish *The Autobiography*, which recounts events only up to the year 1763.

THEMES

Striving for Success

Benjamin Franklin epitomizes the ideal American hero in that he came from humble beginnings, worked hard, and made an almost mythically successful life for himself and his family. He was largely influenced by his father, a maker of soap and candles, whose lowly profession belied the influence he had on his community and his family. He recalls of his father:

> I think you may like to know Something of his Person and Character. He had an excellent Constitution of Body, was of middle Stature, but well set and very strong. He was ingenious, could draw prettily, was skill'd a little in Music and had a clear pleasing Voice, so that when he play'd Psalm Tunes on his Violin and sung withal as he sometimes did in an Evening after the Business of the Day was over, it was extreamly agreable to hear. He had a mechanical Genius too, and on occasion was very handy in the Use of other Tradesmen's Tools. But his great Excellence lay in a sound Understanding, and solid Judgment in prudential Matters, both in private and publick Affairs.

Most of what Franklin said about his father could be applied to himself, except that Franklin's interest in public affairs became a predominant and active part of his life. But this would not be the case had he not applied himself vigorously to the labor of becoming a self-made man. His active life in public affairs came about only after he had become a printer with his own shop, begun a successful newspaper business, published several well-received articles and pamphlets, invented a number of creations to better the lives of those who used them, started a public library and the postal service, created a fire department and sanitation system, and paved and lighted public streets, among other improvements to society. And while he was hard at work, doing what he could to better the lives of the colonists, he decided to strive for moral perfection:

> I wish'd to live without committing any Fault at any time; I would conquer all that either Natural Inclination, Custom, or Company might lead me into. As I knew, or thought I knew, what was right and wrong, I did not see why I might not *always* do the one and avoid the other. But I soon found I had undertaken a Task of more Difficulty than I had imagined.

The difficulty of the task did not turn Franklin from it, however. He lived his belief that "God helps them that help themselves," and as such an exemplar of industry and good fortune, became the prototypical American living the American dream.

Good Works

Franklin provided many models of success that others could, can, and still do emulate. Someone who wants to live a moral life need only follow the plan he describes for mastering his "Virtues and their Precepts." One seeking success in business will also find a robust, dedicated, and practical role model in Franklin. However, his success as a member of society is probably the role that did the most to define the world in which he lived, and it continues to define the modern country to this day.

His life is full of examples of the good works he performed for the betterment of society. In his early twenties, Franklin undertook his "first Project of a Public Nature," North America's first subscription library. He recalls with pride of the libraries that grew from that first one:

> [They] have improv'd the general Conversation of the Americans, made the common Tradesmen and Farmers as intelligent as most Gentlemen from other Countries, and perhaps have contributed in some degree to the Stand so generally made throughout the Colonies in Defence of their Privileges.

As when he was the clerk of Pennsylvania's General Assembly and deputy postmaster, Franklin's public service often served his private interests. By the time he was thirty, his original Junto spawned several satellite groups:

> The advantages proposed were, the improvement of so many more young citizens by the use of our institutions; our better acquaintance with the general sentiments of the inhabitants on any occasion, as the Junto member might propose what queries we should desire, and

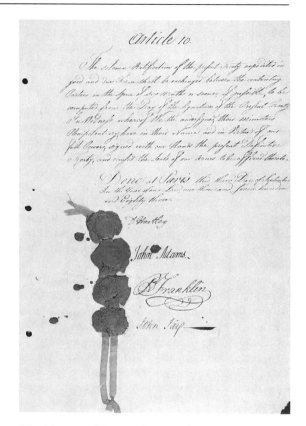

The Treaty of Paris, showing the signature of Benjamin Franklin © *Corbis*

was to report to the Junto what pass'd in his separate club; the promotion of our particular interests in business by more extensive recommendation, and the increase of our influence in public affairs, and our power of doing good by spreading thro' the several clubs the sentiments of the Junto.

Through the Junto, Franklin goes on to regulate the city's constables and build a fire department. He later uses his influence to help establish a college, organize a militia, build a hospital, and pave, clean, and light the city's streets. When it came to useful inventions, such as the Franklin stove, he declined to patent or profit because, "as we enjoy great advantages from the inventions of others, we should be glad of an opportunity to serve others by any invention of ours; and this we should do freely and generously."

In *The Autobiography,* Franklin concludes his section enumerating his public works with this statement:

With these sentiments I have hazarded the few preceding pages, hoping they may afford hints which some time or other may be useful to a city I love, having lived many years in it very happily, and perhaps to some of our towns in America.

His sentiment has been useful to many other towns, in America and around the world. Generous and industrious people from Andrew Carnegie (whose steel fortune endowed thousands of public libraries) to George Washington Carver (who developed but refused to patent thousands of innovative uses for crops grown widely in the U.S. South) to Bill Gates (whose software fortune backs a massive international effort to relieve poverty) have devoted what gifts they could to leave their world better than they found it. All seem to follow in Franklin's wisdom that "Human felicity is produc'd not so much by great pieces of good fortune that seldom happen, as by little advantages that occur every day." The notion that those who can should help those in need is not particular to Americans, but it is part of Franklin's legacy as the original American dreamer that great people have continued to undertake the challenge on a grand scale, with great results.

HISTORICAL OVERVIEW

Franklin's America
The Autobiography of Benjamin Franklin is still considered a literary treasure, two hundred years after its publication, for a number of reasons. First, it provides a close view of eighteenth-century colonial America through the eyes of a man who was not only present for many critical events of the time, but who made several of those events happen. *The Autobiography* is especially prized because a large segment of the population at the time could not read or write, and many of the documents that were written did not survive long enough to be studied by historians. Franklin's descriptions of eighteenth-century life give an intimate view of the intellectual, scientific, political, and religious changes that took place. Specifically, *The Autobiography* reflects eighteenth-century idealism. Franklin's intellectualism and his devotion to scientific inquiry and political advancement reflect the values of the Age of Reason. This eighteenth-century movement focused on the optimistic belief that mankind could be advanced through political and scientific means.

Because Franklin was devoted to the betterment of society, the reader learns much about the cultural and societal needs of the time. His development of a street-cleaning, street-paving, and street lighting system allows the reader to imagine what the streets of Pennsylvania in the 1720s and 1730s must have looked like. His development of the Junto shows how the intellectual elite spent their free time and how important the formation of the group would be to the United States as a whole many years later. For instance, without them, Benjamin Franklin may not have been able to get the University of Pennsylvania built or the idea of colonial unity to be widely supported. Franklin's religious beliefs change throughout the autobiography, which leads readers to ascertain that religious freedom was alive and well in the colonies. Franklin was respected for his religious views, partly because he was intellectually curious and open to a wide range of thought. His scientific experiments and inventions made plain those things eighteenth-century Americans did not have—such as heated rooms before the invention of the Franklin stove—and an understanding of electricity. Finally, the detailed record of his military experiences affords readers the opportunity to trace a proud English American's political dissention with his king, a leader he had previously respected and paid loyal service to. This is key in understanding the historical overview of the times. It is striking to consider a time when Americans, who, for the most part, willingly left the mother country to seek their fortune in a new land, still felt a connection and loyalty to England. Though Franklin does not delve deeply into the American Revolution, it is interesting to read detailed accounts of those events leading up to it.

Though books similar to *The Autobiography* had been written, the autobiographical format had yet to catch on outside the realm of religious tracts in the eighteenth century. This means that Franklin's memoir defined an entirely new literary genre that has gone on to influence every generation after him. It could be said, too, that his insistence on treating the book as a guide to assist others in bettering themselves, as he had done, influenced a whole other genre: the self-help book.

The Enlightenment
The Enlightenment was a seventeenth- and eighteenth-centuryintellectual movement that celebrated the power of human reason. Enlightenment philosophy posits that human beings can ascertain certain objective truths about the universe by

approaching science, government, religion, ethics, logic, and aesthetics systematically. Enlightenment thinkers sought to eradicate tyranny—especially religious and governmental tyranny—and superstition with their methodological approach, believing that irrational thought kept the world from progressing forward. Prominent Enlightenment thinkers include Isaac Newton, Thomas Paine, David Hume, Benjamin Franklin, Jean-Jacques Rousseau, and Immanuel Kant. The Enlightenment and its principles inspired the American and French Revolutions, informed the tenets of classic liberalism and capitalism, and influenced many of the movements of the modern period.

The seeds of Enlightenment can be traced all the way back to the thirteenth century when Thomas Aquinas used Aristotelian logic to defend certain tenets of Christianity. In the fourteenth and fifteenth centuries, a group of French and Italian thinkers known as "humanists" emerged. They declared that proper worship of God involved worship of His finest creation: humanity. To them, anyone who celebrated human intelligence— artists, painters, scholars, architects—celebrated God's glory. Michel de Montaigne, in the sixteenth century, looked to robust non-Christian cultures and realized that morality was relative. He reasoned that non-Christians were not necessarily morally inferior to Christians just because they held different beliefs. This was a monumental shift in thinking at the time, and Enlightenment thinkers were profoundly influenced by the idea that one could borrow philosophies and laws from other cultures to improve one's own.

The Enlightenment was influenced by these philosophical events, but it was years of warfare and repression in Europe—including religious wars, witch-hunts, widespread censorship, and slavery—that finally compelled Voltaire to write about how reason could change the world and Rousseau to espouse "deism." The Enlightenment took hold in France and England in different ways, but both countries were equally affected by it. In France, the movement sparked the Revolution; in England, it caused the power of religion and of the aristocracy to gradually diminish. Intellectual leaders across the Atlantic in America, however, saw the language of Enlightenment as their language, the language of freedom, self-determination, and natural law. The foundations of the Enlightenment are, essentially, the foundations of America. The colonists, responsible for shaping a whole new country, were in a perfect position to put the ideals

of the movement into effect. The "Common Sense" and "Crisis" pamphlets and the Declaration of Independence are proof of how powerfully Thomas Paine, Benjamin Franklin, and Thomas Jefferson were influenced by both the English and French Enlightenment.

Pre-Revolutionary America

The thirteen original American colonies originated with the settlement in Jamestown, Virginia, in 1607. Georgia, the last colony settled, was established by 1732. Each was organized and governed on the authority of the king of England usually through appointed and hereditary governors with often divided loyalties. By Franklin's time, most were established and autonomous enough to resent neglect and meddling from abroad. With England and France warring on two continents by the 1750s—in Europe in the Seven Years War and in North America in the French and Indian War—the British government considered its American colonies a ripe source for fundraising through taxation. This is precisely the conflict that sent Franklin to England in 1757.

By 1763, the American colonies had advanced to the extent that ties with England seemed extraneous. The harder the Americans tried to demand independence, though, the tighter Parliament's grip. For instance, the British government imposed taxes on Americans to cover part of the cost of keeping a standing British army on American soil, supposedly to protect the colonists. In actuality, the colonists could protect themselves and saw that the presence of the "Redcoats" merely infringed on their rights and interests. They bitterly resented having to pay for that. This particular dispute officially began with the Stamp and Sugar Act and ended ten years later with the Boston Tea Party—an act of rebellion carried out by a group of Bostonians who dumped a shipment of British tea into the harbor to protest Parliament's attempt at taxation. England countered with a series of measures known on these shores as Intolerable Acts and ordered that Massachusetts be ruled by British military leader Major General Sir Thomas Gage. Armed revolt soon followed.

This battle for freedom from England was also referred to as the American War of Independence. In his *Autobiography*, Franklin recounts very little of the war that began in 1775 and ended in 1783, despite the fact that he is considered one of its greatest statesmen, was chosen as a delegate of the Continental Congress, and was appointed to the committee that drafted the Declaration of Independence—which he signed after the Revolution was won. His influence prior to, during, and after the war cannot be overemphasized.

In 1774, the first Continental Congress met in Philadelphia and drew up non-importation and non-exportation petitions and addressed them to the king and Parliament. This was an attempt to coerce these entities to repeal the many measures known as the Intolerable Acts. The Congress also encouraged every one of the colonies' cities, towns, and counties to form committees that would serve as local authorities, or foundational revolutionary organizations, that would work closely with overseeing assemblies to take control of the militias. By shaping these forces, the colonists prepared themselves to take control of their country before the British had a chance to organize against them.

CRITICAL OVERVIEW

At least two early readers of Franklin's "Notes of My Life" urged its author to complete and publish the work. Abel James, after having read an early manuscript, wrote a letter to Benjamin Franklin in 1782, positing,

> What will the World say if kind, humane and benevolent Ben Franklin should leave his Friends and the World deprived of so pleasing and profitable a Work, a Work which would be useful and entertaining not only to a few, but to millions. . . . I know of no Character living nor many of them put together, who has so much in his Power as Thyself to promote a greater Spirit of Industry and early Attention to Business, Frugality and Temperance with the American Youth.

Another friend, Benjamin Vaughn, wrote in 1783,

> All that has happened to you is also connected with the detail of the manners and situation of a *rising* people; and in this respect I do not think that the writings of Caesar and Tacitus can be more interesting to a true judge of human nature and society. But these, Sir, are small reasons in my opinion, compared with the chance which your life will give for the forming of future great men; and in conjunction with your Art of Virtue . . . of improving the features of private character, and consequently of aiding all happiness both public and domestic.

The two letters, published in the final version of *The Autobiography* at Franklin's request, do much to dissuade Franklin from believing his "several little family Anecdotes of no Importance to others"

MEDIA ADAPTATIONS

The Autobiography of Benjamin Franklin was released in an unabridged audio CD entitled *The Autobiography of Benjamin Franklin: A Fully Rounded Portrait of the Many-Sided Franklin, Notably the Moralist, Humanitarian, Scientist, and Unconventional Human Being* on December 10, 2005. It is available through The Audio Partners.

should go unpublished. Critics would later deem the work an admirable representation of eighteenth-century literature as well as an important and revolutionary memoir chronicling an entirely new historical era. Even Franklin's wooden prose would, one hundred years later, be praised by the likes of Woodrow Wilson. He writes in an early introduction,

> [*The Autobiography*] is letters in business garb, literature with its apron on, addressing itself to the task, which in this country is every man's, of setting free the processes of growth, giving them facility and speed and efficacy.

The Autobiography has received its share of negative criticism, too. D. H. Lawrence, for one, faulted Franklin's materialism in Lawrence's *Studies in Classic American Literature*:

> Why then did Benjamin set up this dummy of a perfect citizen as a pattern to America? Of course, he did it in perfect good faith, as far as he knew. He thought it simply was the true ideal. But what we think we do is not very important. We never really know what we are doing. Either we are materialistic instruments, like Benjamin, or we move in the gesture of creation, from our deepest self, usually unconscious. We are only the actors, we are never wholly the authors of our own deeds or works. It is the author, the unknown inside us or outside us.

Less specifically, modern critics have taken issue with Franklin's rampant arrogance—an annoying trait especially in one who claims to be wholly committed to humility. Others, including German sociologist Max Weber, disagree with Franklin's blatant capitalism.

Despite the criticism, Franklin's provincial, soil-based prose engagingly chronicles a critical moment in American history while revealing the thoughts of a man who played a major part in its evolution. It is important to note that *The Autobiography* is the first literary account of the American dream. Little wonder the book is often referred to as a uniquely American book, one that has helped define a nation and a people during its emergence.

CRITICISM

Jennifer Jordan Baker

In the following excerpt, Baker argues that the self-promotion of which many critics accuse Franklin is more of a paradigm for American prosperity.

After reading the first installment of Benjamin Franklin's memoirs, Benjamin Vaughan concluded that his friend's life story would offer a fitting paradigm of American upward social mobility. "All that has happened to you," he wrote to Franklin in 1783, is "connected with the detail of the manners and situation of a *rising* people." Vaughan's insistence that Franklin's was a prototypical story of success and self-making suggested that the memoir was representative of the American experience. While the limitations of this prototype are clear to the modern reader—Vaughan spoke specifically of a "rising people" of Euro-American males with access to economic opportunities not available to others—critics have recognized nonetheless a presumption of representativeness in this text. In the words of Mitchell Breitwieser, Franklin "aspires to representative personal universality," creating a rhetorical personality by cultivating "characteristics he felt were in accord with what the age demanded." Franklin's *Autobiography*, according to William Spengemann, attempts to "represent the conclusions of his experience as being universally true and hence applicable to every life, rather than peculiar to his own case."

Recent criticism especially has located this concept of representativeness in the economic and political culture of early America. Michael Warner has maintained that Franklin effaces the particularities of his own personality in order to achieve a "republican impartiality"—refuting his own personal authority and embodying, through

Library Hall in Philadelphia with the statue of Benjamin Franklin in the niche above the door © Lee Snider/Photo Images/Corbis

writing, the legitimacy of a public statesman. Grantland Rice argues that Franklin, by producing and circulating written representations of himself, suppresses the idiosyncrasies of his personality in favor of a disembodied self constituted in print; this "objectified self" (realized in letters, public proposals, treatises, newspaper articles, and, of course, the autobiography itself) takes its cues, he emphasizes, from a burgeoning capitalist economy in which the exchange of goods and money replaces interpersonal relationships.

A different concept of representativeness, I would argue, is at work in this text. In the third section of the *Autobiography*, Franklin recalls that, upon his retirement from the printing business, he repeatedly lent his own name to governmental financial schemes and projects for public improvement. His memoir, by implication, is one of those projects that bears this valuable endorsement. As both a tale of his own rise to wealth and social prominence as well as a more speculative archetype of the success *other* Americans might achieve, the *Autobiography* ultimately operates as a financial instrument—a national letter of credit endorsed by Franklin himself—that attests to the economic promise of America. As with the later public projects that depend upon the visibility, rather than the effacement, of Franklin's name, the efficacy of this national voucher derives from his personal authority. In this sense, the *Autobiography* is representative not as a generic tale of an ordinary American experience but rather as a story of *exemplary* success that uses Franklin's experience to advocate, like a celebrity endorsement, the possibilities of American life.

This representativeness, in fact, takes as its model a philosophy of public credit through which prominent individuals might help ensure the strength of governmental credibility. According to a notion that circulated during the colonial era and later during Alexander Hamilton's tenure as treasury secretary, governmental credit instruments, though technically vouchers for civic fiscal reliability, might be supported by individuals willing to sign instruments and thus lend their names for public credit (I speak of this *theory* of patronage because, in practice, such support was not necessarily successful in countering economic downturns). In the *Autobiography*, an elder Franklin uses his name to support paper financial instruments, and this model applies to his endorsement of all public projects. Having established himself as financial representative, moreover, Franklin encourages the reader to read his *Autobiography* with a speculative spirit. Through early tales of his own rise by means of credit, Franklin emphasizes how vital it is for creditors to support fledgling entrepreneurs; and so these stories illustrate, by implication, the importance of the reader's willingness to credit Franklin's representation of the American experience.

While Franklin does, in the earlier phases of his career, create and exploit an abstract, generalized persona for his own advancement, once he achieves civic prominence, the success of his endorsements ultimately depends upon the particularities of his experience. This is not to say that the later, more visible incarnation is any less a rhetorical persona but rather that it is different in that it trades on Franklin's name. It must, like a bill of credit, assume a measure of personal

authority in order to work effectively. Franklin's individual credibility, in other words, enhances the credibility of America.

Franklin drew a figural relation between his own biography and that of the nation; according to Christopher Looby, he rehearses in the story of his own life "both the past and the (predicated) future of America." Franklin wrote the four parts of the *Autobiography* over the two decades from 1771 to 1790, and the maturation and independence chronicled in the text parallels America's own coming of age. To this thinking I would add that there is, in particular, an analogy drawn between Franklin's own rise on credit as a budding entrepreneur in the first half of the text and the enterprising use of public credit for funding community development in the second half. With this shift, Franklin's role changes: in the first two installments of the memoir, he relies on the willingness of patrons to grant him credit; in the third and fourth parts, Franklin, having benefited from those who invested in him when he was young, lends his patronage to fledgling public projects.

Franklin signals the fact that the *Autobiography* itself is such a project in the opening of part 2, where he inserts personal letters from Abel James and Vaughan, written in 1782 and 1784, respectively. These letters reinforce Franklin's narrative transition from familial letter (an epistle to his son, William) to a document "intended for the public." In particular, the letters emphasize that his memoir itself is a public project that could benefit the new nation. Vaughan's letter, for example, predicts that Franklin's story will not only promote desirable qualities in young businessmen (industry, frugality, and the patience to await one's advancement) but also "tend to invite to [America] settlers of virtuous and manly minds." Vaughan adds, "And considering the eagerness with which such information is sought by them, and the extent of your reputation, I do not know of a more efficacious advertisement than your Biography would give." While Vaughan claims that the *Autobiography* is representative in the sense of being typical of—or "connected to"—the "rising people" of America, his very term "advertisement" suggests another process at work: the publicizing of an extraordinary story designed to arouse desire and patronage. Vaughan's letter identifies the memoir's potential to boost economic confidence and to promote America in the eyes of prospective immigrants; moreover, the letter serves as a fitting prelude to the more publicly oriented sections of the *Autobiography*, in which Franklin—as a protagonist within the narrative and as author of the autobiographical advertisement—works to promote civic ventures.

In part 3, these activities as civic spokesman begin to differ markedly from his earlier public service. In the first two sections, Franklin recalls that in his earlier years he tended to submit project proposals anonymously or under the auspices of a group so as not to arouse suspicions of his own interests: "The Objections, and Reluctances I met with in Soliciting the Subscriptions, made me soon feel the Impropriety of presenting oneself as the Proposer of any useful Project," he writes, explaining his decision to put himself "as much as [he] could out of sight." This strategic self-effacement exemplifies how Franklin, as the critical tradition maintains, uses depersonalized print media to construct a universal, archetypal life. Another well-known illustration of this self-effacement, which comes about a third of the way into part 3, is Franklin's anonymous proposals for an academy. He writes, "I stated their Publication not as an Act of mine, but of some *public-spirited Gentleman*, avoiding as much as I could, according to my usual Rule, the presenting myself to the Public as the Author of any Scheme for their Benefit."

Critics, however, have focused on the narration of events before Franklin's retirement from his printing business, and this conclusion is simply not applicable to the latter parts of the *Autobiography*. Shortly following his anonymous proposal for an academy, Franklin's "usual rule" changes. Five paragraphs later, Franklin recalls that once he "disengag'd" himself from "private Business," a sudden change occurred: "the Public now considering me as a Man of Leisure," he writes, "laid hold of me for their Purposes; every Part of our Civil Government, and almost at the same time, imposing some Duty upon me."

In the narration of events after his retirement from printing in 1748, Franklin's service entails the public endorsement of projects, and his visible connection to such projects supposedly ensures their success; indeed, after his retirement there is no mention of the self-effacement strategies that he describes earlier. As Dr. Thomas Bond discovers when he tries to establish a hospital in

Philadelphia, Franklin's name has become precious currency:

> At length he came to me, with the Compliment that he found there was no such thing as carrying a public-spirited Project through with out my being concern'd in it; "for, says he, I am often ask'd by those to whom I propose Subscribing, Have you consulted Franklin upon this Business? and what does he think of it? And when I tell them that I have not, (supposing it rather out of your Line,) they do not subscribe, but say they will consider of it."

Recognizing that this project will benefit from his signature, Franklin subscribes, enlists other subscriptions, petitions funds from the Pennsylvania Assembly, and even pens and publishes a signed article in its support. On account of this endorsement, according to Franklin, the plan is executed and the hospital soon erected.

While Franklin's retirement from private business may not, in fact, have marked such a clear-cut transition or satisfied those adversaries who accused him of harboring ulterior motives, the text nevertheless sets up the distinction, so crucial to classical republican ideology, between his life as a man of private interests and his life as a civic statesman. His retirement, which seemingly removes him from the business world, affords him the status of "disinterested" and enhances his reputation as civic-minded (his recollection that the public "laid hold" of him for "their purposes" after his retirement effaces his individual agency and emphasizes his status as civil servant). The social prominence he attains later in life transforms his name from a liability to an asset that can be exploited for public ends.

Franklin's text implicitly acknowledges that a candid equation of credit with appearance and perception inevitably unravels the reader's sense of certainty (these uncertainties of printed representation go hand-in-hand with the riskiness of a credit economy). I would argue, however, that it is precisely this economic ethos that works to resolve, rhetorically at least, the problems it raises. If Franklin's relish for credit schemes, inevitably raises doubts about the veracity of the *Autobiography*, it simultaneously encourages a faith in the speculative life that has been promised. In this narrative, doubts are self-fulfilling prophecies that lead to bank runs and financial collapse, and faith in his endorsement, as Franklin's own account demonstrates, keeps expectations in circulation and defers those redemptions that cannot materialize at that moment. As illustrated by Franklin's stories of war-time despair and the croaking Samuel Mickle, financial panic can sabotage potential profits. According to this financial paradigm, printed currency values and the kind of American success recalled in Franklin's memoirs are fictions for the present but may, with the reader's faith, be realized in the future.

The financial mechanisms at work in this text even make irrelevant, again at the rhetorical level, the common criticism that the *Autobiography* is thinly veiled self-promotion. Drawing from his own experience as financier, Franklin depicts a public credibility that is bolstered by his own credibility: the more reputable his own name and success story, the more viable is the American life for which he is a spokesman. By invoking a credit system that intertwines personal and civic interests, he makes self-promotion and national promotion mutually beneficial, enacting, in essence, a Franklinian pragmatism by which one could do good and do well at the same time.

Source: Jennifer Jordan Baker, "Benjamin Franklin's *Autobiography* and the Credibility of Personality," in *Early American Literature*, Vol. 35, No. 3, Fall 2000, pp. 274–93.

SOURCES

Franklin, Benjamin, *The Autobiography of Benjamin Franklin*, Wilco Publishing House, 2005.

———, *The Autobiography of Benjamin Franklin*, 2d. ed., Yale University Press, 2003.

Lawrence, D. H., *Studies in Classic American Literature*, T. Seltzer, 1923; reprint, Penguin Classics; Reissue edition, 1990.

Morgan, Edmund S., "Foreword," in *The Autobiography of Benjamin Franklin*, 2d. ed., Yale University Press, 2003, pp. 1–7.

Weber, Max, *The Protestant Ethic and the Spirit of Capitalism: and Other Writings*, Penguin Twentieth-Century Classics, 2002.

Wilson, Woodrow, "Introduction," in *The Autobiography of Benjamin Franklin*, Century Classics, 1901, p. x; quoted in "Foreword," in *The Autobiography of Benjamin Franklin*, 2d. ed., Yale University Press, 2003, p. 18,

The Big Money

JOHN DOS PASSOS
1936

John Dos Passos's *The Big Money* (1936) argues that the pursuit of the American dream ends in corruption. No matter what good intentions the characters possess, the desire for big money tarnishes, and eventually destroys, their authenticity. Dos Passos illustrates this idea by detailing the personal journey of each character and providing a sketch of an actual public figure whose life parallels, frames, or comments on the fictional characters' lives. For example, Dos Passos tells the story of Charley Anderson, an upstanding young mechanic who earned the Croix de Guerre during the War. Though Anderson starts out a simple mechanic, his longing for the American dream pushes him to a bigger and better career in aviation. Success, greed, and lust quickly lead to Charley's downfall. Dos Passos uses biographical pieces about famed inventors Henry Ford, Frederick Winslow Taylor, and Thorstein Veblen to put Charley's unhappy tale in context. *The Big Money* also showcases Dos Passos's subjective, stream-of-consciousness invention, the Camera Eye. Expressing an autobiographical viewpoint of sorts, the Camera Eye offers a fluid, first-person look at the world.

John Dos Passos is an author from the "Lost Generation," a term Gertrude Stein used to describe American bohemian-modernist writers of the 1920s and 1930s who lived in Europe during World War I and the Depression years. His novel *The Big Money* (1936) marks the end

BIOGRAPHY

JOHN DOS PASSOS

John Dos Passos was born in Chicago on January 14, 1896 and educated around the world. After graduating from Harvard University in 1916, Dos Passos went to study art and architecture in Spain. This worldly schooling inspired Dos Passos's interest in international social and political activity and led to his voluntary participation as an ambulance driver in France and Italy during World War I. Despite his active role in the Norton-Harjes Ambulance Corps, Dos Passos found time to finish his first novel in 1918, the year he joined the U.S. military. Dos Passos continued to write throughout his military career, and his works, in both theme and character, stand as a testament to his experiences in the war. During World War II, Dos Passos broadened his writing career by working as a journalist.

John Dos Passos wrote *The Big Money*, the first novel in his "U.S.A. Trilogy," in 1936. In 1947, his wife of eighteen years died in an automobile accident that left him partially blind. In his later career, Dos Passos leaned toward Communism and became conservative in his political views; some critics claim his work lost impact stylistically after his turn of opinion. In addition to more than forty novels, Dos Passos also wrote travel books, poetry, plays, and political essays. He died on September 28, 1970, in Baltimore.

of that Lost Generation, a time of disillusionment, cynicism, and youthful idealism. Dos Passos, along with his fellow writers, witnessed the horrors of war and contemplated the true meaning of life and humanity, particularly in terms of American materialism and excess. Ironically, due to Dos Passos's changing political views, he became relatively unknown compared to Stein, Ernest Hemingway, Ezra Pound, and other members of the Lost Generation.

The Big Money is the third and final book in a series called the "U.S.A. Trilogy." Alfred Kazin in "Dos Passos, Society, and the Individual" calls *The Big Money* "the most ambitious" of the series. Stylistically speaking, *The Big Money* resembles the other two novels in the trilogy—*42nd Parallel* and *1919*—by telling the stories of Mary French, Margo Dowling, Richard Ellsworth Savage, among others, through a stream-of-consciousness technique and a montage of biographical, journalistic, and fictional pieces. This fragmented style reflects the Lost Generation's uncertainty and search for self in a world where the future was no longer guaranteed. The "U.S.A. Trilogy," published after six years of writing, describes the eternal, and often unsuccessful, quest for the American dream.

PLOT SUMMARY

The structure of *The Big Money* is not divided into traditional numbered or thematically named chapters. In the table of contents, each chapter in the novel is identified by the character whose point of view directs the chapter and comprises a "Newsreel," a "The Camera Eye," and/or a narrative section. The newsreel and camera eye sections emphasize the novel's most important thematic ideas.

Chapter 1: Charley Anderson

Lieutenant Charley Anderson, war ace, returns to America on a ship from France. He looks forward to being home.

In "Newsreel XLIV," the repetition of the lyric *"Yankee doodle"* juxtaposed against capitalized headlines such as "DEADLOCK UNBROKEN AS FIGHT SPREADS" as well as against a journalistic piece about "democratic rights" being trampled shows the crumbling of America from within.

Chapter 2: Charley Anderson

Charley finds a room at a hotel, then gets a drink with his friend Ollie Taylor. At a dinner party, Charley enjoys the company of pretty young Doris Humphries.

In "Newsreel XLV," lyrics also illustrate the power women have over men as a *"St. Louis woman wid her diamon' rings / Pulls dat man aroun' by her apron strings."* This section reveals how women influence men's buying behaviors in their pursuit of *"social prestige."* With this

John Dos Passos Ray Fisher/Time Life Pictures/Getty Images

commentary, headlines reveal violence: a "DAY-LIGHT HOLDUP," a "MAN SLAIN," a "DESPERATE REVOLVER BATTLE."

The "American Plan" begins with the image of Frederick Winslow Taylor, a pioneering efficiency expert. While attending Harvard, "he broke down from overwork [so] the doctor suggested manual labor." Taylor became a machinist and gradually worked his way through the ranks to become chief engineer of Pennsylvania's Midvale Iron Works Plant. Obsessed with production, he developed the "Taylor System of Scientific Management," and although he "increased efficiency" for Bethlehem Steel, he was fired. Eventually, Taylor had a breakdown and died of pneumonia "with a watch in his hand" in 1915 on his fifty-ninth birthday.

"Newsreel XLVI" focuses on men returning from World War I with headlines like "EX-SERVICE MEN DEMAND JOBS." The lyrics, "*No one knows | No one cares if I'm weary | Oh how one knows | No one cares if I'm weary | Oh how*

soon they forgot Château-Thierry," express the emotions of ex-soldiers. Irony comes with the headline "PROSPERITY FOR ALL SEEN ASSURED," as returning servicemen struggle to find their place in this world and "assured" success.

The narrator of "The Camera Eye (43)" is unknown, yet the "eye" offers a string of memories that affect the narrator physically and emotionally; for example his "throat tightens when the redstacked steamer churning the faintlyheaving slatecolored swell" and his "spine stiffens with the remembered chill of the offshore Atlantic." By connecting images of food, the hustle-bustle of the daily commute, and eventually of "shantytowns," the narrator provides a stark contrast between the quintessential image of American "home" and white-collar success to negative, even realistic, images of American life. Finally, life ends "in the old graveyard by the brokendown brick church" and by pulling in one final image of a soldier returning home from

France after many "hated years in the latrines-tench at Brocourt."

"Newsreel XLVII" focuses on prospects society in a series of advertisements: "boy seeking future offered opportunity . . . good positions for bright . . . CHANCE FOR ADVANCEMENT . . . boy to learn . . . errand boy." The lyrics in this section represent the boy's response to these employment calls: "*Oh tell me how long | I'll have to wait | . . . | Do I get it now | Or must I hesitate | . . . | Oh tell me how long.*"

"The Camera Eye (44)" views an "unnamed arrival" from the Foreign Legion returning to Manhattan. In New York, he is in a completely different world and is "stuffed into a boiled shirt a tailcoat too small a pair of dresstrousers too large," as if it is a "forsomebodyelsetailored suit." This young man is offered an "opportunity," because of his supposed skill with a "foreign language," but cannot take it because he is not the man the men offering the job believe him to be—a case of "mistaken identity."

Chapter 3: Charley Anderson

Charley meets his brother Jim, old man Vogel, and his Aunt Hartmann. Jim owns a Ford automobile agency. Charley and Jim visit their dying mother in the hospital. She considers Charley her "prodigal son," because he "made quite a name for himself over there" in the war zone. Jim wants Charley to use his "returnedhero" status, as well as his "connections in the Legion and aviation," to boost business for his automobile shop. But Charley already has "an aviation proposition" with his former commanding officer. Charley's mother dies, and feeling lonely, he visits a girl he once knew, Emiscah. They make love after she becomes upset about her tedious job. Emiscah writes a note telling him she "never loved anybody but him." Not wanting to marry, Charley rejects her.

The family reads the mother's will. While Charley wants to invest in "airplane motors," Jim wants him to invest in a "sure thing": the Ford. Charley decides to sign over his money to Jim, on the condition that Jim lends him four hundred dollars immediately for Charley to invest. Emiscah threatens to kill herself unless he visits her. He plans to lie but, seeing her so "thin and pale," makes another date with her. He leaves town, though he feels a bit guilty.

In "Newsreel XLVIII," industry is taking over America, as shown by the first line, "truly the Steel Corporation stands forth as a corporate colossus both physically and financially." The era's dance halls are portrayed in the lyrics, "*Now the folks in Georgia they done gone wild | Over that brand new dancin' style | Called Shake That Thing.*" There is also tragedy, reflected in the headlines "Woman of Mystery Tries Suicide in Park Lake" and "BOMB WAGON TRACED TO JERSEY," while the headline "LETTER SAID GET OUT OF WALL STREET" foreshadows tragedy to come.

The section "Tin Lizzie" focuses on Henry Ford. Raised on a farm, he believes "big money" can be found with "quick turnover, cheap interchangeable easilyreplaced standardized parts." When machinists are not happy with the way Ford runs production, he gives workers a small "cut in the profits." Eventually the workers turn on Ford and the "strings" he attaches to salaries and profit-making: "cops broke heads, jobhunters threw bricks," and chaos destroyed Ford's property. Later, to raise money to buy out his minority stockholders, Ford makes buyers pay cash on the dollar for cars, rather than using credit. In 1922, Ford becomes "the richest man in the world." However, Ford lowers wages and alienates workers by forcibly preventing them from unionizing. Ironically, in a world changing because of industry, Ford lives out his old age in old-fashioned traditions and "the way it used to be, / in the days of horses and buggies."

"Newsreel XLIX" begins with the lyrics, "*Jack o' Diamonds Jack o' Diamonds | You rob my pocket of silver and gold.*" The newsreel shows the dark product that American industry churned out:

> the men who . . . were fighting their battle for democracy upon the bloodstained fields of France [with] their instruments of murder, their automatic rifles, their machineguns, their cannon that could clear a street two miles long in a few minutes and the helmets that the workers of Gary had produced.

The newsreel also mentions the new business of "purchasing evidence of indebtedness."

Chapter 4: Charley Anderson

Charley returns to New York. He runs out of money and needs to find something to "tide [him] over" until his big plans come to fruition. He dates Doris Humphries and asks her to "hold off on the other guys for a little while" until he becomes financially secure. She declines. Charley joins a poker game at the repair shop where he works and saves some of his winnings. He also dates Eveline Hutchins Johnson, Al's sister-in-law, and at the same time, receives a letter from Emiscah, who asks for money. Not wanting to commit to any of these women, Charley uses his poker winnings to "arrange meetings with agreeable young women."

Charley's fortunes finally improve when he gets a position as a supervising engineer at the Askew-Merritt Company "earning two hundred and fifty a week." Charley has doubts about the men behind the deal.

"Newsreel L" assures that "with few exceptions the management of our government has been and is in honest and competent hands, that the finances are sound and well managed." The headline, "GRAND JURY WILL QUIZ BALLPLAYERS," refers to the 1919 World Series scandal, in which eight Chicago White Sox baseball players deliberately lost the World Series. Other headlines depict industrial progress: "NEWLY DESIGNED GEARS AFFORDING NOT / ONLY GREATER STRENGTH AND LONGER / LIFE BUT INCREASED SMOOTHNESS." As technology becomes more streamlined, people's lives are adversely affected.

"The Bitter Drink" offers a biography of Thorstein Veblen, economist and sociologist. He became famous after writing *The Theory of the Leisure Class* (1899), a satire about American society. He was a "brilliant unsound eccentric" who "suffered from woman trouble." He published several books, including *The Theory of Business Enterprise, The Instinct of Workmanship,* and *The Vested Interests and The Common Man,* which marked a society "dominated by monopoly capital" and demonstrated the "sabotage of life by blind need for money profits." After advocating for the working class and efficiency in production, he died bitter and wanted his life and work to be forgotten.

"Newsreel LI" offers a glimpse of the role of women in society. The contrast between "GIRLS GIRLS GIRLS," and those women offered respectable positions, such as "caretakers . . . cashiers . . . chambermaids . . . waitresses . . . cleaners . . . file clerks" is sharp. However, these jobs for "intelligent young women" do not reflect the "good chance for advancement" and the promise of "good salaries, commissions, bonuses, prizes, and business opportunities" the newsreel claims.

Chapter 5: Mary French

Mary French was raised in a typical American house. After her father loses money in an investment and her brother dies, Mary's family moves to Trinidad where her father becomes a doctor at the mines. When her mother inherits money after Mary's grandfather's death, the family moves to Colorado Springs where Mary feels alienated because the high school girls only "talk about parties and the Country Club and sets of tennis."

Mary attends Vassar and is friends with "lush and Jewish and noisy" Ada Cohn. During Mary's time at Vassar, her parents divorce. Mary and Ada take summer jobs in Chicago "doing settlementwork," but Ada has a "nervous breakdown" over the "way poor people lived." Mary spends the new semester at Vassar attending "lectures about current events and social conditions." Mary returns home when her mother falls ill. She fills in for her father's administrative assistant and finds the job exhausting. In her spare time, she reads *The Theory of the Leisure Class.* One morning, she discovers her father dead. She intends to return to Vassar, but she ultimately decides to stay in Chicago.

Chapter 6: Mary French

Mary attends a lecture by George Barrow and begins dating him. Over the summer, she takes a miserable job as a "countergirl." She quits and eventually gets a job at the *Times-Sentinel* reporting "both sides" of a story involving agitators of a mill strike. Mary conducts interviews, guided by Gus Moscowski, an officeboy for Amalgamated, who shows her "how folks live on fortytwo cents an hour." The squalor upsets Mary. She is fired because she reveals both sides, as assigned. She works with Gus doing publicity for the Amalgamated, or the unionizers. She falls for Gus, but he is arrested "distributing leaflets." When George Barrow returns to town with the Senatorial Investigating Commission, he asks her to be his secretary. She agrees, hoping to defend the striking workers from "inside" Washington.

In Washington, Mary and George develop a relationship. George insists "the workingman is often his own worst enemy." Mary tells George they "are as responsible as anybody for selling out the steelworkers" and she no longer wants to be a "laborfaker," earning her "living off the workingclass." Mary soon realizes she is pregnant, and, fearful George will pressure her to marry him, she thinks about suicide. She heads to New York and begs Ada to help her get an abortion. Eventually she tells George about her predicament in a "specialdelivery letter" and he gives her the address of a doctor. Mary gets the abortion and, not long afterward, seeks new employment.

"The Camera Eye (46)" shows the life of the "walking desperate." It also tells the story of those trying to help those "underdog" unionizers "urging action in the crowded hall." This section also shows the guilt industry leaders feel about laying a false foundation for the American dream: "why not tell these men stamping in the wind that we stand on a quicksand?"

"Newsreel LII" looks at the day's seamy goings on. The "BODY TIED IN BAG" is anonymous, like the "Two Women's Bodies in Slayer's Baggage" and the "Girl Out of Work" who "Dies From Poison."

"Art and Isadora" offers a biographical snapshot of dancer Isadora Duncan. As a young woman, Isadora danced at clubs and onstage in New York where her family ran up bills and neglected rent. They traveled the world, "staying at the best hotels...in a flutter of unpaid bills." She "was the vogue" and was "considered dangerous by the authorities." She returned to America "in triumph" but "found no freedom for Art" there. "At the height of her glory," Isadora's children and their nurse drowned in a freak car accident. Isadora drank heavily, dated many men, tried to commit suicide, and lost her money, but kept dancing. She died when her scarf caught in the wheel of a car and broke her neck.

"Newsreel LIII" asks the question, "ARE YOU NEW YORK'S MOST BEAUTIFUL GIRL STENOGRAPHER?"

Chapter 7: Margo Dowling

"Margie" meets Fred, her drunken father, every night at the train station on his way home. She dreams about escaping her life but has happy memories of summers spent with her father and stepmother Agnes. When Fred gets arrested, Agnes and Margie leave for Brooklyn where Agnes's parents live. Margie does not like Brooklyn, and when Agnes gets a job as a cook, she sends Margie to live at a convent. The convent is dark and oppressive and Margie is thrilled to move to a brownstone with Agnes

and her husband, Mr. Frank Mandeville, an actor with a musical act.

Billed as Little Margo, Margie joins the Musical Mandevilles act. Margie develops a crush on Frank Mandeville and one afternoon, when Frank comes home drunk, depressed over signing a contract to perform on "the filthy stage of a burlesque house," he rapes her, then threatens to kill her if she tells. Margie gravitates toward Tony Garrido, a guitar player from Cuba, and wants to run off and marry him. Tony does not want to get married, but they take the plunge and move to Havana.

"Newsreel LIV" offers a wide view of society, starting with the "morning's trading" and ending with Rudolph Valentino "collaps[ing] . . . in his apartment at the Hotel Ambassador." The section shows celebrities and working-class folk alike falling into despair, as a "RUSSIAN BARONESS [COMMITS] SUICIDE IN MIAMI," "3000 AMERICANS ARE FOUND PENNILESS IN PARIS," and a "*poor girl*" laments her sad fortune in song, despite President Coolidge ironically advocating prosperity "Under His Policies."

"Adagio Dancer" tells the story of actor Rudolph Valentino. After arriving from Italy, he took odd jobs in New York but longed for a life in the "brightlights." The handsome young man eventually ended up on a vaudeville tour where he adopted his new name. Soon, in Hollywood, he got his big break in the film *The Four Horsemen*. Valentino lived the life of luxury and was the object of worship and scandal. He died at the age of thirty-one from complications from a gastric ulcer. His funeral was a chaotic mob scene.

"Newsreel LV" opens with the image of "THRONGS IN STREETS" and the repetitive lyrics, "*Close the doors | They are coming | Through the windows.*" In addition, the "'Physician' Who Took Prominent Part in Valentino Funeral" is "Exposed as Former Convict."

"The Camera Eye (47)" describes the texture of the port as the "sirens boom in the fog over the harbor." The harbor offers opportunity, inviting people to "join up sign on the dotted line enlist" and to "rebuild yesterday." The Camera Eye also sees life on the street: the "old men chewing in lunchrooms," the "drunk bums," and the "two shadows [kissing] under the stoop of the brownstone." These all take on the role of "unidentified stranger," of faceless people trying to eek out an existence.

Chapter 8: Charley Anderson

Charley meets with broker Nat Benton. Charley has been busy in manufacturing and lives with Joe Askew's family. Charley goes to a dinner party at Doris Humphries's apartment. Drunk on champagne, he talks to Doris about marriage, but she rejects him. He finds solace in a prostitute and forces her to pretend she is Doris. Charley, Andy Merritt, and Joe Askew fly "one of the sample planes" to Washington, D.C., "to show off some of [Charley's] patents to the experts at the War Department." Merritt thinks they will need "a separate corporation" to market their new airplane starter. Merritt remains in New York to "negotiate contracts with the government experts," but if those do not succeed, they have "big offers from Detroit" lined up. Charley celebrates their near-success, but he works hard as production ramps up. He acquires "all the Askew-Merritt stock he [can] get his hands on" and discovers the world of credit and debt.

James Yardley Farrell of the Tern Company asks Charley to work for him in Detroit, suggesting that "in a new industry like [theirs] the setup changes fast." Doris evades Charley when he wants desperately to marry her. She writes a letter saying she is marrying someone else. Charley carouses to forget and exchanges his Askew-Merritt stock for Tern stock, bound for Detroit.

"Newsreel LVI" and "The Camera Eye (48)" focus on people traveling, either to check on their fortunes or to seek their fortunes elsewhere after life does not work out as they planned. The lyrics, "*Feel that boat arockin'*" and "*What's that whistle sayin' / All aboard*," are followed by an image of a "LINER AFIRE," then by the refrain of someone "*goin' where there's more.*" The Camera Eye's frequent repetition of the word "westbound" underscores the determination and desperation of the speaker to arrive at his final destination. Lyrics also urge escape: "*get away old man get away.*"

Chapter 9: Margo Dowling

Margo and Tony arrive in Havana. Margo is dismayed by the "fine residential section," which is "full of dust and oily smells and wagons and mulecarts." Tony forgets to translate for Margo, who becomes frustrated. Tony and Margo fight about her unhappiness; when she punches Tony in the eye, the neighborhood teases him. Pregnant,

Margo thinks about killing herself but decides against it. The old women deliver her baby, which is blind and soon dies. Margo writes "desperate letters to Agnes," asking for money and wanting to return home. She visits the consul, and a young man named George offers to help. They have a romantic tryst, and George promises to "write her every day."

Agnes is now the manager of one of Miss Franklyn's tea rooms and takes Margo to a new apartment. Frank makes a pass at Margo, who slaps him soundly and threatens to tell Agnes what happened between them in the past.

"Newsreel LVII" shows how ordinary women were overcome by life's problems while royal women could let the world pass outside their train window, with headlines like "UNHAPPY WIFE TRIES TO DIE," "Society Women Seek Jobs in Vain," and "QUEEN SLEEPS AS HER TRAIN DEPARTS."

Chapter 10: Margo Dowling

Margo goes to work as a chorus girl for Flo Ziegfield and dates Tad Whittlesea, Yale halfback and millionaire's son. Margo considers Tad too much of a spendthrift; he does not seem good enough for her future plans. She dates married casting director Jerry Herman and rejects Tad when he calls. Margo juggles Jerry and Tad. Soon, Jerry grows frustrated with Margo's behavior and breaks up with her. Tad invites her to go on a cruise from Jacksonville to the West Indies. Margo asks Queenie Riggs, a friend from the company, to accompany her, while Tad brings Dick Rogers to complete the foursome. Margo refuses to have sex with Tad on the train to Jacksonville, telling him "Heaven won't protect a workinggirl unless she protects herself." Tad proposes when they arrive at the port in Jacksonville. She does not agree absolutely, but he buys her a ring.

When the boat has engine trouble, they return to Jacksonville where Margo sees Tony at a bar. She finds him unattractive and effeminate. Tony refers to her as "his dear wife," and Tad invites him on their cruise. In the morning, Margo gets a letter with some money from Tad, canceling their trip. Margo takes care of Tony when he becomes ill from too much drinking. He steals her money and jewelry and leaves her with his hotel bill. She contemplates hocking her engagement ring for a bus ticket home.

"Newsreel LVIII" asserts that paradise has been overtaken by industry and progress. The Bay of Biscayne bank stands where "a farmer's hitching-yard" used to be and the Hotel Royal Palm rises from "vegetable patches." The lyrics, "*Lazy River flowing to the southland / Down where I long to be,*" echo this nostalgic look at the past. Also, the contrast between women's expected and unexpected roles in society is shown through the headlines, "WOMAN DIRECTS HIGHWAY ROBBERY" and "GIRL EVANGELS AWAIT CHRIST IN NEW YORK."

"The Campers at Kitty Hawk" recalls the first flight conducted by Orville and Wilbur Wright "and notes that "in two years they had a plane that would cover twenty-four miles at a stretch." But "the Wright brothers passed out of the headlines" in the blur of new inventors, war, and the stock market.

Detroit, that "marvelous industrial beehive," is the focus of "Newsreel LIX." The headlines, "DETROIT LEADS THE WORLD IN THE MANUFAC-TURE OF AUTOMOBILES," "DETROIT THE DYNA-MIC RANKS HIGH," and "DETROIT THE CITY WHERE LIFE IS WORTH LIVING," show a city where progress never sleeps and the American dream is within reach. Song lyrics belie the headlines: "*I've a longing for my Omaha town / I long to go there and settle down.*"

Chapter 11: Charley Anderson

Charley arrives in Detroit for his new job. At a Country Club dance, he meets Anne Bledsoe, his boss's daughter, who enjoys flying. Over the summer, they spend much of their time together. Charley is a success; "As vicepresident and consulting engineer of the Tern Company he was making $25,000 a year." He and Bill Cermak attempt to develop a new motor.

One afternoon on the Farrells' yacht, he proposes to Anne. She cannot commit to an answer. Charley kisses Gladys Wheatley, who is dating Anne's brother. A week after the boat ride, Gladys introduces Charley to her parents. Mr. Wheatley assumes they will marry. Not long after Thanksgiving, Charley and Gladys's engagement, announced at a dinner party thrown by the Wheatleys, hits the papers. They have a son and a daughter right away, and Gladys focuses her energies on the babies, rather than on Charley. Charley kisses his secretary Elsie Finnegan.

Charley and Bill Cermak test out a new motor and have an accident. Bill dies of a skull fracture, while Charley is left with fractured ribs and breathing problems. Bill's widow sues the company for $500,000. Charley invites Nat Benton to go on a fishing trip in the Florida Keys. On his way to meet Nat, he picks up a girl at a sodashop and offers her a ride to Miami; the girl is Margo Dowling. While Charley and Nat are on vacation, the Tern stock plummets. Charley loses big and sells all his airplane stock. To forget his troubles, he has sex with a girl he met once when he was out with Nat. During his interlude, a lawyer bursts in and announces that Gladys is suing him for divorce.

"Newsreel LX" reflects difficulties of marriage: "To young Scotty marriage seemed just a lark, a wild time in good standing. But when she began to demand money and the extravagant things he couldn't afford did Céline meet him halfway?" The tone becomes optimistic with the clip, "speculative sentiment was encouraged at the opening of the week by the clearer outlook," and the lyrics, "*Good-bye east and good-bye west / Good-bye north and all the rest / Hello Swan-ee Hello.*"

Chapter 12: Margo Dowling

Margo returns to New York City. She dates Charley, who "kept offering to set [her] up in an apartment on Park Avenue." She allows him to play some of her money on the stockmarket. Jules Piquot, a "middleaged roundfaced Frenchman" shows interest in Margo. She models for him, but he is "going broke." He has a change of fortune when Vogue decides to photograph his collection. The photographer offers to take pictures of Margo at his studio, which are semi-nudes. Piquot dies owing Margo "back wages"; Margo asks Charley for money. Tony shows up at Margo's after being beaten up by a gang. She asks Charley for more money, but he reveals that he is "hard up for cash, that his wife had everything tied up on him, that he'd had severe losses on the market." She commits Tony to a sanatorium and goes back to her job as an entertainer in Miami.

"Newsreel LXI" suggests that anyone with money can buy paradise, as the "TOWN SITE OF JUPITER SOLD FOR TEN MILLION DOLLARS," and "*like Aladdin with his magic lamp, the Capitalist, the Investor and the Builder converted what was once a desolate swamp into a wonderful city.*"

Florida equates with success, as shown in the "ACRES OF GOLD NEAR TAMPA," specifically "the *spot where your future joy, contentment and happiness is so sure that to deviate is to pass up the outstanding opportunity of your lifetime.*" This dream is in dire contrast to the tragedy as a "GIANT AIRSHIP BREAKS IN TWO IN MID-FLIGHT" and a husband following his "WIFE IN LEAP FROM WINDOW."

Chapter 13: Charley Anderson

Over the years, Charley has grown weary, cynical, and out of shape, despite his nickname as the "boy wizard of aviation financing." He is still carousing. Soon, however, he is out of a job when a deal with Merritt and Farrell falls apart and a patent suit develops. Charley heads for Florida. On the way he meets Margo, who joins him for the rest of his trip south. When they arrive in Florida, Margo suggests they go "on the wagon" and stop drinking so much. The senator sends him a veiled warning via a telegram: Sell stocks because a bill would soon be passed "to subsidize airlines." While the stocks were substantially lower, Charley begins to buy them back in hopes of making a profit. He goes fishing with the senator's friend Judge Homer Cassidy, who, like Charley, also wants to "make a pile" of money.

After a night of drinking, Charley takes a girl named Eileen for a wild ride; he races a train and tries to "beat [it] to the crossin'." Charley and Eileen end up in the hospital after the car stalls on the tracks. Margo visits him and asks for money. She also tells him Eileen's family plans to sue him. His brother Jim flies down to Florida and asks if he has a will. Jim also suggests Charley give him power of attorney.

"Newsreel LXII" debunks the myth of living happily ever after in paradise, as "celery growers [use] a spray containing deadly poison," "banks are having trouble in Florida," a "HURRICANE SWEEPS SOUTH FLORIDA," and "MARTIAL LAW LOOMS."

Chapter 14: Margo Dowling

Agnes comes to Florida after Charley's death, where Margo lives in a house Charley rented for her. Charley's brother is "threatening to sue to get back some securities." Judge Cassidy tells Margo that Charley "left his affairs in considerable confusion." Cliff Wegman arrives and asks Margo to marry him. She declines, not wanting anything to sidetrack her career. Margo has success investing in Miami real estate, but her assets

are not liquid. Tony wants Margo to send him back to Havana. Instead Margo, Agnes, and Tony drive to Hollywood, so Margo can be a movie star.

"Newsreel LXIII" follows the exploits, triumphs, and dangers of celebrity pilot Charles Lindbergh.

The section "Architect" profiles Frank Lloyd Wright. As a young man, he arrived in Chicago with ambition and little money. He landed a job at an architect's office. "The son and grandson of preachers, he became a preacher in blueprints" and sought to rebuild America with a "new clean construction." His life was stormy, as he "raised children, had rows with wives, overstepped boundaries, got into difficulties with the law, divorce-courts, bankruptcy" and projects not completed.

"Newsreel LXIV" offers international snapshots, from "WEIRD FISH DRAWN FROM SARGASSO SEA" and "RUM RING LINKS NATIONS" to "GRAVE FOREBODING UNSETTLES MOSCOW" and "600 PUT TO DEATH AT ONCE IN CANTON."

"Newsreel LXV" reports the stock market crash, along with the lyrics, "*Bring me a pillow for my poor head / A hammer to knock out my brains / For the whiskey has ruined this body of mine / And the red lights have run me insane.*" The newsreel ends with Smythe, who dies in agony after becoming infected from constant exposure to fumes at his job with an oil company.

Chapter 15: Mary French

Mary French lives in Ada's New York apartment rent-free when Ada leaves town for Michigan. Mary works as a researcher for the International Ladies' Garment Workers and Ben Compton, one of the "classwar prisoners released from Atlanta," stays with her. He is shaken by his experiences. After a week, they decide "that they [love] each other." Needing money, Mary asks her mother, now a Republican State Committeewoman, for $500. Ben uses the funds to pay for printing costs to support a strike. Eventually, Mary finds her own apartment and struggles to provide for them. Ben travels frequently to support labor rights. Mary battles for the strike committee; interviewing the strikers and their families, "she only [sleeps] four or five hours a night" and [takes] to smoking a great deal." Her relationship with Ben begins to suffer. Mary moves to Boston, taking a position "on the Sacco-Vanzetti case." She writes articles, makes speeches, and feeds information to newspapermen for other stories. She takes more active roles in protests and has run-ins with the police.

"Newsreel LXVI" and "The Camera Eye (50)" return to the Sacco-Vanzetti case of 1927, about two who were convicted and sentenced to death for the murder of a "paymaster." The lyrics of a labor movement anthem are scattered throughout the newsreel: *For justice thunders condemnation / . . . / Arise rejected of the earth / . . . / It is final conflict / Let each stand in his place / . . . / The International Party / . . . / Shall be the human race.* The Camera Eye begins with an image common to participants of the labor movement: "they have clubbed us off the streets they are stronger they are rich they hire and fire the politicians the newspaper editors the old judges." The Camera Eye ends with the line "we stand defeated America."

"Poor Little Rich Boy" profiles millionaire William Randolph Hearst. Hearst made his fortune in newspapers, married a dancer, and became the governor of New York. But by 1914, "his affairs were in such a scramble he had trouble borrowing a million dollars and politically he was ratpoison," because he sympathized with the Germans and "opposed the peace of Versailles." Hearst retreats to his "castle" in California and dies an eccentric.

Chapter 16: Richard Ellsworth Savage

Dick finds himself strapped for cash; his personal and professional life is "lonely and hellish." He socializes and works with people either who are struggling to achieve their own American dreams or who have struggled and are now successful, like E. R. Bingham. At forty, Bingham was "in the midst of a severe economic struggle" and "was a physical wreck," but ultimately ended up creating what he calls "a healthy American home." Dick drinks to numb his emotions and has sex with two transvestite prostitutes who take his money. He is a hypocrite when he suggests to a colleague that they fire a young man because he "drinks too much" and does not do "serious work."

"Newsreel LXVIII" and "The Camera Eye (51)" present a mosaic of social, political, and international commentaries. Wall Street is "Stunned" but is "SURE TO RECOVER FROM SLUMP." People still long to invest their hard earnings in the American dream but are wary of the market, as shown by a clip from an advice column: "I have

> A WAR-LIKE SOCIETY STRANGLED BY THE BUREAUCRACIES OF THE MONOPOLIES FORCED BY THE LAW OF DIMINISHING RETURNS TO GRIND DOWN MORE AND MORE THE COMMON MAN FOR PROFITS."

saved four thousand dollars which I want to invest for a better income. Do you think I might buy stocks?" The anger and violence of the labor unions continue, as captured in the headlines, "MILL THUGS IN MURDER RAID" and "RADICALS FIGHT WITH CHAIRS AT UNITY MEETING." At the same time, hope remains, as "REAL VALUES [ARE] UNHARMED" and the "PRESIDENT SEES PROSPERITY NEAR." But the Camera Eye shows the hopelessness of American poverty, as "a man halfsits halfflies propped up by an old woman two wrinkled girls that might be young chunks of coal flare in the hearth . . . . without help in the valley hemmed by dark strike-silent hills the man will die."

"Power Superpower" presents a biography of Samuel Insull, who worked for Thomas Edison as an assistant. Not long after getting the company established in electricity, he moved on to gas; "When politicians got in his way, he bought them, when laborleaders got in his way he bought them." Soon, he controlled the light and power companies, "coalmines and tractioncompanies" across the United States, effectively manipulating "a twelfth of the power output of America." But the stock market crash brought him "on his knees to the bankers" and he was "forced to resign" from his companies. Insull and his wife escaped to Canada, then to Europe. Eventually he was forced from Greece and brought back to the United States where he was put on trial. Insull recounted his rags-to-riches story and cried for jury sympathy, earning his "not guilty" verdict.

Chapter 17: Mary French

Mary fills her life supporting the workers' rights, even at the expense of her personal relationships.

"Vag" ends the novel with the image of a hitchhiking vagabond used to hunger, poor health, and jail time. Making his way across the United States, he is abused by the police. He once "went to school," hoping for "opportunity" and a life "bigger than [his] neighbor."

THEMES

The Dark Side of the American Dream

The Big Money deals with the bright illusion of the American dream: In this land of opportunities, everyone can have the lives they want. Jobs are plentiful, home is more than a roof and four walls, and every American can own a Tin Lizzie. World War I has made people weary, wounded, and looking for a better future. Emerging victorious from battles overseas, "America the Beautiful" beckons. But the pursuit of big money does not lead to contentment, companionship, or consciousness. The characters in the novel become numb as one opportunity after another brings them further from personal satisfaction. Mary French, a doctor's daughter from Colorado, goes from one job to the next and ends up an inconsequential worker bee for the labor revolution. Margo Dowling begins as a child actress, marries a man with a drinking problem, and ultimately becomes a mistress and a showgirl. Charley Anderson leaves the war a hero and dies a pathetic businessman after getting hit by a train. Richard Ellsworth Savage is a junior public relations executive looking to make the big money. For them, the American dream is not a possibility but a given. All work hard, sacrificing intimacy and love for success; they only have one goal: money. Unfortunately, money slips through their fingers as quickly as they can make it.

Along the road to achieving their dreams, the characters become sidetracked by lust, greed, and other vices. Dos Passos shows the gradual decay of the American dream as ambition and selfishness lead to bad decisions, tunnel vision, and a loss of direction. Alcohol and sex are used to erase feelings of emptiness and loneliness. The American dream deteriorates, as the quest for a happy ending makes a tragic turn. Like Dos Passos's repeated images of Florida, the American dream glitters like paradise, but is emotional chaos built on water and sand.

Fragments of the American Dream

John Dos Passos's unique storytelling style successfully serves the subject matter of *The Big*

Rudolph Valentino in The Son of the Sheik
© *Bettmann/Corbis*

Money. The years during and after World War I marked a time of social, political, and economic upheaval. Some people struggled to make ends meet on the streets, while others drank champagne as they grew further in debt. The rich could become poor overnight, and vice versa; nothing was solid or predictable. The American dream was falling to pieces, and Dos Passos's fragmented approach captures this inevitable crash. By interspersing poetics with prose and quickly cutting from one character to another, Dos Passos uses the structure of the novel itself to frame its content. The collage of newsreels and use of fictional and nonfictional characters makes the reader feel like a participant in both story and history. Dos Passos wants the reader's experience to echo the characters': At first, the American dream seems whole and hopeful, but by the end the dream has shattered.

In addition, Dos Passos blends genres to illustrate how fiction and nonfiction are intertwined or, more specifically, how fiction may hold a mirror up to truth and reality. Juxtaposing Henry Ford against Charley Anderson or Isadora Duncan against Margo Dowling shows the reader that Dos Passos's story is not simply the made-up musing of an author, but rather a catalyst for the reader to think about patterns, likenesses, choices made, and roads not taken. The constant comparisons and contrasts also demonstrate how successful icons began as ordinary people with flaws, foibles, and big dreams.

HISTORICAL OVERVIEW

The Lost Generation

The Lost Generation refers to a group of American literary intellectuals, poets, artists, bohemians, and writers who lived primarily in Paris but also other parts of Europe from the time period spanning the end of World War I to the beginning of the Great Depression. The term "Lost Generation" is attributed to Gertrude Stein but was popularized by Ernest Hemingway. In Hemingway's book *A Moveable Feast* (published posthumously in 1964), one chapter is entitled "Une Génération Perdue" Since the term is used to describe the generation of youth that came of age during World War I, this generation of youthful idealists who drank too much, had love affairs, sought the meaning of life, and created some of the best American literature is sometimes also referred to as the "World War I Generation." In France, they were known as the *Generation du Feu*, or the "Generation of Fire". Some of the more notable literary figures from this generation are F. Scott Fitzgerald, Ernest Hemingway, and John Dos Passos. Some works representative of this period are *The Great Gatsby* (1925) and *The Sun Also Rises* (1926).

Driving an Ambulance in World War I

Like the characters in *The Big Money*, Dos Passos contributed to American efforts in World War I, a conflict spanning the years between 1914 and 1918. The Allied Powers—France, the Russian Empire, the United Kingdom, and ultimately the United States—defeated the Central Powers, comprised of Austria-Hungary and the German and Ottoman Empires. The United States was reluctant to join the conflict; however, in April 1917, after the passenger ship *Lusitania* and several merchant ships were sunk by German submarines, the United States declared war. Like many of his fellow writers, such as Ernest Hemingway, e. e. cummings, and Somerset Maugham, Dos Passos was an ambulance driver;

it was an exciting, novel occupation for young adventurous men. In addition, many young men longed to jump into battle but did not pass the army's physical fitness test. Dos Passos's near-sightedness was so severe he could not see the largest letter written on an eye chart.

Three main volunteer ambulance groups served the various fronts: the American Field Service (AFS), Norton-Harjes, and the American Red Cross operation in Italy. Wrote Dos Passos prior to his employment, "I'm going to France with the Norton-Harjes as soon as I can take a course in running a machine." According to Steve Ruediger, when Dos Passos arrived on the front and took the driver's seat, he was not an extremely cautious driver; in fact, he was known to take "many chances far beyond the inherent risks of ambulance driving, which many considered risky enough."

Called "The War to End All Wars," World War I introduced modern mechanized weaponry and poison gas to the battlefront and paved the way for wars to come.

The Great Depression

The Great Depression was a devastating economic downturn starting in 1929, though not fully felt until 1930. The start of the Great Depression is often considered to be the New York stock market crash in October 1929, but, no one can really know the definitive reason for its cause. One leading theory is the unbalanced distribution of wealth: Only a very small percentage of the population held the bulk of the wealth in the country while the majority of the population could barely make ends meet. In addition, an oversupply of goods caused by the efficiency of industrialization allowed for tremendous output from factories. This created an environment of too much supply and not enough demand. Because of the large wealth distribution gap between the haves and have-nots, many people could not afford to buy these overabundant products. Those without the means to buy goods relied on credit, thus creating large amounts of debt. These large debts contributed to making the initial recession in 1930 turn into a true depression by 1933. Conservative spending lowered demand for new products. Continuing this spiral, companies predicted poor profits and cut back on capital investments. Banks became more conservative in their lending practices; by

1933, nearly half the banks in the United States had failed. To further complicate matters, the Dust Bowl of the 1930s, which lasted about a decade, combined a drought lasting many years and poor farming practices such as over-plowing and over-grazing. The land was destroyed, and unemployment became rampant as hundreds of thousands of Americans took to the streets in search of basic necessities such as food, shelter, and work. After World War I, the United States was the biggest financier to post-war Great Britain and Germany, so after the depression hit the United States, it eventually trickled to Europe.

CRITICAL OVERVIEW

Dos Passos had a varied and successful career, despite his gradual exile from literary acceptance because of his political views. J. Donald Adams, in a 1936 review in the *New York Times*, praises Dos Passos for his "keen eye for so many different kinds of people." Adams goes on to say that Dos Passos may not be as skilled as some more experienced writers, but he is "one of the ablest naturalistic craftsmen" working in the novel genre. Adams does note Dos Passos's piecemeal style as both ineffective and disruptive to the narrative.

Dos Passos's *The Big Money* beat out Margaret Mitchell's *Gone with the Wind* as the Best Book of 1937, as honored by national writers and critics and reported by the *New York Times*. Mason Wade, in his article "Novelist of America," declares that Dos Passos's "achievement has not yet received the attention it deserves." Wade claims that Dos Passos's work warranted a Pulitzer Prize, because "his five important novels constitute an unequaled portrait of twentieth century America." Wade also extols Dos Passos's "sensitivity and his feeling for language, coupled with his zest for experience" and calls him both a "romantic and a realist."

Vincent McHugh calls Dos Passos's "U.S.A. Trilogy" a "Picaresque Monument to the Past" in the title to his 1943 article in the *New York Times*. Mc Hugh sets the novels "alongside the thesis novels of Upton Sinclair and Theodore Dreiser's *American Tragedy*." He considers the trilogy to be "the most formidable and accomplished novel of the American Twenties and Thirties." But McHugh also agrees with many critics in saying that Dos Passos's characters "lack passion, concentration, hard-packed depth"; however, to McHugh, that lack works with Dos Passos's themes and narratives.

In a 1950 newspaper article, Granville Hicks calls Dos Passos as "a true explorer in his day," but also noted that his "political confusion" led to a decline of "literary mastery." That same year, Martin Kallich in the *Antioch Review* claims that Dos Passos's works follow the trajectory of his political beliefs, particularly marking his change from individualist to socialist to conservative. Two decades later, in May 1971, Alfred Kazin asks, "What Ever Happened to Dos Passos After 'U.S.A.'?" Kazin, writing for the *New York Times*, claims that the "decline of his later fiction" resulted not from his "right-wing National Review indifference to the masses" but from his style change—from controversial social commentary to historical works.

More recently, Dos Passos has gained the recognition many have always thought he deserved. In the *Washington Times* in 1996, George Core claims "Dos Passos did more to forge the modern novel in the United States than any author of his times but Faulkner" and points to "the range of technique and style in 'U.S.A.'" as "breathtaking." Core also notes,

> In its use of fact for the purposes of fiction, "U.S.A." influenced the development of the nonfiction-novel genre as it has been written by Norman Mailer, Truman Capote and others. Indeed, it has influenced this genre as much as it has the standard novel through its technical innovations and sympathy with the down and out.

In 2003, Vincent Balitas of the *Washington Times* argues for Dos Passos's place in the "literary pantheon." He writes, "John Dos Passos was a very intelligent writer whose talent often seems to have been subservient to his political and social agendas. He witnessed firsthand the violence and sheer brutality of war. He saw the corruption of corporate and industrial capitalism, and the lack of justice among the have-nots." Balitas also suggests that Dos Passos's work was vital to the "development of American literature" and while recognizing Dos Passos's flaws, also acknowledges his "innovations" and "historical conscience."

MEDIA ADAPTATIONS

A thirteen-tape unabridged audio cassette version of *The Big Money* was released by Books on Tape in 1984. It is read by Michael Prichard.

CRITICISM

Daniel Aaron

In the following excerpt, Aaron explores Dos Passos's blending of history and fiction, particularly in the cast of characters in his "U.S.A. Trilogy," to vividly capture a moment in the American culture. The Big Money *is the third volume of the trilogy.*

From writer-reporters like Ambrose Bierce, Stephen Crane, and John Reed, Dos Passos had learned how to inject excitement and a sense of urgency into a narrative. By the 1930s he was unsurpassed as a writer of "rapportage," a form of advocacy journalism that simultaneously described, informed, and aroused. It admirably suited his conception of eyewitness novelistic history, what he called "my own curious sort of political agit-prop." As the critic Edmund Wilson pointed out, it had always been Dos Passos's function to take his readers "behind the front pages of the newspapers and provide us with a newsreel of his own" and to convert the abstractions Wall Street, Industry, and Labor into flesh-and-blood persons. Hence rapportage lent itself well to the three devices Dos Passos invented to stitch together the multiple strands of his chronicle: Newsreel, the biographies, and The Camera Eye.

Scattered through the trilogy are the sixty-eight Newsreels, none more than a few pages long. They are made up of snatches from tabloid headlines, popular song lyrics, weather reports, financial predictions, and ephemeral scandals. Artfully inserted to fix in time the episodes of the chronicle, by turn farcical, satirical, and ominous, they also dovetail with the lives of the real and imagined characters. They are the surface noise or static of history and confirm a central

A Model T Ford automobile, aka, Tin Lizzie
E. O. Hoppe/Mansell/Time Life Pictures/Getty Images

proposition in *U.S.A.*, that the debased language of the press signifies a deeper social sickness.

The twenty-six biographies, which stand like observation towers overlooking the flattened narrative landscape, have a comparable function. Dos Passos said he intended these highly stylized sketches or short personal essays to serve "as illustrative panels, portraits of typical or important personalities of the time," and he planted them to "interrupt, and by contrast to give another dimension to the made-up stories which are the body of the book." Each portrait, although sharply individualized, is meant to stand for something more inclusive than the sitter: a type, a cast of mind, a national characteristic. Each reflects some aspect of the historical process and relates obliquely to the occupations, interests, and desires of the invented characters. Together they embody a history of American life and institutions.

Dos Passos's biases are undisguisedly at work in the biographies. His heroes tend to be independent spirits who took risks, held unpopular opinions, or challenged the political and business establishment. The Wright brothers, Luther Burbank, Eugene Debs, John Reed, Randolph Bourne, Thorstein Veblen, and Frank

Lloyd Wright belong to his saving remnant. Less admirable in his eyes are the technical geniuses (besides Edison and Ford, they include Frederick Winslow Taylor, the father of scientific management, and the electrical engineer Charles Proteus Steinmetz), whose accomplishments he acknowledges but whom he presents as the willing or passive creatures of big business. They remind him of "the sorcerer's apprentice who loosed the goblins and the wonder-working broomsticks in his master's shop and then forgot what the formula was to control them by."

Least congenial, for there are no loathsome villains in *U.S.A.*, are the organizers and chief beneficiaries of business and finance. Dos Passos bathes them in irony. Andrew Carnegie, "Prince of Peace," spent millions "to promote universal peace...except in time of war." J. P. Morgan, "a bullnecked irascible man with small black magpie eyes and a growth on his nose," equated American principles with the open shop. Woodrow Wilson "flayed the interests and branded privilege" and then took the nation into a war that "brought the eight hour day, women's votes, prohibition, compulsory arbitration, high wages, high rates of interest, cost plus contracts and the luxury of being a Gold Star Mother." William Randolph Hearst, one-time "millionaire candidate of the common man," backed the "bludgeon rule of Handsome Adolph." In the end all of them are pawns of tendency and no more prescient than their punier counterparts in the narratives.

The same applies to the remembering and reflecting person-voice of The Camera Eye, the author self-observed. The fifty-one internal monologues placed at intervals from the beginning to the end of the trilogy parallel and mesh with events alluded to in the Newsreels and biographies and internalize the surface history. Dos Passos's protagonist (it would be too much to call him a hero) is the only character who actually changes, develops, and learns and who can look back at his earlier selves with a degree of sympathy and humor. Where the invented characters are crushed or crack up, or sell out, the monologist manages to come out whole and undefeated. Without great expectations he's ready to press on. What he's learned about himself and America in his veiled introspections is what *U.S.A.* is all about.

Dos Passos wrote in the prologue to his trilogy: "*U.S.A.* is the slice of a continent...

But mostly," he added, "the speech of the people." We hear this speech in the narratives, the strongest sections of the chronicle. The prevailing language is the American vernacular, directly quoted or expressed in the indirect discourse of the author, who has entered the heads of his twelve main characters and told their stories as if they were prompting him. Out of their intertwining lives he fashions his emblematic history, a fable of America's materialistic success and moral decline conveniently sketched for him in the works of the economist and social critic Thorstein Veblen, the linchpin of *U.S.A.* and the subject of its longest biography.

Dos Passos's Veblen is Socrates reborn, an ironist and dissector of the century who fought "pedantry, routine, time-servers at office desks, trustees, college presidents, the plump flunkies of the ruling businessmen." He took to Veblen as he never did to Karl Marx, whose theories he couldn't comfortably apply to American conditions. *U.S.A.* follows Veblen's "new diagram of a society dominated by monopoly capital" and "the sabotage of production by business." It poses Veblen's alternatives: "a warlike society strangled by the bureaucracies of the monopolies" and forced to "grind down more and more the common man for profits"; and a "commonsense society" managed by competent technicians for the benefit of the people and alert to "the vast possibilities for peace and plenty."

The characters in *U.S.A.* are the victims and beneficiaries of the first alternative. A handful can't or won't adjust to any sort of regimentation. Mac, the radical journeyman printer and feckless picaro in *The 42nd Parallel*, is one example. Joe Williams in *1919*, the unattached and futureless merchant seaman killed in a bar fight in France, is another. Both are anachronisms handicapped by their live-and-let-live attitudes. They belong to a more relaxed lost America, as does Charley Anderson in *The Big Money*. A North Dakota country boy, war hero, airplane designer cum capitalist, Charley is good-natured and democratic, at home in garages and workshops, but once infected by the money bug, he starts to think and talk like a capitalist and to betray his friends.

Most of the other characters are amenable to the standards and values of Veblen's "pecuniary" society and its canon of reputability. They are part of the "servile generation of whitecollar slaves" climbing up and sliding down the social ladder. Dos Passos observes their scramblings with measured detachment yet not without a certain sympathy for their vulnerability. He differentiates those victimized or doomed by their compulsiveness and innocence from the "dead alive," who have anesthetized feeling and prospered at the cost of their humanity. Richard Ellsworth Savage, the most complex character in the chronicle, occupies one of the lower circles in Dos Passos's inferno. Once a poet and rebel (with a good deal of Dos Passos in his background and makeup), he is sensitive and intelligent enough to wince at his own fraudulence but hasn't the strength to sacrifice its compensations.

Savage has no counterpart in Veblen's unfleshed abstractions, but his mentor and tempter J. Ward Moorehouse personifies the type of prudent self-made man Veblen was constantly caricaturizing: "reliable, conciliatory, conservative, secretive, patient, and prehensile." Of all the characters, Moorehouse, master of the burgeoning craft of public relations, archcorrupter of language, is the one best suited to thrive in Dos Passos's Vanity Fair. There are many betrayals in *U.S.A.*, but he is the ultimate betrayer.

Dos Passos was too good a novelist to turn his characters into saints or devils. The worst of them are all too human, the noblest and least selfish warped by their idealism. Mary French drudges her life away for the downtrodden masses, gives herself to a series of unsavory men who "need" her, and eventually hardens into a formula. Self-immolating Ben Compton, strike leader and Marxist revolutionary, gets it in the neck from all quarters and is emotionally crippled by his terrible integrity.

Even as Dos Passos bled for the injured and the insulted and did more than his share of social protesting, one suspects that at no time was he quite at ease with his radical allies, or, for that matter, with group movements of any kind. Blowhards, careerists, and crooks, it seemed to him, sullied whatever cause or party he had supported, particularly the Communist party. He had once classified himself as a camp follower of the party, but that was before Stalinist tactics in the United States and abroad (his disenchantment is anticipated in *The Big Money*) sent him in search of his "real" or "chosen" country. Not long after, he settled down with the ultras of the right (he envisaged them as a beleaguered minority), still a seeker,

still wandering around the globe collecting materials for his books. With a few exceptions his late works were indifferently received.

In retrospect the symptoms of his ultimate rupture with socialists of all varieties were plainly evident: belief in the evil of existing institutions, strong doubts about human goodness, and unwillingness to commit himself totally to any cause. He had "privately seceded" from the United States after the Sacco-vanzetti affair and rejoined it briefly during the early years of the New Deal. But he soon concluded that power had drifted from Wall Street to Washington and that Roosevelt's bureaucrats had lost contact with grassroots America. From there it wasn't much of a jump to the camp of Sen. Joseph McCarthy and others of his ilk, whom he commended for exposing the "Communist Infiltration" of government agencies. Unfortunately his shift to the Republicanism of Robert Taft and Richard Nixon carried little imaginative conviction and inspired pedestrian books. He remained the earnest, decent man he had always been and refused to apologize for what he had said or done. (Asked for permission to quote some wildly anarchistic sentences from his youthful correspondence, he replied: "Go ahead. I wrote them, didn't I?")

Glancing back at his life, one wonders if Dos Passos's long vendetta against coercive institutions wasn't at bottom a cry against the Industrial age itself. From his Harvard days he had been of two minds about a machine civilization full of wonders but dehumanizing. He could evoke it powerfully and poetically, but he doesn't appear to have enjoyed it very much. He had his lighthearted moments, to be sure, but his satire tastes medicinal.

U.S.A. reverberates with the sounds of buses, trucks, cars, trains, airplanes. They speed up the action, and they are also the engines of destruction. The dancer Isadora Duncan (the only woman in the biographies) breaks her neck in a Bugatti when her trailing scarf catches in the wheels; drunken Charley Anderson drives his car through a barrier, trying to beat a locomotive to a crossing, and stalls on the tracks; Anne Elizabeth Trent ("Daughter"), seduced and ditched by Dick Savage, dies in a plane crash. Such incidents suggest that Dos Passos's trilogy might be read as a lament for a simpler and still relatively unmechanized "chosen country."

Of course, it's much more than that: a twentieth-century novel vibrating with history and written by an opinionated man who framed his story in historical time and supplied it with a roaring soundtrack. He wasn't trying to rewrite history as fiction. Historical and fictional elements interact, but they are clearly demarcated. Essentially it is a human comedy in the tradition of two of his favorite authors, Cervantes and Thackeray, and a lengthy exercise in what his old friend the novelist Dawn Powell defined as "man's helplessness against vanity (the vanity of love, greed, lust, power")."

Source: Daniel Aaron, "U.S.A.," in *American Heritage*, Vol. 47, No. 4, July–August 1996, pp. 63–72.

SOURCES

Adams, J. Donald, "John Dos Passos Pictures the Boom Years," in the *New York Times*, August 16, 1936, p. BR2.

Balitas, Vincent, "Writing for His Agendas: John Dos Passos and His Novels of American Life," in the *Washington Times*, September 21, 2003, p. B06.

Core, George, "Dos Passos: His Literary Image Restored," in the *Washington Times*, December 29, 1996, p. B7.

Dos Passos, John, *The Big Money*, Harcourt, Brace, 1936; reprint, Mariner Books, 2000.

Hicks, Granville, "The Politics of John Dos Passos," in the *Antioch Review*, Vol. 10, No. 1, March 1950, p. 85.

Kallich, Martin, "John Dos Passos: Liberty and the Father Image," in the *Antioch Review*, Vol. 10, No. 1, March 1950, p. 99.

Kazin, Alfred, "Dos Passos, Society, and the Individual," in *Dos Passos: A Collection of Critical Essays*, edited by Andrew Hook, Prentice-Hall, 1974, p. 101.

———, "What Happened to Dos Passos After 'U.S.A.'?", in the *New York Times*, May 2, 1971, p. D17.

McHugh, Vincent, "Dos Passos Trilogy Revalued," in the *New York Times*, September 5, 1943, p. BR8.

Ruediger, Steve, "Prose & Poetry—Literary Ambulance Drivers" in *First World War.com*, www.firstworldwar.com/poetsandprose/ambulance.htm (February 12, 2002).

Wade, Mason, "Novelist of America: John Dos Passos," in the *North American Review*, Vol. 244, No. 2, Winter 1937–1938, p. 349.

Black Elk Speaks

JOHN G. NEIHARDT

1932

Black Elk Speaks (1932) is the story of an Oglala Sioux medicine man who lived with his people on the Great Plains through most of the second half of the nineteenth century—an age that saw many bloody conflicts between American Indians and white soldiers and settlers. As a child, Black Elk experienced a vision that he thought would help lead his people through the hardships they were just beginning to endure. Unfortunately, Black Elk's story is ultimately one of broken dreams and unfulfilled visions. Like so many other tribes, the Oglala Sioux's traditional way of life ran counter to the American dream as envisioned by most white Americans in the nineteenth century.

Black Elk Speaks, by John G. Neihardt, is one of the most unusual memoirs ever put to paper. Black Elk, the Oglala Sioux medicine man whose life the book relates, did not speak English. John G. Neihardt, the poet and authority on Plains Indian culture who brought Black Elk's tale to the page, did not speak Sioux. However, the two men recognized each other as kindred spirits, and each played an important part in bringing the book to life.

Neihardt first traveled to meet Black Elk while researching the ghost dance movement of the 1890s for an epic poem he was writing. Hearing that Black Elk had been an instrumental participant in the Oglala ghost dance movement, Neihardt hoped to glean some firsthand

BIOGRAPHY

JOHN G. NEIHARDT

John Gneisenau Neihardt was born on January 8, 1891, near Sharpsburg, Illinois. His family later moved to Kansas, where Neihardt became interested in Greek epic poems, before settling in Nebraska. While ill with a fever as a young boy, Neihardt claimed to have had a vision that convinced him his calling was to write poetry. He published his first book of poetry, *The Divine Enchantment*, when he was just nineteen.

Neihardt continued living and writing in Nebraska, making his home in a town on the edge of the Omaha Indian Reservation. In 1930, while researching the ghost dance movement for his epic poem series *A Cycle of the West*, Neihardt met with Oglala medicine man Nicholas Black Elk; the two became fast friends. Black Elk was sixty-seven years old when he met Neihardt and began telling the story of the first twenty-seven years of his remarkable life, which was published as *Black Elk Speaks* in 1932. He died on November 24, 1950, in Columbia, Missouri, before his story won the wide renown it enjoys today.

Neihardt died in Columbia, Missouri, on November 24, 1973. Neihardt's retelling of Black Elk's life on the Plains, *Black Elk Speaks*, is without a doubt the author's most enduring work.

information for his poem. After first meeting the aging medicine man, however, Neihardt felt that Black Elk's story was an important piece of American history in its own right that needed to be preserved:

> As hunter, warrior, practicing holy man, and indubitable seer, he seemed even then to represent the consciousness of the Plains Indian more fully than any other I had ever known; and when I became well acquainted with his inner world, I knew this to be true.

The two men relied on their children to complete their task: Black Elk's son translated his father's words into English, while Neihardt's daughter recorded a stenographic transcript of the translation. Neihardt later pieced together the transcript, rewriting portions to capture the flavor and meaning of Black Elk's original spoken testimony and to maintain narrative flow. This has led to some criticism that the book is not an autobiography, because many of the specific phrases and sentences in the book originated not with Black Elk, but with his son and with Neihardt. Vine Deloria Jr. in his foreword to the book, argues that such criticism misses the point: "The very nature of great religious teachings is that they encompass everyone who understands them and personalities become indistinguishable from the transcendent truth that is expressed."

Although the book fell into relative obscurity for nearly three decades after it first appeared, a renewed interest in American Indian heritage among readers led to new editions of *Black Elk Speaks* to be published in 1961, 1972, and 1979. More recent editions contain supplemental materials and accounts that help place the creation of *Black Elk Speaks* in a richer historical and literary context. The book remains an essential text for anyone seeking to understand and appreciate the practices and beliefs of the Lakota Sioux, as well as anyone hoping to gain a fuller understanding of the consequences of the westward expansion of the United States in the 1800s.

PLOT SUMMARY

Chapters 1–3

Black Elk Speaks tells the story of Black Elk's early life, beginning with his first childhood memories and concluding in 1890, when he was twenty-seven years old. The text also contains detailed information about Oglala Sioux customs and traditions, as well as first-person accounts of important historical events as witnessed by other living Native Americans. Black Elk sees his tale as one that extends far beyond his own experiences:

> It is the story of all life that is holy and is good to tell, and of us two-leggeds sharing in it with the four-leggeds and the wings of the air and all green things; for these are children of one mother and their father is one Spirit.

Before he begins to tell of his life and his vision, Black Elk makes a pipe offering to the

Black Elk (l) The Library of Congress

Spirit of the World. He also explains the origin and significance of the pipe. According to legend, two hunters were out looking for bison when they saw a woman. One of the hunters recognized the woman as sacred, but the other, being foolish, did not. The foolish hunter approached the woman, and was killed. The woman ordered the other hunter to tell his village she is coming, and to build a large tepee in the center of the nation for her. When the woman arrived, she gave the chief a pipe to help the nation become strong. As she walked away from the village, she transformed into a white bison. Black Elk remarks, "This they tell, and whether it happened so or not I do not know; but if you think about it, you can see that it is true."

After completing the pipe ceremony, Black Elk relates his family history and earliest childhood memories. He is a member of the Oglala Sioux tribe, born in 1863 as the son of a medicine man. When Black Elk is just three years old, Oglala warriors fight back against an encroaching tide of white—or "Wasichu"—soldiers in the area near Fort Phil Kearny, in what is now Wyoming.

Later, Black Elk discovers the reason for the fight: The Wasichus had discovered gold in the area, and "they wanted to have a road up through our country to where the yellow metal was; but my people did not want the road." The fight, known as the Battle of the Hundred Slain, is remembered by Black Elk's older friend Fire Thunder, as is a bloody skirmish the following year known as the Attacking of the Wagons. When Black Elk is five years old, Oglala chief Red Cloud signs a treaty with the Wasichus; white soldiers are removed from the area entirely, and the Oglala people are promised that "our country would be ours as long as grass should grow and water flow."

Around this time, Black Elk begins to hear voices and see visions. His most profound vision occurs when he is nine years old and very ill. In his vision, the six Powers of the World—North, South, East, West, Earth, and Sky—reveal that Black Elk's people shall undergo four generations of increasing difficulties, but Black Elk will have the power to help them survive the hardship and regain their strength.

Chapters 4–7

Black Elk recovers quickly after the vision, and he learns that he had been gravely ill for nearly two weeks. He decides not to share his vision because he fears that no one will believe him. Soon after, the tribe goes on a bison hunt. Black Elk is not yet old enough to hunt, but he rides along with the other boys, pretending to be a scout for the hunters.

When Black Elk is ten, a small group from his tribe travels to Fort Robinson, or "Soldiers' Town" as he calls it, to visit relatives who live in the area with Oglala chief Red Cloud. This is the first time Black Elk sees a Wasichu in person: "At first I thought they all looked sick, and I was afraid they might just begin to fight us any time, but I got used to them." The band stays at Soldiers' Town through the winter and then journeys into the Black Hills. There, Black Elk learns to spearfish from a man named Watanye; this same man tells Black Elk the tale of a Lakota called High Horse and the girl he loved.

According to the story, High Horse fell in love with a beautiful girl from his village. She seemed to like him in return, so High Horse went to the girl's father and offered him horses in exchange for his daughter's hand. The father dismissed High Horse's offer. High Horse's friend Red Deer then devised a plan for High

Horse to steal the girl away in the middle of the night. Red Deer painted High Horse completely white with black circles around his eyes so people would be too scared to chase him during his escape. High Horse entered the family's tepee, but while trying to remain quiet and avoid rousing the girl's parents, he fell asleep. The next morning, the girl found him sleeping next to her and, thinking he was some strange animal, screamed. High Horse fled, and the villagers let him go, believing he might be some sacred creature that would bring bad luck if they killed it.

Crestfallen, High Horse decided he would not return to the village; instead, he and Red Deer went on the war-path. After a few days, they discovered a band from a rival tribe, the Crow. They killed the horse guard and stole all the band's horses—about a hundred in all. They drove the horses back to their own village and up to the entrance of the beautiful girl's tepee. High Horse offered all the horses to the girl's father; finally seeing that High Horse was a man who could provide for his daughter, the father accepted him.

The following year, when Black Elk is eleven, a medicine man named Chips has a vision of soldiers in the area where the Oglala group is camping. Black Elk later discovers that Lieutenant Colonel George Custer—known by the Oglalas as Pahuska, or "Long Hair"—has led his soldiers into the Black Hills and discovered gold there. "Our people knew there was yellow metal in little chunks up there; but they did not bother with it, because it was not good for anything," explains Black Elk.

The small band of Oglalas travels back to Soldiers' Town. Red Cloud and his followers defend the actions of the soldiers, believing the soldiers were trying to remove white settlers from the Sioux territory. Many of the Oglala disagree and start referring to Red Cloud's followers by the derisive name "Hangs-Around-The-Fort." In September 1875, after even more soldiers enter the Black Hills, the Wasichus invite the different Sioux tribes to a council. They want the tribes to lease the Black Hills—which, by treaty, belongs to the Sioux—so the area can be mined for gold. According to Black Elk, "They talked and talked for days, but it was just like wind blowing in the end."

Black Elk and his people leave Soldiers' Town to camp near the Oglala chief Crazy Horse, whose father is cousin to Black Elk's father. Crazy Horse sees things differently than Red Cloud and is willing to fight to keep the Wasichus out of tribal territory. During the winter, messengers track down Black Elk's group and tell them that they must return to Soldiers' Town, or else "there would be bad trouble." The group makes it back to Soldiers' Town in February, while Crazy Horse decides to remain camped on the Powder River. The following month, Black Elk hears that Crazy Horse's camp has been attacked by Wasichu cavalry troops. To Black Elk and his people, the attack is both unprovoked and in violation of Red Cloud's treaty: "These people were in their own country and doing no harm. They only wanted to be let alone." It becomes clear to many of the Oglalas at Soldiers' Town, including Black Elk's family, that the only way to keep their land is to fight for it.

Chapters 8–9

Black Elk's family and several others leave Soldiers' Town in May 1876 to join Crazy Horse. Though he is only thirteen, Black Elk is well trained with both guns and bows, and he is ready to fight the Wasichus if necessary. On the way to meet Crazy Horse at Rosebud River, the group's scouts are fired upon by members of a Wasichu wagon train heading into the Black Hills. The group attacks the wagon train, and although he does not know if any Wasichus are killed, Black Elk is proud that he has participated in his first battle.

When the group reaches the Rosebud River, they find members of many other Sioux tribes have also congregated there. Cheyennes, Hunkpapas, Minneconjous, Black Feet, and others have united to defend their lands against the Wasichus. In June, the congregation holds a sun dance, a traditional festival intended "to purify the people and to give them power and endurance." The sun dance is led by Sitting Bull, considered by many to be the greatest living medicine man. After two days of dancing, scouts report that Wasichu troops are drawing near. Although Black Elk is eager to join in the fight alongside Crazy Horse, he is asked instead to look after the young children in the village. Black Elk's friend, a Hunkpapa named Iron Hawk, fights in the battle against General Crook—known to the Sioux as Three Stars—and his cavalrymen; the Wasichus are also aided by Crow warriors, who are traditional enemies of the Sioux. Although Iron Hawk is at first convinced that his people have lost the battle, he later discovers that the Wasichus and their Crow mercenaries have been soundly defeated.

After the battle against Three Stars, Crazy Horse and his followers move northwest to the area they call Greasy Grass, popularly known as Little Bighorn. Although they won the battle, they travel away from the soldiers, farther into their own territory because, "It was our country and we did not want to have trouble." Soon, however, soldiers led by Pahuska—General Custer—charge deep into Sioux territory to attack the camp. This time, Black Elk is closer to the fighting; he happens upon a wounded soldier on the battlefield and, at the prompting of another warrior, he shoots and scalps the soldier. Black Elk takes the scalp to show his mother, who sings out with pride for his bravery.

Elsewhere in the battle, Black Elk's friend Standing Bear finds himself in the midst of chaos: "There were so many of us that I think we did not need guns. Just the hoofs would have been enough." Iron Hawk, also present at the battle, tells how the warriors pinned down the troops near the river; the soldiers, in desperate need of water, send unarmed men with buckets down to the river. Iron Hawk sees these soldiers and moves in: "I guess they got enough to drink, for they are drinking yet. We killed them in the water."

Chapters 10–14

After the defeat of Custer, Crazy Horse and his followers move east across the Great Plains. Fearing the Wasichus will never stop chasing them, some of the Sioux leave for the safety of soldier-run agencies, while others including Sitting Bull flee toward Canada ("Grandmother's Land"). Many of the Sioux, however, refuse to leave their land: "It was ours already when the Wasichus made the treaty with Red Cloud.... That was only eight winters before, and they were chasing us now because we remembered and they forgot."

Just before winter, Black Elk and his people learn that the Wasichus have bought the Black Hills and all land to the west of the Hills by making agreements with tribe leaders who have stopped fighting and live near the soldiers. More troops battle the last remaining camps of Sioux, who are starving and freezing. In the spring, under Crazy Horse's direction, the last surviving Sioux rebels travel to Red Cloud's Agency, near Soldiers' Town, and vow to stop fighting.

The Wasichus suspect that Crazy Horse remains a threat, so they lure him to Soldiers' Town and place him under arrest. Black Elk and his father follow into Soldiers' Town. Though they do not see it happen, they later hear of Crazy Horse's fate: When the Sioux leader discovered that the soldiers were arresting him, he resisted and was stabbed to death. Black Elk explains, "They could not kill him in battle. They had to lie to him and kill him that way."

After the death of Crazy Horse, the Wasichus force many of the Sioux at Red Cloud's Agency to move east. During the journey, a small band that includes Black Elk's family decides to flee to the north. They eventually reach Grandmother's Land, where some of their relatives already live in a camp led by Sitting Bull. They remain there through two winters. Although they are safe from Wasichu soldiers, the winters are brutal, and many of the Sioux feel homesick for their own lands. In 1879, a very small band that includes Black Elk's family heads south once again.

The group returns to camp near the Bighorn Mountains. Black Elk finds himself increasingly distracted by thoughts of his long-ago vision, and he hears voices all around him that convince him he must do something to help his people. He decides to share his vision with an old medicine man named Black Road. The medicine man tells Black Elk that he must share his vision with people, and the two prepare a horse dance to perform and convey Black Elk's vision.

The entire camp helps to prepare for the horse dance, which takes place around a sacred tepee painted with images from Black Elk's vision. After the horse dance, several people tell Black Elk that they feel healed by the ceremony, and medicine men respect him for his great vision.

Chapters 15–18

The group returns to the area near Soldiers' Town and finds that the Wasichus are building a new camp for the Oglalas to the east. Black Elk and the others journey to the camp, called the Pine Ridge Agency. In the spring, Black Elk experiences another vision; in this vision, two warriors hunt down two dogs and cut off their heads, only to find that the dogs have transformed into Wasichus. He shares his vision with several elders, who all agree that he must perform the vision in a heyoka ceremony, which features foolish characters to amuse and lift the spirits of the viewers. The ceremony is a success: "They were better able now to see the greenness of the world, the wideness of the sacred day, the colors of the earth, and to set these in their minds."

After the heyoka ceremony, the Wasichus move the Oglalas into square gray houses. According to Black Elk, "It is a bad way to live, for there can be no power in a square." Black Elk is approached by a man whose son is ill; using an herb he saw in both of his visions, Black Elk cures the boy. At the age of nineteen, Black Elk becomes renowned for his power to cure.

Black Elk insists that the power does not come from him: "It was the power from the outer world, and the visions and ceremonies had only made me like a hole through which the power could come to the two-leggeds." By sharing another part of his original vision, Black Elk persuades his people to perform two more ceremonies: one to celebrate the power of the bison, and one to celebrate the power of the elk. By performing the ceremonies, he hopes to use the power of his vision to help sustain his people.

Chapters 19–22

By 1883, when Black Elk is twenty years old, all the large herds of bison in Sioux territory have been killed. "The Wasichus did not kill them to eat; they killed them for the metal that makes them crazy, and they took only the hides to sell." Without the bison, Black Elk and his people grow hungry; the situation is worsened when government provisions are frequently stolen by dishonest Wasichus before they reach the Pine Ridge Agency. Black Elk recalls, "There were many lies, but we could not eat them."

After a few more years as a medicine man, Black Elk decides to join a traveling show run by Buffalo Bill Cody. He and a hundred other Oglalas make the journey to New York City, where they perform in Madison Square Garden all winter. Buffalo Bill then moves the show across the Atlantic to London, where they perform for Grandmother England (Queen Victoria). The show travels on to Manchester, where Black Elk and three others are accidentally left behind. They eventually find their way back to London, where they join another traveling show run by a man named Mexican Joe.

After a long run in London, Mexican Joe moves his show to Paris. There, Black Elk meets a Wasichu girl with whom he develops a close friendship; while having breakfast one morning

with the girl and her parents, Black Elk falls unconscious and experiences a vision of his home. When he wakes, he discovers that he has been on the verge of death for three days. The Wasichu girl and her family contact Buffalo Bill, who has brought his show to Paris as well. Buffalo Bill is happy to see Black Elk again, and he arranges for him to return to the United States. When Black Elk finally arrives back at Pine Ridge, he finds everything just as he saw it in his vision. After almost three years, he is happy to be back with his people, and he returns to healing the sick.

Black Elk discovers that the situation at Pine Ridge is worse than when he left. The Wasichus have taken even more Sioux land and have not provided enough food for the people to eat. Black Elk also hears of a sacred man among the Paiute tribe out west; the man, Wovoka, claims to have spoken to the Great Spirit and has seen a vision in which the Wasichus will be swept from the land and the bison will return. That winter, Black Elk's father dies. By the spring of 1890, Wovoka's ghost dance movement—and the ceremony that accompanies it—has spread across the plains; seeing no better prospect for his people, Black Elk decides to participate.

Chapters 23–25

Black Elk spreads the word about the ghost dance to the Brules, a Sioux tribe not far from the Oglala agency. When he returns, the Wasichus decree that the Indians can only perform rituals like the ghost dance for three days each month. An official also secretly reveals to Black Elk that he and another ghost dance follower are going to be arrested. The two flee their camp and stay with the Brules, but they are eventually called back to Pine Ridge by one of their chiefs. After arriving back at Pine Ridge, Black Elk learns that Sitting Bull, who had come south from Grandmother's Land, was killed by Wasichus when he refused to be arrested. Soon after, an ailing Lakota chief, Big Foot, brings the last remaining members of his band, as well as the last of Sitting Bull's people, to Wounded Knee Creek and surrenders to Wasichu soldiers.

At Pine Ridge, Black Elk hears of Big Foot's surrender and sees hundreds of soldiers march off toward Wounded Knee. The next morning he hears cannon fire, and he rides toward Wounded Knee to see what is happening. When he arrives,

BUT THE WASICHUS CAME, AND THEY HAVE MADE LITTLE ISLANDS FOR US AND OTHER LITTLE ISLANDS FOR THE FOUR-LEGGEDS, AND ALWAYS THESE ISLANDS ARE BECOMING SMALLER, FOR AROUND THEM SURGES THE GNAWING FLOOD OF THE WASICHU; AND IT IS DIRTY WITH LIES AND GREED."

he sees Wasichu cavalrymen firing into a gulch filled with women and children. Though he has no weapon, Black Elk and some others decide to charge the cavalrymen to allow the surviving women and children to escape. The tactic works, and Black Elk survives unharmed. Other Sioux arrive and help to push the soldiers back; one of Black Elk's friends witnessed the whole incident and tells what had happened.

That morning, the soldiers had attempted to disarm all of Big Foot's camp. Nearly all the weapons were gathered peacefully, but one man named Yellow Bird refused to give up his gun. A soldier wrestled with Yellow Bird for his weapon but got shot during the scuffle. Almost immediately, soldiers began firing on the unarmed Sioux. The ailing Big Foot, lying infirm in his tepee, was shot right away. Not even the women and children were spared.

Black Elk returns to Pine Ridge with an infant he found still alive at Wounded Knee, but he discovers that his people have fled to avoid the Wasichus. He follows their trail and catches up with them at Clay Creek. The group organizes a war party, and the warriors ride out to meet the Wasichu soldiers. Black Elk is shot during this battle, but he recovers and retreats with some other warriors to a stronghold in the Badlands. The soldiers want to continue fighting, but Red Cloud convinces them to return. Remembering the sight of the massacre at Wounded Knee, Black Elk realizes: "And I can see that something else died there in the bloody mud, and was buried in the blizzard. A people's dream died there. It was a beautiful dream."

THEMES

Spiritual Guidance

Visions of spirits and the spirit world are a recurring theme in *Black Elk Speaks*. Black Elk experiences several visions throughout his life, but the first—at the age of nine—is the most significant. He believes that this vision contains the key to helping save his people from the Wasichus. In that sense, his vision represents his desire to provide a better life and future for his fellow Sioux. Ultimately, Black Elk considers himself a failure for not being able to use his vision to help his people.

Other characters in *Black Elk Speaks* also experience visions. Black Elk tells of a vision passed down from his father and grandfather, originally seen by a holy man named Drinks Water. Long before white explorers had ever visited the Great Plains, Drinks Water saw a vision of a race that would entrap the Sioux and force them to live in "square gray houses," and that there they would starve. Black Elk later points out that his people were indeed moved into square gray houses, and that the government repeatedly failed to provide adequate amounts of food for the Sioux.

Another significant vision in *Black Elk Speaks* is that of Wovoka, the leader of the ghost dance movement. In Wovoka's hopeful vision of the future, the bison return to the earth, as do the deceased loved ones of the surviving Sioux. The Indian territory is wiped clean of all Wasichus, and things are returned to as they were before the coming of the Wasichus. Although Black Elk later supports the ghost dance movement, his first instinct about the popularity of Wovoka's vision is telling: "I thought maybe it was only the despair that made people believe, just as a man who is starving may dream of plenty of everything good to eat."

Each of these spiritual visions represents the idealized potential of the Sioux—or, more broadly, all American Indians—to control their own destiny. This potential is essential to Black Elk's dream of a better life for his people, and when he realizes that the potential is gone, he feels that "the nation's hoop is broken and scattered. There is no center any longer, and the sacred tree is dead."

White headstones mark the graves of soldiers who died in the Battle of Little Bighorn, Little Bighorn National Monument, Montana © *Kevin R. Morris/Corbis*

White Men's Entitlement

In *Black Elk Speaks*, the Sioux try to share their homeland and make room for the Wasichus (white people), but the relationship is soured by repeated instances of broken promises. The history of life in the New World is one of white Europeans never questioning their right to take what they want or use underhanded means to get it. *Black Elk Speaks* is a rare look at the victims of that ugly corner of the American dream.

On several occasions Black Elk mentions Red Cloud's 1868 treaty with the Wasichus, which guarantees that the Sioux could keep their territory "as long as grass should grow and water flow." He quickly points out, "You can see that it is not the grass and water that have forgotten." Their territory is slowly stripped away from them, section by section, until even their reservation is moved to a different location altogether.

After Chief Crazy Horse decides to no longer fight, he is asked to meet with a Wasichu leader at Fort Robinson. According to Black Elk, Crazy Horse is promised that he will not be arrested when he arrives at the fort. However, soldiers immediately move to arrest the Sioux leader, and when he resists, he is stabbed by a cavalryman. Black Elk believes the Wasichus' betrayal is deliberate: "They could not kill him in battle. They had to lie to him and kill him that way."

Later, when the Wasichus take more Sioux land and move the remaining tribes people to a new reservation, soldiers take their ponies from them and promise that the Great Father (the U.S. president) will pay them for the horses. Black Elk notes, "if he ever did I have not heard of it." When the Sioux are placed on reservation lands, unable to hunt for game as they used to, the Wasichus promise to provide adequate food provisions for the Indians. However, the promised provisions are less than enough to feed everyone. According to Black Elk, "There were many lies, but we could not eat them."

Hope for the Future

The dream of a better future is a basic part of the American dream for Americans from all backgrounds. For Black Elk and many of his fellow Sioux, their dearest dream of an ideal future would be a return to the past—a time before the arrival of the Wasichus, when the bison were plentiful and the Black Hills were a sacred place shared by all tribes. Black Elk recalls his early childhood with fondness; though the world of his people is not without troubles, they maintain faith that the Great Spirit will give them the strength to overcome whatever hardships they face.

When the Wasichus begin to enter Sioux territory along the Bozeman Trail, Red Cloud wages a successful campaign to close the road and restore his country to its previous state. He signs a treaty that guarantees a return to the old ways, keeping Wasichus out of Sioux territory. Soon, however, the Wasichus return, and even Red Cloud realizes that they cannot be stopped.

With few exceptions, the prevailing behavior of the Sioux people is not to fight the Wasichus, but to move away in an attempt to continue following the old Sioux ways of living. The Sioux are chased deep into their own territory, and some flee all the way to Canada; however, they find that because the world is changing so swiftly around them, they cannot return to their previous way of life.

The ghost dance movement by Wovoka appeals to Black Elk and others precisely because it promises followers a return to the old ways. Wovoka told of a new world coming in which "there was plenty of meat, just like old times; and in that world all the dead Indians were alive, and all the bison that had ever been killed were roaming around again." When Black Elk finally loses hope for a return to the old ways, he loses hope for the future of his people.

HISTORICAL OVERVIEW

The Battle of the Little Bighorn
At the age of thirteen, Black Elk participated in the Battle of the Little Bighorn, also known as the Battle of the Greasy Grass or Custer's Last Stand. In this battle, the Lakota Sioux and Cheyenne, pursued onto their own territorial lands by U.S. Army troops, were attacked at their camp near the Little Bighorn River in what is now Montana. The soldiers were soundly defeated, though the victory for the American Indians involved was temporary.

In 1876, a large village of primarily Sioux tribes had camped in the area they called Greasy Grass along the Little Bighorn River. Although they were camped deep in their own territorial lands as defined by treaty, some government officials believed that the Indians represented a threat to soldiers and settlers flooding into the nearby Black Hills area. Among the Sioux camped at Greasy Grass were the leaders Sitting Bull and Crazy Horse, who were both considered hostile by the U.S. Army. Three separate detachments of soldiers were sent to engage the Indians where they camped; the most famous of these was the Seventh Cavalry, led by Lieutenant Colonel George Custer—known to the Sioux as Pahuska, or "Long Hair." One of the other detachments, led by General George Crook, was defeated at the Battle of the Rosebud earlier in the year and was not able to push on toward the Little Bighorn camp.

The remaining two detachments had planned to combine forces and attack the Indian camp. However, on June 25, 1876, Custer decided not to wait for reinforcements and plunged ahead with his assault. The army officers discovered too late that they were greatly outnumbered by the Sioux and Cheyenne warriors; this, coupled with a disorganized plan of attack, led to more than half of the Seventh Cavalry being killed, including Custer.

According to Dee Brown, author of *Bury My Heart at Wounded Knee*, "When the white men in the East heard of the Long Hair's defeat, they called it a massacre and went crazy with anger." Although the Sioux viewed their victory at Little Bighorn as an important statement of their resolve to retain their ancestral lands, they were never able to stop the flow of soldiers and settlers into Sioux territory. The following year, Crazy Horse surrendered to U.S. Army forces and was killed during a struggle when soldiers attempted to arrest him at Fort Robinson. Sitting Bull and his followers fled to Canada for several years, but eventually surrendered to U.S. forces in 1881. Like Crazy Horse, Sitting Bull was later killed during an attempt by U.S. troops to arrest him.

The Massacre at Wounded Knee
By 1890, the vast majority of Plains Indians were confined to reservations established by the U.S. government. The death of Sitting Bull, however, sent a small band of Sioux—including many

women and children—fleeing from the agency where the leader was killed. The group adopted a new leader named Big Foot, who led his people south from Standing Rock to try to evade pursuing soldiers and find sanctuary with Red Cloud's people at Pine Ridge. Progress was slow, however, and Big Foot became seriously ill with pneumonia during the journey. The group was eventually intercepted by members of the Seventh Cavalry, the same division that suffered devastating losses more than a decade earlier at the Battle of the Little Bighorn. Big Foot's people, in the custody of the soldiers, camped near Wounded Knee Creek on December 28, 1890.

The following morning, the soldiers ordered Big Foot's people to turn over all weapons before being taken to their new reservation. The disarmament went smoothly at first, until a single warrior refused to give up his gun. In *Black Elk Speaks*, Black Elk's friend Dog Chief identifies this man as Yellow Bird; however, Dee Brown, in his comprehensive work *Bury My Heart at Wounded Knee*, contends that the lone holdout was a deaf Minneconjou named Black Coyote. In any case, a scuffle ensued, during which a shot was fired. This caused the gathered military forces, which had the camp virtually surrounded, to open fire on all the Indians in the camp, including women and children.

Although many of the soldiers involved were awarded medals for their efforts, the events at Wounded Knee were infamous among those who knew the facts surrounding them. Even General Nelson Miles, the commander in charge of the officers who took part in the Wounded Knee incident, considered the event an unjustified massacre. L. Frank Baum, working as the editor of a South Dakota paper called the *Saturday Pioneer*, called the incident "a disgrace to the war department." The incident at Wounded Knee is often considered the final battle of the Indian Wars.

The Ghost Dance Movement

In 1889, a Nevada Paiute Indian prophet named Wovoka—also known as Jack Wilson—claimed to have experienced a vision that could help uplift not only his fellow Paiutes, but all Native American people. In this vision, which reportedly occurred during a solar eclipse, Wovoka claimed that God showed him his ancestors existing in a land of plentiful resources. God assured Wovoka that if his people no longer made war with the whites, they would be able to live in this land of peace and plenty with their ancestors. The vision was recreated by Wovoka and his people as a ceremonial dance, and soon members of other tribes came to see the dance—later called the "Ghost Dance"—and hear of Wovoka's vision.

The dance became wildly popular among many tribes across the western United States, and as it grew, so did the interpretations of Wovoka's vision. For believers among the Sioux tribes of the Great Plains, the vision suggested that all white settlers and soldiers would be erased from their lands, the Sioux's dead ancestors would rise, and abundant herds of buffalo would be restored to the plains within two years. In addition, many warriors believed that if they wore sacred "ghost shirts" into battle, they could not be wounded by the bullets of white soldiers. By 1890, ghost dances were being performed on reservations across the Great Plains; as conditions worsened for the reservation-bound Sioux facing starvation, the ceremonies became more prevalent. The U.S. Army, fearing the movement would lead to a violent uprising, placed a limit on the number of ceremonies that could be performed each month. Ultimately, after the death of Sitting Bull and subsequent massacre of hundreds of Sioux at Wounded Knee in 1890, many Sioux followers lost faith in the power of the Ghost Dance, and the movement faded away as quickly as it had begun.

CRITICAL OVERVIEW

When *Black Elk Speaks* was originally published in 1932, there were few written accounts of the events of the Old West told from the point of view of an American Indian. For this reason, the book was welcomed as a valuable testament from an individual directly involved in many important historical events.

John Chamberlain, in a review for the *New York Times*, proclaims that "the story of Black Elk . . . is one of the saddest and noblest that has ever been told." He notes that Black Elk's description of events from his early life form an "excellent straightforward narrative," and that "years of attrition have sharpened the memory of the ancient Sioux; brooding has greatly magnified his evocative powers." Chamberlain's only criticism is that the account of Black Elk's visions was "amorphous and vague," and he claims, "It is only when this Indian holy man comes to describe his 'visions' that the white-skinned reader is at a loss." However, an unnamed reviewer for the *Boston Transcript* points to Black Elk's descriptions of his visions as one of the book's strengths: "His accounts of his visions, and of the great tribal dances he carried out according to instructions received in these visions—particularly the Horse Dance, a memory of the Great Vision, are uniquely thrilling."

Many reviewers were especially impressed with the authenticity of a narrative that was translated from Black Elk's native Oglala tongue, and therefore required great effort and care to recreate in English. W. R. Brooks, in a review for *Outlook*, asserts that Neihardt's close collaboration with Black Elk "is about as near as you can get to seeing life and death, war and religion, through an Indian's eyes." Paul Horgan, writing for the *Yale Review*, calls the book a "story of the simplest impressiveness," and applauds that both Neihardt and Black Elk "did their jobs with dignity and regard for the past which they both cherish." C. L. Skinner, in a review for *Books*, states, "No unprejudiced reader will doubt that John Neihardt has set down honestly what Black Elk told him, with occasional corroborative statements from Standing Bear, Fire Thunder and Iron Hawk." In a review for the *New Republic*, M. W. Childs expresses a similar sentiment: "Throughout, it is apparent that Mr. Neihardt has set his sensitive poet's mind the task of recording faithfully and without intrusion Black Elk's words. He has been a keen and scrupulous editor."

Later critics have not been quite so kind to Neihardt's methods. G. Thomas Couser in particular leveled numerous criticisms at the book; in his 1989 essay "Black Elk Speaks With Forked Tongue," he argues that Black Elk's testimony in the book is inauthentic because "we see Black Elk not face to face, but through the gloss of a white man—a translation whose surface obscures Black Elk by reflecting the culture of his collaborator." The Bison Books edition of *Black Elk Speaks*, perhaps in an attempt to respond to such criticisms, includes an appendix comparing a passage from Black Elk's original translated transcript to Neihardt's handwritten draft of the same passage. In any case, such criticisms only call into question the book's standing as a

MEDIA ADAPTATIONS

Christopher Sergel adapted *Black Elk Speaks* as a stage play in 1996. It is available from Dramatic Publishing.

An abridged audio recording of *Black Elk Speaks* was released by Audio Literature in 1998. It is available on cassette tape and narrated by Fred Contreras.

genuine memoir and do not diminish its status as an illuminating piece of literature.

Despite positive reviews on its initial release, the book failed to make a significant impact with the public—then in the midst of the Great Depression. As Neihardt notes in his preface to the 1972 edition of the book, "In less than two years the publisher 'remaindered' the edition at forty-five cents a copy and the book was forgotten." However, subsequent editions have proven to be far more successful, much to Neihardt's satisfaction: "The old prophet's wish that I bring his message to the world is actually being fulfilled."

CRITICISM

G. Thomas Couser

In the following excerpt, Couser argues that, despite its reknown, Black Elk Speaks *is not a reliable picture of Lakota culture, but rather suffers as a result of the undue influence of the autobiography's white co-author.*

Alone among similar books, *Black Elk Speaks, Being the Life Story of a Holy Man of the Oglala Sioux,* as told through John G. Neihardt (1932), has enjoyed both popular and critical acclaim. Since the 1960s, it has been something of a cult classic, and until quite recently, scholars and critics extolled it as an authentic and authoritative Native American autobiography—indeed, perhaps the only one.

Euramerican critics set it apart from the narratives gathered lily anthropologists on the basis of its literary merit. It was also cited respectfully by prominent Native Americans: William Least Heat Moon paid homage to it in his bestseller, *Blue Highways* (1982), and it was invoked in the mid-1980s by Sioux attempting to regain control of sacred lands from the federal government. Its status was such that Vine Deloria not only published an edition in 1979, but declined, in his introduction, to inquire into the problems of its genesis, authorship, and editing. It was virtually canonized, then, both as aboriginal autobiography and as Lakota prophesy.

The notion of the text as one that offers a valid, even invaluable, insight into Lakota culture rested for a long time on Neihardt's own account of the collaboration—first offered in his preface to the book and later supplemented in interviews with scholars—and on a reading of the text in isolation from the transcripts. Given the book's reputation as a paragon of Native American autobiography and of bicultural collaboration, its inability to stand up to recent scrutiny is particularly distressing. Despite Neihardt's talent, empathy, and good intentions, *Black Elk Speaks* has proven to be not nearly as reliable as it appears, or was made out to be. In it, we see Black Elk not face to face, but through the gloss of a white man—a translation whose surface obscures Black Elk by reflecting the culture of his collaborator.

The difficulty of rendering a Lakota narrative into English is complicated by the problem of transforming oral into printed materials. Dennis Tedlock has argued that the performative qualities of oral literature—gesture, tone, timing, and sound effects—can be suggested, in freshly recorded narratives, by means of typographical effects, and Dell Hymes has shown how oral literature can be recuperated from transcripts. Neither of these ingenious attempts to recreate oral forms in print helps much with *Black Elk Speaks*, however, because of its complicated ontogeny. Black Elk's Lakota was first translated into idiomatic "Indian English" by his son, Ben Black Elk. In turn, that translation was rendered into standard English by Neihardt, and recorded stenographically by his daughter. Later, at a geographical (and cultural) distance, Neihardt revised and edited the transcripts. The final text is so many removes from its source that the original language and gestures are irrecoverable.

A portrait of an Oglala warrior, His Fights, who took part in the Battle of Little Bighorn © *Corbis*

Thus, a scholar interested in assessing the accuracy, or faithfulness, of Neihardt's "translation" soon reaches an impasse: one cannot compare Neihardt's prose to the original Lakota, which vanished upon utterance.

Neither could Neihardt. Since he spoke no Lakota, and Black Elk spoke no English, the language of *Black Elk Speaks* was produced without being checked either against the original or by its originator. Thanks to Raymond J. DeMallie, however, one can now compare Neihardt's text to the transcripts. A look at them reveals the extent to which Neihardt is responsible for the readability and the dignified and consistent tone of *Black Elk Speaks*—confirming Dell Hymes's argument that literal translations of oral materials are generally most valuable, since "literary" patterns are more often imposed on, than discovered in, native materials. The transcripts reveal that Neihardt was editing in terms of white preconceptions about what Lakota "longhairs" *ought* to be sound like. Even DeMallie, who claims that Neihardt's free translation is likely to be "more faithful to the intended meaning than a strictly verbatim recording," concedes: "In a sense, Neihardt was already 'writing' Black Elk's story by rephrasing his words into English." For this project, Neihardt's vaunted poetic talent may have been a liability rather than an asset.

In addition to the problems inherent in bicultural collaboration, there is the perplexing visionary dimension of *Black Elk Speaks*. Of course, this is one of the features that has caused it to be prized above other Native American autobiographies. It greatly complicates the book, however, making it ghostwritten in two profoundly different and competing senses. As a visionary narrative, it is ghostwritten in the sense that it originates with the ghosts of ancestors and the spirits of the earth, rather than with a living individual. (Black Elk's authorship is that of augmentation: he is essentially a custodian and transmitter of a tribal legacy.) But it is also ghostwritten in the sense that it is conveyed to the page by a surrogate, amanuensis, collaborator—call him what you will. The vision, therefore, if not the entire narrative, is twice mediated: first from his ancestors through Black Elk, and then from Black Elk through Neihardt. (Unlike the poet, the holy man admits that the vision is ineffable and that he is an imperfect vehicle.) In spite of Black Elk's efforts to locate the narrative's authority in a communal and transcendent source, the basis for that authority has slowly but inexorably shifted: from the supernatural to the secular, the tribal to the individual, the Lakota to the English, and the visionary and oral to the written and printed.

DeMallie's publication of the transcripts also makes very clear one of Neihardt's editorial practices—the consistent suppression of Black Elk's awareness of white culture and technology. When this extends to the substitution of descriptive phrases for the names of certain cities, the result is sometimes ironic, if not comic: Omaha becomes "a very big town" and Chicago "a much bigger town." Without knowing what Black Elk's locutions were, we should not make too much of this. But Neihardt's expunging of Biblical phrases such as "many were called but few were chosen" serves to conceal crucial facts about Black Elk (facts still not known to many readers of the book): he became a Roman Catholic early in this century and, more startling perhaps, served as a catechist and missionary to other Sioux for a period of decades thereafter.

It is never easy to identify individual contributions to a collaboratively produced text, but

given the politically sensitive nature of boundaries in the history of white-Indian relations, producers and consumers of bicultural texts need to demonstrate particular tact in this regard. In this case, the efforts of scholars to determine the respective contributions of John Neihardt and Black Elk have yielded especially interesting—and damaging—revelations. For example, in an interview with Sally McCluskey shortly before he died, Neihardt declared that the narrative's very first lines were his own creation: "My friend, I am going to tell you the story of my life, as you wish; and if it were only the story of my life, I think I would not tell it." Here "Black Elk" concedes more than he knows, since his story will be told not so much *in response to* the white man's request ("as you wish") as *in the way that* Neihardt desires (or, in effect, wills).

Thus, the opening uncannily betrays white encroachment on native grounds.

In effect, what we have here is not Black Elk speaking through the passive medium of John Neihardt; it is Neihardt, self-proclaimed author of the book, speaking through the mask of Black Elk (i.e., creating a literary character by means of invented speech). While the opening words appear to be Black Elk's explanation to his collaborator of the distinctively tribal nature of the story he is about to convey, they are in fact Neihardt's justification to his reader of a feature of the text—its tribal focus—that his own editing had already diminished. Moreover, the opening passage brings the text into conformity with mainstream models: Franklin, Thoreau, and Adams—to name a few canonical American autobiographers—all begin their narratives with gambits that deflect the charge of egotism. In the case of Black Elk, the gesture is made necessary only by the preconceptions of his editor about "autobiography."

Intended to correct the impression that he had merely recorded the narrative, Neihardt's interview with McCluskey made it evident that Black Elk's speech had not been translated, but transformed-and at times invented. (Ironically, as DeMallie points out, the text's most frequently quoted passages are ones for which Neihardt has claimed authority.) It also retroactively blurred the boundary Neihardt had originally drawn—by means of the shift from "frame" to "narrative" and by the deployment of first- and second-person pronouns-between his textual space and Black Elk's. Other problematic features of the narrative suggest that what is true in one sense of the opening paragraphs is true in another of the entire text: it is an act of bicultural ventriloquism.

The ending also reveals Neihardt's designs and preconception. In claiming credit for the narrative's organization, in his interview with McCluskey, he asserted that he concluded it with the Battle of Wounded Knee because he considered that to be its most dramatic event. He also acknowledged that he shaped the whole for a white audience: "The translation—or rather the *transformation*—of what was given to me was expressed so that it could be understood by the white world." It should be remembered here that when Neihardt first approached Black Elk, he was seeking material about the Ghost Dance religion for his poem cycle, which was to end with that battle as the climax of white conquest of the West. Though a different book resulted from his visit, the ending was the same; in this sense, at least, it was a foregone conclusion.

The effect of Neihardt's editing is to stop the clock on Lakota life, in both its personal and communal dimensions, and thus to threaten its legacy. Indeed, ending the narrative so *conclusively* with the Battle of Wounded Knee is the literary equivalent of killing off the survivors—a kind of metaphorical genocide. The conclusion encourages white readers to indulge in uncomplicated pathos at the demise of a noble (savage) way of life rather than to compel them to contemplate its tenuous survival in assimilated forms. While Neihardt translates the vision in a compelling—because preternaturally clear—prose, he fails to devise a narrative form that can present it in any but a pathetic and nostalgic way. His book does not entirely transcend that romantic cliché—the song of the dying Indian.

Neihardt's narrative speaks with a forked tongue in several senses. (In the transcripts, though Black Elk complained about the Wasichus' lies, he never uses the phrase "forked tongue.") It speaks with a cloven tongue in the way that all collaborative autobiography does because it conflates two consciousnesses (and in this case languages and cultures) in one undifferentiated voice. It also misleads by not fully acknowledging the extent and the tendencies of its editing. Thus, the book's greatest deception is its most subtle one—its pretense that its own production escaped the cultural imperialism that it condemns. The preface claims that the collaboration was mutual and egalitarian—in effect, that it took place outside of the historical conditions it describes. But the editing is clearly implicated in—and thus encodes—cultural imperialism.

Thus, finally, the text *undoes* what it says: it reenacts the process it condemns. Black Elk repeatedly refers to his present predicament, and his vision points to a distant future, but the narrative produced is largely retrospective. Black Elk's "failure" to narrate events in temporal sequence is "corrected" by Neihardt's editing, and the narrative's truncation severs the tragic past from the present. Black Elk remains marooned in time, and confined to rectangles of print surrounded by white space. His speech is preserved here as Lakota culture is preserved on the reservation: in conditions neither wholly of its making nor freely of its choosing. Neihardt is also caught in a trap of his own creation. In treating the narrative as autobiography (rather than as sacred history), he made it less tribal, but in trying to make it more traditional (editing out evidence of Black Elk's assimilation), he made it less autobiographical (a less accurate expression of Black Elk's life and being), until *Native American autobiography* is revealed to be a misnomer, if not an oxymoron.

Source: G. Thomas Couser, "Black Elk Speaks With Forked Tongue," in *Altered Egos: Authority in American Autobiography*, Oxford University Press, 1989, pp.189–209.

SOURCES

Baum, L. Frank, editorial on the incident at Wounded Knee, in the *Saturday Pioneer*, January 3, 1891; reprinted in *L. Frank Baum's Editorials on the Sioux Nation*, www.northern.edu/hastingw/baumedts.htm (August 31, 2006).

Brooks, W. R., Review of *Black Elk Speaks*, in *Outlook*, Vol. 160, March 1932, p. 194; reprinted in *The Book Review Digest: Twenty-Eighth Annual Cumulation*, H. W. Wilson, 1933, p. 91.

Brown, Dee, *Bury My Heart at Wounded Knee: An Indian History of the American West*, Holt, Reinhart & Winston, 1971; reprint, Owl Books, 2001, p. 297.

Chamberlain, John, "A Sioux Indian Tells a Tragic Story (Review of *Black Elk Speaks*)," in the *New York Times Book Review*, March 6, 1932, p. 4.

Childs, M. W., Review of *Black Elk Speaks*, in the *New Republic*, Vol. 71, June 22, 1932, p. 161; reprinted in the *Book Review Digest: Twenty-Eighth Annual Cumulation*, H. W. Wilson, 1933, p. 91.

Couser, G. Thomas, "Black Elk Speaks With Forked Tongue," from *Altered Egos: Authority in American Autobiography*, Oxford University Press, 1989, p. 190.

Deloria, Vine, Jr., "Foreword," in *Black Elk Speaks*, University of Nebraska Press, 2004.

Horgan, Paul, Review of *Black Elk Speaks*, in the *Yale Review*, Vol. 22, Autumn 1932, p. 206; reprinted in the *Book Review Digest: Twenty-Eighth Annual Cumulation*, H. W. Wilson, 1933, p. 91.

Neihardt, John G., *Black Elk Speaks*, W. Morrow, 1932; reprint, University of Nebraska Press, 2004.

Review of *Black Elk Speaks*, in the *Boston Transcript*, March 9, 1932, p. 2; reprinted in the *Book Review Digest: Twenty-Eighth Annual Cumulation*, H. W. Wilson, 1933, p. 91.

Skinner, C. L., Review of *Black Elk Speaks*, in *Books*, February 21, 1932, p. 3; reprinted in the *Book Review Digest: Twenty-Eighth Annual Cumulation*, H. W. Wilson, 1933, p. 91.

Call It Sleep

HENRY ROTH

1934

Henry Roth's 1934 novel *Call It Sleep* is based loosely on the author's own experiences growing up as a Jewish American in New York City during the early 1900s. In the novel, David Schearl is a young boy who must come to terms with conflicting forces in an effort to forge his own identity. The conflicting forces include intense love for and dependence on his mother Genya coupled with fear and hatred for his unstable father Albert. David must also reconcile his Jewish heritage with both his mainstream American tendencies and his curiosity about other cultures and religions.

The novel is notable for its use of Yiddish both directly and indirectly through character dialogue. Most of the dialogue spoken in the Schearl household is in Yiddish, but it is transcribed for the reader in deliberately formal and elegant phrasing. By contrast, the language David and his friends use in the streets is rough, profane, and so heavily seasoned with dialect that it can be difficult to understand. For example, "W'od id 'ey do t'yuh in de polliss station?" is what one character asks after David returns from a brief episode at a local police station. This turns the table on the reader, clearly illustrating the struggles immigrants face when trying to communicate in a language that is not natively their own. The author does this by transforming Yiddish into easily understood English, and transforming English into a daunting collection of strange sounds.

BIOGRAPHY

HENRY ROTH

Herschel Roth was born on February 8, 1906, in the Austro-Hungarian region of Galitzia (also spelled Galicia), in present-day Ukraine. His family immigrated to the United States while he was still a baby, and as a child he lived for several years on New York's Lower East Side, the setting for *Call It Sleep*.

Roth became interested in writing after being exposed by university friends to authors such as T. S. Eliot and James Joyce, the latter of whose stream-of-consciousness experimentation with language had a profound impact on Roth's own writing. His first novel, *Call It Sleep*, was published in 1934 to excellent reviews but poor sales.

Although Roth still occasionally sold short story to magazines such as the *New Yorker*, he gave up on writing as a primary occupation and became a poultry farmer in Maine. Thirty years after its initial publication, *Call It Sleep* experienced a resurgence in popularity and became a bestseller. Over the next three decades, Roth returned to writing, creating six volumes of a semi-autobiographical series known collectively as *Mercy of a Rude Stream*. Two of the volumes were published prior to the author's death on October 13, 1995, at the age of eighty-nine. Two more volumes were published posthumously. As of 2007, the final two volumes remain unpublished.

Call It Sleep was first published in the middle of the Great Depression, and it was consequently overlooked by many mainstream readers at the time. Although Roth still wrote occasional short stories after the novel's poor performance, he relied on alternate careers to support himself for the next thirty years. It was only in the 1960s, when the novel was rediscovered by critics and readers alike, that Roth was finally able to once again return to writing as more than just a hobby.

Call It Sleep offers a view of the American dream through the eyes of an immigrant child. In addition, the book has earned its place as an enduring document of the Jewish American experience. As Alfred Kazin writes in his introduction to the Picador paperback edition of the novel,

> Though the book was not properly welcomed or understood until it was reissued in paperback in 1964, it has become a world favorite, with millions of copies in print. We can see now that the book belongs to the side of the 1930s that still believed in the sacredness of literature, whether or not it presumed to change the world.

PLOT SUMMARY

Prologue

The year is 1907, a year "destined to bring the greatest number of immigrants to the shores of the United States." On a ferry from Ellis Island to Manhattan, a newly arrived woman and her son travel with her husband, who has already been living in America, working and preparing the home for his family's arrival. They are Jewish and speak to each other in Yiddish. The woman apologizes to her husband, revealing that she could not recognize him when she first saw him at Ellis Island. She tells him that he looks different from when she last saw him in Europe: "Then here in the new land is the same old poverty. You've gone without food. I can see it. You've changed."

The husband is also upset at his wife for not telling the officials that their son is only seventeen months old, which would have saved half the fare they had to pay. The woman argues that the officials would not have believed her because he is so big. The husband asks if she brought the child's birth certificate, but the woman is unsure. The boy wears a straw hat with polka-dot ribbons; the father tells the mother to take it off the boy because it looks silly. When the mother hesitates, the father pulls off the hat and tosses it into the water.

Book 1: The Cellar
Chapters 1–9

Four years later, the boy—whose name is David Schearl—is almost six years old. The family lives in an apartment in the Brownsville neighborhood of New York City. David's father works as a printer; David saves the pages of the daily calendar in their home because his father made it. At the bottom of the stairs leading to their apartment is a cellar door that "bulged with darkness." David fears what lurks behind the door.

One day, David is taken across town by his father, Albert. He is directed to enter, by himself, the printing office where Albert worked, and to ask for his father's personal belongings and final pay. Inside, David is told that Albert nearly killed another employee with a hammer. Several people mention to David that his father is crazy. When David emerges with his father's clothes and money, Albert interrogates him about the people inside. David lies and says the people inside said nothing to him.

Albert gets a new printing job and befriends a foreman named Joe Luter, who hails from the same part of Austria as Albert. Luter is invited to join the family for dinner, and David notices that Luter's presence causes his father to be much more pleasant than usual. Still, David cannot bring himself to like Luter. One night, when Luter has arranged for Albert to go to the theatre alone, Luter returns to the Schearl house to retrieve a package he has forgotten. He makes sly advances toward David's mother—in front of David, who rarely leaves his mother's company—but she politely rebuffs him.

A week later, David's mother takes him to visit their upstairs neighbors, the Minks. Mrs. Mink has a son, Yussie, about the same age as David, and an older daughter named Annie who has a metal brace on one leg. The three children play hide and seek until Yussie is called away to go buy bread. Annie then leads David into a closet to "play bad." He is horrified by what she wants him to do, and he flees to his mother's side in the kitchen. They depart, with David's mother unaware of Annie's actions: "But she didn't know as he knew how the whole world could break into a thousand little pieces, all buzzing, all whining, and no one hearing them and no one seeing them except himself."

David spends the next day avoiding Annie and Yussie. On his way home, he sees a funeral carriage and asks his mother about death and the afterlife. Her answers about what happens to the dead are honest and blunt: "I only know that they are buried in the dark earth and their names last a few more lifetimes on their gravestones."

Chapters 10–16

Luter visits the Schearls for dinner one night but cuts short his visit, and tells them he will not be able to join them for dinner later in the week. After he leaves, Albert reveals that Luter is going to visit a marriage broker, and that Luter has asked Albert to work some overtime at the shop. After dinner, a strange course of events results in David accidentally injuring Yussie, and David subsequently getting beaten by his father with a clothes hanger. David's mother puts an end to the beating, and tells Albert that he will never again strike their son.

Soon after, while David is outside playing with some other boys, he sees Luter enter his family's building while only his mother is home. Immediately after, Yussie confronts David over his injury and challenges him to a fight. The boys all gang up on David, and he strikes one boy to the ground as he flees into his building. Fearful that the boy has been injured, and unable to go to his mother because of Luter, David faces his fear and hides in the cellar: "It was horrible, the dark. The rats lived there, the hordes of nightmare, the wobbly faces, the crawling and misshapen things." After several minutes, David can no longer remain in the cellar and rushes out into the street; he runs away quickly, hoping no one follows.

When he finally grows tired, he begins retracing his route back home. He soon discovers that he is lost, and no one can understand the name of his street, which he pronounces "Boddeh." A woman takes him to the nearest police station, where they eventually figure out the correct street: Barhdee. His mother picks him up soon after and takes him home. Although he never mentions it to her, David cannot escape the thought that his mother "played bad" with Luter when he came to visit.

The next time Luter is expected for dinner, he cancels. David's father detects a sudden change in Luter, as if the man is trying to end their friendship. Soon after, Albert comes home from work with a bandage on his right hand. He has injured it in the printing press, and he blames Luter's coldness for distracting him from his work. He vows never to return to his job and never to work on a printing press again. Yussie stops by, and David makes peace with him and the other boy David had knocked down while fleeing on the day he got lost.

A group of Jewish immigrants take home free matzos, New York City, 1908 © *Corbis*

Book 2: The Picture
Chapters 1–9

Two months later, David's father finds a new job as a milkman, and the family moves to a new neighborhood. They live on the fourth floor of their apartment building; instead of a stairway to the cellar, David is now confronted by a stairway to the roof: "They were inviolable those stairs, guarding the light and silence."

In May, just three months after the family moves in, David's Aunt Bertha—one of his mother's younger sisters—comes to live in America. David's father reluctantly agrees to let her live in the apartment for a while. Bertha is a plump, red-haired woman who always looks messy, sweats profusely, and speaks with a sharp tongue. This last trait results in countless arguments with David's father.

When Aunt Bertha develops severe toothaches, she visits the dentist and discovers she must have six teeth extracted. She begins making frequent visits to the dentist—at first reluctantly, but soon with a strange anticipation. Soon enough she tells her sister that she has met a potential suitor at the dentist's office, a

man named Nathan Sternowitz. Nathan is a Russian American widower with two daughters, aged ten and eleven. When Bertha makes plans to bring him to dinner, David's mother buys a picture of corn stalks and cornflowers to decorate their apartment. She tells David that it reminds her of where she grew up.

One Sunday, while David's father is out, his mother finally reveals to Aunt Bertha a secret she has been keeping since before she came to America. The two women talk in a mixture of Polish and Yiddish; David tries to listen, but can only make out small pieces of their dialogue. He hears enough to understand that his mother had a relationship with a non-Jewish organist at a local church where they lived, and her parents feared a scandal would emerge. Six months later his mother met Albert, and did not speak of the organist again.

Book 3: The Coal
Chapters 1–9

In February, David's father decides that it is time for David to attend a cheder, or religious class taught by a rabbi. The rabbi, Reb Yidel

Pankower, is a stern instructor who strikes his students whenever they make mistakes. David performs well, however, and is especially intrigued when the rabbi tells his students of Isaiah's purification with a fiery coal, brought down to him by an angel.

One day, David is accosted by several white boys who insist on showing him some "magic." They take him to Tenth Street, where there are electrified trolley car tracks, and tell him to throw a piece of metal across the tracks. He does as they command, and the metal ignites in a flash of light. Terrified and awed, David runs to his cheder. He tells the rabbi that he has seen a coal, like Isaiah, in the crack of the trolley car tracks. The rabbi laughs and calls David a fool: "God's light is not between car-tracks." To David, however, the light signifies a great power that the rabbi does not understand.

Book 4: The Rail
Chapters 1–6

Months later, David is told that he must go with his father on a milk delivery route. It is not his father's normal route, and his father does not want to leave the wagon unattended for fear of thieves in the neighborhood. David's job is simply to stay with the wagon while his father makes deliveries within the buildings. While David is sitting with the cart, two men in tatters approach him and attempt to get him away from the cart. When David refuses to move, the men simply take two bottles of milk and tell David that they will pay his father. David knows better, but he is powerless to stop the two. When his father returns, David tells him about the two thieves. His father chases them down with his wagon and beats them with his fists and his horse-whip. He warns David not to tell his mother what has happened.

After the incident, David attends cheder. On his way home, he sees some neighborhood boys trying to capture an escaped canary perched on the house next to his. He later hears the same boys talking about how they had seen a naked woman in one of the apartments while looking for the canary, and he quickly realizes that they are talking about his mother. He flees to the sanctuary of his building's roof and is calmed by the peace he finds there.

Chapters 7–14

The next morning, David returns to the roof. He is surprised when another boy appears on the neighboring roof with a kite. The boy, a Polish American named Leo, seems to befriend David at first even though Leo is older. However, Leo later suggests that he does not want to spend time with David unless David can go skating with him.

Thinking his Aunt Bertha might have skates in the candy shop she has opened with her new husband Nathan, David goes to visit her the next day. He is disappointed when she has nothing for him except candy. While David is there, Bertha asks him to wake up her two stepdaughters, Polly and Esther. He does, and Esther, afraid of the dark, convinces him to go downstairs to the cellar bathroom with her so she can use it. While in the bathroom, Esther tells David he can watch her if he wants, but he does not want to.

Returning home, David discovers that Leo has been looking for him. He visits Leo's apartment, and he is intrigued by the Christian artifacts he sees there. He asks Leo if he can have one, but Leo refuses. After hearing about David's cousin Esther at the candy store, however—and how she wanted David to follow her down into the cellar—Leo offers David a broken rosary if he will take Leo to meet her. David reluctantly agrees to take Leo to the candy store the following morning.

The next morning, David changes his mind and tries to avoid Leo, but Leo catches him. The boys travel to the candy store and sneak into his aunt's yard, where they find Esther. Leo convinces Esther to come into the street and take skating lessons from him, and then he leads her into the basement where he forces himself on her in the dark. David, who has been given the rosary for the part he played, does not know what to do, and he simply hides. Esther's sister Polly hears the commotion and investigates; she is shocked to see a strange boy in the basement with Esther, and threatens to tell their parents. As Esther tries to explain what really happened, David is revealed and runs away to his cheder.

Chapters 15–19

At cheder, David reads for his rabbi and a visiting rabbi. Both are impressed with his abilities, but he breaks down in the middle of his recitation. When the rabbi asks what is wrong, David invents a fantastic story: He has just learned from his Aunt Bertha that his mother is not really his mother. He has also learned that his real father is a non-Jewish organist who lives somewhere in Europe. David is excused from the cheder and runs away. His rabbi decides to visit David's mother and repeat David's story.

Back at the candy store, Bertha and her husband Nathan find out about Leo's assault on Esther. Nathan first blames Bertha, and then decides to go to David's home and tell his mother of the part David played in the affair. Bertha pursues him all the way, trying to stop him.

David finally gets home and discovers that the rabbi is there. The rabbi has told David's parents of his strange tale and learned that David was lying. When the rabbi leaves, however, David's father Albert finally feels that his own longtime suspicions are justified. Albert believes that he is not really David's father, and that much of what David said is actually true. Suddenly Bertha and Nathan arrive at the apartment, with Nathan intending to confront David's parents about their boy's wicked behavior. Bertha attempts to silence her husband, but David blurts out a confession. David's father—no longer believing he is the boy's father—seizes him and begins whipping him with his horse whip. As he does, the broken rosary given to David by Leo falls out of the boy's pocket. David's father sees this as a final confirmation that David is the bastard son of a non-Jew. David's father threatens to kill the boy, to "rid the world of a sin," but David flees the apartment, into the streets.

Chapters 20–21

David takes a zinc-coated ladle from a milk can and travels to Tenth Street, where he had once seen the electrified trolley tracks give off light like Isaiah's coal. He puts the ladle into the tracks, and he is still touching it when the electrical burst hits: "*The hawk of radiance raking him with / talons of fire, battering his skull with / a beak of fire, praying his body with / pinions of intolerable light.*" The resulting electrical burst knocks him out cold. Many of the passersby believe the boy is dead, but a doctor revives him with smelling salts. His ankle is hurt, but otherwise he seems fine. The doctor and a policeman take the boy home on an ambulance wagon. Bertha and Nathan are gone, and the argument between David's parents has cooled. David's

> BEFORE HER THE GRIMY CUPOLAS AND TOWERING SQUARE WALLS OF THE CITY LOOMED UP. ABOVE THE JAGGED ROOF TOPS, THE WHITE SMOKE, WHITENED AND SUFFUSED BY THE SLANTING SUN, FADED INTO THE SLOTS AND WEDGES OF THE SKY. SHE PRESSED HER BROW AGAINST HER CHILD'S, HUSHED HIM WITH WHISPERS. THIS WAS THAT VAST INCREDIBLE LAND, THE LAND OF FREEDOM, OF IMMENSE OPPORTUNITY, THAT GOLDEN LAND. AGAIN SHE TRIED TO SMILE."

father asks his mother if she blames him for David's injury. She tells him, "None foresaw this. No one alone brought it on. And if it's faults we must talk about it's mine as well." The family once again achieves a tentative peace as David closes his eyes: "One might as well call it sleep."

THEMES

Opportunity

One of the driving themes at work in *Call It Sleep* is the theme of opportunity. At the beginning of the novel, the Schearls travel to America in an attempt to seize the opportunities presented by what David's mother calls "the Golden Land." Although the family lives in an area that many would refer to as a slum, and children's luxuries such as roller skates are almost unheard of, the Schearls enjoy many opportunities throughout the novel that they might not experience elsewhere.

Albert Schearl, David's father, is a paranoid man who seems to have a difficult time remaining at a job for any extended period of time. As David learns early in the book, his father is prone to violent outbursts and anxieties that threaten both his co-workers and himself. However, Albert never seems to have trouble finding a new job. Indeed, when he decides to quit the printing business altogether, he simply changes careers and becomes a milkman with a minimum of difficulty. Though this brand of economic opportunity seems to pass without remark in the novel, it represents an important facet of the American immigrant lifestyle during this period.

Similarly, David's Aunt Bertha and her husband Nathan take advantage of the economic opportunities they are presented in America. When she first travels to the United States, Bertha works as a seamstress; when she meets Nathan, he makes children's leggings. Though they have modest means, the two decide to open a candy shop. This significant event happens, with barely a mention, in between the more important events in the novel. The opportunity to start a new business or career is recognized, taken as a given, and frequently exercised by the immigrants in the novel.

Plurality of Cultures

Throughout *Call It Sleep*, David interacts with members of many different cultural and ethnic groups. The novel offers a rich and evocative portrayal of the United States in general, and New York's Lower East Side in particular, as a true melting pot for many of the world's cultures.

One inventive way in which Roth conveys this plurality is through dialect. In addition to accurately depicting the accents of Jewish Americans, the author uses accent and dialect to identify other cultures without the need for further elaboration. For example, when David gets lost and is taken to the police station, the helmeted police officer he meets is clearly Irish American, though this fact is revealed exclusively through his speech with lines like, "Step up close an' do yer dooty, sonny me boy."

This mix of cultures reaches a crescendo at the end of the novel, as David lies unconscious in the street after dropping the dipper on the electrified rail. The spectators from the neighborhood are never described; the reader only hears their voices, just as David would. As Hana Wirth-Nesher indicates in her afterword to the novel, "In the reported speech of the bystanders, Roth makes use of dialect: Yiddish, German, Irish, and Italian, and selective reproduction of other languages, namely Yiddish and Italian." These bystanders all come together in an effort to help David.

Search for Identity

Call It Sleep focuses on the individual's search for identity in two ways. First, the book deals with David's growth from childhood into adolescence, and the challenges of discovering his own identity as a person distinct from his parents. This is difficult, as his father's reputation often precedes him. When David has to pick up his father's final pay at one of the printing offices where his father worked, the other employees comment on how much he resembles his father, though they note that he does not look or act crazy like his father did. As David grows up, he meets new people who do not know him through his parents, and he is finally able to develop his own personality and identity.

The second way in which *Call It Sleep* deals with identity is through David's cultural experiences. Although he is a Jew, David at first has little understanding of what that means. It is only when he attends cheder that he begins to get a sense of the meaning behind Jewish culture and religion. At the same time, he becomes exposed to other religions and cultures, and incorporates elements from these into his own identity. His friend Leo introduces David to Christianity through Catholicism; he is fascinated by the apparatuses of faith such as crucifixes and rosary beads. They seem to represent a mystical power that Judaism does not offer him. Although these elements might seem mutually exclusive to others—such as Leo, who tells David that the Jews are responsible for Christ's death—they become incorporated into David's newly formed identity as a Jewish American.

HISTORICAL OVERVIEW

Manhattan's Lower East Side

Much of *Call It Sleep* is set in the Lower East Side of Manhattan in New York City. The area has a rich history stemming largely from its substantial immigrant population and its unique origins. Although New York City consists of four other boroughs in addition to Manhattan, this area is often considered to be the heart and core of the city from an economic and geographic standpoint.

The island of Manhattan, which is separated from mainland New York by the Hudson, East, and Harlem Rivers, was settled by the Dutch in the 1620s after it was purchased from a local American

Indian tribe by representative Peter Minuit. The settlement was named New Amsterdam, and it operated under Dutch rule until the region was turned over to England fifty years later. The terms of England's annexation allowed the region to retain much of its tolerant cultural heritage, a feature that would later result in the area being viewed as a "melting pot" of various cultures.

The Lower East Side of Manhattan in particular served as the repository for many of the immigrants that journeyed to America in search of freedom and opportunity throughout the nineteenth and twentieth centuries. The island's population peaked around 1910 with well over 2.5 million residents, many of whom lived in tenements found on the Lower East Side. In addition to its substantial immigrant population, the Lower East Side has served as an important center for the arts, as well as a nexus for many activist political movements.

American Immigrants in the Early Twentieth Century

The New York depicted in Henry Roth's *Call It Sleep* is a New York shaped by the rapid influx of immigrants during the late nineteenth and early twentieth centuries. In the novel, Roth refers to 1907, the year in which David and his mother Genya Schearl arrive in America, as "the year that was destined to bring the greatest number of immigrants to the shores of the United States."

Immigration to the United States was negligible prior to the middle of the nineteenth century. After that, Western and Northern Europeans began immigrating to the United States in waves prompted by various economic and agricultural conditions in their respective homelands. For example, hundreds of thousands of Irish immigrants rushed to the United States during the great potato famine that struck their home country during the 1840s.

By the late nineteenth century, the demographics of European immigrants had shifted so that the majority were traveling from Southern and Eastern Europe, most notably Italy and Poland. Nearly all these immigrants entered the United States through New York City and its well-known Ellis Island immigration station, which opened in 1892. Jews from many nations, especially Russia, fled to the United States during the early 1900s to avoid pogroms,

or race-motivated attacks, directed at them by various anti-Semitic groups.

The massive influx of European immigrants was reduced in the 1910s and 1920s when stricter laws were passed by the U.S. Congress, limiting their numbers based first on literacy skills, and later based on quotas established for each originating country. This latter method is still in use today. Despite the popular notion of America as a "melting pot," the population of the United States has never consisted of more than 15 percent foreign-born residents at any time during its history.

CRITICAL OVERVIEW

Call It Sleep was Henry Roth's first novel, published in 1934 when the author was just twenty-eight years old. Critical reception of the book was overwhelmingly positive, particularly for a first novel, but coming as it did in the midst of the Great Depression, the book failed to make a dramatic impact on the reading public and literary scholars until decades later.

One of the novel's most laudatory reviews appeared in a February 1935 edition of *Books*, and was written by F. T. Marsh. Marsh calls the book "the most accurate and profound study of an American slum childhood that has yet appeared." Marsh's praise continues:

> To discerning readers, I believe, for its profound intensity, its rare virtuosity, its sensitive realism, its sheer weight, its power, circumference and depth, this first novel of this Mr. Roth will be remembered for some time to come. I should like to see *Call It Sleep* win the Pulitzer Prize—which it never will.

Other reviewers share many of Marsh's sentiments. A reviewer credited simply as S. A. L., writing for the *Boston Transcript*, calls it "an exceptional book, full of intelligent observation and sympathetic character study." Horace Gregory, in a review for the *Nation*, calls it "a first novel of extraordinary character," and "an experience which few readers of contemporary fiction can afford to ignore." In a review for the *New Republic*, Paul Wren asserts that the book is "packed with rare powers and densities."

Reviewers who were more critical focused primarily on a few specific aspects of the novel. For example, Lewis Gannett, in a mostly positive review for the *New York Herald Tribune*, calls the book "agonizingly real," and cautions, "Some readers who might be drawn to Mr. Roth's book will be shocked by his honest use of street language." In a review for the *New York Times*, H. W. Boynton writes, "The book lays all possible stress on the nastiness of the human animal." He calls the novel "a fine book deliberately and as it were doggedly smeared with verbal filthiness." Joseph Gollomb, writing for the *Saturday Review of Literature*, levels the most serious charges, stating that the book "does violence to the truth" and calling it "by far the foulest picture of the east side that has yet appeared, in conception and in language."

Even with substantially positive reviews, however, the book was published in what Alfred Kazin, in his introduction to the novel, calls "that most unpromising year at the bottom of the Great Depression." As David Kirby notes in his review of *Redemption: The Life of Henry Roth* by Steven G. Kellman, it was a time when "relatively few readers were interested in throwing their disposable cash at an unknown writer, especially one with so troubling a story to tell, and within two years *Call It Sleep* was out of print."

The book was not completely forgotten, however, and a growing interest in the canon of Jewish American literature during the 1960s led to the novel's rediscovery by a new generation of readers. A 1964 paperback edition of *Call It Sleep* became the first paperback reviewed by the *New York Times*, and the book—three decades after its first publication—finally became a bestseller. It has remained steadily popular ever since, and it is considered by many scholars to be an essential classic of Jewish American literature.

CRITICISM

Alfred Kazin

In the following excerpt, Kazin explores Roth's depiction of Jewish immigrants, particularly their language, as they adjust to their new home in New York in Call it Sleep.

Call It Sleep is the most profound novel of Jewish life that I have ever read by an American. It is a work of high art, written with the full resources of modernism, which subtly interweaves an account of the worlds of the city gutter and the tenement cellar with a story of the overwhelming love between a mother and son. It brings together the darkness and light of Jewish immigrant life before the First World War as experienced by a very young boy, really a child, who depends on his imagination alone to fend off a world so immediately hostile that the hostility begins with his own father.

Henry Roth's novel was first published in 1934, at the bottom of the Great Depression. Looking at the date and marveling at this book, which apparently consumed so much of Roth's central experience that he never published another novel, many readers will be astonished. Surely the depressed 1930s produced little else but "proletarian literature" and other forms of left-wing propaganda? A fashionable critic writing in the opulent years after 1945 scorned the 1930s as an "imbecile decade," and explained—with the usual assurance of people who are comfortably off—that the issues in literature are "not political, but moral." Anyone who thinks "political" issues and "moral" ones are unrelated is living in a world very different from the 1930s or the 1990s.

The art fever of the modernist 1920s, in which more first-rate work was produced than in any other single period of American literature, continued well into the 1930s and did not fade until Hitler's war. Henry Roth, twenty-eight when *Call It Sleep* was published, was as open to the many strategies of modernism as he was to political insurgency. (The book owes a great deal to the encouragement of Eda Lou Walton, a remarkable woman who was teaching modern literature at New York University.)

Though *Call It Sleep* was not adequately understood or welcomed until it was reissued in paperback in 1964, it has become popular throughout the world with millions of copies in print. We can see now that the book belongs to the side of the 1930s that still believed that literature was sacred, whether or not it presumed to change the world. Those who identify the 1930s with works of political protest forget that it was the decade of the best of Faulkner's novels, from *The Sound and the Fury* to *The Wild Palms*, Eliot's *Ash Wednesday*, Hart Crane's *The Bridge*, Dos Passos's *U.S.A.*, Katherine Anne Porter's *Flowering Judas*, Edmund Wilson's *Axel's Castle*, Fitzgerald's *Tender is the Night*, Henry Miller's *Tropic of Cancer*, Steinbeck's *The Grapes of Wrath*, Thornton Wilder's *Our Town*,

View of Manhattan, circa 1950 © *Bettmann/Corbis*

Nathanael West's *The Day of the Locust*, Richard Wright's *Native Son*, Hemingway's *For Whom the Bell Tolls*.

What *Call It Sleep* has in common with these works is its sense of art sustaining itself in a fallen world, in a time of endless troubles and of political and social fright. The world was visibly shaking under the blows of economic catastrophe, mob hysteria, the fascist domination of much of Europe, fear of another world war. And no one was likely to feel the burden of the times more keenly than a young Jew starting life in a Yiddish-speaking immigrant family and surrounded by the physical and human squalor of the Lower East Side.

That last sentence could describe Michael Gold in his autobiography *Jews Without Money*, an eloquent but primitive outpouring of emotion that concludes with a rousing call to communism

as the new Messiah. What from the very beginning makes *Call It Sleep* so different from the usual grim realism of Lower East Side novels is the intractable bitterness of the immigrant father, Albert Schearl, toward his wife, Genya, and their little boy, David. The father is an uncompromisingly hostile workingman, a printer by trade, driven from one shop to another by his ugly temper. "They look at me crookedly, with mockery in their eyes! How much can a man endure? May the fire of God consume them!" Roth makes this complaint sound loftier than it would have in Albert Schearl's Yiddish. He has been driven almost insane by his memory and resentment of his wife's affair with a Gentile back in Austrian Galicia. It pleases him to suspect that David is not his son.

This obsession, the dramatic foundation and background of the novel, may not be enough to explain Albert's unrelenting vituperation of his wife and his rejection, in every small family matter, of the little boy. David is not just unloved; he is violently hated by his father. The father shudderingly regards him as a kind of untouchable. The boy not only depends exclusively and feverishly on his mother but, in the moving story of his inner growth, becomes a determined pilgrim searching for light away from his tenement cellar refuge whose darkness pervades the first section of the novel, away from the dark cave in which the father has imprisoned mother and son.

Albert Schearl is at times so frenzied in his choked-up bitterness and grief that the introspection at the heart of his son's character—the boy wanders the neighborhood and beyond in search of a way out—must be seen as the only rebellion open to him. Whatever the sources of Albert Schearl's madly sustained daily war on his wife and son—he is perhaps less a jealous husband than a crazed immigrant unable to feel at home in the New World—Roth's honesty in putting the man's hatefulness at the center of the book is remarkable. It reminds us that the idealizing of the family in Jewish literature can be far from actual facts. Jews from Eastern Europe did not always emigrate because of anti-Semitism. The enmity sometimes lay within the family itself, as has been known to happen everywhere. Instead of sentimentalizing the family situation, Roth turned husband, wife, and son into the helpless protagonists of an obvious and uncompromising Oedipal situation. I can think of no other novel except D. H. Lawrence's *Sons and Lovers* in which mother and son are so fiercely tied to each other. The father is the outsider he has made of himself, and plainly wants to be.

In *Sons and Lovers* (as in lesser works on the same theme) the father is extraneous because he has lost for the mother the sexual charm that first attracted her. In *Call It Sleep* Genya timidly loves Albert for all his brutality. She is prepared to love him more freely if only he would stop berating her, but he is so unremittingly nasty that he virtually forces mother and son on each other. Albert in his daily rage somehow reflects his unconscious bitterness at being held down in "the Golden Land." But it is also clear that, notwithstanding Albert's dominating airs, Genya married him because she had no other choice. Her father had disowned her for her past infatuation with a Gentile.

Albert's war against his wife and son sounds an alarm at the very opening of the novel that continues to dominate these three lives until the last possible moment, when the shock produced when David is burned in a bizarre accident brings about a necessary but inconclusive pause in Albert's war on his family.

The book begins in 1907, the peak year of immigration to the United States. Wife and son have just been delivered from the immigration station at Ellis Island to be greeted by a somber, frowning Albert. Not in the least prepared to be amiable, he is quickly incensed because his wife doesn't recognize him without his mustache.

> The truth was there was something quite untypical about their behavior. . . These two stood silent, apart; the man staring with aloof, offended eyes grimly down at the water—or if he turned his face toward his wife at all, it was only to glare in harsh contempt at the blue straw hat worn by the child in her arms, and then his hostile eyes would sweep about the deck to see if anyone else was observing them. And his wife beside him regarding him uneasily, appealingly. And the child against her breast looking from one to the other with watchful, frightened eyes. . . The woman, as if driven by the strain into action, tried to smile, and touching her husband's arm said timidly, "And this is the Golden Land." She spoke in Yiddish.

Astonished by her husband's haggard appearance, Genya apologizes for not having known him instantly. With the gentleness that she sustains in all the many crises he creates; she says, "You must have suffered in this land." Indeed he has, and will continue to suffer from himself in a way that turns his harshness into their immediate, their most perilous environment. Albert is his wife's only New York. She never attempts to learn English; she is content just to look after her family and is afraid to move beyond the streets of her neighborhood. Her deepest feeling for Albert is not the passion which unsettles him but a concern that comes from a sense of duty. Anything else would be unthinkable to her. Deprived of actual love, since Albert's quarrelsomeness isolates her, she is free to give her entire soul to her little boy.

Call It Sleep is not a naturalist novel, in which character is shaped largely by environment. Jews are generally so conscious of the pressure of history that it was a notable achievement for Henry Roth, coming out of the Lower East Side at a time when it was routine for people to dream of transforming the "conditions" in which they found themselves, to see character as more important than environment. As lower New York in the teens of our century comes alive in David Schearl's anxious but eager consciousness, Roth presents the city not in an external documentary but as formed, instant by instant, out of David's perceptions. David Schearl is portrait of the artist as a very small boy. In this novel we are in the city-world not of *Sister Carrie* but of Joyce's *Ulysses*.

He also shows that Genya's enveloping tenderness toward her son is not just "Freudian," theoretical, but a protectiveness that is a part of Jewish history. Its key is the Yiddish that mother and son speak together. David's English is made to sound effortlessly noble, beautifully expressive, almost liturgical, by contrast with the gutteral street English that surrounds him. We are startled to hear him speak a horrible mutilated street dialect when he is away from Mama. Then he is with strangers; and in this novel of New York, English is the stranger, the adopted language, tough and brazen. It expresses the alienation from the larger world of kids competing with each other in toughness. "Land where our fodders died" becomes a parody of a national hymn that shows how derivative and meaningless the line can be when sung by immigrant street urchins.

The young David, searching for experience beyond his immediate neighborhood, discovers that he is "losted," and he tells a baffled woman who cannot make out where the boy lives, "A hunner 'n' twenny six Boddeh Stritt." Later in the novel David is enchanted by the Polish boy Leo flying a kite from the roof. Like Tom Sawyer encountering Huckleberry Finn, David is astounded by the boy's freedom. Hoping to see this marvel again, David asks, "Yuh gonna comm up hea alluh time?" Leo carelessly explains; "Naw! I hangs out on wes elevent'. Dat's w'ea we lived 'fore we moved."

Maybe street kids once talked this way, maybe not. Roth caricatures the terrible English of the street—a "foreign," external, cold-hearted language—in order to bring out the necessary contrast with the Yiddish spoken at home. This is the language of the heart, of tradition, of intimacy. Just as Roth perhaps overdoes the savage English spoken in the street, so he deliberately exalts the Yiddish that he translates at every point into splendid, almost too splendid, King James English. Even when Albert almost comes to blows with his vulgarly outspoken sister-in-law

Bertha, he cries out: "I'm pleading with you as with Death!" Storming at his son, he menacingly demands "Shudder when I speak to you!" The English doesn't convey the routine, insignificant weight of the word for "shudder" in Yiddish. The people speaking Yiddish in this book are not cultivated people carefully choosing their words. They are hard-pressed, keyed-up, deeply emotional. There is nothing about the lives in the "Golden Land" that is not arduous, strange, even threatening. So they talk as extremely vulnerable Yiddish speakers from the immigrant working class have always done. It is a verbal style, even a routine, in which people expostulate with one another as if they were breaking all the windows in order to let a little air into the house.

Source: Alfred Kazin, "The Art of *Call It Sleep*," in *The New York Review of Books*, Vol. 38, No. 15, October 10, 1991, p.15.

SOURCES

Boynton, H. W., Review of *Call It Sleep*, in the *New York Times*, February 17, 1935, p. 7; reprinted in *The Book Review Digest (Thirty-First Annual Cumulation)*, edited by Mertice M. James and Dorothy Brown, The H. W. Wilson Company, 1936, p. 859.

Gannett, Lewis, Review of *Call It Sleep*, in the *New York Herald Tribune*, February 16, 1935, p. 9; reprinted in *The Book Review Digest (Thirty-First Annual Cumulation)*, edited by Mertice M. James and Dorothy Brown, The H. W. Wilson Company, 1936, p. 859.

Gollomb, Joseph, Review of *Call It Sleep*, in the *Saturday Review of Literature*, Vol. 11, March 16, 1935, p. 552; reprinted in *The Book Review Digest (Thirty-First Annual Cumulation)*, edited by Mertice M. James and Dorothy Brown, The H. W. Wilson Company, 1936, p. 859.

Gregory, Horace, Review of *Call It Sleep*, in the *Nation*, Vol. 140, February 27, 1935, p. 255; reprinted in *The Book Review Digest (Thirty-First Annual Cumulation)*, edited by Mertice M. James and Dorothy Brown, The H. W. Wilson Company, 1936, p. 858.

Kazin, Alfred, "Introduction," in *Call It Sleep*, Picador, 1991, p. ix.

Kirby, David, "Some Called It Sleep," in the *Washington Post*, August 21, 2005, p. BW10, www.washingtonpost. com/wp-dyn/content/article/2005/08/18/AR20050818012 92.html (December 31, 2006).

Marsh, F. T., Review of *Call It Sleep*, in *Books*, February 17, 1935, p. 6; reprinted in *The Book Review Digest (Thirty-First Annual Cumulation)*, edited by Mertice M. James and Dorothy Brown, The H. W. Wilson Company, 1936, p. 858.

Roth, Henry, *Call It Sleep*, R. O. Ballou, 1934; reprint, Picador, 1991.

S. A. L., Review of *Call It Sleep*, in the *Boston Transcript*, February 13, 1935, p. 3; reprinted in *The Book Review Digest (Thirty-First Annual Cumulation)*, edited by Mertice M. James and Dorothy Brown, The H. W. Wilson Company, 1936, p. 858.

Wirth-Nesher, Hana, "Between Mother Tongue and Native Language in *Call It Sleep* (Afterword)," in *Call It Sleep*, Picador, 1991, p. 457.

Wren, Paul, Review of *Call It Sleep*, in the *New Republic*, Vol. 82, February 27, 1935, p. 82; reprinted in *The Book Review Digest (Thirty-First Annual Cumulation)*, edited by Mertice M. James and Dorothy Brown, The H. W. Wilson Company, 1936, p. 858.

Cane

JEAN TOOMER

1923

Jean Toomer's eclectic *Cane* (1923) is a landmark work of African American literature and a classic book of the Harlem Renaissance. Toomer's interwoven collection of sketches, poems, and short stories was embraced by critics and fellow writers, but it did not find a wider audience for many years. While some readers who initially praised the book believed he would be a leading author of his generation, *Cane* was the only book by Toomer to be published commercially in his lifetime. After his death in the late 1960s, he came to be considered a pioneering African American writer, and *Cane* was regarded an important contribution to literature. The book also proved to be inspirational to many African American authors, including Langston Hughes and Alice Walker.

One reason for Toomer's lack of success after *Cane* was that Toomer did not embrace such racial labels. He was of a mixed background, which included white, black, and Jewish ancestors, and he did not want to be labeled by any race whatsoever. He considered such labels limiting and thought of himself as a representative of a new kind of race, a blending, which he emphasized as American. His rejection of the label of "Negro writer" was believed to have hurt his literary career after *Cane* was published.

Inspired in part by his own experiences as the temporary head of a school for African

Americans in Georgia, Toomer was fascinated with racial attitudes and came to some sense of understanding his own and those of others in early 1920s. On his way home to Washington, D.C., from Georgia, Toomer began writing sketches, poems, and stories inspired by his experience in the South. Some of these pieces were initially published in magazines and newspapers such as the *Liberator*, the *Crisis*, the *Little Review*, the *Double Dealer*, and *Broom*, and later became part of *Cane*.

In *Cane*, Toomer explores the folk traditions and culture of the South as well as the physical and psychological oppression of northern society and economic culture. The book is divided into three sections. The first section focuses primarily on the rural South through poems and prose sketches with women at their center. While these women are depicted as strong and independent, they also suffer because of their choices, which defy societal expectations. The second section, which begins with the prose poem "Seventh Street," explores the lives of African Americans in the North—Washington, D.C., and Chicago—who are estranged from nature and their racial community in the South. Their relationships with each other have become unclear and are often interrupted by their own shortcomings or bigger issues in society. Racial identity is also an issue. Toomer added this section at the request of his publisher who thought his book was too brief with just the first section and "Kabnis," the short story, which comprises the third section of the book. In this story, a northern African American comes to the South to teach at a school for blacks but lacks a coherent self-identity. He does not fully comprehend the society and life of the South, loses his job, and spirals downward with sex, drink, and a futile job at a wagon repair shop at which he essentially fails. As in "Kabnis," *Cane* as a whole "was primarily a song for an era that was ending," as Darwin T. Turner writes in his introduction to the 1975 edition of the book.

As was common with literature in the time period in which it was written, both sexuality and primitivism were central themes in *Cane*. While the book was embraced by critics and scholars for its celebration of folk traditions and peasant life, some were offended by Toomer's depiction of women's sexuality. Others embraced its frank and honest take on

BIOGRAPHY

JEAN TOOMER

Born Nathan Eugene Pinchback Toomer on december 26, 1894, the author was the product of the brief marriage between Nathan and Nina Toomer. His planter father was probably the poor son of a slave. His mother was the daughter of a prominent biracial politician, Pinckey Pinchback. Toomer was initially raised in Pinchback's household in a wealthy section of Washington, D.C., where his race was not an issue. From his uncle Bismarck Pinchback, Toomer gained a love of learning and literature. After living in his uncle's household in a black section of Washington, D.C., as a teenager, Toomer spent four years at various universities unable to stick with any of his studies. He then sold cars, was a physical education director, and worked in business.

By 1920, Toomer decided to become a writer. He focused on studying literature and produced a number of unpublished works. During this period, he also briefly took a job in Georgia as the head of a school for African Americans, an experience that inspired *Cane* (1923). His published literary career essentially ended after *Cane* as he refused to be labeled by his black heritage. Toomer then became a disciple of the spiritual leader Georges Gurdjieff and experimented with communal living. He became a Quaker in 1940, a belief system for which he wrote and lectured in the coming years. Though Toomer continued to write, all his future works were rejected by publishers in his lifetime. He died on March 30, 1967, in Doylestown, Pennsylvania.

life in the South, appreciating that Toomer wanted to capture a southern black culture he saw was dying out.

Cane is also noteworthy as a modernist text with complex, sometimes confusing, form and imagery, and touches of the avant-garde. Its experimentalism was the mark of another trend of the era in which it was written; Toomer was particularly influenced by Imagist poets. Some early critics were unsure of its form as well as content.

No matter what critics thought of the work, *Cane* helped shape African American literature in the second half of the twentieth century and beyond. As Tracie Church Guzzio writes in *American Writers*,

> Whatever the degree of its impact, it is clear that *Cane* helped liberate the African American artist by paving the way for exploring new forms and new voices, by revisiting past traditions, and by describing through poetry, rather than propaganda, the richness and humanity of African American life.

PLOT SUMMARY

Section 1
Chapter 1: Karintha
Cane opens with a sketch entitled "Karintha," which focuses on an attractive woman. Toomer writes that men were attracted to her "even as a child." By the age of twelve, she could get away with wild behavior unacceptable in others, but also was rumored to be sexually active, perhaps imitating her parents. This change came when she played house with a young boy. As she grew older, she would sleep with men when she felt like it, and they brought her money. She eventually had a baby: "A child fell out of her womb onto a bed of pine-needles in the forest." Though Karintha continues to live this way and be a beauty at twenty, "Men do not know that the soul of her was a growing thing ripened too soon."

Chapter 2: Reapers
This descriptive poem describes African American harvesters as they prepare their instruments and do their cutting work. A worker's scythe catches a field rat and cuts it, but though there is blood on the blade, they continue to labor.

Chapter 3: November Cotton Flower
This poem is set in the winter when the cotton disappeared, there was drought and desolation, and "dead birds were found / In wells a hundred feet below the ground." Yet when a cotton flower bloomed, people responded not with

Jean Toomer © Bettmann/Corbis

superstitious fear but by embracing its unexpected beauty.

Chapter 4: Becky
This is another sketch about a woman in the South. Becky is a white woman who had two black sons. After she had the first one, she was condemned by other whites in her community, who did not know who fathered the child. Becky faced similar criticism from African Americans, who also did not know the father's name. Still, Toomer writes, "White folks and black folks built her cabin, fed her and her growing baby, prayed secretly to God who'd put His cross upon her and cast her out." Though she was outcast from the community, the railroad boss said she could live on a small piece of land located next to the railroad, while another man donated materials for a cabin, and yet another built the cabin at night—all so their actions could not be known.

When Becky lived in the cabin, she was not seen by the community. However, some citizens secretly left food for her. When her first son was five years old, he began being seen with a little brother in town. Her sons grew up to be bullies who could not hold jobs as adults. They left town after killing two men, and Becky still seemed to be living in her cabin. After awhile, the community was unsure if she was alive or dead and stopped leaving food. One Sunday, the story's unnamed narrator reports passing by the cabin on the road and seeing its chimney fall inside. The narrator is unsure if Becky was under the bricks, despite possibly hearing a groan, but did nothing to see if she was alive or dead. The narrator and his companion, Barlo, quickly left the scene, leaving only Barlo's Bible on the rubble.

Chapter 5: Face

"Face" is a descriptive poem about a strong old woman's face, touching on her hair, brows, eyes, and "her channeled muscles."

Chapter 6: Cotton Song

"Cotton Song" is a poetic song, a spiritual linking of the baling of cotton with God and the judgment day.

Chapter 7: Carma

"Carma" is about a strong black woman. Told from the perspective of a first-person narrator from the North, the story describes seeing her direct a mule-driven wagon down the road. The narrator then tells Carma's story. Her husband is now working on a chain gang because, the narrator believes, of Carma. When he was away from home working, she took on a series of lovers. Her husband found out about her infidelity and beat her. She ran away, taking a gun with her. He heard the gun go off later as she faked her own death. People searched for her, found her, and carried her home. She had no wounds on her body. Because of the deception, her husband slashed the man who found her, landing him in prison.

Chapter 8: Song of the Son

This poem focuses on nature, night, and the sun, emphasizing slaves and their soul's relationship to the soil they work.

Chapter 9: Georgia Dusk

Like "Song of the Son," the poem "Georgia Dusk" emphasizes the land, but one post-slavery where industry and mechanization have taken over.

Chapter 10: Fern

This sketch describes Fern and her story from the point of view of a first-person narrator from the North. He implies that she is half Jewish and half African American. The narrator emphasizes her eyes: "They were strange eyes. In this, that they sought nothing—that is, nothing that was obvious and tangible and that one could see, and they gave the impression that nothing was to be denied." While she slept with some black men when young, they received little from the experience but became obsessed with her. Though they gave themselves to her, Fern began to send them away, seeing herself as above them, and starts abstaining from sex.

Fern then spent her days sitting on her porch, with her eyes gazing at what is around her. It was when Fern was sitting on her porch that the narrator first saw her and was attracted to her. One evening, he walked along her road, stopped by her house, and suggested taking a walk. She is bothered by the peering eyes of her neighbors. Without thinking, he holds her in his arms; she eventually reacts physically, seems to have a spiritual vision, and faints in his arms in the canefield. Though her protectors in the southern community kept their eye on the narrator, he soon returned home but saw her from the train window as he left.

Chapter 11: Nullo

This impressionistic poem describes pine needles falling to the forest floor.

Chapter 12: Evening Song

This first-person poem uses nature imagery intermingled with the narrator's intimate physical description of a woman named Cloine.

Chapter 13: Esther

This sketch begins by describing Esther, another mixed-race female, as a young child. When she is nine, she sees King Barlo, a black man, go into a religious trance on the street. No one is afraid, but instead many in the community watch and listen to his words. After what he says seems to come true, he rides out of town on a black bull. His words and actions impressed Esther. As a teenager, she has related dreams, and by the time she is a young adult, she is working in her grocery store and thinks romantically only of Barlo. When she is twenty-seven years old, he returns to town and she decides she must have him. She goes to the house where he is staying and tells him she has come for him. He rejects her, and Esther understands that Barlo is not what she thought he was. "She steps out. There is no air, no street, and the town has completely disappeared."

Chapter 14: Conversion
This brief poem describes an African religion losing ground and contrasts it with Christianity.

Chapter 15: Portrait in Georgia
Another brief poem, "Portrait in Georgia" discusses the physical appearance of a worn-down woman of the titular land.

Chapter 16: Blood-Burning Moon
This short story focuses on Louisa, a young black woman who works for a white family. Bob Stone, the youngest son of her employers, believed he had "won her." A black field worker named Tom Burwell also loved Louisa. She was stringing both of them along. In the forest, men are processing sugar cane. Tom becomes upset when the men talk about Louisa being with Bob. Tom gets into a physical confrontation with some of the men, then goes to Louisa's house. He tells her he loves her and he would cut Bob if he was involved with her. Louisa denies any involvement with Bob, and they sing together.

Later, Bob thinks about his relationship with Louisa, which he hides from his family despite his certain kind of sexual love for her. He becomes upset at the thought that she was also involved with Tom, and this furor grows when he comes upon the men in the woods and Louisa's duplicity is confirmed. Finding Louisa and Tom together, Bob confronts them. The men get into a physical confrontation. Tom slashes Bob's throat. When they learn what happened, the white men in the town hunt Tom down and beat him. He is burned at the stake. Louisa only sees the full moon, and she believes people, if not Tom, would join her if she sang.

Section 2
Chapter 17: Seventh Street
The focus of Cane shifts from the rural South to the industrialized North. In this first piece in the second section of the novel, Toomer uses poetry and prose to describe city life, jazz, the effects of World War I, and clubs and theaters in the part of town where African Americans live and where metaphorical blood flows. God and religion are also mentioned.

Chapter 18: Rhobert
This brief, obtuse, image-filled character sketch is about a man named Rhobert who is weighed down by the house he metaphorically wears on his head. Such a life physically affects him, but, despite bent legs caused by rickets, he bears his hardships.

Chapter 19: Avey
Another sketch with a first-person male narrator, the story focuses on his attraction since childhood to a young woman named Avey. City boys both black and white admired her, and the narrator went out of his way to get her attention. While they swam and danced together, he believed she would marry a college student who lived on the top floor of her apartment building when he saved enough money. Because the student was gone, she used all the boys in turn until their money gave out. Though the narrator becomes similarly involved and Avey kisses him on the deck of a ship, he does get close to her again for a year later when they are more intimately involved. His opinion of her changes because she seems to have no ambition in life, while he prepares to go to college. His opinion of her as lazy does not change while he is in college. When he meets her again in New York five years later, he tries to reconnect and improve her but then loses his passion for her all over again.

Chapter 20: Beehive
This poem describes a beehive and bees, comparing them to a city and its inhabitants. The narrator sees himself as one of the bees and wants to reconnect with the land.

Chapter 21: Storm Ending
This brief poem describes a thunder storm, which affects the flowers "And the sweet earth flying from the thunder."

Chapter 22: Theater
"Theater" is set at a theater with an African American audience, where the manager's brother, John, is attracted to one of the dancers, Dorris. He watches her as she rehearses, and she notices his gaze. Though they do not speak directly, they make assumptions about each other. Dorris dances for him, and John dreams about her. At the end of the dance, his attraction is dead. Dorris cries in her dressing room.

Chapter 23: Her Lips Are Copper Wire

This impressionistic poem celebrates the telephone and the physical contact of a kiss.

Chapter 24: Calling Jesus

This is a prosaic poem, which explores the concept of a woman's soul as "a little thrust-tailed dog that follows her, whimpering." The dog/soul is left in the vestibule when she comes home at night, but it is free to trail after her. At the poem's end, the narrator reports that "Some one . . . will steal in and cover it that it need not shiver, and carry it to her where she sleeps."

Chapter 25: Box Seat

Dan Moore, a black man, calls on Muriel, a teacher, at the boarding house where she lives. He is in love with her, as his thoughts reveal, but she does not share the same feelings. She admires some of his character qualities but is ultimately not fond of him. Though Muriel is getting ready to go out with her friend Bernice, she spends some time talking to him. He tries to tell her to improve herself and declares his love, then Muriel refuses his advances.

At the theater with Bernice, Muriel watches crude entertainments and thinks about what happened with Dan. He shows up at the theater as well, which upsets Muriel. He watches her more than the entertainment. After two dwarves box, Mr. Barry, one of the dwarves, sings a song and gives a rose to Muriel. She is repulsed, ending Dan's feelings for her. He leaves.

Chapter 26: Prayer

This poem explores divisions within the body, the mind, and the body separated from the soul. The narrator acknowledges that his division and confusion have weakened him.

Chapter 27: Harvest Song

A longer poem, "Harvest Song" is a first-person poem about a reaper harvesting oats in the field all day long. He is tired at night, too tired to bind his cradled oats, and hungry. Toomer writes, "My pain is sweet. Sweeter than the oats or wheat or corn. It will not bring me knowledge of my hunger."

Chapter 28: Bona and Paul

At a school for aspiring teachers in Chicago, a white female student, Bona, is attracted to Paul, a biracial student. Paul struggles with his racial identity, hiding it from the others who question the truth about his heritage.

Paul's white friend and roommate Art has arranged dates for them. Paul's date is Bona. The couple has problems communicating throughout the evening. She tells him that she loves him, and while he is ready to kiss her, she will not because he cannot say he loves her as well.

At Crimson Gardens, Paul feels more disconnected and different. He dances with Bona, but their communication problems continue and she becomes angry with him. Paul keeps her physically near, and their passion is restored by continuing to dance. They leave together before Art and Helen do. However, Bona leaves Paul after he goes back inside to explain his attraction to Bona to the black doorman.

Section 3
Chapter 29: Kabnis

The last section of *Cane* is the story "Kabnis." Ralph Kabnis is a mixed-race teacher who has come south from Washington, D.C., to teach at a school in Georgia. He is unhappy teaching at the school, which educates African Americans. The South in general also does not agree with him.

As the story opens, he is finding it hard to get to sleep, a situation made worse by a noisy chicken in the room next to his. Kabnis kills the chicken, a pet hen on the campus, and does not care about the consequences. While he sees beauty in the night, he can only see ugliness in the South, its culture, and its inhabitants. Kabnis finally falls asleep, looking forward to tomorrow, Sunday.

On Sunday, Kabnis visits Fred Halsey, a prominent local mixed-race man, with Professor Layman, a black teacher and preacher. Layman and Halsey like Kabnis because he is not conceited like other African Americans from the North. The pair tells Kabnis that even though they may be "gentlemen," white people only see skin color.

Kabnis tells them he is contemptuous of the religious practices: "the preacher's hands are in the white man's pockets." He especially does not like the religious services for blacks in the South, finding the shouting uncomfortable.

The conversation turns to Kabnis's boss, Hanby, whom the men do not like, and then to a lynching a year back. Mame Lankins was lynched though she was pregnant. The baby survived her death and was cut out by a white man. He killed the baby and stuck it in a tree with a knife. Kabnis's already edgy state is further agitated when a rock is thrown through Halsey's window with a note. The note seems meant for Kabnis and tells him to return to the North.

Kabnis grows paranoid with every sound when he returns home. He is sure someone is out to get him when Halsey and Layman stop by. Halsey tries to reassure him that no one is after him and that he would have gotten killed already if that was their goal.

Layman and Halsey start a fire to make food, and Halsey passes around some liquor. Hanby, the head of the school, enters just as Kabnis passes the bottle to Halsey. Hanby tells Kabnis he must turn in his resignation tomorrow for drinking in his room. Kabnis is indignant, and Hanby tries to get them all to leave now. Halsey reminds Hanby that he has not paid a bill to Halsey and must do so tomorrow under the same threats that Hanby made to Kabnis. Halsey also says that Kabnis will now work for him doing physical labor.

Kabnis tries to take hold of the situation in his room with Halsey and Hanby, but cannot. Lewis, another black man, comes in. Kabnis learns that the rock and note were meant for him, thrown by other African Americans uncomfortable with his presence. After Lewis and Hanby leave, Kabnis wearily gives in. He will live at Halsey's and work in his shop.

A month later, Kabnis is working at the shop, where wagons are built and repaired. Waiting for lunch, Halsey, Kabnis, and Layman are joined by Lewis, who is planning on leaving town now. It is revealed that Lewis is disliked for his "queer opinions." Their discussion is interrupted by a white customer, Mr. Ramsay, who asks for his hatchet to be repaired. Kabnis is given the task but cannot complete it. His humiliation is furthered by the appearance of Hanby who demands an axle be shaped into a crow-bar.

Halsey's sister, Carrie K., shows up with lunch for Kabnis, Halsey, and Father John, Halsey's father who lives in the shop's cellar. Lewis is attracted to her, and while she initially shows interest, she retreats into propriety. She goes down to the Hole, the shop's cellar, to feed her blind and deaf elderly father. After Lewis asks about her future, Kabnis and Halsey invite

> A STRANGE THING HAPPENED TO PAUL. SUDDENLY HE KNEW THAT HE WAS APART FROM THE PEOPLE AROUND HIM. APART FROM THE PAIN WHICH THEY HAD UNCONSCIOUSLY CAUSED. SUDDENLY HE KNEW THAT PEOPLE SAW, NOT ATTRACTIVENESS IN HIS DARK SKIN, BUT DIFFERENCE."

him to join them for fun with female companions that night.

Later, Lewis, Kabnis, and Halsey are in the Hole with two women named Stella and Cora. Father John is also present. There is tension in the room as all but Father John, drink and talk about town gossip. Kabnis defensively talks to Lewis about who he is, before Halsey sends him to be distracted with Cora. Lying with Cora, his attention is diverted when Halsey begins to talk to Lewis about him. Kabnis spews information about his family, his past, and his opinion of the South. Lewis leaves when the pressure of the situation becomes too much.

The next morning, Halsey has to awaken Kabnis, Cora, and Stella, who are still asleep in the Hole. The women do not want to leave but get up and do so. Kabnis lingers down there, believing that Father John spoke to him in the night. Kabnis talks to him, sharing his opinions of life in the South. Carrie comes down to get Kabnis to go to work. Father John speaks of sin and says that white people make the Bible lie. Kabnis is contemptuous of the old man, while Carrie is reverent. After stumbling around, Kabnis finally goes upstairs to work as the sun rises.

THEMES

Regional Disconnectedness

Throughout *Cane*, Toomer implicitly contrasts the rural South with the urban North, considering the effects of pursuing the American dream of a better life on African Americans. For some, the differences between regions offer a chance to escape, while for others, the differences turn the dream to disappointment. Through many sketches and poems in the book, he shows what they lost by moving north, including the past and a sense of self as well as ties to a specific southern community. This theme is primarily explored in the second section of the book, with the sketches and poems therein, and the third section, which consists only of "Kabnis."

Unlike poems in section 1 such as "Nullo," "November Cotton Flower," "Reapers," and "Cotton Song," which use nature imagery related to the South to establish the rural connection to the land, the poems in section 2 emphasize the fast pace of life in the North as well as its disconnectedness. In "Seventh Street," for example, Toomer describes this differing pace and focus in Washington, D.C.: "Money burns the pocket, pocket hurts / Bootleggers in silken shirts / Ballooned, zooming Cadillacs, / Whizzing, whizzing down the street-car tracks."

More personal disconnectedness can be found in the sketch "Theater," in which a dancer named Dorris catches the attention of the theater manager's brother, John. They never speak but spend much of the sketch judging and imagining what it would be like to communicate and be close with the other. They never connect despite Dorris's dance for him, and Dorris ends up in tears in her dressing room. "Calling Jesus" emphasizes this fact further as a woman is described as literally disconnected from her soul, which follows her around in the form of a small dog.

Toomer talks about the weight of modern living in the sketch "Rhobert." The title character is described as wearing "a house like a monstrous diver's helmet, on his head." While Rhobert is praised for being able to hold up despite having legs weakened from rickets, he is also described as drowning from the pressures of city life and the materialism of modern society. This lifestyle kills his dreams and damages his relationship with his family. The sketch ends by emphasizing the losing battle Rhobert is fighting: "Brother, Rhobert is sinking. / Lets open our throats, brother, / Lets sing Deep River when he goes down."

The theme of contrast finds its ultimate fruition in the final section and story of the book, "Kabnis." The title character, Ralph Kabnis, is an African American teacher from the North living in the South. At the beginning of the story, he is a teacher at a school for African Americans, but he finds life in the South difficult. Kabnis is unhappy with his living quarters, the rules imposed on him at the school, and southern culture in general. Early in the story he prays,

> Dear Jesus, do not chain me to myself and set these hills and valley, heaving with folk-songs, so close to me that I cannot reach them. There is a radiant beauty in the night that touches and . . . tortures me.

As the story progresses, Kabnis shows how disconnected he is, though he has ancestors from Georgia. He states that he does not like how people act in church in the South, offended by their loud proclamations of worship. Though some in the community like and help Kabnis, such as Halsey and Layman, he believes others are out to get him. When a threatening note is thrown with a rock through Halsey's window, Kabnis mistakenly believes it is targeting him. While the others try to set him straight, he cannot accept their explanation of southern behavior. Eventually, Kabnis gives up. He does not fight being fired as a teacher, and while Halsey employs him in his wagon repair shop, Kabnis cannot do the work and is only good for giving into baser instincts. He cannot reclaim what he and his people have lost by living in the North.

Racial Identity

In several sketches in sections 1 and 2, Toomer explores the idea of racial identity, especially as an isolating factor. Several characters in the book are of mixed race and this leads to questions about who they are, what they stand for, and decisions contrary to the norms of their immediate society. While being of mixed race has undoubtedly furthered some American dreams, making it easier to reject part of a heritage that the dreamer finds to be a burden, the abandonment of part of one's self is rarely shown as bringing peace or happiness.

In the first section's "Fern," for example, the title character is implied to be part Jewish and part African American. Initially, Fern gives herself to men and has many admirers. Toomer writes, "As she grew up, new men who came to town felt as almost everyone did who ever saw her: that they would not be denied. Men were everlastingly bringing her their bodies." Eventually, she withdraws herself from sexual activity—a choice at odds with the rest of her community—and comes to be seen as regarding herself as above everyone else; she "became a virgin." She isolates herself at home and stares at the landscape from her porch. The sketch's white male narrator dares challenge this isolation and learns of her anger at the world. While the narrator becomes connected to God and land through holding Fern, she is still isolated and alone at the story's end.

In section 2, Paul in "Bona and Paul" is in some ways more isolated than Fern. A mixed-race student at a school for teachers in the North, Paul hides his racial identity and passes for white among his fellow students. However, many have guessed at his true racial makeup; Helen thinks, "Not one girl had really loved Paul; he fascinated them." Art, his roommate, thinks that he always has to answer questions about Paul's race and wonders, "What in the hell's getting into Paul of late, anyway? Christ, but he's getting moony. Its his blood. Dark blood: moony." Bona, a fellow student who is white, is interested in Paul, and Art arranges for them to go on a double date with him and his love interest, Helen. At Crimson Gardens, Paul, and even Art, feels the stares of those who wonder what Paul is. This situation makes Paul feel isolated even from his own small group. Paul is left alone in the end after he tries to explain himself to the African American doorman; Bona does not wait after she hears who he is. Paul's troubles with racial identity leave him isolated from everyone else.

Power of Womanhood

Many of Toomer's sketches feature prominent women characters. In the first section of *Cane* especially, the sketches explore life in the South through pieces about women who often act in defiance of society's expectations in some way. They often pay a price for their sexual independence, though this pursuit of self is a prominent part of the American dream.

Cane opens with "Karintha," about a woman who men desire and bring their money to, but they "do not know that the soul of her was a growing thing that ripened too soon. . . . they will die not having found it out." "Becky," the next sketch, focuses on a white woman who has two African American sons. While she is publicly rejected by the community, both black and white, for her choices, she spends all her time in her cabin, which some local citizens secretly built for her, while she is regularly fed by others.

"Carma" has even more power. Like Karintha, Carma makes her own sexual choices. She chooses to have numerous affairs while married to her husband, who beats her. However, he ends up on the chain gang for slashing the man who found her when she faked her own death. In "Blood-Burning Moon," Louisa also engenders violence by stringing along two men, one white and one black, each of whom believes that he solely possesses her. Tom and Bob eventually find out about each other, and the white man, Bob, has his rival killed by a mob.

While the title character in "Esther" technically fails to control her sexual destiny—King Barlo is nothing like what she built him up to be her whole life—she also chooses to live her life her way and take risks by even approaching Barlo when he returns to town. In all such sketches in *Cane* women assert their sexual authority without a hint of self-doubt.

HISTORICAL OVERVIEW

Great Migration

Beginning in 1914 as World War I broke out, African Americans moved from the South primarily to large urban centers in the Northeast (New York City, Philadelphia, Baltimore), Midwest (Detroit, Chicago, St. Louis), and West (Los Angeles). The Great Migration, as this movement came to be called, reached an early peak in the 1920s. There are several reasons for this population shift. While the Great Migration was part of a greater trend of urbanization, which was happening throughout the United States in the 1920s, African Americans had more specific motivations for leaving the South.

In many facets of southern life, African Americans faced racial segregation at nearly every turn. Jim Crow laws were southern state laws, which enforced this segregation. For example, in many southern states, African Americans were forced to attend separate schools from white students. They also had separate accommodations in most public places such as trains, buses, libraries, restaurants, and even drinking fountains. In some states, housing restrictions were placed on African Americans who were not allowed to live in certain parts of some communities. In addition, African Americans' right to vote was often limited by such laws, which required a poll tax or literacy test as a prerequisite for casting a ballot.

By the 1920s, the South was still dominated by agricultural and rural communities. Many blacks worked as sharecroppers through the late 1910s, but a boll weevil (a type of beetle) infestation of cotton fields in this time period left the already poor farmers even more economically devastated. The potential for starvation was a compelling factor to seek jobs elsewhere.

The North was believed to be less segregated than the South and held the promise of better employment. World War I temporarily cut down on the number of immigrants from Europe at a time when the number of factory and service jobs increased because of the needs of the war. Many men also left their jobs to serve in the armed forces. Thus more jobs were available in industrial cities in the North for African Americans. Work shortages meant opportunities for many blacks looking for a better life. Labor agents abounded, working to convince blacks to move north and take jobs. Some companies, such as railroad companies, needed workers so badly that they funded some African Americans' travel from the South to the North.

Approximately one million African Americans left the South for the North during the Great Migration, increasing the black population in those cities an average of 20 percent between 1910 and 1930. The Great Migration completely transformed the black population of certain cities. For example, in Detroit the population of African Americans was only 6,000 in 1910. By 1929, the number had increased to 120,000. The Great Migration continued until about 1930 when the Great Depression caused the need for workers in the North to abate.

The effects of the Great Migration on the African Americans who made the journey was profound. While they faced some difficulties adjusting to life in the northern urban centers, workers earned higher wages than they did in the South. Their children received better educations. It also affected blacks left behind in the South. While some white planters and employers tried to prevent blacks from leaving en masse through intimidation and other means, other business owners and farmers promised better pay and treatment to their workers who stayed. There was some change in many whites' attitudes and behavior toward blacks in the South, though racist attitudes continued to dominate.

Harlem Renaissance

One result of the Great Migration was the Harlem Renaissance, a term used to describe a blossoming of African American culture, literature, music, and arts in New York City in the 1920s. Many of the blacks who moved from the South to New York City during the Great Migration settled in Harlem. They developed a change in attitude, becoming what was termed the "New Negro." Discarding the docile slave mentality, the New Negro was smart, eloquent, urban, and confident. Blacks found an expression for this new attitude in cultural forms.

The artists, musicians, and writers who were part of the Harlem Renaissance used their works as social and political critiques and as an expression of what they experienced as African Americans. They wanted to challenge racism and racial stereotypes promulgated by the white community to create a new cultural identity, which would encourage the black race. Many who participated in the Harlem Renaissance, such as painter Aaron Douglas and poet Langston Hughes, were also influenced by a quest to understand their African ancestors.

CRITICAL OVERVIEW

When *Cane* was published in 1923, only about 1,000 copies were initially printed. However, a few critics as well as literary editors and authors embraced the book as a powerful work from the beginning. Such readers responded positively to Toomer's experimental form, artistic structure and style, and his unique take on the subject matter—African American life.

In the introduction to the original printing of *Cane*, Waldo Frank writes, "A poet has arisen among our American youth who has known how to turn the essences and materials of his Southland into the essences and materials of literature." However, not all critics of the time responded as enthusiastically, as some were befuddled by the book's mix of forms. Writing in the *New Republic*, Robert Littell comments, "*Cane* is an interesting, occasionally beautiful and often queer book of exploration into old country and new ways of thinking."

Cane was only reprinted once while Toomer was alive, in 1927. After his death, the book eventually came to be widely read and a significant example of the literature of the Harlem Renaissance

MEDIA ADAPTATIONS

A theatrical presentation of *Cane* was released in 2006 by Chezia Thompson Cager. It is called *Teaching Jean Toomer's 1923* Cane, and it is available on compact disc from the Spectrum of Poetic Fire.

of the 1920s. *Cane* found widespread audience in the 1960s with the coming of the Black Arts movement when both students and scholars rediscovered the book and Toomer, and claimed him as an important black author. In 1965, Robert Bone acknowledged that it was one of the leading works of the Harlem Renaissance. In his article "The Harlem School," Bone claims, "Jean Toomer belongs to that first rank of writers who use words almost as a plastic medium, shaping new meanings from an original and highly personal style."

Over the years, such critics and scholars have praised *Cane* for its realistic depiction of life in the South and of African Americans. Toomer received critical kudos because he resisted the stereotypical depictions of African Americans that were common at the time. Yet some of the book's content was controversial, including Toomer's depiction of women, especially in the book's first section, and his exploration of their sexuality. Others noted the prideful way he depicted women.

Cane's form was an issue as well. There has been some critical debate over exactly what kind of book *Cane* is. Some critics call it a novel, though Toomer himself rejected this label. It has been described variously as one prose poem or even a cycle of short stories. Dismissing this controversy in the *New York Times*, prominent African American author Alice Walker writes,

> Some critics called the book a novel, some called it a prose poem, some did not know what to call it; but all agreed that "Cane" was original, and a welcome change from earlier fiction that took a didactic or hortatory position on black and interracial American life.

Toomer's book continues to be regarded as a significant work into the early twenty-first century. As Karen Jackson Ford asserts in *Split-Gut Song*, "Through lyricism and impressionism, Toomer achieves an accuracy of representation that exceeds realism. Either way the argument is made, realism or 'higher' realism, *Cane* is valued for its authentic depiction of African America."

CRITICISM

William Dow

In the following excerpt, Dow explains how, by speaking from and to different points of view in the different sections of Cane, *Toomer emphasizes the individuality among people often assumed to share a common perspective.*

> "I want great art. This means I want great design." Jean Toomer, "Open Letter to Gorham Munson"

Part of Toomer's "great design" in *Cane* is that his text, like any written text and paralleling any oral performance, is by someone and to someone. It is, then, a social transaction that does not present what is said to the exclusion of who says it to whom and for what purpose. Although *Cane*'s characters receive relatively brief treatment, the identity of the novel's narrator is presented in more fully developed terms, both as a process of consciousness and unconsciousness and as a subject impinged on and affected by interactions with his characters and narratee. The narrator renders his "individuality" through a socialized interdependence based on forms of direct address and a creative negotiation of narrative authority. Toomer's radically new formal transgressions, which follow his radical positions on race and culture, speak to the need to understand *Cane* in terms of both stylistic function and thematic expression.

My purpose here is to trace Toomer's self-reflective narrators in the three sections of *Cane* in order to show how Toomer raises the issue of "social transaction" implied by the choice of narrative method and by the identification of narrator, narratee, and reader. In effect, Toomer does not assert cognitive authority but concentrates instead on articulating modes of narrative authority and patterns of feeling that directly modify not how we understand the world so much as how we engage it. He suggests

Sugar mill workers processing sugar at the California and Hawaiian Sugar Refining Company, Crockett, CA, circa 1900 © *Michael Maslan Historic Photographs/Corbis*

that there are modes other than "race" that afford significant ways of resisting the dominant cultural emphases on difference. I want to show how these concepts and modes are inflected by the geographical movements of the book, what shifts in the identification of narrator and narratee are implied by shifts in the nature of the communal experience in *Cane*'s three sections, and how the subjectivities of characters, narrators, and real and implied readers have been shaped by different communal experiences. *Cane* is a productive rewriting of "race," allowing for the recognition of multiple authentic African American voices, identifications complicated by class, gender, and geography, and greatly enriched by the significant modulations in narrative address that Toomer undertakes.

An emblem of the last geographical movement in *Cane*, "Kabnis" signals the narrator's return to rural Georgia from the urban environments of Washington, D.C. and Chicago, and thus the novel comes full circle. Unlike the narratees in the preceding parts, the narratee in Part Three is not represented by a character, nor is he

mentioned explicitly by the narrator. Instead, the emphasis shifts: the intervening narrator and the character Kabnis point to the autobiographical Toomer: "Toomer places himself at the center of 'Kabnis'"; the narrator tells his "story." But for both the narrator and Kabnis, their desires, their subjectivities, cannot be satisfactorily articulated until they find a means with which to mediate them. Paralleling Kabnis's struggles to do so, the narrator commingles the private with public in "Kabnis," using a self-addressed and autobiographical "you" and a tone of voice that runs the gamut from the stridency of the orator to the tenderness of the poet: "Shadows of pines are dreams the sun shakes from its eyes." He can be nurturing: "Dead blind father of a muted folk who feel their way upward to a life that crushes or absorbs them. (speak, Father!)." He can be sardonic: "[Hanby] is well dressed, smooth, rich, black-skinned Negro who thinks there is no one quite so suave and polished as himself," and he can be merely a neutral describer of actions: "He stands by the hearth, rocking backward and forward. He stretches his hands out to the fire." On the one hand, "Kabnis" renders a kind of individual and communal tragic subjectivity in which the narrator dramatizes the forces destroying the folk culture and causing racial oppression. On the other, "Kabnis" is as much about the narrator's self-exploration (and Toomer's own) as it is a portrayal of communal subjectivities and experience.

"Kabnis" brings a new shaping of subjectivities, most notably those of the narrator and Kabnis. The narrator integrates into Kabnis strong undercurrents of irony, parody, and the burlesque, and casts the story into a kind of mock-epic form. Unlike Carma, Fern, and Karintha whose minds the narrator cannot penetrate, the narrator does know the mind of Kabnis. Yet the subjectivity the narrator produces (his own and Kabnis's) creates a mysterious and elusive atmosphere, particularly in the context of Kabnis's many roles: as a protagonist in the drama, as an educated outsider, as a poet who wants to become the "lips of the south," as "a ridiculous pathetic figure in his showy robe." The first section in the drama portrays Kabnis's isolated subjectivity, which is countered in the following sections when Kabnis comes into contact with the community. With communal contact, mostly among Sempter's black men, Kabnis searches for the security of self, and the identity of a racial self, in others.

But Kabnis fails to find this self and to integrate into the community of "peace." Instead, he feels "suspended a few feet above the soil whose touch would resurrect him." Although he dreams of giving words to the South, he can neither reconcile the cultures of North and South nor, even in moments of heightened self-consciousness, face his racial past. Indeed, Lewis confronts Kabnis with the memory of the past he can either deny and let "die an impotent and meaningless death, or use . . . to become a sustaining, spiritual force behind a reawakened sense of race consciousness":

Lewis: The old man as symbol, flesh, and spirit of the past, what do you think he would say if he could see you? You look at him, Kabnis.

Kabnis: Just like any done-up preacher is what he looks like to me. Jam some false teeth in his mouth and crank him, an youd have God Almighty spit in torrents all around th floor. Oh, hell, an he reminds me of that black cockroach over yonder. An besides, he aint my past. My ancestors were Southern blue-bloods—

Lewis: And black.

Kabnis: Aint much difference between blue and black.

Lewis: Enough to draw a denial from you. Can't hold them, can you? Master; slave. Soil; and the overarching heavens. Dusk; dawn. They fight and bastardize you. The sun tint of your cheeks, flame of the great season's multi-colored leaves, tarnished, burned, Split, shredded; easily burned. No use.

Despite such denials. Kabnis, from a certain perspective, represents the narrator of the first two sections who tries to become integrated into the community and must humble himself and suffer humility in his attempt to do so. Kabnis's intense loneliness, his consuming self-centeredness, and his various "denials," elations, and disintegrations are parts that the narrator later tries to bring together into a "soft circle," a spirit of individual and communal consciousness.

In addressing the community and the narratee the participant-narrator resorts to an invocatory, imperative form: "Night winds fare the breathing of the unborn child whose calm throbbing in the belly of a Negress sets them somnolently singing. Hear their song." "The night winds in Georgia," the narrator urges, "are vagrant poets whispering," and the "weird chill of their song," a song which serves as a refrain for "Kabnis," must be listened to:

White-man's land
Niggers sing.
burn, bear black children
till poor rivers glory
In Camp Ground.

Moreover, as in Parts One and Two, lyricism, "White paint on the wealthier houses has the chill blue glitter of distant stars," interfuses with speculation and uncertainty to dominate the descriptions: "it seems huge, limitless in the candle light"; "Someone is coming down the stairs." The narrator, as part of his self-examination, struggles to discover and interrogate reality, and at times casts doubt not only on his own declarations and predispositions but on the literal reality of his characters' perceptions. This doubt spreads to the narrator's reliance on the narratee's assent and approval. The narrator's earlier confidential attitudes toward the "you," which "encourage actual readers to see themselves reflected in that pronoun" are in this section conspicuously absent.

What replaces this particular narrator-you relationship is Toomer's use of a self-addressed you. Kabnis directs his inner thoughts to "God Almighty, Dear God, Dear Jesus," then to a self-reflective self. "Get up you damn fool. Look around. What's beautiful there?", before addressing his own feelings. "Oh no, I won't let that emotion come up in me. Stay down. I tell you." He later returns to a remonstrative self. "Come, Ralph, old man, pull yourself together." In this section the comments of an omniscient narrator, "Kabnis' mind clears," alternate with Kabnis's various addresses to Jesus, "Jesus how still everything is," and to himself, "Come, Ralph, pull yourself together...You know, Ralph, old man, it wouldn't surprise me at all to see a ghost." Hence the text accommodates a variety of "you's" as it earlier accommodated a variety of "I's." But Kabnis's "you" is self-directed, revealing, insofar as a character-speaker emerges in the text. Kabnis's solipsism and his failure to resolve his differences with the community.

Toomer wished to create "a new idiom which could introduce a greater diversity of perspective and voices, and elements that his lyrical narrative, his poetical or realistic descriptions could not include." But stylistic diversity is, to say the least, everywhere, in *Cane*. The narrator, wishing to engage the "you" and to establish a relation between the narratee and actual reader in Part One, can use the "you's" to substitute or disguise a self-referential "I" in Part Two. The narrator in this section, though less reflective than in the first section, continues to foster sympathy for real-world sufferers and continues to assume that his narratees are in perfect sympathy with him. The narrator in Part Three works against the grain of the protagonist's discourse, providing it with a meaning that, though not explicitly articulated, is (silently) conveyed to the reader behind the protagonist's back. Through such narrative interventions and a posturing of the "you," the narrator emphasizes the fact that the author *exists*, in all his ambiguities, complexities, and failures, and is very much *in* the text.

What is the purpose of *Cane*'s diverse narrative stances and strategies? As Toomer said of *Cane*, "There is nothing about these pieces of the buoyant expression of a new race" and the stories emphasize that socially one's "position here is transient." But paralleling Toomer's "spiritualization of experience," there is a social configuration, evoked by the narrator, which includes a consciousness that the stories, poems, and dramatic form of the text involve the reader in acts of judgment, call for social transactions, and create spaces in which racial meanings are

renegotiated. *Cane*'s poems can be seen in this light, in which direct address and invocatory voices take the form of a spiritual, "Cotton song": "Shackles fall upon the Judgement Day / But lets not wait for it", an imagistic lyric, "Her Lips Are Copper Wire": "and press your lips to mine / till they fare incandescent," or a communal hymn, as in "Harvest Song":

> O my brothers, I beat my palms, still soft,
>   against the stubble of my
> harvesting. (You beat your soft palms, too.)
>   My pain is
> sweet. Sweeter than the oats or wheat or corn.
>   It will not
> bring me knowledge of my hunger.

Hence there is a constant tension between conflicting strategies: between the narrator's self-reflectiveness, whereby the story draws attention to its status as art, and forms of narrative, whereby the story is concerned with its informational, thematic contents. Self-reflectiveness as a mode of exercising narrative authority has the signal advantage that it cannot be deceptive: the artistic "folk song" being laid claim to cannot be mistaken for anything but what it is. So, it is significant that the mode adopted by the narrator of *Cane*, for which he takes responsibility, is self-reflectiveness. It remains for the narrator to incorporate into his own art of narration the advantages of artistic indirection with the certainty of effects. Finally, unlike the storytelling in many modernist texts, *Cane* does not drive the teller out of the tale. Rather, as part of Toomer's "intimate connection of things," the narrator is an essential clement in mediating between his self-designation, his own spiritual life and survival, and that of his fictional communities, narratee, and readers. To this end, social interdependence and its racial implications in *Cane*, even if non-transcendent and derived from "a knowledge of [Toomer's] futility to check solution," become the heart of a "great design."

Source: William Dow, "'Always your heart': the 'Great Design' of Toomer's *Cane*," in *MELUS*, Vol. 27, No. 4, Winter 2002, pp.59–89.

SOURCES

Bone, Robert, "The Harlem School," in *The Negro Novel in America*, rev. ed., Yale University Press, 1965, pp. 65–94.

Ford, Karen Jackson, "The Scratching Choruses of Modernity," in *Split-Gut Song: Jean Toomer and the Poetics of Modernity*, The University of Alabama Press, 2005, pp. 2–29.

Frank, Waldo, "Foreword," in *Cane*, University Place Press, 1967, pp. vii–xi.

Guzzio, Tracie Church, "Jean Toomer," in *American Writers*, Supplement 9, edited by Jay Parini, Charles Scribner's Sons, 2002.

Littell, Robert, Review of *Cane*, in the *New Republic*, December 23, 1923, p. 126.

Toomer, Jean, *Cane*, Boni & Liveright, 1923; reprint, Liveright, 1975, reissued 1993.

Turner, Darwin T., "Introduction," in *Cane*, Liveright, 1975, reissued 1993, pp. ix–xxv.

Walker, Alice, "The Divided Life of Jean Toomer," in the *New York Times*, July 13, 1980, sec. 7, p. 11.

Chronicle of the Narváez Expedition

The *Chronicle of the Narváez Expedition* (1555) is Alvar Núñez Cabeza de Vaca's account of his years as a survivor of a doomed Spanish mission, lost in what is now the southern part of the United States. The expedition landed at present-day Tampa Bay, Florida, and moved from Florida to Texas, Arizona, New Mexico, and Mexico. The *Chronicle* is the first published book by a European about what was to became the United States. Originally published in Spanish as *La relación que dio Aluar Núñez Cabeza de Vaca de lo acaescido en las Indians en la armada donde yua por gouernador Pamphilo de Narbeaz* in 1542, revised and expanded as *La Relacion y comentarios del gouernador Aluar Núñez Cabeza de Vaca* in 1555, the book fueled interest in exploring and conquering North America among its original readers. Cabeza de Vaca included information about gold and copper, as well as other metals and minerals in the area, objects of desire for many an explorer who followed him.

Cabeza de Vaca was a member of an expedition that left Spain in 1527 headed by Pánfilo de Narváez, who was to be the governor of what the Spanish called La Florida. Even before arriving there, the voyagers dealt with many problems, including a hurricane that sank two of its ships. At Narváez's insistence, most of the expedition party moved inland to explore and claim territory. Only Cabeza de Vaca and three others

ALVAR NÚÑEZ CABEZA DE VACA

1555

of the original crew who took the inland journey made it back to Spain alive.

The text of the *Chronicle* details the author's often challenging experiences as a member of the expedition. Cabeza de Vaca spent many years moving through territory not previously seen or explored by Europeans, suffering from soul-crushing hunger, thirst, and physical pain. He was among the first white men to see bison, and he writes about the many Indian tribes he encountered and lived with, their social customs, and the local land, flora, and fauna. Eventually, Cabeza de Vaca and the three other men remaining from the original expedition found other Spaniards and reached Mexico City in 1536, and they were able to return to Europe in 1537.

The *Chronicle* was originally written for the king of Spain as a private report in 1537. Cabeza de Vaca was trying to convince his king to name him governor of La Florida, but the position went to Hernando de Soto. The author later received his own governorship in South America in 1540. In 1542, the *Chronicle* was published in Spain to a limited circulation. The 1555 version of the *Chronicle* became more widely read. It was a more elaborate, detailed second edition, and focused on improving Cabeza de Vaca's reputation after his own governorship in South America proved a failure and landed the author in jail. The *Chronicle* was first translated into English in 1851 by Thomas Buckingham Smith, around the same time the United States gained territory from Mexico after the Mexican-American War.

While in many senses the expedition at the heart of the *Chronicle* was a failure, the book describes a triumph of perseverance. Though all of their possessions were lost and he and his companions often lacked food and water, they were able to adapt to the environment as well as many aspects of the Indian way of life. Cabeza de Vaca repeatedly emphasizes that he lived as naked as many of the Indians for much of his journey; they did what they had to do to survive. As the natural riches and native cultures Cabeza de Vaca encountered sparked the European imagination and drive to claim and conquer, the *Chronicle* is a critical link in the chain of events that shaped the modern North American political, social, and economic landscape.

BIOGRAPHY

ALVAR NÚÑEZ CABEZA DE VACA

Born between 1485 and 1492 probably in Jerez de la Frontera, Spain, Alvar Núñez Cabeza de Vaca was a member of a distinguished family. Pedro de Vera, his maternal grandfather, was involved with conquering the Canary Islands. Cabeza de Vaca served several stints as a soldier fighting in Italy and Spain for both King Carlos V and for four Dukes of Medina Sidonia.

In 1542, Cabeza de Vaca traveled with the party of the new governor of Florida, Pánfilo de Narváez, to explore the new Spanish territory. The expedition was a complete debacle, with only the author and a few others surviving the inland journey. Cabeza de Vaca wrote of his years of hardships in *Chronicle of the Narváez Expedition* (*La relación*), first published in 1542 and updated in 1555.

Before publication of the book, Cabeza de Vaca had already returned to the Americas to serve as governor of the Río de la Plata beginning in 1541. This experience was also disastrous, ending in mutiny. In 1544, he returned to Spain as a prisoner charged with corruption and spent eight years in jail. He wrote another memoir about the experience in *Comentarios*. Cabeza de Vaca died in 1559 or 1560 in Spain.

PLOT SUMMARY

Prologue: Holy, Imperial, Catholic Majesty

As *Chronicle of the Narváez Expedition* opens, Alvar Núñez Cabeza de Vaca addresses the king of his country, recognizing that it is in his service that the author has gone on his travels. He concludes, "this is the only thing that a man who left there naked could bring back with him."

Chapter 1: When the Fleet Left Spain and the Men Who Went with It

On June 27, 1527, the Narváez expedition leaves Spain. It is headed by Pánfilo de Narváez, who is to serve as the governor of the part of North America that includes the Cape of Florida. He has with him five ships and about six hundred men, including the author, who is the expedition's treasurer and head of legal issues.

On a governor-ordered trip to buy supplies in a port city in Trinidad, Cabeza de Vaca barely escapes death as a hurricane hits. The author and about thirty men are on shore while the hurricane rages, and they are the only survivors from the two ships that were originally sent for supplies. The governor arrives with his ships a few days later, in early November 1527. The expedition remains in the port of Xagua until February 1528 as many of the survivors are now afraid to sail in winter.

Chapter 2: How the Governor Came to Xagua and Brought a Pilot with Him

When they sail again, they continue to face storms as they head toward Florida. The expedition finally reaches Florida on April 12, 1528, and sails along the coast until they reach a bay inhabited by Indians.

Chapter 3: How We Arrived in Florida

Alonso Enriquez, the expedition's comptroller, trades for food with the Indians. The next day, the governor and the men, including the author, go ashore. Narváez claims the land in the name of the king of Spain. Cabeza de Vaca reports that the Indians want them to leave, but they do not do anything about it except to leave themselves.

Chapter 4: How We Went to the Interior

Two days later, the governor decides to start exploring the land. On the second trek inland a few days later, a small party captures four Indians, who take the group to their village. They find items from Castile and New Spain, as well as some gold. The Indians tell them about a distant place called Apalache, which has a great deal of gold and other valuables. The expedition plans to take some of these Indians as guides and go there.

The governor meets with a few of the leaders of the expedition and lays out his plan to move inland while his ships remain sailing along the coast until they reach a certain harbor. Cabeza de Vaca vehemently disagrees with the plan. He wants to go back on the ships and look for a better place to make port. The others believe some should travel on land along the coast until they reach the harbor and the ships and the rest of the expedition should follow. The governor selects the second plan and heads the land expedition.

The governor wants Cabeza de Vaca to take charge of the ships, but he will not. Cabeza de Vaca writes, "I refused to accept because I felt sure that he would never see the ships again, nor the ships him." The author insists on taking the inland journey with the governor.

Chapter 5: How the Governor Left the Ships

Starting off on May 1, the governor and his party of three hundred men travel for fifteen days along the coast. They have to cross a swift river, a task that takes a day. On the other side, they find Indians and eventually obtain food in their village. After spending time searching for a harbor and finding none, the party continues to look for Apalache.

About a month later, they meet an Indian chief who is the enemy of the Apalache and is willing to aid the Christians (the author's term for the members of his expedition). The party crosses another river, deep and swift, and lose their first man, who drowns with his horse. They eventually reach Apalache without letting the Indians therein know of their presence. The party has suffered on their long, arduous journey and are happy to reach their destination.

Chapter 6: How We Got to Apalache

Cabeza de Vaca leads the small party to enter the Apalache village. Though attacked by the Indian men, the hostile ones soon retreat. The author describes what they find in the village, including a significant amount of corn.

Chapter 7: The Lay of the Land

After describing the area surrounding the village and the attacks on them by the Indians, Cabeza de Vaca reports they stay for nearly a month. Learning that there is another, more prosperous Indian village called Aute to the south and closer to the sea, the expedition moves there. This excursion also experiences Indian attacks, during which the second Spaniard dies. When they reach Aute, the Indians are gone and their lodges burned, but their crops are still intact.

Cabeza de Vaca soon takes a party of fifty men to look for the sea. They find an inlet but determine that the seacoast is still far off. Returning to Aute, Cabeza de Vaca and his party find many of the men, including the governor, are ill and had been attacked by Indians the previous night.

Chapter 8: How We Left Aute

Though weak from the horrible conditions and extreme illness, the whole party goes to the inlet spot Cabeza de Vaca has found. There is little hope of surviving there. They decide to build ships to leave, using local wood and plants and materials they had brought from Spain. They build five boats between early August and late September, during which time they raid local Indian villages and eat all but one of their horses to survive. The expedition—now just 242 men—finally leaves what they call the Bay of Horses.

Chapter 9: How We Left the Bay of Horses

After a week of sailing along the coast, they encounter Indians in canoes near an island. The Christians take the five canoes abandoned by the Indians as well as the food supplies they find in lodges on the island. For a month, the party sails in this manner, "plying the coast toward the River of Palms" (westward along the Gulf of Mexico), with their supplies dwindling. Finding a small island, they set anchor there, where an intense storm prevents their departure for six days. There is no fresh water, and several men die from drinking saltwater. Even though the storm has not stopped, they decide they must sail on.

They decide to follow an Indian canoe they encountered earlier, which leads them to an Indian village. Though they exchange corn for fish there, they soon fall under attack again. The governor is hurt, and they return to the boats. Traveling farther, they encounter more Indians who offer to get them water as long as one man, Doroteo Teodoro, comes with them. Teodoro takes a black man from the expedition and some containers for water; and the Indians leave two of their own as hostages. The Indians return the vessels but neither the two Christians nor the promised water.

Chapter 10: On the Skirmish We Had with the Indians

The next morning, the Indians want the two Indian hostages left with the expedition to be returned to them, but the governor will not do so until the Christians are returned. Sailing on, the Christians find a cape, a freshwater river, and a bay with many islands. Collecting fresh water from the river, they try to near the river's shore but are unsuccessful because of the sea's movement.

The boats start drifting apart from each other into deep water. When Cabeza de Vaca's boat nears the governor's, he asks for instructions. He recounts that "He answered that this was no time for orders; that each one should do the best he could to save himself." The governor tells him to row to shore but will not help Cabeza de Vaca's boat, which is full of weak men. Instead, Cabeza de Vaca's boat travels with the boat headed by Captains Peñalosa and Tellez. When a storm overtakes them, the Peñalosa/Tellez boat is lost. Eventually, the men on Cabeza de Vaca's boat become increasingly ill. Death seems near for all one night, but in the morning they finally reach shore, on November 6.

Chapter 11: What Happened to Lope de Oviedo with Some Indians

After eating, the most physically robust man, Lope de Oviedo, does some exploring. He learns that they are on an island. "A hundred Indian archers" follow Oviedo back, and the men are terrified since only three of them can even stand up. Though the Indians are ready to attack, the Christians appease them with beads and trinkets. The Indians promise to bring food the next day.

Chapter 12: How the Indians Brought Us Food

The Indians feed the men for several days, until Cabeza de Vaca and his men decide to continue on their voyage. They strip naked to get the boat out of the sand. Two waves across the bow overturn the boat, drowning several men. The rest make it back to shore, having lost everything. "We were in such a state that our bones could easily be counted and we looked like death itself," Cabeza de Vaca writes.

The Indians again bring them food, but they are afraid of the white men's changed appearance.

Though some of the men do not want Cabeza de Vaca to ask the Indians to take them to their village, the author decides that this is the only way to survive. The Indians take care of them. Cabeza de Vaca explains, "In the morning they again gave us fish and roots, and treated us so well that we were reassured, losing to some extent our apprehension of being sacrificed."

Chapter 13: How We Learned About Other Christians

After noticing an unfamiliar trinket one Indian has, Cabeza de Vaca learns that there are other Christians nearby. They turn out to be Captains Dorantes and del Castillo and their crews, safe and in the care of other Indians. They try to repair their boats, but the weather and lack of clothing compel most of the men to remain there for the winter.

Chapter 14: How Four Christians Departed

Many die that winter, and five men who stay on the coast resort to cannibalism as they face starvation. Of the eighty men from both boats, only fifteen are still alive. The Indians begin dying from sickness and blame the Christians for their illness. Though the Indians are planning to kill the remaining Christians, one of their own dissuades them, arguing that if the Christians had such power more of them would have survived. They call the island the "Isle of Misfortune." The author also describes some of the Indians' social customs, including body piercings, division of labor, and mourning and marriage rituals. In April, the Christians and the Indians go to the mainland and celebrate and feast on blackberries for a month.

Chapter 15: What Happened to Us on the Isle of Misfortune

Describing more Indian customs on the island, Cabeza de Vaca also relates that the Indians essentially force the Christians to act as medicine men. Their method of healing is to breathe on their patients, make the sign of the cross over them, and pray. He also describes the Indians' clothing and organization, noting: "They are very liberal toward each other with what they have. There is no ruler among them. All who are of the same descent cluster together."

Chapter 16: How the Christians Left the Island

In the spring, Dorantes and Castillo organize a meeting of the fourteen expedition members who are still alive on the island. By this time, Cabeza de Vaca is on the mainland, ill and perhaps near death. Most of the men from the island try to visit him there, but he is too sick to see them. Dorantes and Castillo, and ten others who are healthy enough to try, leave the island. Cabeza de Vaca reports that he ran from the Indians from the island because they made him work too much. He went to live among the Charrucans, mainland Indians who live in the forest. He had more freedom to move around as he became a trader, operating inland and along the coast among the Indians. Despite an improved life, he continues to suffer physically from the conditions. He writes, "I spent nearly six years in this country, alone with them and as naked as they were."

Cabeza de Vaca remains so long because another Christian, Lope de Oviedo, still lives on the island. It takes the author that long to convince him to leave and look for other Christians. As they travel along the coast, they learn some Indians have killed a few of their compatriots for fun, but three are still alive, barely surviving the ill treatment. Oviedo decides not to stay on but chooses to return with some women of the Deaguanes Indians. Cabeza de Vaca stays, the lone Christian among the brutish Quevenes Indians.

Chapter 17: How the Indians Arrived with Andrés Dorantes and Castillo and Estevanico

Some Indians from a different tribe than the Quevenes lead Cabeza de Vaca to Dorantes, Castillo, and Estevanico. The author convinces Dorantes and Castillo to escape and go to "a country of Christians." To facilitate this plan, Cabeza de Vaca agrees to be a slave to the Indian family holding Dorantes until the spring, when the Indians harvest and live off of prickly pear. The author also learns of the tragic fate of most of the rest of the expedition, most of whom died from illness, starvation, or violence, and many of whom resorted to cannibalizing the dead. Esquivel, the last to survive by cannibalism, was taken by an Indian and lived to tell Figueroa his tale.

Chapter 18: Esquivel's Account, Related by Figueroa

The fates of the expedition survivors passed from man to man until it thus reached Cabeza de Vaca. He begins this chapter by further describing the lot of others from the expedition, including how Dorantes, Castillo, and Estevanico, a Moorish slave of the Spaniards, came to be where they are as slaves. He also includes further information about the Indians' life and customs, including the Marianes Indians killing of all female infants lest they bear children who will become enemies of the tribe. He notes, "They are great liars and drunkards, and drink to become intoxicated. They are so accustomed to running that, without resting or getting tired, they run from morning till night in pursuit of a deer." He also describes a cow-like animal, probably buffalo, as being numerous, large, and delicious.

Chapter 19: How the Indians Separated Us

Because of a conflict between the Indians, the first prickly pear time did not allow the men to escape as planned. Cabeza de Vaca and the others have to live with the Indians for another year, and he is treated badly. A year later, despite the Indians separating the four Christians, they meet up again at the next year's prickly pear time.

Chapter 20: How We Fled

The four men manage to flee, and they eventually find welcome shelter with the Avavares Indians. The Avavares already know about the Christians from their trade with other tribes that had held them captive previously. The Avavares believe the Christians are medicine men.

Chapter 21: How We Cured Several Sick People

The Indians ask Castillo to heal their headaches. He makes the sign of the cross over each patient; the healing works, and many soon demand the same treatment. The four decide to stay the winter with these Indians. While hunting with them for food, Cabeza de Vaca gets lost for five days and is feared dead for a time.

Chapter 22: How the Following Day They Brought Other Sick People

More Indians seek healing from Castillo. Using the same technique, he heals five paralyzed people. When they are healed, Indians from a number of tribes ask Castillo to heal them. The author explains:

> We all prayed to [God] as well as we could to restore them to health and he, seeing there was no other way of getting those people to help us so that we might be saved from our miserable existence, had mercy on us.

Soon, all four men are healing the Indians. The Indians tell a tale about a demon who terrorized them a decade or more before, and the Christians convince them that if they would "be Christians, like ourselves, they would not have to fear that man." The Avavares like the idea.

The four stay with the Avavares for about eight months, before moving on and staying with other tribes. Of the Fig Indians, Cabeza de Vaca notes, "they judge the seasons by the ripening of fruit, by the time that fish die, and by the appearance of the stars, and in all of this they are very clever and expert." They remain naked and hungry, for food is scarce. They begin to make items such as arrows, nets, and lodge matting under contract for the Indians, as well as items for barter.

Chapter 23: How We Departed After Eating the Dogs

After eating two dogs they acquired in barter, the four continue to travel on a trail, eating what they can find. They stay with another group of Indians who treat them very well. "Our departure pained them greatly, and we left them in tears."

Chapter 24: The Customs of the Indians of That Land

Cabeza de Vaca describes more of the culture among the Indians, focusing on women, marriage, interpersonal disagreements, and warfare.

Chapter 25: How Ready the Indians Are with Weapons

Cabeza de Vaca continues his discussion of the way Indians live. He praises their skill with bows and arrows, and their fearlessness in the face of European weapons. "Horses are what the Indians dread most, and the means by which they will be overcome." He advises on tactics against the Indians in battle and commends their physical capabilities, writing, "Their eyesight, hearing, and senses in general are better, I believe, than those of any other men on earth."

Chapter 26: On Nations and Languages

Cabeza de Vaca describes the location of various tribes and Indian languages, listing the Cavoques, Han, Charruco, Deguenes, Mendicans, Quevenes, Marianes, Guaycones, Yguaces, Atayos, Decuba-daos, Quitoles, Chavavares, Maliacones, Cultal-chulches, Susolas, Comos, Camolas, Figs, and Cuchendados, all of whom they have encountered since landing at the Isle of Misfortune. He also talks about how they produce a smoke from a certain leaf that makes them intoxicated, and homosexual marriage found among some tribes.

Chapter 27: How We Moved and Were Received

The next group the Christians stay with also do not want Cabeza de Vaca and his group to leave but make them a feast and try to convince them to stay. The Christians depart despite their hosts' efforts, get lost, and find a new tribe who greets them eagerly. The Christians work as healers for these Indians as well. The situation is repeated with the next tribe as well.

Chapter 28: On Another New Custom

The four continue to travel from Indian village to Indian village, seeing mountains and nearing the sea. They are followed by groups of Indians, who steal from the new Indians they encounter. This situation displeases Cabeza de Vaca, but the new tribes they visit learn to hide their belongings. The group continues to cross the country inland instead of along the coast, eventually losing their Indian escorts who do not want to take the route the four have chosen. When they come upon a lodge, they "were welcomed with tears and deep sorrow [because] they already knew that, wherever we arrived, the people would be robbed and plundered by those in our company." The Indians are relieved when the Christians arrive unaccompanied, and they are shocked the next day when they are plundered by the white men's prior companions. The myths around the men grow as looters advise the looted:

> In consolation, the robbers told them that we were children of the sun and had the power to cure the sick or kill them. . . . They also enjoined them to treat us with great reverence, be careful no to arouse our wrath, to give us all their possessions, and to guide us to where there were many people, and that wherever we should come to they should steal and rob everything the others had, which was the custom.

Chapter 29: How They Steal from One Another

The four Christians persist in their journey, again with more Indians following them, and continue to receive food and gifts. Cabeza de Vaca performs crude surgery on one Indian who has a long arrowhead lodged near his heart. The author successfully removes it, bringing him and his traveling companions much fame. They learn that there is copper in the ground in another location, which the author believes to be near a different sea than the one they have come from.

Chapter 30: How the Manner of Reception Changed

As their travels continue, the Indians begin giving them their possessions when Cabeza de Vaca and his companions enter their homes. The four distribute the goods among the many Indians who follow them and have already lost their possessions. The group continues to travel through a mountainous desert, across a river, and to a plain. They decide to go north. After an event when many of the Indians fall sick and die, and which the Indians believe is the result of the Christians' displeasure with them, they travel on. The four eventually reach an Indian village with permanent housing. These Indians greet them with lodgings already prepared for them and feed them well with beans and squash. They do not raise corn because the weather is too dry, and they ask the Christians to pray for rain. These Indians advise them not to travel north, because food is so scarce they will not eat for weeks if they go that way.

Chapter 31: How We Followed the Corn Trail

The Christians travel in the direction of the sunset for many days along a river and through a plain between mountain ranges without much food. They finally reach an Indian village with permanent housing, which has the corn they seek. The four then continue their journey, passing through similar villages with an abundance of corn and beans. The group receives many gifts of food, hides, blankets, coral, turquoise, and even emeralds while being asked by the Indians to bless them. The author comments that the women of these tribes are treated better and dressed better than those they had previously encountered. They exert authority over those Indians who travel with them and are able to communicate with a number of tribes. They also share their faith and explain the concepts of God and heaven to the Indians. "These people are well made and apt to follow any line that is well traced for them," Cabeza de Vaca notes of the Indians' acceptance of Christianity.

Chapter 32: How They Gave Us Hearts of Deer

In the village where they were given the emeralds, "they also gave Dorantes more than six hundred open hearts of deer." The Christians call the place, "the village of the hearts." While still in that settlement, Castillo notices that an Indian is wearing a sword belt buckle around his neck, and the four learn that Christians had been there previously, but left by the sea. Cabeza de Vaca writes, "We gave God our Lord many thanks for what we had heard, for we were despairing of ever hearing of Christians again."

They learn that Indians have abandoned their villages and are hiding in the mountains because of these Christians, whom the Indians fear because they destroyed villages and kidnapped many people. The author describes their reaction:

> This filled our hearts with sorrow, seeing the land so fertile and beautiful, so full of water and streams, but abandoned and the places burned down, and the people, so thin and wan, fleeing and hiding.

Yet these same remaining Indians give Cabeza de Vaca and his companions blankets and food, and show them respect. He writes, "it clearly shows how, in order to bring these people to Christianity and obedience unto Your Imperial Majesty, they should be well treated, and not otherwise." Cabeza de Vaca learns that some other Christians have recently passed through the area. He also notes that there are indications of valuable metals including copper, gold, and iron in the area.

Chapter 33: How We Saw Traces of Christians

Knowing that the other Christians are nearby, Cabeza de Vaca, Estevanico, and eleven Indians follow the trail to find them, reaching them a day later. He writes, "They stared at me for quite a while, speechless. Their surprise was so great that they could not find words to ask me anything." Cabeza de Vaca is taken to their commander, Diego de Alcazar, who is having problems capturing Indians. He has Alcazar certify when he met them and what state he was in when they found each other.

Chapter 34: How I Sent for the Christians

After the four are reunited and the Indians in hiding are brought forth, the group headed by Alcazar asks Cabeza de Vaca to instruct the Indians to bring them food, which he does. The two groups then come in conflict as Alcazar's group wants to enslave the Indians, an idea Cabeza de Vaca and his men detest. The Indians do not want to leave the four until they find other Indian companions for them, another concept Alcazar's group does not understand. The Indians trust Cabeza de Vaca and his companions but not the other Christians. The author finally persuades the Indians to return to their lives, though the other Christians deceive Cabeza de Vaca and his companions by leading them around in a manner that prevents communication with the Indians, who indeed are enslaved.

Chapter 35: How Well the Chief Magistrate Received Us on the Night of Our Arrival

When the four meet the Chief Magistrate of Culiacan, Melchor Diaz, he apologizes for the actions of the Alcazar group and wants Cabeza de Vaca and his friends to convince the Indians to return. The four do the best they can with a few Indians who are brought there, but many of the Indians cannot be found because they are hiding in the woods from the Christians. Diaz then speaks in the name of the four, invoking God and telling them to serve Him so they can be friends. The Indians agree to become Christians and return home.

Chapter 36: How We Had Churches Built in That Land

An agreement is reached where the Indian will build churches, put up crosses, and allow children of chiefs to be baptized, while the Christians vow not to raid or enslave the Indians. The four move on to the village of San Miguel, where Alcazar reports the Indians have upheld their end of the bargain and returned home. The author makes a special note in his narrative to his king of the religious customs of the Indians:

> In the two thousand leagues we traveled, on land, and by sea in boats, in the ten months more after our rescue from captivity that we

> " BESIDES SUFFERING GREAT FATIGUE AND HUNGER, THE BACKS OF MANY AMONG US WERE COVERED WITH WOUNDS FROM THE WEIGHT OF THE ARMOR AND OTHER THINGS THEY HAD TO CARRY, AS OCCASION REQUIRED. BUT TO FIND OURSELVES AT LAST WHERE WE WISHED TO BE AND WHERE WE HAD BEEN ASSURED SO MUCH FOOD AND GOLD WOULD BE HAD MADE US FORGET MANY OF OUR HARDSHIPS AND WEARINESS."

untiringly walked across land, nowhere did we come upon either sacrifices or idolatry.

Cabeza de Vaca and his companions eventually travel to Compostela. They eventually reach Mexico, where they receive a warm welcome from the authorities.

Chapter 37: What Occurred When I Wished to Return

After wintering in Mexico, Cabeza de Vaca sails to Vera Cruz, then Havana. Near Bermuda, the ship he is on gets temporarily lost in a storm but continues across the Atlantic. When they pass the island of Corvo, a French ship tries to take them over, but they are saved by the Portuguese navy. The ship finally reaches Lisbon, Portugal, on August 9, 1537.

Chapter 38: What Happened to the Others Who Went to the Indies

Cabeza de Vaca relates what happened to the three ships originally left behind when the first went ashore in Florida: The ships sailed, hugging the coast and looking for their captain and crew for a year, then returned home.

THEMES

Righteousness of Purpose

Cabeza de Vaca's perspective as an observer trying to understand the environment and the Indian culture and beliefs is important to the thematic understanding of the *Chronicle*. The author's absolute faith in the righteousness of his king and his god permeates his narrative, and foreshadows the attitude of the Europeans who would follow him into the New World. While he appreciates the landscape and the people he encounters, he does not question whether they should be subject to his country and their religion, and he uses his account to both tempt his countrymen and advise them about how to pursue conquest of this new world.

In one sense, *Chronicle of the Narváez Expedition* underscores the importance of the frontier as an opportunity to explore the unknown and seek opportunity. The original purpose of the governor's mission is to establish claims in Florida and much of what is now the southeastern United States. While the governor does state this fact when his expedition first lands, exploration falls to survival as the primary goal. However, Cabeza de Vaca never forgets that he is an explorer and regularly describes the landscape, social customs of the Indians, and other aspects of the various Indian tribes. The episodes in which Cabeza de Vaca and his three companions act as medicine men, healing any sick Indian with prayer, making the sign of the cross, and breathing on the patient, underscores the author's faith in Christianity as a protective and transforming force in this frontier. He also notes when they learn about precious metals, and where they believe gold, copper, and other such desired objects can be found. Though the text focuses on the difficulty of the journey, Cabeza de Vaca also writes to stimulate interest in what else can be found in this part of the world for future Europeans—those who would arrive on these shores to pursue what would become the American dream.

Survival

One of the major themes of *Chronicle of the Narváez Expedition* is how Cabeza de Vaca and some of his companions are able to adapt to the environment and overcome many hardships to survive—a theme that would define countless other American dreams in the five hundred years to follow. Traveling from what is now Florida westward, the author reports that over time many from the expedition die from various causes, including drowning, hunger and thirst, Indian attack, and illness. The four who make it home to Spain survive by recovering from illness, enduring thirst and hunger, befriending Indians who help them along the way, and moving in the direction to find other Christians. Despite overwhelming odds, they are able to adapt to their environment, persevere, and survive. They keep pressing forward to find their Christian brethren and return home, while the author also is able to note much about the Indians and the environment.

Cabeza de Vaca writes about a number of occasions when he makes choices that allow him to survive in spite of his environment and the hardships therein. After being separated from the governor and many of the other members of the inland expedition in the boats soon after leaving the Bay of Horses, Cabeza de Vaca takes tenacious action after tenacious action to ensure survival. Facing hostile Indians on the island in chapter 11, he gives them beads and bells as a sign of friendship. This action leads to the Indians calling off any attack and bringing food to the weak men. In the next chapter, the author dismisses the concerns of some of his group and asks these Indians to take them to their homes. This action ensures the survival of the group, though the move is a risky proposition. The Indians could attack them or sacrifice them, but instead they keep a number of the men alive for a significant time.

While the actions of Cabeza de Vaca and his companions are motivated by their drive to survive, their actions and circumstances change them as well. For the author and the three men who make it to the safety of their countrymen after years of wandering, the landscape and environment push them to their limits and transform what those limits are. After having to push the boat out of sand in chapter 12, Cabeza de Vaca reveals that he and many others in his group lived naked like the Indians for much of the rest of the time they are there. The author refers to this fact several times in the text. They also learn to deal with being hungry, thirsty, and ill, as well as recovering from these conditions. The survivors do whatever they have to, including temporarily submitting to being enslaved, to survive when nearly everyone who went on the governor's inland expedition loses his life.

When they have a chance to eat something, no matter how foreign, they generally take it. While Cabeza de Vaca reports in chapter 12 that he cannot bring himself to eat horsemeat and rarely ate fish during the time the boats are being built, he later admits that he ate the dogs that he and his three companions acquire in

trade. He eats raw corn when he has to, as well as many other roots, prickly pear, blackberries, raw meat, and even the scrapings from skins he is processing for tanning. Even some of the Indians are surprised how they adapted eating only irregularly. In chapter 31, Cabeza de Vaca writes,

> While traveling with them we used to go the whole day without food, until nighttime, and then we would eat so little that the Indians were amazed. They never saw us tired, because we were, in reality, so inured to hardships that we no longer felt them.

By the end of their journey, the Indians feel protective of the four, who basically live like they do, while the white men the four have been seeking barely recognize them as their countrymen.

HISTORICAL OVERVIEW

Pre-European Native Americans

At the time of Cabeza de Vaca's journey in North America, the area and its indigenous peoples were relatively unknown to European explorers. American Indians, as the native peoples came to be called, lived in separate tribes with different languages and dialects of common languages as well.

The total population of the Indians in the whole of the future United States at this time is unknown, though in Florida alone it is believed there were about 100,000 native peoples before European contact. The highest concentration of native peoples could be found in the Pacific Northwest, along the Mississippi River, and in the basin of the Alleghenies where timber was readily accessible. There were also significant settlements along the Rio Grande River in New Mexico and Arizona as well as parts of the northeast. Southern Texas, California, and much of northern Mexico were only sparsely populated because of the hot, dry climate.

Most Indian tribes were autonomous and fought with each other to obtain spoils or tribute. Within each tribe, land was owned communally, not individually, and there were no written laws. Custom was the primary means of organizing tribal society, and shamans often held the most power. In terms of religion, Indians practiced animism, the belief that spirits formed the world and could manifest themselves anywhere. Indians in the southeast and southwestern portions of the United States primarily subsisted on agriculture, though hunting was the primary occupation of some tribes in Texas. Indian tribes who lived near the coast of the Caribbean Sea relied on fishing as their source of food.

Spanish in North America

The first Europeans to settle in North America were Spaniards, who used the general term "the Western Indies" to describe the area. After Christopher Columbus's early expedition in the last decade of fifteenth century, others in the employ of Spain visited North America regularly in the late 1400s and early 1500s. Spain established its first colony in the Americas in the larger Antilles in 1493.

Within sixty years, Spain had colonies in present-day Mexico and locations south through Central and South America. Some colonies were located on the coast, but the Spaniards established locations inland as well. Parts of North America also came under Spanish control. Juan Ponce de Léon first reached Florida in 1513, looking for the legendary fountain of youth, not to mention riches. The goal of the Narváez expedition a few years later was to establish a colonial presence in La Florida.

Other Spanish explorations of North America followed. Hernando de Soto explored the southeastern portion of the future United States from 1539 to 1542. Francisco Vásquez de Coronado was the first to travel around and conquer parts of the southwest and Great Plains in the early 1540s. From 1542 to 1543, Juan Rodriguez Cabrillo led an excursion up the California coast.

Only one Spanish settlement of significance was established in the future United States, located in St. Augustine, Florida. Some conquistadors failed, such as Lucas Vázquez de Ayllón who unsuccessfully tried to start a colony in what is now South Carolina in 1526. This colony began with five hundred men, women, and children, both Spanish and slaves, but three hundred of them died within three months and the colony was abandoned.

The Spanish monarchy controlled the conquered parts of North, South, and Central America as a dominion of the Spanish crown. Royal permission was needed to explore and establish colonies. The crown held tight control over the colonies, to the point of deciding who was allowed to come to the area. The interests and needs of the Spanish nation were put over anyone who lived in the North American colonies, including Spanish colonists.

Spain was primarily interested in the Americas as a source of precious metals. Spain once had its own rich supply of gold and silver, but it had been mined out by the Romans when they occupied the country before the Dark Ages. Many Spaniards believed that the Americas would provide a rich source of gold, silver, and other metals. They mined such metals beginning in the sixteenth and through the seventeenth century, primarily in South America, until the supply of raw materials began to give out.

In pursuit of this wealth, Spaniards had to cope with the Indian population. At first, there was some debate among the Spanish over whether or not Indians were even humans. The Spanish eventually accepted Indians as human but saw them as childlike and in need of guidance to become the equals of whites. The Indians were also used as a source of labor for the Spanish colonists, who enslaved many native peoples.

CRITICAL OVERVIEW

The original critical opinion of the *Chronicle of the Narváez Expedition* is unknown, save that it influenced its readers to look to North America as a place full of potential for gaining wealth through gold as well as other metals and minerals. It was only available in Spanish and Italian until the mid-nineteenth century, when translations were made into German, French, and English. By the twentieth century, a number of English versions were available.

Many modern readers of English translations find the book exhilarating. Reviewing a new translations of the text, a critic in the *National Geographic Adventure* comments, "The book is as exciting and short as the trip was arduous and long. Cabeza de Vaca writes with breathless energy of the marvels he saw and the sufferings he endured."

Most critics acknowledge that the *Chronicle* was important in the launching of further exploration of North America. Tom Noel of the *Rocky Mountain News* writes in a review of the same translation, "Cabeza de Vaca's journey and his 1542 book about it launched a great American myth—that some fabulously rich American Indians lived in the Golden Cities of Cibola."

MEDIA ADAPTATIONS

Cabeza de Vaca (1991) is a film directed by Nicolás Echevarría, featuring Juan Diego, Daniel Giménez Cacho, and Roberto Sosa. The screenplay is loosely based on Alvar Núñez Cabeza de Vaca's *Chronicle of the Narváez Expedition*. The film depicts Cabeza de Vaca living among the Iguase Indians, emphasizing his mental state and the changes he undergoes because of his experience. *Cabeza de Vaca* is available on DVD from New Concorde DVD.

Haniel Long's *Interlinera to Cabeza de Vaca* (1936), later published as *The Power Within Us*, is a lengthy prose poem broken up into short stanzas. It describes the poet's interpretation of the thoughts and emotions of Cabeza de Vaca on his journey. A version of *The Power Within Us* was published in 2006 by Kessinger Publishing.

George Antheil's "Cabeza de Vaca: A Cantata Based On the Experiences and letters of Alvar Nunez, 'Cabeza de Vaca'" (1961) is a score for oboe, piano, and percussion inspired by *Chronicle of the Narváez Expedition*. Another version, called "Cabeza de Vaca," was written in 1955 for chorus and orchestras.

Some critics believe that the *Chronicle* was more a novel than a factual account, especially the 1555 edition. This edition was expanded in part to help Cabeza de Vaca's reputation in light of the aftermath of his failed governorship in South America. Stephen Petty writes in his paper "Cabeza de Vaca: A Model for Multiculturalism," "The text is novelistic in that the subjective experience is allowed to enter an official report: this is an intimate tale of survival and salvation as it addresses the large themes that dominated the Old World–New World encounter."

Despite such concerns, many critics praise the ethnographic work Cabeza de Vaca did in the book. They note his key eye for observing Indians, their customs, nature, and the landscape. They also laud him for making an effort to understand the Indians and emphasize the importance of respecting, not enslaving, them. While Louis Werner of *Americas* is one critic who praises Cabeza de Vaca's ethnographic work, the critic also admits "the book's veracity is today contested by scholars, many of whom read the tale more as a confabulation of magic realism than a true account of actual events."

CRITICISM

Scott Pollard

In the following excerpt, Pollard traces modern Latin American literature to Cabaza de Vaca, whom he credits with first separating the American persepecive from the European.

> Yet if the only form of tradition, of handing down, consisted in following the ways of the immediate generation before us in a blind or timid adherence to its successes, "tradition" should positively be discouraged. We have seen such simple currents lost in the sand; and novelty is better than repetition. Tradition is a matter of much wider significance. It cannot be inherited, and if you want it you must obtain it by great labor. It involves, in the first place, the historical sense, which we may call nearly indispensable to anyone who would continue to be a poet beyond his twenty-fifth year; and the historical sense involves a perception, not only of the pastness of the past, but of its presence; the historical sense compels a man to write not merely with his own generation in his bones, but with a feeling that the whole of the literature of Europe from Homer and within it the whole of the literature of his own country has a simultaneous existence and composes a simultaneous order. This historical sense, which is a sense of the timeless as well as the temporal and of the timeless and of the temporal together, is what makes a writer traditional. And it is at the same time what makes a writer most acutely conscious of his place in time, of his own contemporaneity. (T. S. Eliot, "Tradition and the Individual Talent")

The boom that took place in Latin American narrative after WWII not only produced a large and diverse group of highly talented writers and a great quantity of experimental, technically advanced works, but it began (and only began) to gain exposure—in the United States, Europe, and even in Latin America itself—for a literature that had previously only been known to a few people in academic and cultural circles. Furthermore, this boom was a continent-wide, international Latin American phenomenon, and the writers involved in it saw it as a means by which Latin American literature and culture could become a force within the international mainstream, and used it to garner political, critical, and economic power. With its aid, Latin America would move beyond a ghettoized, impoverished, third world existence, and no longer be subordinated to the whims and machinations of the first world. For the Argentine author Julio Cortazar, this boom was a catalyst for a Latin American identity: "Finally, what is the boom but the most extraordinary dose of consciousness for the Latin American pueblo, a part of its very identity? What is this dose of consciousness but a very important part of our disalienation?"

This search for identity arose out of the ascendance of the middle class in Latin America and the correlative improvement in the quality of education in the decade prior to the war. What resulted was a higher literacy rate and a greater need for an active publishing industry. For the Uruguayan critic Emir Rodriguez Monegal, "The generation of readers that began to take shape in 1939 had the advantage of more universities and secondary schools, more libraries, more bookstores and magazines; there were, over all, Latin American publishers that not only translated and adapted universal culture but that also promoted national and Latin American culture." All this activity spawned a multinational publishing industry that not only spanned the limits of the continent (from Sudamericana in Argentina to Joaquin Mortiz in Mexico) but became international (Seix-Barral in Spain). Now Latin American writers were read throughout the continent by a much broader readership. Moreover, reprints of older, long out-of-print works augmented this new narrative, and reinforced the sense that a new, independent cultural identity had been born in Latin America.

Ironically, though, these post-war authors found no "literary fathers" among their immediate predecessors. They rejected the criollismo and costumbrismo—patterned after nineteenth-century European realism—that had become standard fictional paradigms in Latin America. As they saw it, these literary forms fostered a sense of regionalism and/or nationalism that had effectively isolated the author within the borders of his or her own country and severely limited intellectual and imaginative stimuli. And since

their predecessors had, for all intents and purposes, mined the nation and the region for all it was worth—at least within the limits of realism—the "boom" authors felt asphyxiated and turned outward in search of new stimuli, which they discovered in the form of international modernism. There is perhaps no better indicator of this turn than the fact that a majority of these authors have spent much of their time abroad. The Cuban Alejo Carpentier lived most of his life in France, as did Cortazar. The Peruvian Mario Vargas Llosa lived in Paris and London. The Columbian Gabriel Garcia Marquez wrote One Hundred Years of Solitude in Mexico and has spent much of his life in Europe. All actively sought the mainstream centers of Western culture: places they had read about as they were growing up, places that had captured their imaginations and to which—trapped in the Latin American "provinces"—they felt a great deal of cultural allegiance. It is here, caught between the margin and the mainstream, national and international allegiances, that the post-war Latin American writer begins to fashion a new cultural identity.

If we believe T. S. Eliot—a disaffected North American—such an identity necessarily fits "within" an overarching European tradition. Literature produced in Latin America may give rise to a broad-based hemispheric culture or a set of national cultures, each with its own peculiar traits, yet either way all remain inextricably bound to and rooted in Europe: simultaneity is always enacted within a Eurocentric horizon. Certainly, the post-war boom authors cultivated such an "historical sense," yet they were not comfortable simply buying back into a European tradition. If they did not adhere to the "successes" of their own preceding generations, neither did they want to be mere adherents to the mainstream. For Eliot, "every nation, every race, has not only its creative, but its own critical turn of mind." This critical turn may, as Eliot sees it, trumpet the "peculiar essence" of nation or race while ignoring the greater tradition of which it is a part, or through "great labor" it may "obtain" that tradition. The boom authors put in the long hours necessary to claim Europe as their own, yet they were not satisfied with the given horizon. Instead, they worked to create a revamped tradition that would mirror and privilege their geographical and intellectual remove from the mainstream. To put it more simply, they would create a tradition that could move outside the boundaries of Europe. To illustrate, I want to look at three self-styled literary histories by Alejo Carpentier, his fellow Cuban Jose Lezama Lima, and the Mexican Carlos Fuentes. These authors do not merely not acquiesce to the traditional centers of power in Europe and the United States; they actually revise Western literary history itself so as to endow Latin American narrative with a privileged place within it. From this perspective, postwar Latin American narrative is not only a part of the modernist canon but extends that canon into the postmodern. La nueva narrativa becomes a central player in world literature because it is not merely a repetition, secondary and redundant, but something truly "new" in the international literary marketplace. And as might be expected from a young, ambitious group of authors who would make a bid for Old World recognition yet are novices on its center stage, the claims they make for inclusion in a mainstream tradition are based on their very newness, in which the New World plays the most significant part, as both the place and the "tradition" that grounds their identity—an anchor for their foray back to Europe.

For Carpentier, Lezama Lima, and Fuentes, literary history is essentially baroque. Originally, the baroque was an aesthetic that consciously set out to break with classicism. In regard to Latin America, it is best to conceive of it as a generic trope—a break with convention—which is expressed as an antagonistic relationship between margin and center. Initially, the New World was meant to be nothing more than an extension, a simple ornament, of the Old. Colonial policy not only demanded dependency, but the maintenance of a strict, Eurocentric identity as well. The New World was never supposed to become independent and autonomous. In *Questing Fictions*, Djelal Kadir notes that Europe and Spain imagined the New World long before the western hemisphere was discovered:

> The most commonly recalled of these structures comprise the antipodean speculations of Parmenides, reauthorized by Aristotle—the notion that the oikoumene, man's home in the cosmos, the world, must have a counterballast; Plato's mythological Atlantis; the New World prophesied by the biblical Book of Revelations—a new earth, a millenial kingdom, the eschatological other world; the Hermetic Utopia of Hermes Trismegistus' Adocentyn, later become Tomasso Campanella's City of the Sun.

Christopher Columbus took with him this long history of utopias when he sailed in quest of India, and they provide the ur-narrative from

which Latin America was originally conceived. Yet Columbus (re)discovered neither India nor Europe's idealized vision/extension of itself, and it is this error that "founds" Latin America's difference: "America, as 'premeditated creation' of European history, as 'a chapter in the history of European utopias,' contends with the previously mentioned structures of its founding by constantly refinding those inventive frames, appropriating them." Latin America defines itself as this "errant quest": the mistaken journey whose end is irrevocably deferred because it cannot find the utopia it had hoped to discover in the New World, yet a journey that never ends, for utopian desire is as irrevocable as the deferment of its realization. Correlatively, as the quest errs in search of the ideals that motivate it, it wanders through what Kadir calls the "abysmal void" of the New World. "Horrified" by that emptiness, utopic desire attempts to fill it by reproducing those absent ideals—a Eurocentric hermeneutic—but it only succeeds in supplementing them.

Among the narratives of conquest and exploration, the *Naufragios [The Shipwrecks] of Alvar Nunez Cabeza de Vaca* may best exemplify this peculiar brand of horror and errancy. In the ingenious, revisionary synthesis he achieves between Old and New Worlds, Cabeza de Vaca stands as one of the first true Americans. Moreover, if we look at him as a writer, he is a predecessor to and paradigm for the likes of Carpentier, Fuentes, and Lezama Lima. Correlatively, it might be interesting for us to think of these postmodern writers as "versions" of their colonial antecedent.

Cabeza de Vaca wrote to claim his own rightful credentials as an explorer, to please the Spanish government, and to secure another royal appointment. He wrote to salvage his own success from the failed expedition of Panfilo de Narvaez, which erred quite a bit, ultimately leaving only a few survivors stranded on the coast of Texas. Needless to say, without these errors, there would be no Naufragios. Yet, in spite of the conventional political purpose of the narrative, Cabeza de Vaca produces something unique, redefining Eurocentric notions of humanity and culture while placing Old and New Worlds on a near egalitarian footing. His retelling of his ten years amongst the Indians of the southern United States and northern Mexico is a deft attempt at cultural bridging that refuses to subordinate the New to the Old, the American to the European. In spite of shipwreck, death, hunger, cannibalism, enslavement—in spite of being stripped of the trappings of European civilization and having every justification for suffering what we call today "culture shock"—Cabeza de Vaca, unlike a "humanist" like Juan de Sepulveda, treats the Indians he encounters as fully human rather than subhuman, and their cultures as worthy of study and recording rather than exploitation and destruction. Yet he was not one to be acculturated. When he became a healer for the Indians, though they saw him and his companions as semi-divine shamans from the "land of the sun," he sees himself as a good, Christian faith healer, conduit of God's will. In an unknown land, Cabeza de Vaca finds that Christianity has resonance; correlatively, throughout the narrative, he constructs a perspective that insists on the essential continuity between Old and New Worlds.

This perspective comes most clear near the end of the narrative when it is sorely tried by Spanish greed, exploitation, and duplicity. When he witnesses the devastation caused to the coastal Indians by the Spanish attempts to enslave them, Cabeza de Vaca sympathizes with the Indians without condemning the Spanish incursion. Pursuing diplomacy, he wins promises from the Spaniards that they would cease and desist, but those promises are quickly broken. Again, Cabeza de Vaca does not denounce their actions. Instead, still living by his wits, he comes up with a scheme to convert the Indians, for if they are Christians and if they build churches—that is, if they act as humans in the eyes of the Spaniards—then they will not be enslaved. Through this ingenious solution, Cabeza de Vaca not only provides a hopeful closure for his narrative but offers proof

of the viability of his perspective. He is the perfect explorer, for, unlike Panfilo de Narvaez, what he discovers is that the New World can be colonized. Just what Spain wanted to hear. Yet Cabeza de Vaca was radically transformed by his experiences. He opened himself up to other cultures and peoples, sympathized with them, then redefined his Eurocentric notions of humanity to account for their alterity. Out of the "horrors" of his experience, Cabeza de Vaca fills the New World with his own peculiar version of Christianity. He may reconfirm Spain's colonial vision, but not without letting a little air into it to make room for the differential nature of American reality—revision and supplement.

Source: Scott Pollard, "Canonizing Revision: Literary History and the Post-modern Latin American Writer," in *College Literature*, Vol. 20, No. 3, October 1993, pp. 133–47.

SOURCES

Cabeza de Vaca, Alvar Núñez, *Chronicle of the Narváez Expedition*, translated by Fanny Bandelier, A. S. Barnes, 1905; revised and annotated by Harold Augenbaum, Penguin Books, 2002.

Noel, Tom, "De Vaca's Journey Unveils Wonders," in the *Rocky Mountain News*, January 17, 2004, p. 3D.

Petty, Stephen, "Cabeza de Vaca: A Model for Multiculturalism," www.library.txstate.edu/swwc/cdv/further_study/multiculturalism.pdf (September 24, 2006).

Review of *The Narrative of Cabeza de Vaca*, in *National Geographic Adventure*, Vol. 5, No. 6, August 2003, p. 30.

Werner, Louis, "Truth & Fiction Chart a Miraculous Journey," in *Americas* (English ed.), Vol. 48, No. 4, July–August 1996, p. 22.

Common Sense

THOMAS PAINE

1776

Thomas Paine's *Common Sense* (1776) may have been the first American bestseller, rousing the colonial spirit for American independence throughout the early Revolutionary War. Certainly Paine did not originate the argument for independence, but his timing of articulating it could not have been better. His pamphlet was first published, anonymously, in January 1776, after hostilities between the colonies and Great Britain had already begun. The pamphlet gained immediate popularity, with up to 150,000 copies circulated in its first year, and it underwent numerous reprintings. People passed copies to friends and family members in addition to reading them out loud to those who could not read themselves. With British laws becoming more restrictive by the day and with colonial trade showing great potential, the small collection of states was ready to throw off its parent country and make its own governing decisions. Paine's ideas helped illustrate how life could be in an independent land, and why a republican government suited the new colonies much better than a hereditary monarchy.

Thomas Paine only lived in America for a relatively short time, but his impact on the emergence of the United States is incalculable. Born in England, Paine did not arrive in the then British colonies until his late thirties and after trying his hand at several different occupations. Frustrated with his career opportunities, Paine traveled to the colonies with little more than an

BIOGRAPHY

THOMAS PAINE

Born in 1737 in England, Paine was the son of a Quaker corset maker. After trying his hand at the family business, he became bored and looked for other opportunities. His wife and child died in childbirth when Paine was in his early twenties. He tried a variety of jobs including seaman, tax collector, English teacher, and shop owner. He married again in his thirties, but he and his second wife soon separated. Still frustrated professionally, Paine moved to the American colonies at Benjamin Franklin's encouragement in late 1774 and quickly became a successful political writer. He published anti-slavery arguments and edited *Pennsylvania Magazine* in 1775.

His (literally) revolutionary *Common Sense* appeared in early 1776 and was followed by his *American Crisis* papers—sixteen in all over the next seven years. With these texts, Paine helped lead unsure and weary colonists to their destiny of self-governing Americans. Despite the many opportunities available to him because of his well-received writing, he continued to travel and seek new opportunities. He tried to make a career as an inventor in England in the late 1780s, but he turned his attention to the revolution in France in the 1790s. He was wrongly imprisoned as a royalist sympathizer in France in 1793, and he returned to the United States at the invitation of Thomas Jefferson in 1802. Paine died an outcast in New York City in June 1809. His obituary in the *New-York Evening Post* read, "He had lived long, did some good and much harm." Paine was buried on his farmland when denied burial in the Quaker cemetery. Oddly, Paine's remains were disinterred by a friend wanting to give him a more austere burial in England, but were then lost. Paine's home still stands today in New Rochelle, New York, where a monument and museum honor his contributions to American society.

---

introduction from Benjamin Franklin. But quickly, Paine set his rhetorical abilities to work for the colonial cause against the British government. He began by writing for a magazine in Pennsylvania, but, at the urging of some of the founding fathers, he began publishing political pamphlets. After Paine's writings became widely circulated throughout the colonies, citizens who were formerly interested in reconciling with the throne became emboldened to declare their independence. Paine's powerful arguments not only convinced colonials that they should separate from Britain but, more importantly, the style of his arguments reached a mass of people. Paine was undeniably intelligent and astute, but his true genius rested in his ability to communicate ideas to regular people.

Paine continued writing throughout his life. Soon after *Common Sense* made a name for its author, he began publishing the *Crisis* papers. Beginning with the famous line, "These are the times that try men's souls," Paine's text has become mythic in American culture; George Washington is said to have read this piece to his beleaguered, freezing troops on Christmas Eve 1776 to hearten their spirits before attacking and defeating the British army in a battle on Christmas day. After the new republic was settled, however, Paine remained restless. He continued writing but left America for England. He dabbled in hobbies, including attempting a new model for an iron-arched bridge. Politics could not let Paine go, however, and after becoming linked with a high-level scandal, he was charged with sedition and fled to France. Impressing a third country with his rhetorical abilities, Paine found himself seated in the French government only to be jailed during the Reign of Terror of the French Revolution. With the help of American ambassador James Madison, Paine was released from prison and traveled back to the United States. But he faced a frosty reception in America because of his most recent publication, *The Age of Reason*, which was perceived to be critical of Christianity. After the respected status Paine enjoyed during Revolutionary times, it is surprising that he spent his last years under public derision in the country he helped establish. Paine died before public opinion would turn his way again, but history has been kind to his memory. With centuries of admirers, historians have, in the last decades of the twentieth century, become even more interested in his contributions to the early American republic. Paine's writings helped convince the mass of Americans that they could survive without British rule; he so emboldened the young nation that his words still describe the independent spirit that defines the American persona.

PLOT SUMMARY

Introduction

Paine begins by proposing to his readers that they have the right to question the King of England because his policies affect their lives. Paine emphasizes that people should question ideas even if they have been long accepted as true, and that the concerns of the colonies will prove to be universal concerns as they involve oppression and liberty, tyranny and freedom. He concludes by establishing that his interests have not been compromised by any political party but are only focused on a reasonable argument.

Of the Origin and Design of Government in General. With Concise Remarks on the English Constitution

Paine establishes the basis for government in society by illustrating how a hypothetically new group of people would first gather to form a society and then organize to form a government. "Government even in the best state is but a necessary evil," Paine writes, and as such, communities often create the vehicle for their own suffering. Governments are necessary because people cannot be trusted; if they were consistently moral, they would not need a governing body but as they are not, they need a system to ensure their security. In the beginning, people band together as a society to meet their needs. Then, they form a government to protect themselves from each other's worst motives. These early governments initially include every member of society and are therefore completely representative. As communities grow, members must be elected to represent the larger groups within the governing body. Because the representatives live with the groups that elected

Thomas Paine The National Portrait Gallery

them, it remains in their self-interest to represent their group fairly. Somehow, Paine argues, the English government has strayed far from this originating model of representative government.

Paine begins to analyze the British government to show how it has drifted away from promoting liberty for its people. At its outset, the British system of government was beneficial. "The more simple any thing is, the less liable it is to be disordered, and the easier repaired when disordered; and with this maxim in view I offer a few remarks on the so much boasted constitution of England"; Paine argues that the British structure has gotten too complicated and thus flawed. Examining each part of the British government, Paine concludes that it has become too separated from the people to represent their freedoms fairly. The king's position, for instance, is a contradiction as it both separates him entirely from his subjects and yet requires him to decide upon their fate. And the established checks on the king are ineffective. Proponents of the system exhibit more of a general national pride rather than actual pride in the governing structure itself. Paine proposes to investigate the constitutional system, in detail, to determine the errors inherent in it.

Of Monarchy and Hereditary Succession

Paine begins with examples from Biblical times to establish how monarchies first, and hereditary monarchies second, are evil forms of government. He argues that differences in status, such as rich and poor, are man-made structures because humankind was equal at creation. However, evil is not necessarily the cause of such distinctions, but evil is often the result of them. But the separation into king and subject is completely unnatural, and until there were kings, there was peace; pride and competition comes with monarchies. Kings only encourage idolatry by requiring humans to revere other humans. God never intended for monarchies to exist, Paine writes, using scriptural evidence to bolster his point. God does not endorse a form of government that raises one human to a higher status than others. Israel only receives a king after begging God for one. When Israel asks Gideon to be king, he refuses, chastising them for wanting a ruler other than God. God presents his people with a king but foretells the curse that monarchs will be to humankind. Paine quotes God saying, in 1 Samuel, "ye shall cry out in that day because of your king which ye shall have chosen, AND THE LORD WILL NOT HEAR YOU IN THAT DAY." Paine brings his argument to a point, stating that the scriptures are clear on this subject; either God disapproves of monarchs, or scripture is in error.

Even with the occasionally good monarch, Paine argues, the addition of a hereditary element to monarchies contradicts all logic. First, how can anyone be certain that the son of a king will be as worthy of the position as the father? Each generation is different, and thus the kingship may be inappropriate for some in the lineage. Second, a group should have the ability to choose its own governor. If that group chooses a king, one scenario is presented. However it is inappropriate for that group to then force its choice on subsequent generations, which is the exact circumstance presented by a hereditary monarchy. It is inappropriate to rob future citizens of the right to choose their government representative by establishing a royal bloodline. England's hereditary monarchy began by force, as William the Conqueror took control with violence. Of that originator of the current British monarchy, Paine writes, "A French bastard landing with an armed Banditti and establishing himself king of England against the consent of the natives, is in plain terms a very paltry rascally original." In the same way hereditary monarchies are passed down from father to son, so is original sin; the parallel is not coincidence, according to Paine.

Being raised royal also breeds an aberrant perspective on life, one that is out of touch with regular society. Young and old kings present a further dilemma as well, because age does not restrict a person from becoming a monarch. As such, whomever the young or old king has as a confidant can often manipulate matters of state. Not only does hereditary monarchy not make sense, it also creates nothing good in a society. England has suffered wars and corruption at the hands of its hereditary monarch, even though proponents claim that inherited royalty eliminates civil unrest. Kings often make their personal quarrels matters of state, and thus conflict increases rather than decreases. God never intended anything but a representative republic, Paine argues, stating, "monarchy and succession have laid (not this or that kingdom only) but the world in blood and ashes. 'Tis a form of government which the word of God bears testimony against, and blood will attend it." England seems to be progressing toward a republic as it incorporates representatives of the people, but the persistence of the monarchy corrupts the entire government.

Thoughts on the Present State of American Affairs

Reconciliation with the British government does not make any sense as it will only prolong a flawed situation that must end at some point in the future. Even though there has been much discussion of the British relationship with the colonies, no effective solution has been found. If the colonies do not take strong action, they will be remembered by history for their weakness. Independence is a worthy cause, Paine argues. "'Tis not the concern of a day, a year, or an age; posterity are virtually involved in the contest, and will be more or less affected, even to the end of time, by the proceedings now." Once fighting began, the colonies entered a new phase where reconciliation is no longer a possibility.

Paine determines to examine the arguments in favor of reconciling with England. One view holds that the relationship was beneficial in the past so it will be again in the future. Paine counters that the past is no good indicator of the future. Plus, he disagrees that the colonies benefited from the relationship in the first place because of their strong trade opportunities. The colonies do not need England to survive because of the rich commerce available to them. Another perspective argues that England has been good protection. To this, Paine counters that the protection has only been according to England's interest, not the colonies'. When connected with Great Britain, America not only gains the parent-country's allies but her enemies as well. Without Great Britain, the colonies would be at peace with France and Spain, for instance. Paine next contradicts that the colonies have no relationship with each other save through England by asserting that, in fact, they only have enemies, not friends, because of England. To the claim that England is the colonies' mother-country, Paine counters that far from a parent, England is rather a "monster" more than a "mother," for "even brutes do not devour their young." If anything, Europe is the colonies' parent, Paine reasons, because people move to America from all parts of Europe, not just England. Some say that England and America should reconcile because, if united, they could be a world power, to which Paine replies that the colonies have no need for being such a power. If trade is the goal, the colonies want to make friends with the rest of the world rather than antagonize it.

Paine asserts that there are no benefits to reconciliation, especially because of the commercial opportunities available to the colonies. To maximize trade, America should have no special relationships with any part of Europe, England included. If England engages in a war with a country, then the colonies will also be at war, thus cutting off a trade option. "Every thing that is right or natural pleads for separation," Paine writes, even the geographical distance between England and North America. Nature must not have meant for the nations to be connected if they are so far apart on the map.

The colonies' independence is inevitable, Paine argues. If separation does not occur soon, the future will inherit the same problems the colonies face now. Those who want to reconcile often have personal motives for doing so, or have not suffered injury from British rule. But, Paine reminds, many have been victims of violence and injustice. Paine makes a personal plea, asking if his readers had suffered the death of a loved one or significant loss of property, would they still wish to reconcile? Appeals for change have repeatedly been

ineffective, and it is unreasonable to hope that England will alter its restrictive policies toward the colonies. He uses a vivid example of the folly of "the doctrine of reconciliation":

> But let our imaginations transport us a few moments to Boston; that seat of wretchedness will teach us wisdom, and instruct us for ever to renounce a power in whom we can have no trust. The inhabitants of that unfortunate city who but a few months ago were in ease and affluence, have now no other alternative than to stay and starve, or turn out to beg.

Commerce remains a key reason to separate from British rule. With England physically distant from the colonies, its guidance on trade matters would be nothing less than unreasonable. Trade will suffer due to England's foreign relationships, which only underscores the injustice of having to share the profits of that trade with the king. America will eventually rule itself; it is much larger in size than England and it is an isolated landmass. Both these elements make it impossible for an external government to effectively control America. He makes this argument:

> To be always running three or four thousand miles with a tale or a petition, waiting four or five months for an answer, which when obtained requires five or six more to explain it in, will in a few years be looked upon as folly and childishness—There was a time when it was proper, and there is a proper time for it to cease.

If the separation is inevitable, then why should the current society leave the fight to its children? Why squander the opportunity the colonies have to start over and install a representative government, Paine asks. The colonies face the unique possibility of creating a truly representative government, free from the corruption of a hereditary monarchy.

Any hope that England could rule the colonies fairly is undercut as Paine explains how the king has no incentive to regulate the colonies' trade appropriately. The king must protect the mainland of England, and so he will make policies that bolster Britain and not America. The King retains a veto power over all colonial matters, which leaves them to the mercy of a foreign ruler. This situation remains unacceptable to Paine. Paine finally addresses the fear that, if the colonies declare independence, there will be outbreaks of unrest, and civil war may ensue. He asserts the true threat to order will be if the colonies remain subject to the British throne.

He predicts that the day a compromise and reconciliation is reached will be the day of colonial revolt. Too many citizens have suffered serious loss of property and even death to stand by quietly and accept anything but independence.

With the introduction, "If there is any true cause of fear respecting independence, it is because no plan is yet laid down," Paine details his own plan for the new government of independent colonies. He proposes a charter to establish the system, which will be a sacred bond to protect the freedom of society. There will be a president to lead the government, and there will be a unicameral, or one-house, system to support the president. The colonies will send representatives to the congress, and the president will be regularly elected from those representatives. Each colony will have the opportunity to present candidates for president, on a rotating basis.

Paine states that the opportunity to reconcile has passed and it is now time to demand independence. "There are injuries which nature cannot forgive," he writes, "As well can the lover forgive the ravisher of his mistress, as the continent forgive the murders of Britain." Independence is not only geographically and culturally inevitable, Paine argues, but it is divinely inspired. God intended for the colonies to rule themselves as a democratic republic. And that republic will become a haven, Paine predicts, for all the oppressed in the world: "O! receive the fugitive, and prepare in time an asylum for mankind."

Of the Present Ability of America With Some Miscellaneous Reflections

Paine asserts that the time to declare independence has arrived. Circumstances are ripe for the fight, with unity and size working in the colonies' favor. The population of the colonies is in the perfect situation to begin a new government. They are just the right mass to be highly unified in their fight against the British, and so should pursue independence right away. Furthermore, the colonies do not have debt to hold them back. It is the present citizens' duty to settle this matter for the future, and not leave it as a burden to their children, "leaving them the great work to do, and a debt upon their backs from which they derive no advantage."

The colonies should begin immediately by preparing an adequate navy to aid in the fight, and Paine lists the specific resources the colonies possess to do just that. Natural resources are plentiful for shipbuilding, and there is enough money to finance a navy large enough to battle the British. Concerns about failure can be alleviated because the navy can be sold for funds if necessary. Even without declaring independence, the colonies would need to build a navy, Paine proposes, because they cannot rely on England to protect them adequately. Even though England has a large and formidable fleet of ships, the colonies only need build enough ships to protect their ports. England's navy has other responsibilities besides fighting the colonies, so the entire fleet will not be available. As such, the colonies have an opportunity for victory, Paine argues.

The colonial navy will have uses beyond fighting for separation. During peacetime, the colonies can employ their ships for trade: "To unite the sinews of commerce and defence is sound policy," he writes, "for when our strengths and our riches, play into each other's hand, we need fear no external enemy." The colonies' resources are great, both in natural products such as hemp, iron, and land itself as well as in intellectual power such as knowledge and motivation. The conflict between the countries will only escalate as America grows, so why put off the inevitable separation? Where England's army suffers from lack of energy (because the soldiers are comfortable and seek personal gain), the colonial army benefits from the deep desire for independence. If the colonies take advantage of these favorable elements, they can choose and form a new kind of representative government. Paine urges the colonies not to let this opportunity pass by. This new government can be a haven for religious differences and can be truly representative.

Paine concludes with some final motivations for the colonies to declare their independence. First, there is no mediator that could effectively reconcile the colonies with England. Both Spain and France would compromise their own self-interests to get involved in the conflict, so they cannot be unbiased mediators. Second, independence would stimulate a robust commercial market in the colonies, which would help establish the republic. Finally, Paine asserts that colonial citizens know they should pursue independence, and so they should begin right away. Paine explains:

> Until an independence is declared, the Continent will feel itself like a man who continues putting off some unpleasant business from day to day, yet knows it must be done, hates to set

"IN AMERICA, THE LAW IS KING. FOR AS IN ABSOLUTE GOVERNMENTS THE KING IS LAW, SO IN FREE COUNTRIES THE LAW *OUGHT* TO BE KING."

about it, wishes it over, and is continually haunted with the thoughts of its necessity.

THEMES

The Evils of Hereditary Monarchies

Paine spends much of his writing arguing against the objectionable nature of hereditary monarchs in general, and one hereditary monarch in particular: King George III of England. Although the colonies directed most of their anger toward the British Parliament for enacting extremely binding commercial restrictions on them, Paine sought to add King George to the list of British offenders. He builds a detailed argument throughout *Common Sense* for why monarchies are not good governments to begin with, but hereditary monarchies are extremely corrupt. He even argues that hereditary monarchs are both unnatural and un-Christian.

Monarchs cannot sustain a just society, claims Paine, because one person cannot fairly make decisions for an entire community. A monarch is not accountable to anyone and thus generally serves his own interests rather than those of his people. Paine says that monarchs are even opposed by God in the scriptures; Israel only received a king after begging for one. And even then, God presented the monarch with a curse, predicting that the subjects would regret the day they asked to become subjects of an earthly master. Kings and queens, even if occasionally good to their people, demand the kind of submission only appropriate for God, Paine argues. People should not worship an earthly leader; they should instead have a government that worthily represents their interests.

If monarchies are inherently flawed, Paine believes that hereditary monarchies are inherently corrupt. Having kingships passed down within a royal family presents so many challenges

to rationality that Paine vehemently opposes the practice. Choosing a society's leader based on birthright disregards any actual skill or capacity for the position, Paine argues. No matter how unsuited one is for government leadership, bloodlines still allow the person to assume the throne. Further, the longer a royal family continues, the less connected to the community they become. They are entirely separated from their subjects and thus cannot know the needs of the people they serve. Paine also illustrates his own disgust for the kind of arrogance a royal family can cultivate in its habits of luxury and ego-gratification.

Paine presents a spirited case for why hereditary monarchies should be banished from the British colonies. He describes why the colonies should terminate ties with the English monarchy and begin self-rule. He additionally illustrates why America, once independent from Britain, should not institute a monarch or a hereditary monarchy in their new society. America has the opportunity, he asserts, to rid itself of old, corrupt forms of government in order to start a new republic.

The Inevitability of American Independence

Paine bolsters his argument for colonial independence by making the case that America will ultimately be self-ruling, whether it occurs in 1776 or whether it occurs some other time in the future. Geography tops Paine's list for why the colonies should split from British rule; because the American continent exists so far from Great Britain, it will eventually be independent. No outside force will be able to permanently control such a large, isolated land mass as North America, Paine argues, and so the colonies should recognize the strength of their bargaining position. Furthermore, if the split is inevitable, Paine asserts that the colonies should take advantage of their opportunity to shape the future. Why saddle the next generation with shouldering the fight and responsibility for an independent nation when the problem can be solved presently? Paine argues that the timing for establishing a new government could not be better, and so the colonies should stand up and fight for a new, free republic. Appealing to a sense of duty and a sense of destiny, Paine rallies colonial citizens to provide a better future for their children. Who knows when as good a chance for victory will present itself, he says.

Paine seemed to anticipate the kind of unique country America would become, appealing to his readers in a language of freedom and independence that the entire world could admire.

Emerging American Capitalism

A main reason Paine believes the colonies could survive independently of Great Britain is the emerging commerce associated with North America. In the short time the Europeans were settled in the colonies, they were constantly discovering new natural resources. "Tar, timber, iron, and cordage are her natural produce," Paine writes, just to name a few of the products ripe for international trade. Because of the emerging market available to the colonies, Paine argues that independence is financially critical as well as morally correct. First, England will not be able to effectively regulate American trade from such a far distance; considering the travel-time involved in simple communications, trade would presumably be hampered. Second, with all of the Crown's alliances already established, Paine argues that there is no motivation for England to promote the colonies' interests. England will make decisions according to its own material gain and national defense rather than according to what would be best for the colonial market. Finally, Paine emphasizes the need to keep all European markets open to trade with the colonies. As England already had quarrels with France and Spain, for instance, those relationships would be detrimental to trade. As an independent country, the colonies could promote their own trade relationships and not inherit the alliances and enemies of England. Paine makes a strong case for the colonies to protect their great commercial potential by eliminating English restrictions. The capitalist success America becomes over the next two centuries is apparent in Paine's arguments, proving the accuracy of many of his assumptions.

Representative Government for the New Republic

Because hereditary monarchies are not appropriate for the emerging colonial government, Paine suggests a representative government instead. Besides railing against the Crown, he also criticizes the complicated Parliamentary system in England as ineffective. Bureaucracy and corruption make the seemingly representative system actually serve special interests. And since the British government retains an inherited monarchy, any progress toward a representative republic is corrupted. Because the colonies will be starting with a blank slate, Paine encourages them to create a new kind of truly representative government. He recommends a fairly elaborate construction of a one-house system with a president, not the two-house system the United States eventually adopts. Paine's structure, however, places representation as the highest priority. Because he believes government to be only a necessary evil and not an institution to be needlessly expanded, Paine believes that the people's voice should be able to guide the government on all matters. The worst part of England's system, Paine argues, is that it lost touch with the people it supposedly serves and protects. Paine's ideas for a new American republic place the people back in the priority position and make the wellbeing of the community more important than the selfish desires of the rulers themselves.

HISTORICAL OVERVIEW

The American Revolution

Paine's writings entered an already-charged political environment. The British colonies were in direct conflict with their parent-country, Great Britain, over their own governing. Some colonies were more affected by restrictive British laws than others, and those most affected began protesting their treatment. Most famously, protesters in Boston staged the "Tea Party" in 1773 when they threw what they believed to be unfairly regulated tea into the Boston Harbor. After such demonstrations, the British government instituted what became known as the Coercive Acts in order to punish the colonies. These pieces of legislation extremely restricted colonial trade, taxed their property, and installed British law enforcement, all without providing colonial representation in Parliament. With all these issues building up tensions among colonial citizens, hostilities had already broken out when Paine published *Common Sense*. The first battles erupted in 1774 at Fort William and Mary in New Hampshire and in 1775 at Lexington and Concord in Massachusetts. Although in hindsight it can appear inevitable that America defeated Great Britain to become a successful, independent nation, the future was not so clear toward the end of the eighteenth century. Colonial citizens were not united in their point of view on British government, with some willing to reconcile with the throne and some unwilling to cause trouble in the first place. Paine's writings became so important specifically because of the conflicted perspective among the colonies. His passionate argument helped bring some unity to the independence movement and helped continue to rouse spirits throughout the Revolutionary War. The last major battle of the war took place in 1781 when the French helped the Americans defeat the British forces at Yorktown.

Plain Language in Literature

Paine's arguments in *Common Sense* can only be considered well-reasoned and detailed. But his large impact on the colonies is due to the combination of his logical appeal with his incredibly accessible language. Although influenced by various philosophers such as John Locke, Paine articulates his ideas in writing that everyday people could understand. Void of complicated language or obscure allusions, Paine's words use common language and recognizable examples to persuade his readers that America should be independent. Straightforward statements and ordinary vocabulary mark Paine's style. And his arguments are backed up with examples from contemporary politics and the Christian Bible, both sources most people during Paine's time could readily recognize. This plain style was no accident for Paine, who believed strongly in the power of the masses. Not only did Paine's words empower the average colonial citizen, but so did his ideas. He believed that every member of society deserved governmental representation and that monarchies and social aristocracies were unjust. Paine sought to give regular people a voice by providing them with reasonable, understandable arguments for colonial independence. His success can be measured not only in the high sales of his writings, but also in the way his readers reproduced his arguments on their own. Paine was an uncommonly persuasive writer, certainly, but he was also an irrepressible champion of the average citizen. American ideals of common people finding success in a democratic country can be traced as far back as Paine's earliest writings encouraging independence.

CRITICAL OVERVIEW

Although Paine lost America's favor in the final years of his life, he has since become one of the most celebrated patriot writers in the country's history. During the Revolution and soon after, Paine's writings were enormously popular. *Common Sense* not only sold an unprecedented number of copies, but it also helped establish Paine as a valuable national asset. Several members of the Continental Congress encouraged Paine to continue writing for the colonial cause, and so his works continued to spur on the fight for American independence.

Some, Like John Adams, had some reservations about the government Paine outlined; In "Revolution with Pen and Ink," William Kashatus defends him:

> Paine wasn't a constitutional theorist. His task was tearing down governments, not creating them. While Congress eventually adopted his suggestion for a unicameral legislature and incorporated it into the Articles of Confederation, it proved to be a dismal failure, just as Adams had feared. Yet at the same time, Common Sense convinced many Americans who had previously been neutral on the subject of independence that a monarchy could no longer address their needs and that they should separate from England.

Reflecting on Paine in 2002, Lewis Lapham notes his power and relevance still today. "To read Tom Paine is to encounter the high-minded philosophy of the eighteenth-century Enlightenment rendered in language simple enough to be understood by everybody in the room," he claims. He goes on:

> [Paine wrote] in what he knew to be "the undisguised language of historical truth," leveling a fierce polemic against the corrupt monarchy of King George III that serves (226 years later, and with no more than a few changes of name and title) as a fair description of the complacent oligarchy currently parading around Washington in the costume of a democratic republic. Were Paine still within reach of the federal authorities, Attorney General John Ashcroft undoubtedly would prosecute him for blasphemy under a technologically enhanced version of the Alien and Sedition Acts.

Perhaps perceiving his threat to governments, even ones that owe him for their very existence, conservative American politicians looked down on Paine for centuries. Harvey Kaye explains:

> Conservatives certainly were not supposed to speak favorably of Paine, and for 200 years, they had not. In fact, they had for generations publicly despised Paine and scorned his memory. And one can understand why: Endowing American experience with democratic impulse

MEDIA ADAPTATIONS

The Giants of Political Thought: Common Sense, The Declaration of Independence, & The Federalist Papers was released as an audio recording in 1998. Narrated by Craig Deitschman, it is available in a set of four audio cassettes from Sound Ideas.

Common Sense was released as an audio recording in 2002. Narrated by George Vafiadis, it is available on compact disc from Commuter Library.

Common Sense and the Declaration of Independence was released as an audio recording in 2006. Narrated by Craig Deitschman, it is available on compact disc from Knowledge Products.

---

and aspiration, Paine had turned Americans into radicals, and we have remained radicals at heart ever since.

Since his lifetime, scholars study Paine's work from many angles and in many eras. Thomas Edison, for instance, was a Paine enthusiast and helped cement his standing in American culture by participating in the Paine Memorial groundbreaking. In an article in *American Heritage* in 2005, Kaye argues that Paine is the most underrated Founding Father, and all the others are overrated as a result:

> Until we build the monument to Thomas Paine on the Mall in Washington, D.C., authorized by Congress in 1992—that is, until we officially admit Paine into the top rank of the Founding Fathers—I will continue to contend that all the usual suspects, yes, all of them are overrated.... [Paine] he not only turned America's colonial rebellion into a revolutionary war but also, to the chagrin of the more conservative of the patriots, defined the new nation in a democratically expansive and progressive fashion and projected an American identity charged with exceptional purpose and promise.

Because his work appeared in pamphlet form and enjoyed mass popularity, Paine is sometimes regarded as a propagandist rather than a philosopher. As Paul Collins writes in the *New Scientist*, Paine's texts "were radically democratic writings deemed so dangerous that, for decades after his death in 1809, British booksellers were prosecuted for selling them." There is no doubt that Paine's writings reached a wide audience, both physically, intellectually, and emotionally. As Neal Ascherson claims in "The Indispensable Englishman, "Thomas Paine has had far more influence upon the thinking and acting of the human race than any other English writer except Shakespeare."

CRITICISM

W. E. Woodward

In the following excerpt, Woodward describes Common Sense *as the catalyst that set the American Revolution in motion, and contends that Thomas Paine, its author, is thus the godfather of the country.*

It was Thomas Paine who brought all these tangled revolutionary impulses to a head and sent them moving in the direction of independence. He wrote a thin book, or pamphlet, called *Common Sense* in which he pointed out the folly of a strong, self-reliant people taking orders from a nation across the sea; and he showed also that many of the British rules and regulations concerning the Colonies were utterly senseless, and could have been conceived only by stupid officeholders who lacked all sound ideas of America and its people.

Paine was the first author in our history to reach the whole American public. His book was an extraordinary best seller, and its keynote was American Independence.

One may read *Common Sense* from cover to cover in three hours; it contains only twenty-five thousand words. Paine, who was always a most painstaking writer, spent the entire autumn of 1775 in writing and revising the pamphlet. Simplicity and force were two of the vital principles of his creative literary work. He reasoned that if an argument did not carry force and conviction there was no sense in printing it at all; furthermore, if it were so intricate in style and expression that only the learned could gather its full import most of its possible readers were thus excluded.

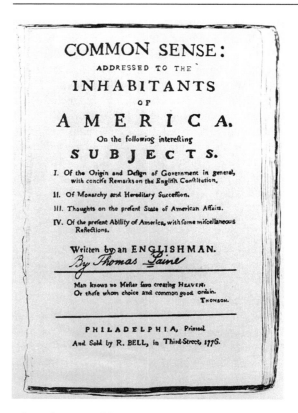

The title page of Common Sense, *1776* © *Corbis*

In the eighteenth century learning and literature were pompous. They were speckled with quotations from Greek and Latin authors. To prove his scholarship, and as a matter of self-respect, an author was moved to refer familiarly to Plato and Aristotle, to Catullus and Cicero, even if his argument concerned nothing more important than the right to catch fish in a pond.

But in *Common Sense* there is not even one quotation from the classics; Paine wrote in the English of the people, in the language that men use as they go about their daily business.

In September of 1775 the North Carolina Provincial Congress disclaimed any thoughts of rebellion. As late as January, 1776, New York, New Jersey, Pennsylvania and Maryland instructed their delegates in Congress to vote against independence if the matter was brought up.

James Truslow Adams says, in The Epic of America: "In Boston the upper class, almost without exception, were strongly opposed to it [to independence], and more than half the upper class throughout the whole colony. It was the same in New York, where the bulk of the property owners were Loyalists. In Pennsylvania, a majority of all the people were not only against war and independence in the beginning, but remained so throughout the struggle."

Nevertheless, despite this show of loyalty to Great Britain, half-formed, misty thoughts of a movement toward independence were in the back of the minds of many men. But they were doubtful of such a radical step. When once taken it could not be recalled, and one hesitates naturally at making a decision with such momentous consequences.

The situation may be compared to that of a chemical process where several diverse elements are brought together to form a single compound. They are all present but they will not unite until a catalyst is added to them.

The catalyst of the situation that has just been described was Thomas Paine. He was the godfather of America. It was he who inspired the Declaration of Independence.

The publication of *Common Sense* was like the breaking of a dam which releases all the pent-up water that stood behind it. The reprinting presses ran night and day to fill the demand for the thin pamphlet. Men read it in the streets, standing still on the narrow sidewalks, rapt in attention, while people passed to and fro. It was read aloud by schoolteachers and patriotic speakers to audiences of unlettered laborers. In the Continental Army the officers read it while their men stood at attention, listening to every word.

As soon as its authorship was known, within a few weeks after it had first appeared, Thomas Paine became a famous man overnight. A Maryland subscriber to the *Pennsylvania Evening Post* wrote a letter to that newspaper in which he said, "If you know the author of *Common Sense* tell him he has done wonders and worked miracles, made Tories Whigs and washed blackamoors white. He has made a great number of converts here."

On April 1 of that year (1776) George Washington said in a letter to Joseph Reed:

My countrymen, I know, from their form of government and steady attachment heretofore to royalty, will come reluctantly to the idea of independence, but time and persecution bring many wonderful things to pass; and, by private letters which I have lately received from Virginia, I find Paine *Common Sense* is working a wonderful change there in the minds of men.

Sir George Trevelyan says, in his *History of the American Revolution*:

> It would be difficult to name any human composition which has had an effect at once so instant, so extended and so lasting. . . It was pirated, parodied and imitated, and translated into the language of every country where the new republic had well-wishers. . . According to contemporary newspapers *Common Sense* turned thousands to independence who before could not endure the thought. It worked nothing short of miracles and turned Tories into Whigs.

In April the North Carolina Provincial Congress, that until then had disclaimed any thought of rebellion, instructed its delegates to vote for independence at the forthcoming meeting of the Continental Congress in Philadelphia. At the September session of the previous year (1776) this body had given explicit instructions to its delegates to vote against independence.

Among the South Carolina delegates to the Continental Congress was Christopher Gadsden, a resolute patriot who stood for independence. Early in February he returned to Charleston, taking with him a copy of *Common Sense*. In the South Carolina Convention he rose and read many passages from Paine's pamphlet and proposed a resolution to the effect that South Carolina, united with the other Colonies, should declare for independence.

"This declaration," says William Henry Drayton in his *Memoirs*, "came like an explosion of thunder upon the members. There had been no intimation of such a purpose, there was nothing in the resolution of the Continental Congress to suggest such a purpose. That the controversy with the mother country might lead to such a revolutionary attempt had been anticipated and dreaded by many from its very inception, but few at the time were prepared to meet the issue. John Rutledge warmly reproved Colonel Gadsden, pronounced the opinion treasonable, and declared he abhorred the idea." Paine, the author of the pamphlet, was denounced and cursed. Even the few who were ready for independence regretted Gadsden's sudden and inopportune declaration.

Gadsden's resolution was voted down. But less than a month later the South Carolina Convention resolved to establish an independent government for South Carolina, with a president instead of a royal governor. It was further resolved to elect a general assembly, and instead of the royal governor's privy council there was to be a legislative council of thirteen members.

This proceeding inclines one to believe that after the "explosion" at the February meeting others besides Christopher Gadsden had been reading Thomas Paine *Common Sense*.

When the Declaration of Independence came before the Continental Congress on July 4 of that year the South Carolina delegates voted for it, together with the delegates of all the other Colonies except New York.

New York delegates refrained from voting on July 4, as they had no authority from their Colonial assembly to vote for independence at that time, but such instructions were received later and they cast their votes for the Declaration on July 9.

The Tories, or Loyalists, constituted a strong minority in all the Colonies. In some of them, in New York and Pennsylvania, for example, they were sufficiently influential to be a distinct menace to the independence movement. The Tories were conservatives, or reactionaries. They wanted no change, or only minor changes in the relation of the Colonies to Great Britain. They feared that separation from the mother country would lead to disaster, and the vexatious laws and regulations imposed on the Colonies by the king and his government seemed to them a lesser evil than those lying quietly hidden in the background of independence.

Many of the Tories were wealthy; it was, indeed, a party of rich landowners, exporters, merchants and professional men, such as college professors, clergymen and lawyers. The common folk included in the Tory classification were, in most cases, tenants or debtors or servants of well-to-do Loyalists.

The Tories were convinced that the independence of the Colonies, if it ever came about, would lead to mob rule, anarchy and disorganization, with "the illiterate trash," as they called the common people, sitting on top of the heap. And, of course, all private property would be seized or destroyed.

Their fears were wholly groundless, but they could not see far enough in the future to perceive that the ghost lying in wait for them on the dark road was only a flapping white sheet. The social system that followed the Revolution was certainly not governed by a mob. It was not even a democracy but an aristocratic republic. The Tories would have been as safe within it as if they were living in the shadow of St. James Palace.

Yet as late as November 24, 1778, after the French had joined the Colonials and the British were losing the war, the French minister at Philadelphia wrote to his government:

> Scarcely one quarter of the ordinary inhabitants of Philadelphia now here favor the cause [of independence]. Commercial and family ties, together with an aversion to popular government, seem to account for this. The same feeling exists in New York and Boston, which is not the case in the rural districts.

To counterattack the revolutionary movement the Loyalists distributed innumerable pamphlets and subsidized newspapers and public speakers. Some of their arguments sound exceedingly strange to a twentieth-century reader. "If I must be enslaved," Samuel Seabury wrote, "let it be by a King at least, and not by a parcel of upstart, lawless Committeemen. If I must be devoured, let me be devoured by the jaws of a lion and not gnawed to death by rats and vermin." Jonathan Boucher declared that "a rebel is worse than the worst prince, and a rebellion worse than the worst government of the worst prince that hath hitherto been."

The anonymous author of *Plain Truth*, a Tory pamphlet, wrote that "Independence and slavery are anonymous terms." A startling idea! If that be true, it would certainly be interesting to have the writer's definition of freedom, which he failed to give.

"God is a God of order and not of confusion," wrote another pamphleteer, "and he commands you to submit to your rulers, and to be obedient to the higher power for conscience sake." The Reverend John Bullman, a Tory divine, preached a number of sermons against the Whigs and the independence movement. In one of them he put forth this specimen of Tory wisdom:

> Every idle projector, who perhaps cannot govern his own household, or pay the debts of his own creating, presumes he is qualified to dictate how the state should be governed, and to point out the means of paying the debts of a nation. Hence, too, it is that every silly clown or

illiterate mechanic will take upon him to censure the conduct of his prince or governor and contribute as much as in him lies to create and foment these misunderstandings which, being brooded by discontent and diffused through great multitudes, come at last to end in schism in the church, and sedition and rebellion in the state; so a great matter doth a little fire kindle.

The appearance of *Common Sense* and its wide circulation among people of all classes and conditions was a major disaster to the Tory cause. Their leaders, and the secret agents of Britain, encouraged writers in their pay to answer its arguments. As a result a swarm of pamphlets appeared bearing such titles as *A Friendly Address*; *An Englishman's Answer*; *The Congress Canvassed*; *Patriots of North America*; and *True Interest of America*. All of these effusions are pompous, windy, dull and unconvincing.

Source: W. E. Woodward, "Paine Writes a Bestseller," in *Tom Paine: America's Godfather*, E. P. Dutton, 1945, pp.66–84.

SOURCES

Ascherson, Neal, "The Indispensable Englishman (American Political Theorist and Author Thomas Paine)," in the *New Statesman* (U.K.), January 29, 1999, pp. 25–27.

Collins, Paul, "The Arch Revolutionary," in *New Scientist*, Vol. 50, No. 2, 2004, p. 51.

Kashatus, William C., "Revolution with Pen & Ink (The Influence of Thomas Paine's 'Common Sense')," in *American History*, Vol. 34, No. 6, February 2000, p. 53.

Kaye, Harvey J., "The Lost Founder: Thomas Paine Has Often Been the Forgotten (and Sometimes the Ostracized) Founding Father. It's Time to Start Remembering—and Celebrating," in *The American Prospect*, Vol. 16, No. 7, July 2005, pp. 34–38.

Lapham, Lewis H., "Uncommon Sense," in *Harper's Magazine*, Vol. 305, No. 1826, July 2002, pp. 7–9.

Paine, Thomas, *The Crisis*, 1776–1783, in *Paine: Collected Writings*, The Library of America, 1995, p.91.

——, *Common Sense*, 1776, in *Paine: Collected Writings*, The Library of America, 1995, pp. 6, 34, 36, 38, 46.

Seymour, Gene, Steven Lubet, Michael Barkun, Mark Rotella, David Thomson, and Harvey J. Kaye, "Overrated Underrated.(Historical Events and People)," in *American Heritage*, Vol. 56, No. 5, October 2005, pp. 60–74.

Daisy Miller

HENRY JAMES
1878

Exploring the conflict between concepts at the heart of the American dream—personal freedom and the social limitation others want to place on that freedom—*Daisy Miller* was a smashing success when originally published in 1878. It remains one of the most popular books written by author Henry James. The short novel established James's reputation as an author on both sides of the Atlantic, and he went on to further explore complex women in such celebrated novels as *The Portrait of a Lady* (1881).

James had two significant inspirations for the tale he told in *Daisy Miller*. In the fall of 1877, he heard a story in Rome about a somewhat ignorant, unknowing American mother new to the ways of Europe. The mother allowed her daughter to befriend a Roman man, whom she introduced to new friends they met in the city. Because of their poor social choice, the mother and daughter suffered social outfall and were ostracized by other Americans living in the city. James also had a free-spirited cousin, Minny Temple, who, though dead for several years, was an inspiration for Daisy and many of his early female heroines.

Daisy Miller was written early in 1878 while James was living in London. After being initially rejected by an American publisher, the novel was originally published as *Daisy Miller: A Study* in two parts by a British periodical, the *Cornhill Magazine*, in the summer of 1878. The story

proved to be immediately popular. Because James failed to secure the American rights to the work right away, *Daisy Miller* was pirated by periodicals in Boston (*Living Age*) and New York (*Home Journal*) that same summer. An authorized American edition was finally put out that fall by Harper's, which also sold well. Over the years, *Daisy Miller* was republished several times in book form, with James making a number of alterations and revisions each time. The author made major revisions with the so-called New York Edition, published by Scribners in 1907–1909, which is the text used for the discussion here.

Though social mores and attitudes have changed significantly since the late nineteenth and early twentieth centuries, *Daisy Miller* continues to be a popular and relevant story. Filtered through the conflicted perspective of Frederick Winterbourne, an American expatriate who lives in Geneva, Switzerland, James describes the last months of the socially naive, essentially innocent Daisy Miller. Daisy has come to Europe with her mother, Mrs. Miller, and younger brother Randolph. The family does not know what they are doing in Europe. The Millers do not appreciate the culture, art, and monuments yet are rich enough to live in fine hotels for months on their trip abroad. While staying in Vevey, Switzerland, Daisy meets Winterbourne, who is both charmed and bewildered by the flirtatious young American woman who does not follow social norms. He enjoys her nonconformity to a point—especially when she is focused on him—but wants to curb it as well. Winterbourne sees that she lacks education and cultivation, and, especially after the scene shifts to Rome, he wonders if she lacks scruples, too.

In Rome, where the Millers and other Americans vacation in the winter, Daisy spends most of her time with an Italian man, Giovanelli, who is not regarded as her social equal. The pair is also often alone, creating a social scandal among the Americans as well as their European counterparts. While Winterbourne's aunt, Mrs. Costello, has disapproved of the Millers since Vevey, the family's new friend, Mrs. Walker, also comes to disdain Daisy because of her continued disregard for propriety. While Winterbourne shares their concerns and comes to see her as more common than he initially thought, he remains protective of her because of her attractive, stubborn naivety. When Winterbourne finds Daisy and Giovanelli alone at

BIOGRAPHY

HENRY JAMES

Born in New York City on April 15, 1843, James was raised on both sides of the Atlantic. His grandfather had founded a business that made him wealthy, while his father used his money to live in Europe for a significant time during James's childhood. James received his education in New York as well as London, Paris, and Geneva. Returning to the United States in 1860, James briefly studied art and attended Harvard Law for a term. When his family moved to Massachusetts in 1864, James decided that he wanted to be an author and began publishing stories and reviews anonymously. He published his first signed story in 1865 in the *Atlantic Monthly*.

From 1869 to 1875, James moved back and forth between the United States and Europe as he worked on his writing career, publishing his first novel *Atlantic, Watch and Ward* in 1870. After settling in London in 1876, James wrote *Daisy Miller* in 1878, which established him as an author of note. As he continued to write, he was influenced by his status and experiences as an ex-patriot. James eventually made London his primary home, though he returned to the United States on occasion and continued to travel. After becoming a British subject in 1915, he died in London on February 28, 1916, after a series of strokes.

the Colosseum late at night, he finally loses respect for her. After her death, caused by picking up a fever (actually malaria) there, Winterbourne comes to understand that she really was just a spontaneous and innocent flirt. His relationship with Daisy does not change him in the long term except that he realizes that he no longer understands young American girls.

As James has written her, Daisy believes she does not have to follow social rules; her mother seems to have never enforced discipline of any kind upon her or Randolph. A physical embodiment of something essentially America, freedom, she charms Winterbourne with this attitude, but chafes every time someone tries to impose any guidance on her, even for her own safety. Such a free nature leads to a close relationship with Mr. Giovanelli and excursions to tourist spots in Rome, but also to her death.

While James shows the intoxicating effects of freedom, he also emphasizes how Americans embrace rules and can be as intolerant abroad as at home. Daisy shows the world a new way to live, but she is rejected for it. In *Daisy Miller: A Dark Comedy of Manners*, Daniel Mark Fogel claims, "In his title character, Daisy Miller, . . . James created the paradigm of a central American myth, the myth of the American girl as free, spontaneous, independent, natural, and generous in spirit."

While readers and critics embraced *Daisy Miller* when it was initially published, the novel eventually came to be seen as one of James's major works. Though the way of thinking about manners and women has changed over time, James's book and his literary creation remain powerful. Carey H. Kirk writes in *Studies in Short Fiction*, "In *Daisy Miller* James has designed a story that will continue to challenge readers' interpretive skills and cause their attitudes toward Daisy and Winterbourne to vacillate for a considerable time to come."

PLOT SUMMARY

Part 1

Daisy Miller opens with a description of the town of Vevey, Switzerland, and a certain hotel therein, Trois Couronnes. Both are popular with the many American tourists who visit in the spring. Frederick Winterbourne is introduced. He is a twenty-seven-year-old American expatriate who lives in Geneva, Switzerland, and is staying at the hotel while visiting his aunt, Mrs. Costello. She lives in Vevey and is staying at the same hotel. Because his aunt had one of her headaches this particular morning, Winterbourne is free to spend his time as he wishes.

In the course of his wanderings, Winterbourne is asked for a lump of sugar by a nine-year-old American boy, Randolph Miller. He tells Winterbourne of his love of sugar and American candy, though his mother does not want to him to have

Henry James AP Images

any. Their conversation is interrupted when Randolph's elder sister, Annie P. Miller, commonly known as Daisy, appears. James describes her as "strikingly, admirably pretty." Though Winterbourne initially subscribes to social mores that dictate that he should not speak to a young unmarried woman, he tells her that Randolph and he have met.

Daisy ignores Winterbourne and asks her brother where he got the pole with which he is playing. Winterbourne learns that they are going to Italy, but when they finally begin to converse, she does not know exactly where they are going. Because Daisy says little, Winterbourne observes what she reveals about her personality and appearance as he continues to try and start a conversation. He eventually finds out that she, her mother, and her brother are going to Rome for the winter, and that Daisy does not think of him as a "real American," but a German.

As Daisy opens up more to Winterbourne, he learns that she is from New York state. Randolph informs him that their father, Ezra, is at home in Schenectady tending to his successful business. After Daisy allows Randolph to go play, she tells him that her brother does not like

Europe, has had little in the way of other boys to play with, and has not been receiving any education. Daisy also informs Winterbourne that her brother is going to college.

Winterbourne is intrigued by their conversation: "She addressed her new acquaintance as if she had known him a long time. He found it very pleasant. It was many years since he heard a young girl talk so much." Daisy tells him more about where they have been and her society life in the United States. Winterbourne grows more intrigued by her and her talkative innocence. He believes that she is "a pretty American flirt."

When Daisy asks Winterbourne if he has been to the Château de Chillon, he says yes and offers to take her and, a moment later, her mother there. Daisy decides that she can go with him alone as their courier (a paid guide/travel helper) Eugenio and her mother stay with Randolph at the hotel. Winterbourne is glad about the excursion. Their conversation is interrupted by Eugenio, who tells her that lunch is ready. Daisy asks for assurance that they will go, and Winterbourne wants her to meet someone who will speak for him. Daisy says that "we'll go some day," and leaves with Eugenio.

Part 2

When Mrs. Costello's headache abates, Winterbourne asks her if she saw the Miller family in the hotel. His aunt does not think highly of them. She tells him, "They're horribly common .... They're the sort of Americans that one does one's duty by just ignoring." Mrs. Costello is especially harsh in her judgment of Daisy, whom she believes "has an intimacy" with Eugenio. When Winterbourne tells her of his plans to take Daisy to the castle, his aunt expresses more disapproval. Mrs. Costello refuses to even meet Daisy.

Despite his aunt's feelings on the matter, Winterbourne remains intrigued. That night around ten o'clock, he finds Daisy walking around the garden. They talk about their respective evenings. Her mother does not sleep much while her brother does not like to go to bed nor sleep. Daisy has also learned some information about his aunt and wants to meet her. Winterbourne tells Daisy that his aunt has a headache every day and cannot, but Daisy understands that Mrs. Costello does not want to make her acquaintance. This fact does not upset Daisy much but makes her think his aunt is quite "exclusive."

Daisy sees her mother and insists on introducing Winterbourne to her. Mrs. Miller initially ignores Winterbourne to tell Daisy about Randolph's actions. Winterbourne is eventually drawn into the conversation as they tell of a time in Dover when Randolph would not go to sleep at all. Winterbourne brings up the matter of the castle, and Mrs. Miller acquiesces to Daisy going alone with him. Daisy immediately wants him to take her out in a boat to the château, though it is eleven o'clock, and Winterbourne agrees.

Winterbourne and Daisy's plans are stymied by the appearance of Eugenio, who agrees with Mrs. Miller that Daisy should not go out in a boat at the time. Daisy chafes at Eugenio's insistence on propriety but is amused that he and Winterbourne are both prepared to "make a fuss," she says, "That's all I want—a little fuss!" Her interest in the trip ends when Eugenio announces that Randolph is asleep. Daisy goes inside with Mrs. Miller and Eugenio.

Two days later, Daisy and Winterbourne make the steamer trip to the castle unaccompanied. Winterbourne gives her a tour, and she is impressed by his knowledge. Daisy wants him to be Randolph's teacher, but he tells her he must soon return to Geneva. This information upsets Daisy, who believes that a woman must be involved. She wants him to come to Rome that winter; Winterbourne already has plans to visit his aunt there. Daisy tells him, "I don't want you to come for your aunt. I want you just to come for me." Winterbourne only promises to be in Rome. When he tells his aunt of what has transpired during the day, Mrs. Costello is unimpressed and dismissive of Daisy.

Part 3

In January, Winterbourne goes to Rome to visit his aunt. She had already written him about the Millers, especially Daisy's actions. She reports that Daisy has become "very intimate with various third-rate Italians." Mrs. Costello tells him that Daisy spends much time alone with such men, many of whom she believes are fortune hunters. Because Mrs. Miller has not acted to stop Daisy, the aunt dismisses the whole family as "vulgar."

The information imparted by Mrs. Costello tempers Winterbourne's previous wish to see Daisy right away. He is jealous about the other men she has been seeing:

He had perhaps not definitely flattered himself that he had made an ineffaceable impression upon her heart, but he was annoyed at hearing a state of affairs so little in harmony with an image that had lately flitted in and out of his mediations.

Instead of seeing Daisy right away, Winterbourne visits other friends. When he calls on an American woman he knew from Geneva named Mrs. Walker, he is surprised by the arrival of the three members of the Miller family. Daisy continues to flirt with Winterbourne, offended that he has not come to see her yet and not believing he arrived only yesterday. While Daisy then focuses her attention on the hostess, Winterbourne talks to Randolph and Mrs. Miller. She tells him of their illnesses and why they came to Europe. Mrs. Miller also declares that Rome is not what she expected, and Randolph interjects his dislike of the city.

When Mrs. Miller starts talking positively about Daisy's many gentleman admirers, Daisy starts talking to Winterbourne again. He remembers that he came directly to Rome without stopping in other Italian cities to see her, and the memory stings because of her attitude toward him. Daisy then asks Mrs. Walker if she can bring "an intimate friend of [hers], Mr. Giovanelli, to her party," which Daisy already planned to attend. Though like all of Daisy's gentleman friends, Mrs. Miller has not met him, Mrs. Walker agrees that he can come.

As the Millers take their leave, Daisy is going walking to the Pincio while her mother and brother return to the hotel. Mrs. Walker tells her not to go, believing it unsafe by the amount of late afternoon traffic, while Mrs. Miller worries about Daisy catching an illness that has been going around Rome. When Mrs. Walker learns that Daisy is going to meet Mr. Giovanelli, the hostess begs the young lady not to go. "Gracious me, I don't want to do anything that's going to affect my health—or my character either!" Daisy protests. To satisfy them, Daisy has Winterbourne escort her there.

Walking to the Pincio, Daisy asks Winterbourne why he had not come to see her. She points out that he visited Mrs. Walker when Winterbourne again states that he just arrived in Rome. Daisy tells him about their hotel as they arrive at the gardens. She wants Winterbourne to help her find Giovanelli, but he refuses. Winterbourne also will not leave her alone there. The matter

is solved when Daisy spots Giovanelli resting against a tree.

After Winterbourne sees Giovanelli, he refuses to leave Daisy alone with him. Daisy does not take his attitude well, stating, "I've never allowed a gentleman to dictate to me or to interfere with anything I do." Winterbourne does not see Giovanelli as a gentleman, and tells Daisy to listen to one—himself. By this time, Giovanelli has seen them and approaches. Daisy makes the introductions, and she holds one on each side as they walk together. "Giovanelli of course had counted upon something more intimate—he had not bargained for a party of three; but he kept his temper in a manner which suggested far-stretching intentions."

In Winterbourne's eyes, Giovanelli is nowhere near a gentleman such as himself, only an imitation at best. Winterbourne has a hard time understanding why Daisy cannot look down upon him. Because she cannot, he wonders if she is really a "nice girl." Winterbourne starts wondering if he should be thinking less of her because of her actions and attitude. Yet, "Daisy at any rate continued on this occasion to present herself as an inscrutable combination of audacity and innocence."

After walking in this manner for about fifteen minutes, a carriage with Mrs. Walker inside pulls up near them. She summons Winterbourne and tells him that Daisy's behavior—walking alone with the two men—is scandalous. "Fifty people have remarked [on] her," Mrs. Walker claims. Winterbourne defends Daisy, declaring her "innocent." Mrs. Walker will not let the subject drop, and also denounces Mrs. Miller for her lack of action. Mrs. Walker wants Daisy to get into the carriage, drive around for a bit, and go home to save her reputation.

After introducing Giovanelli to Mrs. Walker and complimenting her carriage, Daisy refuses to get inside and resents being treated like a child. Winterbourne finds the scene uncomfortable and his discomfort only increases when Daisy asks him what he thinks. He tells her truthfully that she should get inside. Daisy responds, "I never heard anything so stiff! If this is improper, Mrs. Walker, then I'm *all* improper, and you had better give me right up."

Mrs. Walker asks Winterbourne to get in the carriage. Though he wants to stay with Daisy, Mrs. Walker says she will never speak to him again unless he rides with her. After saying his goodbyes to Daisy and Giovanelli, he tells Mrs. Walker, "That was not clever of you." Winterbourne emphasizes that angering Daisy will not help the situation and that she does not want to hurt anyone. Mrs. Walker informs him that Daisy has been acting this way for a month, flirting indiscriminately and scandalously. His hostess also wants him to have nothing more to do with Daisy. Winterbourne refuses, and Mrs. Walker drops him off near where Daisy and Giovanelli are. After witnessing the pair from afar in a moment of friendly familiarity, he walks toward his aunt's home.

Part 4

For the next three days, Winterbourne tries to talk to Mrs. Miller, but she is never at home. Despite the tensions with Mrs. Walker, he goes to her party, where he finds Mrs. Miller also in attendance and alone. Mrs. Miller tells him that Daisy is dressed and ready to go to the party, but she is playing on the piano and singing with Giovanelli at the hotel. Mrs. Walker vows not to speak to Daisy when she comes.

Daisy arrives after eleven in the evening with Giovanelli, immediately approaches Mrs. Walker, and explains her tardiness. Mrs. Walker is short with her. Giovanelli sings a handful of songs for the party. Daisy also talks familiarly with Winterbourne, referring to the incident several days earlier. She thinks it would have been "unkind" to leave Giovanelli as the walk they went on had been planned for some time.

Winterbourne tries to point out the impropriety of the situation, but Daisy does not care. He also tells her he wishes to be the only one she flirts with; Daisy believes he is "too stiff." Winterbourne continues to impress upon her that Giovanelli might not interpret her flirtations the same way an American would, yet Daisy still will not hear of it. She believes that she is only close friends with Giovanelli and blushes when Winterbourne suggests they are in love with each other.

Giovanelli has completed his performance, and he asks Daisy to have tea with him in the other room. They stay there until they take their leave. When Daisy and Giovanelli do depart, Mrs. Walker turns her back on them. Mrs. Miller does not understand the snub, but Daisy does. Mrs. Walker tells Winterbourne that Daisy will not be coming to her house again.

Because of this tension, Winterbourne begins going to the Millers' hotel. On the rare occasions that they are home, Giovanelli is almost always there as well. Daisy's actions do not change when both men are present:

> Winterbourne reflected that if she was seriously interested in the Italian it was odd she shouldn't take more trouble to preserve the sanctity of their interviews, and he liked her the better for her innocent-looking indifference and her inexhaustible gaiety.

Winterbourne realizes that there is little to be jealous about and she is nothing but lightness. Winterbourne also realizes that her primary interest is in Giovanelli.

Some time later, Winterbourne is walking with his aunt at Saint Peter's when he spies Daisy and Giovanelli together. Mrs. Costello notes that Daisy and her paramour are the reason her nephew has been "preoccupied." She also comments that others have noticed that relationship. In addition, Mrs. Costello believes that Eugenio arranged their meeting in the first place and will be paid off if Giovanelli marries her. Winterbourne discounts his aunt's theories, informing her he had Giovanelli checked out and that he is "a perfectly respectable little man." Giovanelli, however, does not have much social standing. Winterbourne does not believe Giovanelli has hope of such a relationship with Daisy.

After a time, his aunt sits down outside of Saint Peter's and other Americans talk to her. They all comment negatively on Daisy and her scandalous actions. Watching Daisy leave with Giovanelli, Winterbourne feels pity for her for how low she has sunk in the eyes of others. He even tries to communicate about the situation with Mrs. Miller on an occasion when he knows she is alone. Mrs. Miller believes Daisy and Giovanelli are essentially engaged; Giovanelli promised to tell her if that happens.

Winterbourne does not see Daisy socially any more as the people they know in common have shut her out. He is torn inside between admiring her defiance and thinking of her as ignorant and shallow. Winterbourne knows he has no chance to help her because she focuses totally on Giovanelli.

Several days later, Winterbourne happens upon them at the Palace of the Caesars. Daisy remarks on what she perceives as Winterbourne's loneliness. She also states that Winterbourne believes she spends too much time with Giovanelli. Winterbourne emphasizes to her that everyone thinks this way and if she goes to see most people, they will treat her as Mrs. Walker did. Daisy does not like this cruelty. She teases him about their alleged engagement, and tells him first that she and Giovanelli are, then that they are not.

A week later, Winterbourne comes upon them again at eleven o'clock at night inside the Colosseum. He does not see them at first as he focuses on quoting Lord Byron's "Manfred," but when he does, he hesitates to approach. Winterbourne is finished with her: "She was a young lady about the *shades* of whose perversity a foolish puzzled gentleman need no longer trouble his head or his heart."

Just as Winterbourne is about to leave, Daisy sees him, and he walks over to her and Giovanelli. When Winterbourne learns that she has been there for some time, he tells her that she is putting herself at extreme risk for catching the "Roman fever." He reprimands Giovanelli for allowing her to take the risk, but the Italian tells Winterbourne that Daisy does not care. Giovanelli agrees with Winterbourne that she should be taken home and should take preventative pills. Daisy does not believe she will be sick, but she goes along.

Though Winterbourne does not mention finding Daisy and Giovanelli at the Colosseum, other Americans soon learn of her latest scandalous episode. Daisy soon becomes quite ill with the sickness. Winterbourne calls on the family repeatedly during her ill-health, but Giovanelli disappears. Mrs. Miller informs Winterbourne that in a lucid moment, Daisy told her to tell him that she was never engaged to Giovanelli.

Within a week, Daisy dies of the illness, perniciosa, and she is buried in a Protestant cemetery in Rome. Giovanelli is among the mourners. He is quite saddened by the loss. He tells Winterbourne, "She was the most beautiful young lady I ever saw, and the most amiable." A moment later, he adds, "Also—naturally!—the most innocent." Giovanelli further confides in Winterbourne that he thought for a moment she might marry him, but he now understands she would not have.

After the burial, Winterbourne leaves Rome. He reunites with his aunt the following summer in Vevey, where the Millers are still a topic of conversation. Winterbourne tells Mrs.

> WINTERBOURNE WONDERED HOW SHE FELT ABOUT ALL THE COLD SHOULDERS THAT WERE TURNED UPON HER, AND SOMETIMES FOUND HIMSELF SUSPECTING WITH IMPATIENCE THAT SHE DIDN'T FEEL AND DIDN'T KNOW....THEN AT OTHER MOMENTS HE COULDN'T DOUBT THAT SHE CARRIED ABOUT IN HER ELEGANT AND IRRESPONSIBLE LITTLE ORGANISM A DEFIANT, PASSIONATE, PERFECTLY OBSERVANT CONSCIOUSNESS OF THE IMPRESSION SHE PRODUCED."

Costello that he finally understands her death-bed message now as a call for "esteem." He soon returns to live in Geneva and resumes his interest "in a very clever foreign lady."

THEMES

Freedom

One of the primary themes explored in *Daisy Miler* is that of freedom. Daisy's American dream is her unflagging belief that she should be free to act however she pleases without regard to what anyone else thinks, Americans or otherwise, nor any social norms, American or European. It is her innocent, if not naïve, belief that she can endlessly flirt and spend time alone as an unmarried woman with any unmarried man she chooses that both attracts and befuddles Winterbourne. Her unabashed embracing of her personal freedom leads to condemnation from other Americans in Switzerland and Italy, including Winterbourne's aunt Mrs. Costello and Mrs. Walker.

From the moment Daisy is introduced in the garden of the hotel in Vevey, she acts as she pleases. The narrator notes that Winterbourne "had begun to perceive that she was really not in the least embarrassed." Daisy easily talks to Winterbourne without a hint of self-consciousness and he recognizes that she is a flirt. She almost immediately suggests they go to a nearby castle alone. Later, in part 2, Daisy even wants to take a rowboat there that night. Though Daisy will not go once her mother is free to join them, Winterbourne and Daisy make it there several days later on a steamer.

Daisy continues to exercise her freedom in Rome. Much to Winterbourne's consternation, Daisy spends her time with an Italian man named Mr. Giovanelli. Though other Americans, including Winterbourne, think of him as their social lesser, Daisy chooses to be alone with him at various sites in Rome, both during the day and at night. Even though this action puts her on the social outs with people like Mrs. Walker and even Winterbourne at times, Daisy does not doubt that she can act any way she wants.

She does not care about consequences; she only cares about being herself. When Winterbourne and Giovanelli become concerned that she might catch Roman fever (malaria) by being at the Colosseum late at night, Daisy agrees to leave but dismisses their concerns. She tells Winterbourne as her carriage pulls off, "I don't care whether I have Roman fever or not!"

Daisy's mother, the only parental figure traveling with her, does not attempt to squelch her daughter's freedom or question her choices. Mrs. Miller allows her daughter to act as she pleases and does not try to meet the men Daisy spends time with in Switzerland or Rome. Even Eugenio, their trip coordinator, does not have a chance of modifying Daisy's actions and attitudes.

However, there are consequences to Daisy's freewheeling actions, whether she likes it or not. There are social snubs from women like Mrs. Walker and Mrs. Costello. Daisy is judged and looked down upon by other Americans abroad as well as the workers from the hotels. More importantly, Daisy dies because of her defiance. Though the others try to convince her not to go out for danger of catching a dread disease, she does go out, contracts the illness—malaria—and dies a week later. While Daisy acts as freely as she wishes while alive, it ends up costing her life.

Social Status and Mores

Though Daisy lives as freely as she can, she still embraces some sense of social status. Another part of the American dream is defining one's self from everyone else while fitting into a social stratum by embracing its norms and mores. When Daisy first meets Winterbourne in Vevey, she tells him that she is disappointed by the lack of "society" in Europe. Daisy states, "I'm very fond of society and I've always had plenty of it." She goes on to explain that she is socially active in her hometown of Schenectady as well as in New York City, and has been given parties by both gentlemen and young lady friends.

The society that Daisy could not see early in *Daisy Miller* condemns her and her mother for the way Daisy chooses to live her life. Though some of their fellow Americans recognize that the Millers have some social standing because of their money and background, Daisy's actions, her mother's inactions, and even Randolph's often out-of-control behavior lead to negative social judgments. Others Americans, such as Mrs. Costello, dismiss them outright. In part 2, she tells her nephew, "They're horribly common.... They're the sort of American that one does one's duty by just ignoring." While Mrs. Costello calls Daisy "a young lady" later in the same conversation, her opinion of the Millers, Daisy especially, does not improve over the course of the book, despite her nephew's feelings. She does not like Daisy for ignoring what she believes are social norms to be followed to the letter.

In Rome, Mrs. Costello's disapproval only increases as Daisy becomes close to an Italian gentleman, Mr. Giovanelli, who people generally consider to be her social lesser. Daisy's stubborn insistence that she is free to do as she wants compels Mrs. Walker to grow frustrated as well. While Mrs. Walker wants to help the Millers, especially Daisy, she does not want Mrs. Walker's version of social help.

The only reason Mrs. Walker takes her carriage to the Pinicio is to save Daisy's reputation when she is seen walking with both Winterbourne and Mr. Giovanelli. Mrs. Walker tells Winterbourne, "That crazy girl musn't do this sort of thing. She musn't walk here with you two men. Fifty people have remarked [on] her." When Daisy refuses Mrs. Walker's version of help and then shows up at Mrs. Walker's party later with Giovanelli, Mrs. Walker condemns her as unwelcome in her home. Becoming a social outcast does not seem to affect Daisy in the least.

Winterbourne has the more challenging relationship with social status and social mores. While he embraces the values of his aunt and Americans of her ilk in Europe, he also sees the absurdity of living strictly by the rules. After becoming charmed by Daisy because she ignores society's rules as he knows them, Winterbourne is happy to break them himself. He talks to her, an unmarried woman, as an unmarried man, without an escort, and even takes her on an excursion under the same circumstances.

What compels Winterbourne to retreat to his previous way of thinking is the presence of competition in the form of Giovanelli. Winterbourne wants to be the only object of Daisy's flirtation, but when he learns she is very friendly with someone from a lower social stratum, his social mores change as he becomes jealous. Winterbourne sees the problems with Daisy's free actions in terms of social norms, and he tries to intercede for her benefit several times.

Despite Winterbourne's jealousy, he also sees the absurdity of some social attitudes. When Mrs. Walker drives up in the aforementioned carriage and speaks to Winterbourne that way, he bristles: "Winterbourne—suddenly and rather oddly rubbed the wrong way by this—raised his grave eyebrows. 'I think it's a pity to make too much fuss about it.'" Though Winterbourne does not like nor trust Giovanelli, he supports Daisy in his own way until the end. After her death, Winterbourne realizes that his error in his belief about Daisy and society's rules: "She would have appreciated one's esteem." He finally understands his own American dream about this part of his life, though the writer implies it is forgotten when he returns to Geneva.

HISTORICAL OVERVIEW

Changing Role of Women in American Society

In the late nineteenth century, women's position in American society was changing in some social strata. By 1880, 2.6 million women were employed in the United States, primarily in domestic work, though an increasing number found employment in manufacturing jobs, especially as the twentieth century loomed. While middle and upper class women generally did not work outside the home, rising incomes, better nutrition, and the increased availability of consumer items changed how they lived their lives as well. More leisure time was available to many women to enjoy emerging mass culture (sports, circuses, arts, and entertainment) as technological advancements resulted in many time-saving devices in the home and some industries.

As women's lives changed in the United States, they demanded more political rights. Women's suffrage, or the right to vote, was a war that saw significant battles in the 1870s. Susan B. Anthony tried to vote in 1872, but courts would not allow it. She took a new tactic in 1878 when she convinced California Senator A. A. Sargent to introduce a constitutional amendment allowing women to vote. The amendment died in committee on this occasion, but the movement continued. Supporters of such an amendment, such as the National Woman Suffrage Association, helped get it reintroduced in committee and even to the Senate floor, but the amendment did not pass until the early twentieth century. Women had more luck gaining the vote on the state level. By 1890, nineteen states allowed women to vote on certain issues.

Victorian Morals and Etiquette

In the late nineteenth century, Americans were greatly influenced by and often practiced Victorian morals and etiquette. The era was named for Britain's Queen Victoria, who reigned from 1837 to 1901, and the morals had their foundation in her country. The beliefs were derived from the image projected on the queen and her husband, Prince Albert, but often had little basis in the reality of the lives of the royal couple.

Victorian morals and etiquette were strict and often defined by social status. Self-control was important to Victorian Americans, as was the display of good character, propriety, and respectability. Respectable people did not talk or write about their emotions or sexual feelings. For instance, it was considered improper by many in Victorian society to use the word "leg" when both men and women were present.

Women were idealized, often received less of an education than their male counterparts, and were expected to be sexually pure. A woman's primary purpose was raising a family and maintaining a home, and she was to act accordingly. They were not to show off their bodies in any way, nor wear makeup. Their actions were considered reflections on their families. If a woman erred, as Daisy did in Rome, it reflected poorly on her family, who also had to pay a social price.

Transatlantic Tourism

Until the 1870s, Americans making tourist visits to Europe were relatively uncommon because of the limitations of travel. While the family of Henry James made a number of these jaunts while he was a child, the advent of passenger steamships in post–Civil War America made such excursions more common and affordable for Americans. Mass transit such as railways and cable cars also became more common in the 1870s, aiding the tourist experience in both the United States and in Europe. It is said that the popularity of *Daisy Miller* increased American tourism abroad in following decades. It was not only families making sometimes years-long trips through key locations in Europe as the James family did decades earlier: American students also began going abroad more often to study at European universities and art schools in this time period.

CRITICAL OVERVIEW

When *Daisy Miller* was first published in England in 1878, the story was immediately popular on both sides of the Atlantic. Copies even found their way to America before the novel could be published there. When officially published in the United States, *Daisy Miller* sold 20,000 copies in just a few weeks. The story was reprinted fives times between 1880 and 1902 alone, and James regularly revised the work. He even wrote an unsuccessful dramatic version, *Daisy Miller: A Comedy in Three Acts*, in 1883.

Daisy Miller was generally well received by critics in the United States when published in the late 1870s. Initially, the novel was praised for its style, cleverness, and realism. It was often originally read as a mild social satire, a cautionary tale of what can happen to an independent, free young lady, especially when abroad, if she is not careful in the company she keeps. Some women readers were offended by his depiction of an American girl. Such women did not believe they were like Daisy and they believed James gave foreigners the wrong impression about what American ladies were really like. Readers in London found Daisy and Randolph amusing examples of Americans and their poor behavior. Yet the novel was also said to influence the increase of American tourism in Europe in the 1880s and 1890s.

Later critics realized that the novel was key in the development of the concept of the "American Girl" as a popular figure in American literature in the late 1800s. Though a pinnacle of James's early period as a writer, some critics saw Daisy was not a particularly well-developed character. Some critics found the depiction of Daisy as flat, primarily because she is seen through Winterbourne's eyes. Over time, critics and readers changed how they interpreted *Daisy Miller* and its characters' actions as culture, manners, and attitudes toward women evolved. The book remained popular, however, as the issues of stereotyping, assumptions, convention, and self-deception remain part of the human condition even if the rules of society and social taboos, especially for women, have changed.

In a 1992 article in the *Sunday Times* (London), Roy Hattersley discusses the larger clash of cultures depicted by James's book:

> Superficially, James's writing confirms the impression of a socialite's concern with manners rather than morals. His novel Daisy Miller an early commercial success describes the tragedy that engulfed a young American girl who defied European conventions. The book's popularity was, in part, based on prurient speculation about the nature of Daisy's relationship with the Italian friend who keeps the reckless rendezvous in the moonlit Coliseum. But the story concerns something far more important than the line that divides innocence from indiscretion: Daisy Miller is a casualty of the conflict between the old world and the new.

During the twentieth century, *Daisy Miller* also came to be regarded as one of James's masterpieces, a reputation that continues into the twenty-first. Describing the importance of the book, Daniel Mark Fogel writes in *Daisy Miller: A Dark Comedy of Manners*,

> Not only was the publication of *Daisy Miller* a pivotal moment in James's career; it also may be said to be a turning point in the development of American literature. . . . [W]ith *Daisy Miller* he conferred on our national literature a stature in the wider world of letters that it had never before enjoyed. At the same time he gave enduring form to some of the foundational myths of modern American literature.

Today, *Daisy Miller* remains relevant to critics and readers alike. As Scott Eyman notes in his review for the *Palm Beach Post*:

> I hadn't read Daisy in about 25 years and was struck by how little it had dated in the 130 years since it was written. James hit on something

MEDIA ADAPTATIONS

Daisy Miller (1974) is a film version of James's story. Directed by Peter Bogdanovich, it stars Cybill Shepherd as Daisy. Though this adaptation of the novel received poor reviews, it follows the basic premise of the book. It is available on DVD from Paramount.

profound about the innocence of the American character, as well as the potential for destruction that innocence carries with it—you can see Daisy Millers in every mall in America.

CRITICISM

Robert Weisbuch

In the following excerpt, Weisbuch considers the nature of American masculinity and how Winterbourne's expatriate status complicates the reader's understanding of such an ideal.

Our questions about Winterbourne may resolve into a single, gigantic problem: What is it to be a man? In the American decades before the Civil War, a new definition of manhood was getting fashioned, and with a rapidity possible only in a new nation formed at a late stage of Western civilization. Industry, and the changes it effects in social organization and individual personalities, came pell-mell upon an America just learning to know itself. "Here, as in a theater," wrote James Russell Lowell, "the great problems of anthropology . . . are compressed, as it were, into the entertainment of a few hours." An extremely insecure aristocracy, for instance, is barely established before it finds itself rudely jostled. "The older ideologies of genteel patriarchy and artisan independence were being challenged by a new middle-class ideology of competitive individuals," writes David Leverenz, adding, perhaps a bit too simply, "The new middle-class won, and its ideology of manhood as competitive individualism still

pervades American life." The significantly absent Mr. Miller is one such winner, remaining behind in what Winterbourne imagines his Italian rival would consider "that mysterious land of dollars." But Winterbourne's confusion over Daisy suggests that commercially energetic America is a mystery to him as well, for Winterbourne is one of the losers in this redefinition of manhood. We know that he had been "put to school" in Geneva by his parents at about the age of Daisy's brother Randolph. Familial wealth is the implication, supported as well by the circumstances and snobbery of Winterbourne's aunt. That is, Winterbourne comes from a shaky displaced aristocracy that has found a shaky home in Europe. In England, Leverenz notes, "a similar class conflict . . . had ended with the gentry reestablishing control by 1870," and although we might wish to complicate this assertion—labor certainly has some claims on an approved manhood in Victorian fiction—the defeat of the many socialist revolutions across Europe by forces of royalty in the 1840s did make the continent a more comfortable site for monied lassitude. America, Fenimore Cooper had written decades earlier, "possesses neither the population nor the endowments to maintain a large class of learned idlers," idlers such as Frederick Winterbourne lifelong "student."

Thus Winterbourne's permanent vacation in Geneva is a choice; he has chosen not to enter into his own time and into the fray of "competitive individualism." This gives particular point to Daisy's characterization of Winterbourne's speeches as "formal" and "quaint." Winterbourne's lectures to Daisy on the nature of who is and is not a gentleman add to the anachronistic lexicon by which he seeks to assert his class superiority.

Winterbourne is willing to compete only by standards that rely on a code of behavior closely allied with inherited caste. He refuses free market competition and this refusal has everything to do with his romantic behavior. When Winterbourne abandons Mrs. Walker's carriage, apparently enlisting in Daisy's cause, he spies her with Giovanelli behind the same parasol prominent in his own first flirtation with her at Vevey, and the narrator's phrasing implies a major moment in Winterbourne's advance-retreat scenario: "This young man" (and the epithet focuses the issue of manhood) "lingered a moment, then he began to walk. He walked—not towards the couple with the parasol; towards the residence of his aunt, Mrs. Costello"—where he can take his revenge

The ruins of the Colosseum, Rome, Italy © David Ball/Corbis

in the sure condemnation of Daisy she will provide. He had done just the same on his arrival in Rome when he heard of Daisy surrounded by the moustaches; he will do the same differently when he hears of Daisy and Giovanelli in company again, retreating more aggressively to tell momma, informing Mrs. Miller that her daughter is "going too far." When he does confront Daisy directly, it is as a parent, not a lover, lecturing her on propriety to the point that Daisy for once evinces resentment. She notes that Winterbourne has failed to offer her tea as a gentleman suitor should; and to his "I have offered you advice," Daisy rejoins, "I prefer weak tea!" suggesting the degree to which Winterbourne dilutes his romantic presence by his learned condescension. In the Colosseum, when Winterbourne indicates to Daisy his condemnation, he does so by opting out of competition, telling her that "it makes very little difference whether you are engaged or not." Daisy, echoing the phrase, soon says "I don't care . . . whether I have Roman fever or not." In the tale's sentimental causality, Winterbourne's

renunciation of interest in Daisy causes Daisy's renunciation of life. As he enters the Colosseum Winterbourne recalls Byron's description of it in *Manfred*, but he might better have recalled Manfred's confession that he killed his beloved, "Not with my hand but heart, which broke her heart, / It gazed on mine and wither'd" (II. ii. 118–19). Winterbourne would rather kill than compete, and his response to challenge, tallying with the response of his class in arenas other than the romantic, is refusal and disdain.

"You needn't be afraid. I'm not afraid," Daisy tells him when he is forced to admit that Mrs. Costello will not meet her, and we sense that Winterbourne fears more generally. Yet it is unanswerable whether he takes his aristocratic stance because he is afraid—of a world of change, of impulses in himself that would force him to choose against his lifelong choice of class—or whether he is afraid because he has chosen an aristocratic stance that demands the loss of what he calls "instinct."

This is not to argue that James is, by contrast, glorifying the ascendancy of the mercantile class in America. As many readers have noted, the disorder of the Miller family, and forms of naiveté that approach the callow in Daisy herself, serve James as a harsh critique upon this class. Mr. Miller's absence from the family journey suggests a gendered distinction good for no one, as the man remains home making more money while the wife and children "get culture" (though never getting it at all). The son, Randolph, is "hard" as the lumps of sugar he criticizes, charmless, uncontrollable, and oddly "aged" with a voice "not young." Europe to Daisy is "perfectly sweet," the Colosseum "so pretty," all with a reductive condescension that is the sweet echo of Randolph's jingoist convictions that American candy and American men are "the best." Their mother suffers from a bad liver that is the equivalent of Mrs. Costello's headaches, these figures of opposing classes both substituting a narcissism of the body as pain for healthful purpose. The Millers too display a familial entropy that is a low result of the democracy that has advanced them. Mrs. Miller "is always wearing my things," Daisy laughs as her mother appears wrapped in Daisy's shawl, but it's a significantly unfunny inversion of roles. Daisy is as much an unofficial orphan as Winterbourne, and the absence of appreciation and authority in her own family may well draw her to the paternalistic, culturally authoritative, and quaint Winterbourne.

Winterbourne cannot meet the challenge, however, for he and his female advisors are part of a fragile, essentially nouveau, American aristocracy that is not real aristocracy at all any more than these expatriates are real Europeans. The problem is less class division and prejudice than it is class confusion and anxiety. Winterbourne and his ilk make hyperbolic any true European conventions in order to stake a nervous claim to beyond-Miller status. "Real" Europe is problematic in itself as, in a commercial age, filthy lucre makes embarrassing appearances amidst the leisure of the European upper class. As early as the second sentence of the tale, the narrator notes of Vevey that "the entertainment of tourists is the business of the place." The highest status hotel in Vevey, where the Millers reside, was built on the site of an old castle, both a reason for its status and a sign of the capitalist transformation of society. An actual establishment, its name, the "Trois Couronnes," implies both nobility and coins. The mishmash of the commercial and the aristocratic in Europe is one reason why its poetry-inspiring history is portrayed in the tale as dead-in-life, miasmic, not so much informing the present as sickening it.

Winterbourne too is financial, however much he wishes to disdain the world of economic struggle. As Ian Kennedy points out, when the narrator tells us that Winterbourne "had imbibed at Geneva the idea that one must always be attentive to one's aunt" just after he has described Mrs. Costello as "a widow with a fortune," James uncovers the savage, selfish underpinning the Genevan ideal of duty and of Winterbourne's fidelity to it and to his aunt. In a sense, attendance upon his wealthy aunt is Winterbourne's job.

He has yet another, and Daisy points to it when, at Chillon, she senses that Winterbourne is returning to Geneva because of a liaison. Bravely turning her hurt to a sally, she taunts, "Does she never allow you more than three days at a time? . . . Doesn't she give you a vacation in summer? There's no one so hard worked but they can get leave to go off somewhere at this season, I suppose." No champion of freedom like Byron's Bonnivard, this prisoner of Chillon yet shares that hero's terrible adjustment to the loss of liberty.

Even this momentary intimation of Winterbourne as prostituted makes his contempt for Giovanelli broadly hypocritical. On meeting the Italian, Winterbourne decides that "he is only a clever imitation" of a gentleman and he makes this claim in terms of labor: "He is a music-master, or a penny-a-liner, or a third-rate artist." Winterbourne himself is, by occupation, no more and something less; and if Giovanelli indeed has "practiced the idiom" of speaking in English "upon a great many American heiresses," one expects that Winterbourne has had to adapt to a few adopted idioms himself: "He had known, here in Europe, two or three women—persons older than Miss Daisy Miller, and provided, for respectability's sake, with husbands—who were great coquettes—dangerous, terrible women, with whom one's relations were liable to take a serious turn." Who is the imitation of a gentleman? Giovanelli, by the unemployed Winterbourne's account, turns out to be a "perfectly respectable little man" who is in fact a *cavaliere avvocato*, and this gentleman lawyer ends by entering a plea for a true perception of Daisy's innocence. Just as the Italian takes Winterbourne's resigned place as amoroso in the narrative, though never in Daisy's affections, so too he takes Winterbourne's place finally in the reader's regard. Giovanelli is not Winterbourne's gigolo opposite so much as his double, and finally his better.

This then is the economic Winterbourne: an emigrant out of fear of practicing the American ideal of equal competition, an unemployed idler whose sense of aristocratic breeding is prostituted by fortune hunting. We must recall that Winterbourne is no confirmed villain, at least not until the final words of the tale when he refuses the true illumination, the grace of understanding his own character that Daisy's death has afforded him. His very attraction to Daisy is proof of a residue of possibility in him and of a desire for a non-Genevan self-reformation. But the forms this attraction takes have everything to do with the class alliances Winterbourne had made; and when we ask, given such choices, what kind of manhood emerges, the answers constitute an encyclopedia of misogyny.

Source: Robert Weisbuch, "Winterbourne and the Doom of Manhood in *Daisy Miller*," in *New Essays on Daisy Miller and The Turn of the Screw*, Cambridge University Press, 1993, pp. 65–89.

SOURCES

Eyman, Scott, "130-Year-Old *Daisy Miller* has Aged Quite Well," in the *Palm Beach Post*, July 21, 2002, p. 8K.

Fogel, Daniel Mark, *Daisy Miller: A Dark Comedy of Manners*, Twayne Publishers, 1990, p. 3.

Hattersley, Roy, "Good Behaviour; Literature," in the *(London) Sunday Times*, (November 22, 1992, p. 6.

James, Henry, *Daisy Miller and other Stories*, Oxford University Press, 1909; reprint, 1985.

Kirk, Carey H., "*Daisy Miller* : The Reader's Choice," in *Studies in Short Fiction*, Vol. 17, No. 3, Summer 1980, pp. 275–83.

Norton, Mary Beth, et al., *A People & A Nation: A History of the United States, Volume II: Since 1865*, 3d. ed., Houghton Mifflin, 1990.

Death of a Salesman

ARTHUR MILLER
1949

If but one text were chosen as the embodiment of the failure of an American dream, *Death of a Salesman* would be it. Arthur Miller's 1949 play is widely considered his masterwork and established him as a leading American play-wright. Though it is also considered one of the most important plays of the twentieth century, it only took Miller six weeks to write. Originally produced on Broadway, the first production of *Death of a Salesman* was directed by Elia Kazan and starred Lee J. Cobb. It ran for 742 perform-ances, and won Miller the Pulitzer Prize, several Antoinette Perry "Tony" awards, the Donaldson Award, and a New York Drama Critics' Circle award.

The drama focuses on Willy Loman, a sixty-three-year-old New York City–based salesman whose career and life have been an illusion of success. Willy has reached a breaking point. After working for thirty-six years for the same company as a somewhat successful traveling salesman, he has been reduced to working on commission, feels weary, and, during the play, is fired after asking to be placed in a job in the New York office. Willy relies on his neighbor and "only friend" Charley for the funds to cover his family's expenses, yet he resents Charley's support.

Willy's turmoil is compounded by his fam-ily, and his consciousness often drifts to the past. While his wife, Linda, is endlessly supportive, she also knows that Willy exaggerates about his

successes. Willy's younger son, Happy, lives a life similar to Willy's. Hap claims he is the assistant buyer at a retailer when he is only an assistant to the assistant buyer. Hap also finds his identity in his romantic and sexual conquests, even at work. Willy's elder son, Biff, is a failure in Willy's eyes for working on farms and ranches in the West making only a few dollars per week. Biff has returned home for a visit and, as usual, they cannot see eye to eye.

There is tension between them because Biff has some understanding of his father's failures. Also, Biff gave up on his dreams as a senior in high school when he discovered that his father had been having an affair while traveling for work. The betrayal resonated with Biff his whole life and created a sense of distrust between father and son. In the end, Willy believes that only killing himself will solve his family's problems, financial and otherwise. An insurance policy will allow his mortgage and other bills to be paid in full and give Biff and Hap the funding to start their own business.

In addition to exploring the internal life of the common man in whose life Miller saw tragedy, he was inspired to write this portrait of Willy's self-delusion and overtiredness by many salesman he knew in his family and growing up in his Brooklyn neighborhood in the 1920s and 1930s. Such men had a sense of outrageous importance in a world where they were basically ignored or irrelevant. A seventeen-year-old Miller even wrote a short story about one such salesman he met during the course of a summer job. This salesman fails to sell anything during the course of one day and is also treated poorly by every potential customer. Miller's mother found the story, "In Memoriam," after *Death of a Salesman* was produced.

In the play, Miller explores themes about the American dream of success and the expectations that can come from an unrealistic interpretation of what that means. Willy wants to believe that he is a smashing salesman and well liked by everyone; the reality, however, is far from the optimistic truth he publicly promotes, and he knows it on the inside. Embracing the materialism and commercialism of American society, superficial symbols of the good life, only adds to Willy's distress.

Willy has always encouraged his sons to think and live the same way, often to their detriment. Despite this sometimes dysfunctional relationship, Miller also emphasizes the substance

BIOGRAPHY

ARTHUR MILLER

Miller was born in New York City on October 17, 1915, the grandson of Jewish immigrants from Poland. Miller's father worked as a women's coat manufacturer, and he was raised in a middle-class household until his father lost his business during the Great Depression. The family then moved to Brooklyn. After graduating from high school in 1932, Miller worked in a warehouse to save money so that he could attend the University of Michigan, where he learned to write. He won several prestigious Hopwood Awards for works he wrote there as a student. With degree in hand, Miller returned to New York City. He held odd jobs and wrote radio scripts while establishing himself as a playwright.

At the age of thirty-three, Miller had his breakout success when *Death of a Salesman* debuted. Miller continued to produce socially relevant plays including *The Crucible* (1953), which was inspired by his own dealings with the House of Representative's Un-American Activities Committee hearings in the 1950s. Though Miller's new works were not as popular after the 1960s, he continued to write until his death from heart failure at the age of eighty-nine on February 10, 2005, in Roxbury, Connecticut. Miller's last play, *Finishing the Picture* (2004), was produced shortly before his death.

and value of families like the Lomans. Willy and Linda want the best for their sons, and vice versa, but they do not always know what that means or the best way to accomplish this goal. Willy's suicide is his gift to his family for their continued well-being because he believes it is all he has left to give, as he has become irrelevant.

While ostensibly about the American dream and its failures, *Death of Salesman* has transcended its time, country, and culture of origin. The play has been continuously staged around the world to enthusiastic audiences, even in Communist countries. Miller himself supervised a Chinese-language production in Beijing, China, in 1983.

Miller explained to *Newsweek*'s Jack Kroll in 1999, "The theme of the brutality of the system toward man—this goes down everywhere, in France, Germany, Italy, Spain, Sweden, Argentina." In an obituary for Miller, who died in 2005, *Hollywood Reporter* quoted him as saying, "I couldn't have predicted that a work like *Death of a Salesman* would take on the proportions it has. Originally, it was a literal play about a literal salesman, but it has become a bit of a myth—not only here but in many parts of the world." In the half-century between Loman's death and Millers's, the playwright saw his American everyman become universal.

Arthur Miller AP Images

PLOT SUMMARY

Act I

When *Death of a Salesman* opens, sixty-three-year-old Willy Loman is returning to his home in New York City late at night. His wife, Linda, is awakened by his entrance as Willy, a traveling salesman, has come back early from his sales trip. When she questions why, Willy tells her, "I'm tired to the death. . . . I couldn't make it. I just couldn't make it, Linda." While Linda tries to reassure her husband that he just needs to rest, Willy tells her that he nearly got into a car accident while he was driving.

The couple talk about what he should do about his job. Willy's territory is New England, and Linda tells him to ask his boss, Howard, if he can work in New York. Willy and Linda also talk about their adult sons, Biff and Happy, who have spent the night in their old room. Linda questions why Willy chastised Biff earlier in the day. At the age of thirty-four, Biff makes little money working on farms out west. Willy agrees with his wife, "Biff Loman is lost. In the greatest country in the world a young man with such—personal attractiveness, gets lost. And such a hard worker." Willy promises to talk to Biff in the morning.

After Linda goes upstairs to bed, Willy talks to himself and eats in the kitchen. Biff and Happy, who were awakened by their parents' conversation, begin to talk in their room. Happy is worried about Willy driving as Happy has noticed Willy has a habit of not focusing on

the task. Happy also tells Biff that Willy has been talking to himself regularly.

As the brothers reminisce about the past, Biff asks why his father ridicules him. Happy asks about Biff's life and what his future holds. Biff has held many jobs over the years and does not want to be limited by business life but does not find working in the West satisfying either. Biff tells Happy, "every time I come back here I know that all I've done is to waste my life." Happy's life is not much better. He works in retail, has his own apartment, and sleeps with many women, including the girlfriends of several executives at his company. Yet Happy is lonely.

Biff thinks his only shot at success is Bill Oliver. Biff once worked for him many years ago, and he hopes Oliver will lend him thousands of dollars to buy a ranch. The brothers' discussion is interrupted by Willy talking loudly to himself as if his sons were still young. Biff and Happy worry about their mother hearing Willy's ramblings before going to sleep.

In the kitchen, Willy continues to talk to his absent sons as if they were still young. The teenage versions of Biff and Happy appear as the scene shifts to the past when Willy returned home from a sales trip one time. Willy gives the boys a punching bag, and he is not particularly upset to learn that Biff "borrowed" a football from his school's locker room. Willy brags to his sons about his sales trip and his popularity in certain New England cities. He tells his sons, "I have friends. I can park my car in any street in New England, and the cops protect it like their own."

As Willy talks to Biff about his upcoming big football game, Bernard interrupts their conversation. Bernard, the son of Willy's close friend and neighbor Charley, is younger than Biff and is supposed to be helping him with math. Bernard tells Willy that Biff's math teacher is threatening to flunk him, preventing him from graduating and accepting an athletic scholarship. Willy dismisses Bernard and his concerns. He tells Biff that he will succeed in life, and Bernard will not.

Young Linda enters and the boys leave. Willy exaggerates his amount of sales to Linda, but he is forced to be truthful with her. The family's bills are a higher amount than what Willy has earned. He tells her he will do better next week in Hartford but also tells her, "people don't seem to take to me." Willy continues, "I know it when I walk in. They seem to laugh at me." Linda encourages him, telling him that he is good-looking and worshipped by his boys.

As young Linda praises him, The Woman appears, dressing. After Willy praises his wife, he moves into the space with The Woman. Willy is having an affair with her, one that she initiated. She is dressing to leave the room, and, as she does, the scene returns to young Linda speaking highly of him. Bernard reappears in the house looking again for Biff so they can study for the Regents, a state exam. Willy again dismisses Bernard's concerns, for which Linda states her support. Willy gets angry again, telling his wife of Biff, "You want him to be a worm like Bernard? He's got spirit, personality."

The scene shifts back to present day. Happy comes downstairs and questions his father about his return. Willy tells his son he regrets not joining his brother Ben in Alaska when Ben wanted him to come as part of a potential business deal. Confused, Willy says that Ben "Walked into a jungle, and comes out, the age of twenty-one, and he's rich!" Hap tries to help, but Willy does not listen. Charley comes in and Happy goes upstairs.

Charley also tries to help Willy by listening and playing cards with him, but Willy is insulted by his offer of a job. For every statement or comment Charley makes, Willy is defensive. Willy's brother Ben enters the scene, a figment of Willy's imagination. As Willy and Charley keep playing cards, Willy talks to both of them. Ben is impatient with Willy. Willy tells Charley that Ben died a few weeks ago in Africa. Ben is talking to Willy about coming to Alaska, a land of opportunity, and asks about their mother, who lived with Willy until her death some time ago. Charley becomes upset by Willy's nonsensical talk and leaves.

As the scene returns again to the past, Ben has arrived at Willy's house. Willy has not seen his brothers for many years, and he has questions about their father who left when Willy was a toddler. Ben left the family at the age of seventeen to look for their father in Alaska. He went in the wrong direction and landed in Africa where he made his fortune.

At Willy's prompting, Ben tells Biff and Happy about their grandfather, a flute salesman and inventor. To prove a point to Ben, Willy sends his sons "hunting" to a nearby construction site to steal supplies for a rebuilding project. Charley comes over and warns Willy that his sons will be caught by the watchman and arrested for what they are doing. Ben insists on leaving, despite Willy's longings for approval.

The scene returns to present day. Linda enters the kitchen and tries to convince Willy to come to bed. He asks her about the diamond watch fob Ben gave him many years ago, but Linda reminds him that he pawned it over a decade ago to pay for a correspondence course for Biff.

When Willy goes outside to take a walk in his slippers, his sons come downstairs and express their concern about him to their mother. Linda asks Biff why he argues with his father when he returns home. Biff has no real answer, nor does he have one about his plans for the future. The situation grows tenser. Linda tells Biff she will not tolerate his disrespecting his father: "Either he's your father and you pay him that respect, or else you're not to come here." Biff informs her and Happy that Willy does not really respect her.

Linda grows more indignant about her sons' attitude toward their father. She tells them that he is great, but tired. Linda also informs them that after working for the same company for thirty-six years, they have taken him off salary and put him on commission only. Additionally, Charley has been giving Willy fifty dollars a week so it looks like he is earning money, but these funds do not cover the bills.

Biff offers to move home and help out, but Linda does not want to be around the fighting such a move would involve. Biff reminds her that Willy threw him out of the house, and tells her why he did so: "Because I know he's a fake and he doesn't like anybody around who knows!" While Biff still is willing to stay, Linda tells them that Willy has tried to kill himself several times. He has had a number of car accidents and nearly killed a woman. He also has tried to kill himself in the cellar with a rubber tubing device on the gas pipe that feeds the hot water heater.

Biff promises to stay in New York, get a job, and do well. Happy reminds Biff that he has taken off in the middle of the work day without covering himself in the past, something he cannot do if he is to succeed. Willy enters as Biff declares they should leave the city. Willy is again defensive about what he perceives is an insult by Biff, but becomes intrigued when Biff tells him that he is going to see Bill Oliver the next day to ask for the money to start a business.

Though Willy is initially dismissive of Biff's efforts because he does not believe that Biff has a serious plan, Happy believes they should start a family-owned sporting goods store. Willy and Biff become enthusiastic about the idea. Willy tries to give Biff advice on how he should handle the meeting with Oliver, but Biff grows angry when Willy yells at Linda for adding her own comments. Biff tells him not to speak that way to Linda.

Upstairs in Linda and Willy's bedroom, Linda wonders if Oliver will remember Biff. Willy is sure of it. Biff and Happy come into the room, to say goodnight. Willy continues to give unwanted advice, so Biff leaves. Willy gets into bed and remembers when Biff was a young, strong athlete. As his parents go to sleep, Biff removes the suicide device from the gas pipe.

Act II

Mid-morning the next day, Linda is serving Willy coffee. The boys have already left. Willy believes Biff will succeed at his meeting and imagines a future with a home out in the country. Linda tells Willy to ask for an advance of about two hundred dollars from his boss, Howard, to pay many bills that are due, including one for the

insurance premium before it lapses. Before he leaves to meet with Howard, Linda tells him to meet his sons for dinner at a restaurant. Willy is hopeful when he leaves home. After Willy leaves, Biff calls. Linda tells him that she is excited that the gas pipe device is gone; she is disappointed to learn that Biff removed it, not Willy.

In Howard's office, Willy tells his employer that he does not want to travel anymore. He desperately tries to convince Howard to give him a job and small salary in New York. Willy reminds Howard that he was close with his father and helped name him. Howard tells him that there are no jobs available in New York. Willy will not accept the answer and tells him how he got into the business in the first place. Willy eventually yells at Howard, who grows impatient. Howard tells Willy to calm down, then he leaves for a bit.

Howard returns a moment later when Willy gets upset after having accidentally turned on Howard's recording machine. Willy says he will continue working on the road, but Howard will not take him back. Howard tells Willy to bring in his samples, take a rest, and come back later.

Willy remains in Howard's office after Howard leaves again. Ben returns and the scene shifts to the past. Willy tells Ben that nothing in his life is working out. Ben offers him a job in Alaska taking care of a business interest he has there. While Willy is enthusiastic, young Linda does not share it. She tells Ben and Willy that Willy is succeeding in New York "well enough." Ben leaves.

Young Biff has already entered the scene. Willy bragged about Biff's future to Ben before he left. Biff is going to play a big football game at Ebbetts Field that day. Happy will carry Biff's helmet to get into the clubhouse; Biff allows Bernard to carry his shoulder guards so he can get in, too. Willy and Linda are getting ready to watch their son play, and Willy gets annoyed when Charley feigns ignorance about the day's big event.

Back in present day, Willy shows up at Charley's office. Bernard is there, and he keeps Willy busy while Charley and Jenny, his secretary, work. Willy brags about Biff's deal, then asks Bernard why Biff did not do well. Bernard tells him that Biff's failing math, then not going to summer school to make up the class, hurt him. Even Willy does not know why Biff refused to go to summer school that year.

Willy asks Bernard if it was his fault. Bernard remembers that Biff was ready to go to summer school when he left for a month and went to see Willy in New England. When Biff returned, he was not the same and gave up. Bernard asks if something happened in Boston, but Willy becomes defensive. Charley enters and Bernard prepares to leave. Charley brags to Willy that Bernard is going to argue a case before the Supreme Court in Washington. Willy is impressed and does not understand how Bernard could be this successful.

Charley hands Willy fifty dollars. Willy asks for enough to cover his insurance premium, and he promises to pay him back. Charley again offers him a job in New York at fifty dollars per week, but Willy is insulted. Willy tells Charley that he already has one, then that he was fired. Charley does not understand why Willy cares if everyone likes him or why Willy will not take a job with him. Willy will not tell him his reasoning, and Charley gives enough to cover the insurance payment. Willy calls Charley his "only friend," and leaves close to tears.

Happy arrives at the restaurant first, bragging to the waiter Stanley about his brother's seemingly imminent business deal. When Biff enters, Happy is flirting with a female patron, the Girl/Miss Forsythe, and lies to her about his and his brother's occupation. He asks her to find a friend and come back and join them.

After she leaves, Biff tells him what happened that day. Biff waited for six hours to see Oliver, without luck. When Oliver left his office at five o'clock and Biff caught his attention for a moment, he did not remember Biff. Biff tells Happy that he got angry, went into Oliver's office, and stole his fountain pen. Biff wants Happy's help telling their father the truth about what happened, but Happy wants him to lie and tell Willy only good news.

The boys have not settled their disagreement when Willy arrives. Willy asks Biff what happened. While Biff starts to lie and Happy builds on it, Willy grows excited and will not let Biff finish telling him what happened. Frustrated, Biff tells Happy, "I can't talk to him!"

The scene shifts between past and present. Young Bernard tells the family that Biff failed math. Willy is angry at young Biff for flunking. Interspersed is Biff's explanation of what happened at Oliver's office, including the theft of the pen. Willy is appalled and Biff tries to tell him

that he stole it unintentionally. Biff promises his father he will be successful and tells him that Oliver talked to a partner about his idea. Biff says that he cannot go to a lunch meeting with Oliver and his partner the next day because of the stolen pen; Biff later confesses that there is no such appointment. Willy grows angry at his son and hits him.

Another scene from the past is then interspersed with the restaurant scene. Willy is with The Woman, while Miss Forsythe and her friend, Letta, arrive and join the party. Willy is drawn to The Woman who is telling him to answer the door. After Willy drifts off to the past, Happy starts to make plans with Miss Forsythe and Letta for the evening, meaning to just abandon Willy at the restaurant. Biff is insulted, telling Hap, "I sense it, you don't give a . . . damn about him." The brothers argue, and Biff leaves. Hap leaves with Miss Forsythe and Letta, denying Willy is his father and claiming that Biff will catch up.

Shifting to the past again, Willy and The Woman are dressing and talking about their affair. There has been a knock at the door, which Willy is reluctant to answer. After sending her to wait in the bathroom, Willy finds Young Biff at the door. He tells his father that he failed math and cannot graduate. Young Biff wants him to talk to his teacher, and Willy is ready to go home immediately to take care of the situation.

Willy tries to get rid of Biff by sending him downstairs to check out, but The Woman comes out of the bathroom before Biff leaves. Willy then tries to hide what she is doing there; Biff does not accept his explanations. Biff tells his father to forget helping him with his grades, and that he will neither go to summer school nor the University of Virginia. Biff yells at him, "You fake! You phony little fake!", and leaves as his father orders him to come back.

In the present, Willy returns to the dining room in the restaurant with Stanley standing over him. The waiter tells Willy that his sons have left and left word that Willy should go home. Willy asks Stanley where a seed store is, saying, "I don't have a thing in the ground." He leaves in search of seeds for a garden.

The scene comes back to the Loman kitchen late at night. Hap and Biff have returned and find their mother waiting up for them. Happy has flowers for her, but she knocks them out of his hands when she hears that they left their father for two women. Angry with both Linda and Hap, Biff wants to see Willy. Linda wants both of her sons to leave and not return. She tells them, "You're a pair of animals! Not one, not another living soul would have had the cruelty to walk out on that man in a restaurant!"

Happy removes himself from the situation by going upstairs. Biff expresses his self-hatred by admitting they left him talking to himself in the bathroom. He still demands to talk to Willy even though Linda tries to prevent it. The mother and son go outside to watch Willy planting a garden.

As Willy plants his seeds, Ben walks in. Willy tells him Linda has suffered and offers Ben a deal related to his insurance policy. Willy is implying to his brother that he will kill himself so his family can have the $20,000 benefit. Ben believes the move will be seen as cowardly to his family, but Willy enthusiastically believes it will be the right thing to do and his funeral will be packed with those he has worked with as a salesman. Willy hopes his suicide will impress Biff, especially.

After Ben leaves, Biff tells his father that he is leaving again and not coming back. Biff makes Willy come inside and talk to Linda about his decision, which Linda supports. Biff wants his family to forget he exists, and he tries to get Willy to shake his hand so he can leave. Willy refuses and accuses Biff of acting out of spite. Biff finally confronts him with the suicide device from the gas pipe, which Willy denies knowing anything about.

The family confrontation grows more heated as Hap joins in. Biff calls his brother a liar, and he admits to spending time in jail. Biff also tells Willy, "I never got anywhere because you blew me so full of hot air I could never stand taking orders from anybody!" Biff opens up about his recent revelations, but Willy cannot accept Biff's pessimistic truth. Biff nearly attacks his father with the truth about their lives, which Willy also cannot stomach. Biff breaks down and cries, begging to be free of fake dreams.

After Biff goes upstairs, Willy realizes that his son loves him and believes $20,000 would help him with his goals. Ben appears again, encouraging Willy to take action. Willy sends Hap and Linda to bed. When Ben disappears, Willy does not know what to do. His family eventually hears the car driving away quickly. The act ends with the family, Charley, and

> " I AM NOT A LEADER OF MEN, WILLY, AND NEITHER ARE YOU. YOU WERE NEVER ANYTHING BUT A HARD-WORKING DRUMMER WHO LANDED IN THE ASH CAN LIKE ALL THE REST OF THEM!"

Bernard leaving the house and going to Willy's grave.

Requiem

At the grave, Linda says she does not understand why Willy killed himself. Happy is similarly confused. Charley and Biff have a better understanding of Willy and his motivations. Biff tells them, "He never knew who he was." Happy is ready to prove his father's death was not in vain, but Biff realizes his brother still does not understand. Left alone at his grave, Linda asks for her dead husband's forgiveness and tells him, "We're free. . . . We're free."

THEMES

Pursuit of the American Dream

The primary theme of Miller's *Death of a Salesman* is Willy's unfailing yet skewed belief in the American dream of success. Willy believes that being a profitable, money-making self-made man is key to living a successful life. He constantly harps on his sons, especially Biff, that they must be successes in business, even though Biff only values this goal to any degree because of his father. Willy and Hap believe they are successes in Willy's definition of the term, at least publicly. Willy brags to Linda about his prowess as a traveling salesman, but in reality he never makes as much money as he says he does. Similarly, Hap claims to be an assistant retail buyer, when in fact he is an assistant to the assistant buyer. Happy's success lies more in his sexual conquests than actual business dealings.

Willy secretly knows he has become a failure, but he hides it with his public bravado. At sixty-three, he has been taken off salary at the company for which he has worked for thirty-six years and put on straight commission. He cannot make money as a traveling salesman under this structure. Charley, his only friend and neighbor, gives him fifty dollars per week to cover his expenses and make it look to Linda like Willy is making money. She knows the truth about the funds as well as the fact that he has been thinking about killing himself. Willy will not let on to anyone about his failures, nor will he allow Charley to give him a job. Willy even scorns Charley for helping him. He needs the American dream to be true for his life to have validation, because the pursuit of wealth has been the major goal of his life.

Yet Willy's pursuit of success and the American dream is not exactly pure. He lies to everyone about his achievements, a habit that Hap enthusiastically embraces. In addition to inflating the amount of money he makes, Willy also repeatedly emphasizes how well liked he is around New England and how important he is; both statements are essentially untrue, at least at present time, and probably always have been.

Willy encourages his sons to share this false, self-inflated optimism. Biff's passing math is unimportant to his father, but Biff's popularity based on athletic skills is highly valued. Willy allows young Biff to get away with stealing a football from his school to practice, and he encourages both of his sons to appropriate building supplies from a nearby construction site when his brother Ben visits. As adults, the sons continue to act badly. Biff still cannot stop stealing. Hap wants to lie about Biff's meeting with Oliver to keep their father happy, while Biff wants to give up the false front. Biff does his best to be honest with his father no matter what the cost.

Though Biff does not believe it, he is living the American dream in one sense that his father cannot. He has left the fast life of the city and unsuccessful stints at business to live in the West and work on farms and ranches. While he is not paid much by his father's standards and still has problems holding a job, Biff also must engage in hard, honest labor in such environments. Returning home to the arguments makes him distressed, while working out west makes him more free to pursue his happiness.

Charley and his son Bernard are even greater examples of the American dream of success made good in *Death of a Salesman*. Their actions speak louder than words, and neither wealth nor popularity are their only pursuits in life. Charley tries to help Willy, while Bernard did all he could to get Biff to pass math, graduate from high school, and take one of his athletic scholarship offers. Willy believed that Biff would succeed in life while Bernard would fail solely because of his son's good looks and personality. As Willy learns when he is quite desperate to borrow money from Charley, Bernard has achieved the American dream: He is married with two sons, has a successful career as a lawyer, is about to argue a case in front of the U.S. Supreme Court, and has time for leisure pursuits. Bernard is everything Willy wishes he and his sons were.

Importance of Family

Throughout *Death of a Salesman*, Miller emphasizes the importance of family, especially father-child bonds, as a key relationship in the American dream. Charley seems to be a decent father who taught his son Bernard the proper values. Family ties are also at play in Willy's career, as he works for a family operation. He began his salesman career for Howard's father, and helped name Howard. While Howard has not treated Willy well, he emphasizes the importance of his family to Willy by sharing recordings of his children's voices.

The Loman family is dysfunctional to be sure, but not for lack of caring for each other. Willy wants his sons to be successes and, though his means of promoting this idea in their life is often misguided, there is never any doubt that he cares about them. This situation goes both ways. Hap and Biff idolized their father as boys. As adults, they are both concerned about their father's mental state. Biff is especially troubled by his father's suicidal thoughts and actions. They act as best they can to help him and their mother with this situation. Yet the sons make mistakes as well. Hap and Biff abandon their father at the restaurant after he wanders off in the haze of the past again; Hap even denies that Willy is his father to the two women he just met.

There is a significant fissure in the Loman family structure. Biff gave up on his academic and athletic dreams when he found out his father was having an affair with another woman on the road. Willy's failure as a husband made Biff question his father's other values. While it seems that Biff never told Hap or his mother what he saw, Biff does not like Willy's sometimes poor treatment of Linda. Biff's difficulties with his father stem from Willy's infidelity; Linda does not always understand why Biff is standing up to Willy when her husband treats her poorly. Despite such problems, every member of the Loman family wants to do right by its other members. Willy even assumes killing himself is doing right by his family, in a misguided notion that money is worth more than honest relationships.

Materialism

Another, darker aspect of the American dream explored in *Death of a Salesman* is the concept of materialism. Willy, Linda, and Hap, more so than Biff, want to own the best of everything associated with the good life, no matter what the cost economically or personally. One reason for Willy's distress is the amount of payments he owes on consumer items such as refrigerators, cars, washing machines, vacuums, and the like, as well as upkeep on said items. He also has a mortgage that is nearly paid off as well as a life insurance policy about to lapse for nonpayment. The Lomans have lived beyond Willy's salary for some time, embracing materialism as a physical embodiment of Willy's economic success.

Because Willy is not the success he tells everyone he is, this situation leads to increasing problems for him and his family. If they had budgeted their money and not bought items on the market because of advertising—Linda explains why they bought their refrigerator because "They got the biggest ads of any of them!"—the family's financial situation might be different when Willy loses his job. As it stands, he sees the only way to help his family is to kill himself. That way, they will get the $20,000 from their insurance policy, pay off debts, and perhaps start a business. Even Linda recognizes that "We're free" at the play's end. However, this freedom has come at a price. A few lines earlier, she tells Willy's grave that "I made the last payment on the house today. Today, dear. And there'll be nobody home."

HISTORICAL OVERVIEW

Post–World War II Prosperity

After World II ended in the mid-1940s, the United States' economy greatly improved and Americans experienced prosperity as they never

had before. Years after the Great Depression, the war led to increased industrial production in support of the war effort. Because workers could not spend much of their earnings during the war years as only limited commercial consumer items were being produced, Americans had about $140 billion in savings by 1945. Businesses responded by converting war-time industry to producing products many Americans wanted. Businesses also invested significant amounts of money into new materials and equipment, about $300 billion, and created new technologies. For the first time in decades, many Americans had money to spend and an excess of products and services from which to choose.

Not all Americans saw these economic benefits. Poor Americans suffered because of high inflation that did not allow them to save money. In 1946 alone, the inflation rate was 18.2 percent. Because of government policy support of big corporate farms, smaller farmers often lost out in the post–World War II economic boom. Migrant farm workers regularly received the lowest pay of any American job category. Unskilled laborers and clerks were not much better off. Strikes and labor unrest was common in this time period in many major industries.

Post–World War II Uncertainty

For the victors in World War II, the post-war period saw a tension-filled conflict arise between two major former allies: the United States and the Soviet Union. While Europe was recovering from the economic, physical, and psychological devastation of the war, the United States took on a greater international leadership role. Though the Soviet Union was similarly weakened by the war, Joseph Stalin, the country's dictator, ensured that the country's military remained strong.

Within a few years after World War II's end, the United States and the Soviet Union became locked in an international battle for dominance. The two emerged as dueling superpowers, with each country working for sway over other smaller countries. The resulting stand-off was not only political but ideological as well, as the United States promoted democracy while the Soviet Union pushed its version of Communism.

The "battles" of the Cold War began as soon as World War II ended. By the end of the war, the Soviet Union occupied a number of countries in

Eastern Europe, such as Poland, Romania, East Germany, and Bulgaria. The Soviets took control of most of these countries while driving back the Germans. Instead of ceding control of such countries to their people at war's end, the Soviet military remained in control and Soviet-run Communist governments were put in place. These countries were behind the so-called "Iron Curtain" and formed the Soviet bloc.

By 1947, the Soviet Union was attempting to do the same thing to Greece and Turkey. U.S. President Harry S. Truman responded with the Truman Doctrine, which stated American would act to contain the Soviets and prevent them from taking control of any more countries. The United States government showed it would follow the doctrine by giving $400 million in economic aid to Greece and Turkey. The United States also organized the Berlin airlifts of 1948 and 1949. These airlifts ensured the western-controlled portion of the German city would remain free from Communist influence.

The Cold War continued to escalate in the 1950s and eventually became an arms race as well. Both the United States and the Soviet Union soon had nuclear bombs; there was a looming threat that one or both countries would use them. The uncertainties created by the Cold War left many Americans feeling anxious about their future as well as the future of the world. Such feelings continued until the Cold War ended in 1991.

Consumerism

As businesses grew in the post–World War II period, corporations gained power in shaping American society and how Americans who had money spent it. Mass culture was also pushed by radio programs, movies, and, in a few short years, television by advertising for products made by such corporations. Goods highlighted in such advertising and programs also became more widely available to Americans. Everything from cars to electrical appliances to potato chips could be purchased nearly everywhere in the United States because of an improved national distribution network.

Though wages also were on the increase in this time period, many American consumers, especially the growing middle class, were tempted to spend more than they made. New forms of consumer credit became easily available and popular. There was short-term consumer

credit such as loans for automobiles. This practice became common in post–World War II America; until this point, most cars were cash purchases. In 1946, Americans owed about $8.5 billion in short-term credit; by 1958, that figure increased dramatically, to $45 billion.

Many of Willy Loman's financial problems came from problems with owing too much on short-term credit. Many of the Lomans' household items and services were purchased on credit, and keeping up with payments proved difficult for Willy. Many Americans found their identity in the amount of consumer products they owned, used, and consumed.

Long-term consumer credit, such as home mortgages, also saw a major increase in the late 1940s and 1950s. Many Americans bought homes in the post-war housing boom. In 1946, Americans owed about $23 billion in long-term credit; by 1958, that figure increased to nearly $120 billion. Willy also has a home mortgage, but unlike his short-term credit problems, his home is nearly paid off.

CRITICAL OVERVIEW

Death of a Salesman was lauded by critics and audiences from its first production in 1949. It is said that businessmen wept during the original Broadway run. Robert Garland of the *New York Journal American* writes of the play's opening night:

> Here's my true report that yesterday at the Morosco, the first-night congregation made no effort to leave the theatre at the final curtain-fall of Arthur Miller's *Death of a Salesman*. It's meant to make known to you the prevailing emotional impact of the new play.

William Hawkins of the *New York World-Telegram* compares it to "the finest classical tragedy." Writing in the *New York Post*, Richard Watts Jr. concludes, "*Death of a Salesman* emerges as easily the best and most important new American play of the year."

Other critics of the original production found the ideas Miller explored to be universal. In the *New York Times*, Brooks Atkinson declares:

> It is so simple in style and so inevitable in theme that it scarcely seems like a thing that has been written and acted. For Mr. Miller has looked with compassion into the hearts of some

MEDIA ADAPTATIONS

A film version of *Death of a Salesman* in 1985, featuring the same cast as the Broadway revival of 1984. Dustin Hoffman stars as Willy Loman, John Malkovich plays Biff Loman, and Kate Reid appears as Linda. It is available on DVD from Image Entertainment.

ordinary Americans and quietly transferred their hope and anguish to the theatre.

Miller, *Death of a Salesman*, and its characters continued to garner such critical kudos long after its premiere, as the play turned into an international phenomenon. By the 1984 Broadway revival, Willy Loman (played by Dustin Hoffman), is called "a classic American part in one of the sentimental icons of our theater" by Lloyd Rose in *The Atlantic*.

On the fiftieth anniversary of the first production of *Death of a Salesman* in 1999, the play's power was still evident, even by critics who took issue with some aspects of the drama. Writing in *Time*, Richard Zoglin asks, "Why does this depressing, sometimes overwritten, painfully familiar play still move us in almost every incarnation? . . . The chief reason, of course, is Willy Loman, that all-American victim of his own skewed recipe for success." Zoglin ends his conflicted piece by noting,

> That it continues to fascinate us is testimony to Miller's ability to pack so much—heartbreaking family drama, an Ibsenian tragedy of illusions shattered, an indictment of American capitalism—into one beaten-down figure with a sample case. After 50 years it still makes the sale.

Other critics believe the play's universality has only increased over time. David Klinghoffer of *National Review* claims, "Now that women routinely labor outside their homes, we are all Willy Loman." The critic also concludes, "A man's descent to failure too horrendous to contemplate. Whatever line of work you are in, we are all salesmen, selling our products, our services, our selves."

CRITICISM

Granger Babcock

In the following excerpt, Babcock examines how Willy's failure is a product of the fallacies of his masculine, individualistic, American success fantasy.

Most critics recognize that Arthur Miller intends Willy Loman as a victim of "society." But Willy's construction as a victim is interpreted within the parameters of a self-generated individual and is used as the main reason conservative critics deny *Salesman* tragic status. As a victim, the argument runs, Willy has no understanding of his situation; he is, in the words of Dan Vogel, "too commonplace and limited." Unlike Oedipus, Hamlet, or Lear, Willy is incapable of self-knowledge and is, therefore, not tragic but pathetic: "he cannot summon the intelligence and strength to scrutinize his situation and come to some understanding of it." Even liberal critics like Thomas Adler and Ruby Cohn, who are generally sympathetic towards Willy, tend to judge his character harshly; in their estimation, he is either a "victim of himself and his choices," or he "has achieved neither popularity nor success as a salesman, and has failed as a gardener, carpenter, and father." Willy's problem (or part of his problem), then, according to these critics, is that he accepts his fate; he does not possess the vision, volition, capacity, strength, knowledge, or pluck to fight against the cultural forces that shape his life.

The underlying assumption of these arguments is that Willy *can* change his life—with a little hard work, perhaps—but that he *will* not. Behind these judgments is a model: the national subject, or what I will call the masculine unconscious. This model can also be described as the autonomous, active male subject that determines and makes itself, as well as the liberal subject, the rugged individual, or the exceptional American. Whatever linguistic sign the masculine unconscious uses to communicate itself, it is wholly other to the subject, and it is given to the subject by the publicity apparatus of capital. Miller calls this other the "law of success":

> The confusion of some critics viewing *Death of a Salesman* . . . is that they do not see that Willy Loman has broken a law without whose protection life is insupportable, if not incomprehensible to him and to many others; it is a law which says a failure in society and in business has no right to live. Unlike the law against incest, the law of success is not administered

Scene from Death of Salesman *with Lee J Cobb* Columbia/The Kobal Collection

by statute or church, but it is very nearly as powerful in its grip upon men.

As C. W. E. Bigsby notes, "Willy Loman's life is rooted in America's past." More precisely, his identity is rooted in models from two different periods of American capital, which are conflated in his mind. Willy's father represents the unfettered and unalienated labor of mercantile capital. His brother Ben represents the accumulative processes of monopoly capital. Both figures are mythic; that is, both figures embody an heroic past that is disseminated by the symbolic practices of capital and reproduced in individual men. Together, Miller suggests, they represent the (his)tory (not an history) of the (white) race in America. Or, as Irving Jacobson suggests,

> What Willy Loman wants, and what success means in *Death of a Salesman*, is intimately related to his own, and the playwright's, sense of the family. Family dreams extend backward in time to interpret the past, reach forward in time to project images of the future, and

pressure reality in the present to conform to memory [ideology] and imagination.

Willy desires to be like his father because his father is like other successful men, other "great" inventors; his father is a model citizen—he has amassed a fortune. His father is like America's first model citizen, Ben Franklin, who "invented" electricity and the lightning rod. His father is like Thomas A. Edison and B. F. Goodrich, both rich and famous because of their inventions. Nevertheless, given the mercantile economy in which Miller locates Willy's father, it is unlikely that he could have produced a "gadget" that earned him more in a week than Willy earns in his lifetime. This type of event was more common (but still relatively isolated) in the period of capital Ben represents (monopoly capital) when "great" inventors like Edison and Goodrich did earn more money in a week (by producing technology for an emergent industrial economy) than a salesman could earn in thirty-five years. The figure of Willy's father exists simultaneously in

Willy's "mind" with the figures of Edison and Goodrich. The simultaneity of the Franklin-Edison-Goodrich-father Loman narrative produces a fusion of the individual stories, which erases the specific history of the individual figures by marginalizing their differences; this fusion, again, is produced by the publicity apparatus of capital. Through the other, that is, Willy plugs himself into the success narrative as he rereads his family history.

Historically, as C. Wright Mills notes, "for men in the era of classical liberalism, competition was never merely an impersonal mechanism regulating the economy of capitalism, or only a guarantee of political freedom. Competition was a means of producing free individuals, a testing field for heroes; in its terms men lived the legend of the self-reliant individual." Whether or not what Mills argues is historically representative, it is safe to assume that in a decentralized economy (an economy without the hierarchy of industrialized structures), individual competition through labor was a way for many to create mobility and wealth. However, as the economy became more centralized and hierarchical, competition, as Willy says, became "maddening" because it did not yield the same results (imagined or otherwise) as it did for men of Willy's father's and Ben's generations.

In Willy's time, in fact, competition has become warlike. After returning from a selling trip, for instance, Willy tells his family he "Knocked 'em cold in Providence, slaughtered 'em in Boston." Willy's gift to his sons on his return from this same trip is a punching bag with "Gene Tunney's signature on it." "[I]t's the finest thing for the timing," he tells his apprentices. Elsewhere, Willy describes business as "murderous." When Biff goes to ask Bill Oliver for a loan, Willy's advice is "Knock him dead, boy." The violence of Willy's language echoes the ruthlessness of his model, Ben—the same man who attacks Biff: "Never fight fair with a stranger, boy. You'll never get out of the jungle that way." Willy's desire to emulate Ben's power thus leads him to bring "the spirit of the jungle" into his home, where it reveals itself as what Sartre calls "counter-finality." His positive intention of providing his boys with a model for success results in the negative legitimation of theft and fantasy.

Miller problematizes Willy's pedagogy by suggesting that even sanctioned expressions of masculinity involve theft. In the scene which follows Ben's fight with Biff, for example, Willy has his sons start to rebuild the front steps because Willy doesn't want Ben to think he is just a salesman; he wants to show Ben that Brooklyn is not Brooklyn ("we hunt too"); he wants to show Ben what kind of stock his sons come from: "Why, Biff can fell any one of these trees in no time!" Instead of providing the materials to rebuild the front stoop, however, Willy directs his sons to "Go right over where they're building the apartment house and get some sand." Charley warns Willy that "if they steal any more from that building the watchman'll put the cops on them." Willy responds, addressing Ben, "You shoulda seen the lumber they brought home last week. At least a dozen six-by-tens worth all kinds of money." This, of course, is a parody of Ben's logging operations in Alaska, but it also suggests that the individualism that the success ideology sanctions legitimates theft, just as that ideology legitimates the expropriation of foreign land and mineral resources. This is made even clearer in the following lines, when Willy excuses his sons' behavior because, as he says, "I got a couple of fearless characters there." Charley counters: "Willy, the jails are full of fearless characters," and Ben responds, "And the stock exchange, friend!" Again, these lines suggest that Miller recognizes that even legitimized expressions of masculine behavior, practices and beliefs that the American publicity apparatus valorizes, involve theft.

A further example of Miller transforming the success ideology into theft is found in the scene where Biff "borrows" a football from his high school locker room so that he can practice with a "regulation ball." Willy, predictably, laughs with Biff at the theft and rewards the action by saying, "Coach'll probably congratulate you on your initiative!" Initiative, even in Franklin's day, is one of the key elements of masculine autonomy, and here Miller insists that initiative is a form of theft. Later in the same scene, Biff tells his father, "This Saturday, Pop, this Saturday—just for you, I'm going to break through for a touchdown." Happy then reminds Biff that he is "supposed to pass." Biff ignores Happy's warning and says, "I'm *taking* one play for Pop (italics mine). This taking is a pattern that will eventually take over Biff's life, for as Biff tells Willy at the end of the play, "I stole a suit in Kansas City and I was in jail... I stole myself out of every good job since high school!" More important for Miller, however, is that this one moment of taking represents a typical moment in the dominant version of American masculinity. Biff's "theft" of the play is another instance of his initiative, another example drawn from the headlines which celebrate individual achievement. For a moment in Willy's mind, Biff is like Red Grange or Gene Tunney. As he tells Charley, "When this game is over . . . you'll be laughing out the other side of your face. They'll be calling him another Red Grange. Twenty-five thousand a year." What is lost in Biff's taking, however, is the team. Biff's initiative, and his desire to place himself above the goal of the team, jeopardizes the collective goal of the team—to win the City Championship.

The final confrontation occurs two scenes later when Biff tells Willy "you're going to hear the truth—what you are and what I am." Biff rejects Willy's "phony dream" because

> I ran down eleven flights with a pen in my hand today. And suddenly I stopped . . . I saw the things that I love in this world. The work and the food and time to sit and smoke. And I looked at the pen and said to myself, what the hell am I grabbing this for? Why am I trying to become what I don't want to be? What am I doing in an office, making a contemptuous, begging fool of myself, when all I want is out there, waiting for me the minute I say I know who I am!

This is an assertion of Biff's desire against Willy's desire and the fantasy that Willy's desire constructs. Because Biff recognizes that his father's dream is false, that his father has been positioned by the law of success to believe in the autonomous male, he is in a position to resist (at least partially) the ideology. Biff does not believe in the version of universal citizenship that Willy believes in. Biff recognizes that he is "a dime a dozen," that he will never be B. F. Goodrich or Thomas Edison or Red Grange or J. P. Morgan or Gene Tunney. He attempts to resist the ideology of the success narrative because he doesn't want to be other; he doesn't want to be number one: "I am not a leader of men, Willy, and neither are you. . . . I'm a dollar an hour, Willy. . . . A buck an hour." Willy, a believer to the bitter end, insists that he is exceptional: "I am Willy Loman, and you are Biff Loman." At this point there is a complete repudiation of the success fantasy: Biff screams, "Pop, I'm nothing! I'm nothing, Pop," and he begins to hug his father and cry.

Source: Granger Babcock, "'What's the Secret?' Willy Loman as Desiring Machine," in *American Drama*, Vol. 2, No. 1, Fall 1992, pp. 59–83.

SOURCES

"Arthur Miller dies; Pulitzer for *Salesman*," in the *Hollywood Reporter*, Vol. 387, No. 45, February 14, 2005, p. 4.

Atkinson, Brooks, "*Death of a Salesman*, a New Drama by Arthur Miller, Has Premiered at the Morosco," in the *New York Times*, February 11, 1949.

Garland, Robert, "Audience Spellbound by Prize Play of 1949," in the *New York Journal American*, February 11, 1949.

Hawkins, William, "*Death of a Salesman* Powerful Tragedy," in the *New York World-Telegram*, February 11, 1949.

Klinghoffer, David, "Undying Salesman," in the *National Review*, Vol. 51, No. 4, March 8, 1999, p. 54.

Kroll, Jack, "Rebirth of a Salesman," in *Newsweek*, Vol. 133, No. 8, February 22, 1999, p. 51.

Miller, Arthur, *Death of a Salesman: Text and Criticism*, edited by Gerald Weales, Bantam Books, 1951; reprint, Penguin Books, 1996.

Rose, Lloyd, Review of *Death of a Salesman*, in *The Atlantic*, No. 253, April 1984, p. 130.

Watts, Richard, Jr., "*Death of Salesman* A Powerful Drama," in the *New York Post*, February 11, 1949.

Zoglin, Richard, "American Tragedy," in *Time*, Vol. 153, No. 6, February 19, 1999, p. 77.

The Declaration of Independence

THOMAS JEFFERSON

1776

Perhaps the greatest of the great documents of American culture is the Declaration of Independence, which was adopted on July 4, 1776. It is a comparatively brief essay because it was intended to summarize the grievances of the American colonists against the British Crown, thus providing justification for the American separation from England. Foremost among the Declaration's associations with the American dream is its firm statement about the "inalienable rights" of all people, including "life, liberty, and the pursuit of happiness." Over time this phrase has become a simple summary of what this country stands for and a statement of the basic principles of American democracy. It is these words, more than any others, that have drawn immigrants from all over the globe and served to instill in all citizens the fundamental concept of what the United States stands for. It is in the pursuit of these principles that Americans have fought and died in wars, organized and advocated for civil rights, and pursued political office.

To fully appreciate the Declaration of Independence, it is necessary to understand the background of its composition. England established colonies in North America in the early seventeenth century; for more than 150 years, the inhabitants of these colonies, for the most part, were quite content to remain tethered to the "Mother Country." They considered themselves Englishmen and entitled to the same rights as

their brethren thousands of miles across the Atlantic Ocean, an idea shared by the vast majority of British inhabitants. However, the colonists gradually developed an interest in self-sufficiency; they wanted to control their own economic and political affairs, which for the most part were firmly dominated by the government in England.

Nevertheless, there was no widespread, organized agitation for independence until after the French and Indian War, the American name for what Europeans termed the Seven Years' War. Much of the fighting took place in North America, and American militia supplemented the British army and its Indian allies against the French, who also fought alongside certain native tribes. The war ended in 1763 and resulted in the almost complete removal of French authority in North America; from that point on, the British were unquestionably the dominant Europeans on the continent. However, the British government decided that the colonies were not paying their share of the war's cost, and various taxation plans were introduced to rectify the situation. The colonists were enraged, particularly as they had no direct representation in the British Parliament. Eventually the political arguments turned violent, and by 1775 the American colonies were in open revolt against the Crown.

In spite of the fighting that had broken out, many colonists still held out hope for a peaceful resolution to the conflict. By the summer of 1776, however, leaders of the Patriot movement were convinced only independence from Great Britain would be satisfactory. The Continental Congress realized that a formal declaration of independence stating the reasons for severing ties with England was necessary. While a number of Patriot leaders collaborated in drafting the ideas of the Declaration, it fell to Virginia representative Thomas Jefferson, a gifted author, to compose the final draft so familiar to Americans today.

It is not surprising that Americans who remained loyal to the Crown did not embrace the Declaration of Independence, and a careful analysis of the document reveals certain argumentative weaknesses. For example, while Jefferson enumerates the causes of the need for the declaration, he does not provide specific instances of Royal interference with colonial rights. There is no effort to name which British soldiers are accused of harming colonists, nor

are the accusations of the revocation of colonial charters—legal recognition of their existence—supported by any evidence or proof. This lack of evidence is a curious omission in a document prepared by a lawyer. Of course, Jefferson did not intend for his declaration to be a formal legal document; he intended for it to serve as a brief explanation of the reasons the colonies intended to leave the British Empire. Excessive legal jargon or detailed evidence, therefore, would have made the document much longer and less likely to make an impression on the average reader.

More troubling, perhaps, to modern readers is the fact that many of the rights defined in the declaration have not always been fully protected by the federal government. The phrase "all men are created equal" is somewhat sexist; the word "people" would be more inclusive of women. Yet women could not vote, seek political office, or hold most jobs in the eighteenth century—an imbalance of equality not corrected until well into the twentieth century. The Declaration appeared at a time when many Americans, including the document's author, owned slaves. Even when African Americans were free, their rights were generally ignored. For that matter, only men who owned property were allowed to vote or run for office in most parts of the infant nation, pointing to either the literalness or hypocrisy of Jefferson's famous phrase.

The phrase "Life, Liberty, and the pursuit of Happiness" has also been restricted in many ways over the years. For example, if all people are guaranteed "Life," why does this country still allow capital punishment? If everybody is at liberty and free to do whatever he or she sees fit, why were interracial marriages illegal in some states until the 1960s? Why is same-sex marriage illegal in most states today? The answer, of course, is that notions of individual liberty were very different in 1776 compared to modern times. Yet it is important to remember that these principles of liberty have gradually expanded in the wake of the Declaration and the publication of the nation's other "Great Documents." Whenever a group of Americans finally achieves its rights—or whenever a new concept is assumed to be a "right" of every American—freedom and democracy are promoted and expanded. Although it can be a long and painful process, the expansion of freedom in democracy within our nation continues as we

BIOGRAPHY

THOMAS JEFFERSON

Thomas Jefferson was born on April 13, 1743, in Virginia. Upon his father's death in 1757, young Thomas inherited five thousand acres of land; eventually he built his famous house, Monticello, on a portion of this land. Jefferson was an incredibly brilliant and dedicated scholar, eventually mastering such areas as architecture, horticulture, archeology, and several foreign languages. In addition to his accomplishments as an author, Jefferson was an inventor; later in life, he founded the University of Virginia, the first college in the United States not formally associated with a specific religious denomination.

Trained as a lawyer, Jefferson held a number of political offices; he served in the Virginia Colonial legislature and as governor of his native state during the latter stages of the American Revolution. After independence was achieved, Jefferson served as secretary of state under George Washington and vice president under John Adams before being elected the third president of the United States in 1800. As president, Jefferson oversaw the Louisiana Purchase of 1804, which greatly increased the size of the United States, and launched the Lewis and Clark expedition, which explored the newly acquired territory and paved the way for its eventual settlement. "The Sage of Monticello," as he has been called, remained interested in public affairs during his retirement. He died on July 4, 1826, the fiftieth anniversary of the adoption of his most important achievement.

Jefferson is buried at Monticello beside his wife; he designed his own gravestone, an obelisk upon which he insisted only three of his many accomplishments be listed: his authorship of the Declaration and the statute of Virginia for religious freedom, plus his title as "Father of the University of Virginia." As quoted by Noble E. Cunningham Jr., Jefferson chose these endeavors "because by these, as testimonials that I have lived, I wish most to be remembered." Interestingly, John Adams, also a signer of the Declaration and a former president, and a friend of Jefferson's despite their political differences, died the very same day.

---

attempt to perfect the ideals of Thomas Jefferson's Declaration of Independence.

PLOT SUMMARY

The Declaration of Independence is a comparatively brief work, consisting of only thirty-two paragraphs, most of which consist of a single, long sentence. As Lee A. Jacobus observes in his analysis of Jefferson's rhetoric in *A World of Ideas*, Jefferson incorporates causal analysis, "a method associated with legal thought" that indicates Jefferson's legal background. Put simply, the Declaration consists primarily of a list of causes that have encouraged the colonies to sever official ties with Great Britain. Jefferson also makes excellent use of parallelism, the construction of sentences so that they are relatively equal in length and structure. One interesting aspect of Jefferson's emphasis on parallelism is the use of "He" and "For" as the first words of paragraphs 3 through 29. This device is called anaphora, which Jacobus defines as "the technique of repetition of the same words at the beginning of successive lines." Ultimately it is Jefferson's mastery of structure and organization that emphasizes the power of his stirring assertions of colonial rights and explanations for declaring independence.

The Declaration of Independence begins with its famous and oft-quoted introduction:

> When in the Course of human events, it becomes necessary for one people to dissolve the political bands which have connected them with another, and to assume among the powers of the earth, the separate and equal station to which the Laws of Nature and of Nature's God entitle them, a decent respect to the opinions of mankind requires that they should declare the causes which impel them to the separation.

The signing of The Declaration of Independence, by John Trumbull Public Domain

This introduction essentially states that it is necessary when a group of people decide to declare themselves independent "a decent respect to the opinions of mankind" requires them to explain why. The document then outlines the philosophy of government that will become the basis for the American system: "We hold these truths to be self-evident, that all men are created equal, that they are endowed by their Creator with certain unalienable Rights, that among these are Life, Liberty and the pursuit of Happiness." It claims that governments are formed by men "to secure these rights," and thus derive "their just powers from the consent of the governed." People therefore have the right to amend or abolish altogether any government that does not protect their fundamental rights.

The Declaration acknowledges that such radical changes should not come about if the complaints about the government are "light and transient. . . . But when a long train of abuses and usurpations, pursuing invariably the same Object evinces a design to reduce them under absolute Despotism, it is their right, it is their duty, to throw off such Government, and to

provide new Guards for their future security." It claims that the history of the current king (George III, who is never mentioned by name in the Declaration) "is a history of repeated injuries and usurpations" against the rights of the American states. After introducing the evidence with this phrase—"To prove this, let Facts be submitted to a candid world"—the document sets forth a list of the king's offenses.

All of the eighteen charges that follow start with the word "He," indicating that the king, personally, has committed these crimes against the colonies. The first three are that He "refused to Assent," "has forbidden his Governors to pass," and has "refused to pass" laws needed for the public good in the colonies. The Declaration next mentions that the king has interfered with the rightful legislative processes in the colonies by calling legislative sessions "at places unusual, uncomfortable, and distant," "dissolv[ing] Representative Houses," and refusing "for a long time, after such dissolutions, to cause others to be elected," which exposed the colonies "to all the dangers of invasion from without, and convulsions within."

The seventh charge is that the king has also limited immigration to the colonies, thereby keeping their populations from growing. The eighth and ninth charges deal with his interference with judicial processes in the colonies, namely that the king has refused to establish a local judiciary and that he appoints all judges and sets their salaries, which assures their loyalty to the Crown at the expense of the colonists' rights.

Next, the accusations turn to the presence of British army troops in the colonies:

> He has erected a multitude of New Offices, and sent hither swarms of Officers to harrass our people, and eat out their substance.

> He has kept among us, in times of peace, Standing Armies without the Consent of our legislatures.

> He has affected to render the Military independent of and superior to the Civil power.

The thirteenth charge is the longest, including nine sub-charges regarding his "Assent to . . . Acts of pretend Legislation." Following these charges, the document enumerates certain instances in which the king has supported Parliamentary legislation that has infringed upon the rights of the colonists. The Declaration points out that "large bodies of armed troops" have been quartered in the homes of private citizens without their consent, and that troops who commit crimes against the colonists have been protected from punishment for their misdeeds. The king has also supported Parliament in restricting colonial trade with other countries, imposing taxes on the colonies "without our consent," and suspending the "benefit of Trial by Jury." The Declaration notes that citizens have been transported to England to face trial and that colonial charters have been revoked, which undermines "the Forms of our Governments."

In the last five of the enumerated charges, the Declaration points out that the king is in the process of waging war on the colonies and "has plundered our seas, ravaged our Coasts, burnt our towns, and destroyed the lives of our people." As part of his campaign against the colonies, the king has hired "foreign mercenaries"— primarily German troops—to assist in the subjugation of the rebels, forced Americans to take up arms against their neighbors, and encouraged his Indian allies to wage war on the less populous settlements on the frontier.

Having completed his list of royal offenses, Jefferson insists that the colonists have consistently

> WE HOLD THESE TRUTHS TO BE SELF-EVIDENT, THAT ALL MEN ARE CREATED EQUAL, THAT THEY ARE ENDOWED BY THEIR CREATOR WITH CERTAIN INALIENABLE RIGHTS, THAT AMONG THESE ARE LIFE, LIBERTY, AND THE PURSUIT OF HAPPINESS. THAT TO SECURE THESE RIGHTS, GOVERNMENTS ARE INSTITUTED AMONG MEN, DERIVED THEIR JUST POWERS FROM THE CONSENT OF THE GOVERNED."

"Petitioned for Redress in the most humble terms," to no avail. This lack of consideration indicates that the king "is unfit to be the ruler of a free People." Furthermore, the Declaration claims, the colonists have appealed directly to the English people, counting on their sense of "native justice and magnanimity" to provide relief. However, these "British brethren . . . have been deaf to the voice of justice and of consanguinity," which further indicates the necessity for separation. The Declaration adds that the English will be considered with the rest of the world as "Enemies in War" and "in Peace Friends." The Declaration concludes with a lofty announcement "That these United Colonies are, and of Right ought to be Free and Independent States." Because the formal links to England have been severed, the States now claim the right "to levy War, conclude Peace, contract Alliances, establish Commerce," and otherwise function as an independent nation. Finally, the document announces that the signers of the Declaration "mutually pledge to each other our Lives, our Fortunes, and our sacred Honor" in defense of freedom and independence.

THEMES

Fundamentals of American Government

Perhaps the most important element of the Declaration of Independence is its clear statements of the fundamental principles of the American idea of democracy and freedom. By condemning the excesses of the British king and his Parliament, Thomas Jefferson draws attention to the natural rights of all people. The phrase "all men are created equal" is a statement that implies all people have the same rights, with no person having greater freedom or power simply by virtue of social rank, such as an aristocratic background. Because of the God-given right to "Life, Liberty, and the pursuit of Happiness," all people are entitled to live without interference from the government and are free to strive for whatever it is that will make them content. Jefferson reiterates the principle that people should control the government, not vice versa; they should choose their own leaders and elect their own representatives.

Among the specific trespasses against the colonists' "self-evident" rights, the Declaration charges that the king refused to "Assent to Laws for establishing Judiciary powers," "made Judges dependent on his Will alone," and "sent hither swarms of Officers to harrass our people, and eat out their substance." Furthermore, "He has kept among us, in times of peace, Standing Armies without the Consent of our legislatures," and "He has affected to render the Military independent of and superior to the Civil power." Among the "pretended Legislation" the king is accused of assenting to are " imposing Taxes on us without our Consent," and "depriving us in many cases, of the benefits of Trial by Jury." Protections from precisely these infringements are set forth in the U.S. Constitution and Bill of Rights, which, together with this document, form the very foundation of the United States government.

Together, the Declaration of Independence, the Constitution, and the Bill of Rights are the American "Charters of Freedom," which define American social and political culture. From these works, our very concept of American government is derived. All three Charters were drafted by leading Patriots, but none of them were aristocrats or members of royalty; furthermore, ratification by the states was required before the Constitution and Bill of Rights became law. Thus the circumstances of the Charters' creation symbolize the rise of democracy and representative government, because the consent of private citizens was necessary for ratification. The documents are also revered icons, significant not just for the ideas they contain but also for the very fact that these ancient papers continue to physically exist after more than two

hundred years. Since 1952, the Charters of Freedom have been displayed in a specially designed rotunda in the National Archives, located in Washington, D.C.

Founding Fathers: The First Patriots

One of the most interesting contributions to American culture associated with the Declaration of Independence is the idea of the "Founding Fathers," the group of men who signed the Declaration and who have become symbols of American patriotism. Several other figures from the Revolutionary period are considered Founding Fathers but did not sign the Declaration, including George Washington and Alexander Hamilton. The Founding Fathers continue to inspire patriotism and public service among Americans. These men are considered the personification of the American dream: They were bold, they gambled big and won, and they inspired Americans to follow in their footsteps for the dozen or more generations since they lived.

Fifty-six Patriots signed the Declaration, including future presidents Thomas Jefferson and John Adams. Elbridge Gerry, who would become vice president under James Madison, and from whose name we get the word "gerrymander," which refers to redrawing Congressional districts for political purposes, also signed the document. Benjamin Harrison of Virginia fathered William Henry Harrison, who was eventually elected president but died after only a month in office; his great-grandson, also named Benjamin Harrison, was elected president in 1888.

Many of the other signers would serve as legislators, governors, and other elected officials of their respective states. Among the most notable signers is John Hancock, a Revolutionary leader from Massachusetts, who was the first to sign the Declaration and the only one to do so on July 4, 1776. Hancock served as president of the First Continental Congress and was later governor of Massachusetts. Another famous signer was Benjamin Franklin, the Philadelphian scientist, inventor, and author whose face now graces the $100 bill. Franklin is considered one of the most important of the signers because he influenced so many of the others—and members of the public—to support the Revolution. Franklin also helped secure French recognition of the rebellious colonies, a decision that ultimately brought France into the war as an American ally. Samuel Adams, cousin of John Adams, was one of Massachusetts's most active supporters of the independence movement and organized several protests against British authority, including the so-called "Boston Tea Party" of December 16, 1773. Richard Henry Lee of Virginia composed the resolution of independence contained in the Declaration's last paragraph, which Jefferson subsequently included in the final draft. Caesar Rodney of Delaware rode all night on July 1, 1776, to cast his tie-breaking vote in favor of the Declaration of Independence. Benjamin Rush of Pennsylvania was a physician who later became an outspoken humanitarian and advocate for the abolition of slavery. Charles Carroll of Maryland was the only Catholic among the Founding Fathers; upon his death in 1832 at the age of ninety-five, he was the last surviving signer of the "Declaration of Independence."

Over the years, several myths have developed in regard to the Founding Fathers. For example, John Hancock is reputed to have signed his name in such large letters because he wanted King George III to be able to read it without having to wear his glasses. As a result, the phrase "John Hancock" has become a slang term meaning signature. However, other documents in Hancock's name, some written before the Declaration of Independence, are signed in a similarly exaggerated manner. Benjamin Franklin is credited with discovering the nature of electricity after flying a kite during a thunderstorm, but evidence suggest that Franklin did not actually hold the kite string as indicated in popular legend. It is also commonly supposed that Thomas Jefferson wrote the Declaration of Independence by himself, but other members of the Continental Congress contributed material and revised Jefferson's draft. In modern times, the Internet has served to promote various myths about the signers; a persistent forward that shows up in people's e-mails around Independence Day includes a tremendous amount of misinformation. Titled "The Price They Paid," the mailing claims that five of the signers were captured and tortured by the British (false), two had sons killed in combat (only one), and nine died of "wounds and hardships" suffered in combat (none died in combat, though Button Gwinnet of Georgia died of wounds sustained in a duel with a fellow American officer).

HISTORICAL OVERVIEW

Origins of the Declaration of Independence

The Declaration of Independence contains ideas from a variety of sources. Certainly the English philosopher John Locke influenced Jefferson, although to what degree has become a point of debate among scholars. There is no doubt, however, that the famous phrase, "Life, Liberty, and the pursuit of Happiness" in the Declaration is a paraphrase of Locke's assertion that men have a natural right "to preserve their lives, liberties, and fortunes." Thus Jefferson differs slightly from Locke in emphasizing the importance of wealth and ownership. Jefferson was also influenced by the great thinkers of the Enlightenment, a time when major innovations in science, art, and philosophy appeared. In addition to the Englishman Locke, Jefferson read deeply among the works of the Scottish Enlightenment writers, such as David Hume and Francis Hutcheson. His religious views were derived in part from Henry St. John Bolingbroke, to whose writings Jefferson was exposed by his teacher, Dr. William Small. From Bolingbroke Jefferson developed his belief in the regularity of the cosmos and thus a natural explanation for God. Bolingbroke also criticized many of the principles of Christianity and was a Deist, meaning he believed God created the universe but has no daily contact with it. Jefferson himself became a Deist, and debate over his and the other Founding Fathers' intentions toward the role of religion in the life of the new republic remain heated today.

Although the Declaration of Independence is certainly influential, it was not the only or even the first "declaration" of American rights to be written during the Revolutionary period. In *American Scripture: Making the Declaration of Independence*, Pauline Maier identifies at least ninety "declarations" published in individual colonies or towns in 1776; in some cases, these declarations were made prior to the one in Philadelphia adopted on July 4. Both Virginia and New Jersey divorced themselves before July 4, and Maryland proclaimed her independence two days later. All of these documents, as well as the "official" Declaration of Independence, were influenced by the English Declaration of Rights, also known as the Bill of Rights, which was approved in 1689. In many ways the English Declaration is similar to the American Declaration; indeed, Jefferson and the other patriots were

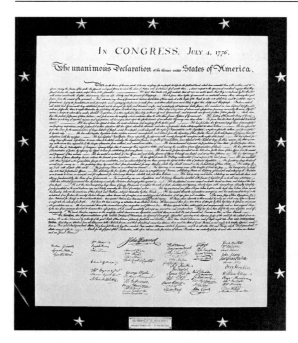

Facsimile of the Declaration of Independence
© Corbis

inspired to declare independence in part because of what they perceived as violations of their rights as Englishmen. Among the important ideas in the English Bill of Rights is the right of Englishmen to petition the king for redress of grievances and freedom from taxation not approved by Parliament. These and other concepts found their way into the Declaration of Independence and later the Constitution of the United States.

Impact of the Declaration of Independence

The Declaration of Independence is undoubtedly one of the most important and influential documents in American history, but it has also had an impact on other countries' histories as well. Jefferson's most famous work became the basis of the French Declaration of the Rights of Man and Citizen, which the French National Assembly adopted in 1789. Drafted by the Marquis de Lafayette, a French nobleman who had fought for American independence and who later became a leading proponent of republicanism in his own country, the Declaration of the Rights of Man and Citizen was in many ways inspired by the American Declaration. In fact,

Lafayette shared the document with Jefferson himself, who offered suggestions and advice. However, as Pauline Maier notes, Lafayette's document more closely resembles "American declarations or bills of rights, not the Declaration of Independence." Lafayette's declaration also differs significantly in that it outlines the duties of French citizens to the Crown as well as their rights.

Throughout the nineteenth century, the American Declaration was cited as the inspiration for various movements to reform governments. When countries in Latin America broke away from Spain, they declared their independence with documents similar to Jefferson's masterpiece. To a large extent, the American Civil War (1861–1865) was justified by the rebellious southern states because they felt Abraham Lincoln's government threatened their rights in a manner similar to that of King George III's oppression of the American colonies. The Declaration of Independence has also been mentioned in connection with modern revolutions. The Communist leader Ho Chi Minh, for example, justified his efforts to unify Vietnam with principles he identified in the Declaration. In 1997, the United Nations Educational, Scientific, and Cultural Organization (UNESCO) adopted the Universal Declaration on the Human Genome and Human Rights, an important statement of the rights of people all over the world to expect justice regardless of their genetic condition. On the eve of the twenty-first century, then, the potential of science to revise the very definition of "human" inspired UNESCO to declare its support for human rights before troubling questions of genetics could ignite controversy in light of future discoveries or innovations, not after the fact.

Preservation and Promotion of the Declaration of Independence

According to Pauline Maier, "during the first fifteen years following its adoption...the Declaration of Independence seems to have been all but forgotten." It seems not to have been accorded the almost holy status it now enjoys in this country until well into the nineteenth century, although Maier notes a tribute to the document and its author, then residing in France, as early as July 4, 1789, sent to him by his fellow Americans. To a degree, the Declaration was downplayed in the early years of the country because the Federalist party, then largely in control of national politics, were Jefferson's political opponents on the one hand, and were slightly embarrassed by the document's strong anti-British sentiment, which was bad for international commerce by the early 1800s, on the other. After the War of 1812 and the decline of the Federalist Party, the Jeffersonian-influenced Republican party (not precisely the modern Republican party) began to promote the document and Jefferson's reputation. After both Jefferson and fellow ex-president and signer John Adams died on the fiftieth anniversary of the Declaration's adoption—July 4, 1826—interest in the document exploded. By the 1850s, Jefferson's assertion that "all men are created equal" was being used to promote the abolition of slavery. Abraham Lincoln incorporated the Declaration into his political philosophy and specifically referred to it in his Gettysburg Address of 1863. As this document took its rightful place among the acknowledged great documents of American history, the Declaration itself was further enshrined in the hearts of the nation.

For many years there was comparatively little effort made to prevent the ravages of time from affecting the Declaration of Independence. The original document, printed on relatively cheap parchment and with a poor quality of ink, was roughly handled and indifferently preserved for many years. Technological shortcomings and unsophisticated notions of archival preservation techniques further limited appropriate care of the Declaration. It was not until the 1920s that serious efforts to preserve the document got underway. In 1952 the Declaration was permanently displayed in the National Archives in Washington, D.C., There it is sealed in an airtight case; various instruments measure temperature, humidity, and other conditions that might harm the revered statement of the American dream of liberty.

CRITICAL OVERVIEW

Reaction to the Declaration of Independence varied depending on the attitudes and personal convictions of the people who read it. Upon receiving word of the Declaration on July 10, George Washington ordered it read to his troops. To the Continental Congress, he wrote, "I trust the late decisive part they (Congress)

have taken, is calculated for that end, and will secure us that freedom and those privileges, which have been, and are refused us, contrary to the voice of Nature and the British Constitution." Washington also informed his soldiers that in the wake of the Declaration he hoped "this important Event will serve as a fresh incentive to every officer, and soldier, to act with Fidelity and Courage, as knowing that now the peace and safety of his Country depends (under God) solely on the success of our arms." Not surprisingly, citizens who remained loyal to the Crown were less supportive of the Declaration. Thomas Hutchinson, a former governor of Massachusetts, published his *Strictures Upon the Declaration of the Congress at Philadelphia* shortly after the document was widely distributed. Hutchinson concluded that Jefferson's charges against King George III were "false and frivolous" and suggested the criminality, not the justification, of the revolt, according to Pauline Maier in *American Scripture*.

Scholars of the Declaration of Independence have provided the most useful observations about the document. Garry Wills's landmark 1978 study, *Inventing America*, explores in great detail the influences on the Declaration. Among his most startling claims is that Jefferson was inspired as much or more by such philosophers as Francis Hutcheson and David Hume instead of John Locke, the great thinker whom historians had traditionally credited as being Jefferson's primary intellectual influence. In discussing the "Scottish thinkers" that he considers more relevant to the composition of the Declaration, Willis concludes that "Jefferson drew his ideas and words from these men, who stood at a conscious and deliberate distance from Locke's political principles." As Noble E. Cunningham Jr. points out in his 1987 book *In Pursuit of Reason*, "the Declaration of Independence was to become the most cherished document in American history, not solely because of its proclamation of independence but also because of its affirmation of the political principles that would undergird the new American republic." In *American Scripture* (1997), Pauline Maier asserts that the Declaration was "at once a legacy and a new conception, a document that spoke both for the revolutionaries and for their descendants, who confronted issues the country's fathers had never known or failed to

MEDIA ADAPTATIONS

A Broadway musical based on the signing of the Declaration of Independence, called *1776*, debuted in 1969, and was adapted for film in 1972. The play was revived for another Broadway run in 1997. Sherman Edwards wrote the music and lyrics to accompany the book by Peter Stone. Peter H. Hunt directed both the Broadway production and the movie. The original 1969 cast recording is available on compact disc from Sony. The film version is available on DVD from Sony Pictures. The 1997 revival cast recording is available on compact disc from TVT.

The Giants of Political Thought: Common Sense, The Declaration of Independence, & The Federalist Papers was released as an audio recording in 1998. Narrated by Craig Deitschman, it is available in a set of four audio cassettes from Sound Ideas.

Readings of *The Declaration of Independence, the Constitution of the United States, and the Bill of Rights* were released as an audio recording in 2004. It is read by Terry Bregrey and available on compact disc from Audio Bookshelf.

Common Sense and the Declaration of Independence was released as an audio recording in 2006. Narrated by Craig Deitschman, it is available on compact disc from Knowledge Products.

---

resolve, binding one generation after another in a continuing act of national self-definition."

CRITICISM

Stephen E. Lucas

In the following excerpts, Lucas champions The Declaration of Independence *as a literary and rhetorical masterpiece.*

The Declaration of Independence is perhaps the most masterfully written state paper of Western civilization. As Moses Coit Tyler noted almost a century ago, no assessment of it can be complete without taking into account its extraordinary merits as a work of political prose style. Although many scholars have recognized those merits, there are surprisingly few sustained studies of the stylistic artistry of the *Declaration*. This essay seeks to illuminate that artistry by probing the discourse microscopically—at the level of the sentence, phrase, word, and syllable. By approaching the *Declaration* in this way, we can shed light both on its literary qualities and on its rhetorical power as a work designed to convince a "candid world" that the American colonies were justified in seeking to establish themselves as an independent nation.

The text of the *Declaration* can be divided into five sections—the introduction, the preamble, the indictment of George III, the denunciation of the British people, and the conclusion. Because space does not permit us to explicate each section in full detail, we shall select features from each that illustrate the stylistic artistry of the *Declaration* as a whole.

The introduction consists of the first paragraph—a single, lengthy, periodic sentence:

> When in the Course of human events, it becomes necessary for one people to dissolve the political bands which have connected them with another, and to assume among the powers of the earth, the separate and equal station to which the Laws of Nature and of Nature's God entitle them, a decent respect to the opinions of mankind requires that they should declare the causes which impel them to the separation.

Taken out of context, this sentence is so general it could be used as the introduction to a declaration by any "oppressed" people. Seen within its original context, however, it is a model of subtlety, nuance, and implication that works on several levels of meaning and allusion to orient readers toward a favorable view of America and to prepare them for the rest of the *Declaration*. From its magisterial opening phrase, which sets the American Revolution within the whole "course of human events," to its assertion that "the Laws of Nature and of Nature's God" entitle America to a "separate and equal station among the powers of the earth," to its quest for sanction from "the opinions of mankind," the introduction elevates the quarrel with England from a petty political dispute to a major event in the grand sweep of

People view the Declaration of Independence at the hall of the National Archives, Washington, D.C. © *Bettmann/Corbis*

history. It dignifies the Revolution as a contest of principle and implies that the American cause has a special claim to moral legitimacy—all without mentioning England or America by name.

Rather than defining the *Declaration*'s task as one of persuasion, which would doubtless raise the defenses of readers as well as imply that there was more than one publicly credible view of the British-American conflict, the introduction identifies the purpose of the *Declaration* as simply to "declare"—to announce publicly in explicit terms—the "causes" impelling America to leave the British empire. This gives the *Declaration*, at the outset, an aura of philosophical (in the eighteenth-century sense of the term) objectivity that it will seek to maintain throughout. Rather than presenting one side in a public controversy on which good and decent people could differ, the *Declaration* purports to do no more than a natural philosopher would do in reporting the causes of any physical event. The issue, it implies, is not one of interpretation but of observation.

The most important word in the introduction is "necessary," which in the eighteenth century carried strongly deterministic overtones. To say an act was necessary implied that it was

impelled by fate or determined by the operation of inextricable natural laws and was beyond the control of human agents. Thus Chambers's *Cyclopedia* defined "necessary" as "that which cannot but be, or cannot be otherwise." "The common notion of necessity and impossibility," Jonathan Edwards wrote in *Freedom of the Will*, "implies something that frustrates endeavor or desire. . . That is necessary in the original and proper sense of the word, which is, or will be, notwithstanding all supposable opposition." Characterizing the Revolution as necessary suggested that it resulted from constraints that operated with lawlike force throughout the material universe and within the sphere of human action. The Revolution was not merely preferable, defensible, or justifiable. It was as inescapable, as inevitable, as unavoidable within the course of human events as the motions of the tides or the changing of the seasons within the course of natural events.

Investing the Revolution with connotations of necessity was particularly important because, according to the law of nations, recourse to war was lawful only when it became "necessary"— only when amicable negotiation had failed and all other alternatives for settling the differences between two states had been exhausted. Nor was the burden of necessity limited to monarchs and established nations. At the start of the English Civil War in 1642, Parliament defended its recourse to military action against Charles I in a lengthy declaration demonstrating the "Necessity to take up Arms." Following this tradition, in July 1775 the Continental Congress issued its own Declaration Setting Forth the Causes and Necessity of Their Taking Up Arms. When, a year later, Congress decided the colonies could no longer retain their liberty within the British empire, it adhered to long-established rhetorical convention by describing independence as a matter of absolute and inescapable necessity. Indeed, the notion of necessity was so important that in addition to appearing in the introduction of the *Declaration*, it was invoked twice more at crucial junctures in the rest of the text and appeared frequently in other congressional papers after July 4, 1776.

Labeling the Americans "one people" and the British "another" was also laden with implication and performed several important strategic functions within the *Declaration*. First, because two alien peoples cannot be made one, it reinforced the notion that breaking the "political bands" with England was a necessary step in the course of human events. America and England were already separated by the more basic fact that they had become two different peoples. The gulf between them was much more than political; it was intellectual, social, moral, cultural and, according to the principles of nature, could no more be repaired, as Thomas Paine said, than one could "restore to us the time that is past" or "give to prostitution its former innocence." To try to perpetuate a purely political connection would be "forced and unnatural," "repugnant to reason, to the universal order of things."

Second, once it is granted that Americans and Englishmen are two distinct peoples, the conflict between them is less likely to be seen as a civil war. The Continental Congress knew America could not withstand Britain's military might without foreign assistance. But they also knew America could not receive assistance as long as the colonies were fighting a civil war as part of the British empire. To help the colonies would constitute interference in Great Britain's internal affairs. As Samuel Adams explained, "no foreign Power can consistently yield Comfort to Rebels, or enter into any kind of Treaty with these Colonies till they declare themselves free and independent." The crucial factor in opening the way for foreign aid was the act of declaring independence. But by defining America and England as two separate peoples, the *Declaration* reinforced the perception that the conflict was not a civil war, thereby, as Congress noted in its debates on independence, making it more "consistent with European delicacy for European powers to treat with us, or even to receive an Ambassador."

Third, defining the Americans as a separate people in the introduction eased the task of invoking the right of revolution in the preamble. That right, according to eighteenth-century revolutionary principles, could be invoked only in the most dire of circumstances—when "resistance was absolutely necessary in order to preserve the nation from slavery, misery, and ruin"—and then only by "the Body of the People." If America and Great Britain were seen as one people, Congress could not justify revolution against the British government for the simple reason that the body of the people (of which the Americans would be only one part) did not support the American cause. For America to move against the

government in such circumstances would not be a justifiable act of resistance but "a sort of Sedition, Tumult, and War ... aiming only at the satisfaction of private Lust, without regard to the public Good." By defining the Americans as a separate people, Congress could more readily satisfy the requirement for invoking the right of revolution that "the whole Body of Subjects" rise up against the government "to rescue themselves from the most violent and illegal oppressions."

Although the *Declaration* begins in an impersonal, even philosophical voice, it gradually becomes a kind of drama, with its tensions expressed more and more in personal terms. This transformation begins with the appearance of the villain, "the present King of Great Britain," who dominates the stage through the first nine grievances, all of which note what "He has" done without identifying the victim of his evil deeds. Beginning with grievance 10 the king is joined on stage by the American colonists, who are identified as the victim by some form of first person plural reference: The king has sent "swarms of officers to harass *our* people," has quartered "armed troops among *us*," has imposed "taxes on *us* without *our* consent," "has taken away *our* charters, abolished *our* most valuable laws," and altered "the Forms of *our* Governments." He has "plundered *our* seas, ravaged *our* coasts, burnt our towns, ... destroyed the lives of *our* people," and "excited domestic insurrections amongst us." The word "our" is used twenty-six times from its first appearance in grievance 10 through the last sentence of the *Declaration*, while "us" occurs eleven times from its first appearance in grievance 11 through the rest of the grievances.

Throughout the grievances action is instigated by the king, as the colonists passively accept blow after blow without wavering in their loyalty. His villainy complete, George III leaves the stage and it is occupied next by the colonists and their "British brethren." The heavy use of personal pronouns continues, but by now the colonists have become the instigators of action as they actively seek redress of their grievances. This is marked by a shift in idiom from "He has" to "We have": "*We* have petitioned for redress ...," "*We* have reminded *them* ...," "*We* have appealed to *their* ...," and "*We* have conjured *them*." But "*they* have been deaf" to all pleas, so "We must ... hold *them*" as enemies. By the conclusion, only the colonists remain on stage to pronounce their dramatic closing lines: "*We* . . . solemnly publish and declare . . ." And to support this declaration, "*we* mutually pledge to each other *our* Lives, *our* Fortunes and *our* sacred Honor."

The persistent use of "he" and "them," "us" and "our," "we" and "they" personalizes the British-American conflict and transfigures it from a complex struggle of multifarious origins and diverse motives to a simple moral drama in which a patiently suffering people courageously defend their liberty against a cruel and vicious tyrant. It also reduces the psychic distance between the reader and the text and coaxes the reader into seeing the dispute with Great Britain through the eyes of the revolutionaries. As the drama of the *Declaration* unfolds, the reader is increasingly solicited to identify with Congress and "the good People of these Colonies," to share their sense of victimage, to participate vicariously in their struggle, and ultimately to act with them in their heroic quest for freedom. In this respect, as in others, the *Declaration* is a work of consummate artistry. From its eloquent introduction to its aphoristic maxims of government, to its relentless accumulation of charges against George III, to its elegiac denunciation of the British people, to its heroic closing sentence, it sustains an almost perfect synthesis of style, form, and content. Its solemn and dignified tone, its graceful and unhurried cadence, its symmetry, energy, and confidence, its combination of logical structure and dramatic appeal, its adroit use of nuance and implication all contribute to its rhetorical power. And all help to explain why the *Declaration* remains one of the handful of American political documents that, in addition to meeting the immediate needs of the moment, continues to enjoy a lustrous literary reputation.

Source: Stephen E. Lucas, "The Stylistic Artistry of *The Declaration of Independence*," in *Prologue*, The U.S. National Archives and Records Administration, Vol. 22, Spring 1990, pp.25–43.

SOURCES

Cunningham, Noble E., Jr., *In Pursuit of Reason: The Life of Thomas Jefferson*, Louisiana State University Press, 1987, p. 349.

"Declaration of Independence," on *NARA: The National Archives Experience*, www.archives.gov/national-archives-experience/charters/declaration_transcript.html (January 8, 2007).

"George Washington and the Declaration of Independence, 1776," on *The Learning Page*, The Library of Congress, memory.loc.gov/learn/features/timeline/amrev/north/independ.html (January, 8, 2007).

Hutchinson, Thomas, "Strictures upon the Declaration of the Congress of Philadelphia," October 15, 1776, on the *Homepage of Dr. William Cutler, History Department, Temple University*, astro.temple.edu/~wcutler/H67/Hutchinson.htm (January 11, 2007).

Jacobus, Lee A., *A World of Ideas: Essential Readings for College Writers*, 6th ed., Bedford/St. Martins, 2002, p. 77.

Maier, Pauline, *American Scripture: Making the Declaration of Independence*, Vintage Books, 1997, pp. 106, 208.

"The Price They Paid," on *Snopes.com*, www.snopes.com/history/american/pricepaid.asp (January 8, 2007).

"Project Profile: Charters of Freedom," on *Save America's Treasures*, www.saveamericastreasures.org/profiles/charterfree.htm (January 8, 2007).

Wills, Garry, *Inventing America: Jefferson's Declaration of Independence*, Doubleday, 1978; reprinted by Mariner, 2002, p. 239.

Elbow Room

JAMES ALAN MCPHERSON

1977

"Elbow Room" (1977), a short story about a biracial couple, is part of a collection that made James Alan McPherson the first African American man to win the Pulitzer Prize for fiction. His stories and style are greatly influenced by his upbringing in the segregated South, as well as his philosophy that there are only human topics, not "black" or "white" ones, allowing McPherson to present a deep understanding of both points of view. His humanistic take on life, which is expressed in many of his stories and captures an era perhaps lost in American history.

Like many of the tales in *Elbow Room*, this short story focuses on characters in difficult situations who must struggle to find success for themselves. The author also explores social, cultural, and political tensions in America in the 1960s and 1970s, including racial tensions, where black and white America meet as the Civil Rights movement slowed and the idealism of the counterculture movement and Vietnam War resistance faded. Critic Patsy B. Perry enthuses that the story "involves acknowledgement and acceptance of several styles and values, an acculturation allowing for many different ways of viewing the world."

"Elbow Room" centers on Paul Frost and Virginia Valentine, a biracial couple who have left their small communities in Kansas and Tennessee, respectively, for life in California. They face problems both individually and together as they challenge the status quo in American society in

BIOGRAPHY

JAMES ALAN MCPHERSON

Born in September, 16, 1943 in Savannah, Georgia, McPherson was the son of James, an alcoholic master electrician, and Mable, a domestic worker. McPherson credits his childhood exposure to Savannah's varied cultural history and his later exposure to both African American and white communities with molding his personal, humanistic values and capability to see beyond racial barriers. These ideals flourish in McPherson's writing, which he began while an undergraduate student in the 1960s.

McPherson won first prize from the *Atlantic* for his story "Gold Coast" in 1965 and became a contributing editor to the magazine after earning a master's degree in creative writing in 1969. That same year, he published his first collection of short stories, *Hue and Cry*, which is full of frantic characters trapped in difficult situations, often race-related, reflecting complexities of life in the United States.

McPherson followed *Hue and Cry* with his second short story collection, *Elbow Room* (1977), which was also a critical success. After winning the Pulitzer Prize in 1978 as well as other significant awards including a MacArthur "genius" grant, McPherson did not publish another book for twenty years. Instead, he focused on teaching at the college level, returning to publishing with two collections of essays *Crabcakes: A Memoir* (1998) and *A Region Not Home: Reflections from Exile* (2000). As of 2006, McPherson teaches creative writing at the University of Iowa.

several ways. Paul refuses to serve in the military during the Vietnam War, while Virginia sees the world through the Peace Corps and returns to a United States where she finds it hard to maintain her idealistic expectations.

The couple meets and marries in California, further challenging the norms of American society.

Paul, still an idealist, finds protection and support in Virginia, who has had her idealism stripped away by her post–Peace Corps experiences in the eastern United States. In turn, Virginia can show her softer side to Paul, which is usually masked by her outer strength and swagger. While neither's family supports their marriage initially, Virginia's family soon comes around. Paul's father, on the other hand, refuses to accept Virginia and remains convinced the marriage will not last.

The story's narrator is an African American writer and friend of Paul and Virginia. Throughout his narrative, his literary editor often interrupts and interjects questions, requests for clarification, and suggestions about the story. The narrator is skeptical about Paul and Virginia's relationship, as well as about Paul's effect on Virginia's life and stories, but he comes to see that Paul is committed to his values and challenging the status quo. While Paul struggles to find the meaning of race in his life, his family, and in society, the couple stays together, has a child, overcomes difficulties with Paul's father, and integrates their lives with their families'. Virginia also remains true to herself and her ideals, not allowing Paul's father or anyone else to control her and her family.

"Elbow Room" is the last story in *Elbow Room*, the last book McPherson would publish for twenty years. Some critics believe that this story hinted at the path the author would take. David Streitfeld of the *Washington Post* comments, "The final story in *Elbow Room* . . . is about a fellow who can no longer make sense of the interracial marriage of two friends. He loses, in fact, his belief in narrative." While McPherson eventually returned to writing books, he believed the time and style of stories like "Elbow Room" had passed. He told Streitfeld, "The languages I used for those short stories is dead. I noticed this back in the '70s. The language of civic discourse is gone."

PLOT SUMMARY

"Elbow Room" opens with an italicized editor's note in which the unnamed editor expresses his or her frustrations with the story's narrator. Among other things, the editor notes that the narrator "flaunts an almost barbaric disregard for the moral mysteries, or integrities, of traditional narrative modes," and says, "This flaw in his discipline is well demonstrated here."

James Alan McPherson © *Corbis*

Section 1

The story proper begins with background information on Paul Frost, who grew up in a small town in Kansas and went to school in Chicago. After being called for selective service and refusing as a conscientious objector, he did alternate service at an insane asylum. He came to believe that many of the hospital's residents were not insane, and finally told a patient so, asking, "So what are you *doing* here?" When the patient asked him, "What are *you* doing here?" Paul became unnerved. He soon moved to Oakland, California, for a second year of alternative service at another hospital. Paul eventually married Virginia Valentine, an African American woman from Warren, Tennessee.

Section 2

The focus in "Elbow Room" shifts to Virginia's background. She left her small Tennessee town and joined the Peace Corps when she was nineteen years old and traveled the world for the next three years. Of her, the narrator says, "She had a talent for locating quickly the human core in people. And she had great humor. . . . She began calling herself 'nigger' in an affirmative and ironic way." Virginia used these skills, even enhanced them, while working in locales such as Ceylon, India, Senegal, Egypt, and Tanzania. Returning to the United States and settling in the Northeast, Virginia found many kindred spirits who had similar experiences and looked at the world in a new way. Soon, however, these people's attitudes began to change and they drifted apart: "People began to feel self-conscious and guilty." Virginia was not prepared to give up the fight to affect change and moved to California, "Like a wounded bird fearful of landing with its wings still spread, she went out to the territory in search of some soft, personal space to cushion the impact of her grounding."

Section 3

The narrator, an African American man, tells his story. He went west to find more stories to tell. Like Virginia, he found the Northeast suffocating, explaining, "Ideas and manners had coalesced into old and cobwebbed conventions." This shift backward included race and social class as well. He relates this social turn of events to his need for stories. The editor interjects and questions the narrator's discussion of caste restrictions and stories:

> *What have caste restrictions to do with imagination?*
>
> Everything.
>
> *A point of information. What is your idea of personal freedom?*
>
> Unrestricted access to new stories forming.

The narrator focuses on Virginia and Paul. He prizes Virginia and her stories, but he neither understands nor trusts Paul's motivations for marrying her and perhaps claiming her life's stories for himself. He notes Virginia's odd wardrobe choices, and writes, "I recognized it as the disguise of a person trying to deflect attention away from a secret self." The narrator admits that he came to realize that Virginia is hiding her "secret self" behind her stories and strong, swaggering persona. Paul, the narrator understands, finds that strength attractive, as he left his family, their profitable business life, and values behind when he married her. The narrator explains how he understands what Paul and

Virginia see in each other. McPherson writes, "Paul Frost was a very lucky innocent. Virginia Valentine was protecting him to heal herself."

Paul's brother travels from Kansas to serve as best man at the wedding, though Paul's parents do not come. Virginia's parents come from Tennessee, and long since having given up on trying to convince her to return home, support the marriage with their presence and gifts from home. At the reception, the narrator talks with her father, Daniel Valentine, who is still uncomfortable with his daughter and her choices. He tells the narrator about the family pride he had passed to his daughter, as well as the warning he had given Paul about not mistreating Virginia. "He said this to me as one black man to another, as if he owed me reassurance," he says. At the end of their conversation, Mr. Valentine admits they are a "fine couple."

Paul and Virginia build a happy life living in an apartment in San Francisco's Mission District. They both work, and Paul also works on his degree at a community college. The narrator admires how they choose to live and pick their friends, noting, "They were the most democratic people I have ever seen. They simply allowed people to present themselves, and they had relationships with Chicanos, Asians, French, Brazilians, black and white Americans." Nonetheless, the narrator also believes this ideal society is doomed to fail, that the situation in San Francisco will soon be the same as it is elsewhere in the country.

The narrator reports that Paul faces pressure from his family, primarily his father, in Kansas. His father believes that Paul will eventually leave Virginia, and he promises to support his son when he does. They have disagreements over the telephone, with Paul calling his father bigoted. "Nothing was ever resolved, but the discussions were most rational." When the narrator has dinner one night at Paul and Virginia's, Paul explains that his father is small-minded, a product of his environment, and does not understand African Americans. Though Virginia is less sure, Paul tells the narrator that he believes his father will come to understand his wife, and he will take her to Kansas someday.

Though the narrator acknowledges this story is not his, he cannot resist putting himself into the matter. The narrator tells Paul that he believes society's forces will come and compel him to change, but before this happens, Paul should "force the reality of your wife into your father's mind and run toward whatever cover it provides." Because Paul still does not understand and seems almost angry, the narrator continues to drive his point home, using a mask that Virginia brought back from Ibadan as the center of an example, with this scenario:

> You are a dealer in art. . . . You want to sell this mask by convincing your best customer it is beautiful and of interest to the eye. Every other dealer in town says it is ugly. How do you convince the customer and make a sale?

Paul becomes enraged and orders the narrator to leave. Virginia supports him, saying, "Go away! Please, go *away*! No matter what you think, this is my husband!" The narrator exits, acknowledging that their story was not yet ready to tell.

The editor interrupts again. The editor believes the previous section was opaque, and asks for explanation. The narrator explains that he was challenging Paul's beliefs and way of looking at the world, but Paul did not want to be so confronted. The narrator concludes, "I think he understood enough to know that he was on a moral mission."

A few weeks later, Virginia calls the narrator to defend her husband and his actions. She tells him, "One thing I learned from traveling is you accept people the way they are and try to work from there." She then invites him to join her and Paul at a New Year's Eve mass at an Episcopal cathedral. The narrator describes the scene inside the church where many types of people are present. He also relates an incident in which a man sitting behind the three of them tells Virginia, whom he assumes is a man, "if you're too *dumb* to take your hat off in church, get out!" Paul turns around and defends her to the stranger with "fierce eyes" and an arrogant tone. The narrator notices a change in Paul's voice, noting, "I thought to myself, *This one's a man.*"

The narrator reports that Paul throws himself into understanding his history and other points of view in the new year. He becomes upset when he is twice called "nigger" by children in February. Paul calls the narrator and asks what that term means to him, but hangs up on the narrator after receiving a flippant answer. The narrator believes Paul should find his own meanings. A short time later, Virginia learns that she is pregnant. Paul tells the narrator that his father was upset by the news.

The narrator says that he moves away from Virginia and Paul after Christmas because he finds better stories to tell from a man who has been recently released from prison after fifty years. The narrator describes his interactions with this man, including a party thrown by the man's benefactress. The editor again interjects, stating that this section does not serve a purpose, is unclear, and should be cut. The narrator admits to the lack of focus, but that the point of the section is that "There was no focus. There was no control. The hands of a great clock seemed to be spinning wildly."

The narrator believes that everyone was surrendering at the time, noting, "There was a feeling of a great giving up." Even Virginia, he states, no longer controls nor exists inside her stories because of her advancing pregnancy. He writes, "There was no longer the sense of the personal epic." Paul also suffers a personal crisis of identity and self, no longer spending time with white men. He finds work as a landscaper, reads philosophy and the Bible, and is quite alone. The narrator seems to admire Paul at this point, but will not intrude on the development of Paul's story. He writes,

> I never once heard him say to Virginia, "I don't understand." For the stoic nature of this silence, considering the easy world waiting behind those words, one could not help but love him.

By June, Paul's parents reach out to their son and daughter-in-law. Paul's mother confides that her ethnic heritage is not all white, while his father eventually agrees to accept Virginia and the baby at their home. Virginia is insulted by this gesture, not wanting her child to be seen as "an honorary white." The narrator learns about the dispute from Virginia as they visit a Japanese tea garden in the summer. She says, "I'm black. I've accepted myself as that. But didn't I make some elbow room, though? I mean up *here*?" She indicates that she means she had to make room in her mind to accept herself. She expresses more feelings about race and relating to the world, but the narrator realizes that he is no longer interested in their predicament. She talks about the changes in Paul, and he listens a little longer as out of a sense of obligation.

Later in the summer, the narrator spends time with Paul walking through San Francisco. They do not say much, though the narrator twice points out black men he believes to be "niggers." When the narrator pushes the issue, Paul accuses the narrator of believing that he is a bigot. The narrator explains that he believes Paul is a

> THE FATHER ACCUSED THE SON OF BEGINNING TO THINK LIKE A NEGRO. THE FATHER ACCUSED THE SON OF BEING DELUDED. THE SON ACCUSED THE FATHER OF BEING NARROW-MINDED. THE SON ACCUSED THE FATHER OF BEING OBTUSE. NOTHING WAS EVER RESOLVED, BUT THE DISCUSSIONS WERE MOST RATIONAL."

product of his Kansas background, but a still-defensive Paul insists that there is more to him and his children will be even better. The narrator can only see the situation this way: "They will be black and blind or passing for white and self-blinded. Those are the only choices." After they part and the narrator begins to walk way, Paul reminds him that he has been fighting society's prejudice and offers his own definition for *nigger*: "It's what you are when you begin thinking of yourself as a work of art."

Two months later, the narrator reports that he tries to contact the couple before moving back East, but finds they had moved away. Six months after moving himself, a letter from Kansas arrives. In it is the birth announcement for Paul and Virginia's son, Daniel, and three pictures. The first shows a pink newborn with black hair. The second shows a brown-skinned four-month-old. The third shows Paul, Virginia, Daniel, and Paul's parents, with Virginia and Paul looking sure of themselves. On the back of the picture is written, "He will be a *classic* kind of nigger." The editor asks for clarity about a comment written on the back of the photo, but the narrator cannot fully explain. The narrator reports that he tried to call them in Kansas, but they had already left for Tennessee. He believes the boy's story will be bold and perhaps strong. The editor still wants an explanation for the comment.

THEMES

Challenging the Status Quo

Throughout "Elbow Room," the two primary characters consistently challenge the status quo in American society. The country was born of people searching for a better way of life than the one they fled from, and that value remains a vital part of the American dream. Paul Frost, a white man from a small town in Kansas, first leaves home, then refuses to serve in the military during the war. The author writes, "He returned home briefly and confronted his family and the members of a selective service committee. These were people who had watched him growing up. They were outraged at his refusal." Paul's own silence at this outrage affects him at the time but does not deter him from making other such choices.

Though Paul's challenges to the status quo cause him considerable angst and much study to understand, he remains on his path. Virginia is never unsure of hers. McPherson depicts her as stronger and more confident than Paul. Like Paul, she left a small town, and she saw the world as a Peace Corps volunteer. Even in the Peace Corps, she challenged the status quo. Virginia takes her attitude back to the United States and finds similarly minded people in the cities of the Northeast for a time. As many people there give up the fight to change the American status quo, Virginia moves to California so she can continue. The narrator states,

> Virginia, like many of the more stubborn, abandoned the East and ran off to California. Like a wounded bird fearful of landing with its wings still spread, she went out to the territory in search of some soft, personal space to cushion the impact of her grounding.

She meets and marries Paul in California. In their marriage, they continue to defiantly challenge society's norms.

For the narrator of "Elbow Room," Paul and Virginia's challenging the status quo is a fragile example of the times: The times have changed and may yet change back. Virginia fled to California because she saw people enlightened in the Peace Corps reverting back to form. The narrator expects the reversion to reach California as well, but the narrator understands by the end that Virginia and Paul will continue to challenge the status quo in the long term. McPherson ends the story with the narrator's optimism that Paul and Virginia's child will make more progress than either of his parents, because "The mother is a bold woman. The father has a sense of how things should be."

Racism

"Deciding then that Hindus were more 'black' than anyone she had ever seen at home, [Virginia] began calling herself 'nigger' in an affirmative and ironic way." In doing so, Virginia attempts to disarm, or even empower, the most degrading term of American racism to suit her own purposes. She has experienced racism longer (her entire life) and from more points of view (in the Peace Corps) than her husband; she has more tools and tactics to fight it. Paul seems never to have considered race at all before he fell in love with a black woman, and he struggles to make sense of it throughout the story. While Paul suffers from identity issues and searches for greater understanding after the marriage, he is uneasy in his new position in the world. Initially, Paul's father believes that the marriage will not last and promises to support him when it ends. Paul will not accept his father's limited world view, but continues to challenge his father's opinion of him, his marriage, and later, his child with Virginia.

When she is pregnant, Virginia will not let her father-in-law accept her child as what she terms "an honorary white." To her, his father must accept Paul, Virginia, and their child for who they are, nothing less. She will not accept the space he tries to carve out for them in his life until he fully accepts his black daughter-in-law and black grandchild without trying to downplay their racial identities. She says, "I'm black. I've accepted myself as that. But didn't I make some elbow room, though?" She will not accept anything less than Paul's father doing the same.

The narrator seems to resent, or at the very least suspect, Paul's quest to understand the racial issue, as if the fight against racism were strictly the providence of its victims. As he says himself after upsetting Paul at dinner, "I had confronted him with his color and he became white." Although Virginia calls herself, her friends, and her husband all "nigger" at some point in the story, the narrator bristles when Paul tries to make sense of the word and its impact. As the couple prepares for parenthood and withdraws from the exciting life in which the narrator first saw such potential for drama, he loses interest in them. His attitude seems to shift at the end, however. Conflict between Paul and Virginia interests him as a writer and serenity does not, but he also sees a different story in the future generation. He concludes: "I will wager my reputation on the ambition, if not the strength, of the boy's story."

The Melting Pot

Another theme present in this story of the American dream is that of the melting pot, in which new cultures, ties, and traditions are created as old ones blend together. The narrator spends much of his story focusing on Paul and Virginia, their marriage, and their future child—the evolution of a family unit. However, once they become a family with a baby on the way, the narrator loses interest in their story and moves on, though he is curious enough to try and track them down after they all leave California. He sees hope in the future by what Paul and Virginia have created together.

Another way the bridge between old and new ways is emphasized in the story is in the relationship between Paul and Virginia and their families, especially their fathers. Though the fathers question the marriage and Paul's father does not believe it will last, Paul and Virginia still care what their parents think. They want acceptance from their parents but will not compromise the couple's firmly held beliefs.

Paul and Virginia invite them all at the wedding, though only Virginia's family and Paul's brother actually come. Virginia's family is initially reluctant, but accepts her decision. Paul's family is more difficult. He does not give up on his father even though they disagree about racial—and hence personal—issues. Though his father is upset to learn that Virginia is pregnant, Paul's father does not cut off contact. McPherson writes, "both sets of parents began making gestures." In the end, there is reconciliation on all sides, and Paul and Virginia's son is apparently welcomed with his parents in both sets of grandparents' homes.

Idealism

A sense of idealism also pervades "Elbow Room." Idealism in this sense means living or trying to live up to high standards or principals, which is the very "dream" part of the American dream. The narrator is idealistic in the kinds of stories he is looking for, and he finds unique qualities to the ones he tells, despite losing interest in the story of Virginia and Paul at times.

In section 2, the narrator plainly states that "Virginia's quest was an epic of idealism." This quest is leaving the small community of Warren,

Tennessee, and soaring to the world as a member of the Peace Corps. She learned much about "different ways of looking at the world" and brought that back to the United States. Every choice Virginia has made has been to live up to this sense of idealism, including moving to California and marrying Paul Frost. She sees in Frost something unbroken as she once was before she was disillusioned, something she is trying to regain in her relationship with him. The narrator writes:

> She was an eagle with broken wings spread, somewhat awkwardly, over the aristocratic soul of a simple farm boy. Having his soul intact made him a vulnerable human being. But having flown so high herself and having been severely damaged, she still maintained too much grace, and too complete a sense of the treachery in the world, to allow any roughness to touch the naked thing.

Thus, Paul is almost more idealistic than Virginia because his dreams and visions are still possible to him. He values Virginia's strength, which gives him a safe place to explore his own identity as an idealist. As a couple, the early days of the marriage had idealistic aspects to it: "Both of them were learning Spanish from their Chicano neighbors. They chose their friends carefully with an eye to uniqueness and character. They were the most democratic people I have ever seen."

Furthermore, Paul will not let his small-minded father ruin his marriage to Virginia. Though the narrator emphasizes that Paul does not necessarily understand the complexity of racial issues presented by his marriage, Paul works hard to maintain his idealism in the matter. By the end of "Elbow Room," it seems he has successfully worked through them. In doing so, he revives Virginia's idealism as well.

HISTORICAL OVERVIEW

Peace Corps

Founded by an executive order from President John F. Kennedy in 1961, the Peace Corps was intended to help the United States win the political support of third-world countries during the Cold War. Peace Corps volunteers helped developing countries by working in humanitarian aid programs to improve such areas as their agriculture, transportation, education, public health, and communications capabilities. By 1963, more than seven thousand young Americans had volunteered for the Peace Corps, serving in forty-four countries; by 1974, volunteers were serving in sixty-nine countries. Although budget cuts had the Peace Corps shrinking since the 1980s, President George W. Bush pledged to expand the organization as part of the Global War on Terror.

Counterculture Movement

By the early 1960s, a burgeoning counterculture movement was emerging in the United States. Led by the young baby-boom generation, it was a reaction to the conservative, socially repressed, suburban ideals of much of white America as they developed in the post–World War II consumer boom. Originally centered in college towns like Berkeley, California, and Ann Arbor, Michigan, the movement could soon be found in nearly every city identified with a university. Generally supporting the left side of the political spectrum, dubbed the New Left, the counterculture found a voice in groups like Students for a Democratic Society as well as Berkeley's Free Speech Movement.

Members of the counterculture movement questioned authority and establishment values and tried to affect social change through their actions, including teach-ins, protests, and marches. For example, they supported the Civil Rights movement, which had been making progress in the 1950s through the early 1970s in changing laws and increasing rights of African Americans. Some hippies, as certain members of the counterculture movement were called, essentially dropped out of mainstream society by embracing alternative institutions such as communal living, freer expressions of sexuality, drugs such as LSD and marijuana, and rock music. The counterculture movement lost steam by the mid-1970s as its proponents aged and the Vietnam War ended; some of its values became part of mainstream American society.

Resistance to the Vietnam War

One major focus of the counter-culture movement was resistance to America's increasing role in the Vietnam War. Though initially led by students, Americans of all ages eventually became involved in such protests against the war and the United States' involvement. Beginning in 1950, United States played a limited role in supporting first the French and later Vietnamese non-Communist forces against Vietnamese communists led by Ho Chi Minh, who were trying to control the whole of Vietnam. In the United States, protests against

American involvement in Vietnam grew louder and more organized when President Lyndon B. Johnson decided the United States would take a leading role in fighting the war with the non-Communist South Vietnamese. Johnson began committing tens of thousands of U.S. troops to the conflict in 1965. By 1969, there were over half a million U.S. troops in Vietnam.

Many Americans did not support the war in Vietnam or the draft that compelled young American men to fight in it. They pointed out that the increased number of troops did not translate into any type of victory. Americans also saw how desperate the conflict was as reports from the war were televised on news broadcasts each evening. Beginning in the mid-1960s, nationwide protests, including several marches on Washington, D.C., with thousands of people participating, demonstrated American discontent with involvement in Vietnam.

Throughout the war, the United States used the selective service draft to find enough men to fill the massive troops requirement. "The acceleration had begun when Johnson announced a doubling of draft calls in July 1965. From calling about 16,000 draftees each month, [Selective Service] began calling 40,000," according to military historian George Q. Flynn. One way men showed their resistance was by protesting and/or refusing to serve in the U.S. military when drafted. A draft lottery instituted in 1969 gave more fuel to the voices of dissent as it seemed to work against men born later in the year.

To avoid serving in the military, many men fled to Canada and Sweden. Others obtained deferments or exemptions by getting married, attending college, training to join the clergy, and joining the National Guard or the Peace Corps. Men could also avoid service by obtaining exemptions as medically unfit. Conscientious objectors could do alternative service such as Paul Frost does in "Elbow Room," by working in health care or taking care of certain other civilian needs for a certain period of time, usually several years. During the war as a whole, over two hundred thousand men were formally accused of violating laws related to the draft.

Interracial Marriage

Through the early twentieth century in the United States, many states had passed laws which prohibited marriages between the races. Breaking many of the anti-miscegenation (the

mixing of the races) laws was considered a fel-
ony, and even those who performed such marriages could face serious charges. As late as 1965,
a Virginia trial court put an interracial couple in
jail for marrying. Two years later, the U.S.
Supreme Court overturned the conviction of
this couple in the case *Loving v. Commonwealth
of Virginia*. As a result, anti-miscegenation laws
were ruled unconstitutional in the United States.

At that time, seventeen states had such anti-
miscegenation laws on the books, concentrated
in the southern part of the United States. As such
laws were repealed in those states, interracial
marriages increased. According to the U.S.
Census Bureau, in 1960, there were 157,000
mixed-race marriages in the United States, 0.4
percent of all marriages in the United States. By
1980, the number increased to 997,000, representing 2 percent of all marriages.

According to a 2006 article in the *Journal of
Black Studies*, African Americans were largely
accepting of interracial relationships much earlier
than whites, but that white Americans are becoming more accepting of interracial relationships:

> In 1972, 76% of African Americans in a Gallup
> poll said they approved of interracial marriage,
> while less than 30% of Whites at the time
> approved of such marriages. During the 25-
> year period ending in 1997, the Gallup poll
> data showed only a slight increase for African
> American endorsement of interracial marriage,
> from 76% to 83%. Whites' endorsement dur-
> ing the same 25-year period shows a dramatic
> increase from about 28% to 67%.

Despite the 1967 Supreme Court ruling and
changing American opinions, it was not until
2000 when the last state, Alabama, overturned
its state law against interracial marriage.

CRITICAL OVERVIEW

Like the collection that contains "Elbow
Room," this story was praised by critics for its
honesty, carefully crafted narrative style, and
drawing of characters who are trying to know
and understand themselves and the situations in
which they find themselves. Margo Jefferson
comments in a 1977 *Newsweek* review of the
collection, "The ambitious title story is a clinical
examination of a young interracial couple's
efforts to form a relationship free of the cliches
of American racial history. They are seen
through the eyes of a black writer engaged in a

similar battle to free himself." While many of
McPherson's stories in *Elbow Room* are about
life in the United States about white and African
American culture through a black point of view,
this story in particular is lauded for being
observant of social tensions of the time.

Herman Beavers is another critic who believes
the stories in *Elbow Room* found their power in
reflecting the loss of idealism as the Civil Rights
era and the Black Power movements lost steam. He
also argues that "Elbow Room" shifts when
Virginia becomes pregnant, showing there is a
way out of this loss. He writes, "The story, which
deals with the interracial marriage of Virginia
Valentine and Paul Frost, functions as a racial
allegory meant to suggest that redemption will
come only with the kind of courage and love
bound up in the birth of a child."

Not every critic appreciated McPherson's
sometimes esoteric take on the subject matter.
While the reviewer in the *New Yorker* calls the
collection as a whole full of "deeply felt short
stories," this story in particular is one which the
critic believes "tell[s] the reader ... a bit more
than he wants to know about the ideological or
artistic problems that confronted the narrator."

CRITICISM

Jon Wallace

*In the following essay, Wallace examines how the
intensely metafictive quality of McPherson's narrative enhances and redefines the short story's
complex discussion of race and identity.*

As the epigraph to the title story of his
Pulitzer Prize winning book *Elbow Room*,
James Alan McPherson quotes a passage from
In the American Grain in which William Carlos
Williams declares that one challenge faced by
American pioneers was to settle a new land without relying entirely on old values: "[Daniel]
Boone's genius," says Williams, "was to recognize the difficulty as neither material nor political but one purely moral and aesthetic." Like
Boone, McPherson recognizes the importance
of moral and aesthetic problems: specifically,
the moral and aesthetic problems of storytelling,
which he considers a very serious business
indeed. In fact, another quotation that would
be equally useful as an introduction to "Elbow
Room" is Joan Didion's simple but profound

A mask from Nigeria © *North Carolina Museum of Art/Corbis*

observation that "We tell ourselves stories in order to live." In much of McPherson's work and in Didion's essay, "story" can be read to refer simultaneously to fictional narratives and to ideological stories—myths which we use to order the world and define ourselves. Although such myths can be expressed in the form of a coherent series of assumptions about the nature of the world and persons (as in the world view of modern science), they generally take the form of dramatic mythical narratives (Genesis, for example) that serve as the bases of more abstract formulations. Hence the relevance of morality and aesthetics, for what McPherson implies in "Elbow Room" is that neither meaning nor identity should be considered material or political matters, that is, structures *necessarily* imposed upon us from without by external "realities." They should instead be recognized for what they always are: human creations whose validity can be measured not only by standards of realism and objective truth (if such truth is possible), but also by the sense of coherent purpose that they provide. Moreover, the plausibility of a given story or ideology is as much a matter of form as content. We don't live by a story simply because its theme or idea makes sense; we accept it because it appeals to us as a satisfying "new coherence" or dramatic structure. In short, all stories (all the myths that justify all abstract ideological values) are inventions, like fictional stories, that we live by because we find them both morally and aesthetically compelling.

All of which is to say that the protagonist of "Elbow Room" is neither Paul nor Virginia Frost, nor is the real story their struggle to live sanely and lovingly in a racist culture as a white man and black woman. The protagonist is the narrator, and the real story is about his struggle to find a form for their story—a form that will be, first, morally satisfying insofar as it will do justice to them as human beings seeking to define themselves in their own terms, and second, aesthetically satisfying insofar as it will engage and sustain our attention. The tempting alternative, one that the narrator succumbs to several times, is to explain—and exploit—them in terms appropriate to *his* story, not theirs.

McPherson dramatizes his narrator's moral and aesthetic struggle in both the frame and story-within-a-story of "Elbow Room." In the frame story, the narrator resists the conventional structures of an editor, who claims in his introduction that the

Narrator is unmanageable. Demonstrates a disregard for form bordering on the paranoid. Questioned closely, he declares himself the open enemy of conventional narrative categories. When pressed for reasons, narrator became shrill in insistence that "borders," "structures," "frames," "order," and even "form" itself are regarded by him with the highest suspicion.

The narrator's anti-establishment commitments are clear, arguing as he does for creative freedom from the conventional ideological constraints advocated by his editor. In their first exchange, the editor interrupts the narrator's discussion of a time when, after a short period of freedom (presumably in the sixties), "caste curtains" were again drawn in this country "resegregating all imaginations." During this time, the narrator tells us, he was obliged to go out in search of stories "to complete my sense of self." This search was often risky, due to the distrust that was then separating people:

Yet not to do this was to default on my responsibility to narrate fully. There are stories that *must* be told, if only to be around when fresh dimensions are needed. But in the East, during that time, there was no thought of this. A narrator cannot function without new angles of vision. I needed new eyes, regeneration, fresh forms, and went hunting for them out in the territory.

A point of information. What has form to do with caste restrictions?

Everything.

You are saying you want to be white?

A narrator needs as much access to the world as the advocates of that mythology.

You are ashamed then of being black?

Only of not being nimble enough to dodge other people's straight-jackets.

Are you not too much obsessed here with integration?

I was cursed with a healthy imagination.

What have caste restrictions to do with imagination?

Everything.

A point of information. What is your idea of personal freedom?

Unrestricted access to new stories forming.

Have you paid strict attention to the forming of this present one?

Once upon a time there was a wedding in San Francisco.

Insofar as he asserts the need for "new angles" and "new eyes," "fresh forms" and "unrestricted access to new stories forming," the narrator speaks as a literary subversive attempting to resist the editor's formal "straightjackets."

But once we leave the frame story and enter the story, or stories, of the wedding couple—Paul Frost and Virginia Valentine—we find the narrator becoming an editor in his turn, one who is interested primarily in form, not in people as creatures in time struggling to live sanely and lovingly. "Virginia I valued for her stock of stories," he writes. "I was suspicious of Paul Frost for claiming first right to these. They were a treasure I felt sure he would exploit." In these lines the narrator's moral and aesthetic interests clash. Good stories should be both somehow "moral" (purposive, idealistic) and aesthetic (dramatically engaging); but, McPherson would have us remember, so should story tellers. Indeed, the purpose of all good stories is to broaden and deepen awareness so that people can, among other things, learn to accept themselves and each other. As sensitive as the narrator is to his own sense of self, he nevertheless fails to "relate" to others without "intruding," as if he were literally "writing" them into *his* story. For example, after listening to Virginia talk about how Paul's father had refused to accept their marriage, the narrator confesses that "It was not my story, but I could not help intruding upon its materials. It seemed to me to lack perspective." He then proceeds to pontificate on the themes of time, media, and selfhood in a language hardly intended to express or encourage sympathetic understanding:

> Time out here is different from time in the East. When we say "Good afternoon" here, in the East people are saying "Good night." It's a matter of distance, not of values. Ideas that start in the East move very fast in media, but here the diversity tends to slow them down. Still, a mind needs media to reinforce a sense of self. There are no imaginations pure enough to be self-sustaining.

Angered by what he takes to be condescension, Paul declares: "I don't understand what you're talking about." We have been in such situations before in *Elbow Room*: a defensive protagonist attempting to order the world to his satisfaction, usually as a means of escaping its human entanglements. This seems to be the narrator's motive in "Elbow Room," but we cannot be sure. What we do know is that he can be aesthetic to a fault, preoccupied with form at the expense of human involvement. His main goal seems to be to follow Paul and

Virginia as an observer in order to make something artful out of them.

Shortly after the above exchange, the narrator again intrudes, this time as an interrogator. Pointing to an African mask on the wall of Paul and Virginia's apartment, he asks if Paul thinks it is beautiful. Paul says, "It's very nice. Ginny bought it from a trader in Ibadan. There's a good story behind it." The narrator presses the point, asking again if Paul thinks it is beautiful. Growing angry, Paul answers yes. The narrator then poses a problem:

> You are a dealer in art. You have extraordinary taste. But your shop is in a small town. You want to sell this mask by convincing your best customer it is beautiful and of interest to the eye. Every other dealer in town says it is ugly. How do you convince the customer and make a sale?

As theoretically useful as the question might be as a means of exploring racial differences, it is not an appropriate one, given the human context. Psychologically, Paul is hardly in a position to deal with such bewildering racial puzzles—a fact that the narrator understands but does not act upon: "You have enlisted in a psychological war," he tells Paul shortly before the latter orders him out of the apartment. "I left them alone with their dinner," he then adds, concluding the scene. "It was not my story. It was not ripe for telling until they had got it under better control."

Psychological war is everyone's story in "Elbow Room." What it involves at bottom is a struggle of self-creation in which individuals oppose the power of culture in an attempt to transcend its limited and limiting definitions. Immediately after the scene in Paul and Virginia's apartment, the editor interrupts, declaring that an

> *Analysis of this section is needed. It is too subtle and needs to be more clearly explained.*
>
> I tried to enter his mind and failed.
>
> *Explain.*
>
> I had confronted him with color and he became white.
>
> *Unclear. Explain.*
>
> There was a public area of personality in which his "I" existed. The nervous nature of this is the basis of what is miscalled arrogance. In reality it was the way his relationship with the world was structured. I attempted to challenge this structure by attacking its assumptions too directly and abruptly. He sensed the intrusion

and reacted emotionally to protect his sense of form. He simply shut me out of his world.

Unclear. Explain.

I am I. I am we. You are.

Clarity is essential on this point. Explain.

Despite his detailed understanding of the personal and social implications of Paul's and Virginia's stories, the narrator eventually loses interest. After a conversation with Virginia in which she talks about her ideal of selfhood, he writes:

> Inside myself I suddenly felt a coolness as light as the morning mist against my skin. Then I realized that I was acting. I did not care about them and their problems any more. I did not think they had a story worth telling. I looked away from her and said, "Life is tough, all right."

With a cliché he writes them off, convinced that they and their child have essentially two choices: black isolation or self-destructive white compromise—entrapment within conventional social categories. His decision reveals the extent of *his* isolation—his essentially defensive commitment to aesthetic rather than moral values. Losing interest in Paul's and Virginia's ability to live "fresh forms," the narrator walks away in despair, "convinced there were no new stories in the world."

But Paul and Virginia, committed as they are to each other, and to ideals of selfhood that go beyond merely aesthetic form, succeed in proving him wrong. Broadened and deepened by her flight into the hearts of other countries, and other people, Virginia becomes "a magic woman" who could speak "with her whole presence in very complicated ways. She was unique. She was a classic kind of narrator." Virginia is also a woman capable of human intimacy and commitment—a trait evident in her relation to Paul, whom she resolves to protect against all psychological dangers. Paul himself is also magic, in his own subdued Kansas way. Willing, as the narrator notes, to confront "the hidden dimensions of his history" in order "to unstructure and flesh out his undefined 'I,'" Paul marries Virginia, fathers a son, and eventually convinces his father to accept his family. More importantly, at least as far as the theme of the story is concerned, he constantly grapples with the issue of his identity, realizing that the question "Who am I?" can never be answered conclusively:

> And many times, watching him conceal his aloneness, I wanted to answer, "The abstract white man of mythic dimensions, if being that will make you whole again." But the story was

still unfinished, and I did not want to intrude on its structure again. The chaos was his alone, as were the contents he was trying desperately to reclaim from an entrenched and determined form. But to his credit it must be said that, all during this time, I never once heard him say to Virginia, "I don't understand." For the stoic nature of this silence, considering the easy world waiting behind those words, one could not help but love him.

In the concluding lines of the story, the narrator describes his response to a photograph recently sent to him of Paul and Virginia, their baby, and Paul's parents. On the back of it are the words "He will be a *classic* kind of nigger." The editor intrudes to demand a clarification of this comment. "I would find that difficult to do," writes the narrator,

> It was from the beginning not my story. I lack the insight to narrate its complexities. But it may still be told. The mother is, after all, a country raconteur with cosmopolitan experience. The father sees clearly with both eyes. And when I called Kansas they had already left for the backwoods of Tennessee, where the baby has an odd assortment of relatives. I will wait. The mother is a bold woman. The father has a sense of how things should be. But while waiting, I will wager my reputation on the ambition, if not the strength, of the boy's story.

Comment is unclear. Explain. Explain.

The narrator, himself partially transformed by Paul and Virginia's story, realizes that there is no explanation beyond the story of "Elbow Room" itself, beyond the texture of its language, images, tone, and syntax—in the feel of verbal formulations designed to make new eyes and new selves by modifying old forms, social and linguistic. Or, in terms of another metaphor, there is no explanation beyond the play of opposites that is the story: the editor and the narrator, the narrator and Paul, Paul and Virginia, male and female, and even the aesthetic and moral dimensions of stories that interact to generate a meaningful form. Paul? His son? Both? can become "classic" only by going beyond such antithetical classifications to a synthesis that subsumes them. Since such a synthesis does not yet exist, we cannot explain it, only sense it as a possibility somewhere beyond, or between, the lines of our current public and private stories—in a place beyond definitions, where there is room for everyone.

Source: Jon Wallace, "The Story Behind the Story in James Alan McPherson's "Elbow Room", in *Studies in Short Fiction*, Vol. 25, No. 4, Fall 1988, pp. 447–52.

SOURCES

"About the Peace Corps," *Peace Corps*, www.peacecorps.gov (November 1, 2006).

Beavers, Herman, "James Alan McPherson," in *Dictionary of Literary Biography, Volume 244: American Short Story Writers Since World War II, Fourth Series*, edited by Patrick Meanor and Joseph McNicholas, Gale, 2001, pp. 246–53.

Jacobson, Cardell K. and Bryan R. Johnson, "Interracial Friendship and African American Attitudes about Interracial Marriage," in the *Journal of Black Studies*, Vol. 36, No. 4, March 2006, pp. 570–84.

Flynn, George Q., *The Draft: 1940-1973*, University of Kansas Press, 1993, p. 170.

Jefferson, Margo, "Black Manners," in *Newsweek*, October 17, 1977, p. 116.

McPherson, James Alan, "Elbow Room," in *Elbow Room*, Little, Brown and Company, 1977; reprint, Griot Editions/Quality Paperback Book Club, 1996, pp. 215–41.

Perry, Patsy B., "James Alan McPherson," in *Dictionary of Literary Biography, Volume 38: Afro-American Writers After 1955: Dramatists and Prose Writers*, edited by Thadeious M. Davis and Trudier Harris, Gale 1985, pp. 185–94.

Review of *Elbow Room*, in the *New Yorker*, November 21, 1977, p. 230.

Streitfeld, David, "Lost and Found; Success Was the Best—and Worst—Thing to Happen to Author McPherson," in the *Washington Post*, March 9, 1998, p. B1.

"Table of Race of Wife by Race of Husband," U.S. Bureau of the Census, www.census.gov/population/socdemo/race/interractab1.txt (July 5, 1994).

"Vietnam Online," *American Experience*, PBS Online, www.pbs.org/wgbh/amex/vietnam/index.html (November 1, 2006).

Finding My Voice

MARIE G. LEE

1992

Finding My Voice (1992) is a familiar American coming-of-age story from an unfamiliar perspective. In her debut novel, author Marie G. Lee, the American child of Korean immigrants, explores questions of belonging, pressure (from both parents and peers), and racism for a girl like herself in modern small-town America. Through her protagonist, Ellen Sung, Lee examines what it feels like to be an outsider and how the assimilation process started by immigrant parents is completed by their children. In this novel, Ellen must navigate the expectations of friends and family while trying to figure out who she is.

Finding My Voice reflects Lee's own experiences as a high school student and a member of the only Korean family, indeed the only family of color, in the small Minnesota town in which she was born and raised. The author admits to including autobiographical elements to the story but says the primary character, Ellen Sung, is fictional. In an autobiographical sketch published in the *Eighth Book of Junior Authors and Illustrators*, Lee explained:

> It wasn't me, but someone very much like me. Perhaps James Baldwin was right when he said that novelists always write their first novel about their own lives because they have years of accumulated gunk to get off their chest. Well, that's exactly what I did: I wrote my heart out.

The inspiration for *Finding My Voice* came from a time Lee drove with her father through a

BIOGRAPHY

MARIE G. LEE

Marie G. Lee was born in April 25, 1964, in Hibbing, Minnesota. Her parents were immigrants from Korea who came to the United States a decade earlier. Like the Sungs in *Finding My Voice*, her family was the only Korean family in town and her father worked as a doctor. Lee liked to dream and read as a child, often more than she enjoyed making friends. She was drawn to books with alienated characters, such as S. E. Hinton's *The Outsiders* (1967). Lee also began writing when she was quite young, though she did not share her stories and poems with anyone until she was much older.

Entering Brown University to become a doctor, Lee changed her academic focus and earned a degree in economics in 1986. To please her family, she then pursued a professional career, first as a consultant at Standard and Poor's, then as an editor at Goldman Sachs. Because Lee still felt drawn to writing, she began working on books, including her debut *Finding My Voice* (1992), in her spare time. By the early 1990s, Lee was focusing on writing full time. She drew on her own experiences as a Korean American to create characters who are outsiders because of their race in a number of novels for young adults and younger readers. She has published several other novels, including *If It Hadn't Been for Yoon Jun* (1993), *Necessary Roughness* (1996), *F Is for Fabuloso* (1999), and *Somebody's Daughter* (2005). As of 2006, she is a visiting lecturer at Brown University.

number of small towns in Minnesota on the way to go skiing. In one particular community, Lee observed two football players in their letterman jackets walking down the street, and she thought it would be interesting to write about such communities and the importance of the letter jacket.

In the story, Ellen's father wants her to go to Harvard, like her older sister, and become a doctor—his American dream of success. Throughout the novel, Ellen works on understanding her parents while defining herself and what success means to her, getting a boyfriend, and dealing with racism. Ellen shudders at the racist comments directed at her throughout the story, but she does next to nothing until the novel's end.

When cheerleader/star gymnast Marsha Randall's racial taunts lead to violence, Ellen finally stands up for herself. Over the course of the novel, Ellen becomes more self-confident and sure of some of the choices she is making as an individual. She does not let the physical scars from Marsha's attack deter her from leaving her Minnesota hometown, seeing the larger world, and going to Harvard.

Kirkus Reviews endorsed the book, finding that *Finding My Voice* "is filled with searing truths about day-to-day racism.... Honestly rendered, and never didactic, the story allows readers first to flinch in recognition, and then to look into their own hearts."

Finding My Voice won the Best Book Award from the Friends of American Writers. The young adult novel also received several other honors such as being named the Best Book for Reluctant Readers by the American Library Association in 1992 and a Children's Choice citation by the International Reading Association in 1994.

PLOT SUMMARY

Chapter 1

As *Finding My Voice* opens, Korean American Ellen Sung is getting ready for her first day of her last year of high school. Ellen is unhappy that her mother has included litchi nuts in her lunch. Though Ellen does not want to be different, she is grateful her mother prepared the lunch. On the way to the bus stop, however, Ellen dumps the nuts in a garbage can.

As Ellen boards the school bus, a popular boy named Brad Whitlock pushes her and says, "Hey chink, move over." No one says anything, and Ellen becomes upset by the comment. She arrives at school and meets up with her best friend Jessie. Jessie can tell something is wrong, but Ellen does not share the incident.

In chemistry class, Ellen sits with her friend Beth. Ellen also notices that Tomper, a popular jock, is in the class. He greets Ellen and later tells her he will go to her first gymnastics meet. Ellen also has Tomper and Beth in her last class of the day, English composition. In this class, Ellen has to partner with Mike Anderson, a rather unintelligent but popular hockey player, for a vocabulary project. She helps him while noting the reaction he gets in class because of his popularity.

Chapter 2

At dinner that night, Ellen feels the pressure created by the success of her older sister, Michelle. Michelle was an excellent student in high school and now attends Harvard. Ellen's parents ask her about school. She is tempted to tell them what happened on the bus and daydreams about how they would react: "With all this stress I think Ellen should worry less about grades and more about having a fun senior year and making friends," she imagines her mother saying. But she does not tell her parents about the incident. Ellen's father always eats Korean food and Ellen and her mother always eat American food.

Chapter 3

At school, Jessie wants Ellen to go to a keg party. Though Ellen thinks it will be hard to get permission to stay out late that Friday, she agrees to go. In chemistry class on Friday, Tomper asks if Ellen will be at the party. That night after dinner, Ellen gets permission to go to a movie with Jessie.

Many high school students are at the party. Tomper fills Ellen's and Jessie's cups from the keg. Jessie notes that Marsha Randall, a cheerleader and captain of the gymnastics team, and her friends are drinking V-8 juice instead of beer because of their participation in sports: "'What a bunch of showoffs, those cheerleaders,' Jessie says, probably loud enough that Marsha and her friends can hear." Ellen says that she "admire[s] how Jessie says exactly what's on her mind." When Ellen goes with Jessie to get another beer, Ellen notices that Marsha is putting beer in her V-8 can. Tomper starts talking to Ellen and guides her to a dark spot where they

can see the stars. He kisses her—her first kiss, she admits—but Ellen soon has to go home.

Chapter 4

In chemistry class on Monday, Tomper leaves before she can talk to him. He is also elusive around English class. Tomper works with Marsha on a class assignment, and Ellen notices that the two seem very friendly. In the locker room before gymnastics practice, Ellen overhears Marsha tell others that she is pursuing Tomper. "When I watch her during practice—her beautiful hair and long strong body—I can't see how Tomper could possibly like me if he can have *her*," Ellen thinks.

Chapter 5

Working in the chemistry lab, Ellen accidentally breaks a pipette. When Ellen offers to pay for it, the teacher, Mr. Borgland, tells her, "You Orientals are always trying to save money." Learning she is Korean, Borgland adds, "You Koreans WOK your dogs!" and laughs. Ellen is mortified by him and what he has said. Ellen cries as she prepares to leave school, and Jessie insists that Ellen come home with her. Learning what happened, Jessie is outraged by Borgland's racist remarks. She believes Ellen should tell the principal. Ellen will not because she believes it will not change anything. Ellen also does not want to deal with her parents' reaction.

Chapter 6

Ellen responds to Borgland's comments by studying harder and glaring at him occasionally. Ellen and Jessie are unhappy that Brad and Marsha have been selected as candidates for homecoming king and queen, but during gymnastics practice, Ellen congratulates Marsha on her nomination. The gymnastics coach, Barbara, tells Ellen that she will be competing in junior varsity in two events at the meet the next day. At the meet, Tomper and Jessie are there to show support for Ellen. She does well on the balance beam and floor events, winning the former and placing second in the latter. Ellen stays to cheer for Beth and the rest of the varsity squad. They are impressed that Marsha can perform a difficult move called a "Valdez" on the beam. After the meet, Tomper speaks to Ellen, but he leaves holding hands with Marsha. Ellen realizes that she has feelings for him. She thinks, "Books, Tomper, letter jackets, parties, friends. Where do I fit into this mess?"

Chapter 7

Mrs. Klasten, the English teacher, announces in class that Ellen has set a record: "She's gotten a perfect score on the weekly vocab tests to date—six weeks!" After class, Tomper finds Ellen and congratulates her. At home that night, Ellen shares her triumph with her parents. Her father only cares that the achievement will matter to colleges. Her parents also want to know what colleges she will visit and interview with, besides Harvard. "Father seems to be living in a universe made up of only a few neat and orderly images: books, Harvard, good grades, being a doctor or lawyer," Ellen observes. "I think of my head and its chaotic crush of ideas, worries, joys, and I wonder how I came to be so different from my father."

Chapter 8

At gymnastics practice, Ellen asks her coach to help her learn a Valdez on the low beam. After practice, Marsha walks by Ellen and says, "Hey ching-ching-a-ling. Ah-so." Ellen again feels horrible and starts to cry. Beth leaves with her. As they pass Marsha and her friend Diane again, Marsha says, "Ching chong Chinaman." Beth stands up for Ellen, but Marsha makes another racist remark. Ellen does not understand why she is being picked on and starts to feel ill.

At home, Ellen's parents are gone for the weekend. She thinks about Marsha, remembering that she heard that her tormentor is unintelligent. Ellen thinks that leaving Arkin, her hometown, will help, and she decides to apply to Harvard, Brown, and Wellesley. The next morning, Ellen snoops around her father's study. As she wonders about why their family lives in Arkin, she finds two small scrapbooks with articles about her father. She learns that her father came to America after the Korean War and had an internship in California. She also finds pictures of her father's relatives and her mother in her wedding dress as well as many letters in Korean, a language she does not read.

Chapter 9

Ellen and her mother fly east to visit the colleges. Ellen first goes to Wellesley, a women's college. While her mother stays in town, Ellen stays overnight with a student named Caitlin. Ellen observes at dinner that students focus on social lives, not classes. Ellen's mother next drives them to Boston, and Ellen goes to her interview at Harvard. During the interview, she tells her interviewer, Jeff Rose, that she is looking for a more diverse environment and that she has suffered from racial taunting. Later, Michelle gives her advice and the sisters study together in the library. Finally, Ellen and her mother drive to Rhode Island to visit Brown. This interview also goes well, and Ellen stays overnight with a student-athlete named Betsy. Flying home with her mother, Ellen is unsure which college is right for her. She thinks, "is the question where would I be happiest going or where would Mom and Father be happiest sending me?"

Chapter 10

In calculus class, Ellen realizes that she is not doing well on a test. She hopes to distract herself from her worries in gymnastics practice, but Marsha again taunts her with a racial slur. Ellen decides to say something to her coach. Ellen tells Barbara she is thinking of quitting because of what has been said to her. Barbara dismisses Ellen's concerns, saying, "I don't know what you're talking about—and you don't have to name names—but I'm sure they don't mean it." Then Barbara tells her that she might be used as an alternate on varsity in an event soon, and that she does not want her to quit. Ellen decides to stay with the team.

At home that night, Ellen is doing calculus homework when Tomper calls. She is surprised by his call, which is ostensibly about an English assignment. They talk for a few minutes and she feels happy about the attention. The next day at school, Ellen gets her calculus test back. Her grade is a D-plus, the worst grade she has ever received. She then has to give a book report in English class on *The Bell Jar*, which receives praise from both the teacher and classmates including Tomper and Mike. That night, her father asks about her calculus grade. She tells him it was a B-minus, and he tells her she will not be allowed to do gymnastics or go out until her grade is an A.

Chapter 11

At school, Ellen asks her calculus teacher for tutoring help and the sessions clarify what is unclear to her. Barbara is unhappy with Ellen's leave of absence from gymnastics. She will not guarantee a place on the team for Ellen. Though Jessie wants Ellen to go to the hockey game on Friday night, Ellen tells Jessie that her parents want her to focus on her studies. At home that night, Ellen's father wants to read her college applications before they are sent, though Ellen has already asked her English teacher for assistance. She agrees to accept his help, "because there is no other answer."

Chapter 12

Mrs. Klasten is especially impressed with the epigraph in Ellen's essay:

> Like Homer's Odysseus, my parents set sail from home to a new land. Maybe like Odysseus, one day they'll return home. But where will I go? Born on the journey, I'm not sure where I belong.

Mrs. Klasten tells Ellen that she has the talent to be a writer. Ellen insists that she wants to be a doctor. She submits the applications in December after her father reads them. He only notes that they are mistake free.

Though Ellen's parents are gone for the weekend, Ellen tells Jessie she cannot go out but has to stay home and study. Just as she starts, Tomper calls and asks if he can come over. She agrees. He finds kimchi in the refrigerator and asks if he can try it. He is impressed by the taste of the Korean dish, and he encourages Ellen to try it for the first time. She asks him about his dating Marsha, and he tells her they only went on a few dates. Tomper kisses Ellen, who tells him, "You can't just come over out of the blue and expect me to be glad you want to kiss me." He responds, "It's just so much simpler here, where it's just you and me."

Chapter 13

On Monday, Ellen has another calculus test, which she aces. That Friday, she gets permission to go out with Jessie. They get dropped off at the Pizza Palace, where they see Rocky Jukich. Jessie suggests that Rocky give them a ride to Erie, a nearby town. Rocky, the girls, and his friends meet up at a bar that they know serves underage drinkers. Playing foosball, Jessie flirts with a guy Ellen dubs "Ickyteeth." His friend Mitch becomes partners with Ellen in the game. Ellen soon wants to leave, so Ickyteeth and his friend give them a ride back to Arkin. Mitch forces a kiss on Ellen when they drop her off at her house. When Ickyteeth laughs at the situation, Jessie slugs him and gets out of the car as well.

Jessie spends the night at Ellen's house. They talk about what happened. Jessie admits to Ellen that the trip to Erie was a bad idea. Ellen thinks, "If I'm going to go to college next year, I'm thinking, I'm going to have to quit acting like such an immature little kid. If I didn't like being with those guys, I should have said something."

Chapter 14

Ellen's father allows her to return to the gymnastics team. Though Ellen competes on varsity, she does not earn a letter. Though she does not like conflict, she asks Barbara why she was not given one. Barbara tells Ellen it was because she failed to take part in enough meets and informs her that her general dedication to the team was a criterion. Ellen wonders how much more she could have done and remembers that she worked hard on school so her parents would allow her to participate in the first place. She remembers her sister's advice that good grades would make everything else all right, but she thinks, "Getting all A's didn't get me the letter jacket I wanted so badly, and it didn't protect me from some bad men in a bar. . . . I think of how all my life Mother and Father have treated good grades like the answer to life. They aren't." At home, Ellen throws away her pictures of gymnasts, hoping that her parents are right.

Chapter 15

At school, Ellen earns a 4.0 grade point average on her first semester report card. Tomper offers to help her carry her belongings home after school, then asks her on a date for Friday. Though she considers asking her parents for permission to go, Ellen chooses to lie instead. On Friday, Ellen goes to Jessie's house before the date, and Jessie helps her get ready. Tomper takes her to a movie and the Pizza Palace. When Brad sees Ellen and Tomper together, he stares at the couple "as if Tomper is bringing in his pet tarantula." Tomper kisses her at the end of the date, and says, "I don't know what took me so long, El. I must be really stupid."

Chapter 16

Ellen and Tomper continue dating. One day, Ellen's happiness is tempered because Tomper wants to talk to Ellen after school. When they meet, Tomper asks her why she is hiding him from her parents. Ellen tells him it is because Michelle did not date in high school and she does not want to risk their saying no. Tomper wants her to be honest with them. He says he will pick her up at her house on Friday for a party.

Chapter 17

Ellen waits until she's eating dinner with her parents on Friday night to tell them about Tomper. Her parents question her desire to date. Ellen says she wants to go and points out that she has earned all A's. When Tomper arrives, he is polite to Ellen's parents, but Ellen's father will not shake his hand. The parents allow them to leave together, and they go to a party for his hockey team. As Tomper and Ellen leave the party, Brad bumps into her and she thinks he makes another racist comment. At home, Ellen's parents are waiting for her and she thanks them for the opportunity. She is hurt by her father's silence, but she reminds herself that she has not done anything improper.

Chapter 18

Ellen is nervous about her college applications in the spring. She learns that she was accepted to Harvard and Wellesley, but put on a waiting list for Brown. A few weeks later, her father asks her why Ellen has not sent in her acceptance to Harvard. Ellen is unsure if she wants to go to Harvard or Wellesley. When Ellen thinks about the decision herself, she thinks about regrets over what happened during the school year with the racist remarks and decides to go to Harvard. Lee writes, *"One day, I think to myself, I will figure out how to please my parents without silencing my own voice."*

Chapter 19

At high school graduation, Beth is the valedictorian. When Ellen's name is called, a male voice among the seniors utters a racial slur. Ellen feels horrible for her parents and believes it was Brad. Her parents do not act any differently when they allow her to go to Mike's graduation party. When Ellen returns home, her father is waiting for her. He heard the comment and he tells her about the racism he and Ellen's mother experienced when they first came to the United States. Ellen's father also shares information about his own past and what made him want to come to America. Ellen comes to understand why he puts so much emphasis on grades and education. Although he graduated from Seoul National University, he tells Ellen, "soon I realized that no matter how well a person is educated in another country, an immigrant must fight for work, especially if his skin is not white."

Chapter 20

During the summer, Ellen spends much of her time with Tomper, Jessie, and Mike. One day, the four go to a drive-in movie before heading to Jessie's cabin. Ellen learns that Mike and Tomper are no longer friends with Brad because of his problem with Ellen being Asian. The four then spend the night at Jessie's cabin. Tomper and Ellen sleep in the same bed. In the morning, Ellen and Jessie talk about Jessie's future. Jessie wants to believe there is more to life than parties, marrying, and having kids.

Chapter 21

Two weeks before Ellen is set to go to Harvard, she goes to a party at Mike's cabin with Tomper and Jessie. During the party, Marsha comes up to Ellen, pushes her, and spews more racist comments. Marsha also tells her that she is not worthy of Tomper. Ellen shouts back, "You're so ignorant! You are a racist idiot!" Marsha scrapes Ellen's face with her fingernails, and Ellen punches her in the mouth. Marsha falls and then attacks Ellen with a beer bottle. Ellen does not know what happened, but finds herself on the ground. When Ellen regains consciousness, she is with her parents at the hospital the next day. Ellen has stitches all over her face from Marsha's attack. Ellen's father credits Tomper with helping manage Ellen's injuries. Ellen sees her face and is appalled by her appearance.

Chapter 22

A few days later, Ellen is back at home and her mother tells her they have to go to the police station. Ellen gives her statement, but she declines to press charges against Marsha. She tells the officer, "It's not going to change things." After Ellen's stitches are removed, she begins to pack for college. Though her parents believe she could wait a semester to enter Harvard, Ellen wants to go in the fall as planned. Her mother seems proud of her decision. A few days before her departure, Ellen says goodbye to Tomper with a date at the Sand Pits. He sheds a tear as they end their relationship. The last night before she leaves, Ellen spends time with Jessie. Jessie gives her a poem about friendship.

Chapter 23

Ellen leaves for Harvard. Her parents, Jessie, Tomper, Beth, and Mike all see her off at the airport. She waves from the plane to all of them, and she imagines them waving back as her plane

> HE WOULD NEVER TELL US WHAT LIFE WAS LIKE IN KOREA OR WHY HE AND MOM LEFT. FROM WHAT I'VE LEARNED IN MY HISTORY CLASSES, EMIGRATING FROM A COUNTRY LIKE KOREA WASN'T AS SIMPLE AS DECIDING TO GO, PACKING YOUR BAGS, AND MAKING RESERVATIONS ON THE BOAT."

rises in the sky. "After all that's happened to me this year, the pain was worth it," she thinks as she leaves Arkin.

THEMES

Assimilation

One concept explored in *Finding My Voice* is the idea of assimilation. Assimilation is the process by which one group, in this case Ellen and her family, takes on traits of and becomes part of the larger culture. Ellen's parents are natives of Korea, while their daughters were born and raised in the United States. Ellen knows little of her Korean heritage, and she cannot speak or read the language. Her parents have told her little about their past. They are the only Koreans in a town that is primarily Scandinavian in extraction, leaving them somewhat culturally and socially isolated.

Ellen's parents have assimilated less than their daughters, though Mrs. Sung is more assimilated than her husband. Ellen's father, a local doctor, insists on eating Korean food. Ellen explains, "I know that sometimes he likes to sample 'American' things, but when he does, he takes exactly one bite, one package, or whatever, because by and large he finds American food very weird." Ellen's mother prepares American-style meals for herself and Ellen, while her husband eats Korean dishes.

Ellen's mother also seems more open to new experiences, as shown when Ellen allows Tomper to pick her up for a date. Mr. Sung does not understand why his daughter would want to date in high school. He will not even shake Tomper's hand, nor will he talk to him when he

picks up Ellen. Mrs. Sung also questions Ellen's desire to date, but she is more open and welcoming to Tomper. Ellen later reveals that her mother compliments Tomper's appearance.

Ellen is the most assimilated of the three, but she also faces the most difficulties in the story. She finds it hard to fit in both at home and at school, and not just because of her parents and their different values. Ellen has become American in the sense that she does place value on participating in gymnastics and having a social life when her parents do not and cannot understand why it is important to her. But she also values hard work and is proud of her academic achievements, despite her parents' uncompromising strictness related to her academic success.

Striving for Success

Success is an important theme in *Finding My Voice*, and an important part of the American dream for Mr. Sung. Both of Ellen's parents, but especially her father, want Ellen to be academically superior, earn all A's, go to Harvard, and become a doctor. They want her to follow in the esteemed footsteps of her sister, Michelle, who is a pre-med student at Harvard, and her father, who works as a doctor in town. For much of the book, Mr. Sung only speaks to Ellen in reference to her grades, college applications, and decisions about which university to attend. Ellen does not understand why her father is so focused on her academic success.

When Ellen initially decides to go to Harvard, she is unsure if she is going for them or for herself, though she eventually embraces her attendance there as a symbol of her success. Ellen has a revelation about the matter while talking to her father after graduation. He opens up about the struggles he faced coming to the United States and having his prestigious degree from Seoul National University mean less because it is not American. He tells her, "So now you and your sister can do more than I or your mother ever could: you will graduate with degrees from Harvard, and nobody can say anything to you, because everyone knows Harvard."

Ellen explains her epiphany: "All this time I thought I was getting those grades for him and Mom. And Mom and Father just wanted to set me up for a better life." Such understanding and learning more about her parents' past from her father makes Ellen appreciate her success all the more. These feelings of self-worth come into play when she finally confronts the racism she has faced throughout the book.

Racism

If the American dream is that anyone can succeed, its dark shadow is that some people will always try to hold others down. That ugly truth reveals itself in the racist remarks directed at Ellen throughout the novel. While she is an American and the United States is the only country she has ever known, her classmates and even a few educators remind her that she is racially different from them, as the only Asian in a school full of white students. All the racist remarks made by students like Brad and Marsha, as well as the chemistry teacher, refer to Ellen's Asian heritage, though most are derogatory terms for natives of China, not Korea.

Ellen is confused by the racist comments and nearly always reacts to them by shutting down. Jessie and Beth stand up for her when an incident happens in front of them, but it is not until Ellen has experienced personal growth in the book that she stands up to a tormentor herself. When Ellen does take Marsha on shortly before she is to leave for Harvard, she finds herself in a physical fight. At its end, Marsha injures Ellen by breaking a bottle on her head, which leaves Ellen with outward scars showing the inner pain she has suffered. Ellen does not let Marsha's attack limit her or change her decision to go to Harvard in the fall, nor does she press charges against Marsha because she does not think it will transform Marsha or the racist thoughts of others. The racism Ellen experiences makes her more determined to succeed and ultimately more sure of who she is.

HISTORICAL OVERVIEW

Korean Americans in the United States

The first significant numbers of Koreans came to the United States in 1903, with about eight thousand Koreans going to work on Hawaiian sugar plantations between 1903 and 1905. Immigration numbers had an early peak during and after the Korean War in the early 1950s, when many students, orphans left parentless by the war, and wives of servicemen were allowed to immigrate to the United States.

More Koreans, and Asians in general, began moving to America in large numbers when immigration policies were reformed with the Immigration and Naturalization Act of 1965. The number of immigrants from North and South Korea continued to increase in the 1970s through the 1990s, and often included entire families due to the changes in immigration law. By the 1990 census, nearly 800,000 Korean Americans were living in the United States, with about 73 percent born in Korea. About one-tenth of these people were also adoptees primarily raised by white families and without Korean names.

The greatest concentration of Americans with a Korean heritage could be found in several major cities including Los Angeles and Anaheim, California; New York City; Washington, D.C.; and Chicago, Illinois. Significant numbers of Korean Americans also lived in New Jersey, Texas, and Maryland. Some of the bigger cities had Korean-focused communities or neighborhoods, so-called "Koreatowns." Because these "Koreatowns" were often in depressed parts of these cities, Korean American businesses and consumers often helped rejuvenate such neighborhoods.

Many Koreans came to the United States looking for personal freedom and better economic opportunities for themselves and their children. Because Koreans often immigrated as whole families in the late twentieth century, there were often different rates of assimilation within families. Korean-born parents often were slower to adopt the American culture, and they continued to embrace Korean values and speak their native language. Their children were often more Americanized and used English as their primary language. Such a dichotomy sometimes lead to intergenerational conflicts within families about cultural identity.

By the early 1990s, Korean Americans were making an impact on American culture in small, but significant, ways. In 1992, the first Korean American was elected to Congress when Chang-Jun "Jay" Kim was elected to represent the state of California. He was born in Seoul, South Korea, in 1939, and came to the United States in 1961. Kim previously served on the city council and as mayor of Diamond Bar, California. Two years later, comedian Margaret Cho became the first Korean American to star in her own television series, the short-lived situation comedy *All-American Girl*. In 1995, Chang-rae Lee became the first Korean American writer to receive the PEN/Hemingway Award.

CRITICAL OVERVIEW

Like many of Lee's novels, *Finding My Voice* was generally well received when it was published in 1992. It has been praised for being one of the first such books to represent the experience of an Asian American young adult. Writing in *Kliatt*, Barbara Shepp calls the book "well-written" and "believable." She concludes, "It has a mature and sensitive presentation of many teen issues, a likable main character, and a satisfying resolution that does not rely on pat answers."

A number of critics were moved by the depiction of Ellen, as well as the relationship between Ellen and her parents. The *Publishers Weekly* reviewer comments, "If Lee's story line is somewhat familiar, her portrayal of her heroine is unusually well-balanced." While Libby K. White of *School Library Journal* calls Ellen a "likable, gentle teen," she is one critic who finds that "The portrayal of her parents is not as satisfying." However, White does commend the way Lee depicts their evolution in the face of Ellen's social and personal growth.

The themes of *Finding My Voice* and Lee's handling of them also garnered critical acclaim. Writing in the *Bulletin of the Center for Children's Books*, Betsy Hearne notes that "Lee has detailed the strain of ethnic 'difference' ... and the insecurity it breeds." Penny Blubaugh of *Voice of Youth Advocates* says, "This is a sensitive coming-of-age story that should provoke anger and thought."

CRITICISM

A. Petruso

Petruso is a freelance writer who has degrees in history and screenwriting. In this essay, Petruso argues that most of the white characters in Finding My Voice *are profoundly undeveloped and presented with an element of reverse racism.*

Marie G. Lee's *Finding My Voice* resonates with readers who have been hurt by racism, but it is less likely to spark any recognition or enlightenment among readers who may have inflicted those injuries. In Melinda L. de Jesús's article "Mixed Blessings: Korean American Identity and Interracial Interactions in the Young Adult Novels of Marie G. Lee," she analyzes four of Lee's young adult books, including *Finding My*

> WHILE LEE ACCOMPLISHES HER GOAL IN SHOWING READERS HOW THROWN OFF ELLEN IS BY SPOKEN RACIAL SLIGHTS, BORGLUND IS MERELY A CARICATURE OF A CASUAL RACIST, NOT A FULLY FORMED CHARACTER."

Voice. De Jesús praises Lee's depiction of Korean Americans and their identity through the filter of teen drama. However, de Jesús also notes a flaw in Lee's books, claiming "While her Asian American readers will most likely find much to identify with in her novels, non–Asian American readers of color cannot help but notice how her non-Asian characters remain largely undeveloped." Later in the same article, the critic comments, "Asian American children will be empowered by these novels—but what will they learn about non-Asian teens of color from Lee's works?"

These exact critiques do not seem to apply to *Finding My Voice* because there are no non-white characters depicted therein save Ellen Sung and her family. However, de Jesús's observed flaw of Lee's books applies to *Finding My Voice* as well because Lee's white characters are extremely flat and undeveloped. They often act without motivation and Lee does not give any sense of their background. Because the novel is told from Ellen's first-person point of view, the development of the other characters is necessarily sifted through her perspective. But as an author, Lee does not work in much detail about any character except Ellen. Even Ellen's parents are portrayed nearly as superficially as Ellen's friends, fellow students, educators, and tormentors.

One element of the story weakened by Lee's shallow characterizations is the racism Ellen experiences. In an article published in the *ALAN Review*, Lee writes,

> I wrote *Finding My Voice* with the hope that it would be interesting not only to the teen who has ever felt different and/or been a victim of harassment, but also the teen who might potentially be the harasser. I want readers to know, through the character of Ellen, that behind every racial slur there's a person.

Readers of *Finding My Voice* know almost nothing about why the harassers pick on Ellen, other than because of her different race. Though behind every speaker of racist remarks there is also a person, readers would not know this fact from the way Lee depicts them in her book.

There is no explanation for the motivation of one of the adults who says racial slurs to Ellen. At the beginning of chapter 5, Mr. Borglund, Ellen's chemistry teacher, makes remarks about "Orientals," the way they handle money, and Koreans "woking" dogs to her after she breaks a pipette and offers to pay for it. This incidence of racism comes out of nowhere because readers have no knowledge of who Mr. Borglund is other than a high school chemistry teacher. Is he just ignorant? Having a bad day? Reacting to some ancient hurt of his own? He is never shown saying anything racist again, and it is hard to understand what his motivation is for speaking that way to her. While Lee accomplishes her goal in showing readers how stunned Ellen is by spoken racial slights, Borglund is merely a caricature of a casual racist, not a fully formed character.

Among Ellen's peers, there are two fellow students who use racial slurs to and about her. Brad Whitlock is depicted in much the same way as Borglund. Brad is a popular high school senior who suddenly starts calling Ellen "chink" on the bus the first day of school. Ellen admits she is befuddled by Brad's remark, thinking of the comment and who said it: "And why Brad Whitlock, the popular guy who had never before even bothered to acknowledge my existence all these years at Arkin High?" Readers are left to wonder as well.

Brad repeats his racist phrase several times, including at their high school graduation. At the beginning of chapter 16, he is depicted confronting Tomper about dating Ellen. Tomper's friend and Jessie's boyfriend Mike tells Ellen in chapter 20 that Brad told Tomper that he should not date Ellen because of her race. Mike admits he initially rationalized Brad's behavior. After believing that his long-time hockey buddy was "just playing around," Mike tells Ellen he had an epiphany: "After I got to know you, Ellen, and saw what a nice girl you are, I started realizing that Brad really did mean a lot of what he said, that he really did hate."

These scenes are the sum of Lee's depiction of Brad and his racism. Readers have no idea why Brad feels this way or what his motivation is for abruptly starting to pick on Ellen. There is no information on his background or the pressures and insecurities he might feel because of her. Arkin is depicted as a homogenous community, yet readers have no idea where Brad fits in in terms of social class, parental influence, academic and emotional intelligence, and the like. Lee depicts him like a dog who has suddenly gone mad and picked one target, Ellen, on the first day of school.

The reasons for Marsha's racist remarks and negative attitude toward Ellen may be a bit clearer than Mr. Borglund's and Brad's. Marsha is a talented gymnast, cheerleader, and homecoming-queen candidate. The first instance of Marsha's racism against Ellen occurs in chapter 8 after gymnastics practice. Ellen has started learning a difficult move called a "Valdez," which Marsha had been the only gymnast on the team to perform until then. After Ellen has some success with Marsha's prized move, Marsha insults her with several remarks related to Ellen's race. Marsha later cuts Ellen down with racist remarks after another gymnastics practice when Ellen stands in her way.

In addition being threatened about competition from Ellen in gymnastics, Marsha is jealous of Ellen over Tomper's attention. After learning that Tomper kissed Ellen at the party in chapter 3, Marsha begins pursuing him, and Tomper and Marsha date briefly. Marsha's racial taunts turn to physical violence after Tomper and Ellen become romantically involved, in a violent fight with Ellen at the book's climax in chapter 21. While painful to Ellen, Marsha's racism is at least framed more realistically than anyone else's in the book. Marsha is a girl who acts out against Ellen because of resentment, insecurity, and jealousy.

Lee's depiction of Marsha's racism touches on another issue in *Finding My Voice*: Ellen's own jealousy. Ellen finds Marsha pretty, and often comments on Marsha's perfectly beautiful appearance while putting herself down in comparison. Ellen is jealous of Marsha's appearance as well as her athletic talent. One reason for Marsha's success in gymnastics, Ellen reveals at the beginning of chapter 8, is that Marsha has been doing gymnastics since she was a kindergartener, while Ellen's parents did not allow her to start gymnastics until the ninth grade. Ellen clearly finds plenty to admire about her nemesis.

In other ways, Ellen feel superior to Marsha, and indeed to their fellow students. At the party in chapter 3, Jessie tells Ellen that Marsha could not complete basic math problems like dividing fractions. Later, Lee reveals that Marsha wanted to study to be a dental hygienist but could not get into a program. Most of the white characters are depicted as lazy, stupid, and/or directionless. With the exception of Beth, none of Ellen's peers is academically motivated or regarded as intelligent. Throughout *Finding My Voice*, Lee implies no white student is interested in going to college other than hockey players going on to pursue their sport, and Beth, the only person regarded as Ellen's academic and intellectual equal. Beth is the only other girl in Ellen's calculus class and a whiz at the subject. Beth is also Ellen's lab partner in chemistry, her friend on the gymnastics team, and the class valedictorian.

Ellen's best friend Jessie is a talented pianist, but she plans to go to business college instead of pursuing music as a career. Ellen sees Mike Anderson as a hockey player with no brains, and she judges him for it: "*He might be popular,* I'm thinking, *but he's sure not much to look at in the I.Q. department.*" Mike is redeemed somewhat by dating Jessie, revealing he regrets the incident on the bus with Brad, and by no longer being friends with Brad. Mike and Jessie talk of getting married, and Ellen knows their lack of ambition for anything beyond small-town will end their friendship soon.

Other than Beth, Jessie, and Mike—none of whom has ambitions as grand as Ellen's dreams of being a Harvard-educated doctor—it seems that no one in Ellen's class is going to college. Tomper, Ellen's boyfriend, plans to join the army like his father did. While Arkin might be a simple small town, it is hard to believe that there are not children who are interested in discovering and fulfilling their potential. Not to mention others who are motivated for their children to have a better life through a college education. Such depictions make the novel unbelievable, and while perhaps intended to increase sympathy for Ellen, they make her isolation seem more self-imposed than a cruel twist of fate.

Lee also depicts Ellen and her family as academic and social superiors. No other parents mentioned in the book—and only a few parents are mentioned at all—support their children or encourage them in any way. For example, Jessie gets access to liquor after she graduates and is never depicted as being supervised. Her mother was killed by a teenage drunk driver some time earlier, and Jessie's father does not seem to play an active role in her life. Tomper's parents allow him to smoke as his older brothers did, tell him only to stay out of jail, and do not encourage any kind of academic success. When Tomper comes over to Ellen's home in chapter 12, he reports having to make Rice-a-roni by himself at the age of five.

Lee is obviously trying to highlight cultural differences between the Sung family and the white people in town, but there is no balance to her portrayal. There are success-oriented white parents everywhere, although some value other measures of success besides academics and prestigious colleges. This depiction of white parents as disengaged is highlighted by the conspicuous absence of Beth's parents in the novel, even though she is an academic achiever and a friend of Ellen's. Ellen says that her parents do not value her participation in gymnastics at all because they do not understand how it fits into her getting into Harvard. Do Beth's parents support her at gymnastics meets or her academic triumphs? Do they encourage her and support her? Adding such details would have added balance to the depiction of white parents in Lee's novel.

The bigger point in *Finding My Voice* is that Ellen cannot know or understand others until she comes to know herself, finds her voice, and accepts its power. Yet readers are taken on this journey of self-discovery without a road map of understanding the white people in Arkin who live around Ellen and her family. Lee could have shown that being an American is more than being white and popular and perfect in the backdrop of the novel. Lee also had a chance to show that even the popular people who are white and seem perfect face the same kinds of challenges Ellen does.

Ellen learns to stand up for herself to her parents and to Marsha, yet readers have no framework to understand why Marsha and Brad emerge as racist cowards. It is satisfying that in the end Ellen embraces Harvard and becoming a doctor as her own dream, a dream whose seed was planted by her parents, whom she comes to appreciate. Perhaps Lee hints at why she draws such superficial characterizations of everyone else through the words of Mrs. Klasten, the

English teacher who encourages Ellen to write: "books . . . give you only the words; you have to use your imagination for the rest."

Source: A. Petruso, Critical Essay on *Finding My Voice*, in *Literary Themes for Students: American Dream*, Gale, 2007.

SOURCES

Blubaugh, Penny, Review of *Finding My Voice*, in *Voice of Youth Advocates*, December 1992, p. 282.

De Jesús, Melinda, "Mixed Blessings: Korean American Identity and Interracial Interactions in the Young Adult Novels of Marie G. Lee," in *Children's Literature Association Quarterly*, Vol. 28, No. 2, 2003, pp. 98–109.

Hearne, Betsy, Review of *Finding My Voice*, in the *Bulletin of the Center for Children's Books*, Vol. 46, No. 2, October 1992, pp. 47–48.

Lee, Marie G., "Autobiographical Sketch," *Eighth Book of Junior Authors and Illustrators*, edited by Connie C. Rockman, H. W. Wilson, 2000, vnweb.hwwilsonweb. com (August, 26, 2006).

———, *Finding My Voice*, Houghton Mifflin Company, 1992.

———, "How I Grew," in the *ALAN Review*, Vol. 22, No. 2, Winter 1995, scholar.lib.vt.edu/ejournals/ALAN/ winter95/Lee.html (November 3, 2005).

Review of *Finding My Voice*, in *Kirkus Reviews*, September 15, 1992.

Review of *Finding My Voice*, in *Publishers Weekly*, Vol. 239, No. 30, July 6, 1992, p. 57.

Shepp, Barbara, Review of *Finding My Voice*, in *Kliatt*, Vol. 29, No. 1, January 1995, p. 9.

White, Libby K., Review of *Finding My Voice*, in *School Library Journal*, Vol. 38, No. 10, October 1992, pp. 143–44.

The Grapes of Wrath

JOHN STEINBECK

1939

The Grapes of Wrath (1939) shines light into the darkest corners of the American dream. It is John Steinbeck's greatest novel and an undisputed American classic, but upon publication, the book garnered immediate attention and fierce controversy. It soared to the top of bestseller lists, sold almost half a million hardcover copies, and received scores of positive reviews. A year later, the book was awarded the Pulitzer Prize. An indicator of its enduring significance is the fact that, since its publication, *The Grapes of Wrath* has sold more than fifteen million copies.

Steinbeck was inspired to write the novel after researching and producing a series of articles for the *San Francisco News* about migrant workers in California. He reported on the hundreds of thousands of families that fled drought- and dust-ravaged farms in the Midwest to earn money as fruit, vegetable, and cotton pickers in California's fertile fields. Masses of fleeing workers endured a treacherous trek west only to find little work and unfair wages when they arrived. The onslaught of desperate, poverty-stricken people created a situation of unrivaled tension, violence, and want. Steinbeck saw the germ of an epic story and began taking notes and plotting its development while he wrote the seven newspaper articles he had been assigned to write.

Steinbeck's masterpiece is more than a tale of the plight of migrant farm workers, though. It

is, according to critic Robert DeMott, "part naturalistic epic, part labor testament, part family chronicle, part partisan journalism, part environmental jeremiad, part captivity narrative, part road novel, part transcendental gospel." In the introduction to the 2006 Penguin Classics edition, DeMott quotes a radio interview in 1939, in which Steinbeck explained,

> Boileau said that Kings, Gods, and Heroes only were fit subjects for literature. The writer can only write about what he admires. Present day kings aren't very inspiring, the gods are on a vacation, and about the only heroes left are the scientists and the poor. . . . And since our race admires gallantry, the writer will deal with it where he finds it. He finds it in the struggling poor now.

Part of what makes *The Grapes of Wrath* such an enduring success is the fact that as history and culture evolve and change, Steinbeck's novel, an ode to the gallant struggling poor, remains steadily and forcefully relevant. Americans still go hungry in a land of great riches. Americans still seek spiritual comfort and the hope that it brings. Americans still understand that if one human suffers, we all suffer. More specifically and somewhat shockingly, migrant farm workers still struggle to make ends meet by doing backbreaking work in unsafe conditions for very little money. Over the decades, *The Grapes of Wrath* has been named by such cultural luminaries as Edward R. Murrow, César Chávez, and Bruce Springsteen as a critical influence on their professional and personal lives. Gerald Haslam, a California writer, says, "The great, the ennobling theme of Steinbeck's work—we are a human family, together in this, and collectively we can transcend life's challenges—reached into me and stretched my soul."

In fact, the novel had an immediate and intense impact on American political affairs at the time of its publication. Steinbeck was branded a communist and a troublemaker by California landowners seeking to discredit his work. Oklahoman political leaders sought to ban *The Grapes of Wrath* for its supposed derogatory view of migrant workers. Others saw the raw, rough language spoken by its protagonists as profane and attempted to censor it. Despite what its detractors had to say, and continue to say about it, *The Grapes of Wrath* is etched into America's collective literary and cultural conscience, while

BIOGRAPHY

JOHN STEINBECK

John Ernst Steinbeck was born on February 27, 1902, in Salinas, California, to parents of modest means. Steinbeck spent childhood summers working as a hired ranch hand, which gave the future author a profound appreciation for the California landscape and its people. Although he took a series of writing and literature courses at Stanford University from 1919 until 1925, he never earned a degree. While living in New York City and working on his first novel, *Cup of Gold*, Steinbeck worked as a laborer and journalist. After the novel was published in 1929, Steinbeck and his new wife moved to Pacific Grove, California, where the author continued to write and publish. Not until the publication of *Tortilla Flat* in 1935 was Steinbeck able to claim financial security and popular success as a writer. The late 1930s found the author writing about the California labor class in *In Dubious Battle* (1936), *Of Mice and Men* (1937), and the novel many consider his finest work, *The Grapes of Wrath* (1939). The book was awarded the Pulitzer Prize in 1940 and served as the basis for the decision to award Steinbeck the Nobel Prize for Literature in 1962. He wrote a total of seventeen novels and was nominated for an Academy Award for screenwriting in his career. Steinbeck died on December 20, 1968, of heart disease in New York City.

the controversy it once created is little more than a footnote.

PLOT SUMMARY

Chapter 1

The Oklahoma soil becomes cracked and parched during a long summer drought. The cornfields dry up and the wind fills the air with dust. The ruined crops lay covered in dust and

John Steinbeck AP Images

the men become silent. Their wives and children look to see if the men will break and are relieved to see that they are "hard and angry and resistant," a sure sign that they will not break.

Chapter 2

Tom Joad has just been released from the McAlester State Penitentiary where he served four years for killing a man. Wearing stiff new clothes, he convinces a driver with a "No Riders" sign on his car to drive him a short way to his family's farm. Having been away and out of touch with his family for the length of his sentence, he is unaware of the fact that most farmers in the area have either been "dusted out" or "tractored out" of their farms. The driver tells him, "Croppers going fast now. . . . One cat' takes and shoves ten families out." The driver talks about how lonely it gets on the road and asks Tom about himself. Tom admits that he has been in prison. "Homicide. . . . That's a big word—means I killed a guy. Seven years. I'm sprung in four for keepin' my nose clean." The driver lets him out along a dirt road leading to the Joad farm.

Chapter 3

A turtle makes its way along the scorching highway. A woman swerves to avoid the creature, but a man in a truck aims to hit it. The turtle flips over, rolls off the highway, and resumes its journey.

Chapter 4

Tom discovers the turtle, wraps it in his coat, and carries it with him. He comes upon a tattered old man that he recognizes as Jim Casy, the preacher who baptized Tom when he was a boy. Casy relates the story of how he decided to stop preaching, saying that his habit of taking girls "out in the grass" after church caused him to feel so conflicted, he began to doubt his faith. After much thought, Casy decides, "Maybe all men got one big soul ever'body's a part of."

Tom tells Casy why he went to jail: "I killed a guy in a fight. We was drunk at a dance. He got a knife in me, an' I killed him with a shovel that was layin' there. Knocked his head plumb to squash." He talks about the niceties of prison, clean clothes and regular meals, and tells a story about a fellow inmate who preferred the conveniences of the jail to life on the outside. When Tom prepares to move on, Casy asks if he can come along. Tom welcomes him, saying his family always thought highly of the man when he was their preacher. When they get to the Joad place they find it deserted.

Chapter 5

Because the farms are tenant-farmed, they are not owned by the farmers that live on them. This means that the landowners and the banks have the right to evict the farmers from the land. They come onto the land and tell the "tenant men" they have to get off the land. "The tenant system won't work any more. One man on a tractor can take the place of twelve or fourteen families," the narrator explains. Some owners are cruel, some are kind, but they all come bearing the same bad news. When the farmers ask what they are supposed to do, the owners suggest they head west to California where there is work. Tractors driven by neighbors earning three dollars a day arrive on the land. They have orders to plow down the property, including the house, whether the farmers have left or not. When the displaced farmer asks who gave the orders to plow his land, that he wants to shoot him, he is told, "I don't know. Maybe there's nobody to shoot.

Maybe the thing isn't men at all. Maybe, like you said, the property's doing it."

Chapter 6

When Tom and Casy find the Joad homestead untouched they assume the neighbors have abandoned the area, too. Muley Graves comes along and explains what has happened to the Joad homestead. He tells Tom that some company has bought up all the land in the area and kicked out all the farmers. He says that Tom's whole family is living with Tom's Uncle John, picking cotton in hopes of earning enough money to buy a car and drive to California. Muley shares the rabbits he has caught with Tom and Casy and, after they eat, they go to the cave where Muley sleeps. They have to be careful the police do not catch them on the land and arrest them for trespassing. Tom is bewildered by the idea of being arrested for sleeping on his own farm and Casy is unable to sleep for thinking of all he has learned that night.

Chapter 7

This section is narrated by a used car salesman. He describes the many ways he cheats poor families seeking transportation for their trek westward. He brags about filling engines full of sawdust to hide transmission problems and replacing working batteries with cracked ones. The farmers are easily duped as they know little about cars and are desperate to buy.

Chapter 8

Casy, Muley, and Tom walk the several miles to Uncle John's house. On the way, Tom describes his uncle's guilt about not calling a doctor when his pregnant wife complained of stomach pains many years prior. When she died, he blamed himself and has never been able to get over the loss. To repent, he performs random acts of generosity, like giving candy to children and bags of meal to needy neighbors. These acts do nothing to assuage his guilt.

Tom is reunited with his family at Uncle John's. Neither of his parents recognizes him at first, and both then express their fear that he has broken out of jail. He explains that he has been paroled and that he will be able to join them on their trip to California. His mother asks, "They didn't do nothin' in that jail to rot you out with crazy mad?" He answers, "I was for a little while. But I ain't proud like some fellas. I let stuff run off'n me." He greets fiery Grampa and Granma Joad and slow brother Noah and they gather to share a breakfast that Casy blesses with a non-traditional prayer. After they eat, Pa Joad shows Tom the truck Tom's younger brother Al helped him pick out. The sixteen-year-old arrives soon after, full of admiration for Tom. Tom learns that his youngest siblings, Ruthie and Winfield, have gone to town with Uncle John and that their sister, Rose of Sharon, has married a neighbor boy, Connie, and is expecting her first child.

Chapter 9

This very short chapter describes how "tenant people" go about preparing for the trek to California. They face the heartbreaking task of deciding which of "their belongings and the belongings of their fathers and their grandfathers" to leave behind or sell to raise money for the trip. The farmers are forced to accept ridiculously low sums for farm equipment and good work horses because the buyers understand that the desperate men are in no position to demand more. Even the most sentimental items must be left behind, sold, or destroyed before the families leave their farms for good.

Chapter 10

Ma Joad tells Tom she is worried about what the family will find in California, although she trusts what the handbill she read says about their being able to find work. Pa Joad returns from town feeling dejected after selling off the family's belongings for a mere eighteen dollars. The family gathers and decides to take Casy with them on the trip. They do not see any point in waiting to pack, so they set about the task immediately. First, they slaughter the pigs and pack the meat in salt. Casy offers to help Ma pack the meat, but she claims it is woman's work. He replies, "They's too much of it split it up to men's or women's work. You got stuff to do." Connie and Rose of Sharon arrive, and the family prepares to leave, then Grampa claims he plans to stay and live off the land. The family laces his coffee with a sleeping tonic, waits until he has fallen asleep, then loads him onto the truck along with the rest of the family and all that they own. Their journey westward begins.

Chapter 11

The land is vacant once the farmers abandon it. Men on tractors come and work the land, but they have no connection to it. "The machine man, driving a dead tractor on land he does not know and love, understands only chemistry; and he is contemptuous of the land and of himself." Gophers, field mice, weasels, cats, and brown owls take over the abandoned farmhouses, which quickly fall apart.

Chapter 12

Highway 66 is packed with families headed to California. They are cheated by salesmen when they try and buy car parts and are met with hostility when they stop at service stations for gas and water. But they also witness moments of hopeful beauty. "The people in flight from the terror behind—strange things happen to them, some bitterly cruel and some so beautiful that the faith is refired forever."

Chapter 13

Tom's brother Al, a skilled mechanic, drives the battered and overloaded Hudson, "every nerve listening for weaknesses, for the thumps or squeals, hums and chattering that indicate a change that may cause a breakdown." Al becomes "the soul of the car." When the family stops to rest, their dog gets hit by a car. Rose of Sharon worries that witnessing something so violent will hurt her unborn child. At the end of a long first day of driving, the Joads pull into a ditch to camp beside Ivy and Sairy Wilson, a couple whose car has broken down. The couple is hospitable and warm, and the Joads are grateful for their kindness. Sairy invites Grampa, who has taken ill, to come and rest in their tent. He dies of a stroke while Casy prays over him and the family is forced to bury the old man along the roadside. Al fixes the Wilsons' car and the two families agree to travel to California together.

Chapter 14

Westerners are nervous about the change they feel coming. The "hunger in the stomach, multiplied a million times" is the cause; the result is a mass migration upon their land. The influx of hundreds of thousands of hungry farmers threaten those "who hate change and fear revolution" because they know that the weak, when united with others like themselves, become strong. "The danger is here, for two men are not as lonely and perplexed as one."

Chapter 15

A waitress named Mae and a cook named Al work at a coffee shop along Highway 66. Mae looks forward to the truckers who stop, for they make her laugh, do not steal, and leave the biggest tips. Two of her favorites stop in for pie and coffee and they talk about the mass migration of Midwesterners on the road. A ragged man and two small boys come in asking to buy a loaf of bread for a dime. Mae initially rebuffs the man, saying she needed the bread for sandwiches. Besides, the loaf would cost him fifteen cents. After Al growls at her to give him the loaf, she gives in and takes ten cents for it. The grimy, tired children eye the candy case and their father asks if the "stripy ones" are penny candy. She gives him two for a penny even though they really cost a nickel each. The truck drivers notice her generosity and leave her a huge tip.

Chapter 16

The Joads and the Wilsons drove for so long, "the highway became their home and movement their medium of expression." After three days on the road, the Wilsons' car breaks down again. Tom and Al leave the family to wait for them while they find parts in a car lot in town. Once they find the parts and fix the car, they make their way to a campsite where everyone can rest for the night. A ragged, bitter man tells an assembled group of campers that he is on his way back East after a disastrous experience in California. Although they've been warned they will not find work, Casy tells Pa that the Joads' experience will be different.

Chapter 17

The many families driving the same road and camping along the same springs begin to form little communities. "In the evening a strange thing happened: the twenty families became one family, the children were the children of all." Codes of behavior, laws, and leaders emerge as well as methods of enforcing those laws.

Chapter 18

The Joads and the Wilsons arrive in Needles, California, and pull up to an encampment beside a river. They still have to make their way across the desert before they get to fertile picking fields, so they decide to stop and rest before moving on. While bathing in the river, a father and son tell the men that they are headed back to where they came from as they cannot earn a living in California. They warn the newcomers that the natives will treat them badly and call them "Okies," which "use' ta mean you was from Oklahoma. Now it means you're a dirty son-of-a-bitch. Okie means you're scum." Noah tells Tom that he is not leaving the river, that he will "catch fish an' stuff" to survive. Ma Joad and Rose of Sharon watch over Granma in a makeshift tent because she is sick and hallucinating. A policeman pokes his head in and rudely demands that they move on. The intrusion is very upsetting to Ma, who becomes even more upset after Tom tells her that Noah has left the family to live by the river. When the Joads pack up to cross the desert that night, they are forced to leave the Wilsons behind due to Sairy's failing health. When the family is stopped for a routine inspection, Ma begs the officer to let them go on as her mother is deathly ill. Once they arrive in the valley, Ma tells the family that Granma died early on in the journey. She had lain with the body all the way through the night.

Chapter 19

Once California belonged to Mexico, but American squatters, hungry for land, stole it away from the Mexicans. Once they owned it, they "imported slaves, although they did not call them slaves: Chinese, Japanese, Mexicans, Filipinos," to work it, then paid them slave wages. Then the Okies came and the "soft" California landowners became afraid and their fear turned to hate for the "strong" Okies: "perhaps the owners had heard from their grandfathers how easy it is to steal land from a soft man if you are fierce and hungry and armed." But the Okies only want to feed their families. They plant secret gardens in fallow fields so their children can eat, but when the plants are discovered by deputies, they are destroyed.

Chapter 20

Ma and Pa Joad are forced to leave Granma's body at the coroner's office because they cannot afford to give her a proper burial. They set up camp at a "Hooverville" where they are treated rudely. Tom meets Floyd, who echoes what Tom has heard all along the way: There are no jobs. Floyd warns Tom that anyone who suggests organizing against the landowners will be arrested, labeled a "red," and placed on a blacklist, which ensures the agitator will never find a job. When a contractor arrives seeking workers, Floyd demands a guaranteed wage and a signed contract, an act of defiance that gets him arrested. When he runs off, the deputy shoots, and hits a woman's hand. Casy knocks the deputy unconscious and takes the blame for the scuffle when the police arrive. Casy is taken to jail and the sheriff tells everyone they have to

clear out as the camp is scheduled to be burned that night. Connie leaves without telling the family, Uncle John gets drunk, and the family prepares to depart. Rose of Sharon is heartbroken that they have to leave without her husband.

Chapter 21

"The moving, questing people were migrants now." The hostility they face in this new land unites them. The Californians band together in an effort to keep the Okies in their place, but that only makes the migrants angrier.

Chapter 22

The remaining Joads find Weedpatch camp, a government facility where migrants live and govern themselves. Exhausted by the events of the day, they settle into their assigned spot in the dark of night. Tom wakes up first, has breakfast with his neighbors, and walks to their worksite where he is hired to dig a ditch with them. When the rest of the family wakes up, they find their new "home" boasts clean grounds and working toilets and showers, niceties the family has never before experienced. The camp manager visits Ma Joad after the men leave to find work. He is very kind to her, which lifts her spirits and makes her feel like a human being again. The Ladies Committee welcomes Ma and Rose of Sharon to the camp by showing them around and explaining the rules. Pa, Uncle John, and Al look for work all day, but return home unsuccessful.

Chapter 23

Migrant people, despite their many hardships, find little ways to amuse themselves and find some semblance of pleasure. They tell stories and jokes, play music, get drunk, and attend prayer meetings. "The migrant people looked humbly for pleasure on the roads."

Chapter 24

Weedpatch camp officials have been warned that the Farmers' Association plans to infiltrate the Saturday night dance, start a riot, and shut the camp down. The chairman of the camp committee hires a band of men to preempt the riot. Tom is one of those men. The night of the dance, the riot is successfully squelched before it has a chance to start and the guilty instigators are thrown out of the camp without incident. Pa says, "They's change a-comin'. I don' know what. Maybe we won't live to see her. But she's a-comin'." To that, one of the campers relates a story about how when five thousand mountain men in Akron, Ohio, joined a union, the city people threatened to run them out of town. The mountain men demonstrated by marching through town with their rifles on the way to a turkey shoot, and marching back through town when they were finished. "Well, sir, they ain't been no trouble sence then." The storyteller suggests they "git up a turkey shootin' club an' have meetin's ever' Sunday," but nobody responds.

Chapter 25

When large landowners monopolize farming, they ruin more than the lives of the migrants. Unable to compete, small local farmers watch their crops fail or go unpicked because they cannot afford to pay anyone to do it. Their debts mount as the crops decay on the ground. "In the souls of the people the grapes of wrath are filling and growing heavy, growing heavy for the vintage."

Chapter 26

The Joads have lived in the government camp for almost a month. Work and food are scarce, so Ma Joad decides the family should leave the next morning and look for work elsewhere. While preparing to leave, a man stops to tell them of peach-picking work up the road. When they arrive, they find mobs of angry people and are told they will be paid just five cents for each box of peaches picked. They are desperate, so they take the job. The entire family picks all day and earns a dollar, which must be spent on food for their dinner that evening. After a meager meal, Tom goes to see what the commotion along the roadside is all about. He finds Casy, who explains that workers are striking in opposition of the two-and-a-half cent per box wage they were being paid. The police come, recognize Casy as the leader of the workers, call him a communist, and kill him by smashing his head with a pick handle. Enraged, Tom picks up the weapon, hits Casy's murderer, then flees after being hit in the face. He makes it back to the family tent and relates the story of what happened when they wake up and discover his wounds the next morning. He is afraid he may have killed Casy's attacker. Ma Joad hides Tom in the back of the truck and they leave the peach farm. About twenty miles down the road, Al sees a sign that says, "Cotton Pickers Wanted." They

park the truck in a ditch away from a row of railroad boxcars that cotton pickers live in. Tom leaves the family to hide out in a culvert down the way and tells Ma to leave food for him whenever she can.

Chapter 27

Migrants hired to pick cotton must buy cotton-picking sacks for a dollar. Before they even pick one boll, they are already in debt. Sometimes there are so many pickers in one field, workers are unable to pick enough to pay for the sack. To counter the crooked owners who rig the scales, workers sometimes load their sack with rocks.

Chapter 28

The job picking cotton provides the Joads a boxcar to live in and more money than they have had in some time. They have enough to buy new clothes, a tin stove, and meat for supper every night. Ruthie accidentally reveals to another child that her brother killed a man and is hiding out in the woods. Afraid that word will get around, Ma Joad finds Tom and tells him that his secret has been exposed. Although it breaks her heart, she is afraid he will be caught and urges him to leave. He tells her he has decided to organize the people like Casy was doing when he was killed, and for her not to worry about him. The Wainwrights and the Joads celebrate the news that Al Joad and Agnes Wainwright plan to wed. The next morning, the two families arrive at a fresh, twenty-acre cotton field only to find a huge gathering of migrants ahead of them. The entire crop is picked before noon. It begins to rain.

Chapter 29

A gusty downpour soaks the land. Unable to work, people sit in wet clothes waiting for the deluge to end. The water gets into the cars, fouling the carburetors. Some are washed away. Sick, hungry, and cold, the people seek relief by huddling in barns, crouching under sheds, and lying under wet hay. Word comes that there will be no work until spring. The women watch their men's faces, looking to see if they will break. They are relieved to see anger there instead.

Chapter 30

The rains continue. Three days into the storm, Rose of Sharon goes into labor. Pa convinces the men to build a dam to keep the rising water from flooding the boxcar. After an uprooted tree

> "WHEREVER THEY'S A FIGHT SO HUNGRY PEOPLE CAN EAT, I'LL BE THERE. WHEREVER THEY'S A COP BEATIN' UP A GUY, I'LL BE THERE.... I'LL BE IN THE WAY KIDS LAUGH WHEN THEY'RE HUNGRY AN' THEY KNOW SUPPER'S READY. AN' WHEN OUR FOLKS EAT THE STUFF THEY RAISE AN' LIVE IN THE HOUSES THEY BUILD—WHY, I'LL BE THERE."

destroys the dam, Pa Joad retreats into the boxcar to find that Rose of Sharon has delivered a stillborn child. After six days of rain, the boxcar begins to flood. The family abandons it and goes in search of dry land. They find a barn sheltering a dying man and a small boy. The man has not eaten in six days and is unable to digest solid food. Ma gives Rose of Sharon a look, and the girl immediately understands that only she can save the man. After asking everyone else to leave, the young girl waves off the starving man's protests, and lovingly suckles him.

THEMES

Protest

The Grapes of Wrath is, at its heart, a protest novel. Steinbeck wrote the book after witnessing firsthand the deplorable situation Dust Bowl migrant families faced in the 1930s. Fueled by outrage, he recorded what he saw. By honestly portraying the situation for what it was, he forced American readers of the late 1930s and early 1940s to see what they would rather turn away from. By framing the characters as archetypes and ordinary heroes, he transformed a particular event in a particular moment in time into a universally moral lesson, one that contemporary readers continue to be influenced by today.

Protest as a way of invoking social and political reform is an inherent American ideal. Examples of individual Americans rebelling against authoritarian forces for the sake of improving society can be traced all the way back to Thomas Paine, one of the first Americans to speak out against injustice. Had Paine and other American revolutionaries not stood up for the greater good, the American colonies would not have become the United States of America. Just as Paine argued for independence from Great Britain, Tom Joad pledges to serve the disenfranchised by standing up to the police and the landowners, just as Jim Casy did. In his famous farewell to his mother, Tom tries to explain what he plans to do now that he understands that "a fella ain't got a soul of his own, but only a piece of a big one." He tells her, "I'll be ever'where—wherever you look. Wherever they's a fight so hungry people can eat, I'll be there. Wherever they's a cop beatin' up a guy, I'll be there." She says she does not understand, and he cannot really explain it, but the reader knows that once Tom leaves his family, he will go on to become an activist, protesting against the indignities forced on desperate workers by forces so large they cannot be seen. Kurt Hochenauer writes in the *Midwest Quarterly*,

> Tom's transition from the private to the public, from an inner, intuitive sense of morality to an outward expression of that morality, parallels the exemplary American man embedded in the rhetoric of one of America's first social rebels, Thomas Paine. As an augmentation of Paine's rhetoric, Tom further mythologizes rebellion and protest as the natural right of all Americans.

In chapter 14, Steinbeck writes, "This is the beginning—from 'I' to 'we.'" This phrase expresses the foundation of organized protest, the transformation of individual anger into community action. When Tom, like Paine, recognizes that he is merely a part of a larger whole, and that the whole shares his frustrations, his pain and anger, he understands that he is no longer alone. Although the forces against him loom large and are, for the most part, invisible, he has dignity and justice on his side. In chapter 20, Tom becomes incensed after Casy is unfairly taken to jail:

> "Ma," he said, "if it was the law they was workin' with, why, we could take it. But it *ain't* the law. They're a-workin' away at our spirits. They're a-tryin' to make us cringe an' crawl like a whipped bitch. They tryin' to break us. Why, Jesus Christ, Ma, they comes a time when the on'y way a fella can keep his decency is by takin' a sock at a cop."

Jane Darwell, Henry Fonda, and Russell Simpson in a scene from the film The Grapes of Wrath © *Corbis*

Tom refers to the larger family of man when he refers to "us" in this passage. As the narrator points out in chapter 17, "twenty families become one family" on the road to California. Once they get there, the families seem to multiply to include the entire human race. By the end of the novel, Tom has become Paine's American man, a man that, according to Paine's *The Crisis* (1776), "can gather strength from distress and grow brave by reflection. . . . but he whose heart is firm, and whose conscience approves his conduct will pursue his principles unto death." Thanks in large part to the examples set by the quietly rebellious Ma Joad and obviously moral Jim Casy, Tom's new identity is forged by his experiences as well as the influence of his activist mentors.

Human Dignity

Tom Joad's transformation is based on his new-found belief that every man, woman, and child deserves to live in dignity, no matter how rich or poor they may be. But Tom is not the only character bent on rising above the shame of his situation. The theme of human dignity is a constant thread running through *The Grapes of Wrath*, and indeed, through the American dream. The Joads and their cohorts do not ask for favors—in fact, many firmly resist favors— but they all stand firm in their belief in their basic human rights to decency, dignity, and pride.

America's Founding Fathers stated the American ideal plainly when they declared independence from Great Britain in 1776: "We hold these truths to be self-evident, that all men are created equal, that they are endowed by their Creator with certain unalienable Rights, that among these are Life, Liberty and the pursuit of Happiness." They defined the ideal of human rights more clearly in 1789 with the Bill of Rights, including the Eighth Amendment to the U.S. Constitution: "Excessive bail shall not be required, nor excessive fines imposed, nor cruel and unusual punishments inflicted." Together, the self-evident truth that all are created equal, the right to pursue happiness, and the protection from cruel punishment guarantee every American the right to stand tall and expect fair treatment; while the Okies get no such treatment, they refuse to bow.

Although they are bewildered and confused, they refuse to be beaten by the unseen forces that have stripped them of their homes and futures. Instead, the migrants infuse their every action with decency and pride, refusing to let their dignity be taken from them, too. When Grampa dies in a stranger's tent on the side of the road, Granma summons all the pride she can muster rather than let the situation defeat her:

> Sairy took Granma by the arm and led her outside, and Granma moved with dignity and held her head high. She walked for the family and held her head straight for the family. Sairy took her to a mattress lying on the ground and sat her down on it. And Granma looked straight ahead, proudly, for she was on show now.

The frequent use of the words *pride* or *proud* signals its increased currency among folks with very little to offer. Without money, prospects, or food, pride is one of the few things the migrants possess. It may sound generic, the same as if a stranger says, "Pleased to meet you" or "It's my pleasure," when these characters say they are "proud." The difference is, when they say they are proud, it is a deep, genuine expression of pride at still being able to do something for another, even (or especially) when they can do so little for themselves. When the Wilsons provide some meager comfort to Grampa and Granma, the two families exchange thanks and pride:

> Pa said, "We're thankful to you folks."
>
> "We're proud to help," said Wilson.
>
> "We're beholden to you," said Pa.
>
> "There's no beholden in a time of dying," said Wilson, and Sairy echoed him, "Never no beholden."
>
> Al said, "I'll fix your car—me an' Tom will." And Al looked proud that he could return the family's obligation."

Later, when Ma thanks Sairy for helping when Grampa died, Sairy says, "You shouldn't talk like that. We're proud to help. I ain't felt so—safe in a long time. People needs—to help." When Ma and Sairy talk about Granma's reaction to her husband's death, Ma says, "Maybe she won't really truly know for quite a while. Besides, us folks takes a pride holdin' in. My pa used to say, 'Anybody can break down. It takes a man not to.' We always try to hold in."

While they value their pride, they do not confuse it with their dignity or decency, which come from a deep sense of righteousness. Early in the novel, Tom explains to his mother how he stayed sane in jail, saying, "I ain't proud like some fellas. I let stuff run off'n me." Later, he tells her, "Ma, they comes a time when the on'y way a fella can keep his decency is by takin' a sock at a cop." More than once in the migrant camps, desperate women seem to prefer suffering in proud, stoic silence to admitting her children are hungry and accepting help. The others do their best to preserve those mothers' pride while doing the decent thing and feeding the hungry:

> "Ain't you got no money, Mis' Joyce?"
>
> She looked ashamedly down. "No, but we might get work any time."
>
> "Now you hol' up your head," Jessie said. "That ain't no crime."

The most striking act of human dignity is illustrated in the final scene, when Rose of Sharon offers of her own body to feed a starving man. The man must relinquish his pride to be saved, but Rose of Sharon is transformed by the act, growing from a selfish child into a life-giving woman in a single, humble, show of kindness. By behaving decently and taking pride in helping others when they have and can do so little for themselves, the migrants maintain their dignity in the face of daily hardships, which gives them the strength to carry on.

HISTORICAL OVERVIEW

The Great Depression

On October 29, 1929, the New York Stock Exchange crashed. This event caused a worldwide economic collapse whose effects would be felt for the next decade. The crash left banks insolvent, caused a drastic downturn in consumer confidence, and left 25 to 30 percent of the workforce unemployed. Economists still speculate about the cause of the Great Depression, though there are obvious contributors. Herbert Hoover, American president at the time, blamed it on the aftereffects of World War I, the unstable American banking structure, rampant stock speculation, and the fact that Congress failed to back many of his economic proposals. Others blamed the crash on too many banks and a glut of production that eclipsed demand due to stagnant workers' wages.

After the crash, the economy was further hampered by a severe drought that laid waste to America's agricultural center. Unemployment continued to rise, foreign banks collapsed, destroying world trade, and American spending came to a screeching halt. The Great Depression and its attendant poverty and desperation provide the historical context for *The Grapes of Wrath*, which was written toward the end of the worst economic period in American history.

The Dust Bowl Years

Concurrent with the Great Depression were the Dust Bowl Years, the decade beginning in 1930 that saw profound agricultural devastation along the southern plains of the United States. Unsound farming practices and years of drought in Kansas, Oklahoma, Texas, New Mexico, and Colorado removed groundcover that served to hold the soil in place. Plains winds whipped the soil into great, billowing dark clouds of dust that would sometimes hang in the air for days. The dust covered everything. It found its way through the doors and windows of homes and blanketed the furniture. Children wore masks on their way to school just so they could breathe. The dirt and dust got into farming equipment, trucks, and automobiles, rendering them useless. Nothing could grow, so farmers wound up losing their farms. Families began packing their belongings and heading west to California where they believed they could find employment as migrant farm workers. Most dreamed of earning enough money to buy a piece of land to replace the farms they were forced to abandon.

The mass migration of unemployed, desperate, poverty-stricken Midwesterners overwhelmed the infrastructure of California. Government relief in the form of housing, food, and medical care was limited and resources were strained. In 1933, in California's San Joaquin Valley, cotton workers joined with the Cannery and Agricultural Workers Industrial Union in the largest agricultural strike in American history. After three people died and

hundreds were injured, workers were granted a 25 percent raise. On April 14, 1935, the worst "black blizzard" happened; the day is still remembered as Black Sunday. That year, Congress established the Soil Conservation Service, which began developing conservation programs to safeguard topsoil and prevent over-farming. By this point, an estimated 850 million tons of topsoil had blown off the southern plains. Farmers were offered incentives for practicing soil conservation farming techniques. By 1936, the migration of workers into California had become so overwhelming policemen began patrolling the borders of Arizona and Oregon in an effort to keep the "undesirables" from entering the state.

In 1939, the year *The Grapes of Wrath* was published, the country began to see its way out of the Great Depression and the Dust Bowl Years. In the fall it began to rain, which brought the lengthy drought to an end. World War II, just a few years away, boosted the American economy by providing jobs to the millions who had been out of work for almost a decade.

CRITICAL OVERVIEW

The Grapes of Wrath became an overnight literary sensation during a particularly troubling and turbulent moment in U.S. history. The country was still reeling from the effects of the Great Depression, yet nearly ten thousand copies a week, at $2.75 each, flew off bookstore shelves for the first year of its publication. The consensus among critics, even those who had problems with the book, was that *The Grapes of Wrath* was a great American epic and a triumphant effort. Some readers, though, found the graphic descriptions of the struggles of migrant farm workers difficult to take. These people accused Steinbeck of fabricating the circumstances he described, so horrified were they by the thought that Americans could be made to suffer so completely at the hands of their own people.

The book, which placed Steinbeck squarely in the middle of the national debate over migrant workers, was also considered to be filthy and profane. In the introduction to the 2006 edition, Robert DeMott quotes Oklahoma Congressman Lyle Boren saying in 1940, "Take the vulgarity out of this book and it would be blank from cover to cover." Steinbeck was committed to representing the migrants authentically, including their rough language and manner of speaking. Having them talk any other way would have drained the book of much of its power, he argued. His portrayal of Californians angered still others. His authentic renderings of the locals and the migrants caused many to ban *The Grapes of Wrath* in libraries and schools across the country. One of the first libraries to call for its censorship was the Kern County Free Library in Kern County, California. According to the resolution drawn up by its board of supervisors,

> John Steinbeck's work of fiction . . . has offended our citizenry by falsely implying that many of our fine people are a low, ignorant [*sic*], profane and blasphemous type living in a vicious and filthy manner, . . . Steinbeck presents our public officials, law enforcement office and civil administrators, business men, farmers, and ordinary citizens as inhumane vigilantes, breathing class hatred and divested of sympathy or human decency or understanding toward a great, and to us unwelcome, economic problem brought on by an astounding influx of refugees, . . . *The Grapes of Wrath* is filled with profanity, lewd, foul, and obscene language unfit for use in American homes, therefore, be it resolved, that we . . . request that . . . *The Grapes of Wrath* . . . be banned from our library and schools.

The points made in the Kern County resolution were echoed by other civic leaders, and the book was banned in several states. The next year, First Lady Eleanor Roosevelt came forward, praised the book, and defended it against such bitter criticism, telling an interviewer, "I have never believed that *The Grapes of Wrath* was exaggerated." In 1940, *The Grapes of Wrath* won the Pulitzer Prize for literature. It later served as the cornerstone for the decision to award Steinbeck with the Nobel Prize in 1962. According to Robert DeMott's introduction of the Penguin Classics 2006 edition,

> In spite of flaws, gaffes, and infelicities its critics have enumerated—or perhaps because of them (general readers tend to embrace the book's mythic soul and are less troubled by its imperfect body)—*The Grapes of Wrath* has resolutely entered both the American consciousness and its conscience. Few novels can make that claim.

The flaws DeMott refer to include the book's "alleged sentimentalism, stereotyped characterizations, heavy-handed symbolism, unconvincing dialogue, episodic, melodramatic plot, misplaced Oklahoma geography, and inaccurate rendering of historical facts." He includes a sampling of the negative reviews, including Philip Rahv in the Spring 1939 *Partisan Review* who concludes, "the novel is far too didactic and long-winded," and cultural critic Leslie Fiedler, on the occasion of its fiftieth anniversary, who calls it "maudlin, sentimental, and overblown."

Whatever the objections to structure, language and topic, critics then and now note the importance of the work as a champion for Americans in need. In 1939, Charles Lee lauds the book:

> In *The Grapes of Wrath*, [Steinbeck] has written as memorable an American novel as I have ever read. Long, superbly angry, lashing with sustained indignation, his story towers above the work of others who have essayed to translate the desperations and dreams of the sharecropper into words. . . . . had he been a novelist Whitman might have told such a story as this.

Another early critic, Fritz Raley Simmons, fears that the now-classic's legacy would collapse under its own weight:

> *The Grapes of Wrath* . . . is not the kind of book that usually makes a best seller. It is terrific writing, but it is the kind of writing that makes one think and think hard. And it is especially disturbing to the kind of people who can afford to buy books.

Despite critical objections and worries for the novel's future, Steinbeck's masterpiece has maintained an unthreatened place among the classics of American literature since it first appeared. Linda Pelzer celebrates its power and relevance in 2000:

> Fifty years after its first publication on 14 April 1939, *The Grapes of Wrath* still gives voice to America's dispossessed. They may no longer be Okies set adrift by dust and Depression, but whether Hispanic migrants working the California fields or Midwestern farmers battling bankruptcy, their plight is no different from the Joads', and no less poignant. . . . [Tom Joad's] words resonate to the deep heart's core of our common humanity, moving us not only to feel the numbing poverty, the torturous suffering, the callous anonymity that constitute life for a vast American underclass but to recognize as well the quiet dignity with which they endure such indignities. Fifty, indeed sixty, years after its first publication, *The Grapes of Wrath* remains a powerful testament to human resilience and solidarity.

MEDIA ADAPTATIONS

The Grapes of Wrath was adapted as a film by Nunnally Johnson in 1940. Legendary director John Ford won an Academy Award for Best Director. The movie stars Jane Darwell, who won the Academy Award for Best Supporting Actress for her role as Ma Joad, Henry Fonda, John Carradine, and Charley Grapewin. It is available on DVD from Twentieth Century Fox.

The Grapes of Wrath was released as an unabridged audiobook in 1998; Dylan Baker narrates the story and voices the characters in this twenty-one-hour recording. It is available on audio cassette from Penguin Audio.

CRITICISM

John J. Conder

In the following excerpt, Conder argues that in The Grapes of Wrath, *Steinbeck endorses the philosophy that economic, legal, religious, and societal forces largely control individual destiny, but lays out a philosophy to rise above those forces and achieve personal freedom.*

The interchapters of Steinbeck's novel create a network of interlocking determinisms through their emphasis on the operations of abstract, impersonal forces in the lives of the Oklahomans. Chapter 5 is especially effective both in capturing the poignancy of the human situation created by such forces and in pointing to the kind of deterministic force underlying the others in the novel. In one fleeting episode a nameless Oklahoman who threatens the driver of a bulldozer leveling his house is told that armed resistance is futile, for the driver acts in the service of the bank, and "the bank gets orders from the East." The Oklahoman cries, "But where does it stop? Who can we shoot?" "I don't know," the driver replies. "Maybe there's nobody to shoot. Maybe the thing isn't men at all. Maybe . . . the property's doing it." Or at least the Bank, the monster requiring "profits all

the time" in order to live and dwarfing in size and power even the owner men, who feel "caught in something larger than themselves."

The vision that appears here has a name: economic determinism. This view does not say that man has no free will. One might indeed find among a group of bank presidents a corporate Thoreau who prefers jail (or unemployment) to following the demands of the system. It merely asserts that most men charged with the operation of an economic structure will act according to rules requiring the bank's dispossession of its debtors when a disaster renders them incapable of meeting payments on their mortgaged property. Far from denying free will, such determinism fully expects and provides for the willed resistance of the Oklahomans. The police take care of that. Nor is this vision without its moral component, though neither the police nor the owner men can be held individually responsible. "Some of the owner men were kind," Steinbeck writes, "because they hated what they had to do, and some of them were angry because they hated to be cruel, and some of them were cold because they had long ago found that one could not be an owner unless one were cold." These anonymous men are not devil figures but individuals performing functions within a system, so the work indicts the system rather than individuals who act in its service. In the case of the Oklahomans, the indictment is founded on a fundamental irony: societies, designed to protect men from nature's destructive features—here a drought—complete nature's destructive work, expelling men from the dust bowl into which nature's drought has temporarily transformed their farms.

By virtue of the instinct for self-preservation, in the camps twenty families become one large family, sharing a single instinct. The animal can come to life on this instinctual level because the animal's anlage is in the separate family, the basic unit through which man fulfills his needs, and the instinctual sense of unity is strengthened by a common set of threatening circumstances issuing in shared emotions: first fear, then anger. In this condition, the "school intelligence" directing its drives is instinctual alone, and hence the human group is more like the school of fish to which Steinbeck refers. Guided solely by instinct, the human group-animal achieves a measure of protection from a hostile social environment, but with instinct alone, it can no more transcend the social

An abandoned farm in Texas showing the ravages of the Dust Bowl in 1938 © *Bettmann/Corbis*

determinism of the body politic than the turtle (which in the novel symbolizes it in this condition) can transcend the machinations of the drivers eager to squash it. Chance alone can save the group or the turtle as both walk, like Tom, one step ahead of the other, living from day to day.

But the group changes, and in this respect the plot goes one step further than the interchapters, which halt with the fermenting of the grapes of wrath. For the plot shows the emergence of a rational group consciousness, first in Casy, then in Tom, whose final talk with his mother, representing the principle of family, discloses that his own consciousness has transcended such limitations. In fact it is mainly in Tom that the group develops a head for its body; for he survives the murdered Casy, and he was from the beginning more clearly a member of the de facto group than Casy, who owned no land. And by stressing how the animal that is the group achieves rational consciousness and (hence) freedom, Steinbeck

harmonizes freedom and determinism in his most important way. The group determined by instinct and circumstance in the interchapters achieves both rational self-awareness and freedom in the person of a member who substitutes the consciousness of a group for a private consciousness and thus gives the group access to the faculty of human will. Tom thus enables it to move from instinct to reason and to that freedom which reasoned acts of the will provide. By having the group consciousness mature in the plot section of his novel, Steinbeck thus unites it to the interchapters structurally and harmonizes his novel philosophically.

And he provides a triumph for the group within the context of determinism, for their attainment of rational group consciousness is itself a determined event because such potential is inherent in the species. Their achieved freedom of will as a group thus is the final term of a socially determined sequence of events that leads to the group's creation, and the group's exercise of it to attain its ends fulfills the historical determinism of the novel. Yet this is not the only hope in these pages, for the prospective triumph of the group provides hope for the triumph of the individual as a whole person.

The Grapes of Wrath is the story of the exploitation of a dispossessed group, and it is difficult not to feel that it will always engender sympathies for the dispossessed of the earth wherever and whenever they might appear. But the novel's indictment of society for what it does to individuals should have an equally enduring appeal; for here its message goes beyond the conditions of oppressed groups and addresses individuals in all strata of complex societies. The condition of individual Oklahomans in fact is an extreme representation of the condition of social man, and in the capacity of individual Oklahomans to change lies the hope for social man.

The migrants' achievement of rational freedom speaks for more than freedom for the group. It tells readers of a vital difference in kinds of freedom. Steinbeck has written, "I believe that man is a double thing—a group animal and at the same time an individual. And it occurs to me that he cannot successfully be the second until he has fulfilled the first." Only the fulfilled group self can create a successful personal self; only freedom exercised by a personal self in harmony with a group self can be significant.

This aspect of the novel's vision depends upon Steinbeck's fuller conception of an individual's two selves. One is his social self, definable by the role he plays in society and by the attitudes he has imbibed from its major institutions. The other is what is best called his species self. It contains all the biological mechanisms—his need for sexual expression, for example—that link him to other creatures in nature. And by virtue of the fact that he is thus linked to the natural world, he can feel a sense of unity with it in its inanimate as well as its animate forms. But the biological element in this self also connects him to the world of man, for it gives him an instinctive sense of identification with other members of his species, just as the members of other species have an instinctive sense of oneness with their own kind.

The species self thus has connections to nonhuman and human nature, and Steinbeck refers to the latter connection when he speaks of man as a "group animal." He views a healthy personal identity as one in which the species self in both its aspects can express itself through the social self of the individual. But society thwarts, or seeks to thwart, the expression of that self. It seeks not only to cut man off from his awareness of his connections to nonhuman nature, it seeks also to sever him from the group sense of oneness with the human species that the individual's species self possesses. Ironically, therefore, purely social man loses a sense of that unity with others which society presumably exists to promote.

The novel's social criticism rests on this view, and its emphasis on grotesques, purely social beings cut off from their connections to nature, both human and nonhuman, portrays an all-too-familiar image of modern man. In too many instances, by imposing mechanical rhythms on human nature, society creates half-men. Its repeated attempts to distort the individual's identity is emphasized by numerous dichotomies between social demands and instinct. Tom tries to comprehend the meaning of his imprisonment for killing in self-defense. Casy tries to understand the meaning of his preaching sexual abstinence when he cannot remain chaste himself. And the point is made by the basic events that set the story moving. A mechanical monster, indifferent to the maternal instincts of the Ma Joads who exercise their species selves in the interest of family solidarity, expels families from their land. The social mechanism thus tries to thwart the demands of the group aspect of the self to remain together. And the same mechanism is responsible for sowing what has become a dust bowl with cotton, rendering it permanently useless for agriculture, thus showing its indifference—nay, hostility—to the connections with nature that the species self feels.

Tom finds no meaning, at the novel's outset, in a system that imprisons him for killing in self-defense, and he discovers the true meaning of the system only after he kills the deuty who murders Casy—a nice bit of symmetry that illustrates his growth in awareness as he perceives, like Casy, that his second killing is also an instinctual response, one of self-defense against the true assaulter, the system, which so thwarts man's instinctual life that it leaves him no choice other than to strike back. This line of meaning is echoed by others: by Ma, who says of Purty Boy Floyd, "He wan't a bad boy. Jus' got drove in a corner"; by the nameless owner men who tell the tenants early in the novel, "You'll be stealing if you try to stay, you'll be murderers if you kill to stay." And it is implicit in Tom's own position at the beginning of the plot: to leave the state violates the conditions of his parole, yet to stay means to break up the family and to face unemployment and possible starvation.

Under such circumstances, it is not surprising to discover that the true prison in *The Grapes of Wrath* is the world outside the prison walls, the real point of Tom's story of a man who deliberately violated parole to return to jail so that he could enjoy the "conveniences" (among them good food) so conspicuously absent in his home. "Here's me, been a-goin' into the wilderness like Jesus to try to find out somepin," Casy says. "Almost got her sometimes, too. But it's in the jail house I really got her." He discovers his proper relationship to men there because it is the place of the free: of men who exercised the natural rights of nature's self only to be imprisoned by the society that resents their exercise. And in fact he can see how the law violates self because he has already seen how religion does. Without the revelations of the wilderness, he would not have had the revelation of the jailhouse; the first is indispensable to the second. Together, they make him the touchstone for understanding the novel's philosophy of self and for measuring the selves of the novel's other characters.

Just as the species self is the ultimate source of freedom for a group, it is the same for an individual. If man can recognize that he is a part of nature by virtue of that self's existence—if he can affirm for this aspect of a naturalistic vision—he can liberate himself from the condition of being a grotesque and, in recognizing his oneness with others, escape the tentacles of economic determinism as well.

Source: John J. Conder, "Steinbeck and Nature's Self: *The Grapes of Wrath*," in *Naturalism in American Fiction: The Clasic Phase*, University Press of Kentucky, 1984, pp.142–59.

SOURCES

The Charters of Freedom," *U.S. National Archives and Records Administration,* www.archives.gov/national-archives-experience/charters/charters.html (October 29, 2006) .

DeMott, Robert, "Introduction," in *The Grapes of Wrath*, Penguin Books, 2006, pp. ix–xlv.

"First Lady's Week," in *Time* Magazine, April 15,1940, www.time.com/time/magazine/article/0,9171,789721,00.html (October 31, 2006).

Haslam, Gerald, "*Grapes of Wrath*: A Book That Stretched My Soul," *CaliforniaAuthors.com,* www.californiaauthors.com/essay_haslam.shtml (October 31, 2006).

Hochenauer, Kurt, "The Rhetoric of American Protest: Thomas Paine and the Education of Tom Joad," in the *Midwest Quarterly*, Summer 1994, pp. 392–404.

Kern County Board of Supervisors, *Resolution 21 August 1939,*; quoted in Lingo, Marci, "Forbidden Fruit: The Banning of the Grapes of Wrath in the Kern County Free Library," in *Libraries & Culture*, Fall 2003, September 29, 2006.

Lee, Charles, "*The Grapes of Wrath*: The Tragedy of the American Sharecropper," in the *Boston Herald*, April 22, 1939; reprinted in *The Critical Response to John Steinbeck's* the Grapes of Wrath, edited by Barbara A. Heavilin, Greenwood Press, 2000, p. 47.

Paine, Thomas, "December 26, 1776," *The Crisis*, www.ushistory.org/Paine/crisis/c-01.htm (November 2, 2006).

Pelzer, Linda C., "Honoring an American Classic: Viking's 1989 Edition of John Steinbeck's *The Grapes of Wrath* (Review)," in *The Critical Response to John Steinbeck's* the Grapes of Wrath, edited by Barbara A. Heavilin, Greenwood Press, 2000, p. 309.

Simmons, Fritz Raley, "Farm Tenancy Central Theme of Steinbeck," in the *Greensboro Daily News,* July 1939; reprinted in *The Critical Response to John Steinbeck's* the Grapes of Wrath, edited by Barbara A. Heavilin, Greenwood Press, 2000, p. 55.

Steinbeck, John, *The Grapes of Wrath*, Viking Press, 1939; reprint, Penguin Classics, 2006.

The Great Gatsby

F. SCOTT FITZGERALD

1925

F. Scott Fitzgerald's masterpiece *The Great Gatsby* (1925) is the quintessential tale of the American dream: the heights a man may reach, the past he can discard, the joy he may (or may not) find, and the tragedy that living the dream may bring him. The novel is set in what Fitzgerald called the "Jazz Age," a period bridging the 1920s and 1930s, and emphasizes the life of pleasure and decadence after the tragedy and horror of World War I. Gatsby's American dream is essentially the "rags-to-riches" story about overcoming poverty and creating a life of pure luxury and indulgence; Fitzgerald's American dream is a dangerous, romantic myth.

Though *The Great Gatsby* is now an undisputed title in the American literary canon, the novel did not sell well when first published and slipped into near oblivion in the following decades. The economic, social, and political hardships of the Great Depression and World War II seem to have turned away those readers who could no longer afford to dream in their daily lives or those readers who, rather like Jay Gatsby himself, knew all too well how quickly dreams and success could shatter.

Middle-class "middle-westerner" Nick Carraway narrates this novel; he is a keen observer of the American fairy tale come to life. As he uncovers more and more about Gatsby and his obsession with Daisy Buchanan, Carraway realizes the high price of materialism, envy, and

BIOGRAPHY

F. SCOTT FITZGERALD

Francis Scott Key Fitzgerald was born in St. Paul, Minnesota, on September 4, 1896, to a furniture manufacturer and salesman. He began writing early, scribbling in the margins of his textbooks and penning adventure stories for the school newspaper. Though his grades were not good enough to grant him immediate admission into Princeton, he managed to talk the administration into accepting him on probation. In 1917, however, he interrupted his education to join the army and wrote his first novel, which the publisher Charles Scribner's Sons praised, but rejected. Fitzgerald met debutante socialite Zelda Sayre when he was stationed in Montgomery, Alabama. When the war ended, Fitzgerald, who had never been sent overseas, joined the advertising business, hoping to make enough money to marry Zelda. Unfortunately, Zelda called off their engagement, not wanting to settle for life on his meager salary.

A year later in 1919, Fitzgerald worked with an editor at Scribner to publish his first novel, *This Side of Paradise*. Propelled by the momentum of his new professional writing career, he also sold short stories to popular markets. Inspired by Fitzgerald's newfound success, Zelda married Fitzgerald. They had a tumultuous relationship that produced one daughter, Frances (whom they called "Scottie"), in 1921. Fitzgerald became an icon of the 1920s, synonymous with both the carefree wealth of the Jazz Age, personified by his masterpiece *The Great Gatsby* (1925), as well as the disaffected American abroad of the Lost Generation, epitomized by his earlier novel, *This Side of Paradise* (1920). After Zelda was diagnosed with schizophrenia in the 1930s, Fitzgerald's star dimmed a bit, and he found himself in Hollywood writing screenplays to pay the bills. He died of a heart attack at the age of forty-four on December 21, 1940, with heart, lung, and liver disease from years of excessive drinking and smoking.

desire. The American dream, like Gatsby's house in the end of the novel, is empty, or may never have existed. The editors of *Readings on* describe Fitzgerald in terms of his famous characters:

> In some ways, F. Scott Fitzgerald was Jay Gatsby: poor dreamer become financially successful, vitally attached to a romantic dream. He was also Nick Carraway, the participating yet detached observer of life, who admired the dreamer's intensity but regretted his fatal flaws.

Ironically, *The Great Gatsby* actually predated the term "American dream" according to critic Jeffrey Louis Decker, who notes that the concept "was not put into print until 1931." In that sense, *The Great Gatsby*'s underlying narrative marks the birth of a myth, one that shaped the definition of success for future American society. Scholar Tara Carter writes,

> Fitzgerald writes about the traditional white American dream which is born out of capitalistic ideals, and, thus, reliant on material acquisitions and attaining high social status.

And while he does a fine job creating shallow, wealthy characters that cause the reader to think twice about the benefits of wealth, he never shows the American dream from a different perspective other than from people residing in a privileged, white world.

Despite its inauspicious beginnings and the multitude of debates that still rage about Fitzgerald's commentary on race, society, and success, Fitzgerald's glamorous novel has made a remarkable place for itself. Not only does the novel have a permanent slot on school reading lists, but the book has been adapted into four film versions, an opera, and a play, performed in Minneapolis in 2006 for the first time since 1926.

PLOT SUMMARY

Chapter 1

The Great Gatsby begins with Nick Carraway introducing himself and providing the reader with background about his prominent family

F. Scott Fitzgerald © *Bettmann/Corbis*

from the "Middle West." After graduating from Yale, Nick decided to go east and learn the bond business, with the "grave, hesitant" approval of his "aunts and uncles" and the financial support of his father. Nick lives in a modest house in West Egg, next to the elegant mansion owned by the enigmatic Jay Gatsby and across the bay from Tom and Daisy Buchanan. Tom, whom Nick knew in college, and Daisy, Nick's second cousin once removed, invite Nick to dinner, along with Miss Jordan Baker, a golf pro. Daisy captivates Nick with her lovely sad air, while Tom makes the biggest impression during the meal with his racist commentary ("It's up to us who are the dominant race to watch out or these other races will have control of things") and his mysterious disappearance during the party. When Daisy follows her husband to the kitchen, Miss Baker tells Nick that Tom has "some woman in New York" who does not "have the decency not to telephone him at dinner time." After Daisy returns, she informs Nick that she heard about his engagement, which he denies as pure rumor. Nick goes home and sees Mr. Gatsby standing outside the mansion looking across the bay; he considers speaking to him, but decides not to intrude on an apparently private moment.

Chapter 2

Nick recounts first meeting Tom Buchanan's mistress, Myrtle Wilson, in her husband's car repair shop, which is looked over by a large billboard bearing the image of a pair of large spectacles and eyes advertising Dr. T. J. Eckleburg, an eye specialist. Nick visits George Wilson's shop with Tom, who makes a date with Myrtle when George's back is turned. After giving her husband her usual story about visiting her sister in New York, Myrtle accompanies Nick and Tom to the city, but she rides in a separate train car to keep up appearances. The three go to the apartment Tom and Myrtle use for their rendezvous where they meet Myrtle's sister, Catherine; Mr. McKee, a photographer who lives downstairs; and Mr. McKee's "shrill, languid, handsome, and horrible" wife. Catherine tells Nick she once went to a party at Gatsby's and comments on his power. Catherine also says that neither Tom nor Myrtle like their spouses and that Daisy is the one keeping them apart. Myrtle agrees and comments that her own husband "isn't fit to lick [her] shoe." When Tom and Myrtle fight about whether Myrtle has the right to mention Daisy's name, Tom breaks Myrtle's nose. Mr. McKee leaves the chaotic scene, and Nick follows.

Chapter 3

Nick receives a formal invitation to one of the huge parties Gatsby throws every few weeks. He does not see Gatsby, but when he asks about his host, the guests are appalled. Nick encounters Jordan Baker, and they meet a drunken man with "enormous owl-eyed spectacles" in the library, who excitedly attests that the books in the library are not simply props: "I ascertained. They're real." Gossip about Gatsby abounds: He may be a murderer, a spy, or a German. Amidst the dancing and gaiety, Nick meets a man sitting at a table with a joyful little girl. Before he introduces himself, the man reveals that he has seen Nick before, possibly in the war when Nick was with the Ninth Machine-Gun Battalion and the man was with the Seventh Infantry. They speak about their experiences in France, and the man invites Nick along on a hydroplane excursion in the morning. The man finally introduces himself as Gatsby, to Nick's surprise. When Gatsby goes inside, Nick demands that Jordan tell him all about Gatsby. Gatsby sends his butler to fetch Jordan, with whom he wishes to speak privately. As the party progresses, Nick notices that most of the remaining party guests, couples, are fighting. Jordan returns from her meeting with Gatsby and says she "just heard the most amazing thing," but does not reveal the secret. Chaos ensues in the parking area when a car is stuck in a ditch, and the parting guests blame the owl-eyed drunk from the library, though he denies involvement. As Nick leaves the party and looks back at the empty house, he gets the distinct feeling of loneliness. At the end of the chapter, Nick says, "I am one of the few honest people that I have ever known."

Chapter 4

Nick chronicles the tide of upper-class guests who come in and out of Gatsby's mansion over the summer. Thus far, Nick has attended "two of his parties, mounted in his hydroplane, and at his urgent invitation, made frequent use of his beach." Gatsby picks Nick up for a lunch date in his shiny, impressive car and, during the ride, addresses the gossip, saying: "I don't want you to get a wrong idea of me from all these stories you hear." Gatsby admits he is from a wealthy California family and was educated at Oxford. After his family died, he inherited a fortune, traveled the world, and went to war, where he received a medal "For Valour Extraordinary" in Montenegro and tried to "forget something very sad that happened to [him] a long time ago." Nick does not necessarily believe Gatsby, but he is fascinated nonetheless. On the way to lunch, Gatsby gets pulled over for speeding, but the policeman lets him go without a ticket after recognizing the powerful man he had stopped. At lunch, Gatsby introduces Nick to Mr. Meyer Wolfsheim, a New Yorker involved in shady business deals. Wolfsheim mistakes Nick for a man "looking for a business gonnegtion," but Gatsby quickly tells him that Nick is not the man. Tom shows up at the restaurant where they are having lunch, but before Nick can introduce Tom to Gatsby, Gatsby disappears.

Nick recalls an afternoon with Jordan when she tells him about Daisy Buchanan's (then Daisy Fay) relationship with Gatsby. On the day of Daisy's wedding, Jordan found Daisy drunk and wanting to change her mind about marrying Tom. She married Tom and had a daughter, but she apparently never forgot about Gatsby, whom she had known as an officer from Camp Taylor when she was eighteen. At nineteen, she had intended to run off to the city with Gatsby before he left for the war, but Daisy's mother stopped her. Two summers later, she was engaged to Tom Buchanan. Jordan found out later that Tom was cheating on Daisy: After he got into a car accident, the newspapers reported that the girl with him, a chambermaid at the hotel where the Buchanans were staying, broke her arm. Jordan tells Nick about Daisy's odd reaction when Jordan mentioned that Nick lived next door to a man named Gatsby. Finally, Jordan reveals Gatsby's secret: Gatsby wants Nick to invite both him and Daisy over to his house so they can reunite.

Chapter 5

Nick tells Gatsby that he has agreed to help him meet with Daisy. Gatsby asks Nick to do some "confidential" business for him, but Nick declines. On a drizzly day, Gatsby and Daisy meet at Nick's; Gatsby pretends to arrive after Daisy, though he had already waited an hour. Nick tries to disperse the awkwardness by having them help him prepare tea and cakes, but he decides to leave them alone to sort out their personal conflict. When Nick returns, Daisy looks upset, but Gatsby appears as if "a new well-being radiated from him." Gatsby invites Nick and Daisy to his home. During the tour, Gatsby tells them, "It took me just three years to earn the money that bought it." Confused, Nick reminds Gatsby that he said he had inherited his money. Gatsby admits his money was lost in the war and that he regained it through drug and oil business. He brings up the business proposition a second time, but Nick does not get the chance to answer. Daisy admires the mansion while Gatsby admires Daisy. Gatsby shows off his massive wealth and material possessions. After watching Gatsby and Daisy, Nick realizes that Daisy has not measured up to Gatsby's fantasy of her, noting, "No amount of fire or freshness can challenge what a man will store up in his heart."

Chapter 6

A reporter comes to the mansion to question Gatsby. The truth about Gatsby is revealed to the reader. He was born James Gatz to "shiftless and unsuccessful farm people." Gatsby changed his name when he was seventeen. He was living hand-to-mouth as a clam digger and salmon fisher when Dan Cody's yacht "dropped anchor in the shallows along shore." Gatsby was enamored with the beautiful boat and the success it symbolized, and a few days after meeting the rich old man, he joined Cody's yachting crew. Gatsby yachted around the world with Cody, and when Cody died, he willed his money to Gatsby. However, Gatsby only received twenty-five thousand dollars, while Cody's young mistress Ella Kaye got the rest of the millions. Gatsby does not reveal this version of the truth to Nick until much later.

Nick spends his time dating Jordan, but he eventually visits Gatsby. Gatsby has another party where Gatsby introduces Tom and Daisy to a variety of celebrities. Daisy and Gatsby dance while Tom amuses himself at another table. As the party winds down, Nick waits with Tom and Daisy as their driver brings the car around. Tom is edgy about Gatsby, wondering if he made his money by bootlegging. He vows to find out more. Gatsby tells Nick he does not think Daisy enjoyed the party. He is also disappointed that he and Daisy do not connect like they used to and wishes they could "repeat the past." Gatsby flashes back to "one autumn night, five years before" when he kissed Daisy. Nick finds himself caught up in Gatsby's sentimentality.

Chapter 7

When the mansion lights do not come on one Saturday evening, Nick gets concerned and visits Gatsby. A new butler answers the door and turns Nick away. Nick learns that Gatsby fired his old servants and replaced them with people who could not be bribed, explaining, "I wanted people who wouldn't gossip. Daisy comes over quite often—in the afternoons." Eventually Gatsby calls Nick and informs him that the servants are contacts of Wolfshiem. He also tells Nick that Daisy wants Nick to lunch at her house the next day; Jordan Baker would attend as well. Nick is suspicious of the gathering.

When Nick and Gatsby arrive at the Buchanans', the phone rings for Tom. Jordan whispers to Nick that it is "Tom's girl" calling, but Nick reassures her that Tom is discussing a "bona-fide deal" with someone. Daisy kisses Gatsby when her husband ducks out to make drinks for the guests. Soon after, Daisy shows off her daughter to the little party. In the heat of the day, Daisy tells Gatsby that he "look[s] so cool"; Tom begins to recognize the relationship between them and suggests they all go to New York. As they wait for Daisy and Jordan to get

ready, Gatsby remarks to Nick that Daisy's voice "is full of money." As Daisy and Gatsby ride toward the city in the same car, Tom tells Jordan and Nick that Gatsby is not who he claims to be. They stop at George Wilson's repair shop for gasoline. In making small talk, George says he and his wife "want to go west," a comment that surprises Tom. Nick realizes that George knows his wife has been having an affair but does not know with whom. Nick sees Myrtle spying on them from the second floor of the shop. Based on her expression, it seems she believes Jordan is Tom's wife.

Tom's relationships both with his mistress and his wife are unraveling. The five decide to rent "the parlor of a suite in the Plaza Hotel" for the afternoon where they drink and talk. Tom tries to poke holes in the story of Gatsby's past by bringing up the fact Gatsby is "an Oxford man," which obviously Tom does not believe. Gatsby explains that he only attended the university for five months; some soldiers were given the chance to go after the war. After Gatsby's smooth response, Tom announces that he knows about Daisy and Gatsby and that he will not allow Gatsby to disregard "family life and family institutions." Gatsby insists that Daisy never loved Tom, and at first, Daisy agrees. Tom is furious and calls Gatsby a liar. Gatsby forces Daisy to admit she never loved Tom, but then she changes her mind. Tom's indiscretions with other women are brought into the argument, and Gatsby informs Tom that Daisy intends to leave him. Tom brings up Gatsby's dark dealings with Wolfshiem, including bootlegging and gambling. Gatsby does not deny the charges and tries to explain himself to Daisy, who retreats inside herself. Tom tells Daisy to go home with Gatsby, telling her, "Go on. He won't annoy you. I think he realizes that his presumptuous little flirtation is over." Nick, Jordan, and Tom follow in another car.

As the argument among the five winds down and they head home, the narrative switches scenes to George Wilson's repair shop. George has locked Myrtle upstairs. He tells Michaelis, who runs the coffee shop nearby, that "she's going to stay there till the day after tomorrow and then we're going to move away." Later, Michaelis sees Myrtle run outside, yelling at George. She gets killed when hit by a car coming from New York, a car that does not stop. Not long after the accident, Tom, Nick, and Jordan drive past the garage and wonder about the gathering crowd;

they stop out of curiosity. Someone in the crowd describes the vehicle as a "big yellow car. New." Tom recognizes the car as Gatsby's. When Tom, Nick, and Jordan arrive at the Buchanans', Gatsby talks with Nick alone and acts cagey about the ride home, asking "Did you see any trouble on the road?" Soon after, Gatsby confesses that he thought the woman had been killed, but Nick sees that he cares more about Daisy's reaction to the accident than the accident itself. Gatsby admits that Daisy was driving the car. Nick wonders what Tom would think if he knew Daisy had been the driver who hit Myrtle.

Chapter 8

The next day, Nick visits Gatsby at the mansion. He advises Gatsby to leave town. Gatsby refuses, wanting to make sure Daisy is all right. Nick tells the reader that Gatsby told him the story of Dan Cody that night and also talked about first meeting Daisy. As an officer, Gatsby had visited Daisy's home and had become enthralled by its mystery and hers. Because of his impoverished background, he decided to "let her believe that he was a person from much the same strata as herself—that he was fully able to take care of her." But in reality, he could not pursue Daisy. While he was at war, he tried desperately to get home to her, but could not. Daisy was confused about her identity without him and turned to Tom Buchanan. After becoming Gatsby's confidant, Nick compliments Gatsby, saying, "They're a rotten crowd. You're worth the whole damn bunch put together."

Nick's narrative returns to the night of the hit-and-run accident and tells what happened after they left the garage for the Buchanans', a story he learns from the neighbor Michaelis. Michaelis stayed with George all night to help him deal with the tragedy. George reveals to Michaelis that Myrtle "had come from the city with her face bruised and her nose swollen" a few months earlier. George also hints to Michaelis about Myrtle's other strange behaviors recently. George believes Myrtle ran out to speak with the man driving the fancy car that killed her. In addition, George tells Michaelis that he confronted Myrtle about her affair.

The afternoon after the accident, Nick, the chauffeur, the butler, and the gardener find Gatsby's body in the pool, mortally wounded. George's dead body lies nearby.

> HE MUST HAVE FELT THAT HE HAD LOST THE OLD WARM WORLD, PAID A HIGH PRICE FOR LIVING TOO LONG WITH A SINGLE DREAM."

Chapter 9

Two years later, Nick can still remember the day he found Gatsby. Rumors swirl about Gatsby and the murder. At the inquest, Myrtle's sister Catherine insists Myrtle was not Gatsby's lover and "was completely happy with her husband." The newspapers cast George as "a man deranged by grief" over his belief that his wife had been unfaithful. Nick calls Daisy, but she and Tom went away and "left no address." Nick tries to get in touch with Wolfshiem but has no luck. When Nick finally receives a note from the man, the message is cold and selfish. A shady business associate of Gatsby's phones Nick, mistaking him for Gatsby. Unexpectedly, Gatsby's father, Henry Gatz, shows up after reading about his son's death in the paper. Gatz mourns his son's "big future." Later, Nick receives a call from one of Gatsby's so-called friends who does not take the time to express condolences; he simply wants a pair of tennis shoes he had forgotten during a visit. Nick travels to New York where he sees Mr. Wolfshiem, who informs Nick that he "made" Jay Gatsby, but he cannot come to his funeral because of the risks involved. When Nick returns to the mansion, Gatz shows him a worn photo of the house that Gatsby had sent him; obviously Gatsby's father was proud to show the world what his son owned. Gatz also presents a book, *Hopalong Cassidy*, which Gatsby read as a child. Inside the book, Gatsby had made a schedule that showed his motivation and ambition for the future. Only a handful of people attend Gatsby's funeral: Nick, Owl Eyes, Mr. Gatz, and the minister.

Nick sees the jewels, sparkles, and glitz of the American East as empty, grotesque, and cold. He attempts closure with Jordan Baker, though she has already moved on to an engagement with another man. Nick runs into Tom, who reveals that the day Gatsby was murdered, he told George that Gatsby owned the car that killed Myrtle. "They were careless people—Tom and Daisy," Nick decides. "They smashed up things and creatures and then retreated back into their money or their vast carelessness or whatever it was that kept them together." Before Nick moves back to the "middle-west," he visits the mansion one last time and realizes that Gatsby's dreams had eluded him.

THEMES

Perception as Reality

The Great Gatsby illustrates the tragic cost of the American dream. In the end, both Jay Gatsby and Myrtle Wilson lose their lives in the pursuit of success, or at least the appearance of success. For them, the American dream means being able to exchange their impoverished pasts for the good life. Unfortunately for them, the good life is a masquerade.

Jay Gatsby, formerly James Gatz, is murdered as a direct result of the secret affair between Tom Buchanan and Myrtle Wilson. George Wilson, enraged by his wife's illicit relationship with Tom and inspired by the godly artificial eyes of Dr. T. J. Eckleburg, mistakes Gatsby for his wife's lover. However, Gatsby's untimely death can also be attributed to his lifelong quest to erase his humble origins and become someone respectable enough for Daisy Buchanan. For Gatsby, that chameleon-like ability to control outside perceptions was tantamount to his new beginnings, as well as his unexpected end; if people knew the true Gatsby, he would never have achieved his financial power or social reputation, but he might have kept his life. To everyone in the novel, Gatsby was someone different: ambitious boy, former lover, wealthy businessman, con man, success story, murderer. "Who is this Gatsby anyway?" Tom asks, alluding to the fact that no one knows anything about Gatsby except for rumors from the grapevine and dubious "facts" provided by Gatsby himself. Of course, Gatsby did not create his identity alone; after Gatsby's death, Meyer Wolfshiem, a Jewish crime boss also in hot pursuit of the American dream, tells Nick of Gatsby, "I made him . . . raised him up out of nothing, right out of the gutter."

By the same token, Myrtle Wilson dies because of her dream of a more worldly and sophisticated existence. This story arc is foreshadowed early in the novel when Myrtle goes with Tom and Nick to New York. When she arrives in the city, Myrtle's physical change reflects her social aspirations:

> She had changed her dress to a brown figured muslin which stretched tight over her rather wide hips. . . . At the news-stand she bought a copy of *Town Tattle* and a moving picture magazine, and in the station drug store, some cold cream and a small flask of perfume. Upstairs in the solemn echoing drive she let four taxi cabs drive away before she selected a new one, lavender-colored with grey upholstery.

Later, in the apartment that Tom and Myrtle use for their trysts, Nick notes,

> Mrs. Wilson . . . was now attired in an elaborate afternoon dress of cream colored chiffon, which gave out a continual rustle as she swept about the room. With the influence of the dress her personality had also undergone a change. The intense vitality that had been so remarkable in the garage was converted into impressive hauteur.

Myrtle finds her life with George Wilson too banal. She believes, like Gatsby, that the trappings of wealth will give her a new identity and, subsequently, a new status in society. Though she tells Mrs. McKee that she only wears her cream-colored chiffon when she does not care about her appearance, the statement is clearly ironic. She feels powerless as Mrs. George Wilson, as if her life is as in need of repair as the cars in her husband's shop. But as Tom Buchanan's lover in the city, she sees endless possibility in the material things; she can dispose of a dress on a whim and easily acquire another without a second thought. She can change whenever she likes, traveling from George's rags to Tom's riches on an afternoon train.

They crave money and status because they believe that happiness will follow; misery and destruction, however, are all their quests achieve. In effect, Gatsby's and Myrtle's deaths show a dark side to striving to achieve the American dream.

The Price of Success

The American dream is an ideal: a picture-perfect life with everything one could want behind a white picket fence. Life behind the fence is happy, peaceful, and, above all, moral. Wealth and success has been achieved through hard work and straight shooting. However, the characters in *The Great Gatsby* show that in order to reach social and financial success a person might have to sacrifice his ethics by telling lies, oppressing others, or breaking laws.

Many characters in the novel lie to get what they want. For Myrtle Wilson, the truth gets in the way of her personal goal: to become a woman of class. She hides her affair with Tom Buchanan because the truth would prevent her from living life in the city as the well-kept mistress of a wealthy man. As Tom's lover, she can live a better life than George can provide.

Of course, to become Jay Gatsby, James Gatz had to lie to the public, in essence creating the illusion of the American dream from the ground up. The only way Gatsby can be with Daisy is by building a social mystery around his identity and involving himself in illegal dealings. In this way, the younger Gatsby mirrors Fitzgerald himself: just as Fitzgerald could not woo his beloved Zelda without some form of viable income, Gatsby the soldier cannot woo Daisy.

Tom Buchanan's American dream is about entitlement and excluding those not entitled. When he looks down on Gatsby for his connections to con man Meyer Wolfshiem, the American dream becomes a measure of morality. In Tom's eyes, Gatsby's accomplishments and possessions are tainted by how he acquired them. Early in the novel, Tom Buchanan claims that "civilization's going to pieces" and believes the "white race . . . will be utterly submerged." Racist ideas appeal to Tom: For him, the American dream is being usurped by "other races," and he sees himself as "standing alone on the last barrier of civilization." Though Tom is having an affair with a married woman and is married himself, he stands as a moral judge not only for Gatsby, but also for society at large. Tom does not think all men should have an equal shot at the American dream and looks down on those whom he deems undeserving. He is jealous of his status as one of the deserving because it is his by inheritance, not achievement, and thus more difficult to justify.

Meyer Wolfshiem is one of those men Tom Buchanan wants to deny entrance to the club. As a Jewish businessman with shady dealings, Wolfshiem represents "those other races" who will eventually "submerge" the white race. To Tom, Wolfshiem is not worthy of what America has to offer because of his ethnicity, which is a bigger flaw than his immorality. In addition, Wolfshiem "made" Gatsby, as Wolfshiem tells Nick late in the novel, alluding to Tom's biggest fear that the lower classes and races will eventually prevail by "making" each other into American success stories.

HISTORICAL OVERVIEW

Jazz Age

Fitzgerald coined the term "Jazz Age," naming a time after World War I when the public longed for frivolity, decadence, and pleasure despite the national prohibition on alcoholic beverages. Women had won the right to vote in 1920, the same year that Prohibition went into effect, and were reveling in their newfound strength. In Fitzgerald's own words, "It was an age of miracles, it was an age of art, it was an age of excess, and it was an age of satire." Modernism burst onto the scene during this period, as did many modern technological conveniences. The bold lines of Art Deco became popular, along with the free-form style of Jazz music. This musical trend gets ironic treatment in chapter 3 of *The Great Gatsby* when the orchestra leader announces, "At the request of Mr. Gatsby," that he will play "Vladimir Tostoff's *Jazz History of the World.*" Tostoff is an imaginary composer whom Fitzgerald cynically references to show how jazz is rivaling classical music as the soundtrack for the rich. As the sound of pleasure, danger, and eroticism found in the seamy lower class, jazz gave the newly wealthy a vicarious thrill. For them, jazz symbolized one version of the American dream: the journey from rags to riches in the traditional face of old money.

World War I

Like Jay Gatsby and Nick Carraway, Fitzgerald was part of the American military effort in World War I, which lasted from 1914 until 1918. France, together with the Russian Empire, the United Kingdom, and ultimately the United States, enabled the Allied Powers to defeat the Central Powers, comprised of Austria-Hungary and the German and Ottoman Empires. The United States did not want to enter the conflict at first. However, after the 1915 sinking of the passenger ship *Lusitania* as well as several merchant ships by German submarines, the United States declared war in April 1917. Though Fitzgerald never fought overseas "in wet, grey little villages in France" like Gatsby and Carraway, he did join the army in 1917. Known as "The War to End All Wars," World War I introduced modern mechanized weaponry and poison gas to the battlefront and paved the way for wars to come.

Prohibition

In *The Great Gatsby*, Tom Buchanan suspects that Gatsby is a bootlegger and accuses him of using his chain of drug stores as a front for illegally selling grain alcohol. In December 1917, the Eighteenth Amendment to the U.S. Constitution was passed, prohibiting the "manufacture, sale, or transportation of intoxicating liquors" in the United States, but the amendment did not officially go into effect until January 16, 1920. Prohibition fostered illegal brewing and selling of alcohol, particularly by groups of gangsters and corrupt government officials. Prohibition also provided the seed money and profit to develop organized crime, suggested in *The Great Gatsby* through Wolfshiem's shady dealings. The Twenty-first Amendment repealed national Prohibition but allowed states to control the purchase and sale of alcohol.

CRITICAL OVERVIEW

In 1922, Fitzgerald wrote to his publisher, "I want to write something *new*—something extraordinary and beautiful and simple & intricately patterned." In an advertisement dated April 19, 1925, in the *New York Times*, Charles Scribner's Sons, publisher, claims "Scott Fitzgerald has done it!" Also on that date, Edwin Clark, a critic for the same newspaper, writes:

> The philosopher of the flapper has escaped the mordant, but he has turned grave. A curious book, a mystical, glamourous story of today. It takes a deeper cut at life than hitherto has been enjoyed by Mr. Fitzgerald. He writes well—he always has—for he writes naturally, and his sense of form is becoming perfected.

But his contemporary public did not agree; in actuality, the novel did not sell well, despite testimonial advertisements from social celebrities. It was not until the 1940s that *The Great Gatsby* was read with excitement and appreciation. Arthur Mizener, in the January 1946 *Sewanee Review*, says, "Fitzgerald's great accomplishment is to have realized in completely American terms the developed romantic attitude." Along these same lines, John Berryman in the Winter 1946 *Kenyon Review* calls *The Great Gatsby* "a masterpiece," defining the term as "a work of the literary imagination which is consistent, engaging, and dramatic, in exceptional degrees." Reflecting on the

book thirty-five years after it was published, Mizener declares:

> Almost for the first time Fitzgerald created with that voice an image of The Good American of our time in all his complexity of human sympathy, firm moral judgment and ironic self-possession. We can now afford to turn our attention to such things—because, whatever disagreements we may have over Fitzgerald's work as a whole, there remain few doubts of the greatness of "Gatsby" or of its imaginative relevance to American experience.

In the 1960s, as America entered a state of political and social turmoil, some critics such as Tony Tanner in his 1965 book, *The Reign of Wonder*, tried to make Fitzgerald and his work relevant to the times, noting, "Into the figure of Gatsby [Fitzgerald] put much of what he admired in America. . . . There is something in Gatsby's generous, ideal aspirations which transcends their sordid base and survives their squalid destiny." By 1980, Charles Scribner III states confidently in his new introduction to the novel, "It now rests far above the shifting winds of literary fortune."

Today, many scholars possess varying notions of Gatsby's true nature, many of which are explored in *Readings on* The Great Gatsby. Robert Ornstein, with his article "Gatsby is a Classic Romantic," claims the novel illustrates the futile and "unending quest of the romantic dream," while in "Gatsby is a Sinister Gangster," Thomas Pauly discusses Gatsby as an "upscale, stylish" thug. Brian Way finds the "social comedy" in Gatsby, theorizing that "Gatsby is a Profoundly Comic Character." At the same time, Giles Mitchell has given Gatsby's personality a "clinical analysis" with his stance that "Gatsby is a Pathological Narcissist." These vastly different approaches to the title character in Gatsby reflect Fitzgerald's own characterization of Gatsby: He is an invention not only created by himself, but by others as well.

However, in his preface to Scribner's 1995 "definitive, textually accurate edition" of *The Great Gatsby*, Matthew Bruccoli argues that Fitzgerald did accomplish his goal of creating something "extraordinary and beautiful and simple," calling the book a "masterpiece." He also declares the book "the defining novel of the Twenties, which have become trivialized and vulgarized by people who weren't there." He goes on to explain the novel's and its protagonist's "greatness":

MEDIA ADAPTATIONS

The 1974 film version of *The Great Gatsby* was directed by Jack Clayton and stars Mia Farrow as Daisy and Robert Redford as Gatsby. It is available on DVD and VHS from Paramount.

Director Robert Markowitz made a television version in 2000 with Academy Award–winner Mira Sorvino as Daisy. It is available on DVD and VHS from A & E Home Video.

In 1999, the New York Metropolitan Opera House debuted the novel adaptation as an opera by John Harbison and Murray Horowitz. A recording is available on CD from Naxos.

It has become convenient to refer to *The Great Gatsby* as "the great American novel." If this phrase means anything, it means that the novel is a great work of fiction with defining American thematic qualities and that James Gatz/Jay Gatsby is the great American character. ... Gatsby is a self-made—indeed, self-invented—man. He believes in the American dream of success, ... he fulfills it; ... he is betrayed by it. The appellation *great* as applied to Gatsby reverberates with irony. He is truly great by virtue of his capacity to commit himself to his aspirations.

CRITICISM

Meredith Goldsmith
In the following excerpt, Goldsmith explores the ways Gatsby attempts to "pass" for a member of the Anglo-American leisure class by adopting its styles and mannerisms.

The Performative Apparatus of Americanization
Fashion makes explicit the imitative trajectories of narratives of both passing and Americanization. In *Autobiography of an Ex-Coloured Man*, the gift of tailor-made clothing allows the ex-coloured man to reconstitute himself as white, while Cahan's David Levinsky "was forever watching and striving to imitate the dress and the ways of the well-bred American merchants with whom [he] was, or trying to be, thrown." The imitative qualities of Gatsby's clothing—like that of the novel's other sartorial social climbers—ironizes his efforts at originality. As Gatsby exposes the contents of his armoire to Daisy, for example, his clothing compensates for his lack of familial lineage. Figuring his closet as a kind of Fort Knox, with "bricks" of shirts "piled a dozen feet high," Gatsby appropriates images of might to mask the deficiencies of his origins. If in his "hulking cabinets" Gatsby attempts to approximate Tom Buchanan's brutish economic and physical mastery, Gatsby's acquisition of his clothes signals his alienation from it. Significantly, Gatsby is unaccountable for his own sartorial style, relegating the job to a middleman: "I've got a man in England who buys me clothes. He sends over a selection of things at the beginning of each season, spring and fall." Allowing Dan Cody to outfit him with a new set of clothes, Gatsby, like Levinsky and the ex-coloured man, capitalizes on his homosocial, professional, and personal associations to facilitate his social mobility.

Like his clothing, Gatsby's efforts to transform his physical appearance also suggest his bodily alienation from the Anglo-American leisure class. We remember that Gatsby watches mesmerized as Daisy raises his "pure dull gold" brush to her blonde hair. The monosyllabic description of the brush, with its lack of serial commas, suggests an inimitable quality ostensibly matching Daisy's own perfection. But as Gatsby notes to Nick, "It's the funniest thing, old sport ... I can't—when I try to—." Gatsby's near-speechless moment as he watches Daisy brush her hair, emphasized by its dashes, calls attention to hair itself, another link between *Gatsby* and the fiction of passing and Americanization. Hair lies on a bodily boundary, occupying a liminal position between self and world, and alterations to male hair certify the self-transformation in narratives of both passing and Americanization. For example, the loss of David Levinsky's sidelocks on his first day in America effects his symbolic transformation into an American. When the ex-coloured man vows to live as a white man, he claims that he will "change his name, raise a mustache, and let the world take [him] for what it would." As a child, the narrator exploits the light/dark contrasts of his skin and

Robert Redford and Mia Farrow in a scene from the 1974 film The Great Gatsby *Getty Images*

hair to convince himself that he is white: upon learning of his mother's blackness, the ex-coloured man "notice[s] the softness and glossiness of [his] dark hair that fell in waves over my temples, making [his] forehead appear even whiter than it really was." Fitzgerald's depiction of Gatsby's hair casts class mobility in the terms of the manipulation of both self- and external perception both Johnson and Cahan's narratives suggest. While Gatsby's hair "looks as if it were trimmed every day," Nick accentuates the continuities between Gatsby's body and the objects around him, noting that his own lawn has been "well-shaved" by Gatsby's gardener. During Gatsby's tenure as Dan Cody's assistant, he styles his hair in a dashing pompadour, making himself "just the sort of Jay Gatsby that a seventeen year old boy would be likely to invent." Like Cahan's David Levinsky and Johnson's ex-colored man, Gatsby's changes to his hair style encode his efforts at self-revision on the body for the external gaze.

In the *Gatsby* manuscripts, Fitzgerald underscores the class and gender implications of hairstyle, linking Gatsby's style choice more closely to those of Daisy's. At Gatsby's second party, Daisy and Tom encounter the Star. The Star's eagerness to copy Daisy's haircut flatters Gatsby; Daisy, refusing to be "the originator of a new vogue," claims that being imitated would "spoil it for me." Reversing the norms of fandom, in which audiences yearn to resemble those on screen, here the star yearns to appropriate Daisy's perfection. However, for the working actress to imitate the woman of leisure threatens the boundary between the classes that the Buchanans deem essential: the Star is sustained by publicity, from which Daisy must protect herself to preserve her class position. The circulation of men's images may enhance their reputation, while it threatens those of women: the reproduction of Gatsby's image, whether through news, rumor, or legend increases his power; Tom's scandals land him in the papers but fail to unseat him from his class position.

However, the circulation of the female image harbors particular dangers, evoking the historical connection between public women, actresses, and prostitutes. Fitzgerald links Daisy and the Star through parallel kissing scenes: when Gatsby recalls kissing Daisy on the Louisville street in 1917, the author uses the same images of whiteness, moonlight, and flowers that he distributes around the director's embrace of the Star. For Daisy to admit such parallels, however, is impossible: the circulation of Daisy's image would force her into uneasy familiarity with the actress, endangering both her class and sexual position.

While Fitzgerald might be expected to draw a contrast between those aspects of "personality" that may be externally manipulated—like possessions, clothes, and hair—and those more ostensibly a function of the body—like physical characteristics, Fitzgerald renders just such characteristics the function of imitation and repetition. While Gatsby's smile, for example, first appears to harbor singularity, Fitzgerald ultimately reveals it too as a reproducible commodity:

> He smiled understandingly—much more than understandingly. It was one of those rare smiles with a quality of eternal reassurance in it, that you may come across four or five times in life. It faced—or seemed to face—the whole external world for an instant, and then concentrated on *you* with an irresistible prejudice in your favor. It understood you just so far as you wanted to be understood, believed in you as you would like to believe in yourself and assured you that it had precisely the impression of you that, at your best, you hoped to convey.

The passage enacts the movement from mass audience to individual viewers; metonymizing the smile until it stands in for Gatsby, Nick allows himself to bask in its glow. Stepping out of the role of mass viewer for a moment, Nick experiences a moment of communion with Gatsby, feeling that that their relationship, like Gatsby's with Daisy, is "just personal," liberated from the realm of objects.

However, Gatsby's smile works as a commodity that extends his social power, recalling that of David Levinsky, who develops a "credit face" to solicit investments despite his own lack of capital. Like Levinsky, Gatsby's smile enables him to elicit trust, facilitating his economic rise. Like an advertisement in its use of the second person, the passage reports Nick's seduction by Gatsby's charisma, marketing Gatsby's smile to the reader as if it were a commodity. In the

manuscript, however, Fitzgerald transformed Gatsby's face into an art object: "He was undoubtedly one of the handsomest men I had ever seen—the dark blue eyes opening out into lashes of shining jet were arresting and unforgettable." The transition from the language of art—with its aura intact—to that of reproducible object or advertisement suggests Fitzgerald's increasing awareness of the problem of commodity aesthetics. As Daisy remarks later in the novel, Gatsby "resemble[s] the advertisement of the man," although Tom prohibits her from telling us precisely which one. In her identification of Gatsby's nonspecificity, Daisy gets it closer to right than she knows: even Gatsby's seeming uniqueness is bound up with his likeness to a set of commodified representations.

Fitzgerald's collapsing of the boundary between the frankly imitative and the ostensibly authentic links the character at the very top of the novel's economic and racial hierarchy—Daisy—with Wolfshiem, who resides on or near the bottom. *The Great Gatsby* links Daisy and Wolfshiem by contrasting the ostensibly innate class superiority of her voice with the openly imitative aspects of both his and Gatsby's. Most memorably, of course, Daisy's voice metaphorizes the seeming innateness of her class position, while Gatsby's near-Victorian formality recalls the immigrant struggle to master American speech and etiquette, poignantly presented in Cahan's *Rise of David Levinsky*. In addition, Meyer Wolfshiem, the novel's worst speaker, creates a degraded copy of English through his transformation of "Oxford" into "Oggsford" and "connection" into "gonnegtion." Fitzgerald appears to endorse a kind of vocal nativism, in which the decline of English mimics Tom's anxieties about the decline of "Nordic" superiority.

However, where Daisy's "thrilling voice" ostensibly evokes her aristocratic class and racial position, Jordan senses in it the conflict between repression and desire, noting that "perhaps Daisy never went in for amour at all—and yet there's something in that voice of hers." Fitzgerald's manuscripts reveal the conflict between class, gender, and sexuality that Daisy's voice harbors: when Gatsby comments on Daisy's voice, Nick first responds, "She loves you. Her voice is full of it." Nick's sentimentalization of Daisy, notably absent from the novel's final version, reads her voice as the vessel for her suppressed emotions; Gatsby, who has forcibly assimilated the trappings of the leisure class, assesses it more coldly, interpreting the richness of her voice as a signifier of the class position she works to sustain.

Similarly, Wolfshiem's immigrant diction, which Fitzgerald takes such care to differentiate from the Anglo-American norm, reiterates one of *Gatsby*'s signal themes. In a novel whose plot turns on causal uncertainty—notably, Nick reads the fixing of the World Series as something "that merely *happened*, the end of some inevitable chain" (emphasis added)—references to "connection," or the lack thereof, suggest the repression of causal links necessary to the maintenance of both the Buchanan and Gatsby worlds. The word "connection," reshaped by Wolfshiem's immigrant accent, becomes literally unspeakable, underscoring the economic and homosocial imperatives underlying the novel's ambiguous causal linkages. Wolfshiem's business "gonnegtions" link men for profit, exposing the conflation of economic and gendered power that is partially responsible for Myrtle's death. Wolfshiem's interest in forging "gonnegtions" registers his mastery of American mores of class and gender rather than his failed imitation of them.

Reading *Gatsby* in tandem with narratives of racial passing and ethnic Americanization complicates Fitzgerald's class politics, transforming Gatsby's persona into one in which the ostensibly biological imperatives of "race" and the supposedly more fluid boundaries of class are complexly and ambiguously intermingled. Inauthenticity, the trope of identity in passing and Americanization fiction, emerges as close to the norm for almost all of *Gatsby*'s characters, even those whose class and ethnic status are usually considered unshakeable. Where this section has located *Gatsby* in respect to African-American and Jewish-American ethnic literary texts of the 1910s, the next section situates it in relation to the racial and ethnic performance culture of the era, which lends Gatsby's West Egg parties their "spectroscopic gayety."

Source: Meredith Goldsmith, "White Skin, White Mask: Passing, Posing, and Performing in *The Great Gatsby*," in *Modern Fiction Studies*, Vol. 49, No. 3, Fall 2003, pp. 443–68.

SOURCES

Bender, David, et al., eds., *Readings on* The Great Gatsby, Greenhaven Press, 1998, pp. vii, ix, xi, 15.

Berryman, John, "F. Scott Fitzgerald," in the *Kenyon Review,* Winter 1946, pp. 103–12; excerpted in "Fitzgerald, F. Scott (1896–1940)," in *Modern American Literature,* Vol. 1, 5th ed., St. James Press, 1999, p. 369.

Bruccoli, Matthew, "A Brief Life of Fitzgerald," *F. Scott Fitzgerald Centenary,* www.sc.edu/fitzgerald/biography.html (December 4, 2003); originally published in *F. Scott Fitzgerald: A Life in Letters,* Scribner, 1994.

Bruccoli, Matthew, "Preface," *The Great Gatsby,* Scribner, 1995, pp. vii–xvi.

Carter, Tara, "The Migrant in New York: In Pursuit of an American dream in Rudolph Fisher's 'The City of Refuge' and F. Scott Fitzgerald's *The Great Gatsby,*" *SMACK!,* www.uiowa.edu/~smack/archive/smack1.2/2ess2.htm (September 10, 2006).

Clark, Edwin, "Gatsby's Scott Fitzgerald Looks Into Middle Age," in the *New York Times,* April 19, 1925, www.nytimes.com/books/00/12/24/specials/fitzgerald-gatsby.html (October 11, 2006).

Decker, Jeffrey Louis, "Gatsby's Pristine Dream: The Diminishment of the Self-Made Man in the Tribal Twenties," *NOVEL: A Forum on Fiction,* Vol. 28, Autumn 1994, pp. 52–71.

Fitzgerald, F. Scott, *The Great Gatsby,* Scribner, 1925; reprint, 1995.

First World War.com-A multimedia History of WWI, www.firstworldwar.com (September 7, 2006).

Mizener, Arthur, "*Gatsby,* 35 Years Later," in the *New York Times,* April, 24, 1960, www.nytimes.com/books/00/12/24/specials/fitzgerald-gatsby60.html (November 1, 2006).

———, "Scott Fitzgerald and the Imaginative Possession of American Life," in the *Sewanee Review,* January–March 1946. pp. 66–67; excerpted in "Fitzgerald, F. Scott (1896–1940)," in *Modern American Literature,* Vol. 1, 5th ed., St. James Press, 1999, p. 369.

Mitchell, Giles, "Gatsby is a Pathological Narcissist," in *Readings on The Great Gatsby,* Greenhaven Press, 1998, pp. 61–67.

Ornstein, Robert, "Gatsby is a Classic Romantic," in *Readings on The Great Gatsby,* Greenhaven Press, 1998, pp. 33–40.

Pauly, Thomas H., "Gatsby is a Sinister Gangster," in *Readings on The Great Gatsby,* Greenhaven Press, 1998, pp. 41–51.

Scribner, Charles, III, "Introduction," in *The Great Gatsby,* Scribner, 1980, p. xx.

Tony Tanner, *The Reign of Wonder,* Cambridge University Press, 1965; excerpted in "Fitzgerald, F. Scott (1896–1940)," in *Modern American Literature,* Vol. 1, 5th ed., St. James Press, 1999, p. 370.

Way, Brian, "Gatsby is a Profoundly Comic Character," in *Readings on The Great Gatsby,* Greenhaven Press, 1998, pp. 52–60.

House Made of Dawn

N. SCOTT MOMADAY

1968

A powerful look at the alienation one Native American experiences, *House Made of Dawn* (1968) is regarded as the beginning of the Native American renaissance in literature. The first novel by highly regarded Native American author N. Scott Momaday, *House Made of Dawn* surprised everyone when it won the Pulitzer Prize for fiction in 1969. This marked the first time an American Indian was given this award. Momaday did not believe it initially when he was called with the news, and even the publisher had forgotten it had published the novel.

Momaday began writing what became *House Made of Dawn* several years earlier as a series of poems. It gradually evolved into stories, before being published as a novel in 1968. Momaday had previously published excerpts in the *Southern Review*, *New Mexico Quarterly*, and *The Reporter*.

Like Abel in the novel, Momaday grew up on Indian reservations, where his parents—his father was a Kiowa Indian while his mother was part Cherokee—worked as educators. He learned much about several Native American cultures throughout this childhood, and he appreciated the land, language, and oral traditions of American Indians. Momaday drew on this familiarity while writing the book, the title of which comes from a Navajo religious ceremony song, "House Made of Dawn."

In *House Made of Dawn*, Momaday explores complex ideas about American Indian identity,

language, landscape, and cultural conflict in a lyrical, stream-of-consciousness style. His sometimes fractured and circular narrative includes folk tales and legends. The novel also features poetic language and movement, influenced by Momaday's primary focus as a writer: poetry. Momaday uses both first-person and third-person points of view and moves around in time with flashbacks to explicate the depth of Abel's pain.

The plot of *House Made of Dawn* focuses on Abel, a Jemez Pueblo Indian, and his loss of identity as he returns first to his native community after serving in the U.S. military during World War II. While Abel participates in native rituals, he feels no connection to them. He soon kills an albino man, and is sent to prison. Abel's alienation grows deeper after his release from prison. He is sent to Los Angeles, where he is even more alienated than at home. While Abel has friendships with other Native Americans there, especially Ben, he feels even more disconnected from the land, the people, both white and Indian, and himself. Abel finally returns home to New Mexico again after taking a brutal beating in Los Angeles. He is able to reconnect to his home.

Throughout *House Made of Dawn* are flashbacks from Abel's childhood, which was stained by the deaths of his mother and brother from alcoholism. Abel was raised by his grandfather Francisco, who participates in native religious rituals as well as in the Catholic Church run by Father Olguin. Religion, faith, and ritual play prominent roles in the book; Tosamah connects the faiths in his Los Angeles church for Native Americans. While his grandfather tried to pass on to Abel the importance of tribal rituals, including a sacred tribal run through the valley, it is not until his grandfather's death after his return from Los Angeles that Abel can begin to heal both in body and spirit.

Critics praise the novel for its depth, though many believe that its meaning was misunderstood by some early reviewers and readers. *House Made of Dawn* garnered scholarly attention by the 1980s and earned comparisons to works by William Faulkner as well as James Joyce. Martha Scott Trimble in *N. Scott Momaday* explains its power:

> [*House Made of Dawn*] is a complex, symbolic expression of how language and culture tend through their own territorial imperatives to

BIOGRAPHY

N. SCOTT MOMADAY

Born February 27, 1934, in Lawton, Oklahoma, Momaday is the son of Alfred, a Kiowa artist and art teacher, and Mayme, a one-eighth Cherokee teacher and writer. When Momaday was two, the family moved to New Mexico where his parents worked as teachers among the Navajo and Pueblo Indians. He grew up on several Indian reservations in the Southwest and learned about the art, language, literature, and history of many tribes. After earning his bachelor's degree in political science from the University of New Mexico, he spent a year in law school in Virginia, where he met William Faulkner, an influence on his writing.

Momaday began writing poetry while teaching on a New Mexico reservation. On the basis of his work, he was admitted to Stanford, where he continued to compose poetry while earning his master's and doctoral degrees. While teaching at various universities, Momaday wrote poetry and fiction. His first book, *House Made of Dawn* (1968), was influenced by tribal traditions. It was the surprise Pulitzer Prize winner in 1969. Though Momaday followed it with *The Way to Rainy Mountain* (1969), he found it hard to write for years because of the expectations set by the prize; his next work of fiction was 1985's *The Ancient Child*. He is the founder and chairman of the Buffalo Trust, a nonprofit foundation for the perpetuation and development of Native American culture and heritage in Santa Fe, New Mexico. As of 2006, Momaday continues to teach and write.

encompass one, sometimes to a point of isolation... *House Made of Dawn* transcends any Indian problem; that the novel is a universal statement does not make the effect of Momaday's portrayal of the deculturation of an Indian youth any the less lamentable.

PLOT SUMMARY

Prologue

House Made of Dawn opens with a description of a beautiful landscape in the past: "There was a house made of dawn. It was made of pollen and rain and the land was very old and everlasting.... The land was still strong. It was beautiful all around." Abel is running on the road in the valley at dawn. Momaday writes, "Against the winter sky and the long, light landscape of the valley at dawn, he seemed almost to be standing still, very little and alone."

Section 1: The Longhair: Walatowa, Cañon de San Diego, 1945
Chapter 1: July 20

The first section starts with a description of the land near the Jemez pueblo in Walatowa, New Mexico. Francisco drives his horse-drawn wagon along the river and on the road to San Ysidro. He remembers his past as a runner participating in "the race for good hunting and harvests." Francisco passed the best runner in 1889, the same year he killed fourteen deer. He is on his way to the meet the bus bringing his grandson, Abel. Abel stumbles off the bus, drunk. He does not recognize his grandfather, who puts him on the wagon.

Chapter 2: July 21

Abel sleeps off his drunkenness at his grandfather's for a day. The next day, Abel goes out in the early morning and checks out the scenery.

Abel has memories of his childhood. He did not know his father, a member of some Native American tribe. When Abel was five years old, he played with his brother Vidal and lived with his mother, a Jemez Pueblo Indian, and already elderly grandfather. His mother died that October. As Abel grew older, he herded sheep, observed a prayer ritual when his brother died, and, by seventeen, he was hunting and having sex after a dance in town.

Later, Abel saw an eagle carrying a snake in its talons at dawn. Because of what he saw, he went on a hunt with the Eagle Watchers Society. He helped kill rabbits for bait and participated in a ceremony of purification. He caught a female eagle and kept it bagged. When he looked into the bag, he saw the great bird: "Bound and helpless, his eagle seemed drab and shapeless in the moonlight, too large and ungainly for flight. The

N. Scott Momaday Ulf Andersen/Getty Images

sight of it filled him with shame and disgust." He killed the eagle.

Though Francisco did not understand, Abel left the town and this life behind.

Returning to the present, Abel can remember these parts of his life, but not what happened after he left nearly as well. His only clear memory of fighting in the war involves regaining consciousness on a battlefield strewn with bodies. He was nearly run over by a tank. As daylight breaks, Abel watches a car drive into town.

At the mission in town, Father Olguin is saying mass. Francisco attends the service. The woman who was driving the car, Mrs. Angela Martin St. John, walks in the middle of the mass. She approaches the priest after the service. A visitor to the area, she needs wood cut for her wood stove. Father Olguin promises to send someone to help her.

At Francisco's, Abel still has not eaten. He watches his grandfather and others working the fields. Abel feels somewhat at home for the moment.

Chapter 3: July 24

Abel goes to Angela's house to chop her wood. He charges her $3. Angela watches him work, amazed at his body and his physical work. She is pregnant and hates her body. After he cuts up part of the wood, she puts some in the fire. Father Olguin stops by to invite her to come to town for the feast of Santiago celebration.

Chapter 4: July 25

On the hot day, the myth of Saint James is re-enacted in town. The priest escorts Angela to the Middle in town to watch the ceremony and games. Abel is among the participants who try to grab a rooster from a hole in the ground as they ride by on horseback. Angela is impressed by the scene. An albino finally gets the rooster and remains on his horse, and then beats Abel with the rooster, killing the bird.

The event makes Angela weary. After she goes home, Father Olguin stays up late reading the journal of Fray Nicolás from the mid-1870s. While the journal is primarily about religion, Fray Nicolás also mentions the birth of the albino, Juan Reyes Fragua. Inspired by the letter Fray Nicolás wrote, Father Olguin decides that "tomorrow he would become a figure, an example for the town."

Chapter 5: July 28

After describing the lay of the land, including its geography and wildlife, and the never-changing life in town, the narrator reveals that Abel feels out of place: "he tried to pray, to sing, to enter into the old rhythm of the tongue, but he was no longer attuned to it." He even finds it difficult to talk to his grandfather. Abel does find some connection as he walks in the canyon to finish the job at Angela's house.

Angela has been thinking about Abel, wondering when he will return. Angela is out to have a mineral bath. Abel cuts the wood and waits for her return, which does not come until after dark. She makes him coffee and talks to him as he listens. She senses that he knows their lovemaking is inevitable, which makes her excited and nervous. They do make love. Francisco is working the fields at the same time. Weary and thinking of the past, he hears whispers in the corn. When he hears something new and alien, he becomes excited.

Chapter 6: August 1

Father Olguin feels good about his life and work, fitting in the town's pace of life. The arrival of Angela had excited him, but she is now keeping her distance. He takes this gesture as a sign of respect. On this day, he decides to visit her, surprising her. The priest tells Angela about the town. Angela listens to him as well as the rain she can hear coming down some distance away. Father Olguin catches her not listening to him, and Angela is embarrassed when she is expected to respond and does not.

When the priest returns to town, he is more easily annoyed by people, especially children. The storm passes over Angela's house and she enjoys the cleansing event:

> She closed her eyes, and the clear aftervision of the rain, which she could still hear and feel so perfectly as to conceive of nothing else, obliterated all the mean and myriad fears that had laid hold of her in the past.

There is another celebration in town, enjoyed by a crippled old man who appreciates the sounds, people, and smells. After passing by a Catholic shrine, he takes part in ceremonies in the kiva (a ceremonial chamber built of wood, wire, and greenery). When he comes out of the kiva, the rain is coming down on the town.

At night, after the rain ends, Abel, the albino, and others are at Paco's bar. Many are drunk. Outside, Abel talks to the albino, called the "white man," and stabs him several times. Momaday writes, "He could not think; there was nothing left inside him but a cold, instinctive will to wonder and regard." Abel watches as the albino dies.

Chapter 7: August 2

There is a procession through town. Francisco takes his wagon to the fields, and says his grandson's name several times. Momaday writes, "He knew only that he was alone again."

Section 2: The Priest of the Sun: Los Angeles, 1952
Chapter 1: January 26

It is several years later in Los Angeles. The "Priest of the Sun," also known as Rev. Big John Bluff Tosamah, is preaching at his Pan-Indian Rescue Mission. The preacher emphasizes the importance of words to children. He talks about his grandmother who was illiterate but could tell stories, and compares her to white men's changing relationship with language. Tosamah also relates this oral literature back to St. John and the Word of God.

Abel is in Los Angeles and again having a hard time adjusting. He does not understand the sea, which is not part of his life experience.

Abel wakes up cold and in pain, unable to open his eyes. He had been drunk, but the effects of alcohol are wearing off. He is near the sea, by a fence and some docks in an industrial area. His hands are broken. Abel remembers that his body was once great until he hurt his back falling off a horse. He only became sick when he began drinking.

Abel reflects back six years to his trial. He is disassociated from the event. Father Olguin testified, saying that Abel was not murdering the albino. The priest explained, "I mean that in his own mind it was not a man he killed. It was something else." Abel only talked about it once and would not speak of it again.

Returning to the present, Abel is awake, coughing blood. When he hears voices near him, he hides in the brush. He remembers what prison was like, then reflects back further as he tries to understand when his life went wrong:

> He tried to think where the trouble had begun, what the trouble was. There was trouble; he could admit that to himself, but he had no real insight into his own situation. Maybe, certainly, *that* was the trouble; but he had no way of knowing.

Abel also thinks about his recent life in Los Angeles with Milly, a white social worker whose personal quizzes are interspersed in the text, and his friend Benally, also known as Ben. While living with Ben, he and Milly become lovers.

Painted for his prayer meeting, Tosamah describes peyote. He is holding a ceremony with peyote and all forty-four people present ingest the drug. There is an ebb and flow to the emotion in the room. Some of the participants speak, offering praise and thanks and describing their visions; Ben mentions the "house made of dawn."

Abel realizes how badly he is hurt; his face is cut and his hands are mangled and broken. He wonders who will find him. While he is in this state, he reflects back to his life as a child. After his mother died, Abel and Vidal, his brother, visited fat Josie for comfort. "He was a child who did not laugh," and she made a fool of herself to amuse him. Francisco did not approve.

After his brother died, he only visited her one more time, and she danced in the kitchen.

At Abel's trial, a white man named Bowker talked about Abel and what happened to him when he served in the war. Bowker found him alive on the field when they thought he was dead. He saw Abel nearly get hit with a tank. Bowker described Abel dancing while being shot at by the enemy. Abel remembers a time when he and Vidal had guns near the river. They shot geese, and one landed in the river. These memories are mixed with Abel telling Milly about the birds. He promises her that he will get a job, and they will go to the beach.

Milly was lonely when Abel was not there, and she knew he was drunk somewhere. Milly had lived in Los Angeles for four years, but no one knew the real her until Abel, who was as lonely as she was. She thinks back to her childhood; her father was an unsuccessful farmer who loved her. She left when she was seventeen years old, and never saw him again. She went to school, worked as a waitress, got married, and had a daughter named Carrie. Her husband left her, and her daughter died at the age of four.

Abel forces himself to get up. After sneaking a ride on the back of a truck, a man sees Abel and is horrified. Dizzy and in agony, Abel has visions of going to the beach with Milly and Ben.

Chapter 2: January 27
Tosamah's sermon describes the geography and weather of his home. He talks of his grandmother, her past, and the history of her tribe. Tosamah tells of the time he made a pilgrimage to her grave, describing the landscape, including Devils Tower. His grandmother had practiced Indian rites since childhood, but became a Christian as well. Her home had seemed big when he was a child but was much smaller when he returned there after her death.

Section 3: The Night Chanter: Los Angeles, 1952
Chapter 1: February 20
Ben describes when Abel left Los Angeles. Ben had given him his only coat. Though Ben is cold in the rain, he is concerned about Abel. Abel had a broken nose and hands, and Ben is worried that no one on the train would help him.

After getting money owed to him and buying wine, Ben returns home. He remembers how Milly fit in with Abel, adjusting to his comfort level without question. He also reflects on last night when Ben, Abel, and other Native Americans went on a hill, got drunk, and danced around the fire with drums and flutes. Ben and Abel watched, happy, then went off by themselves. Ben talked about what they would do in the future, emphasizing plans they made while Abel was in the hospital. Abel believed what Ben said, and Ben began to as well. Ben also sang "House Made of Dawn" so only Abel could hear:

> Your offering I make
> I have prepared a smoke for you.
> . . .
> Restore my body for me,
> Restore my mind for me.
> . . .
> Happily I recover

Ben knew from the beginning that Abel would not make it in Los Angeles because he was unwilling or unable to change. Ben also believes that Tosamah did not understand Abel, though he warned Ben about him. On an earlier occasion, Ben was sitting on the hill by himself and Tosamah gave him his interpretation on of what "they" did to Abel. Ben thinks Tosamah did not understand Abel because he did not grow up on a reservation and is educated. Tosamah did not have the same fear as Abel and Ben.

Ben describes how he met Abel. He was working on the line in a factory and Abel was hired there. Ben showed Abel the ropes, befriended him, and offered him a place to stay. It took a while before Abel would talk to anyone, and when he did, he did not reveal much about himself. Ben found they had a lot in common.

Ben believes that Abel had a hard time adjusting to life. He tried for two months, but the pressure and questions from his parole officer, his relocation officer, and others were hard on him. They did not like that he drank and caroused. He was told he had to stay out of trouble or go back to prison. Ben covered for him, but they did not understand Abel's situation or how to talk to him.

After a twelve-hour workday, Ben and Abel went to Tosamah's and played poker. Though they had to be at work early, Abel would not leave. Tosamah started picking on Abel indirectly, mocking the "*longhairs* and the reservation and all"; Abel tried to attack him but was too drunk. His pride hurt, Abel would not go

back to work for two days. Ben told their boss he was sick, but Abel stayed drunk and passed out.

When Abel returned to work, the foreman was hard on him. Momaday writes, "Finally he just dropped everything and looked at Daniels hard, like maybe he was going to hit him or something, and walked out." Abel started drinking, borrowing money from Ben, then Milly. He could not keep another job. Abel still had fun going to the beach with Ben and Milly.

Ben remembers stories Abel told him of his childhood. Sitting at home, Ben wonders where Abel is. Ben remembers another time, when Ben and Abel were coming home from Henry's. They were being loud, and Martinez came out of a dark alley to stop them. He takes all of Ben's money and uses a stick to beat and bruise Abel's hands. Abel could not let the incident go, and often got drunk and became angry.

For work, Ben sometimes had to make deliveries on the company truck. If he had to travel far, he would pick up Abel and take him along. One time, Ben went to Westwood with Abel. Ben grew angry when Abel forced him to wait so he could watch a woman. It was Angela. "She was going to help him, he said. She liked him a lot, and, you know, they fooled around and everything, and she was going to help him get a job and go away from the reservation, but then he got himself into trouble," Ben recounts. Abel stopped looking for work.

Ben sees Los Angeles as a city of activity and promise. He sees the material possessions and friendly people. He believes the Relocation people are all right despite what Tosamah says. Abel started hating everyone and everything. He even got angry at Ben and Milly. No one was allowed to help him. Ben reached his breaking point one day and told Abel to get out. After the drunk Abel left, Ben worried, especially when Abel did not come back for three days.

Ben finally found Abel on their stairs nearly dead. Abel was covered in blood and broken. Ben called an ambulance and rode to the hospital with him. Calling in sick at work, Ben stayed with Abel. He even called Angela, who visited Abel in the hospital two days later. She told him about her son Peter:

> Peter always asked her about the Indians, she said, and she used to tell him a story about a young Indian brave. He was born of a bear and a maiden, she said, and he was noble and wise. He had many adventures, and he became a

> THEY MUST KNOW THAT HE WOULD KILL THE WHITE MAN AGAIN, IF HE HAD THE CHANCE, THAT THERE COULD BE NO HESITATION WHATSOEVER. FOR HE WOULD KNOW WHAT THE WHITE MAN WAS, AND HE WOULD KILL HIM IF HE COULD. A MAN KILLS SUCH AN ENEMY IF HE CAN."

great leader and saved his people. It was the story Peter liked best of all, and she always thought of *him*, Abel, when she told it.

On the hill before Abel left, Ben prayed. He told Abel to look out for him and what they would do there in the future. Ben recalls, "We were going to see how it was, and always was, how the sun came up with a little wind and the light ran out upon the land."

Section 4: The Dawn Runner, Walatowa, 1952
Chapter 1: February 27
Returning to third-person voice, the narrator describes the landscape in winter. Father Olguin is older and had made his peace with the town. He feels some exclusion and estrangement, but he is doing good works and is a good example to others.

Abel visits his grandfather's home each morning for six days. Francisco is dying. Abel listens to him talk every morning before Francisco becomes comatose every afternoon. Abel cannot think of anything to say to him, but he takes care of him and ensures there is a fire.

There are stories of Francisco's past. He took his grandsons to Campo Santo so they could learn the whole of the black mesa's shape. As a young man, he explores caves and mountains. At night a bear came upon his camp and spooked his horse. He did not kill the bear then but continued his journey at sunrise. He caught up with the bear and killed it. In another story, Francisco needed to go to the fields. He sent Vidal there, and he took young Abel to the valley to hear the men running. In a different vignette, Francisco challenged a runner and bested him.

Chapter 2: February 28
At Francisco's, Abel wakes up in the middle of the night. His grandfather has died. Abel takes care of his appearance, dressing him and performing rituals. Abel then goes to Father Olguin's and tells him of Francisco's passing. Abel leaves, waits for the runners in the valley, and joins them. Though broken, he runs on singing "House Made of Dawn" under his breath.

THEMES

Alienation
Much of *House Made of Dawn* focuses on the alienation Abel feels as he tries to fit into both the primarily Native American community he grew up in as well as the white-dominated city of Los Angeles after he is released from prison. To be alienated is to feel isolated or withdrawn, as if one does not belong where he or she is. In the novel, Abel first senses that he is different as a child: "His father was a Navajo, or a Sia, an outsider anyway, which made him and his mother and Vidal somehow foreign and strange." He left his home to serve in the military during World War II and almost died. His alienation grows deeper when he returns home the first time. When he arrives, Abel stumbles off the bus drunk and cannot even recognize his own grandfather, Francisco. While he participates in the feast of Santiago celebration, he has a hard time finding any connection to the life in the town, even with Francisco. The author writes,

> His return to the town had been a failure, for all his looking forward. He had tried in the days that followed to speak to his grandfather, but he could not say the things he wanted; he had tried to pray, to sing, to enter into the old rhythm of the tongue, but he was not longer attuned to it. And yet it was there still, like memory.

This sense of alienation leads to his murdering the albino, called the "white man," a trial, and jail time. After his release from jail, Abel moves to Los Angeles and finds work in a factory. Though he has friends in Ben and Milly, he is close to them only relatively. While Abel knows other Native Americans, such as Tosamah, Ben believes they do not understand Abel either. After Abel is humiliated at a card game, his sense of alienation in Los Angeles increases. He retreats into drink, loses his job and his way, and ends up beaten with a broken face and hands. Ben believes the reason for Abel's failures in Los Angeles is his very nature. Ben explains,

> You could see that he wasn't going to get along around here.... You know, you have to change. That's the only way you can live in a place like this. You have to forget about the way it was, how you grew up and all. Sometimes it's hard, but you have to do it.

While many people embrace the American dream, others, like Abel, feel alienated from it and American society as a whole because of their background and experiences. It is only when Abel returns home a second time, takes care of his grandfather until his death, and runs again in the valley that his sense of alienation begins to show signs of easing.

Cultural Conflict

Throughout the narrative of *House Made of Dawn* is a sense of cultural conflict, a consequence of the melting pot that makes up America and the American dream. In addition to Abel's sense of alienation—a personal type of cultural conflict—Momaday emphasizes tensions between white and Native American people and society as well as within native culture. For example, Abel remembers that he was presumed dead after a battle in World War II, but he survived only to be nearly hit by what he recalls as a "machine." At his trial, a white man named Bowker who served with him remembers the story slightly differently. Bowker emphasizes Abel's otherness when describing Abel's actions when he jumped up and was nearly hit by the tank. Bowker says, "He was giving it the finger and whooping it up and doing a g—dam *war dance*, sir.... And there *he* was, hopping around with his finger up in the air and giving it to that tank in Sioux or Algonquin or something."

While there are other cultural conflicts based on quick misunderstandings—such as Milly adjusting her way of dealing with people to fit Abel's personality and Abel short-circuiting Angela's desire to bargain a price for cutting her wood—other conflicts in the story are born of deeper, long-term differences. Father Olguin, for example, serves the community as a Catholic priest. Yet members of the Native American community, such as Francisco, practice both Catholicism and Indian rituals, and do not seem close to the priest.

The priest relates well to white visitor Angela, even escorting her to the feast of Santiago, but he does not share the same ease with the everyday people who form his constituency. In the last section of the novel, Father Olguin finally accepts that even his shining life example will not allow him to overcome cultural differences nor result in full acceptance by the community. The author writes, "he had come to terms with the town.... [T]here was the matter of some old and final cleavage, of certain exclusion, the whole and subtle politics of estrangement, but that was easily put aside."

The cultural conflicts between white and Native cultures are more obvious in Los Angeles. Abel's difficulties are not understood by Milly, his white supervisor, or even the public officials who brought him there. Ben, however, understands what Abel is going through. Ben even realizes that some American Indians who live in Los Angeles share this cultural misunderstanding. One night, Tosamah warns Ben about Abel, but Ben believes that Tosamah's more privileged background does not allow him to grasp Abel and his alienation. Ben says of Tosamah, "He's educated, and he doesn't believe in being scared like that. But he doesn't come from the reservation. He doesn't know how it is when you grow up out there someplace." Cultural conflict is often born of such misunderstandings.

The Land

In *House Made of Dawn*, Momaday also emphasizes the importance of the physical landscape, especially in the scenes set in Abel's home community and in several of Tosamah's sermons about his grandmother. Such connections to the land that the United States is built upon has been a vital part of the American dream since the country was founded. Momaday describes the geography of the area around Abel's reservation as well as its wildlife and how it changes through the seasons. Francisco is very connected to this land, which he works as a farmer as well as with animals. In the flashbacks, Abel and his late brother are described in similar terms as Abel participates in an eagle hunt and shoots geese with Vidal. Their grandfather also taught them about the land and its seasons.

For Abel, Los Angeles does not fit physically, in part because this land is coastal. Momaday describes him as not understanding the sea, and he nearly dies beside it after being beaten up. It is only when Abel reconnects with the land as a runner in the valley, an event described at the beginning and end of the novel, that his healing can begin. His grandfather had run when he was young, and he showed young Abel the runners many years back. This running through the land is Abel's salvation:

> Pure exhaustion laid hold of his mind, and he could see at last without having to think. He could see the canyon and the mountains and the sky. He could see the rain and the river and the fields beyond.

HISTORICAL OVERVIEW

Native Americans in the United States from the 1940s to the 1970s

During World War II, 44,000 Native Americans served in the U.S. military, though their total population only numbered about 350,000. While Indians were drafted—they had become recognized as citizens of the United States in 1924, and thus eligible—about 40 percent had volunteered, according to a 1942 survey. In the service, Indians were fully integrated. Because of the labor shortages around the United States caused by the war, many other Native Americans left reservations to work in factories and other high-paying jobs. About 40,000 American Indians worked in war industries, including an estimated 12,000 women.

When Native American soldiers returned to their reservations, many faced difficulties. Some tribes welcomed the return of these soldiers as heroes, such as the Navajo. Other tribes were less hospitable. The Zuni Pueblo, for example, wanted their returning soldiers to undergo purification before coming in contact with members of their tribe. Either way, many Native American soldiers lost any status they had gained in the opinion of whites while serving in the military when they returned to civilian life.

After World War II, many Native American soldiers received a monthly subsistence check for $90 on a temporary basis. They also received some education in agriculture. Despite such efforts, former soldiers left their reservations and moved to urban areas. Between 1941 and 1950, the number of American Indians living in cities went from 24,000 to 56,000. After the end of World War II, many Native Americans lived in San Francisco and Los Angeles, California. However, most were unable to find regular employment and had a third of the median income of white men. Despite such economic and social difficulties, some Native Americans found solace in groups that formed across tribal lines in the cities.

Federal policies regarding Indians continued to change in the 1950s. In 1953, the federal government released itself from all responsibilities for Native American tribes and their land in a policy called "termination." With a new congressional resolution, Native Americans became full citizens of the United States. They were no longer wards of the United States and no longer received financial subsidies. The reservation system was also ended, and tribal lands were distributed to individuals in the tribe. This redistribution led to reservation land being available and sold to non–Native Americans as well.

Beginning in 1954, the United States government began a program to settle more Native Americans in cities. This was a voluntary program, but it had poor results and ended in 1960. Many Native Americans resented the attempts to assimilate them into mainstream society. Because of the failure of these changes, the policy of termination was reversed by the federal government in the early 1960s.

Inspired in part by the success of the African American civil rights movement, Native Americans became activists, adopted the slogan "red power," and began demanding more rights by the mid-1960s. In 1964, Native Americans went to Washington, D.C., and wanted to be included in President Lyndon B. Johnson's War on Poverty. By this time, Native Americans were the poorest minority group in the United States. In the late 1960s, they began demanding preference in hiring practices. Native Americans also wanted to be reimbursed for land confiscated by both federal and state government in violation of treaties. They went to court to challenge violations of land and water-rights treaties, winning the first in a long line of victories in 1967.

Native Americans formed groups to reach their goals. One of the best-known groups is the American Indian Movement (AIM), founded in 1966. AIM ensured government funds reached other organizations operated by Native Americans. The group also ensured Native Americans in cities received support. AIM was also involved in deliberate action. AIM took over Wounded Knee, South Dakota, in 1973.

This village was the site of a nineteenth-century massacre of Sioux Indians by white soldiers. By taking over the village, AIM members wanted to highlight the poverty and alcoholism engulfing the reservation located around Wounded Knee. The siege ended after seventy-one days when a Native American was killed and another wounded. The federal government also agreed to look again at treaty rights for Native Americans as part of the agreement made to end the siege.

Wounded Knee was not the only confrontation initiated by Native Americans in this time period. In 1969, two hundred Native Americans calling themselves "Indians of All Tribes" landed on Alcatraz Island, seized the abandoned federal prison there, and held it for nineteen months. As at Wounded Knee, the activists wanted to highlight the poor living conditions on Native American reservations that resulted in an average life expectancy of only forty-four years in 1970. The U.S. government's forced removal of the activists in 1971 ended the seizure of the island in the San Francisco Bay. Such actions resulted in some long-term positive changes as the U.S. government passed several acts in the 1970s and 1980s that gave Native Americans more control over their education and better medical care. They also had continuing legal success in reclaiming tribal rights.

CRITICAL OVERVIEW

When *House Made of Dawn* was originally published in 1968, it garnered mixed reviews. Soon, however, the novel came to be seen as Momaday's masterpiece. Scholars later embraced the book as one of the most important novels of the twentieth century.

Initially, *House Made of Dawn* did receive some praise from critics for its use of language. *Publishers Weekly* calls it "a beautiful and moving tale" and noted, "Its intricately conceived pattern ... is executed with easy lyricism." Similarly, Marshall Sprague of the *New York Times Book Review* writes that the novel is "as subtly wrought as a piece of Navajo silverware," but also believes "There is plenty of haze in the telling of this tale—but that is one reason why it rings so true." (Later, such reviews were dismissed by scholars who believed that such critics did not understand the cultural background of

the characters nor the author of the book as well as the tribal tradition that informed the book's imagery.)

Early critics who reviewed the book negatively found *House Made of Dawn* hard to follow, if not obscure and confusing in its structure and lacking of a plot line. While Joan W. Stevenson of *Library Journal* praises the book for being "Strong in imaginative imagery, descriptive detail, and evocation of the natural world," she also notes, "this book will tax readers accustomed to definite plot lines and vivid characterization." The *Kirkus Service* comments, "Momaday's writing ... is detailed and explicit ... and one's sympathies are aroused in a general way but we remain, finally, uninvolved in his tragedy."

Some reviewers were surprised when *House Made of Dawn* won the Pulitzer Prize in 1969. The *Times Literary Supplement*'s critic was one who was shocked by the award. While lauding Momaday's "considerable descriptive power," the critic also believes "the rhetoric is a bit too facile, smacks somewhat of campus creative-writing, and on occasion creates a nebulosity opaque enough to count as self-parody."

Over the years, the book's reputation changed and deepened. By the 1980s, *House Made of Dawn* became the focus of scholarly critiques. Within a decade, the novel was regarded as the hallmark of the Native American renaissance in literature. The book was regularly used in literature courses at universities, though it has also been the subject of at least one potential banning in Round Rock, Texas, in the mid-1990s, for its explicit love scenes. Momaday was not offended by the attempt, telling Starita Smith, Daniel J. Vargas, and Taylor Johnson of the *Austin American-Statesman* the effort was "silly and kind of amusing, but it sells books. It should happen every once in awhile to keep the publishers happy."

In addition to finding new meaning in the book's connection to Native American spirituality and oral traditions, scholars analyzed Momaday's aesthetic and descriptions as well. Many critics and scholars emphasized the importance of language and Momaday's descriptions. The way various facets of the novel were interpreted also changed. For example, one source of critical debate was interpreting the meaning of Abel's stabbing the albino. A few saw the albino as representative of a pagan tradition in conflict with the Catholic rites in which

MEDIA ADAPTATIONS

House Made of Dawn was adapted as a movie in 1987. Momaday shares the screenwriting credit with Richardson Morse, who also directs. It stars Larry Littlebird as Abel and Mesa Bird as Grandfather. It is available on VHS from New Line Home Video.

Abel was raised. Many others interpreted the albino as a symbol of white oppression or as a symbol of cultural conflict between white and native cultures. Alan R. Velie in *Dictionary of Literary Biography* interpreted it as such: "Momaday uses the term *white man* to describe the albino, and the murder is rendered in sexual terms—a sort of macabre double entendre."

No matter what the interpretation, many critics found *House Made of Dawn* intriguing. Martha Scott Trimble, in *N. Scott Momaday*, comments,

> We may resolve many of the mysterious things unique to *House Made of Dawn*, but Momaday, in making his points about the range of relationships between cultures, wishes to leave at least the non-Indian reader with an abiding sense of what he does not know.

CRITICISM

Matthias Schubnell
In the following excerpt, Schubnell considers the novel's central dilema as the struggle between individual and community, specifically in the mediation between the two in order to derive a satisfyingly whole sense of identity, and how this relates to Native American cultures in times of crisis.

Abel is struggling to find an identity within his own tribe long before he comes into direct contact with the culture of modern America. From a developmental point of view his experience is universal: it is the struggle of a young man to establish a stable position in his community. From a historical perspective his crisis reflects a crisis of his culture which denies its young tribal members accommodation to changing conditions.

Abel's problem grows out of a generation conflict within a tribal community in which the ancient traditions tend to lose their meanings for young Indians in their confrontation with the cultural tradition of modern America. The old generation of traditionalists tends to exert pressure on young tribal members in order to assure the perpetuation of the old ways. This can lead to a conflict between communal obligations and the search for a new Indian identity which must include the benefits of modern society.

Abel cannot simply adopt the traditional customs of his tribe as would have been natural in a community unaffected by the encroachment of an alien culture. He turns his back on the Indian world and enters modern America. Here, under the influence of an unsympathetic environment, Abel's conflict is aggravated. He shows all the symptoms of identity confusion: estrangement from both the tribal and the Anglo-American cultures, sexual and emotional disturbance in his personal relationships, and an inability to channel his aggression appropriately.

His return to the native community suggests that Indian cultures are capable of overcoming such crises, not by isolating themselves but through an adherence to basic traditional values and by the selective acceptance of new elements from other cultures. This strategy, which has been a strength of American Indian societies throughout the period of contact with other cultural groups, must be continued. In giving an account of the developmental crisis in the protagonist's life history Momaday makes a statement about Indian life in a period of increasing cultural and economic pressures. *House Made of Dawn*, then, is a novel about an individual and a communal search for identity.

Abel grows up in a world where the preservation of old values counts more than progress. Even today Pueblo life revolves around a complex system of religious ceremonials based on a solar calendar, whose keeper is the cacique, the Pueblo medicine man. According to his observation of the course of the sun, the cacique determines all the essential events of tribal life, the planting, harvesting, and the religious ceremonies.

Ruins of pre-Columbian Peublo Indian cliff dwellings in Mesa Verde National Park Eliot Elisofon/Time and Life
Pictures/Getty Images

In *House Made of Dawn* the old man Francisco functions as the teacher and guardian of the traditional Pueblo way of life. He represents the old generation of the tribe which possesses the cultural heritage and strives to preserve it by handing it down to the next generation. Francisco teaches his grandsons, Abel and Vidal, to observe the sun. He tells them that "they must know the long journey of the sun on the black mesa, how it rode in the seasons and the years, and they must live according to the sun appearing, for only then could they reckon where they were, where all things were, in time." In revealing the connection between the sun, the landscape, and the rhythms of Indian life, Francisco roots the two boys in the old ways of the tribe. Francisco's teachings are central to their development as well as the perpetuation of Jemez tradition.

Under the guidance of old man Francisco, Abel is raised according to the tribal patterns of his people and acquires a deep feeling for his environment. Typical of Abel's consciousness is his natural attitude toward death: ". . . he knew somehow that his mother was soon going to die

of her illness. It was nothing he was told, but he knew it anyway and without understanding, as he knew already the motion of the sun and the seasons." Abel is at the center of Indian life. He herds sheep, takes part in a deer hunt, and participates in the ceremonial activities of his tribe.

Despite this seeming harmony with the tribal world, however, Abel somehow remains a stranger within his community. Not only during his time away from the reservation but also while growing up among his own people, he lives in a state of isolation. He was born into his position as an outsider: "He did not know who his father was. His father was a Navajo, they said, or a Sia, or an Isleta, an outsider anyway, which made him and his mother and Vidal somehow foreign and strange." Tribal communities are not necessarily homogenous entities as they are often perceived by outsiders; within the tribe subgroups may exist which do not meet the full acceptance of the majority. The early deaths of his mother and brother increase Abel's isolation. He is left with his grandfather, Francisco, as his only other relation.

Preoccupied with Abel's conforming to the tribal tradition, Francisco monopolizes his education. He forbids him to find a substitute mother in Josie, one of the women in the village. The lack of family ties prevents Abel's full integration into the native community. As Abel approaches adolescence he finds it increasingly difficult to accept tribal patterns and the domineering authority of his grandfather.

It is common for young people at this stage of personal development to question the way of life which adults in their families or communities expect them to adopt. Momaday shows in his novel the severity of the conflict between a budding individual and a rigid tribal pattern which depends for its perpetuation on the absence of individual awareness. He reveals how the crisis in Abel's personal development reflects a crisis in Pueblo culture.

Pueblo traditionalists maintain that in an age of growing pressure from outside the tribal culture can only survive in isolation. Even though technical attainments of Anglo-American culture have been adopted for their obvious usefulness, Pueblo communities are very reluctant to allow any interference that could dilute traditional tribal life. This inevitably leads to tremendous pressures in the educational processes of young Indians. A culture which depends for its survival on the adoption of age-old patterns by the next generation not only shelters against influences from the outside but also ignores or even suppresses the individual needs of its members. Thus a generation conflict is almost unavoidable....

Abel's decision to leave the Pueblo community grows out of the realization that he cannot find an identity simply by adopting the teachings of his grandfather. Momaday shows by means of a few central events that Abel has no choice but to step out of the limiting realm of his native village in order to remain true to himself.

Momaday stresses the young Indian's position between two cultures by means of Abel's shoes. The shoes are typical of the white man's fashion in the city and therefore conspicuous to traditional Indians. In some Pueblo communities tribal rules demand that shoes or boots can be worn only if the heel is cut off, to avoid injury to the sacred earth on which the community's existence depends. Abel, however, does not share this orthodox view; to him the shoes are simply objects of good craftsmanship, admirable in their own right, like "the work of a good potter or painter or silversmith." As Abel steps out of his native community, he is wearing these shoes, having waited "a long time for the occasion to wear them." In this situation they signify the world he is about to enter, and as Abel realizes this he grows anxious and afraid:

> But now and beyond his former frame of reference, the shoes called attention to Abel. They were brown and white; they were conspicuously new and too large; they shone; they clattered and creaked. And they were nailed to his feet. There were enemies all around, and he knew that he was ridiculous in their eyes.

Despite Abel's fears of what awaits him in the alien world of modern America, his departure is a necessary step toward his understanding of himself.

Abel's withdrawal from the tribe is the result of a disturbed communication between the old and the young generation. Anxious to preserve the ancient tribal ways, the old members of the pueblo have grown blind to the needs of the young.

In referring to the cyclical concept of time Momaday demonstrates his belief in the inherent potential of American Indian cultures to survive historical crises. That the new rise of the old culture should take place an hour before the dawn seems unimportant in the narrow context of this passage. In the larger context of the novel, however, it becomes most significant: Abel's celebration of the funeral rites for his grandfather "a while...before the dawn" is not only the moment when he finds his way back to his tribe but also, from a historical perspective, the point where Jemez culture gains new impetus in its struggle to survive a period of cultural encroachment and oppression. Like the Bahkyush people who had once journeyed along the edge of oblivion and recovered to become eagle hunters and rainmakers, Abel, who is associated with this group as an eagle hunter, also returned from the edge of the void to become a dawn runner. As the Kiowas' migration from the north of the American continent to the south and east was "a journey toward the dawn" which "led to a golden age," the positive outcome of Abel's migration between two worlds can be seen as a hopeful beginning of a new period of Pueblo culture.

In much the same way as the reference to the cyclical concept of time indicates the potentially positive resolution of the historical crisis in Indian culture, the cyclical structure of the novel justifies a hopeful reading of Abel's future.

At the close of the book Abel returns to the personal wholeness and harmony with the universe which were his main strengths at its beginning. Indeed the cyclical concept of tribal history and the cyclical movement of Abel's personal history interconnect at the end. Abel, whose dilemma is the product of historical crisis in Indian culture, overcomes his identity conflict and symbolically resolves the communal crisis of his tribe. Momaday's own comment on *House Made of Dawn* points in this direction: "I see the novel as a circle. It ends where it begins and it's informed with a kind of thread that runs through it and holds everything together" ["An Interview with N. Scott Momaday," *Puerto del Sol* 12, No. 1 (1973)] This race, then, is a race for identity, both personal and communal. It finds its final resolution in the ceremonial race which shows Abel reconciled with his native culture and the Indian universe.

Many alienated characters in recent American fiction—Ralph Ellison's *Invisible Man*, Faulkner's Joe Christmas in *Light in August*, and John Updike's Rabbit Angstrom in *Rabbit Run*—are running away from something and have no viable alternative to which they can turn. Abel is unique in that his running manifests an act of integration, not a symbol of estrangement. Momaday himself suggested this reading of the symbol by referring to its cultural context: "The man running is fitting himself into the basic motion of the universe ... That is simply a symbolism which prevails in the southwestern Indian world."

Abel's running at dawn, singing the words of the Night Chant, marks the end of his struggle for identity. He has finally returned to his place in the house made of dawn. He has found the right words to articulate himself and he has a vision of the appropriate path to wholeness. The novel's final scene is charged with mythological overtones: according to a Pueblo emergence myth, Iatik, the corn mother, after creating the present world, called on the people to emerge from the previous world underground. As they entered their new environment they were blind. Then, the story [as related by Richard Erdoes in *The Rain Dance People*] goes on to explain, "Iatik lined them up in a row facing east and made the sun come up for the first time in this new world to shine upon them. And when its rays shone upon the eyes of the people, they were opened and they could see."

In the primordial setting of dawn over the Jemez Valley, Abel too "could see at last without having to think. He could see the canyons and the mountains and the sky. He could see the rain and the river and the fields beyond. He could see the dark hills at dawn." His new vision and voice are expressions of his communion with his native tradition and raise the hope that he may become the living link between the ancient past and a promising future for his tribal culture.

Source: Matthias Schubnell, "The Crisis of Identity: *House Made of Dawn*," in *N. Scott Momaday: The Cultural and Literary Background*, University of Oklahoma Press, 1985, pp.101–39.

SOURCES

"Exhibition," in the *Times Literary Supplement*, No. 3508, May 22, 1969, p. 549.

Momaday, N. Scott, *House Made of Dawn*, Harper & Row, 1968; reprint, Perennial Library, 1989.

Morgan, Thomas D., "Native Americans in World War II," in *Army History: The Professional Bulletin of Army History*, No. 35, Fall 1995, pp. 22–27.

Review of *House Made of Dawn*, in the *Kirkus Service*, Vol. 36, No. 7, April 1, 1968, p. 421.

Review of *House Made of Dawn*, in *Publishers Weekly*, April 1, 1968, p. 34.

Smith, Starita, Daniel J. Vargas, and Taylor Johnson, "Author Labels Round Rock Censorship Effort 'Silly,'" in the *Austin American-Statesman*, December 7, 1994.

Sprague, Marshall, "Anglos and Indians," in the *New York Times Book Review*, June 9, 1968, p. 5.

Stevenson, Joan W., Review of *House Made of Dawn*, in *Library Journal*, June 15, 1968, p. 2522.

Trimble, Martha Scott, *N. Scott Momaday*, Boise State College, 1973.

Velie, Alan R., "N. Scott Momaday," in *Dictionary of Literary Biography*: Volume 143: *American Novelists Since World War II, Third Series*, Gale Research, 1994, pp. 159–70.

John F. Kennedy's Inaugural Address

JOHN FITZGERALD KENNEDY

1961

On January 20, 1961, John Fitzgerald Kennedy delivered one of America's few standout inaugural addresses and one of the finest speeches in American history. By invoking the American dream and extending its promise to the rest of the world, Kennedy's speech was an inspirational call to action that resonates even today.

It is no coincidence that the 1961 inaugural address is continually compared to Abraham Lincoln's second inaugural address as well as the "Gettysburg Address," both of Woodrow Wilson's inaugural addresses, and several of Franklin Delano Roosevelt's and Winston Churchill's finest speeches—Kennedy looked to these gifted orators and their wise and beautiful words for inspiration. According to Thurston Clarke in his book, *Ask Not: The Inauguration of John F. Kennedy and the Speech That Changed America,*

> [Kennedy] knew this speech represented an extraordinary opportunity to present himself, as he chose to be seen, for the pages of history, and few presidents in the twentieth century cared more about history, or its perspective, than John F. Kennedy.

The power of Kennedy's inaugural speech lies in its brevity and lyrical succinctness—qualities common among Wilson's, Lincoln's, and Churchill's most remembered speeches. Like the times reflected in these previous speeches, the late 1950s and early 1960s were fraught with crisis. The cold war had been escalating

since the mid-1940s, and the U.S. civil rights movement was reaching a fever pitch. Marked by an idealistic tone that elevated the speech above pessimistic cold war rhetoric, Kennedy's inaugural address relied on the hope and optimism of a new generation, one he believed would turn the experiences of the past into tools to change the future.

Though some skeptics continue to debate whether Kennedy or his principal speech writer, advisor, and confidant, Ted Sorensen, should be credited with the inaugural's authorship, most contend that even if Sorensen was its primary draftsman, the speech was pure Kennedy. Clarke writes,

> On close examination, the Sorensen material that Kennedy incorporated into his speech turns out to be largely a compilation of ideas and themes that Kennedy had been voicing throughout his adult life, expressed in words that Sorensen had drawn from Kennedy's writings and extemporaneous speeches. In short, one finds that Kennedy was more than the "principal architect" of his inaugural address; he was its stonecutter and mason, too, the man whose beautiful language, either dictated by him or channeled through Sorensen, cemented together the grand ideas of his speech.

Those grand ideas, coupled with their eloquent expression, included, first and foremost, Kennedy's call for a reduction in cold war tensions, and, secondly, in Clarke's words, an extension of "the promises and guarantees of the Declaration of Independence to the entire world." A combination of crisis and idealism formed the basis of the inaugural address and set the tone for Kennedy's administration, which included the formation of the Peace Corps in 1961 and the acceleration of America's space program as well as the Cuban Missile Crisis and the Bay of Pigs. In *American Orators of the Twentieth Century: Critical Studies and Sources*, Theodore O. Windt Jr. points out,

> The idealism was counterbalanced by a mood of critical urgency. He described the world he faced in somber words: "In the long history of the world, only a few generations have been granted the role of defending freedom in its hour of maximum danger. I do not shrink from the responsibility—I welcome it." Thus do the two major themes of his administration merge in his Inaugural Address.

The facts that Kennedy was the youngest elected president, the first Catholic president, and the first president born in the twentieth century made for a winning combination the day of

BIOGRAPHY

JOHN FITZGERALD KENNEDY

John Fitzgerald Kennedy was born in Brookline, Massachusetts, to Joseph P. and Rose Fitzgerald Kennedy on May 29, 1917, the second of nine children in a wealthy, prominent family in business and politics. Kennedy was educated at Choate Academy, Princeton University, Harvard College, and Stanford Business School. In 1940, Kennedy published *Why England Slept*, a book based on his Harvard senior thesis. A year later, he joined the navy. In 1943, Kennedy was injured when a Japanese destroyer attacked the patrol torpedo (PT) boat he was commanding. He was awarded the Purple Heart and spent the rest of the war recovering from his injuries.

Kennedy was elected to the U.S. House of Representatives in 1946, and the U.S. Senate in 1952. In 1954, he married Jacqueline Bouvier, with whom he had three children: Caroline, John Jr., and Patrick, who died a few days after his birth. Kennedy wrote *Profiles in Courage* between 1954 and 1955. The book was published in 1956, the same year Kennedy began pursuing the 1960 Democratic presidential nomination. In 1957, *Profiles in Courage* won the Pulitzer Prize for biography. Kennedy was forty-three years old when he was elected president, which made him the youngest person elected president in U.S. history. He was also this country's first Catholic president and the first president born in the twentieth century. He delivered his inaugural address on January 20, 1961. He was assassinated in Dallas, Texas, on November 22, 1963.

his inauguration, but, during his election campaign, many equated his youth with inexperience and his religion as loyalty to the Vatican over the Constitution. These factors contributed to Kennedy's narrow defeat of Republican Vice President Richard M. Nixon in one of the closest presidential elections in United States history:

Out of nearly 69 million popular votes cast, Kennedy's margin over Nixon was a mere 118,550 votes. The enduring passionate response to Kennedy's inaugural address all but blocks from the collective American memory that nearly half the country voted for Nixon in 1960.

PLOT SUMMARY

Kennedy, a scholar of history, begins his speech by addressing several of the dignitaries in attendance: "Vice President Johnson, Mr. Speaker, Mr. Chief Justice, President Eisenhower, Vice President Nixon, President Truman, reverend clergy, fellow citizens," referring to Lyndon Baines Johnson, the new vice president; Sam Rayburn, Johnson's mentor, the Speaker of the House; Earl Warren, the chief justice; Dwight D. Eisenhower, the outgoing president; Richard M. Nixon, the outgoing vice president and Republican candidate for president against Kennedy; and Harry Truman, the only other former president at the proceedings. Using the phrase "fellow citizens" to refer to the rest of his audience goes back to the first inaugural address, on April 30, 1789, when George Washington began his speech, "Fellow Citizens of the Senate and of the House of Representatives."

He begins his remarks with a nod to another famous phrase:

> We observe today not a victory of party, but a celebration of freedom—symbolizing an end, as well as a beginning, signifying renewal, as well as change. For I have sworn before you and Almighty God the same solemn oath our forebears prescribed nearly a century and three quarters ago.

This portion of the speech echoes Winston Churchill's V–E Day speech on May 8, 1945, in which he said, "This is not a victory of a party or of any class. It's a victory of the great British nation as a whole."

Next, he alludes to both scientific advancements and the threat of nuclear war, which alternately thrilled and terrified his contemporaries, saying, "The world is very different now. For man holds in his mortal hands the power to abolish all forms of human poverty and all forms of human life." Then he invokes the belief in the Americans' divine righteousness in their aims: "And yet the same revolutionary beliefs for which our forebears fought are still at issue

around the globe—the belief that the rights of man come not from the generosity of the state, but from the hand of God." He ends with a statement to temper the previous fearsome reference to nuclear annihilation with the hopeful notion that larger, more generous forces are at work in the universe.

The next segment begins, "We dare not forget today that we are the heirs of that first revolution." Echoing the phrase "revolutionary beliefs" from the previous section, Kennedy emphasizes the historical significance of the country's revolutionary beginnings. He goes on to boldly state his vision of the country's mission to uphold those principles of the American Revolution:

> Let the word go forth from this time and place, to friend and foe alike, that the torch has been passed to a new generation of Americans—born in this century, tempered by war, disciplined by a hard and bitter peace, proud of our ancient heritage—and unwilling to witness or permit the slow undoing of those human rights to which this nation has always been committed, and to which we are committed today at home and around the world.

Kennedy had read and repeated these ideas throughout his life. The imagery of a passing torch recalls the first Olympiads as well as George Washington's reference to the "sacred fire of liberty" in his first inaugural address. The notion of a new generation echoes the slogan Kennedy used in his 1946 congressional campaign, "The New Generation Offers a Leader." Fourteen years later, Kennedy responded to Harry Truman's concern that he lacked the maturity to be president in a televised press conference, saying, "It is time for a new generation of leadership, to cope with new problems and new responsibilities."

He continues his declaration of his vision and determination:

> Let every nation know, whether it wishes us well or ill, that we shall pay any price, bear any burden, meet any hardship, support any friend, oppose any foe, to assure the survival and the success of liberty.

Kennedy's gift for imbuing speeches with lyricism and rhythm is evident in his alliterative phrasing here. The efficacy of his idea, though, does not rely on this poetic device. The message that Americans and their freedoms will be protected under his leadership rings loud and clear, as does the warning to potential enemies of the American way of life.

In his book *Sounding the Trumpet: The Making of John F. Kennedy's Inaugural Address*, scholar Richard J. Tofel describes the next portion of the address this way:

> A series of messages expressly directed at audiences around the world—Western allies, newly independent former colonies, what we would today call Third World peoples, Latin America, the United Nations, and, finally and most significantly, the Soviet Union.

The series begins, "To those old allies whose cultural and spiritual origins we share, we pledge the loyalty of faithful friends." The phrase "we pledge" is repeated in a litany of varied promises to "those new states whom we welcome to the ranks of the free," to "those peoples in huts and villages across the globe struggling to break the bonds of mass misery," because, "if a free society cannot help the many who are poor, it cannot save the few who are rich."

Kennedy the historian goes on to echo a phrase that resonates in American rhetoric when he refers to the United Nations (UN) as "our last best hope in an age where the instruments of war have far outpaced the instruments of peace." In his first inaugural address in 1801, Thomas Jefferson said, "this Government, the world's best hope." Kennedy had used variations of phrase—also found in Abraham Lincoln's 1862 message to Congress and Eisenhower's 1957 inaugural address—in speeches in 1954, 1960, and 1961. He pledges American support to the UN, "to prevent it from becoming merely a forum for invective, to strengthen its shield of the new and the weak, and to enlarge the area in which its writ may run."

The litany of promises ends as the new president makes a request of "those nations who would make themselves our adversary":

> that both sides begin anew the quest for peace, before the dark powers of destruction unleashed by science engulf all humanity in planned or accidental self-destruction... remembering on both sides that civility is not a sign of weakness, and sincerity is always subject to proof. Let us never negotiate out of fear. But never let us fear to negotiate.

Kennedy, grounding his ambitious aims in realistic qualification, cautions:

> All this will not be finished in the first one hundred days. Nor will it be finished in the first one thousand days, nor in the life of this administration, nor even perhaps in our lifetime on this planet. But let us begin.

After outlining the exhaustive and monumental challenge of "creating a new endeavor," a "new balance of power," and a "new world of law, where the strong are just and the weak secure and the peace preserved," Kennedy invites the nation and the world to join him in setting their feet upon the path of change, regardless of how long it might take for change to come. Once more, Kennedy borrows from the masters by invoking Franklin Delano Roosevelt's initial "Hundred Days" in office, as well as Winston Churchill's June 1940 speech to the House of Commons, which reads in part, "Let us therefore brace ourselves to our duties, and so bear ourselves that, if the British Empire and its Commonwealth last for a thousand years, men will say, 'This was their finest hour.'"

In the next section, Kennedy begins his call to strategic action.

> In your hands, my fellow citizens, more than mine, will rest the final success or failure of our course. Since this country was founded, each generation of Americans has been summoned to give testimony to its national loyalty. The graves of young Americans who answered the call to service surround the globe.

Once again, Kennedy references a generation; this time, though, he uses the word to remind his "fellow citizens," his "generation," of those generations past who gave "testimony" to their "national loyalty." The words "In your hands" and "more than mine" echo Lincoln's first inaugural address while "the graves of young Americans" mirror the "Gettysburg Address" ("It is for us the living, rather, to be dedicated here to the unfinished work which they who fought here have thus far so nobly advanced.")

The urgency increases in the following section:

> Now the trumpet summons us again—not as a call to bear arms, though arms we need; not as a call to battle, though embattled we are—but a call to bear the burden of a long twilight struggle... against the common enemies of man: tyranny, poverty, disease, and war itself.... Can we forge against these enemies a grand and global allianace,... that can assure a more fruitful life for all mankind? Will you join in that historic effort?

The origin of the trumpet metaphor is unclear, though Tofel argues that it is from First Corinthians 14.8, "For if the trumpet give an uncertain sound, who shall prepare himself to

LET EVERY NATION KNOW, WHETHER IT WISHES US WELL OR ILL, THAT WE SHALL PAY ANY PRICE, BEAR ANY BURDEN, MEET ANY HARDSHIP, SUPPORT ANY FRIEND, OPPOSE ANY FOE TO ASSURE THE SURVIVAL AND THE SUCCESS OF LIBERTY."

the battle?" General Maxwell Taylor alludes to the verse in the title of his 1960 book, *The Uncertain Trumpet*, which Kennedy read and admired. Regardless of its origin, Kennedy's metaphor makes plain the fact that his inaugural is, at its heart, a call to action.

As the speech reaches its crescendo, Kennedy revisits both the energy and idealism of his generation and the fire metaphor previously invoked in the phrase, "the torch has been passed to a new generation of Americans."

> I do not believe that any of us would exchange places with any other people or any other generation. The energy, the faith, the devotion which we bring to this endeavor will light our country and all who serve it—and the glow from that fire can truly light the world.

Then comes the climax, the most resonant line of the speech, and indeed of Kennedy's political career: "And so, my fellow Americans: Ask not what your country can do for you—ask what you can do for your country." Clarke calls it "the master sentence that was a distillation of his philosophy and experience, the chrysalis of countless campaign speeches, and the logical and emotional climax of his inaugural address." The memorable words are repeated in a similar directive, this time to "My fellow citizens of the world." Kennedy tells those listening outside the United States, "Ask not what America will do for you, but what together we can do for the freedom of man."

The final words of Kennedy's inaugural address follow custom and call on God to bless and assist citizens of America and the world.

> With a good conscience our only sure reward, with history the final judge of our deeds, let us go forth to lead the land we love, asking His blessing and His help, but knowing that here on earth God's work must truly be our own.

THEMES

Freedom

Kennedy begins his inaugural address with the words, "We observe today not a victory of party but a celebration of freedom." The lofty idea of freedom is a suitable one to invoke during any presidential inaugural address, but world events at the time of Kennedy's inauguration—the spread of communism, the very real threat of nuclear war, and the escalating violent and non-violent events related to the American civil rights movement—lent a sense of gravity to the notion of freedom because so many Americans were either living without it or were threatened with its loss. Kennedy makes it clear throughout the rest of his speech that freedom is not something one is handed but something that must be fought for. He reminds his listeners, "We dare not forget today that we are the heir of that first revolution." He refers, of course, to the American Revolution that secured America's freedom from British rule—a battle that paved the way for the American dream.

He extends the ideals of the American dream to all the world's people, saying, "Americans [are] unwilling to witness or permit the slow undoing of those human rights to which this nation has always been committed, and to which we are committed today, at home and around the world."

He then addresses "those new states whom we welcome to the ranks of the free." These new states include newly independent former colonies around the world. To them he pledges, "our word that one form of colonial control shall not have passed away merely to be replace by a far more iron tyranny." He specifically pledges to help Latin American countries and adds this warning:

> This peaceful revolution of hope cannot become the prey of hostile powers. Let all our neighbors know that we shall join with them to oppose aggression or subversion anywhere in the Americas. And let every other power know that this hemisphere intends to remain the master of its own house.

In *Ask Not: The Inauguration of John F. Kennedy and the Speech That Changed America*, Thurston Clarke writes of the notion that emerging economies should be protected from communism:

> There was nothing new about this idea—Woodrow Wilson, Henry Luce, and others had voiced it before him—but it was ideally

John F. Kennedy giving his inauguration speech Getty Images

suited to a time when the United States and the Soviet Union were competing for the allegiance of eighteen new Asian and African nations, and when the United States was offering only a sterile anticommunism, while the Soviets were promising an ideology that appeared to have transformed their once backward nation into a superpower in four decades.

Improvement

Speaking at a time of great American prosperity and tremendous global anxiety, Kennedy foreshadows his administration's efforts to alleviate human suffering, saying early in his address, "man holds in his mortal hands the power to abolish all forms of human poverty." He goes on to outline his philosophy of assistance for the needy, which would come to life in the form of the Peace Corps, established by Kennedy's executive order just forty days after his inauguration, on March 1, 1961:

To those people in huts and villages of half the globe struggling to break the bonds of mass misery, we pledge our best efforts to help them help themselves, for whatever period is required—not because the Communists may be doing it, not because we seek their votes, but because it is right. For if a free society cannot help the many who are poor, it cannot save the few who are rich.

To our sister republics south of the border, we offer a special pledge: to convert our good words into deeds—in a new allegiance for progress—to assist free men and free governments in casting off the chains of poverty.

It is clear that he hopes to establish strong Democratic societies by helping establish strong economies in the struggling world, and by doing so, to curb the growth of communism. As such, Kennedy aims to improve both the world's economic and political situation through the same means. He goes on to say, "The energy, the faith, the devotion which we bring to this endeavor will light our country and all who serve it—and the glow from that fire can truly light the world."

Sacrifice

The call to action, sacrifice, and service is a prominent theme in Kennedy's inaugural speech. He lays out lofty goals for the country, but he does not claim that they will be easy to achieve. He prepares Americans for a struggle in pursuit of difficult but worthy aims. He also invokes the many who have sacrificed in the past for equally difficult and worthy endeavors:

> In your hands, my fellow citizens, more than mine, will rest the final success of our course. Since this country was founded, each generation of Americans has been summoned to give testimony to its national loyalty. The graves of young Americans who answered the call to service surround the globe. Now the trumpet summons us again . . . to bear the burden a long twilight struggle, year in and year out, . . . a struggle against the common enemies of man: tyranny, poverty, disease, and war itself. . . . I do not shrink from this responsibility—I welcome it. I do not believe that any of us would exchange places with any other people or any other generation.

After uttering the most famous line in his speech, "And so, my fellow Americans: Ask not what your country can do for you—ask what you can do for your country," he adds, "My fellow citizens of the world: Ask not what America will do for you, but what together we can do for the freedom of man." By extending the promise of freedom to the whole world, Kennedy invites the whole world to imagine it, and to fight for it.

Idealism

Kennedy buoys his vision of threat, work, and sacrifice with several grand references to American idealism—borrowed from the revolutionaries who shaped this country and laid the foundation for the American dream.

> We dare not forget today that we are the heirs of that first revolution. Let the word go forth from this time and place, to friend and foe alike, that the torch has been passed to a new generation of Americans—born in this century, tempered by war, disciplined by a hard and bitter peace, proud of our ancient heritage—and unwilling to witness or permit the slow undoing of those human rights to which this nation has always been committed, and to which we are committed today at home and around the world.

This passage is the first to promise hopeful change in the face of great adversity. In it, the American Revolution serves as the backdrop and the inspiration for "a new generation of Americans" committed to the ideal of freedom. But it is Kennedy's inspirational tone in phrases like "Let the word go forth," "the torch has been passed," and "proud of our ancient heritage" that speaks to his belief in the possibility of change. This powerful hope is echoed in the following passage:

> Let every nation know, whether it wishes us well or ill, that we shall pay any price, bear any burden, meet any hardship, support any friend, oppose any foe to assure the survival and the success of liberty.

Again, Kennedy strikes an idealistic tone by promising success in the face of all adversity. By echoing the idealistic American "can-do" spirit, he connects with and assures Americans and citizens of the world that threats to their liberty will be met with great resistance.

Kennedy's idealism is most effectively communicated by his use of the words "we" and "us." This infers that he shares with his fellow Americans and world citizens the same goal—freedom from "tyranny, poverty, disease, and war itself." But when Kennedy shifts the focus from "we" to "you," he makes a hugely optimistic leap. When he asks, "Will you join in that historic effort?", he reveals his belief that if he asks, many will. When he tells his "fellow Americans: Ask not what your country can do for you—ask what you can do for your country," he again reveals his optimism for the future.

HISTORICAL OVERVIEW

The Cold War

Kennedy's entire political career took place in the shadow of the cold war and the nuclear arms race with the Soviet Union. It is little wonder then that his inaugural address emphasizes the battle for freedom in an "hour of maximum danger." His pledge that the American people would "pay any price, bear any burden, meet any hardship, support any friend, oppose any foe to assure the survival and success of liberty" is a direct reference to the war between the communist world and the free world.

The Yalta Conference, a 1945 meeting between Winston Churchill, Franklin D. Roosevelt, and

Joseph Stalin ("The Big Three"), is widely recognized as the beginning of the cold war. Roosevelt sought Soviet assistance in the Pacific War; Churchill sought free elections in Eastern Europe; and Stalin sought to establish a base of Soviet influence in Eastern Europe for the sake of Soviet national security. Together, they attempted to devise an agenda regarding governance of postwar Germany. Roosevelt, who would die of a massive cerebral hemorrhage two months later, was accused of "selling out" at Yalta because his negotiations with Stalin led to Soviet expansion into Japan and Asia. Stalin later violated the terms of the agreement and formed the Soviet Bloc. At the time of the conference, the Soviet military, nearly three times as large as Eisenhower's forces, were established all over Eastern Europe. It was at Yalta that Churchill and Roosevelt understood the actuality of Soviet power.

After World War II ended, the Western democracies fought with the Soviet Union over their widespread takeover of East European states. In 1946, Churchill warned that an "iron curtain" was falling over the middle of Europe and Stalin divined the occurrence of a third World War sparked by "capitalist imperialist" Western forces. His assertion deepened the rift between the United States and the Soviet Union.

The cold war, which lasted from 1945 to the early 1990s, was defined by constant East-West competition, conflict, and tension brought about by military buildups, proxy wars, ideological differences, and a massive nuclear arms race. In an effort to contain communism, the United States established alliances with Southeast Asia, the Middle East, and Western Europe. Although the Soviet Union and the United States never fought one another directly, the Korean War, the Cuban Missile Crisis, and the Vietnam War were all direct results of the cold war that waged between the two countries for decades.

The 1950s

In the decade leading up to Kennedy's presidential election, the United States experienced an era of great prosperity. For the first time in almost thirty years, the American economy resembled the economic livelihood of the 1920s, a credit-based boom time in U.S. history. The homecomings of American G.I.s from World War II throughout the decade led to the baby boom. Young families made their homes in suburbs across the country and the nation looked toward a hopeful future.

But there were internal conflicts, too. The civil rights movement grew in strength and urgency throughout the decade. In 1954, the Supreme Court overturned the 1896 *Plessy v. Ferguson* ruling that made "separate but equal" segregated facilities legal. The case of *Brown v. Board of Education of Topeka* outlawed these facilities and called for the integration of schools. Despite the ruling, African Americans had to fight for access to public services, the political process, and private dignity, especially in the South. Civil rights leaders staged various acts of civil disobedience throughout the 1950s, including "sit-ins," nonviolent marches, and boycotts, such as the watershed Montgomery Bus Boycott.

International conflicts that affected the United States during this time include the end of European colonialism in Asia and Africa and, most directly, the Cold War and its related nuclear arms race. The decolonization of East Asia and Africa began in earnest at the end of World War II. The process was largely nonviolent, though highly volatile in a political sense. The Soviet Union, whose leaders took a Marxist-Leninist view of colonialism, saw it as the pinnacle of capitalism and encouraged colonized territories to seek independence, especially during the progression of the Cold War. Because many nationalist movements in countries such as Cuba, Guatemala, Indochina, and the Philippines were allied with communist groups, the United States feared they would be influenced by the Soviet Union. This led to increased competition between the two countries, especially in this time of heightened decolonization throughout the world. The fear of both the threat and the spread of communism were heightened by the reluctance of Asia, Africa, and Latin America to choose sides in the conflict. Meanwhile, the United States and the Soviet Union began pursuing a course of nuclear rearmament.

Competition between the two superpowers began with geopolitical, economic, and ideological differences that led to costly defense spending in both countries and a nuclear arms race; because the Soviet Union and the United States were stockpiling nuclear weapons, other countries felt the need to increase their own inventory of nuclear warheads. This Cold War would bring the two nations to the brink of nuclear war,

John F. Kennedy talking to Peace Corp volunteers in Washington, D.C., 1962 © *Bettmann/Corbis*

especially after Soviet leader Nikita Khrushchev and Cuban leader Fidel Castro formed an alliance in 1959 after the Cuban Revolution.

CRITICAL OVERVIEW

According to Theodore O. Windt Jr. in *American Orators of the Twentieth Century*, Kennedy's January 20, 1961, speech is "one of the few truly memorable Inaugural Addresses in U.S. history." Its elegant lyricism, its power, and its idealism called Americans to action and inspired real change. In *Ask Not: The Inauguration of John F. Kennedy and the Speech That Changed America*, Thurston Clarke mentions the great writers, thinkers, and admirers who later revealed how touched and impressed they were by the speech. He quotes James Reston's *New York Times* editorial the day after the inauguration:

> The evangelical and transcendental spirit of America has not been better expressed since Woodrow Wilson and maybe not even since Ralph Waldo Emerson.... For, like all true

expression of the American ideal, this was a revolutionary document.

Eleanor Roosevelt sent Kennedy a handwritten note that read, "I think 'gratitude' best describes the kind of liberation & lift to the listener which you gave.... I have reread your words several times & I have been filled with thankfulness." Speechwriter Mike Feldman, after hearing the speech, "was inspired to read every previous inaugural and came to the conclusion that the only one possessing a similar inspirational quality was Abraham Lincoln's second." Clarke also writes that Kennedy's own wife Jacqueline compared the speech to "Pericles' Funeral Oration and the Gettysburg Address." Novelist Carson McCullers, in a message written to the president for a commemorative scrapbook of the inauguration, wrote,

> I think that I have never been moved by words more than I was by your inaugural address.... It reminded me of the great speeches of FDR and Winston Churchill. Indeed, it is one of the greatest addresses of our age.

The January 21, 1961, *New York Times* published snippets from editorials from papers across the country to give their readers a sense of the national response to the inaugural address. From the article entitled, "Editorial Comment Across the Nation on President Kennedy's Inauguration" comes this opinion from Albany's *Times Union*: "The Inaugural will be recalled and quoted as long as there are Americans to heed his summons." From the *Sun* in Baltimore, Maryland:

> The Inaugural address was somber without despair, firm without bellicosity, bold without arrogance.... Eloquence without substance is nothing. The address has substance.... We may have caught a glimpse into the nature of the young, cool and still somewhat mysterious new President of the United States.

And from the Salt Lake City *Tribune*:

> His eloquent phrases reveal him as a determined man who does not flinch from the awful responsibilities of leadership.... (He) made a fine start.... May the response to his forthrightness and courage echo across the land.

In his own commentary, Clarke writes,

> The speech is generally acknowledged to have been the greatest oration of any twentieth-century American politician. It was also the centerpiece of an inauguration that would turn out to be one of the great political events of that century, a moment when Americans would step through a membrane in time, entering a brief, still seductive, era of national happiness.

Kennedy's inaugural address still inspires transcendent praise from cultural and political luminaries from around the globe, but the most resounding response to the speech came from people whose lives were changed by Kennedy's inspirational call to action. According to Clarke, James Meredith, "a black U.S. Air Force veteran," requested an admission application from the all-white University of Mississippi "the evening after Kennedy spoke." After being denied admission, Meredith launched a campaign that included writing letters to the Justice Department and filing suit with U.S. District Court demanding to be admitted. While he was attempting to register for classes on September 30, 1962, a riot broke out on the university campus. On October 1 of that year, flanked by U.S. Marshals, Meredith finally became the university's first black student. That moment in civil rights history is just one of many moments inspired by Kennedy's memorable speech.

MEDIA ADAPTATIONS

Many audio recordings of Kennedy delivering his inaugural address are available on the Internet, including through the History Place at www.historyplace.com/speeches/jfk-inaug.htm and through American Rhetoric at www.americanrhetoric.com/speeches/jfkinaugural.htm.

Kennedy's inaugural speech is also included on the DVD *Vintage JFK*, a collection of Kennedy video footage. This fifty-minute DVD is available through Quality Information Publishers.

One of Kennedy's greatest achievements, the formation of the Peace Corps, is another living testament to the optimism of the inaugural address and the passion it inspired in many young people. Kennedy planted the seeds of the Peace Corps in a presidential campaign speech delivered at the University of Michigan on October 14, 1960. At two o'clock in the morning, Kennedy challenged the students to join his effort of affecting positive global change. On November 1 of that year, at a speech in San Francisco, Kennedy reiterated his intent to form an organization that he then dubbed the "Peace Corps." Since its inception by Kennedy's executive order on March 1, 1961, the Peace Corps has trained over 182,000 volunteers who shared Kennedy's vision of contributing to society. These volunteers have served in 138 countries around the globe. Those volunteers, and countless others moved to public service in the generations since Kennedy issued his challenge to his own generation, cite the phrase that begins "ask not" as the one that has inspired them most.

SOURCES

Churchill, Winston, "Their Finest Hour," June 18, 1940, reprinted in *The History Place*, www.historyplace.com/speeches/churchill-hour.htm (November 21, 2006).

———, "To V–E Day Crowds," May 8, 1945, reprinted in *The Churchill Centre* www.winstonchurchill.org/i4a/pages/index.cfm?pageid = 428 (November 21, 2006).

Clarke, Thurston, *Ask Not: The Inauguration of John F. Kennedy and the Speech That Changed America*, Owl Books, 2005, pp. 7, 10, 13, 206–209, 214.

"Editorial Comment Across the Nation on President Kennedy's Inauguration," from the *New York Times*, January 21, 1961, select.nytimes.com/gst/abstract.html?res=F60815FE385B147A93C3AB178AD85F458685F9 (November 21, 2006).

Jefferson, Thomas, "First Inaugural Address," March 4, 1801, reprinted in *Bartleby.com*, www.bartleby.com/124/pres16.html (November 21, 2006).

Kennedy, John F., "Ask What You Can Do for Your Country," January 20, 1961, from *American Heritage Book of Great American Speeches for Young People*, edited by McIntire, Suzanne, John Wiley & Sons, 2001, pp. 200–203.

Lincoln, Abraham, "Gettysburg Address," November 19, 1863, reprinted in *Abraham Lincoln Online*, showcase. netins.net/web/creative/lincoln/speeches/gettys burg.htm (November 21, 2006).

Reston, James, "Editorial," in the *New York Times*, January, 22, 1961; quoted in Thurston Clarke, *Ask Not: The Inauguration of John F. Kennedy and the Speech That Changed America*, Owl Books, 2005, p. 206.

Tofel, Richard J., *Sounding the Trumpet: The Making of John F. Kennedy's Inaugural Address*, Ivan R. Dee, 2005.

Washington, George, "First Inaugural Address," April 30, 1789, reprinted in *National Center for Public Policy Research*, www.nationalcenter.org/WashingtonFirstInaugural.html (November 21, 2006).

Windt, Theodore O., Jr., *American Orators of the Twentieth Century: Critical Studies and Sources*, edited by Bernard K. Duffy and Halford R. Ryan, Greenwood Press, 1987, p. 247.

Little House on the Prairie

LAURA INGALLS WILDER

1935

Laura Ingalls Wilder's *Little House on the Prairie* is a classic work of children's literature by one of the best-known American children's authors. Published in 1935, *Little House*, as it is commonly known, is the third in a series of books by Wilder that describe the pioneer experiences of the author and her family as they move from Wisconsin through several western territories and states, before finally settling in what became De Smet, South Dakota. (One book, *Farmer Boy*, depicts the childhood of Wilder's husband, Almanzo.) While the series is autobiographical, the so-called "Little House" books are considered works of historical fiction as Wilder altered and embellished some aspects of their lives.

Little House is set in the early 1870s, when Charles ("Pa") and Caroline ("Ma") Ingalls took their three young daughters, Mary, Laura, and Carrie, to Indian territory in what is now part of Kansas. The family left Wisconsin, the setting for the first "Little House" book *Little House in the Big Woods*, because Pa felt the area was becoming too populated and driving out wildlife. Settling on a lonely part of the prairie on the edge of the Osage Diminished Reserve, Pa believed that the federal government would soon open up the land for settlement by whites and push the Indians further west, a prospect he saw no problem with. By getting there ahead of most everyone else, he would have the pick of the land.

In *Little House on the Prairie*, Wilder tells how she and her family journeyed there and built a life. With the help of the few white neighbors in the area, Pa constructs a house and stable for their horses and digs a well. Wilder describes his process and craftsmanship in detail. After a cattle drive passes through, Pa acquires a cow and calf. To feed and support his family, Pa hunts local game and collects furs. He trades some of his furs for a plow and seeds so he can begin farming in their first full spring in the area. While the days are filled with work just to survive, there are a few moments of happiness, such as when Pa plays his fiddle, when Pa takes his older daughters to the creek and the deserted Indian camp, and when Mr. Edwards brings them Christmas presents from Santa. There are also scary moments as when sometimes-hostile Indians enter the home and take food and supplies and when the whole family falls ill with malaria.

No matter what happens to the Ingalls family, they exhibit a hardy pioneer spirit as they pursue their American dream. They essentially risk their lives for a chance at owning land in virgin territory. Though the several other white settlers in the area aid each other so they can achieve this same goal, Pa and his family have to be essentially self-reliant because these neighbors are several miles away. There is little social interaction outside of the family as well as much uncertainty because of the presence of potentially hostile Indians for significant portions of the year. In the end, however, Pa's gamble does not pay off, and the family leaves before the U.S. government can force them to. At the time, the government decided not to make the Indians leave at this time, but instead make the white settlers move out of Indian territory. The American dream of the Ingalls family has to find another home.

When *Little House on the Prairie* was originally published in 1935, it was an instant success and has remained in print ever since. Though quintessentially American, the book has been translated into at least forty languages. Despite Wilder's sometimes controversial depiction of Indians and white Americans' negative attitudes toward them, *Little House* remains an important, influential work of American literature. In *Children's Literature Association Quarterly*, Charles Frey writes, "In the strength of its writing, the color and variance of its lively incidents, and its deep, deep affection for the life of all being, *Little House on the Prairie*

BIOGRAPHY

LAURA INGALLS WILDER

Born February 7, 1867, in Pepin, Wisconsin, Wilder was the second of four daughter born to Charles and Caroline Ingalls. As described in her primarily autobiographical historical fiction books, commonly called the "Little House" series, Wilder spent her childhood on the American frontier, moving from Wisconsin westward before the family settled in De Smet, South Dakota. She began writing during her childhood, beginning with themes and poetry. After marrying Almanzo Wilder in 1885, Wilder continued the practice as much as she could while raising her daughter, Rose, and helping her husband farm.

The Wilder family moved to Mansfield, Missouri, in 1894. Wilder then spent most of her time working on the new family farm and volunteering. By 1911, Wilder focused attention on writing again. She began by writing essays about farm life, which were published in the *Missouri Ruralist*, and later contributed to other periodicals. Rose Wilder encouraged her mother to write about her pioneer childhood. Wilder's first effort, childhood-encompassing *Pioneer Girl*, was rejected by publishers in the early 1930s. With the aid of her daughter, Wilder rewrote the story into the well-known series of which *Little House on the Prairie* (1935) is the third volume. With the success of the books, Wilder became a widely acclaimed, popular writer. She died February 10, 1957, in Mansfield, Missouri.

stands and will stand as writing for children that has few equals and no superiors."

PLOT SUMMARY

Chapter 1: Going West
Little House on the Prairie opens with the Ingalls family preparing to leave the Big Woods of Wisconsin and move west. The family consists

of Pa and Ma, and their three young daughters, Mary, Laura, and Carrie. Pa is moving the family west to Indian territory because of the increased number of people in the Big Woods, which he believes keeps away wild animals. "He liked a country where the wild animals lived without being afraid."

At the end of winter, Pa sells their house and packs most of their possessions in a covered wagon. Leaving early one morning, they say good-bye to their relatives and start on their journey. They stop in Pepin to trade furs for goods, cross a frozen lake, and spend the night in an abandoned cabin. During the night, they hear the ice breaking up in the lake—they crossed just in time.

Their journey takes many monotonous days as they travel through Minnesota, stopping to camp each night on their way to Kansas. The weather is often hard, but they cross the Missouri River on a raft. One day, Pa trades their tired horses for two quick mustangs, whom Mary and Laura name Pet and Patty. Laura's legs sometimes ache from being cooped up in the wagon, but she feels ashamed when she complains.

Chapter 2: Crossing the Creek
The family comes across a creek with high, fast-running water. Though the situation has a potential for danger, Pa decides to cross the creek at its ford. As Pa prepares the wagon for the crossing, Laura worries about the family bulldog, Jack. Pa will not let the dog ride in the wagon, but makes him swim on his own.

As the wagon enters the water, Ma drives Pet and Patty as Pa guides the horses in the water. The girls obediently lie down in the wagon. The wagon makes it safely to the other side, but Jack is missing. Pa feels bad for not letting Jack ride in the wagon, and he looks for him to no avail. The family continues their journey on the prairie without their companion and guard dog.

Chapter 3: Camp on the High Prairie
After Wilder provides details of how they camped outdoors on the prairie, Pa talks to Ma about staying in this area. One night, they hear wolves howling nearby and wish Jack was there. As Mary and Laura get ready for bed, eyes appear near the camp. It is not a wolf advancing on the camp, but Jack. They are happy to see

their tired dog, finish their nightly rituals, and go to sleep.

Chapter 4: Prairie Day
After going through their morning routine while camping on the prairie, Mary and Laura explore near the wagon. They find abundant wildlife, including jackrabbits and gophers. When lunchtime nears, Mary and Laura pick flowers for Ma and return to the wagon. As they eat lunch, Laura tells Ma she wants to see a papoose now that they are in Indian territory. Ma does not want to see Indians at all. Pa returns from his own exploratory expedition with fresh game and enthusiasm for the area. He plays his fiddle and sings after they eat a satisfying meal. "When at last Laura set down her plate, she sighed with contentment. She didn't want anything more in the world."

Chapter 5: The House on the Prairie
Packing up the wagon again, the family travels for a few hours to the spot Pa has picked out for a house. It is located near a creek bottom and an old trail as well as within sight of the Verdigris River. Ma and Laura make a tent of the canvas wagon cover while Mary watches the baby. Pa spends days hauling logs up from the creek bottom, then builds the walls for a house. While building the cabin's walls with Ma's help, a log falls on her. She sprains her ankle, halting work on the cabin and stables while she recovers.

While hunting one day, Pa returns early with news that they have a neighbor only two miles away. The bachelor Mr. Edwards has agreed to help Pa finish their cabin in exchange for Pa's labor on his house. The men finish the house, except the roof, in one day. Mr. Edwards stays for dinner, then dances to Pa's fiddle playing until he goes home.

Chapter 6: Moving In
Though the house does not have a roof or floors, Pa tells them to move in for safety reasons. While the girls clean out the wood chips and Ma, Mary, and Laura move the family's things inside, Pa puts the wagon's canvas over the structure as a make-shift roof. Pa was happy with where they were. He tells Ma, "We're going to do well here, Caroline. This a great country. This is a country I'll be contented to stay in the rest of my life." Though they settle their things inside, the family still has to cook outside by campfire because Pa has not built the fireplace yet.

Chapter 7: The Wolf-Pack

The day after Pa and Mr. Edwards build a stable for Pet and Patty, Pet delivers a colt. They name the mule Bunny because "it looked like a jack rabbit." One Sunday, Pa rides Patty to explore the prairie. By suppertime, he still has not returned and the family's animals are restless. Suddenly, Patty and Pa appear streaking to the family's home. He rides her there quickly because he encountered the largest wolf pack he has ever seen.

Over supper, Pa tells them they have neighbors. The Scott family lives only three miles away, while two bachelors are residing six miles farther. He also found a family from Iowa sick with "fever 'n' ague" (malaria), and had to go back to the bachelors' to get them the help they needed. It was on his way back that he encountered the fifty-strong wolf pack who surrounded him and Patty. Though nervous, Pa and the horse did not run from the pack. As soon as the wolves went into the creek bottom, Patty ran home.

After dinner, the girls go to bed. Wolf howls wake Laura up, and her father shows her the wolves, which now ring the cabin and stables. Wilder writes, "She had never seen such big wolves. The biggest one was taller than Laura." Feeling safe guarded by Pa and Jack, Laura goes back to sleep.

Chapter 8: Two Stout Doors

In the morning, Pa builds a door for their house without nails. He uses pegs in the place of nails, leather straps for hinges, and a stick for a lock. Laura helps him build the door and hang it in the doorway. The next day, they build a similar door for the barn, except that the latch is replaced by a chain, which he padlocks at night.

Chapter 9: A Fire on the Hearth

When the time comes to build the fireplace, Pa takes Mary and Laura with him when he goes to gather the rocks he needed. While Pa digs them out near the creek bottoms, the girls play nearby. Because it is warm, Laura nearly sneaks a foot in the water without her father's permission. Catching her, he tells his daughters they can only wade in shallow water, which Laura does.

In the afternoon, Pa constructs the fireplace. He uses rocks and mud to build it on the outside of the house. He starts on the chimney that day as well and completes it the next day using the

stick-and-daub method the rest of the way. Once the outside is completed, he cuts a hole in the wall for the fireplace. When the mantel is done, Ma puts a little china woman they brought from Wisconsin on it. That night, Ma cooks supper in the fireplace. The family eats dinner inside on a table and log chairs that Pa quickly put together.

Chapter 10: A Roof and a Floor

Laura and Mary spend many a day doing chores and experiencing the nature outside. Ma admonishes the girls for not keeping their sunbonnets on and for "getting to look like Indians" with their tan skin. Laura wants to see Indians, and Pa promises she will sometime soon. He is now ready to put a roof and floor on the house. Pa borrows nails from Mr. Edwards to complete the roof. Pa plans on paying him back when he makes the trip to Independence, Missouri, which is forty miles away. Pa also makes a puncheon floor.

Chapter 11: Indians in the House

One day, Pa takes his gun and goes hunting. He leaves Jack chained to the stable as a guard dog. Laura and Mary try to comfort the unhappy dog. As they do so, two Indian men go into the house where Ma and Carrie are alone. Laura wants to do something and considers freeing Jack. Because Pa said not to free Jack, Mary and Laura sneak into the house. The Indians, wearing fresh skunk skins, force Ma to make them cornbread. They eat and leave.

After the Indians are gone, Ma makes cornbread for dinner. When Pa comes home, Ma tells him what happened. As Pa skins the rabbit and dresses the hens, Laura admits to Pa that she thought about turning Jack loose. He tells Laura and Mary in a severe tone of voice to always obey because if Jack had been free, "He would have bitten those Indians. Then there would have been trouble. Bad trouble."

Chapter 12: Fresh Water to Drink

After Pa makes the bedstead, Ma stuffs the mattress with grass instead of straw tick. Their bed looks cozy when it is complete. Pa plans on building a bed for the girls later, but he builds a locked cabinet for the cornmeal and other supplies right away. He then begins digging a well. When he reaches the point where he needs help, Pa arranges for Mr. Scott to help him. Pa will help Scott build his well later on.

The cast of Little House on the Prairie *Getty Images*

Every morning before the men go down into the hole, Pa lights a candle and sends it to the bottom. As long as the candle stays lit, it is safe to go down. Mr. Scott scoffs at the daily practice. One morning, Scott goes down in the well before Pa finishes breakfast. When Pa goes outside, he finds Scott passed out at the bottom of the well hole. Though Ma worries about her husband's safety, Pa goes down to get Scott from the bottom of the well while Ma helps work the rope to pull him up. Scott now believes in sending the candle down to check each morning.

The men continue to work hard day after day, digging deeper and deeper. They finally hit quicksand, then the well is full of water. "The water was clear and cold and good. Laura thought she had never tasted anything so good as those long, cold drinks of water."

Chapter 13: Texas Longhorns

One night, a cattle drive passes by the little house. Pa agrees to help the cowboys keep the cattle out of the ravines in the creek bottoms as they pass through in exchange for beef. When the job is done, Pa is given a cow and her calf in

addition to beef. The family is happy to have the cow and its milk. Though the cow is still wild, Pa is able to get a tin cup's worth of milk from her that day.

Chapter 14: Indian Camp

One hot midsummer day, Pa takes Mary and Laura to the abandoned Indian camp in a prairie hollow. They find ashes from a campfire and moccasin tracks. After Laura finds the first Indian bead, Laura, Mary, and Pa spend the afternoon gathering the beads. When they go home, supper is being prepared. Mary immediately gives her beads to Carrie. Though Laura does not want to, she also gives her beads to Carrie. They make a necklace for their baby sister, but Laura is still jealous. Wilder writes, "often after that Laura thought of those pretty beads and she was still naughty enough to want her beads for herself."

Chapter 15: Fever 'n' Ague

While Ma and Laura pick blackberries, they are bitten by mosquitoes. Swarms of the pests are everywhere at night, preventing Pa from playing fiddle. First, Mary, Laura, and Pa become sick, then Ma falls with the illness, too. The family is sick for days, with aches and cold and hot flashes. When Mary cries out for water one day, Laura gets out of bed, crawls across the floor with Jack's help, and gets Mary her water.

Another day, Laura wakes up and is being given medicine by Dr. Tan, "a doctor with the Indians." The family is being taken care of by Mrs. Scott. All the settlers in the area are sick with what was called fever 'n' ague, malaria carried by the mosquitoes. Mrs. Scott is caring for all the ill families in turn, while Jack had first brought Dr. Tan into the house. Dr. Tan works for the Indians and was going to Independence, Missouri, when the dog stopped him. He is helping all the ill settlers now, too.

When Pa feels better, he retrieves a watermelon from the creek bottom. Mrs. Scott believes that the watermelons caused the sickness, but Pa thinks it was the night air that is the culprit. He eats much of the melon he retrieved with little effect on him.

Chapter 16: Fire in the Chimney
When the weather turns colder, Pa goes out hunting one day. Ma and the girls build a fire and sit inside. Ma finds the chimney was on fire outside, and she deals with the situation. Because Laura cannot help her, she goes inside to find a burning stick has rolled under Mary's skirts as she holds baby Carrie on the rocker. Laura pulls both of them in the rocking chair away from the fire, and throws the burning stick back in the fire. Ma comes in, observes what Laura did, and uses water to douse the fire inside. She is proud that Laura had saved them.

Chapter 17: Pa Goes to Town
The house feels empty when Pa leaves to go to Independence. When Mr. Edwards stops by to check on them and do the chores, Jack chases him to the top of the woodpile. Jack has to be locked inside the house every time Mr. Edwards comes. Mrs. Scott visits on the second day and tells Ma that she hopes the rumors of Indian troubles are false. A cold wind picks up on the third day as the family worries about Pa driving back. On the fourth day, Pa comes back late in the night, after Mary and Laura try to wait up for him. He tells them about his journey, and despite the harsh weather, brings back squares of glass for the home's windows in tact. Wilder

writes, "Everything was all right when Pa was there. . . . He would not have to go to town again for a long time."

Chapter 18: The Tall Indian
As autumn settles in, Indians ride by the house all the time on the trail. Pa says, "I thought that trail was an old one they didn't use any more. I wouldn't have built the house so close to it if I'd known it was a high road." Jack does not like the Indians and has to be chained to the house or the stable at all times. Ma also is not fond of the Indians, but Pa considers the ones that live nearby "peaceable enough."

During the early winter, Pa sets traps and catches animals for their fur. He is saving the furs to trade in the spring. One day when he has gone hunting, two Indians nearly take all the furs as well as the cornbread and tobacco. They drop the furs before leaving, much to Ma's relief. The furs are going to be traded for a plow and seeds. Later, Pa tells Laura that the Indians will be forced by the government to move west because white settlers have moved to the area.

Chapter 19: Mr. Edwards Meets Santa Claus
As Christmas nears, Mary and Laura wonder how Santa Claus will find them in Indian territory. Because of the strong creek current, it seems that neither Santa Claus nor Mr. Edwards, who has been invited to spend the day with them, will come. Despite telling them that Santa will not be coming, Ma has Mary and Laura hang their stockings before going to sleep. Mr. Edwards arrives in the morning, having swum across the creek. He brings Christmas gifts for the girls from Independence, where he claims to have met Santa Claus. In each stocking is a tin cup, peppermint candy, a little cake, and a penny. They feast that happy Christmas with Mr. Edwards.

Chapter 20: A Scream in the Night
During the winter, the wind howls all day and night. One night, they are sure they hear a woman scream. Unsure if the sound came from the Scotts', Pa goes out to check on them. It takes several hours for him to come back. When he does, he says the scream is from a panther. Mary and Laura are not allowed to go outside until Pa kills the panther. Several days of hunting the panther prove fruitless. Pa meets an

Indian in the woods who indicates that he had killed the big cat.

Chapter 21: Indian Jamboree

At the end of winter, Pa goes to Independence to trade his furs. Expecting his return on the fifth day, Mary and Laura are playing outside when they hear loud, unexplainable sounds coming from the Indian camp. Though the sounds come and go, Ma keeps everyone inside except when they do chores. When Pa comes home with supplies, he tells them the Indians are having a jamboree. He also brings news from Independence: "He said that folks in Independence said that the government was going to put the white settlers out of the Indian territory," but Pa does not believe it.

Chapter 22: Prairie Fire

In the spring, Pa begins breaking up the prairie sod with his plow. He is planning to grow sod potatoes and sod corn this year. One day, black clouds near the house as a prairie fire is coming. Ma and Pa go into action to save their buildings with Laura's help. Ma fetches water while Pa plows a furrow around the house, then sets a deliberate small fire on the side away from the house. They beat the fire out with wet sacks. Their actions guide the main fire away from the house.

After the fire, Mr. Scott and Mr. Edwards come to talk to Pa. They believe the Indians might have set the fire deliberately, but Pa does not think so. The number of Indians gathering in the Indian camp make Mr. Scott nervous; he thinks they might be taking action against the settlers. Pa thinks they are getting ready for their spring buffalo hunt.

Chapter 23: Indian War-Cry

While Pa returns to his plowing, the Indians gathered in creek bottoms grow louder. There is yelling between the Indians. One night, Indian drums beat all night long. The Indians no longer come by, but stay together in the creek bottoms. There is a general sense of unease on the prairie. Wilder writes, "It didn't feel safe. It seemed to be hiding something." Mr. Scott and Mr. Edwards talk about building a stockade, but Pa does not think it would help to display fear.

Late one night, Laura and her sisters are awakened by the Indians' war cry. Pa tells them that the Indians are talking with each other about war, but the soldiers at nearby forts will

> "NO MATTER HOW THICK AND CLOSE THE NEIGHBORS GET, THIS COUNTRY'LL NEVER FEEL CROWDED. LOOK AT THAT SKY!" LAURA KNEW WHAT HE MEANT. SHE LIKED THIS PLACE, TOO. SHE LIKED THE ENORMOUS SKY AND THE WINDS, AND THE LAND THAT YOU COULDN'T SEE TO THE END OF. EVERYTHING WAS SO FREE AND BIG AND SPLENDID."

protect them. The war cries continue for many nights as the family stays inside the house every day. After the loudest night, Laura wakes up in the morning to find many Indians using the trail to go west.

A few days later, Pa goes to the Indian camps and finds nearly all of them deserted. He then meets an Osage Indian in the woods who tells him that all the Indian tribes but the Osages want to massacre the white people in their territory. An Osage leader would not let that happen, and the other tribes left. Wilder writes, "No matter what Mr. Scott said, Pa did not believe the only good Indian was a dead Indian."

Chapter 24: Indians Ride Away

The next morning, the Osage Indians leave the creek bottoms and go west. Pa spies the Indian leader, Du Chêne. The family watches the Indians leave. Laura likes watching the ponies and the Indians of all ages. She makes eye contact with a papoose, and tells her father she wanted one. The family stays there the whole day, not eating supper, until all the Indians have passed.

Chapter 25: Soldiers

After the Indians leave, life continues to blossom on the prairie. As Pa plows, Ma, Mary, and Laura plant a garden. Soon, Pa is able to plant corn and potatoes on his plowed field. This activity ends when Mr. Scott and Mr. Edwards inform them that the federal government is going to send soldiers to remove them from their homes, which are still in Indian territory. Pa does not want to be removed in that way, so he is leaving now and going north. He gives Scott the cow and calf, and after dinner, prepares the covered wagon for the journey north.

Chapter 26: Going Out
The next morning, the Ingalls family packs up the wagon and leaves for Independence, Missouri. As they leave, Pa says, "It's great country, Caroline. But there will be wild Indians and wolves here for many a long day." They travel out the way they came in, stopping to camp along the way.

THEMES

The Pioneer Spirit
Because Pa feels that the Big Woods in Wisconsin are becoming too crowded, he moves his family west to Indian territory. One common component of the American dream involves taking risks to achieve such success in life. Pa takes the risk because, though the Indian territory is not yet open to white settlers, he believes it will be soon. By being among the first settlers in the territory and exhibiting pioneer spirit, he puts himself and his family in position to have claim on the best land when the federal government opens it to settlement.

Living in Indian territory is not easy, as the Ingalls family finds out during the time they are there taking the risk. Some of the Native Americans in the area resent the presence of the white settlers. They come into the house and demand or steal food and supplies. At the end of *Little House on the Prairie*, the Indians prepare for a spring buffalo hunt and discuss killing the whites. While this threat does not come to pass, it makes life tense for the few settlers in the area.

Because neighbors are limited in number and the nearest town, Independence, is forty miles away, every day life is full of risks. While building the walls to the house, a log rolls on Ma. Though it is only a sprain, anything worse could have been devastating to the family. Even worse, the whole family falls ill with malaria during the summer. Their dog Jack drags a stranger to the house, Dr. Tan, who gives them medicine and helps save their lives.

In the end, Pa's gamble does not pay off. After receiving conflicting information for several months, the family learns of the government's decision that the white settlers must leave the Indian territory; they will be removed by force if necessary. Pa will not wait for this indignity, so the family leaves. Though they are not successful this time, the family is none the worse for wear and has gained a mule in the process.

Self-Reliance
Another aspect of the American dream explored in *Little House* is self-reliance. Essentially alone on the prairie where he has chosen to take his family, Pa relies on himself for nearly everything and only uses the help of neighbors on a labor exchange basis. He chooses the place where they will build their home. He builds the home by himself, first with the help of his wife, then with the aid of Mr. Edwards. Pa builds the stable the same way. Though Laura helps Pa construct the doors for the house and stable, Pa himself constructs the roof. He reluctantly uses nails lent by Mr. Edwards, and he pays him back as soon as he makes the trip to Independence. Pa builds the floor and furniture by himself as well.

To support and feed his family, Pa hunts game. He collects furs to trade for goods as well as a plow and seeds. When he obtains the plow and seeds, he begins working the prairie sod. Ma, Mary, and Laura plant a garden. They also collect blackberries when they are ripe. In addition to cooking all the family's meals, Ma also does the family's sewing and makes all their clothes. The Ingalls family gets whatever it wants or needs through its own labor.

Good Neighbors
Though the Ingalls family is essentially self-reliant, they do rely on the help of others at times, and they help others in turn. This supportive action makes the American dream possible as neighbor aids neighbor, especially when a crisis is at hand. The most obvious instance of the importance of neighbors helping each other is when families fall ill.

In chapter 7, "The Wolf-Pack," Pa goes out exploring the prairie and finds a family from Iowa sick with malaria being take care of by their youngest children. Though he is late getting back to his own family, Pa goes back to other men he met earlier in the day, two bachelors, so they can care for the ill family. When the Ingalls family and other families in the area come down with the same illness later on, Mrs. Scott travels from house to house with the Indian physician, Dr. Tan, taking care of the sick.

The labor exchanges mentioned above also help everyone achieve their American dream. Mr. Edwards is a bachelor and happily helps Pa build the home and stable first so his family can have shelter. In addition to lending Pa nails to complete the roof, Mr. Edwards labors for the family in another way. He risks his life to cross the swollen creek at Christmas to deliver gifts from Santa to Mary and Laura. If Mr. Edwards had not done so, the girls would not have had much of a Christmas that year. His actions as a friend and neighbor to the Ingalls family helps make their time on the prairie endurable.

Joy in Everyday Life

No matter what happens in *Little House on the Prairie*, the Ingalls family finds joy in everyday life around them. To achieve the American dream is to endure sometimes trying, if not boring, circumstances. Though they are isolated on the prairie, the Ingalls family never complains about the tedium of every day life. Only Laura has moments of rebellion, but she is usually obedient and also consistently helps her family.

Much of the text of *Little House* consists of breathtaking descriptions of the landscape, weather, and wildlife the Ingalls experience daily on the prairie. Pa loves the big sky overhead, while Mary and Laura enjoy the antics of small animals such as gophers, water bugs, and frogs. Ma and Pa go about their daily lives without complaint or resentment; they are depicted as generally being happy where they are. There are also unexpected findings when the Ingalls explore life away from their immediate home environment.

One day, for example, Pa takes Mary and Laura to the Indian camp, described in chapter 14, "Indian Camp." On their way there, they see beautiful foliage; once at the camp, Pa points out the moccasin tracks and other remains from the Indians' last stay. Their excursion is highlighted by finding and collecting loose Indian beads. Wilder writes of the Laura finding the first bead, "She picked it up, and it was a beautiful blue bead. Laura shouted with joy." After finding the first one, the hunt for more beads define a lovely afternoon and a necklace for Carrie. While such excursions are rare in the book, they help make life on the endless prairie interesting.

HISTORICAL OVERVIEW

The Frontier Era

Little House on the Prairie, and all of Wilder's "Little House" books, takes place in the era of westward expansion in the United States. By promising free land to settlers, the U.S. government lured people west. The promise began with the Homestead Act of 1862, which granted land ownership to migrants who remained on the 160 acres of claimed land and worked it for a certain number of years. Many took the government up on the offer for various reasons. For example, some settlers saw it as a means of ending a cycle of poverty or a second chance at success. Others just wanted the land for free. Either way, holding onto one's claim and surviving often brutal conditions was difficult. People had to build their homes, lives, livelihoods, and communities from scratch. They also faced social isolation during the years the farms and communities were being developed.

Despite such conditions, many Americans believed in the West and what it represented. Pa, for example, saw it as a land of possibility and escape where he could make a living away from the over-populated Big Woods. He takes a risk by going to Indian territory in or near Kansas in *Little House on the Prairie* because he has faulty information that the federal government will be opening up the Indians' land to settlers soon. By being among the first in the area, he hopes to stake the best claim. The lack of reliable, efficient communication between Washington, D.C., and the West lead to problems, however. Throughout the book, Pa wants to believe the area will be open soon, but he receives conflicting reports. In the end, the government declines to release the Osage territory and force the Indians westward. The family decides to leave before soldiers forcibly remove the settlers.

The frontier still held an attraction for Pa and others despite this particular failure in *Little House*. Westward expansion began in earnest in the early 1860s and was aided by the 1869 completion of the transcontinental railroad. Hundreds of thousands of people went to Kansas, Nebraska, Texas, and California in the 1870s and 1880s. For Americans, the western frontier symbolized hope, individualism, and self-confidence gained from conquering the wilderness. Some Americans were lured west not by the promise of free land but by the promise of prosperity created by exploiting virgin mineral and lumber resources. Many, however, were farmers and ranchers. Between the years 1870 and 1900, there were more acres settled and cultivated in the United States than between 1620 and 1870.

The Great Depression

Little House on the Prairie was published in 1935, at the height of the Great Depression. After the prosperous, sometimes frivolous 1920s came to an end with the stock market crash of October 1929, the United States fell into an economic depression unmatched in the twentieth century. Between 1929 and 1933 alone, 100,000 businesses failed, and corporate profits went from $10 billion in 1929 to only $1 billion in 1933. Farm incomes also fell dramatically as lower prices resulted in less profits.

As companies went out of business, more and more Americans found themselves out of work. In the beginning of 1930, there were four million Americans out of work; by 1933, this number reached thirteen million, or 25 percent of the American workforce. Many people who had not lost their investments and/or savings in the 1929 crash often became economically devastated as they spent their funds to survive as the Great Depression lingered. Banks were also particularly unstable in this time period, and several thousand shut their doors. One of President Franklin D. Roosevelt's solutions to the economic crisis was the New Deal legislation in the early and mid-1930s. These programs helped revive the economy and put Americans back to work. They gave hope after the failed presidency of Herbert Hoover in the late 1920s and early 1930s.

There was social and cultural fallout as the Great Depression affected all Americans. Families faced serious strains as widespread unemployment affected familial relationships. People put off marriage and married couples put off having children because of the economic distress. While the divorce rate fell in the 1930s, it became more common for husbands and fathers to simply abandon their wives and families. The families that did stay together spent more time in close quarters, as there was less money for recreation. The result was often an increase in family tension. Many American also ate poorly because they could not afford to eat as well as they should, resulting in widespread malnutrition and disease.

Wilder's "Little House" series was popular when it was published in the 1930s because of what it represented in these harsh times. By looking back to a time of American triumph, promise, and prosperity, Wilder's books brought a beacon of hope to readers in these dark years. Yet Wilder herself began writing the books after the stock market crash when her family's savings were wiped out. She was looking for economic security for the entire family, as were many Americans in this time period.

CRITICAL OVERVIEW

Since its publication in 1935, *Little House on the Prairie* has been popular with both readers and critics. Originally, one reason for it appeal to readers was a sense of nostalgia. In the mid-1930s, the United States was in the middle of the Great Depression. *Little House* looked back to a simpler, happier time and place in American history. Despite the economic problems of the 1930s, this book and other books in the series sold well.

By the 1950s, *Little House*, as well as all eight books in the "Little House" series, was considered a classic work of children's literature. Though some critics have noted inconsistencies with the story and questioned the author's sense of geography, the book has continued to be praised for how it depicted a strong sense of family and familial love at its center. Critics also praised how the family was depicted as hard working, resourceful, and courageous in the face of potential disaster.

Other critics believed that Wilder skillfully made what must have been a monotonous daily life experience quite interesting. Charles Frey writes in *Children's Literature Association Quarterly*, "It's surprising that the writer's skill and interest so rarely flag. The very consistency of interest and liveliness of detail, indeed, might seem almost to camouflage what must have been an often-dreary sameness of days."

While *Little House* has been beloved for generations, there also have been two major areas of debate. Beginning in the 1980s, some critics and Native Americans decried Wilder's depiction of Native Americans as well as the anti-Indian attitudes expressed by characters

MEDIA ADAPTATIONS

Little House on the Prairie was loosely adapted for a television series that originally aired from 1974 to 1983. The series centered on one place, Walnut Grove, Minnesota, though the Ingalls family actually moved a number of times. Despite its liberties with Laura Ingalls Wilder's series of books, the television series was an immensely popular celebration of television's version of pioneer life. The series starred Michael Landon as Pa and Melissa Gilbert as Laura. Each season, as well as several related television movies and specials, is available on DVD from Imavision.

Little House on the Prairie (2005) is a television miniseries based on the book of the same name by Laura Ingalls Wilder. Unlike the television series, this miniseries remains relatively faithful to the source, describing the young Laura's experiences living in Indian territory in the 1870s. Directed by David L. Cunningham, *Little House on the Prairie* stars Cameron Bancroft and Erin Cottrell. It is available on DVD from Buena Vista Home Entertainment.

such as Ma and the Scotts. Of the controversy, Wayne Scott writes in the *Oregonian*, "Early settlers such as the Ingalls seem more ignorant than innocent...more destructive than pioneering. Behind the pioneering spirit depicted in the story, there was forced exodus, destruction and genocide inflicted on Native Americans." Several libraries and classrooms in South Dakota, Minnesota, and Louisiana have banned the book as a result.

Other critics have debated how much of a role Wilder's daughter, Rose Wilder Lane, played in the composition of *Little House*. Some critics believe that she wrote most, if not all, of the text, that she was essentially her mother's ghostwriter. Others believe Lane was her mother's sounding board, collaborator, or just the editor as her mother claimed.

Despite such criticisms, *Little House* and the other books in the series remain important works of American literature. Complimenting Wilder's writing style, Ann Hyman of the *Florida Times Union* writes, "Wilder tells her stories of people and places and events that she experienced as she remembers them, no frills, plain storytelling, almost journalism, in the voice of her times and from the perspective of a child." In *Writers for Children*, Fred Erisman emphasizes the books' historic importance and declares, "Artistic in their artlessness, the 'Little House' books speak quietly but eloquently for the simple virtues of industry, responsibility, and family cohesiveness."

CRITICISM

Anita Clair Fellman

In the following excerpt, Fellman contends that Laura Ingalls Wilder and her daughter consciously emphasize the American ideal of self-sufficiency in the Little House *books as a statement to Americans seeking relief from the Great Depression.*

Laura Ingalls Wilder's books, ostensibly a record of the actions and values of her pioneer family, are part of the frontier myth; I would even argue that they are a key means by which the myth gets perpetuated generation after generation, as children read them in school, borrow them from the library, or perhaps get the boxed set for Christmas or a birthday. The myth selects out portions from the vast array of pioneer experiences and projects them as the entire picture. In its focus on the individualism inherent in the settlers' values, for instance, the myth ignores the struggles to form community in regions with the ceaseless coming and going of populations. In its emphasis on self-sufficiency and on the bounty of the land, it leaves out the shaping role of government, the close economic ties of the West to the industrial order, and the dependence of many settlers upon wage labor.

The *Little House* books do this as well. Out of the fullness of the Ingalls's lives, Laura Ingalls Wilder and Rose Wilder Lane, her daughter and collaborator, selected elements that convey a certain portrait of their family. Their vision of the frontier was created by memory, by their

Covered wagons on the Plains going West
© *Bettmann/Corbis*

gender, by the dynamics of the relationship between them as mother and daughter, by their politics, by their livelihoods, by the "frontier longings" that they shared with many of their contemporaries in the 1920s and 1930s, and by their awareness, as literate Americans, of the frontier thesis.

Although the myth tells us that a novice sat down at the age of almost sixty-five to write with instinctive artistry the story of her childhood, Wilder actually had spent fifteen years (1911–25) writing for the *Missouri Ruralist* and other regional papers and, with Lane's help, had published several articles in *McCall's* and *Country Gentleman*. Although her daughter was unsuccessful in rousing her to devote much attention to writing for national periodicals, in 1925 Wilder began researching family stories with the idea of writing some pioneer anecdotes. Her mother's death in 1924 clearly spurred her to this effort, but she may have been inspired as well by the flood of writings on the frontier that appeared in the 1920s and by Lane's keen freelancer's eye for what was current in publishing. David Wrobel surmises that "the image of the frontier . . . provided a kind of solace for some in

the uncertain postwar years." Unlike writings on the frontier that had appeared in the Progressive Era, the "longing[s] for wilderness and pioneer virtues" that permeated writing on the frontier in the 1920s "were less frequently accompanied by concerns over the dangers of excessive individualism in a postfrontier world than they had been in those earlier decades." Sometime in the late 1920s Wilder at last began writing an adult-level autobiography, which she called *Pioneer Girl*. Lane, acting on her mother's behalf, was never able to find a publisher for the autobiography, partly because the market for such writings was well saturated, but the two women used the manuscript as the source for the Little House books during the 1930s and early 1940s.

Numerous scholars have pointed out recently that men's and women's writings on the frontier differ and that our perception of the frontier as a place of conquest, escape to freedom, lawlessness, individualism, and concern for autonomy emerges from males' imagined notions of the West. Women's imagined Wests, though sharing aspects of the dominant visions, also embrace, in tension with them, "the making of the garden, the building of the home (town, city), the clearing of the land— the sustaining of the human community." Wilder's West, possibly even more than most female accounts, embodies the tension between the two visions. Her depiction of the frontier does not include a romanticization of violence but does portray some lawlessness as a natural consequence of laws and policies that were inappropriate and foolish. Certainly it is Wilder's father, Charles Ingalls, who is portrayed as the parent with the urge to strike out ever further west and her mother, Caroline Ingalls, as the one who wants to settle down somewhere with access to a church and a school for her girls. Nonetheless, it is Laura, the daughter who shares her father's vision, with whom we are invited to identify and whose long process of socialization into acceptance of feminine values we witness with ambivalence. Furthermore, Caroline Ingalls's attachments to extended family, friends, and community are downplayed; her immediate family forms virtually her entire world, and her commitment to self-sufficiency matches that of her husband. While Laura is being trained for female social roles, she is also being tutored in moral autonomy as the basis for her freedom and independence, regardless of circumstance.

At some point in her life Wilder became aware of the frontier thesis of American development, or at least had absorbed its major tenets. In 1937 when she and Lane were midway in the Little House series, she was invited to speak at a book fair in Detroit. Her talk is filled with language expressive of Turner's formulation of stages of frontier development, of the progression from barbaric to civilized: "I began to think what a wonderful childhood I had had. How I had seen the whole frontier, the woods, the Indian country of the great plains, the frontier towns, the building of railroads in wild, unsettled country, homesteading and farmers coming in to take possession. I realized that I had seen and lived it all—all the successive phases of the frontier, first the frontiersman, then the pioneer, then the farmers, and the towns. Then I understood that in my own life I represented a whole period of American History." Wilder goes on to describe western Minnesota as "too civilized for Pa," who decided that they should push west to an unsettled part of Dakota Territory. The wording of this talk suggests that Wilder was not simply telling her family's story, but as a matter of course filtered her narrative through a lens, the frontier thesis, that she shared with her contemporaries. In other words, she was a historical actor interpreting her experiences through the mythological frontier.

In addition to the influences of her gender and the context in which she produced her manuscript, Wilder's emotional makeup and her turbulent relationship with her daughter, Rose, helped dictate her view of frontier values. I have discussed the implications of their mother-daughter relationship and their livelihoods for their political ideology elsewhere. Here let me say briefly that the two women remained central in each other's emotional lives until the younger woman was well into middle age. Wilder was a much less expressive person than Lane, but each sought affirmation from the other in ways that the other could not provide, and each concluded that overdependence upon another person was futile and self-defeating. Their preoccupations with autonomy rather than attachment colored their views on emotional and material self-sufficiency and on the dangers of dependence upon government.

Although artistic goals clearly shaped the two women's work on the *Little House* books, Wilder and Lane also had political aims in mind.

Mother and daughter, writing in the midst of the Great Depression, were profoundly anti–New Deal. They were opposed to the expanding role of government, feeling that individuals were capable of overcoming hardships on their own and that when government intervened in people's lives, it did so in crude, blundering ways that did more harm than good, as with the farm programs that paid farmers to plow their crops under. In 1936, as grasshoppers descended on the Wilders' Missouri farm, Wilder wrote to her daughter that they were doing what they could to kill them but were futilely battling a judgment of God: "We as a nation would insult Him by wantonly destroying his bounty. Now we'll take the scarcity and like it" (Wilder Papers, folder 19, microfilm roll 2).

As the 1930s progressed, Lane became more and more of a political individualist, maintaining that society was only a meaningless abstraction. She believed that the remarkable energy that had transformed the young United States, and was increasingly affecting the world, stemmed from Americans' rejection of authority and their acceptance of the responsibility that comes from individuals standing on their own two feet, dependent upon no one. Her political ideas, which later contributed to the resurgence of libertarianism in the United States, are most fully expressed in *The Discovery of Freedom*, published in 1943, the same year that *These Happy Golden Years*, the last of the original eight Little House books, appeared. She had been working out her ideas in the 1930s, however, in articles published in *The Saturday Evening Post* and other magazines, as well as in her best-selling novel *Free Land* (1938). Among the many examples of her intellectual influence is the career of the late Roger Lea MacBride, her "adopted" grandson, who ran for president on the Libertarian Party ticket in 1976.

There is strong evidence from their correspondence that Wilder was in agreement with many of Lane's ideas. Wilder left the Democratic Party and opposed Roosevelt, and she frequently commented to Lane that the two of them regarded the events of the day in the same way. She was also filled with unaccustomed praise for *The Discovery of Freedom*. Wilder was less well read and not as politically sophisticated as her daughter, but in crucial ways she had tutored her daughter in the belief in the emotional self-sufficiency that was a corollary to the economic self-sufficiency that Lane advocated. Together, as the two women thought through their family history, deciding what from *Pioneer Girl* to incorporate, what to delete, and what to elaborate in the *Little House* books, they melded their anti–New Deal politics with the meaning they made of the Ingalls and Wilder family experiences. Thus, part of the artistry of the books is based on a self-conscious, particular vision of frontier life.

A number of sources support this assertion. One is the text of *Pioneer Girl*. This work of nonfiction is much less adorned than are the children's books, and one can see not only where Wilder and Lane have changed the facts of the Ingalls's lives between it and the Little House series but also how they have enhanced certain aspects to present a consistent picture of family self-sufficiency and ingenuity. The information in *Pioneer Girl* has been supplemented by Wilder's biographers (Zochert; Anderson). Another source is the Little House books themselves, with their artful juxtaposition of challenge, deferred gratification, and family good feeling. A final source is correspondence between Wilder and Lane about the writing of the books. Ironically, as the overall purpose of what they were creating became clear to them, Wilder began to urge her publisher to stress that the stories were true; indeed, she told her bookfair audience in Detroit that in every story in the series "all the circumstances, each incident are true" (Raymond to Wilder, Dec. 22, 1936, Correspondence, Laura Ingalls Wilder Series; Anderson, *A Little House Sampler* 220). Lane both instructed her mother on the distinction between overarching truthfulness and mere accuracy of detail and insisted to others that the *Little House* books "are the truth and only the truth" (Lane to Wilder, Jan. 21, 1938; Mortensen, "Idea Inventory").

Source: Anita Clair Fellman, "Don't Expect to Depend on Anybody Else," in *Children's Literature*, Yale University Press, Vol. 24, 1996, pp.101–16.

SOURCES

Erisman, Fred, "Laura Ingalls Wilder," in *Writers for Children*, Charles Scribner's Sons, 1988, pp. 617–23.

Frey, Charles, "Laura and Pa: Family and Landscape in *Little House on the Prairie*," in *Children's Literature Association Quarterly*, Vol. 12, No. 3, Fall 1987, pp. 125–28.

Hyman, Ann, "*Little House* more than children's book," in the *Florida Times Union*, June 25, 2000, p. G-4.

Scott, Wayne, "In My Opinion—Revisiting Wilder's 'Little House' Books," in the *Oregonian*, April 12, 2005, p. B09.

Wilder, Laura Ingalls, *Little House on the Prairie*, Harper Trophy Edition, 1971; originally published in 1935.